To my parents
GERMAINE and HENRY MULLER
WEITZENHOFFER

General Techniques of Hypnotism

ANDRE M. WEITZENHOFFER, PH.D.

*Professor of Psychiatry and Behavioral Sciences
Department of Psychiatry and Behavioral Sciences
University of Oklahoma Health Sciences Center
Oklahoma City, Oklahoma*

GRUNE & STRATTON
A Subsidiary of Harcourt Brace Jovanovich, Publishers
New York   San Francisco   London

Grune & Stratton, Inc.
111 Fifth Avenue
New York, New York 10003

Distributed in the United Kingdom by
Academic Press, Inc. (London) Ltd.
24/28 Oval Road, London NW1

Library of Congress Catalog Card Number 56-8597
International Standard Book Number 0-8089-0523-6

Printed in the United States of America

Contents

PART I. FOUNDATIONS

PART II. WAKING SUGGESTIONS

PART III. HYPNOSIS AND HYPNOTIC SUGGESTIONS

Preface

THE PRESENT WORK had its inception in 1948 when I conceived the idea of writing a definitive treatise on hypnotism. It was to be one of a three volume set dealing respectively with the foundations, the techniques, and the applications of hypnotism. For a number of reasons, the publication of such a treatise became impractical. Instead, what was intended to be the first part was published separately in a much abbreviated version under the title of "Hypnotism: An Objective Study in Suggestibility" (John Wiley and Sons, Inc., 1953). The present text corresponds to what would have been the second part of the projected treatise. It deals nearly exclusively with the *general techniques* of hypnotism, that is, with those techniques that underlie the production of hypnotic phenomena in general and which are applicable to most situations, as contrasted to the specialized techniques which have been developed in specific fields of applications such as psychiatry and dentistry. In its emphasis on techniques, the present book differs essentially from my previous work which is devoted to empirical facts and to theory. It does not presuppose any prior knowledge of hypnotism or require any collateral reading. However, inasmuch as the material is directed toward professionals in medicine, psychiatry, psychology, dentistry, and other allied fields, the book as a whole does presuppose a rather high level of training, some sophistication, and a definite maturity on the part of the reader. It is a technical text written for professional workers.

In writing this book, I have tried to produce a text which could serve for teaching introductory and advanced courses in hypnotism at the graduate level in universities. At the same time, realizing that there are relatively few such courses actually available and that they are often geographically inaccessible to many potential students, I have also tried to write a text which might serve as a surrogate for those courses. Although I doubt if a book can ever fully replace a supervised course of training, it is my hope that the present work will prove to be a reasonably satisfactory substitute.

In the past, students of hypnotism have learned to hypnotize largely by trial and error and the rote memorizing of stereotyped procedures with little opportunity to gain an understanding of what they were doing. One of the major aims of this work is to give the student a working understanding of hypnosis and hypnotic phenomena. The central theme throughout the text is that hypnotic hypersuggestibility is a multifactorial entity, an expression of three or more distinct and mutually interacting processes which also interact with various expressions of the subject's personality. The effective induction and utilization of hypnosis must be based upon an individualistic approach in which all elements of the process are accorded their proper place. In particular, recognition must be given to the psychological make-up of the subject or patient, especially his needs and defenses, as well as to the psychophysiological processes presumed to underlie hypnotic phenomena. Consequently, tailoring hypnotic techniques for each individual is emphasized over the use of stereotyped methods of induction and utilization of hypnosis. Such an approach calls for a thorough understanding of the dynamics of the situation. For this reason, I have presented the various techniques against the background of a rationale derived from the available experimental data and from as unified a theory of hypnosis as possible. It is the main function of chapter 2 and of more limited discussions placed at strategic points in the text to develop such a rationale.

I would like to make it clear, however, that I do not claim every aspect of each known technique of hypnotic induction or utilization can be derived from the known properties of suggestibility and hypnosis or from theory. Nor do I mean to imply that we must not look elsewhere for a criterion of what constitutes an effective technique. There are unfortunately still too many imponderables in the domain of hypnotism to allow this. But to the extent that one can base on, or at least relate techniques to experimental and theoretical knowledge, I believe it is fruitful to do so.

The fact that this text has been written to serve a wide range of professional interests and training has presented certain problems with regard to the use of technical language as well as the kind of information which should be included. The needs of a dentist, a research psychologist, a general practitioner, and a psychiatrist, to name but a few, are not the same. To serve each group more satisfactorily, it has seemed necessary to include material which might be of special interest and use to a limited readership. Such material has often been presented in a highly technical and specialized language, as this was the only adequate way of handling it. However, where certain aspects of it might be of interest to a wide audience, I have not hesitated to repeat it in less technical language, even though this might seem repetitious to some readers.

One of the fundamental premises I have followed is that the only way to learn how to hypnotize effectively is through actual practice. This has led me to present from the very start many of the techniques of hypnotism in the form of demonstration-experiments to be carried out by the reader. These demonstrations have been carefully chosen in order to illustrate various fundamental points and to bring out important facts as well as to afford actual practice in the acquisition of essential techniques. In order to make the text as much of a substitute as possible for actual classroom instruction, the basic demonstration have been described in great detail, the reader being told exactly, word for word, what to say, what to do, and how to and when to say or do it. On the other hand, since many features specific to a given technique or demonstration are essentially duplicated in other situations, I have not felt it necessary to do the above with each and every technique described in the text. This, for one thing, has made it possible to cover a much greater number of techniques than would otherwise have been possible.

The present book aims to present a comprehensive coverage of general techniques. It is to be expected that, depending upon his needs and background, each reader will find certain chapters of greater interest or value to him than others. A few recommendations might be made in this regard.

For a *brief, introductory course* in hypnotic techniques, on the order of a primer, the reader should study the following chapters: 1, 2, 3 (only the sections on the Chevreul pendulum, backward postural sway, and arm (hand) levitation), 4 (only the sections on hand clasping, eye catalepsy, and catalepsy of the arm), 5 (optional), 6, 7, 12 and 15 (optional).

On the other hand, the reader who already has a basic knowledge of techniques and who wishes to widen his knowledge regarding these—that is, who needs an *advanced course*—can limit himself to the following material: 2, 8, 10, 13, 14, 15 (optional).

Chapter 2 probably will be found rather difficult by some readers, particularly those who have had no previous contact with the hypnotic literature. Reading it is not absolutely essential, but I believe most serious students will profit considerably by studying it carefully. Since many references are made to its contents in the remainder of the text, it is advisable that every reader at least familiarize himself with it by a quick perusal. Actual detailed study of the chapter can wait until the rest of the book is completed, or it can be done piecemeal with the other chapters.

Some readers may feel overwhelmed by the size and coverage of this book. It should be kept in mind, however, that there are really only a small number of basic techniques which must be mastered, and that the greater percentage of existing techniques are variations. It may be felt by some that I should have limited myself to the former. But sooner or later they most likely will want to know about these variations. Also it has been my aim to offer a comprehensive coverage of available techniques. Had I limited myself to the very basic ones, this aim could not have been accomplished. Finally,

I believe that most students will find that having information on these variations, which are typical applications of the principles underlying hypnosis, will help them to better understand these very principles. To offset the feeling of confusion that might arise from access to too many procedures, I have made certain recommendations in appropriate places in the text with regard to the choice of a procedural method. As a further help, the two plans of study mentioned earlier have been suggested. On the other hand, I wish to emphasize that the coverage of techniques aims at being *representative* and not encyclopedic. There are roughly five or six thousand books and articles dealing with hypnotism, animal magnetism and suggestion. A book of this size could hardly begin to encompass the mass of available material. Undoubtedly there will be some readers who will fail to find in the text some specific technique, fact, or discussion in which they are interested, but on the whole I believe that this work can be offered to the specialist as well as to the nonspecialist with the confidence that it will serve either group satisfactorily.

I am considerably indebted to Dr. Bernard E. Gorton who wrote for this book the section dealing with Dr. Schultz's "autogenic training." I owe a note of thanks to Drs. Max L. Hutt, Leonard M. Lansky, George K. Levinger, and Walter R. Reitman for their constructive criticisms of the early drafts of this work. Adrian Rook Tieman and Miriam Gallaher were most capable editorial assistants and readers. Nor would I forget the excellent work of my secretary Joan Strong Warmbrunn. Finally, to my wife I owe a very special vote of thanks and appreciation for the manifold ways in which she helped to produce this book.

I am indebted to the National Science Foundation and the National Institute of Health which, by their generous grants in the form of fellowships, gave me in the past few years much of the freedom necessary for bringing this work to completion. To the Center for Advanced Study in the Behavioral Sciences I am especially grateful for making it possible for me not only to devote my full time to the final work on this book, but also to have access to much needed editorial and secretarial assistance.

André M. Weitzenhoffer

Center for Advanced Study in
  the Behavioral Sciences
    Stanford, Calif.
      July, 1957

Acknowledgment

I WOULD LIKE to make the following acknowledgment of courtesies extended to me. The following authors and publications generously gave me permission to use quotations:

The International Journal of Psychoanalysis and Dr. Herman Nunberg for material taken from his article, "Transference and Reality," International Journal of Psychoanalysis, 1951, XXXII, 1-9.

The American Psychological Association for quotations from J. W. Friedlander and R. T. Sarbin, "The Depth of Hypnosis," Journal of Abnormal and Social Psychology, 1938, 33, 281-294, and from L. W. Davis and R. W. Husband, "A Study of Hypnotic Susceptibility in Relation to Personality Traits," Journal of Abnormal and Social Psychology, 1931, 26, 175-182.

The Ronald Press Company for several quotations from John G. Watkins, "Hypnotherapy of War Neuroses," 1949.

Acta Psychiatrica et Neurologica Scandinavica for the material from E. F. Wagner, "Induction by Means of Folding Hands," Acta Psychiatrica et Neurologica Scandinavica, 1951, 26, 90-94.

Mr. Raphael H. Rhodes for the quotation from his book, "Therapy Through Hypnosis," Citadel Press, 1952.

Random House for the quotation from Sigmund Freud, "The Basic Writings of Sigmund Freud," 1938.

The American Psychiatric Association for several quotations from the article by B. Stokvis, "A Simple Hypnotic Technique with the Aid of Colour-Contrast Action," American Journal of Psychiatry, 1952, 109, 380-381.

Grune and Stratton, Inc. and Drs. J. Bordeaux and L. M. LeCron for permission to reproduce the "LeCron-Bordeaux System for Indicating Depth of Hypnosis," from their book, "Hypnotism Today," 1947; and Dr. Lewis R. Wolberg for the many quotations from his two works, "Hypnoanalysis," 1945, and "Medical Hypnosis," Volume I, 1948.

The Houghton Mifflin Company for two definitions quoted from Warren's "Dictionary of Psychology," 1934.

The Journal Press for material from the following articles: R. W. White, "An Analysis of Motivation in Hypnosis," Journal of General Psychology, 1941, 24, 145-162; H. Hoagland, "The Mechanism of Tonic Immobility ('Animal Hypnosis')," Journal of General Psychology, 1928, 1, 426-447;

M. V. Kline, "A Visual Imagery Technique for the Induction of Hypnosis in Certain Refractory Subjects," Journal of Psychology, 1953, 35, 227-228; and Dr. Milton H. Erickson for the many lenghy quotations from his writings, especially from: "The Method Employed to Formulate a Complex Story for the Induction of an Experimental Neurosis in a Hypnotic Subject," Journal of General Psychology, 1944, 31, 67-84; "A Study of Clinical and Experimental Findings on Hypnotic Deafness: I. Clinical Experimentation and Findings," Journal of General Psychology, 1938, 19, 127-150; "The Induction of Color-Blindness by a Technique of Hypnotic Suggestion," Journal of General Psychology, 1939, 20, 61-89.

The International University Press for quotations from C. Fisher, "Studies on the Nature of Suggestion," Parts I and II, Journal of the American Psycho-Analytic Association, 1953, 1, 222-225, 406-437.

The University of Pennsylvania Press for quoted material from E. D. Snyder, "Hypnotic Poetry," 1930.

The Woodrow Press, Inc., for quotes from J. G. Watkins, "Trance and Transference," Journal of Clinical and Experimental Hypnosis, 1954, 2, 284-290, from M. H. Erickson, "The Development of an Acute Limited Obsessional Hysterical State in a Normal Hypnotic Subject," Journal of Clinical and Experimental Hypnosis, 1954, 2, 27-41, and from L. M. LeCron, "A Method for Measuring the Depth of Hypnosis," Journal of Clinical and Experimental Hypnosis, 1953, 1, 4-7.

The Psychoanalytic Quarterly for material from I. Macalpine, "The Development of the Transference," Psychoanalytic Quarter, 1950, 19, 501-537, and from M. H. Erickson and L. S. Kubie, "The Successful Treatment of a Case of Acute Hysterical Depression by a Return under Hypnosis to a Critical Phase of Childhood," Psychoanalytic Quarterly, 1941, 10, 583-609.

The Journal of Nervous and Mental Diseases for a quotation from M. H. Adler and L. Secunda, "An Indirect Technique to Induce Hypnosis," Journal of Nervous and Mental Diseases, 1947, 106, 190-193.

Part I.
Foundations

Preliminary Remarks

THIS BOOK is about hypnotic techniques, but we shall deal with "hypnotism" in a much broader sense than is etymologically implied by the term.* The topic of this book is more correctly stated as the *control and use of suggestibility*. In this frame of reference, hypnosis is merely a special aspect of suggestibility, since it appears to be an induced psychophysiologic state characterized by hypersuggestibility. It is this property which primarily concerns the hypnotist. Actually, there seems to be a fundamental difference between "hypnosis" and "suggestibility" in as much as the former is a *state* of the organism, and the latter is a characteristic property, actually a *capacity*.

So-called "waking suggestibility" and hypnotic suggestibility are on a continuum. However this is not the only reason why we should be concerned with suggested waking phenomena—there are some very practical reasons for so doing. Although it is true that suggestions usually have their greatest effectiveness in the hypnotic state, there are many instances in practice when a hypnotist must forego the advantages of trance induction, yet he may still use suggestions effectively; and the modern method of inducing hypnosis requires the use of waking suggestions. Indeed, one does not so much learn how to hypnotize, as how to give suggestions. Thus, the hypnotist not only works within the hypnotic state, but must also work within the waking state. He transcends the boundaries of hypnosis proper. Properly speaking then, one should speak of suggestibility phenomena in general, and of hypnotism in particular. However, by convention, we will continue to refer to hypnotism when we mean to include under this heading suggestibility phenomena not dependent on the presence of a hypnotic state. This will be emphasized by speaking of "waking" as contrasted to "hypnotic" phenomena.

In one sense, almost anyone can learn to hypnotize. Indeed, at first glance, hypnotizing is extremely simple. Any individual able to memorize and recite a specific pattern of words can "learn" to hypnotize *some* individuals to *some*

---

*There has been a recent trend toward using "hypnosis" as synonymous with "hypnotism." Inasmuch as the former refers to a state of the individual, the two terms will be differentiated in this book.

3

degree. Trance induction depends so little upon the physical presence of a hypnotist that it is possible to induce hypnosis by playing a recording of the proper suggestions to a subject who may never have met the person who made the recording.

Let the reader beware of this apparent simplicity! I have not stated that *all* individuals could be hypnotized, or that the induced trance could be of the deepest kind. Here is where difficulties arise. The problem is not to learn to hypnotize per se, but rather to learn to hypnotize *effectively*. This involves much more than reciting a formula or patter.

THE DANGERS OF HYPNOTISM

Most professional men agree that hypnotism can be dangerous, but rarely if ever are the dangers specified. What are they then? First of all, as far as it is known today, hypnosis per se is no more dangerous than natural sleep. There is no evidence that hypnosis in itself weakens the will, damages the nervous system, or in any other way adversely affects the mental and physical well-being of individuals. The danger lies in its *misuse;* especially in the mismanagement of subjects or patients before they are hypnotized, during the induction of a trance, in the hypnotic state, and following hypnosis.

Managing hypnotic subjects would be a relatively simple problem if individual behavior were highly predictable. The hypnotist rarely, if ever, knows an individual well enough to predict with certainty his every reaction to suggestions or to hypnosis. The psychotherapist is probably in the best position to predict reactions, the nonprofessional in the worst. In most circumstances the majority of individuals submitting to hypnosis present no major problems. Unfortunately, there is a certain appreciable percentage who will react in such a way as to cause all sorts of difficulties; furthermore, the best behaved subject will occasionally become unexpectedly difficult to handle during hypnosis. These difficulties may range from minor emotional outbursts to full-fledged convulsive seizures. Posthypnotic difficulties may include mild to severe headaches, with vertigo and nausea; various degrees of depression; persistent drowsiness and perseveration of other suggested effects; and neurotic and psychotic episodes; arising immediately or only much later. These incidents sometimes occur in spite of every precaution taken, but in the majority of cases they can be ascribed to flagrantly improper management of the subject. Mismanagement is least likely to occur with qualified, clinically oriented hypnotists; is found too often with professional research workers who look upon their subjects more as guinea pigs than as human beings; and is a constant occurrence with amateur and stage hypnotists. Unfortunately, a warning does not prevent undesirable reactions. Once an untoward reaction has been initiated, it is of the utmost importance to notice it and to counteract it as early as possible. One must know what measures to take, and when and how to take them. A sound grounding in the behavioral sciences as well as in hypnotism is a minimum requirement, clinical orientation and training is much to be desired—only then is a hypnotist fully equipped to handle hypnotic phenomena. I can only agree with the majority of professional workers, that there is no place for the amateur or stage hypnotist.

RESPONSIBILITIES OF THE HYPNOTIST IN THE SUBJECT-HYPNOTIST INTERRELATIONSHIP

Freud[65] once remarked that hypnosis endows the hypnotist with an authority which was probably never possessed by even priest or miracle man. Such authority carries a proportionate amount of responsibility. Freud was referring here to the ability he believed hypnosis gave the hypnotist to alter the mental and physiological status of the individual. This alone makes hypnosis a great responsibility, but the question goes much deeper.

First, there is the matter of the trust which the subject places in the hypnotist. Hypnosis requires cooperation to an unusual degree. The subject who submits to hypnosis is seemingly being asked to relinquish his capacities for reality-testing, his ability to control the real and the mental world and, in essence, much of his adult individuality—genetically speaking, the subject is asked to regress to a more primitive, child-like level of organization. This is no small request to make of any person, whatever his motivation. The hypnotist must go a long way, indeed, to justify such implied faith.

There is inherent in the hypnotic setting a great potential for the rapid development, by the subject, of strong positive feelings toward the hypnotist which further complicates the situation. It is this mechanism which seems to bring about and intensify the subject's extreme cooperation. These feelings not only render the subject extremely receptive to suggestions, but often give him an extraordinarily forceful, even overpowering, affectively-toned motivation to carry them out. Furthermore, these sentiments have a tendency to perseverate into the subsequent waking (nonhypnotic) state, extending the hypnotist's influence.

The recognition of this characteristic of the hypnotic interrelationship is not new. Jones[95] credits Bertrand,[11] a mesmerist, as being the first to point out specifically that the nuclear element in the subject-hypnotist interaction is the thorough occupation of the subject's mind with the thought of the operator. Just what form this thought takes was not specified. Moll[127] and Janet,[92] among others, amplified this notion, calling attention to the fact that this preoccupation with the hypnotist is associated with strong sentiments toward him which tend to continue into the waking state.

Just what are these feelings? They vary some, but the most typical ones are a strong affection for and a child-like trust in the hypnotist. Janet noted the strong resemblance between these manifestations and those of erotic love, but he also emphatically denied that they were the same. At a later date, orthodox psychoanalysts took the opposite stand, insisting on the sexual nature of this affection.

All of the cases on which Janet, a male, reported were women. It is difficult to tell what percentage of Freud's cases were female, but it is my impression that most were. Would a similar effect have been observed had hypnotist and subject population been predominantly of the same sex? This is an important question for which no satisfactory answer is available. On the other hand, that the above should exist even in such a restricted situation is sufficient cause for serious consideration.

Although the observations of Janet and others were made on mentally ill individuals undergoing psychotherapy, there seems to be little question of the generality of the phenomenon. It is my impression from my own experience with relatively well-adjusted, physically healthy subjects, that these manifestations occur to a considerable extent in this group too, although the feelings which develop seem to be much less intense, and certain morbid elements are absent. I have not been able to ascertain satisfactorily whether the feelings that develop differ in male and female subjects.

To reiterate, hypnosis, as a two-person interaction, is anything but a casual relationship. It places the subject in an especially vulnerable position. This fact puts hypnosis in a special category, and puts the hypnotist in a position of great responsibility during and following hypnosis.

Thus far we have only looked at the hypnotist-subject interaction from the subject's point of view. How does the hypnotist perceive and react to the situation? He is not immune to the development of special feelings, even strong ones, toward his subjects. Something akin to "countertransference," if nothing more, would be expected to occur on some occasions at least.* Hypnotists do indeed show affective reactions to the subject's behavior (i.e., anger, irritation, etc.). Furthermore, some hypnotists develop feelings of possessiveness and affection toward their subjects. However, whether or not the hypnotist develops the near-erotic feelings that Janet found in his subjects remains unknown. As will be seen later (page 59), it seems that hypnosis activates and/or satisfies certain needs in some subjects. It is likely that something similar is true of the hypnotist. Although data is lacking, it is my general impression that an individual's becoming a hypnotist and his pre-

---

*According to Macalpine[117] countertransference is indeed an obligatory and essential part of hypnosis.

ferred *modus operandi* are both sometimes reflections of basic personality problems; in many such instances hypnosis is used as a means of morbid satisfaction.

The fact that the hypnotist is himself susceptible to parataxic distortions and that his use of hypnosis may play a primary part in his need-system raises a serious question regarding who should be a hypnotist. Whatever the requirements of the perfect hypnotist may be, they probably will vary with the intended use of hypnosis. There is a considerable difference in the intimacy, the degree or intensity, and the general quality of the interrelationship which exists in hypnotherapy, in a hypnotic experiment and in the production of anesthesia for a tooth extraction. What may be a substandard qualification in one instance may be fully satisfactory in another. Whatever the particular need may be, and until such time as the necessary criteria can be developed and enforced, one can only point out some of the reasons why the use of hypnosis is a very serious matter and hope that every aspirant and veteran hypnotist will see it as his duty to rate himself in respect to his qualifications and, having done so, to act accordingly.

No matter what uses a person makes of hypnosis, sooner or later he will find himself sought out by various individuals who see in hypnosis a panacea for their problems, real or imaginary. Possibly because of the particular relationship which seems to arise between subject and hypnotist, subjects at times seem prone to seek help from the hypnotist in other areas. It is only too easy to acquiesce to such demands, especially when they are, as is often the case, persistent and appealing. It cannot be overemphasized that under no circumstances should a hypnotist expand his activities beyond his fields of specialization, unless adequate supervision can be secured. Preferably, the proper specialist trained in hypnotic techniques should take the case over completely. Not unique to hypnotism, this holds true for any specialized service, but there is a greater temptation for the specialist who uses hypnosis to take over functions for which he is not qualified. This is particularly true in areas of psychosomatic disturbances and in other situations where psychotherapy is indicated.

The ramifications of the hypnotist's responsibilities are many. One topic of considerable controversy at times, is whether a person may become more suggestible in a nonspecific manner once he has been hypnotized. More particularly, does he become more susceptible to hypnosis as a consequence? It is fairly well established that this does take place with respect to the original hypnotist, but there is little information on the extent to which such an increased susceptibility generalizes to others. There are reasons to suspect that this may occur, and in the absence of definite evidence to the contrary, it is every hypnotist's responsibility to protect his subjects against such a possibility. He can best do so by giving suggestions to the subject which are specifically aimed at counteracting any general increase in suggestibility. At the same time this should not be done in such a way as to prevent another competent hypnotist from benefiting by this enhanced susceptibility or from being able to hypnotize the individual in question.

The increase in the subject's responsiveness to the hypnotist as a result of having been hypnotized, or even having been given many waking suggestions, poses another serious problem. To what extent, as a consequence, is the subject likely to be too easily influenced by the hypnotist in interactions other than frankly suggestive ones? Is he not likely to be unduly influenced by whatever the hypnotist says or does, even though this may not be intended? On occasions, subjects have spontaneously voiced uncertainty about whether or not they were free of influence when interacting with me in what was intended to be a nonsuggestive situation. These were, by the way, individuals capable of developing very deep trance states. I do not know whether or not they had a real basis for this feeling. It is important that the possibility exists. There are many situations in practice where such a condition is not particularly important because there is little or no opportunity for future interaction (e.g., childbirth or a tooth extraction). In other instances, such as in certain forms of therapeutic guidance, this condition may even be an advantage. However, where the condition seems contraindicated, it should be counteracted by appropriate suggestions. In any event, the hypnotist should remain aware of his potential for influencing subjects outside the hypnotic situation and take appropriate precautions. This is particularly true immediately following dehypnotization. The hypnotist's need to monitor his speech and action in the presence of his subjects, particularly when they are hypnotized, must be emphasized. Hypnotized persons can be vulnerable and sensitive to all sorts of cues emanating from the hypnotist, and it is easy to inadvertently give a suggestion or introduce changes in one which is being given, with possible disastrous results for the subject.

A hypnotist must keep careful track of all suggestions given to the subject and make certain that their influence is completely removed before the subject leaves, unless there is a specific reason for retaining their influence.

A particularly delicate situation frequently arises when a patient or experimental subject is to attend more than one hypnotic session and certain instructions are to be given in this regard. The ideal way of making sure that the instructions will be carried out and that the subject will keep his future appointment would be to give the instructions to him while he is hypnotized. However, even if they are given as instructions, and are not intended to be suggestions, they may become associated with a posthypnotic effect, and the hypnotist is faced with the question of to what extent he has the right to influence a person's behavior outside the hypnotic situation. This is a matter that each hypnotist must decide for himself. There are situations which warrant enforcing the instructions in the above manner, but where there are no good reasons for doing so, instructions should be given with considerable circumspection to avoid undue posthypnotic effects. For instance, if a hypnotized subject is told "When you come back next Thursday you will have no difficulty in visualizing a black circle on the wall as soon as I clap my hands twice," the intention being merely to prepare the subject for this particular effect, inadvertently he was also given a suggestion to "come back next Thursday." This sort of indirect suggestion may not be effective in all cases, but it can be expected to have an influence in some instances. Since the reaction cannot be predicted it is necessary to guard against it at all times. It is best to give the hypnotized subject only necessary instructions in hypnosis; all others should be given in the waking state, at a time when his suggestibility is as normal as possible.

These are some of the responsibilities every hypnotist must face. Many of these are common sense ethics. Unfortunately, too often they are ignored through sheer negligence and laxity. The best general rule of conduct for hypnotists is that they should take every precaution that they would want taken were *they* the subject.

HYPNOTISM, A SCIENCE AND AN ART

In the past, hypnotism has been associated with the realm of the occult and quackery. Today, however, we know that it is neither, that it is a legitimate scientific topic. It has been the subject of a great many scientific investigations in the last half century, particularly in the last 20 or 30 years.[191] Although there are still many questions about hypnotism that remain unanswered, and new ones will probably arise as time passes, definite strides toward an understanding have been made. Today we are beginning to be able to formulate a body of laws and properties and an entirely new perspective has arisen in regard to hypnotism and its applications.

Within reason, it is possible to approach hypnotic techniques rationally, making use of a number of principles and properties of suggestibility and psychodynamics. On the other hand, the success of any given technique also depends upon the hypnotist's basic ability to speak and act at the most effective time and in the most effective manner. No formula can substitute for the hypnotist's perspicacity, insight and experience. Even deeply hypnotized individuals will occasionally be unresponsive to suggestions. Circumventing the underlying resistance is often largely a matter of skill, ingenuity and insight on the part of the hypnotist. It is for such reasons that hypnotism, although it has gained the status of a scientific subject, also remains an art.

HYPNOTISM AS PSYCHOLOGY

Hypnotism and the whole field of suggestibility are a part of psychology. It is not particularly surprising, therefore, to find that a good hypnotist is, above all, a good psychologist, although perhaps more at the applied than academic level. Looking upon hypnotism as part of psychology supplies a useful frame of reference with which to approach hypnotic phenomena. That a good background in psychology is a valuable addition to the hypnotist's armamentarium has, as its basis, more than a psychologist's bias toward his specialization.

LEARNING TO HYPNOTIZE

Like the mastery of any other skill, learning to hypnotize possesses at least three basic requirements: (1) receiving competent instruction; (2) having opportunity to acquire practical experience, preferably under supervision; and (3) acquiring sufficient knowledge in related areas.

Of these requirements the first two are essential, the third is certainly to be recommended. Whether it is essential or not depends largely upon what the individual plans to do with his training. It does not really belong in a course in hypnotic techniques but constitutes the content of one or more collateral courses in such fields as general psychology, abnormal psychology, psychiatry, psychotherapeutics, psychosomatic medicine and dentistry, physiology and medicine proper.

Clearly, this type of training would best be obtained in a university lecture-laboratory course, possibly with a combined practicum phase. There are a few universities presently offering such courses, and the reader is strongly recommended to take advantage of such instruction if possible. The extent to which one becomes skilled in the use of hypnotism bears a direct relationship to the extent of practice one has had—a point too often disregarded. Since practice is so intimately related to the general method of studying the material of this book, it will be more satisfactorily considered in the general discussion of training.

HOW TO USE THIS BOOK

The chapters which follow consist of a series of exercises or demonstration-experiments and short pertinent discussions or commentaries. The exercises have a threefold purpose:

1. They contain typical suggestions designed to produce certain specific and basic suggestibility phenomena of practical importance. By memorizing and learning to use these suggestions, the trainee will acquire a good portion of his basic skills.

2. They are designed to lead the trainee to discover and demonstrate certain general principles of suggestibility and suggestions.

3. The suggestions are to serve the trainee as basic models for the designing of specific suggestions in his own field.

PLAN OF STUDY

To profit most from this book, the reader should follow closely the order of the chapters and the order of the exercises within each chapter. In general, the study of the material in each chapter should involve four phases for best results.

Memorizing. The reader should at first memorize thoroughly one of each kind of suggestion discussed in the chapters. Later this will not be so necessary. At the same time the reader must keep in mind the fact that the skillful use of suggestions involves more than a mere recitation of any given suggestion. Actually, the *pattern* and *content* of the suggestions, more than the actual words, are what is crucial. He should also pay close attention to the memorizing of the parts that call for various intonations, gestures, postures and manipulations of the subject.

Practice Without Subjects. Learning a suggestion means also learning complex coordinations of movements and speech. Although a mere recitation of suggestions can bring about the desired effect in many instances, most situations, as will be seen later, require that the hypnotist must do a number of other things while giving suggestions. It is essential that such activities be an integral part of the suggestion situation, and that the entire procedure be as smooth as possible.

Since intonation, inflection, speed of delivery and voice volume are crucial factors, the reader should practice giving suggestions aloud as much as possible, giving the proper characteristics to his delivery. A tape or wire recorder is a useful adjunct here.

Giving suggestions usually requires that the hypnotist be standing near the subject, often in a specified position; it also requires certain motions on his part. Therefore, from the start, the trainee should imagine that he is actually suggesting to some other person and act accordingly. Role-playing is extremely useful here. As practice progresses, the trainee should imagine himself faced with different situations and change his suggestions appropriately.

If possible, the trainee should practice near a full-length mirror, or even better, near several mirrors strategically placed, so that he can check his appearance. Another effective method with a mirror is to use your reflection as a subject, addressing suggestions to it. Of course, the trainee will be unable to stand behind the subject as some of the instructions call for, but using the mirror in this fashion gains him two advantages: he can see how he would appear to the subject, and the practice situation gains more reality.

Finally, another effective method, which has the advantage that it can be used at any time, is to visualize yourself giving suggestions to a subject. Go through the process step by step, vividly, imagining the entire situation—see the subject and yourself, hear yourself giving suggestions, see the subject responding. Correctly done, this should take the same amount of time as it would in actuality. It is best to proceed at a normal pace although it is possible to speed up imagined action. Try this practice many times, introducing variations in the subject's responses and matching your suggestions to these situations.

The following instructions for a demonstration (which you will be asked to perform later) clarify the above steps.

This demonstration is known as "suggested postural sway." The words in larger type indicate that they should be said with increased emphasis as indicated by the type used. This emphasis is partly obtained by a rise in voice volume. Conversely, smaller type will indicate a decrease in voice volume or emphasis. Emphasis is also obtained by enunciating each word in a passage in a staccato fashion. This technique should be used primarily on material printed in large capitals. An increase or decrease in tempo will be indicated accordingly in brackets. In general, relative length of pauses between words will be indicated by the punctuation. Just read the following —do not attempt to carry it out.

Place yourself behind the subject, about a foot away. Speak to him in a normal tone of voice as follows:

> I want you to stand before me, feet together, arms and hands hanging by your sides. . . That's right, just as you are now. Try to be relaxed. Now in a few moments you are going to experience a tendency to *fall backward*. . . Do not resist, but let yourself fall if you feel like falling— I am right behind you and will catch you right away, just like this. [*While saying these last words, place your hands on the subject's shoulders and pull him firmly, but gently backward, stepping at the same time one step or so backward and allowing him to fall only a very short distance. Note whether the*

subject tends to resist, and particularly if he moves or steps back at all to preserve his equilibrium.] . . .There, I did not let you fall very far, did I? [*If the subject seemed to resist, particularly if he tended to step back, say the following— otherwise omit the next sentence and go on to the one after.*] I think you were a little scared I would let you fall, because you resisted. Next time we try this don't move your feet [*if he did*]. . . Just let yourself go. I will catch you right away. Okay?. . . .Now stand straight, feet together, head up. [*Nearly always the subject will tend to hold his head slightly downward, in normal position. Gently, tilt his head up slightly.*] Close your eyes and think of falling backward. Think that a force is pulling you backward. In a few moments you will feel something pulling you backward. . . There is a force pulling you backward. You feel a force pulling you backward. You are falling backward, falling backward. A force is pulling you backward. Do not resist, let yourself fall. You cannot help yourself. [*Very often the subject will begin to sway or show other signs of responding earlier in the suggestions. If so, you should cut the suggestions short and pass on to the next part right away. If, on the other hand, the subject is slow in responding or shows overt resistance, you should delay the last part and repeat the earlier first part of the suggestions. If the subject resists, it often helps to interpose in the suggestions: "The more you resist, the less you can help from falling backward."*] You are falling backward, falling, falling, *falling*, FALLING, FALLING. . .FALL! [*You will often have to alter this last phase considerably, cutting it short, or lengthening it, depending on how the subject responds, and particularly* DEPENDING UPON WHAT YOU ANTICIPATE HIS NEXT RESPONSE OR EXPERIENCE WILL BE.]

This then is a typical suggestion. First, you should memorize it. In the process of memorizing, you should also try to memorize the directions for delivery of the suggestions—keeping in mind that there are no set rules in this matter and that on occasions you may find it preferable to alter the directions or omit them. On the whole, the pattern of suggestions given in this book usually will be found as effective as any.

After you have memorized the above suggestion fairly well, read it aloud once (if you have not done so already), then try reciting from memory. Imagining the subject is before you, go through the motions indicated as best you can. At first you may feel awkward, do not let this deter or worry you. As you continue practicing the suggestions, imagine various situations in which you might be using them and make any appropriate changes. For instance, assume the subject is resisting, or that he is responding strongly very early in the suggestions (some subjects will actually start swaying in the experiment as soon as they begin thinking of falling backward). Try to be critical of yourself at all times. Remember that everything you do and say is part of the suggestions, hence learn to coordinate your statements and motions, tone of voice, etc., as smoothly as possible.

How long should you continue this form of training? This will vary with the individual—some learn faster than others. Furthermore, as you progress in your training, less work is required. At first you should plan on practicing each suggestion *at least* once a day for a week.

As you will note in subsequent chapters, many of the exercises and demonstrations are of two kinds: autosuggestions and heterosuggestions. You should do each of these, first taking proper precautions as indicated. The experiments in autosuggestion will give you an invaluable insight into the responses of the subjects. As already indicated, one of the most important aspects in giving suggestions is *to be able to anticipate* what the subject is going to feel or do next. Having experienced the effects of suggestions yourself will be of great value and it will enable you to better empathize with the subject.

In regard to effective autosuggestions, the best results will generally be obtained if you concentrate on the suggestions and make no attempt to analyze your sensations or responses. Think continuously of the effect that is to be induced—do not stop and wait for it to happen. A continuous stream of suggestions is crucial, here as well as in giving heterosuggestions. Furthermore, and this is important, do not stop as soon as you become aware of a response—on the contrary try to build it up. Your aim is to obtain a complete response, and not just a sign of it. In using autosuggestions, try to feel the expected effect as much as possible. Imagine what is to happen as vividly as possible. Feel it happening. Try to recall the feelings associated with similar experiences in the past, and try to re-experience them in your mind. Thus, if you are giving yourself suggestions of falling backward (be sure to have someone behind you ready to catch you), try to feel yourself falling backward—see yourself falling in your imagination—try to create in your mind the feelings associated with falling backward.

Practice with Subject. Practice with actual subjects is the best. *It should be done under competent supervision*, insofar as possible. The subjects need not all be highly susceptible or even susceptible to hypnosis at all. Much valuable practice can be secured by working with individuals who are incapable of developing a trance state. I refer to such practice as "mock hypnosis" and to such subjects as "pseudo" hypnotic subjects. The borderline between actual and pseudosubjects is hazy and, in a strict sense, unreal or at least arbitrary. From the moment an individual agrees to submit to the possible influence of suggestions he is a subject. Many beginning students of hypnotism mistakenly believe that the only good practice is that done with susceptible subjects. The supply of susceptible individuals is not always adequate for sufficient practice if practice is limited to this group alone. Practice with pseudosubjects affords additional opportunity to go through the various steps of a procedure exactly as with any other subject. In addition, even though a person is not, or is only mildly, susceptible, he or she can simulate the suggested responses and, with practice, can give a good approximation of a real hypnotic session. With planning before each practice session, a pseudosubject can present the hypnotist with a variety of situations. With some students mock practice is useful in helping them to acquire poise and fluency, because they tend to feel more at ease in such a situation. It also affords an opportunity to acquire some degree of proficiency without running the danger of losing a potentially "good" subject through faulty technique. It can be an excellent source of information on whether one speaks too loud, too low, too fast or too slow; whether one is too authoritarian or too permissive; too self-conscious or too hesitant. Here, as in other fields, proficiency comes only from a wide variety of experience. Every effort should be made to get practice with as many different individuals as possible. The inclusion of pseudosubjects helps considerably to attain this goal.

Polishing. As you go through the other phases of your training take note of your mistakes and weakness as well as of your strong points. In future practice try to take these into account. Repeat the procedures under as many different conditions as possible until you know every aspect and can easily adapt them to any situation. Make certain you understand the reasons for each step of the technique you use. Always analyze the suggestions that you plan to give before using them. The better you understand the process of hypnosis and suggestion, the more proficient you will become. Finally, watch professional hypnotists at work. Try to discover both their weaknesses and their strong points.

Order of Lessons and Exercises

This book is aimed at giving the optimum training to the reader. It is very important that the reader should proceed in order from chapter to chapter and from exercise to exercise, except when otherwise specifically indicated (e.g., Preface). The reader should do the experiments of each chapter *before* reading the discussion section at the end. This also applies to answering the various questions asked throughout this book. The full answer to some questions will have to be delayed until later. The reader is strongly advised to keep going back over earlier material as he progresses through the book and to re-examine it in the light of his newly acquired knowledge and experience.

The preface contains specific recommendations regarding which chapters are considered essential and which optional. The reader will also find there a reading plan for using this book as a *beginner's text* and *as an advanced text*.

ADDITIONAL READING

This book is self-contained and does not presuppose any additional text. However, the broader the reader's knowledge in the fields of psychology and hypnotism, the more effective he is likely to be in the use of hypnosis. Consequently, he is urged to do all the additional reading possible. A selected reading list will be found at the end of this chapter.

EXPERIENCE AND PRACTICE

No matter how comprehensive and detailed a book may be in regard to any technique, there are certain things which can only be gained from long practice and experience. One can become acquainted with the basic techniques and modes of application of hypnosis in a relatively short time with a minimum of effort, but it takes many years and hundreds of subjects and patients to assimilate and master all the techniques. A smooth, well-integrated, poised, highly flexible technique can come only from wide interaction with every type of individual. Self-confidence, one of the most important factors in the use of hypnosis and suggestions, rarely comes from reading a "how-to-do-it" book. It is primarily a by-product of repeated success, of learning what one's limitations are through sheer experience, and of encountering the various pitfalls of hypnotism. Through long and varied experience the hypnotist gradually acquires a certain invaluable sensitivity toward his subjects. This last might be described as a "feel," or as the ability to empathize with the subject. It is this sensitivity which allows the proficient hypnotist to choose the optimal method for a given subject, to alter his technique as needed, to anticipate and counteract difficulties which may arise, and generally to utilize the trance state most effectively.

All of this raises a difficult question. Just how long should one train before qualifying as a professional hypnotist? The successful *supervised* application of hypnosis in one's field of specialization to a minimum of twenty-five cases probably constitutes adequate initial training, provided it is done in conjunction with lectures or reading in the field. In my experience, a one semester course meeting two to three hours weekly seems satisfactory for an elementary course. An additional semester usually serves well to cover the more advanced aspects of hypnotism. Training, whatever form it takes, should include reading, lectures, demonstrations, and an adequate opportunity for supervised practice. I definitely do not believe that lecture demonstrations alone are sufficient. In the final analysis, the only sound criterion of a person's qualifications as a hypnotist is probably his ability to convince a properly chosen board of examiners that he has indeed mastered this field. The dental profession, for instance, has moved in this direction in recent years.

A related question is one of the number of different techniques of inducing hypnosis one should become proficient with. As the reader has probably already become aware, a relatively large number of techniques and their variations are described in this book. He is not expected to master each and every one of them. There are a few basics which he should learn to use well and he should at least try the other ones. More important, however, is that he should know they exist, what they consist of, and what their peculiarities are. More will be said later concerning which specific techniques he should concentrate on at first. The use of hypnosis is an individual matter. Every hypnotist comes in time not only to prefer one or two techniques, but often develops one of his own. It would be unrealistic, therefore, to insist that the reader use any specific method to the exclusion of all others.

EMERGENCIES

A few emergencies can arise in the use of hypnotism. What should you do if the individual with whom you are practicing becomes inadvertently hypnotized before you are trained to handle hypnosis? First, how will you know that the subject is hypnotized? There are no definite signs, unfortunately. (See Moll[126] for one of the best discussions of objective signs.) In some cases the subject may appear to be asleep. In others, he will lack facial expression and have a certain rigidity or automaticism of action. He will tend to act only when told to, otherwise remaining immobile in whatever position he was when last addressed. His tone of voice when speaking will tend to be flat—a monotone. He will tend to answer questions cursorily or in monosyllables. Should this happen, remember that a hypnotized subject will always "wake up" on his own, although this may take some time. You need only make certain that he does not leave the room until he is awakened. In most instances, all you need to do is to tell the subject that when you tell him it is so, he is going to be perfectly normal, fully awake, just as he was before you started giving him suggestions. "Alright," you now say, "you are now wide awake, you feel fine, just as you did before we began." If he fails to wake, a sudden clapping of your hands near him with the sharp command: "Wake up!" or "Wide awake!" will be effective in most instances. Above all, *never get excited* whatever the subject does. *A hypnotized subject can nearly always if not always be controlled by properly given suggestions.*

If you should hypnotize your subject inadvertently before you have had proper training, *do not attempt to experiment* with the hypnotic state. *Wait until you are ready for it.* Be satisfied that you have a "hypnotic subject." If you have access to other subjects, do not use this subject again until you are ready to work with hypnosis proper. Otherwise, familiarize yourself with chapter 7 before using the subject again and continue to do the experiments in sequence.

SELECTED READINGS ON HYPNOTISM

Those of greater importance have been starred (*)

I. BOOKS

A. *Of Historical Interest*

BAUDOUIN, C.: Suggestion and Autosuggestion. London: George Allen and Unwin, Ltd., 1920.

*BERNHEIM, H.: Suggestive Therapeutics (1886). New York: London Book Co., 1947.

BINET, A.: La Suggestibilité. Paris: Schleicher frères, 1900.

*——and FÉRÉ, C.: Le Magnétisme Animal. Paris: Felix Alcan, 1890. (Also translated into English.)

BRAID, J.: Neurypnology. London: George Redway, 1899.

*BRAMWELL, J.M.: Hypnotism: Its History, Practice, and Theory. Philadelphia: J.B. Lippincott Co., 1930.

CHARCOT, J.M.: Note sur les divers états nerveux déterminés par l'hypnotization sur les hystéro-épileptiques. Compt. rend. de l'Acad. d. Sc. Paris, 1882, XCIV, 403-405.

CULLERRE, A.: Magnétisme et Hypnotisme. Paris: J.B. Bailliére et Fils, 1886.

ENNEMOSER, J.: Der Magnetismus. Leipzig, 1819.

FOREL, A.: Hypnotism. New York: Allied Publications, 1949.

*JANET, P.: Psychological Healing. Vol. 1. London: George Allen and Unwin, 1925.

LIÉGEOIS, M.J.: De la Suggestion et du Somnambulisme dans leurs Rapport avec la Jurisprudence et la Médecine Légale. Paris: O. Doin, 1899.

MESMER, F.A.: Mesmerism. (Introduction by G. Frankau.) London: Macdonald and Co., 1948.

*MOLL, A.: Hypnotism. London: Walter Scott, 1890.

*——: Der Rapport in der Hypnose. Untersuchungen über den thierischen Magnetismus. Schriften d. Ges. f. psychol. Forsch. I. Leipzig: Druck von Otto Dürr, 1892.

PHILIPS, J.P.: (Durand de Gros) Cours Théoriques et Pratiques de Braidisme. Paris: Bailliére et Fils, 1860.

*RICHER, P.: Études Cliniques sur la Grande Hystérie ou Hystéro-Épilepsie. Paris: Delahaye et Lecrosnier, 1885.

Schilder, P.: The Nature of Hypnosis (1921, 1926). New York: International Universities Press, 1956.

*SCHMIDKUNZ, H.: Psychologie der Suggestion. Stuttgart: F. Enke, 1892.

SIDIS, B.: The Psychology of Suggestion. New York: D. Appleton Co., 1910.

B. *Experimental and Theoretical*

DORCUS, R.W.: See Section C.

HULL, C.L.: Hypnosis and Suggestibility. New York: D. Appleton-Century, 1933.

KLINE, M.V.: Hypnodynamic Psychology. New York: The Julian Press, 1955.

KUHN, L. and RUSSO, S.: Modern Hypnosis. New York: Psychological Library Publishers, 1947.

LECRON, L.M.: Experimental Hypnosis. New York: Macmillan Co., 1952.

WEITZENHOFFER, A.M.: Hypnotism: An Objective Study in Suggestibility. New York: John Wiley and Sons, Inc. 1953.

C. *Techniques and Therapy*

BRENMAN, M. AND GILL, M.M.: Hypnotherapy. New York: International Universities Press, 1947.

DORCUS, R.W.: Hypnotism and its Therapeutic Applications. New York: McGraw-Hill Book Co., 1956.

RHODES, R.H.: Therapy Through Hypnosis. New York: The Citadel Press, 1952.

ROSEN, H.: Hypnotherapy in Clinical Psychiatry. New York: The Julian Press, 1953.

SCHNECK, J.M.: Hypnosis in Modern Medicine. Springfield, Ill. Charles C Thomas, 1953.

WATKINS, J.G.: Hypnotherapy of War Neuroses. New York: The Ronald Press Co., 1949.

WOLBERG, L.R.: Hypnoanalysis. New York: Grune and Stratton, Inc. 1945.

——: Medical Hypnosis, Vols. I and II. New York: Grune and Stratton, Inc. 1948.

D. *Animal Hypnosis*

MANGOLD, E.: Methodik der Versuche über tierische Hypnose. Handbuch der biologischen Arbeitsmethoden. Abt. VI. Methoden der experimentellen Psychologie. Teil C^1, Heft 5 (Reine Psychologie): Hypnose, Berlin: Urban und Schwarzenberg, 1925.

PREYER, W.: Die Kataplexie und der thierische Hypnotismus. Sammlung physiologischen Abhandlungen, 2te Reihe, H.1. Jena: G. Fisher, 1878.

VERWORN, M.: Beitrage sur Physiologie des Zentralnervensystems. 1. Theil: Die sogenannte Hypnose der Tiers. Jena: G. Fisher, 1898.

VÖLGYESI, F.: Menschen und Thierhypnose. Leipzig: Orell Fussli Verlag, 1938.

E. *Hypnotism in Relation to Social Psychology, Sociology and Anthropology*

BECHTEREW, V.M.: Die Bedeutung der Suggestion in sozialen Leben. Grenzfr. Nervenleben, Wiesbaden, 1905.

STOLL, O.: Suggestion und hypnotismus in der Völkerpsychologie. Leipzig: Veit u. Co., 1904.

II. JOURNALS OF HYPNOTISM

There has been a total of at least 46 periodicals published in the past on hypnotism and animal magnetism. Of these, 21 have dealt with hypnotism proper. At present only three of these are published. The four most important past and present periodicals on hypnotism are the following:

British Journal of Medical Hypnosis, 1950-
Journal of Clinical and Experimental Hypnosis, 1953-
Revue de l'Hypnotisme, 1887-1910
Zeitschrift für Hypnotismus, 1892-1902

III. REVIEWS AND BIBLIOGRAPHIES

(*Note*: Many of the books listed earlier contain excellent bibliographies.)

BIRD, C.: Suggestion and suggestibility: a bibliography. Psychol. Bull., 1939, *36*, 264-283.

COFFIN, T.E.: Some conditions of suggestion and suggestibility: a study of certain attitudinal and situational factors influencing the process of suggestion. Psychol. Monogr., 1941, 53, No. 4.

DESSOIR, M.: Bibliographie des modernen Hypnotismus. Berlin: C. Dunker, 1888.

ERICKSON, M.H.: Hypnosis: A general review. Dis. Nerv. Syst., 1941, 2, 13-18.

GILMAN T. and MARCUSE, F.L.: Animal hypnosis. Psychol. Bull., 1949, 46, 151-165.

GORTON, B.E.: The physiology of hypnosis: A review of the literature. Pts. I and II. Psychiat. Quart., 1949, 23, 317-343; 457-485.

HULL, C.L.: Hypnotism in scientific perspective. Scient. Mo., 1929, 29, 170-185.

JENNESS, A.: Hypnotism. In Personality and the Behavior Disorders, Vol. I. J. McV. Hunt, Ed., New York: The Ronald Press, 1944.

OTIS, M.: A study of suggestibility in children. Arch. Psychol., 1924, 11, No. 70.

PATTIS, F.A., Jr.: The production of blisters by hypnotic suggestions: a review. J. Abnorm. Soc. Psychol., 1941, 36, 62-72.

REVUE DE L'HYPNOTISME: —Many of the issues of this journal contain a bibliographical index of books and papers published since 1880. They contain also reviews of books published in the area from that date until 1910.

SCOTT, W.D.: Suggestion. Psychol. Bull., 1910, 7, 369-273; 1911, 8, 309-311; 1912, 9, 269-273; 1913, 10, 269-270; 1914, 11, 250-252; 1915, 12, 225-226; 1916, 13, 266-268.

STEIN, M.R.: A critical review of an investigation in the psychology of suggestion and hypnosis. J. Abnorm. Soc. Psychol., 1930, 25, 49-56.

WEITZENHOFFER, A.M.: The transcendence of normal voluntary capacities in hypnosis: An evaluation. Personality, 1951, 1, 272-282.

YOUNG, P.C.: A general review of the literature on hypnotism and suggestion. Psychol. Bull., 1927, 24, 540-560; 1931, 28, 367-391.

——: Experimental hypnosis: A review. Psychol. Bull., 1941, 38, 92-104.

Dynamics of Hypnosis

THE PRESENT chapter attempts to explain what hypnosis is, to show how and why the hypnotic state arises under certain conditions, what these conditions are, and what is its relation to suggestibility. Much of what follows is based upon the theory of hypnosis I have developed in my previous work [191] and the facts presented there. Its acceptance by the reader is by no means a requisite for the mastery of the remainder of the material in this book.

Since suggestions play a central role in the use of hypnosis as well as in modern techniques of induction, they seem to constitute a logical starting point. In spite of this central role and of the great many attempts which have been made to define this concept, few, if any, have succeeded in adequately defining suggestion. Although its existence is generally agreed upon, just what distinguishes it as such is another matter. It appears that much of the difficulty in arriving at a satisfactory definition is due to the lack of recognition that it is not so much any single property, as a specific group of properties, which characterizes a suggestion.

NATURE OF SUGGESTION

Suggestions as Stimuli. As I have previously explained,[191] a suggestion is first of all an ideational stimulus. As a stimulus it differs from many other stimuli in that it is always the nuclear element in an interpersonal relation in which it is used to convey an idea from one individual to another with the aim of evoking certain responses. It is characteristic of these responses that their initiation does not involve any conscious volitional effort and that they are neither innate nor acquired adequate responses to the stimulus.

A person giving a suggestion is called the *suggester,* and more commonly, the *operator* or *hypnotist.* The recipient of a suggestion may be called the *suggestee,* but is more commonly known as a *subject.* It is standard nomenclature to speak of a subject who responds well or poorly to suggestions as a *good* or *bad* subject respectively.

The definition of suggestion is by no means simple because of the problem of clearly separating a stimulus acting as a suggestion from stimuli which do not. The very same stimulus which acts as a suggestion in one context can also function in other capacities; similarly a suggested response can also be elicited by other stimulus-situations. To complicate matters still more, in practice, what is usually referred to as a suggestion is really a complex integrated mixture of elements which are not particularly distinguishable one from the other; some of these function as suggestions, and some do not. In addition, what seems to be a complex, *in toto*, response to a suggestion may actually have only part of its elements directly produced by the suggestion.

Conation and Suggestion. An especially important characteristic of suggestion is that the response it elicits is nonvoluntary. The subject *never initiates* the suggested act; the act is *non*voluntary in its initiation; it never involves the conscious, active, volitional participation of the subject. He may voluntarily initiate subsequent behavior, such as when he reacts overtly to a hallucination, but the first action in any suggested behavior sequence is never conscious. On the other hand, it need not be one that the subject cannot appraise or could not control if he wanted to, although this is often the case. But it is an act in which *he is a passive participant*. This is why we speak here of "nonvoluntary" and not "involuntary" behavior. Whether or not the subject can subsequently gain or preserve his potential control over the situation, once events have been initiated, depends upon the extent to which the processes that have been started have carried the situation beyond his control, on whether they are capable of gaining autonomy as they progress, or whether they alter the perceived situation in such a manner that the subject's responses, although voluntary, are nevertheless determined by distorted perceptions.

For instance, in the postural sway situation (see page 98) where it is suggested to the subject that he is falling backward, it is clear that once he has lost his equilibrium there is little he can do to prevent himself from falling and the suggestion must go to completion. Or, consider a subject made to hallucinate that a coin he is holding has become red hot. The reflex response which ensues has a certain autonomy that places the final suggested act outside the subject's control. In fact, the specific avoidance reaction used by the subject in this situation is often so strongly conditioned to the words and/or the ideas of the suggestion that even though he may not have any sensory experiences, he gives reflexedly the proper responses. Finally, consider the subject hallucinating that he is in a cherry orchard during the cherry season. The hallucination may be so realistic that once initiated it will entirely dominate the subject's actions. Within the limits of the hallucination, he has full conscious control of his behavior, but it is also clear that the "reality" of the hallucination allows it to retain the over-all control.

The extent to which this is true is shown clearly in the investigations of suggested antisocial acts.[191]

A few words might be said concerning another aspect of suggestibility which is implicit in what has just been said. One of the conditions required for the efficacy of a suggestion is that the subject does not use his critical faculties, or is rendered unable to use them with respect to the suggestion, at least at the time the suggestion takes its initial effect. This is probably one reason why it is not uncommon to prepare the subject for this beforehand, by instructing him to make his mind a blank, to be completely passive, not to think or to analyze what he is being told, what he feels or what he does. In this regard, suggestions appear to act through a double action, a facilitation of certain processes (to be taken up presently) and a simultaneous inhibition of opposing tendencies such as critical ideation. If this is true, one must ask whether inhibition or abolition of the critical faculties may not be the main character and condition for suggestibility and hypnosis. On the other hand, it may be that the real issue lies in the adequacy of the proposed definition or in what we mean by "critical ideation" and "critical faculties."

Commands and Suggestions. According to the present definition, a command or request is not a suggestion as Hull[85] also emphasized, because it is usual to consider the individual responding as taking a conscious, voluntary part in initiating the response.* That a command is never a suggestion might appear to be a contradiction of fact at first because we constantly see or hear of hypnotists giving "commands" to their hypnotized subjects. But do they? Could it be that what they say to the subject has the same form as a command, but does not function as one? Command or suggestion, what the hypnotist tells the subject is, first of all, a stimulus. As such it may function in any number of ways, depending upon the manner in which it is given, the setting and various antecedent conditions. We are not even dealing here with a command or request functioning as a suggestion, but rather with the same stimulus acting in one of two capacities. Similar remarks can be made with regard to a variety of instructions. Kept clearly in mind, the above will reduce much of the confusion in regard to what does or does not constitute a suggestion.

A further source of confusion is that not all the elements which make

---

*The reader may point out here that there are situations where "commands" elicit automatic responses. The well-trained soldier, for instance, probably does "about face," and other gyrations, at a command without his volition usually taking any part in it. But are we really dealing here with a command or with a stimulus that looks like a command? We could probably also condition a finger retraction to the stimulus "about face" given in the form of a command. Furthermore such a response is an acquired adequate response to the command as stimulus.

up a complex suggestion are suggestive elements. All of the statements made in the process of giving suggestions do not necessarily function as suggestions, nor is that intended. It is true that anything we say or do can probably act as a suggestion, depending on how it is perceived, but this does not mean that it always does. Certain things that are said or done as part of a suggestion are merely intended to integrate the elements into a sensible whole, to give body and structure, but these elements are not suggestions in themselves, even when tied up with the remainder of the material. They may have been introduced to establish a set, to call forth an attitude, to generally set the stage, or to communicate intelligently; at other times their presence is needed merely because the subject must be in a certain position, in a particular place, doing specific things, irrespective of any suggestive effect— we must get the subject to stand up first before we can give him suggestions of falling backward, or to place his hands in a certain fashion before we can give him the so-called "hand-clasping" suggestions. With a given subject this type of instruction does actually function as a suggestion and he finds himself going through the required motions in an automatic manner. Occasionally, a subject, for one reason or another, is led to interpret all statements by the hypnotist as suggestions even though some of them may not have been intended to act as such. If it also happens that this subject perceives the suggestion situation as one in which he will not have to make any conscious effort at any time, but will behave in a sort of automatic, reflexive manner, he may wait passively for the response to occur without his volitional participation. Unless the instructions not intended to be suggestions happen to act as such, one may gain the mistaken notion that the subject is unresponsive and uncooperative.

These considerations apply to commands in that they are often associated with suggestions proper .Thus, we tell an individual: "You cannot get up. You are stuck to your chair. Try to get up!" The last sentence is merely a challenging command to get the subject to test the effectiveness of the suggestion. Conceivably it may have some very indirect suggestive effects, but that is not its main, direct function. Another situation would be when we have the subject hallucinate being in a cherry orchard during the cherry season. We tell him, "Pick up a basket and fill it with cherries." Here we have both suggestions and commands integrated into a single unit. We suggest to the subject that he hallucinate a basket and subsequently fill it with cherries, but in the setting of the cherry orchard, this is also a command. Presumably, two separate neural processes are involved here, but they have the same common end-path. Not infrequently in this sort of situation, the subject will carry out a number of activities which have not been suggested, in addition to the suggested ones, getting a ladder, setting it up against a tree, climbing upon it, and so forth. He may also eat some of the cherries with obvious enjoyment, throwing the stems and stones away, even though this was not suggested, at least not directly. Here we have an elaboration of a suggestion in which the original suggestion or the hallucination and ensuing activity induced by it act in turn as suggestions for other perceptions and activities. Or they may bring the latter about simply through association. In these new perceptions and activities the subject now introduces volitional elements in the form of self-initiated activities appropriate to the suggested situation.*

It is probable that many stimuli function simultaneously as both suggestion and command for the same response, resulting in a synergic effect. This situation is not to be confused with the one discussed previously. In the case of the basket of cherries the commands and suggestions aimed to produce different responses. Here, the command and the suggestion are directed at the production of the same response. For instance, we address an audience and say commandingly "You will all rise now!" This, as a command, instigates certain higher center processes which we refer to as conscious and volitional. These in turn lead to the act, the overt motor activity of rising. Now, if some member of the audience happens to be particularly suggestible, the ideational content of the command may independently give rise to neuromotor activity also leading to the act of rising, but without involving any volition. The result is an enhanced response. There is also the possibility that a sequential type of interaction takes place between voluntary and non-voluntary responses.

Suggestion in the Extended Sense. In practice the boundaries of suggestions are not always too clearly defined. Instructions and commands are usually not suggestions, but there are circumstances in which they do have all their properties. It is convenient to forego an exact distinction when the instructions and commands are made an integral part of the suggestion proper, as is usually the case. In an extended sense, we shall use the term suggestion to denote *any communication, verbal or nonverbal, simple or complex, from the suggestor to the suggestee, aimed at bringing about some experience and behavior at variance with the suggestee's environment or the behavior he would have otherwise exhibited.* It may include, as an integral part, instructions, commands, etc., if these are necessary elements for the effectiveness of the suggestion.

It needs to be emphasized that there are situations when it is really im-

---

*It is possible to argue that no volitional participation is involved and that the entire behavior sequence consists of a chain of suggestion-producing responses. While this may be the case in some instances, there is good evidence that the first alternative is the more usual one.

possible to tell whether a statement has acted as an instruction, command, or a suggestion. When a hypnotized subject is told "Stiffen your arm" and he does this, he may be following instructions in a normal, volitional manner, or he may be responding reflex-like to a suggestion while his thought processes have little to do with the response. The subject himself may not be able to tell which applies. It does not make too much difference practically, so long as the end result is what we seek. For this reason, in practice, the term "suggestion" is used in a very broad sense to include combinations of suggestions proper and instructions of a nonsuggestive character.

Suggestion as Surrogate. This extended definition of suggestion brings up the "as if" character of the elicited response. I have previously[191] subsumed this under the description of the suggestion as a *surrogate* stimulus. By this it was meant that suggestions call forth responses which, under other circumstances (the absence of suggestions), would not take place, but which constitute at the same time an adequate response to other non-present stimulus-situations. This particular view characterizes suggestions rather well in many situations and can be a useful way of analysis; however, there are also instances where the concept must be stretched far more than is desirable in order to make it fit. In retrospect, it now seems more correct to say that certain classes of suggestions can also be defined as surrogate stimuli, but it is a question whether this can be said in all instances.

Suggestion is More than an Ideational Stimulus. Thus far we have dealt with suggestion primarily at a level of definition and description in which we have emphasized its properties as an ideational stimulus. I have tried to point out in what ways a stimulus functioning as a suggestion differs at the observational level from a stimulus not functioning as such, and we have seen that the very same stimulus can have either type of function. To be more concrete and specific, consider the postural sway suggestion. Under most circumstances telling a person that he or she is falling backward simply does not lead to this person falling or even appreciably swaying. Yet under essentially "identical" conditions the very same assertion, word for word, seems to be instrumental in bringing it about. Obviously, there must be something different in the two situations which therefore are not really identical. What is this factor?

Many years ago, Lipps[112] made the important observation that it was not the arousal of certain ideas which was characteristic of suggestions, but rather a psychic effect which resulted from the arousal of these ideas and which normally did not result from the arousal of ideas in general. Lipps went on to develop a theory of selective inhibition which he identified as this psychic effect. In expanding upon these notions, Jones[96] takes the position that this inhibition is the result of the subject's concentration upon the idea of the operator (suggestor or hypnotist). He interprets this concentration on the idea of the operator as consisting of an emotional bond which he calls "rapport." A stimulus which gives rise to ideas is in itself not a suggestion unless "rapport" is present—it is a peculiar attitude on the part of the subject toward the operator and is the missing element we spoke of earlier. Expanding upon this view in a later paper[95] Jones sees suggestions as comprising three processes, an emotional "rapport" between subject and operator, an acceptance of the suggested idea and, finally, the ultimate effect realized by the idea after it has been incorporated into the personality. He identified the first of these processes with Durand de Gros's[40] notion of "hypotaxia," and the second with the latter's concept of "ideo-plasty."

It seems to me that we can agree that something else besides the arousal of ideas occurs in the subject when a suggestion is given, unless this something else is already present. In its most spectacular and extreme form, this additional element is the state of hypnosis. I like to think here in terms of Durand de Gros's hypotaxia which includes hypnosis as well as other induced states.

I think we can also agree that whatever is responsible for this additional element does not reside in the physical aspect of the ideational stimulus, and more specifically in the signs used to arouse the ideas. The conclusion all this leads to is that the extra element has its origin in the attendant conditions associated with the stimulus proper, in the setting in which the stimulus acts. Many things which make up the setting can prepare an individual to be receptive to suggestions—the creation of a positive disposition, a passive, receptive "attitude," a positive affect toward the operator, a cooperative state of mind, transference, and so forth. All are part of what I like to call the *suggestion-situation*, or, for short, suggestion.

When we analyze the postural sway situation more carefully, we see immediately that there is nearly always more than just the statement, "you are falling backward." We usually make it to a person who has specifically volunteered to submit to its influence. In any event, it is usual to precede the suggestion by such instructions as, "be relaxed," "keep your mind a blank," "just listen to what I say," "pay attention to nothing else but my voice," "just let yourself go," and so forth. In many instances the subject is a patient and the hypnotist is a therapist. They may have interacted as such for some time before any suggestioning is attempted, and, as will be seen later, in the giving of suggestions one very frequently, if not always, makes use of all sorts of devices* to bring about receptivity, which serve to alter the subject's perception of the situation, if nothing else. Thus, in the final analysis a suggestion is neither stimulus nor setting per se, but is the *structured totality of the stimulus-setting.* The setting prepares the subject to receive the "suggestion." The suggestion is not just the words or ideas, but a complex process, an entire pattern of interaction, of which the words and signs are only a small part.

In many ways the suggestion-situation is normally structured to bring about the state of receptivity that Durand de Gros, Jones, and others have spoken about. The induction of hypnosis is only one of many ways of doing this and, as will be seen presently, it itself usually involves a prior structuring. Considered in its most general aspects, this structuring or hypotaxia-producing process is an ongoing process in which feedback plays a basic role. It seems unnecessary to expand upon this point at present, it will become increasingly obvious to the reader as he goes further. This state of affairs is not really too surprizing now that we have come to think of responses as being a function of apperception and of the situation as a whole. A response is to a stimulus-situation complex, not to a "stimulus" per se. Suggestion is only a special instance of this observation.

Brief Working Definition of Suggestion. This treatment of suggestion should make it clear why it is difficult to satisfactorily define this concept. It would have been easy to merely state, as one definition does, that a suggestion is an idea which is uncritically accepted and acted upon by an individual. I suspect that properly interpreted this says all that has been stated in the previous pages. But how many readers would have interpreted it in these terms? As an alternative I would like to now offer a somewhat longer definition which is still reasonably brief while preserving some of the major ideas which have been presented.

A suggestion is a stimulus in the form of a meaningful statement or gesture (sign) made by one individual, the suggester, and directed at another, the suggestee, such that the idea or group of ideas it evokes initiates alterations of mental processes or of behavior in the suggestee in the absence of conscious, voluntary participation, and such that these alterations are neither innate nor acquired "normal" (adequate) responses to this stimulus.

To this might be added the following companion definition:

Suggestibility is an individual's capacity to respond to suggestions.

---

*Under "devices" are included certain techniques referred to by some writers as "tricks" or "hocus pocus;" the use of drugs, hyperventilation, physical relaxation, sensory fixation, etc.

THE RESPONSE TO SUGGESTIONS

Subjects, particularly when hypnotized, react in a variety of ways to the statements made to them by the hypnotist. Usually, these statements are to the effect that the subject will have or is having certain experiences, will do certain things, or will both have the experiences and do these things. Some individuals do not respond at all to any suggestion. They have no experiences, nor do they feel any need to carry out any of the suggested acts. These persons are usually said to be *nonsuggestible* (or *insusceptible* to hypnosis*). At the other extreme are two categories of subjects who respond fully to some or all suggestions and who are said to be *suggestible* (or *susceptible* to hypnosis). Those who lose all awareness of themselves and their surroundings, at least to the degree called for by the suggestions, experiencing whatever is suggested very vividly, with a strong quality of reality, including responses intended to be overt;† and those other individuals who also have very vivid experiences, but express many of these in overt motor behavior, performing whatever motions have been suggested. If, for instance, the suggestion is one of being out on a lake catching many fish, the first type will have this very experience but will not show the least sign of it at the time; on the other hand, the second kind will go through the actual motions of casting a line, reeling in the fish, and so forth, while having at the same time corresponding sensory experiences.

Many individuals who do not feel that they have been influenced by the suggestions and who, as a matter of fact, have not shown any sign that they have been, say so, often spontaneously. There is another group who, although they do not feel that they are being or have been influenced by the suggestions, do not volunteer this information, proceeding instead to "act out" the instructions or suggestions as if they were being influenced. They simulate the suggested effects by behaving in the manner they believe is expected. Even when questioned directly about the effects of the suggestions, these subjects often give false reports, not always being aware of doing so. This is the type of reaction to suggestions that some psychologists prefer to call "role playing."‡ It is frequently possible to get these subjects to admit

---

*Because, as will be seen later, there is a close relationship between suggestibility and capacity to become hypnotized.

†In other words, every aspect of the suggestion is hallucinated and kept at the sensory level. These experiences can be extremely real, so much so that the subject may later on have difficulty in reconciling these with his knowledge of where he actually is. Some subjects even refuse to accept them as only hallucinations.

‡One should take care not to confuse "role playing" with another type of situation which

their pretense and to talk about it. One of the interesting facts that is uncovered when this is done is that the suggestions did have some influence after all. Although the individual may stoutly deny that he was ever influenced, there is considerable evidence that the suggestions did have an effect. This influence takes a rather peculiar form, that of a compulsion, often quite strong, to give actuality to the suggested idea, if not through an actual experience, at least symbolically. The subject is frequently aware of the compulsion and can be led to talk about it; in other instances he has no such awareness, although its presence can be demonstrated in various ways.

This compulsion, with its attendant tendency to role play, was not entirely unknown to early investigators. Gibier[68] discussed it in very definite terms, de Rochas[145] also showed that he was well aware of this aspect, referring to Gibier's comments and calling attention to a very interesting report made by a hypnotic subject in 1895, containing a very clear description of compulsive role-playing.

Why do some individuals role play? If a subject is unable for one reason or another to produce certain suggested phenomena, yet feels strongly compelled to do so, role playing, as a compromise solution, may have a certain need-reducing capacity. In other instances, role playing appears to be a defense against ego-threatening aspects of the hypnotic situation.* In many cases the subject's subsequent denial of any influence can be seen as the result of repression. In some cases one can detect certain underlying elements of hostility, where one may suspect that transference, if not responsible for role playing, at least contributes to its character. This is an area where data are very inadequate and much must be left unsaid, although it does seem clear that in most, if not all, instances, role playing is a bona fide response to suggestion as defined earlier, representing a suggestive influence as real as that in a nonsimulated response.

The cases considered thus far represent the extremes in the response domain. In practice every possible gradation and variation is observed.

---

arises fairly frequently where the subject essentially makes an admission of role playing as a form of rationalization of his behavior. Upon being told that he cannot raise his hand he may make some sort of ineffectual attempt to do so, then will declare: "Well, I could really lift it if I wanted to." If questioned about this statement, he may then add that he just does not feel like making the effort, or give some other excuse. If pressed further he may show signs of irritation, may repeat what he has already said, think up something more, or will simply say that he just feels like going along with the suggestion.

*Specific reference is made here (and elsewhere in this section) to hypnosis, not because the feature under consideration is specific to hypnosis, but because it is most clearly observed in connection with it. What is being said in this section is true of suggestion in general.

The experiences which arise from suggestions vary considerably in scope and intensity. The compulsions which are felt also range from none to very weak, to very powerful. Sometimes affect is associated with these compulsions. Many individuals show a combination of role playing and adequate response. This frequently happens with subjects who are anything less than deeply hypnotized. They are apparently sufficiently hypnotized to feel a strong compulsion to produce the suggested phenomena, yet not sufficiently so to produce an adequate response. They usually relinquish their role playing as soon as they reach the deeper states. In some cases, probably more common than one may realize, the role playing takes the form of an exaggeration of a weak adequate response. For instance, the subject reports seeing a very black, sharply delineated circle on a blank card when this is suggested, although actually only a poorly defined, shadow-like, grayish, washed-out image is experienced. Or again, upon being told that his body is so heavy that he cannot get up from his chair, the subject goes fully along with the suggestion although he experiences a real but only relatively slight heaviness and could easily get up. One particular form of role playing which often occurs is when the subject makes no actual effort to test the reality of the suggestion, merely agreeing that the suggestion is effective but shying away from demonstrating it.

It must be noted that this type of behavior is not always indicative of role playing. In many cases it is probably the result of an inhibition of the subject's ability to will himself to counteract the suggestion. It could also be a defense against the ego-threats inherent in the situation—as long as the test is not made the subject can fancy himself still in control of the situation. To test is to face an unpleasant reality. Subjects will often offer all sorts of rationalizations for not testing which, in some instances, may be symptomatic of "passive" hypnosis. Hypnotized subjects are sometimes described[191] as falling into two categories in terms of the quality and strength of their responses: those who develop "passive" hypnosis and tend to be relatively unresponsive, to give weak, partial, abortive responses and generally to show a diathesis for passivity; and those who develop "active" hypnosis who respond rapidly, give strong reactions and carry them to completion.

Other aspects of responses to suggestions will be taken up in connection with various techniques.

NATURE OF HYPNOSIS

HYPNOSIS DEFINED

There are two ways of approaching the definition of hypnosis, descriptively and operationally. Each has its merits and will be used below.

Descriptive Definition. HYPNOSIS IS A CONDITION OR STATE OF SELECTIVE HYPERSUGGESTIBILITY BROUGHT ABOUT IN AN INDIVIDUAL (SUBJECT) THROUGH THE USE OF CERTAIN SPECIFIC PSYCHOLOGICAL OR PHYSICAL MANIPULATIONS OF THIS INDIVIDUAL BY ANOTHER PERSON (HYPNOTIST).

Since, as will be seen in chapter 10, self-hypnosis is equivalent to a two-person interaction in which part of the self appears to take over the role of the hypnotist, the above definition includes the case of self-hypnosis.

Although selective hypersuggestibility is a basic characteristic of hypnosis the above should not be understood to mean that there are no other equally characteristic and fundamental concomitants of this state. But to date they have not been isolated.

Operational Definition. HYPNOSIS IS A CONDITION OF SELECTIVE HYPERSUGGESTIBILITY SPECIFICALLY BROUGHT ABOUT IN AN INDIVIDUAL BY THE USE OF THE COMBINATION AND SEQUENCE OF VISUAL FIXATION UPON A SMALL TARGET-OBJECT AND SUGGESTIONS OF RELAXATION, OF VARIOUS SYMPTOMS OF SLEEP (PARTICULARLY HEAVINESS OF THE EYELIDS), OF CLOSURE OF THE EYES, AND FINALLY OF SLEEP.

In general, suggestions (or procedures) used to produce hypnosis are called *trance-inducing* suggestions (or procedures).

It is customary to use the word "trance" synonymously with "hypnosis." Tradition has also made "waking" and hypnosis polar terms so that it is customary to designate the state of not being hypnotized as "waking." This is an unfortunate choice of word since it also is synonymous with being awake or wakeful as opposed to being asleep. However, it is clear that the hypnotized individual, by not being asleep, is awake, yet by definition is not in a waking state. Although it is usually true that the waking individual is awake and hence that waking and wakefulness become indistinguishable, the two conditions do not necessarily always go together. In line with the above, one speaks of "waking suggestions" and "waking phenomena (or responses)" for suggestions given to non-hypnotized individuals and for the phenomena observed in waking subjects. Conversely, "hypnotic suggestions" and "hypnotic phenomena" are the suggestions given to hypnotized persons and the phenomena which are exhibited by the latter. One also speaks of "waking" a subject, meaning to cancel the hypnotic state or to dehypnotize him. The subject is said to be in a *deep* or a *light* hypnosis when he becomes very hypersuggestible or slightly so respectively. Very deep hypnosis is often called a "somnambulic state" or "somnambulism." A suggestion is said to be *posthypnotic* when it is given while the subject is hypnotized and in such a manner as to come into effect only at some predetermined time after the trance is terminated. Frequently a specific signal is used to activate a posthypnotic suggestion and is referred to as a "post-hypnotic signal." A phenomenon is said to be "posthypnotic" when it takes place in the waking state, or at least after a period of waking has elapsed since dehypnotization, and when it can be unambiguously associated with, or shown to have its genesis in, a previous hypnotic state. Posthypnotic phenomena can be spontaneous or suggested.

Were it not for the spectacular increase hypnosis brings about in the suggestibility of some individuals, it probably would be of little more than academic interest today. But hypersuggestibility is a major characteristic of hypnosis.

Methods for inducing hypnosis abound. A rather comprehensive review of techniques will be found in reference 192 and the reader desiring a quick preview at this time should refer to it. The main purpose of this section will be to examine the mechanics of the hypnotic process, and more specifically the dynamics of trance induction. Utilization of the trance will be explained later.

CONDITIONS FOR HYPNOSIS

Techniques of induction have been classified in various ways. One such divides them into physical, psychic and physiopsychic, with a number of further subdivisions. Another useful classification which will be used in this book distinguishes between four basic techniques, the Braid method, the Classical method, the Standard method (also called Modern method), and the Sensorimotor method.*

As a result of roughly two centuries of using and experimenting with hypnosis, workers have come to agree that certain conditions and proce-dures are capable of bringing about the hypnotic state. Five of these have been known for a long time: (1) Fixation (or concentration) of attention, (2) monotony, (3) limitation of voluntary movement, (4) limitation of the field of consciousness, and (5) inhibition; and they might be called the classical conditions. They have been used extensively in the past to "explain" hypnosis and as a basis for designing methods of hypnotizing. We shall examine whether they really bring about a state of hypnosis in the sense in which we understand it and whether they are mutually independent. Modern research[191] has led to the recognition of a sixth condition which may be designated as (6) successive response to suggestions *or their equivalents*.

The first of these conditions is specific to the Braid method which will be described briefly presently and in more detail in chapter 9. Depending

*The Sensorimotor method and related techniques fall in the Brenman and Gill[21] category of "waking methods," the others being "sleep methods."

upon theoretical biases, any one or any combination of conditions 1 through 5 could be argued as being specific to this method too.[192] Historically, however, condition 1, in the form of visual fixation, has priority. It was the taking of alternate positions regarding the bases of hypnosis which led to the use of the four remaining classical conditions. All five are characteristic of the Classical method. In essence, the Classical method places the subject in environments so structured as to bring about one or more of the conditions; this and this alone presumably brings about the hypnotic state.

A combination of all six conditions, with the sixth playing a dominant role, is characteristic of the Standard method, hence it is often referred to as the Suggestion method. The use of condition 6 alone might be said to be specific to the Sensorimotor method, itself a very recent development in the field of hypnotism. Of the four methods, the Standard method is most widely and frequently used. We shall spend most of our time examining it because it is by far the most effective in the majority of circumstances and throws the most light upon the mechanics and dynamics of hypnosis.

STANDARD METHOD. DYNAMICS OF HYPNOSIS

The first method of induction described in chapter 7 is quite typical of the Standard method. In essence one has the subject focus his attention (possibly by having him fixate a bright object), combined with suggestions aimed at bringing about closure of the eyelids, relaxation and, in general, the experience of various symptoms of natural sleep. Clearly, this method depends initially upon some waking suggestibility, and we may expect that the more suggestible the subject, the more rapid and successful the induction will be. It appears[191] that the suggestibility of the *hypnotized* individual is made up of at least three components or dimensions, the ideomotor, the heteroactive and the dissociative. Alternatively, one can think of these as different kinds of suggestibilities since the possession of any one of the components confers upon the individual a certain degree of responsiveness to suggestions. All three are intimately and dynamically interrelated and contribute to each other's manifestation. It is possible that other components not yet isolated exist, possibly one is a certain "transference" aspect which is exhibited in many hypnotic situations.

In any event, each of these components depends upon the presence of certain psychophysiological processes which we shall hereafter call *basic processes*. At any given instant, these processes may or may not be active in an individual, so that the latter will possess different amounts of each. The presence of these components, it should be added, is not entirely specific to the existence of the hypnotic state, and any or all of these can be found in some individuals who have not been hypnotized. Normally, one who has never submitted to suggestions or hypnotic procedures, or at least has not done so for some time, will possess only the ideomotor component. If others are present, they will be relatively inactive in most instances. *The induction of hypnosis consists then in nothing more than the activation and the enhancement of these components or processes, and, more generally, the creation of conditions which favor their manifestation.*

The process underlying the ideomotor component is called *ideomotor action*, the tendency of thoughts or ideas to be automatically translated, reflex-like, into specific patterns of muscular activity. Ideomotor action is probably a reflex which differs from the more common variety only in that it is elicited directly by higher center activity rather than by afferent peripheral impulses. There is strong evidence in support of the assertion that many waking suggestions act purely through ideomotor action. As stimuli, they evoke corresponding thoughts, images, etc., which in turn act as cue-producing responses, and evoke actual motor responses. Eysenck's investigations of suggestibility have led to distinguish between three types of suggestibilities, *primary*, *secondary*, and *tertiary* suggestibility. Primary suggestibility is specific to hypnosis and certain waking suggestions, such as that of postural sway. Ideomotor action appears most likely to be the process underlying primary suggestibility.[191]

An important property of ideomotor action (*homoaction*) is that, within limits, the elicitation of a submaximal* ideomotor response enhances a subsequent response of the same kind, provided it is elicited within a certain interval of time. If the response of a subject to a suggestion is submaximal, it tends to enhance his response to the same suggestion when repeated within a certain interval of time. Homoaction accumulates with multiple repetitions of a suggestion, the accumulation having an asymptotic limit. It is also believed to decay with time if further suggestions are not given. Since the effect is cumulative, it is possible to start out with a submaximal response, one which may even be too weak to be overt, and enhance it by repetitions of the suggestion until it becomes maximal, or at least overt. Homoaction would appear to be one of the main reasons for using repetition in giving suggestion.

Since repetition is indeed a characteristic feature of suggestions, one

---

*It must be clearly understood that the magnitude itself of the response has no essential function aside from the fact that if the response was maximal to start with it would be impossible, by definition, to observe an enhancement.

is at first prone to conclude that this is the mechanism by which waking suggestibility is converted into hypnotic hypersuggestibility. This, however, is only part of the story for, as we have seen, hypnotic hypersuggestibility is a much more complex phenomenon. Ideomotor action, even when homoactively increased, does not account for all of its properties.

The ideomotor component usually appears to make up the greater part, if not all of the waking suggestibility of individuals when they first come into contact with a hypnotist. There are reasons, however, for believing that when an individual is made to respond to a number of suggestions, a progressively increasing tendency for him to respond to other suggestions arises. We shall call this effect *heteroaction*. It can also be spoken of as a generalization of suggestibility. Several processes probably contribute to it, one of which may be the recently reported phenomenon of *abstract conditioning* which can be briefly described in the following manner: If for *any reason*, a person carries out an act or has an experience when another person makes a statement in which the idea of the act or of the experience is present or implied, and the two events are closely juxtaposed in time, there is created, through a conditioning process, a tendency for the first individual to *reflexively* exhibit motor and sensory responses associated with the ideational content of *other* statements made by the second person. In the case of suggestions the conditioning probably takes place with respect to two aspects of the suggestion-situation, the origin of the suggestion and the fact that the statements are suggestions given in a suggestion setting. That is, conditioning takes place with respect to not just a stimulus, but to the class of stimuli characterized by the fact that each stimulus is a group of ideas emanating from the hypnotist in a suggestion setting; and the conditioned, adequate response is actualizing or giving maximal reality to these ideas. In brief, the subject learns (is conditioned) to give reality within his personal limitations and those of the setting in which he is to the ideas presented by the hypnotist. As we shall see presently, hypnotic behavior probably often becomes strongly motivated and the subject not only learns but becomes strongly compelled to give this reality-producing response. Much of hypnotic behavior is best understood if one keeps in mind that as a rule the subject will try giving reality to the best of his ability to the suggested ideas and, if he cannot, will give the nearest and best possible approximation. This may consist in a vivid hallucination, very exact role-playing, or some other substitute behavior.

Although abstract conditioning is not specific to the hypnotic situation, the latter appears to be particularly favorable for its production and manifestation. It is very significant that this process apparently takes place not only if the initial response is an adequate one, but also if it is a volitional act or if it is brought about by agencies other than suggestion.

Because of the presumed nature of the underlying process, heteroaction is a reflexive process whose action is also superimposed upon or added to homoaction and may be confounded with it. Indeed, it may be that the reported "homoactive" effect of voluntary responses is in reality "hetero-active."

If an individual can be brought to respond to a set of suggestions through such a process as ideomotor action, this can be used as a basis to initiate abstract conditioning and hence bring about heteroaction. As abstract conditioning progressively develops and expands its domain, one observes a growing generalization of suggestibility. This is the key to the process of trance induction by the Suggestion method which I have proposed earlier.[191] Confronted with an individual who usually possesses only a limited innate suggestibility of the ideomotor kind, the hypnotist, in order to increase the corresponding component of suggestibility through homoaction and to bring about overt responses, begins by acting upon the ideomotor process. The goal of induction is to bring about as great a generalization of suggestibility as possible. For this, strong, clear-cut, overt responses are desirable. Many individuals at first give weak, partial, abortive, poorly defined and often nonovert responses. Homoaction serves to eradicate these features. But more basic is the fact that rarely does the subject respond overtly, even partially, to the first statement of the suggested idea. Ideomotor action is strictly at the level of individual neuromotor units and must be built up to encompass large groups of these as well as to integrate their action before overt responses become evident. Once this has taken place in regard to a few suggestions heteroaction sets in and adds its threefold effect, enhancing homoaction for responses already established, bringing additional responses into the subject's repertoire and, by this last, furnishing a new basis for further conditioning. It is, so to speak, a self-generating and self-enhancing process. The subject is now well on the way to becoming hypnotized.

Most individuals do not respond equally well to all suggestions. As will be seen in greater detail later (chapter 6) it is possible to grade suggestions on the basis of the ease with which one can obtain a response to them. From the standpoint of suggestibility this is the same as grading them on the basis of the amount of suggestibility an individual must have to be fully affected by them. It is also possible to choose a set of suggestions requiring different degrees of suggestibility and to give them consecutively to the subject in such an order that each suggestion never requires more sugges-tibility than he has at the time, yet always requires a little more suggestibility than the previous one. According to the theory which has just been outlined such a procedure should be highly favorable to the generalization of suggestibility and should lead to a definite rise in suggestibility. This has been found to be true and many hypnotists use this procedure as a way of preparing subjects, that is, of creating the most favorable conditions for the induction of hypnosis or for the administration of the more complex and difficult waking suggestions.

It has been remarked that homoaction and particularly heteroaction are not specific to adequate responses to suggestions but will also occur when the suggested response is brought about through some other agency, including conscious voluntary effort. This has an important application. It means that if we can get a subject with relatively weak suggestibility to respond by such means we may be able to raise his suggestibility to a point where his responses eventually become entirely determined by the basic processes already discussed. As will be seen later, this is the main rationale for the so-called use of "deception" in hypnotic procedures.

Thus far we have spoken of only two of the three components of hypnotic suggestibility. As the above events progress, a third important process, which I call *dissociation of awareness** probably enters into the picture to give the final touch to the hypnotic state. It appears to be an essential constituent of deep hypnosis and consists in essence in a selective constriction of awareness which excludes all but the hypnotist as a source of stimulation. The focusing of attention, monotony, and the remainder of the classical conditions, if truly effective, would seem to be specifically conducive to this type of dissociation. Of particular interest is the fact that when present in conjunction with the other two basic processes, dissociation of awareness appears to bring about a condition which Kubie and Margolin[103] have aptly described as an extension of the subject's ego into that of the hypnotist. This very likely can serve as a meeting point for nonanalytic and analytic interpretations of hypnosis and suggestibility. Actually, as will be seen shortly, to be in full agreement with psychoanalytic theory one should substitute "superego" for "ego" in the above. For a fuller account

---

*The concept of dissociation, as widely used as it has been, remains a poorly defined notion. By "dissociation of awareness" I mean a segregation or separation off from awareness (or consciousness) of a group of mental processes. I have used the above expression because I conceive of awareness as being a process which can and is continually being associated with or dissociated from other mental activities. In the induction of hypnosis there seems to be a stage during which consciousness is highly constricted or restricted, that is, dissociated from that which would normally constitute its content.

of this still poorly understood aspect of hypnotic induction as well as of the overall theory just outlined, the reader is referred to reference 191.

The final outcome of any trance induction depends largely upon the extent to which each of these processes has taken place. Some individuals may develop each one to a high degree, others may never go beyond heightened ideomotor action, some may show nothing more than weak ideomotor action. In addition to the basic processes there are a number of factors which have a definite influence upon the production of hypnosis and upon the general manifestations of suggestibility. These factors may be altered and manipulated, within limits, in order to enhance the subject's suggestibility. They include the attitudes, expectancies, fears, needs and defenses of the subject. We will have much more to say about these later in more pertinent contexts, but we can point out at this time that this is the reason why instructions and suggestions given during the process of trance induction are not always aimed directly at the three basic processes. For instance, they may be aimed at reducing some of the normal anxiety that subjects feel in a new situation.

It should be emphasized that this description is primarily concerned with the induction of hypnosis by means of the Standard method and it has been implicitly assumed that the subject initially has little else than some capacity for ideomotor action. However, some individuals seem to come to the hypnotist with a certain amount of generalized suggestibility and/or a high capacity for dissociation of awareness. The consequence is that some individuals show a high suggestibility from the very start and hypnosis may be readily induced through a briefer technique. It should be kept in mind, however, that a rapid induction need not indicate that a deep trance will follow. Presumably, a very deep trance requires the presence of dissociation of awareness and possibly more, but on the other hand, eyelid closure and even more complex responses may be readily brought about when hetero-action alone has developed. Usually we expect a subject to develop the hypnotic state in a step-wise fashion, passing through what are often referred to as stages, phases or degrees of hypnosis (chapter 6). There is a possibility that some persons will develop the dissociation of awareness without the other two basic processes being activated. This could account for some cases of so-called "passive hypnosis." On the other hand, as Hull[85] has suggested, some of these cases may be the result of natural sleep being mixed with the hypnotic state.

In summary, the Standard method, which consists of a combination of sensory fixation and sleep suggestions, appears to bring about hypnosis by activating at least three processes, ideomotor action and homoaction, heteroaction (probably in the form of abstract conditioning), and dissociation of awareness, more or less in this sequence. The dissociation of awareness is brought about largely by the concentration of the subject's attention upon the fixation target, the suggestions and the person of the hypnotist. The other two processes are primarily activated by the giving of the suggestions and the subsequent responding of the subject to them. Such factors as attitudes, beliefs, expectancies, and so forth can help or hinder the activation and the manifestation of the basic processes. There exists a complex interaction between processes, factors and between factors and processes in which feedback plays an important role. The reader will find in figure 1 an attempt to present this summary in a diagrammatic form. The heavier arrows indicate the main direction in which the various processes and factors are conceived to have their effects.

To conclude this section a few words should be said regarding post-hypnotic suggestions. Although by definition suggested posthypnotic behavior takes place after the subject has been dehypnotized, the evidence points to the fact that it nevertheless is hypnotic behavior because its initiation is always accompanied by the appearance of a trance state. Furthermore this trance has the remarkable property that it apparently is essentially a reinstatement of the hypnotic condition existing at the time the posthypnotic suggestion was given.* Thus in this sense posthypnotic behavior is really an extension over time of the subject's hypnotic behavior and the posthypnotic suggestion never ceases to be a hypnotic suggestion.

This is also the conclusion to which the theory outlined in this section leads, although on somewhat different grounds. Like any other hypnotic suggestion the posthypnotic suggestion consists of a complex of ideas presented to the subject in the context of a suggestion after he has attained, through abstract conditioning, the habit or tendency of reflexively responding to such a complex by giving the ideas maximal reality. The major difference between hypnotic and posthypnotic suggestions consists of the fact that in the latter the ideational complex includes the additional explicitly stated idea that the response will take place only after the subject has been dehypnotized. Although one is tempted to add to this the notions of latency and of signal as distinctive features, this would be incorrect since both ideas are used in many hypnotic suggestions. The subject's adequate response to the

---

*This was first reported by Gurney[77a] and substantiated by Janet,[91] Fontan and Ségard,[60a] and Erickson and Erickson.[51]

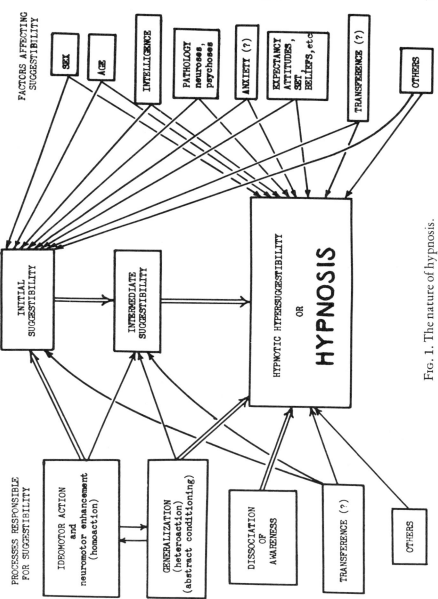

Fig. 1. The nature of hypnosis.

posthypnotic suggestion is the same as that to any hypnotic suggestion, namely, to give reality to its ideational content, hence in particular to give maximal reality to the additional feature.

But what about the spontaneous trance mentioned earlier? Clearly it is not part of the adequate response to the posthypnotic suggestion, although I suppose one might argue that through a rather remote association of ideas the notion of becoming hypnotized again might become implicit in the posthypnotic suggestion. There is, however, a better explanation. To begin, it is clear from what has just been said that abstract conditioning plays a central role in the mechanism of the retention and activation of posthypnotic behavior. Since according to the present theory abstract conditioning is essentially identified with hypnosis, the occurrence of an abstract conditioned response must of necessity bear the earmark of hypnosis. Consequently in this respect posthypnotic behavior should be associated with the characteristics of hypnosis and reinstatement follows ipso facto. Actually, as we have seen, abstract conditioning is only one of a number of dimensions each contributing something to the final character of hypnosis. Other factors also affect this character, whether or not they be dimensions. Thus, for instance, dissociation and transference will usually give the hypnotic state a very distinctive character. The possibility of redintegration would in itself lead us to expect that suggested posthypnotic behavior would show dissociation and transference features closely resembling similar features present in the original trance. In addition the conditions which exist in the learning situation which hypnosis and its utilization constitute are such that associations are really established not between the suggestion as a stimulus and the reality-giving response alone, but between the suggestion and a response complex consisting of the reality-giving response and a variety of co-existing induced effects (hence responses) in the individual. As a consequence one would again observe the presence of various symptoms of hypnosis whenever a posthypnotic act is initiated, and for obvious reasons, they would characteristically have regressive features. A more detailed discussion of this and other aspects of posthypnotic phenomena will be found in a recent article.[197a]

BRAID AND CLASSICAL METHODS. HYPOTAXIA

Thus far we have talked of the Standard method. Discussion of the Sensorimotor method shall be left to chapter 8. We will next take up briefly the two remaining methods. James Braid,[18] as we shall see in greater detail in chapter 9, found that visual fixation on a small bright object by the subject sufficed to bring about the so-called mesmeric trance, now known as hypnosis. I have called this the Braid effect. He soon came to the conclusion that it was not the visual fixation but the attendant concentration of attention which was responsible for hypnosis and that any other way of obtaining a focusing of attention would be just as satisfactory. And indeed so it has been found. Auditory, tactile, and even gustatory and olfactory stimulation, both repetitive and continuous, have been used successfully.

In later years, under the influence of Bernheim, it was denied that concentration of attention was directly responsible for hypnosis. In its stead suggestion was assumed the key to all hypnotic phenomena, including the induction of hypnosis. Accordingly, with some individuals, the prior conviction that sensory fixation brings about hypnosis acts as a suggestion and the phenomenon results. Aside from such an action, sensory fixation presumably leads to mental and sensory fatigue, this in turn predisposes the subject to feeling tired and sleepy, whereupon "sleep" is subtly suggested and ensues. In the case of visual fatigue such attendant symptoms as a burning sensation, tearing, blinking, difficulty in keeping the eyes open, and so on, are particularly effective, all acting as so many suggestions of oncoming sleep. Since the Standard method consists in suggesting, among other things, fatigue and sleepiness, the above symptoms, and closure of the eyes, it is easy to see how visual fixation might work by simply reinforcing the suggestions.

These are certainly possible modes of operation which must be kept in mind. But are they the only way in which sensory fixation brings hypnosis about, or is there an additional, more basic effect? Two questions may be asked: Can hypnosis be induced by concentration of attention alone, and if not, is concentration of attention essential for all trance inductions?

We have to go back to Braid's original descriptions of his experiments to throw light upon the first question. According to these, the Braid effect shows an initial phase during which suggestions are effective, and a later phase in which the subject is unresponsive. Braid speaks of this phase as a state of stupor (or torpor). It also appears from these early reports that, if suggestions of any kind are given at a certain fairly critical time, the Braid effect becomes limited and the stage of torpor is never reached. There is evidence in Braid's writings that the initial phase is one of hypersuggestibility. Now, the Standard method of trance induction possesses a very interesting and important feature. Suggestions are given from the very start while the subject is fixating on the target-object and also concentrating on the words and the hypnotist. This insures that suggestions are always given whenever the critical stage in the Braid effect due to the focusing of attention is reached and consequently the Braid effect is automatically limited to its suggestibility phase. It is for this reason too that one rarely, if ever, observes the second phase when using the Standard method. It is possible, as will be seen later, to bring about a stuporous condition by means of additional procedures when using this induction technique. Conceivably, although not demonstrated, this condition is the same as the second phase of the Braid effect.

It was the first phase of the Braid effect to which Durand de Gros[40] referred when he used the term *hypotaxia* to denote the stage of preparation of the subject to become receptive to suggestions. The stage which followed was that of actual action by suggestions and called *ideoplasty*. The two stages constituted hypnosis proper. Durand de Gros believed that hypotaxia had an organic basis and could be brought about by a large variety of agents. Visual fixation was one, but so were monotonous sounds and suggestions. Indeed, all of the classical conditions for hypnosis were considered to be hypotaxia-producing conditions. Whether there are really five distinct classical conditions, however, is not clear. Their existence has been arrived at consensually rather than experimentally. It is very difficult to set up one of these conditions without producing the others too, and it may well be that we are dealing here only with five alternative ways of describing a single condition. A step toward empirical verification in this area has been made by Lovell and Morgan[113] who studied the effects of regularly recurring sounds upon the human organism. The main effect they noted was the induction of a significant degree of relaxation and that a large percentage of the subjects became drowsy. There may therefore be some basis for believing that monotony, at least, can bring about hypnosis.

To conclude this discussion of the Braid effect, if the latter does exist as a phenomenon apart from suggestion it most likely is identifiable with the dissociation of awareness to which we referred earlier. It was proposed at the time that hypnotic hypersuggestibility consists of at least three components, one due to ideomotor action and homoaction, one produced by abstract conditioning, and one resulting from dissociation of awareness. These might be respectively designated as *ideomotor hypersuggestibility*, *conditional hypersuggestibility*, and *dissociative hypersuggestibility*. All three are forms of hypotaxia. Whereas the Braid method involves only one, dissociative hypersuggestibility, the Standard method makes use of all three. But insofar as hypnosis is a condition of induced hypersuggestibility, any of these processes alone could be used as the basis of a hypnotic condition and we must answer the second question raised earlier negatively. That is, concentrated attention does not appear theoretically to be essential for all trance inductions.

SUGGESTIBILITY CONTINUUM—
WAKING VS. HYPNOTIC SUGGESTIBILITY

It is rather important to have a clear understanding of the relationship suggestibility holds to hypnosis. There exists a controversy of long standing in this regard which seems to have originated with Bernheim,[10] who contended that hypnosis did not have any reality apart from suggestion. This position was quite in contrast to that held by Charcot and his school. The latter saw hypnosis as a pathological manifestation of the nervous system. Equally at the opposite end was Freud[64] who, although a former student of Bernheim, insisted that suggestion is only a "forme fruste" of hypnosis.

There seems to be little question now that hypnotic, or at least hypnotic-like, phenomena can be brought about without going through typical induction procedures. The Sensorimotor method is evidence of this. Definite evidence suggests that it is possible to begin with simple waking suggestions, proceed to increasingly complex ones and, without ever saying a word about sleep, relaxation or anything else usually associated with the induction of a trance state, conclude with a subject in relatively deep hypnosis. That is, the subject passes gradually from waking into hypnosis with no clear transition being evident. The reason why this is possible should be clear from what has already been said—the subject's repeated responses to suggestions raise his suggestibility through homoaction and heteroaction. Although visual fixation of a bright object seems to have been the traditional method for bringing about the dissociation of awareness and is thus incorporated in the Standard method, it most likely is not essential. Braid, who originated this technique, was inclined to believe that visual fixation was merely a device for obtaining a concentration of attention, the all-important factor. The same result can be obtained through auditory stimulation; even the words of the hypnotist can presumably serve for this purpose. One often instructs the subject to pay close attention to the words of the suggestions. Thus, the subject's concentration on the suggestions and other instructions might be expected to bring about some degree of dissociation. I observe that those who are susceptible to hypnosis tend to become progressively more involved in the suggestion situation and to participate more and more completely in it, until they seem to submerge completely in it. In this way an increasing restriction of awareness develops which may or may not be distinct from the focusing of attention just discussed. It is not clear whether this effect is independent of or a function of the subject's growing suggestibility. The monotony of repetition which supposedly induces hypnosis, most likely through the production of the dissociated state, is another possibility.

In any event, this seems to be one sense in which one may say that all hypnotic phenomena can be brought about by waking suggestions. This, however, does not necessarily mean that there is no hypnotic state per se. Thus far, it must be admitted, objective measures aimed at differentiating hypnosis from nonhypnotic conditions have been relatively unsuccessful.[191] Aside from the criterion of hypersuggestibility, there is little basis for making a distinction. For the time being we are forced to fall back upon the statement that if the *full* state of hypnosis is the resultant of three or more distinct basic processes acting sequentially and at the same time, then at any instant the distinction between waking and hypnosis depends upon deciding whether all of the processes have taken or are taking place. We can think of waking and hypnotic suggestibility as constituting a multidimensional continuum. Waking and hypnosis are then simply names for two regions in it, each lying at opposite ends. The boundary separating them is rather indefinite, indeed all one can really speak of is an in-between, borderline region. One might refer to it as partial hypnosis, mixed or hypnoidal state, etc. From a practical standpoint this is probably a matter of small importance since one is usually primarily interested in the extreme regions of the suggestibility continuum. In this suggestibility continuum ideomotor action can be thought of as constituting a sort of common core for suggestion effects in waking and in hypnosis.

One aspect of hypnosis which has probably done more than anything else to confuse the picture in regard to its relation to suggestibility is the fact that, presumably, there are a number of ways to activate the various processes which make up the complex state called hypnosis, of which the Standard method is only one. Not all of the existing methods necessarily activate all of the basic processes, nor the same ones. When they do, the processes which are activated may be in different sequences and activated to different degrees in each case. Braid's method may bring about a condition which has some features common to those of the state induced by the Standard method, while in other respects the two conditions may be quite different. The same is probably true for the Classical method and for methods in which narcotic drugs are employed. It is important not to confound these various conditions, at least not until it has been shown beyond doubt that they are identical in all respects.

In any case, the existence of two or more essentially different methods of producing hypnosis leads to a problem in nomenclature. For reasons of priority I shall designate the conditions described by Braid as the "Braid effect." Alternatively, one might speak of different *types* of hypnosis, as Kline[97] does.

HYPNOIDAL STATE AND HYPNOIDIZATION

It is common practice today to speak of the lowest depth of hypnosis as a *hypnoidal* state as originally defined by Davis and Husband.[36] In a sense this term involves a contradiction because etymologically it implies a condition which is neither waking nor true hypnosis, but lies between the two; yet it is used as a descriptive measure of the depth of hypnosis. Quite apart from this, however, there exists a basic problem regarding its nature and relation to hypnosis.

The term hypnoidal seems to have been originated by Sidis.[168,169] He speaks of hypnoidal states as being intermediate and transitional states between waking, sleep and hypnosis. He also refers to them as *subwaking* states. Phylogenetically speaking, he says the hypnoidal state is the primitive or primordial "rest-state" from which sleep and hypnosis became differentiated. The more primitive an animal is, the more hypnoidal-like is his sleep state. As animals have evolved, sleep has proven to be of value whereas hypnosis has turned out to be either dangerous or valueless, hence it has been eliminated as part of the normal adjustment of the organism. As a consequence, he considers sleep and hypnoidal states as normal, whereas hypnosis and trance states, in general, are seen as subnormal. Although, according to Sidis, the hypnoidal state *is not* hypnosis, it is characterized by suggestibility because of its intermediate nature. In other respects, it is the equivalent of sleep.

The hypnoidal state, says Sidis, can be brought about by any of the following conditions, used singly or in combination, monotony, limitation of voluntary movements and limitation of the field of consciousness. The hypnoidal state is characterized by catalepsy, which may be transient and hardly perceptible. It always gives way to sleep or *hypnosis*. Whether one gets one or the other as a consequence of inducing a hypnoidal state is determined by whether the threshold for stimulation of activity is raised (sleep) or decreased (hypnosis). In turn, the fall in psychomotor threshold is a function of a predisposition to, and the further *cultivation* of, "dissociation" in the individual. If this predisposition and/or "cultivation" is absent, the hypnoidal state passes into natural sleep.

These conditions apply not only to adult humans but, according to Sidis, work equally well on children, even infants, and upon animals of all sorts. This is important because, on the basis of this and other remarks, there can be no doubt that what he calls a hypnoidal state in animals has the same properties as what has generally been included under the expression "animal hypnosis" (see chapter 11). It may be of some significance that Sidis speaks of hypnoidal states in the plural. This implies the possibility that hypnoidal states in animals are not necessarily the same states as those found in man, although this seems rather unlikely from the way Sidis writes about it.

Sidis was very clear on what he meant by "hypnoidal." It is unfortunate that later investigators, such as Davis and Husband, should have chosen to use the same expression to designate a condition which has never been shown conclusively to be the same as the state Sidis speaks of. The consequence is that nowadays it is not always too clear what is being referred to when the word "hypnoidal" is used. Most investigators consider the hypnoidal state of Davis and Husband as an in-between state, bearing many points of resemblance to hypnosis, and which is the same as the condition found in drowsy states, day-dreaming, reverie, states of abstraction and so forth, although here again it has never been demonstrated that such states even involve an enhanced suggestibility as presupposed by definition. In fact, it is not even known whether all of these states are one and the same, or what their exact relation is to hypnosis. The consensus, however, seems to be that when the hypnotic state, as defined on the Davis-Husband scale of hypnotic depth (chapter 6) is attained, many of the characteristics of the above-mentioned states are seen. There is drowsiness, fluttering and closing of the eyelids, a feeling of heaviness and complete physical and mental relaxation, consciousness fluctuates considerably between the waking threshold and a condition of dreaminess, emotional excitement is very low, the subject is very passive, critical thinking is depressed and even abolished and suggestibility is enhanced.

Unfortunately, this still does not resolve the basic question: Is there a hypnoidal state, as defined by Sidis, which partakes of hypnosis, but which is not hypnosis in any sense of the word? No categorical answer seems possible at this time. Whatever evidence Sidis had for maintaining that an essential difference existed between the two conditions was never given by him clearly in any of his writings. Although we may respect his opinion on this matter, it remains an opinion which, by modern scientific standards, is largely unsupported. Neither are the arguments of modern investigators such as Kubie and Margolin[102] or Steger[173] more conclusive. Steger has compiled a list of points of similarity and dissimilarity between hypnosis and the hypnoidal state. After looking these over, I find it difficult to see how she can still claim that there is an essential difference. Individual variations in hypnotic behavior could well account for such differences as

Sidis and others have reported. Even if one could be certain that "animal hypnosis" is not the same as human hypnosis, one could not use this fact, coupled with the identity Sidis claims exists between "animal hypnosis" and hypnoidal states, because one cannot be really sure just what Sidis did produce in his human and animal subjects. There is no adequate evidence to date that the hypnoidal state is the same as hypnosis, but what evidence does exist seems to favor the view that there really is no essential difference.

RAPPORT AND HYPNOSIS

Jones[96] has asserted that "rapport" is the basic force behind suggestion. Similarly, Lipps[112] feels that it is "the relation between suggestor and suggestee . . . by virtue of which the power of suggestion is obtained." Until relatively recently it had been generally agreed among investigators and users of hypnosis that there was a condition called "rapport" which was associated with suggestions and, particularly, with hypnosis and was a very essential part of hypnosis. On the other hand, there had been considerable diversity of opinion as to what rapport is, how it functions and how it relates to hypnosis. In more recent times the need for the concept of rapport has been seriously questioned. One of the reasons for this diversity of opinion probably results from the fact that rapport manifests itself in a great many ways. In his famous work on rapport, Moll[127] begins by remarking that the phenomena which are subsumed under this term are so varied that no single definition is possible, that one can best comprehend its meaning through examples. He then proceeds to devote the next 235 pages of a monograph to the clarification of this concept. Anyone particularly interested in this topic should read his work. For the purposes of the present chapter, something less involved seems indicated.

Since rapport has acquired a number of meanings throughout the years, depending upon the context in which it has been used, it seems valuable to begin by making a distinction between *hypnotic rapport* and other forms of rapport of which we shall say no more. Hereafter, "rapport," as used in this text, will always denote hypnotic rapport unless otherwise specified.

Rapport, as it relates to hypnosis and as understood in the traditional sense, can probably be best described as a condition or state of affinity between subject and hypnotist which is present at the *onset* of hypnosis, of such a nature as to preclude the relating of the subject to any stimulus source other than the hypnotist himself, unless the latter instructs the subject otherwise; or such that the capacity to relate to stimuli originating from the hypnotist is much larger than the same capacity with respect to other stimuli. Moll[127] speaks of "isolated rapport" when the subject responds to only the hypnotist, and of plain "rapport" when the subject responds strongest to the hypnotist but may still respond more weakly to stimuli originating from other sources.

Stated somewhat more concisely, rapport might be said to designate a *differential or selective and enhanced responsiveness of the subject to stimulation by the hypnotist, usually in association with a variable amount of affect, presumed to coincide with the appearance of hypnosis.*

At one time, rapport was considered to be a criterion for the presence of hypnosis. For many investigators it was symptomatic, an attendant phenomenon. For others it was a sine qua non for hypnosis, being the primary condition underlying hypnotic hypersuggestibility. There were also others however, who saw it as an artifact and believed that it was by no means an essential feature of hypnosis or even symptomatic of it. The question whether there can be hypnosis without rapport has been answered positively on three grounds.

Quite early in the controversy the argument was raised that rapport was a suggested phenomenon of hetero- or of autosuggestive character, very much as Charcot's classical symptoms of the "grand hypnotisme," as discussed in chapter 9. But as Moll, among others, remarked, rapport can be observed in situations where the possibility of suggestion can be eliminated. As for the argument that the concentration of attention on the idea of the hypnotist gives rise to an autosuggested idea of isolation, this is not only a rather farfetched explanation, but would require an unjustified revision of the entire concept of suggestion and of associative phenomena, as Moll[126] justly observed.

A second argument offered in support of the notion that hypnosis can be present even though rapport is absent has been based on the notion that rapport can be "broken," meaning that the subject becomes unresponsive to the hypnotist with respect to some or all of his statements. If this can occur without the hypnotic state vanishing, some investigators feel the point would be proven. The only empirical data offered to date in support of this contention is not really pertinent to this question, unless one defines "rapport" to specifically refer to the acceptance and carrying out of a suggestion.[191] Rapport is then said to be "broken" if the suggestion is rejected. This notion of rapport, however, is quite different from the traditional concept. Furthermore, leaving out this consideration, it seems to me that there is a circularity involved in this kind of proof because, if rapport is an essential characteristic of hypnosis, then any syndrome which possesses all the other characteristics or symptoms of hypnosis but this one must be something else than hypnosis by definition.

Finally, some investigators have maintained that since the range of stimuli to which hypnotized individuals respond is highly variable and can be made as inclusive or as restrictive as one may wish through suggestions (provided the depth of hypnosis is sufficiently great), there is really no rapport. This argument, however, is really no argument since Moll has made it very clear that traditional rapport is concerned with relative as well as absolute degrees or specificity of responsiveness.

Additionally, these various arguments against the reality of rapport fail to take into account at least two of its other basic characteristics. First, rapport is not so much concerned with the acceptance or rejection of suggestions as with the identity of the sources of stimulation to which the subject overtly reacts, whether negatively or positively. Secondly, the traditional picture of rapport is one of a condition which arises concurrently with or at the onset of hypnosis, and before any specific suggestions have been made with regard to the subject's range of responsiveness. All in all, attempts to demonstrate that rapport is not an essential part of hypnosis have been rather unproductive.

Attempts to clarify the exact nature of rapport have not been much more successful. A few recent investigators such as Hull[85] have centered their attention upon the relative responsiveness of the hypnotized subject and have interpreted rapport as a form of selective anesthesia. This, however, seems to be a questionable way of looking at rapport unless one qualifies this anesthesia as being a pseudoinsensibility, as Warren does.[187] For as Moll[126] pointed out many years ago, one can often demonstrate that although the subject is not responsive to certain stimuli in an overt manner, he also is not anesthetic to them—in some cases he may even be fully aware of them even though they do not have the power to evoke an overt response.

Other investigators, such as Lipps and Jones,[96] seem to have centered their attention upon the selective aspect of hypnotic hypersuggestibility. This approach seems to come closest to answering the question of what is traditional "rapport," but in so doing it also leads to the rather disconcerting conclusion that there is, after all, really no rapport as distinct from hypnosis per se.

As was explained earlier, when a person is hypnotized a number of processes seem to be set in motion. Two of these processes seem particularly relevant here. One is a constriction of the subject's field of awareness so that every source of stimulation beside the hypnotist is excluded. The other is a specific (classical) conditioning of the subject's responses to the verbal statements of the hypnotist. Either of these processes could be expected to lead to the specificity of response. That is to say, selectivity of responsiveness is an inherent property of hypnosis and is not distinguishable from hypnosis if we take it as being the *total outcome* of manipulations of the subject typical of trance-inducing techniques. Like hypersuggestibility, this selectiveness is an outcome of such manipulations and can be taken as one of the defining characteristics of hypnosis. It seems more correct to state therefore that hypnosis is a state of *selective hypersuggestibility* than to merely say that it is a state of hypersuggestibility.

Much of the confusion and controversy which has arisen in the past in regard to the problem of rapport seems to me to have had its root partly in the failure to recognize this fact. It made it necessary to speak of rapport as distinct from hypnosis and as an attendant phenomenon. Its true nature was hidden with the consequence that all kinds of unnecessary issues had to be raised. But no less important was the failure to clearly separate hypnosis as it manifests itself *at its onset* from the form it later takes when suggestions have been given. The hypnotic state can manifest itself in just about any form one may wish if the proper suggestions are given. The three classical stages of hypnosis described by Charcot are usually considered to be such a case. More recently it has been shown[6] that even sleep electroencephalograms can be brought about in the hypnotic state with proper instructions to the subject, although, as is well known, the electroencephalographic pattern observed at the onset of hypnosis or shortly thereafter cannot be differentiated from the one typical of the nonhypnotized, wakeful individual. This should be kept in mind for the proper evaluation of the few experiments which have been directly aimed at rapport and which have been reported as showing that the latter is not characteristic of hypnosis. As I have previously explained,[191] this conclusion was reached on the basis of behavior preceded by suggestions which, in essence, contained implicit or explicit instructions to the subject to behave as if there was no rapport, or as if rapport had properties other than those ascribed to it by tradition. Clearly, the use of such an adulterated hypnosis does not allow an inference such as the above one.

The conclusion that rapport and hypnosis are really not distinct from one another is exactly the same one reached, on somewhat different grounds, by orthodox psychoanalysis. One of the best presentations of this approach can be found in some of Jones' works. According to the psychoanalytic position, rapport is a focusing or concentration on the *idea* of the hypnotist and consists of a powerful, one-sided, emotional bond, which, Jones and other psychoanalysts argue, is nothing else than a transference manifestation; but according to them, it is only one step further to the conclusion that rapport *is* hypnosis.

It is of considerable interest and significance that the psychoanalytic interpretation emphasizes the subject's concentration of attention as the basis of rapport, for this element is common to the interpretation presented previously. This seems to be the meeting ground for non-analytic and the analytic theories of rapport and hypnosis.

The two approaches differ in the psychoanalytic emphasis on the transference or affective aspect of the subject-hypnotist interaction. Otherwise the conclusion is the same, namely that traditional rapport appears to have been merely a way of describing what we call hypnosis. A few writers, such as Jones, have felt that rapport was really the more fundamental of the two by virtue of being antecedent to hypnosis.* I do not believe one can fully decide this point as yet. If it could be shown that only suggestion can bring about hypnosis, and if the force behind it is rapport, as Jones and Lipps maintain, then one would have to agree that rapport is the more fundamental; unfortunately the necessary evidence is lacking. The only basis for a choice seems to be, at present, which of the two aspects of hypnosis one wishes to emphasize—the interpersonal or the pure stimulus-response interaction.

To go back to the main point of disagreement between the two positions, we have seen that it consists of whether or not the transference or emotional factor was fundamental to rapport or hypnosis. The theory or interpretation which has just been developed does not exclude this factor or say that it cannot play a basic role. But I think one must ask two questions: Are emotional elements of the kind posited by psychoanalysis invariably present in hypnosis (or suggestion) and, if so, to what extent are they responsible for the subject's behavior? Secondly, if such elements are present in some or all instances, are they necessarily transference manifestations?

The first of these questions must be left unanswered for the present. In regard to the second, although it is probably true that transference can give rise to the type of emotional bond and concentration on the idea of the hypnotist that Jones talks about, it is also probably true that affective responses toward any individual, as well as the concentration of attention upon his person, can arise without a transference being involved, even considering the postulated libidinal aspect of the process. Hypnosis is not an everyday variety of interaction. It may be true that, in this particular situation, transference is not only always a present, dominant factor, but is also the basis of all emotional responses toward the hypnotist. This remains to be shown, and the psychoanalytic position does not seem to be entirely justified empirically, although it may be theoretically tenable.

As noted earlier, the recognition of affective elements in the subject-

*This might look like a contradiction of Jones' assertion that rapport is hypnosis; however, one must keep in mind that for Jones it is not so much hypnosis as "suggestion" that concerns one and, as we saw, rapport is the basic force behind suggestion.

hypnotist relationship, particularly with reference to rapport, is not entirely a modern innovation. Moll essentially recognized this in his treatment of sympathy and antipathy. The mesmerists' concept of rapport* indubitably included affective elements of this kind too. Thus, the transference aspect of rapport is really an old story.

For a clear understanding of the literature on hypnosis it must be kept in mind that "rapport" has been used in a variety of ways. It may be of value to briefly summarize in conclusion some of its major meanings. In practice, then, rapport denotes: (1) an elective or selective perception; (2) the transference aspect of the hypnotic interaction; (3) a selective hypersuggestibility; and (4) an intimate, harmonious relationship without specific reference to cause or nature.

HYPNOSIS AND THE LEARNING PROCESS

In the past, learning phenomena have been related to hypnosis in two ways: the effects of hypnosis on learning have been investigated, and attempts have been made to explain suggestibility phenomena in terms of learning principles. For obvious reasons, the first of these approaches will not be of further concern to us.

Hull, probably more than any other person, was responsible for the notion that suggestion phenomena were learned, that is, were acquired responses similar to "habits." He says[85]: "The experimental evidence indicates that whatever else prestige suggestion may be, it at least is a habit phenomenon." Hull was led to make this statement because hypnotic and waking suggestions were found by his associates to "manifest the classical behavior of habituation." He went on to remark that the view he was trying to present in his final evaluation was that suggestion can be reduced "to the strictly physical basis of the associations between stimuli and responses, ideas becoming purely physical symbolic acts."

For Hull too, ideomotor action also plays a basic role in suggestion. Because, in his opinion, it comes into existence through the process of association or conditioning, he is also able to reduce this aspect of suggestion to a habit phenomenon.

A full analysis of this question unfortunately leads into intricacies of learning theory which go quite beyond the scope of this book. The general conclusion which seems to derive from it, however, is that present day learning principles are not adequate to account in full for all of the properties of suggestion, including some of the most basic. A major revision of learning

*For details, refer to Moll's work.[127]

theory would first be necessary before all suggestion phenomena could be entirely included. This is not to say that learning does not play a part in suggestibility. It is clear from the theory presented earlier that this must be so in at least two aspects of suggestibility: that in which ideomotor action enters and that in which abstract conditioning plays a part. On the other hand, these do not appear to be all there is to suggestibility or hypnosis.

In the previous question we asked whether suggestibility per se is a learned response, an acquired association between stimulus and response. There is a more indirect, third way in which learning might enter into the picture.

Many individuals can be "trained," so to speak, to attain a gradually deeper trance state over a period of several hypnotic sessions. Similarly, every subject is not equally capable of initially producing certain phenomena under hypnosis, even though relatively deeply hypnotized. Here again it is often found that one can "train" the subject to perform at a higher level.

In some instances the observed "training" can be ascribed to homo-action, further generalization of suggestibility and possibly to an implicit suggestive effect which has its root in the subject's own experience of having responded to some suggestions.* On the other hand, in most cases, I believe true learning takes place. Many years ago, investigators of learning phenomena discovered that individuals can "learn to learn." A similar phenomenon has been found to exist in the field of visual detection. It seems possible that something like "learning to enter the hypnotic state" can also take place in some or all individuals. It is not difficult to see how this might come about. Entering the hypnotic state involves a special frame of mind. It seems reasonable to assume that the more often and the more completely an individual can experience this frame of mind, the easier and more perfectly he will be able to approximate it on future occasions. We may also expect most subjects to have some anxiety at the prospect of being hypnotized which is likely to interfere with the development of an adequate trance state, but as he repeatedly experiences the hypnotic state as anything but a situation to be feared, the anxiety will lessen and, with the disappearance of this inhibiting factor, hypnotic susceptibility will appear to rise. Similarly, many individuals come to the hypnotic session with preconceived ideas of what the trance state is like. If these ideas are antagonistic to the proper development of the hypnotic condition they must be removed first for the full susceptibility to manifest itself. Here again the subject must learn what is correct and what

---

*One may prefer to say here that such experience creates a favorable set or attitude for subsequent trials, or that there is an autosuggestive effect.

is false; often this involves no more than his learning to discriminate between volitional and nonvolitional suggested activity. These few examples should give the reader an idea of the possible manner in which learning may enter into the so-called "training" of the subject.

Many hypnotists err in assuming that once a person is deeply hypnotized he can easily carry out any reasonable suggestion. Hypnosis may facilitate the acquisition of certain skills, it may make possible some which otherwise would not be, it may enhance previously acquired skills, but the subject also retains many of his basic, waking limitations. Since, however, he also retains his capacity to learn, it may be expected that he can probably acquire or perfect a skill while hypnotized, and should hypnosis facilitate this process, he will do so with unusual efficiency. Thus, improvement in hypnotic performance as a function of trials over time is normally to be expected, as is the particular effectiveness of special training procedures. In some cases it may be merely a matter of lessening inhibitions; in others of extinguishing interfering habits, improving already existing desirable habits, or, finally, teaching the subject a new skill.

To take only one example, let us consider visual hallucinations. Not infrequently one encounters individuals who, although they seem to be hypnotized to a sufficient degree, are nevertheless unable to have satisfactory visual hallucinations. Normally, one would take this fact as evidence that they have not reached a truly deep hypnotic state (chapter 6); sometimes, however, one has other reasons for believing that a deep hypnosis is really present, but that something is preventing the subject from being able to hallucinate. Regardless of the particular cause of this inability, it may be important to obtain an hallucination for one reason or another, and an effort in this direction is warranted. When the trance depth is sufficient, but the subject is unable to hallucinate to a satisfactory degree, it is frequently because this sort of experience is a threatening one for him. The hypnotist's main job here is to render it acceptable to the subject. Above and beyond this, it should be realized that in order to have hallucinations one must, essentially, undo an entire lifetime of conditioning inimical to hallucinating. According to current thinking in psychology, everyone is born with a high potential for hallucinating, indeed, in the very early stages of life, the individual presumably cannot and does not distinguish between the real and the hallucinated world. It is part of the maturation process to learn, not only to discriminate between the real and the hallucinated world, but also to keep the hallucinated world in abeyance. Concurrently, he learns to use verbal symbols in preference to sensory imagery, in his thinking processes.

Thus habits which counter hallucinatory productions are acquired quite early in life and become deeply ingrained. They must be overcome before the individual can hallucinate freely, and in some, maybe most instances, the individual may essentially have to learn what he once could do innately. Much more than this is involved, of course. This brief discussion is intended to help the reader to understand better why one can speak of "training" hypnotic subjects, even in respect to phenomena such as hallucinations.

According to some theories, learning cannot take place unless motivation is first present. As usually stated, drives (or the resulting tension states) must be reduced for learning to occur. Other theorists do not go quite as far, merely agreeing that motivation can be an enhancing factor. In any case, it may be worth looking briefly at this aspect before concluding this section. What kind of motivation or drive, if any, can be related to hypnosis? Some years ago, White[200] examined this question in detail and came to the following conclusion:

> The hypnotic subject is confronted by a situation which must be conceived not as a test but as an unusual kind of personal relationship. The central press is *dominance*, in a form which is at once extreme yet provisional. The character of this press is modified by the particular purpose of the session and by the operator's attitude which may range from coaxing to portentious domination. It is further modified by preconceptions sown in the subject's mind by rumors and literary plots, often too well rooted to be removed by instructions. The press of hypnotic dominance is likely to arouse the need for *deference*, the strength of which correlates positively with susceptibility, or the need for *autonomy*, the strength of which correlates negatively. But there is a great deal of individual variation in the tendencies which are awakened, so that manifest needs like *passivity, exhibition, sex*, or *aggression* may sometimes occupy the foreground. At the same time, hypnosis, by reason of its unusual nature, makes an appeal to certain needs which have become latent as the subject outgrew childhood. There is reason to believe that three latent infantile needs sometimes function as motivating forces favorable to hypnosis: the need for *love*, such as a child feels toward its parents, the tendency toward *passive compliance* in the presence of an elder, and the wish to participate in *omnipotence*. A latent need for *aggression*, on the other hand, works like a manifest one to oppose the operator's purpose.

In still another study,* White found that individuals who exhibit *passive* hypnosis are higher on the needs for succorance and for abasement than individuals of low hypnotic susceptibility, and also show higher anxiety and less superego integration. This constellation of relatively high anxiety, need for succorance and need for abasement is seen by White as defining the syndrome of passivity. On the other hand, individuals who possess this syndrome but, in addition, are also high on the need for deference and low

*In Murray.[130]

on the need for autonomy, are those who exhibit *active* hypnosis. Non-susceptible individuals were found to be low on the needs for counteraction, order and conjunctivity, but to be high on superego integration.

Two of White's points are particularly well taken, even if one may not agree with the needs he emphasizes. First, that the pattern of needs which is involved may be quite complex and will be largely made up of acquired rather than innate needs, and second, that all needs are not favorable to hypnosis.

White speaks of needs which belong to the nomenclature of the Thematic Apperception Test. Two other needs of this type which I believe may also enter into the picture are the need for affiliation and the need for achievement; although these may play a greater part after hypnosis has been induced than before. This notion of an underlying drive behind hypnosis can at least be traced back to Freud for it is implied in the concept of hypnosis as a transference phenomenon, and is much more explicitly stated in his assertion that the basic component of this transference is the masochistic element in the sexual drive. It is not known whether a single constant drive or a small constant group of drives is responsible for the different degrees of readiness shown by individuals entering the hypnotic state, or whether this must be ascribed to differing individual patterns of motives. In any event, although there may exist a small, invariant nucleus of motives underlying hypnosis, there is good evidence that, in addition, individuals bring to the hypnotic situation certain highly specific needs which hypnosis can satisfy. An excellent example of this is to be found in Fliess'[60] patients who spontaneously enter a hypnotic state to retreat from a threatening situation. Even if the set of needs White talks about is not the basic one, some individuals probably do enter the hypnotic state partly or even mainly because one or more of these needs are dominant in him. On the other hand, I do not believe one must, of necessity, posit that hypnosis is a motivated response, at least no more so than the knee-jerk reflex.* A structure as complex as the nervous system is likely to possess certain properties which serve no particular functions but which nevertheless may be made to manifest themselves. Hypnosis may be such a property.

The problem of motivation not only exists in regard to the induction

---

*I realize there are some who would insist upon the knee-jerk reflex as a motivated response. Even so, I think one needs to distinguish between whatever drive is involved here and the type of drives involved in, say, hunger, and particularly in the so-called acquired motive states. For one thing there is a matter of adaptive function. Also, if hypnosis is a vestigial property of the nervous system, as implied by Sidis, it may very well have lost whatever drive was initially attached to it.

of hypnosis, but also in respect to the trance state and its utilization. Unfortunately, this aspect has not been investigated at all and one can only guess that the same needs which are active in the subject's waking life will normally be active in hypnosis. This does not mean, of course, that they may not be counteracted and even displaced. Also certain needs may be enhanced and others which were only latent may now be made manifest. It may even be that needs not previously present may be brought into existence. For instance, when hypnotized many individuals appear to experience some sort of compulsion to carry out the suggestions. When the response is prevented from taking place, the subject usually develops tension which can be reduced only by acting out or removal of the suggestion. This tension can be quite great and does not appear to differ in any essential way from that associated with primary and secondary drives. One form in which this "drive" manifests itself is as an over-riding desire to please or obey the hypnotist. Failure to respond properly may be very painful for subjects who perceive this as a personal failure.

We spoke earlier of the needs which may underlie the capacity to enter into the hypnotic state. We also saw that, within limits, with repeated hypnotizations many individuals become progressively more susceptible to hypnosis. This was interpreted in terms of learning. It is possible that the original and, probably, succeeding hypnoses bring about needs which motivate the subject toward subsequent hypnosis. Many individuals who have been hypnotized seem to seek a repetition of this experience. From a few of these persons I have been able to secure information showing that hypnosis is a definite source of gratification for them; exactly how could not be determined at the time. In any case, this would appear to indicate that some sort of need to be hypnotized can arise in some persons as a consequence of being hypnotized. Such a need might be derived from the more primary need for omnipotence, as White suggests,[200] or from some other need already present. Furthermore, if hypnosis creates in the individual a strong need to carry out suggestions, or a need to please or obey the hypnotist, then the act of successfully carrying out a suggestion can be highly rewarding to the subject. In this circular manner, hypnosis can become a desirable condition by virtue of being the means to another form of gratification.

A cursory and very superficial attempt has been made to indicate the direction one might take in considering the question of the role of needs in hypnosis. Lack of empirical data does not permit us to go further, and a more extensive theoretical treatment does not yet seem warranted. Every user of hypnosis should be aware of the possible part motivation may play in hypnosis and the manner in which it may do so. Later we shall see how the subject's needs can indeed be manipulated to advantage in the production of hypnotic phenomena.

Emphasis has been placed upon essentially "normal" motive patterns. But some individuals who submit to hypnosis are deviants, a fact which may or may not be known to the hypnotist at the time. Such individuals will often come to the hypnotic session with a need system which is morbidly satisfied by the hypnotic experience, or they may subsequently develop such a pathological system. As a consequence, the motivational picture is considerably more complex than we have made it appear, particularly since pathological manifestations may appear even in essentially normal subjects.

TRANSFERENCE AND HYPNOSIS*

Kline's view on the nature of hypnosis referred to earlier is of importance in another respect, for it represents a compromise between the nonanalytic and the orthodox analytic interpretation of hypnosis. According to Kline there are two kinds of hypnosis: "instantaneous hypnosis" induced by means of "psychomechanical" methods, and "non-instantaneous hypnosis" induced by means of "psychodynamical" procedures (transference management). The standard trance-inducing technique about which we have been talking would appear at first glance to belong to the first category. Actually, however, as will soon be seen more clearly, a skillful hypnotist usually makes use of transference management and associated psychodynamic procedures as a matter of course, regardless of the basic trance-inducing technique used.

Hendrik[79] has remarked that transference is an everyday phenomenon. Similarly Nunberg[134] has stated "the tendency to 'transfer' infantile experiences into reality and to act them out can be observed not only in the transference situation but also independently of it." If this is true we would certainly expect to find some transference elements in the more than casual interpersonal relationship which is characteristic of modern† trance induc-

---

*This section, which is very technical, has been included here for the benefit of readers with psychiatric or equivalent training. Its reading is not essential for an understanding of subsequent material. Since the term "transference" has several usages in the literature, it seems best to define it in regard to its use in this book. With one minor alteration (in brackets) Warren's[187] definition appears very suitable. Accordingly, *transference* is "the development of an emotional attitude on the part of a patient toward the analyst, in the form of either an affectionate reaction (positive) or of a hostile reaction (negative), the attitude in either case being derived from earlier relations of the patient with one or both of his parents [or other 'significant others'] and not from the actual analytic situation."

†Modern methods have been singled out, not because the problem under discussion applies only to them, but because it is more significant with respect to them. With few exceptions, the same questions arise also in connection with the older methods.

tion. It seems doubtful then that instances of pure "instantaneous hypnosis" are ever found in practice. Hendrik makes a further remark which seems particularly relevant here. He states that it is the way transference is *utilized* by psychoanalysis that sets it apart from other forms of therapy, and makes transference stand out in it. Perhaps along a similar line of thinking we can say that to the extent one can distinguish clearly between techniques in which transference management plays a role and those in which it does not, one may speak of two categories of *trance-inducing procedures*. Whether two basically different hypnoses correspond to them is another matter. The effective use of transference in one form or another does not necessarily mean that it is responsible for a different kind of hypnosis than that which is obtained when it is not used, nor does it even mean that it must fall into the category of a basic process.

Whether hypnosis is ever anything more than a transference phenomenon is of more than theoretical or passing interest; it is worth briefly examining the question further at this time. I hope to touch upon some of the more salient and basic features and to help clarify the various issues. For more details on some of the finer points, the reader should refer to the original papers mentioned in these pages and to the excellent bibliographies contained in some of them. The discussions by Jones,[95,96] Fisher,[58] Wolberg,[203,204] and especially Macalpine[117] are particularly recommended. Additional references will also be found in Fenichel.[56]

Freud, and nearly every orthodox psychoanalyst, has taken the position that hypnosis is nothing more or less than a transference manifestation. He could not have stated this position more clearly than when he said,[63] "What he [Bernheim] called suggestibility is nothing else than the tendency to transference. . .," and a little later on, ". . .we have to admit that we have only abandoned hypnosis in our methods to discover suggestion again in the shape of transference."* On the other hand, it should be noted that Freud was fully aware that suggestibility is only a circumscribed aspect of a transference phenomenon since it does not include a negative aspect.

This was not Freud's first statement of this identity. The very first hint of this would seem to be a footnote in his "Three Contributions to the Theory of Sex"[62] wherein he remarked more explicitly:

> I must mention that the blind obedience evinced by the hypnotized subject to the hypnotist causes me to think that the nature of hypnosis is to be found in the unconscious fixation of the libido on the person of the hypnotizer (by means of the masochistic component of the sexual instinct).

*Freud seems to be using the terms "hypnosis" and "suggestion" interchangeably here. Actually, he came to think of suggestion as a *forme fruste* of hypnosis,[64] hence as being less basic.

It is, incidentally, the part in parenthesis which has served as the basis for later statements by students of Freud that he advocated that "femininity" is positively correlated with hypnotic susceptibility or suggestibility. At a still later date Freud[64] opined that hypnosis is like "being in love" but with the "absence of directly sexual tendencies." This he felt did not, however, account for the element of overpowering by superior force that he perceived as evident in hypnosis. To account for this element he appealed to his primal horde hypothesis, adding that hypnosis must also involve a revival of coercion by the primal father, that is, a reactivation of instinctual submission. Thus, in his final formulation Freud saw hypnosis as a transference involving both libidinal and submissive instinctual strivings.

In the meantime, Ferenczi[57] had taken up Freud's footnote and expanded upon it. He placed the main emphasis upon the submissive component. He held that the hypnotic influence was derived from the reactivation of childhood reactions to adult authority, hence that the relation was one of submission-dominance. Actually his theory is somewhat more complex than this because he sees this relationship as arising from the reactivation of the Oedipus complex out of which two forms of the child-parent relationship evolve. Corresponding to these there are two forms of hypnosis—a maternal form, based on love; and a paternal form, based on fear.

About this time, Jones[96] too began to formulate his views, although it was not until some time later that he presented them fully developed.[95] His analysis of the matter is unquestionably one of the best. In it he follows Freud quite closely in regarding hypnosis as involving the substitution of the object (the hypnotist) for the ego-ideal (superego), but he also places greater emphasis upon the regressive aspect of the process, and particularly upon the underlying primary-narcissistic element, speaking of a "regression to narcissistic identification."

Apparently much influenced by both Freud and Ferenczi, Schilder,[151] alone, and later with Kauder,[151] stressed four interrelated aspects of the relation of hypnosis to transference in another fine theoretical exposition. They saw hypnosis, first of all, as a goal-inhibited form of eroticism in which both homosexual and heterosexual strivings are present, and in which a masochistic element of passivity, or subjection to authority, plays a major role. More fundamentally, hypnosis is seen as a regression, a return to a more primitive, undifferentiated psychosexual stage, namely that of magical omnipotence. By identifying with the hypnotist and by granting the power of his fantasies to the latter, the subject is able to realize his infantile fantasies of omnipotence. Similarly, Fenichel[56] saw the hypnotized subject as reverting to the phase of passive-receptive mastery of the first two years of life, in which omnipotence is vicariously obtained through introjection of the all-powerful adult (the hypnotist in this case).

In general, it can be stated that from Freud on there has been an essential agreement among orthodox psychoanalysts that the subject-hypnotist interrelationship centers around a regressive libidinal tie associated with, among other things, a change in superego structure. But differences of opinion have arisen in regard to which type of infantile sexuality is involved, the stage of psychosexual development to which the regression returns the individual, the exact *modus operandi* of the regression, and the nature of the superego changes. In regard to the latter, some investigators speak of a displacement by or substitution of an auxiliary or parasitic superego (the hypnotist); others speak of a merging of the subject's original superego with the introjected image of the hypnotist; still others speak of a reactivation of the subject's superego powers, and so forth.

In more recent times there seems to have been a shift toward placing emphasis upon ego regression in addition to the libidinal element. Evidence of this will be found in such papers as those of Brenman,[21,22] and of Kubie and Margolin.[103] The most recent study emphasizing this view is that of Fisher.[58] On the basis of his empirical findings he concludes:

> Suggestibility seems associated with a regression to a narcissistic ego organization, to a pregenital libidinal organization with emphasis on aims of incorporation, and with a more primitive form of object relationship of induced regression.

He believes that he is speaking here of the same thing as Jones's narcissistic identification and Fenichel's passive-receptive mastery stage. He also finds evidence in his data that the suggestion is perceived as an impregnating substance, and that its acceptance is an unconscious gratification. Carrying out the suggestion is erotically symbolic of having a baby. Thus, as Jones has summed up,[95] hypnosis would seem to have a strong erotic, feminine element. At the more mature level, the incorporation and rejection of suggestion centers more about the notion of "good" and "bad" substance. Fisher admits, however, that this particular perception of suggestion on the part of his subjects may have been specific to his experimental procedures and that it is probable that in many instances other perceptions are the dominant factor in the determination of the reactions of subjects. He goes on to point out more specifically that one is probably never dealing with a simple libidinal or ego regression in suggestion effects, but always with a simultaneous regression of id, ego and superego jointly.

He sums up his theoretical position by saying:

> . . .There is nothing specific about the hypnotic state. . . [the] 'hypnotic' phenomena

are brought about as a result of the interaction of constellations of psychic attitudes of the subject toward the physician, and the activity of the latter in the context of a relationship of induced regression.

The final outcome of this interaction, he adds, is determined by which specific ego functions become regressed and by the particular defenses which are aroused by the manipulations of the hypnotist. Fisher stresses the role of defenses in the determination of reactions to suggestions. He is not alone in this. Wolberg,[203] for instance, places a similar emphasis.

One of the most sophisticated discussions and broadest interpretations of this whole question has been given by Wolberg.[203] Although essentially agreeing with the basic tenets of previous workers, he also stresses the fact that hypnosis cannot be fully understood either at the psychological or at the physiological level alone, but must be looked upon as a psychosomatic reaction embracing both types of factors. His basic psychological conception of hypnosis, the aspect we are primarily concerned with here, seems to be that of a dependency relation wherein the hypnotized individual aims to gain gratification of various needs and motives. Wolberg's theory is much less restrictive in regard to motivational aspects than previous ones. Thus, there is no exclusive gratification of any single or even group of motives or needs. Instead, he sees the subject utilizing hypnosis "as an individual experience fitting into the framework of his own personal values and goals."

He also makes a specific distinction between suggestion and hypnosis as follows:

> Suggestion, like hypnosis, is associated with a motivation to gain important objectives through a dependency relationship. The difference between hypnosis and suggestion is that in suggestion the ego operates at a more mature level of integration. We may speculate that the individual who is susceptible to suggestion seeks to attain security and gratification through the agency of a parental figure, or other external authoritative force, consciously, in the same way that the hypnotized subject strives to satisfy these needs in the trance state.

I believe that Wolberg uses "suggestion" here to refer to what I have preferred to call "waking suggestibility." This use of suggestion is, as Macalpine[117] has remarked, the source of much confusion and should preferably be eliminated. Historically it seems to go back to Bernheim who insisted that there is no hypnosis but only suggestion, meaning by this that all of the so-called somatic symptoms described by Charcot (see chapter 10) were suggested artifacts. On the other hand, Freud and Jones, among others, seem to have used this term to designate the totality of suggestibility phenomena. In spite of this, there seems to have been rather general agreement that suggestion, or its equivalent, denotes the specific (usually verbal) instrument used to evoke specific responses through the medium of suggestibility.

Wolberg agrees that in some instances the hypnotist probably does displace the subject's superego or is absorbed as such to varying degrees but, in general, the hypnotist becomes more of a symbol of the subject's superego and is regarded less as a real person. The induction of hypnosis involves a reactivation of the power of the subject's superego rather than a substitution of another, "parasitic," superego. Furthermore, the subject's reactions to induction procedures are variable. Whether they are of defiance, compulsion, surrender or contentment, depends upon his attitudes toward early authority figures and on his character structure developed out of early relationships. In any case, Wolberg emphasizes that the hypnotist is always more than a reanimation of the parental superego. Even in the deepest hypnosis he is also perceived as a *new* authority figure by part of the subject's ego. Wolberg seems to doubt that the hypnotist ever becomes fully introjected in any given hypnotic induction, although he agrees that it is conceivable that over many hypnotizations a partial and gradual incorporation might result.

Mention should be made of some recent papers by Guze[78] and by de Milechnin.[123,124] These authors present the theory that hypnosis consists of the arousal of a primitive, infantile pattern of emotional responses. Pending further clarification of the theory I cannot find any essential difference between it and the psychoanalytic theory. Both basically emphasize a regression to infantile modes of emotional response to significant figures, saying very little else.

This concludes our summary of the major psychoanalytic interpretations on the nature of hypnosis as a transference phenomenon. Generally speaking, orthodox analysts have been rather consistent in their position. Many have felt that there is no essential difference between the two conditions. Although I do not get this impression entirely, Fisher[58] feels that for Macalpine,[117] and Nunberg,[134] among others, the difference reduces entirely to a question of the relative intensity of the regression. It is Glover,[71] I believe, who feels that a distinction should be made between "hypnotic" and "spontaneous" or "analytic" transference, but even in this there does not appear to be any fundamental break with traditional analytic thinking. The one definite attempt at such a break is that of Wolstein.[206] He presents arguments against the notion that hypnosis and transference are the same sort of phenomenon. He points out that the character of the transference is a function of the analytic setting, and the hypnotic character seen in some transference situations is really an artifact brought on by the particular setting used. There is no doubt that the first of these points is true, as has been recognized by a number of Freudian analysts. We have already seen that Wolstein's position was anticipated by Hendrik. Nunberg contends that the only difference between the analyst and the hypnotist is that the former makes use of his special power to teach reality testing to the patient, whereas the hypnotist makes use of the same power to teach the subject to give up reality testing.

Alexander and French[2] have shown that the analytic setting can determine the character of the transference relationship, hindering or facilitating its appearance. Macalpine seems to hold a somewhat similar position. Fisher,[58] following his attempt to examine the question empirically, has arrived at a conclusion which is highly relevant to Wolstein's contention. He states:

> This investigation has shown that if the analyst behaves toward the patient as the hypnotist does toward his subject, the patient will react *in some respects like* a hypnotized person. The crucial factor, therefore, in bringing about 'hypnotic' phenomena *may* be the activity of the physician in the context of a relationship of induced regression. On the other hand, it is possible to induce a hypnotic state, but thereafter act toward the subject, not like a hypnotist in the traditional sense, but like an analyst, as in the so-called technique of hypnoanalysis. Under the circumstances the subject will behave more like a patient in analysis, i.e., regressive phenomena will be less marked and there will be a greater preservation of the ego and superego functions mentioned earlier. (Italics mine.)

The word "like" in the Fisher quotation is the crux of the problem. Fisher may have intended a much stronger statement by this, implying identity between the two types of elicited behavior rather than a resemblance, but it is significant that he also specified that the likeness is only "in some respects," and that the crucial factor "may" be the activity of the physician. In other words, he appears to be uncertain of the identity, and certainly, in my opinion, his data do not point to anything more than a similarity. We are faced here with essentially the same question that has been raised by the "role taking" theorists in another context. Does the individual act as if he were hypnotized, or is there really a condition of hypnosis? I believe Wolstein is saying that the proper structuring of the transference (or analytic) situation can elicit hypnotic-like behavior which has in the past been mistakenly interpreted as actual hypnosis. There is also a danger that in structuring the situation so as to produce hypnotic-like behavior one may actually create hypnosis—inducing conditions quite apart from the transference. It is quite possible that in some of the instances referred to there were elements of hypnosis induced in addition to, perhaps in spite of, the transference because of this very structuring. In the absence of proper controls, the dangers of confounding are great.

Another argument of Wolstein is that, while it is true that some transference manifestations do appear to resemble posthypnotic suggestions, many others have no traits in common with hypnotic phenomena. Unfortunately, this argument is not as strong as it may first seem because one should realize that just as structuring the transference situation could give the subject's behavior the appearance of hypnosis, it is also true that a hypnotic situation can be so structured as to give the subject's behavior the appearance of waking behavior.[191] Consequently, if hypnosis and transference are the same, one might well expect to observe the sort of thing Wolstein talks about. Finally, he claims that although proper structuring of the transference situation can lead to hypnotic-like (or rather, post-hypnotic-like) behavior, there is evidence that certain transference phenomena *cannot* be made to occur by manipulating the subject's suggestibility. Unfortunately Wolstein does not make it clear what he specifically means by "manipulating suggestibility" and hence, depending upon this meaning, his argument may or may not be entirely relevant to the question at hand. In any event, his statement has weight only if the relation between transference and hypnosis is a symmetric one, as it would be were we faced with a true identity. Actually, it is by no means certain that this is the case. If transference should turn out to be more fundamental or inclusive than suggestibility, and I believe there is an intimation of this, for instance, in Jones' works, then we would expect to find that some transference manifestations might not be duplicated in hypnosis even though hypnosis were an aspect of transference, and in this sense was transference.

In final evaluation then, Wolstein's arguments do not prove the non-identity of transference and hypnosis, although they do raise some questions regarding relationship.

So much for theory. Just what are the empirical facts? The evidence for the analytic point of view is not particularly convincing, far less so than is the theory itself. It is true that there exist many case reports in the literature but, aside from a few and for the most part inadequate experiments, there is really little to go on at the empirical level. Many of those who uphold one view or another do so largely because of their identification with one particular viewpoint in personality theory or psychotherapy. Others claim to have substantiating empirical data but base their ideas upon case material and their interpretation of the latter within the framework of their therapeutic orientation. Thus much of the so-called evidence concerning the transference nature of hypnosis is derived from dream material, fantasies, various reported subjective feelings, some acting out and so forth, all interpreted and obtained according to analytic principles and methods from patients being hypnotized. This approach may be excellent for the purpose of therapy, but it has serious experimental limitations. Worst of all, much reported data come from very small samples, often of one!*

Depending upon the manner in which the therapist or experimenter interprets material, substantiation has been obtained for just about every point of view. Thus if the patient produces erotic material in which the therapist-hypnotist is a dominant figure, it is often concluded that Freud or Schilder are confirmed, and conversely, failure to find certain other elements is pointed out as evidence that some other theorist is wrong. The case of Ferenczi's theory exemplifies the danger and weakness of this type of approach. One finds evidence to support it in the available data only sporadically. Ferenczi formulated his theory on the basis of the type of family interaction typical of the society he lived in. His conception of the hypnotic transference was undoubtedly well suited for the latter. It is ill-suited for the present American culture and particularly for certain subcultural groups within it. Are we then to infer from the data that Ferenczi was wrong?

There are a few direct experiments relevant to the problem. Some investigators have felt that, if the analytic theory is correct, susceptibility to hypnosis and suggestibility in general should be a function of the sex of the hypnotist. Eysenck[54] and Weitzenhoffer and Weitzenhoffer[197] have therefore attempted to determine what influence the sex of the hypnotist might have. These investigators were unable to find any evidence of an effect. White,[200] after reviewing existing information relevant to this question, also concludes that the evidence is negative. It has also been felt that the sex of the subject should be a determinant. Here again the reported evidence[191,197] does not support the theory.

There are, however, a number of reasons for not accepting such failure to support the hypothesis as definitive. The most obvious reason is that many of the experiments have been too restricted in scope. In many respects, too, the experimental and therapeutic situations are not comparable. It is one thing to deal with seriously disturbed individuals, and another to deal with less disturbed or normal persons. The manner of measuring suggestibility, that is, whether it is a waking test, response to trance-inducing suggestion, or response to hypnotic suggestion, could conceivably make some difference. Then, too, there is the matter of allowing time for the transference to be initiated and to develop fully, although presumably in hypnosis this is very

---

*It can of course be argued that even with such samples many occurrences of the same kind of data give statistical significance, or at least some theoretical importance. There is some truth in this, provided certain conditions are observed. Unfortunately there is no evidence this was the case in most of the reports in question.

rapid.[117] Finally, the personality of the hypnotist and his approach to men and women could be of influence on their respective responsiveness.

One particular aspect of the problem which until now had been over-looked is the fact that the important sex element might be *femininity* versus *masculinity* rather than *femaleness* versus *maleness*. That is, the psychological rather than the physical characteristics of women and men might be the main determinant of their respective susceptibility. Indeed, orthodox psychoanalytic theory suggests that the more psychologically feminine an individual is, the more suggestible and susceptible to hypnosis he should be. Weitzenhoffer and Weitzenhoffer[197] have recently reported an investigation of this question. No evidence could be found that the relative femininity of the subject had any significant degree of influence.

Similarly in respect to the influence of the sex of the hypnotist. What may really count is how masculine or feminine the operator is perceived to be by the subject, and not just his physical sex. This aspect was also tentatively explored by Weitzenhoffer and co-workers. Thus far the results have been negative, but certainly far from being definitive.

On the positive side, Rosenzweig and Sarason[146] found that there *may* be an erotic element relating "impunitiveness" to hypnotizability. Just what this signifies is unclear, and in any event represents only a small effect. Speyer and Stokvis[172] studied the fantasies reported by a male physician who had been consecutively hypnotized by first a female, then a male hypnotist. They feel they have evidence from this which supports the traditional claims. Lorand[112a] reported a somewhat similar study, also claiming positive evidence. Some of the defects of this sort of study have already been mentioned: both leave much to be desired in respect to controls, and one can hardly generalize from a single case. For all we know they may have been atypical.

To date, the best investigation of the relationship of transference to hypnosis and suggestibility has been reported by Fisher.[58,59] It can serve well as a model for future investigations in this area, although it is not without flaws. One of the difficulties that arise in drawing inferences from the reported data, as Fisher admits, is that there is some question as to the extent one can generalize from the highly specific situation in the experiment. Essentially, Fisher attempted to find out whether individuals in therapy long enough to have developed a transference, or who showed evidence of it, would be more suggestible as a consequence and whether such an enhancement would be comparable to that of hypnotized individuals. Furthermore, if this were the case, would the suggestion situation have specific significance, transference-wise, for the subjects? Although somewhat equivocal, his results do lend some support to the analytic position. Yet, taken as a whole, the investigation falls short of demonstrating the identity of, or even a causal relation between, transference and hypnosis.

We can only state, to date, that the question remains unresolved, although I believe there are clear indications that transference manifestations may play a much more important part in hypnotic phenomena than the non-analytically oriented person might suppose. Just exactly what this part is, is another matter. It certainly should be investigated more intensively and carefully.

There is one aspect in this controversy which has been largely overlooked, yet which may be of considerable, even crucial importance, and which weakens the present analytic position. With the exception of the Speyer, Stokvis, and Fisher reports, the affirmative view that transference and hypnosis are identical has been upheld by individuals using hypnosis in therapy as a result of observations made on their patients. Indeed, Freud himself was very insistent upon confining the use of the term "transference" to the psychoanalytic *therapeutic* situation. Inasmuch as transference is to be expected in most, possibly all, psychotherapeutic interactions, it should be a foregone conclusion that it is usually present *when hypnosis is used for therapy*, particularly since hypnosis is often not used in the first few interviews. Furthermore, as was pointed out earlier, it is likely that there is a transference component in the prehypnotic interaction of subject and experimenter even when therapy is not intended. Unless proper precautions are taken, as Fisher attempted to do in his investigation, any specific contributions made by hypnosis to the total transference will be confounded with those arising from the therapeutic process or the experimental situation itself. Indeed, the problem of interaction between measures is extreme, and it may be that separating transference from hypnotic phenomena (should they be distinct) is a near impossibility.

It should be remarked that Freud's insistence that transference has meaning only in the context of therapy is not consistent with his assertion that hypnosis is only a transference manifestation, for there is no question that he meant this identity to apply to hypnosis regardless of whether it was produced in a therapeutic or nontherapeutic situation. I do not think that there is any question that hypnosis is basically the same thing in either case. If hypnosis is transference, then it would seem of necessity that the concept of transference must be extended to situations other than therapy, as Hendrik and Nunberg have suggested. This is a modification which I am presently inclined to accept.

I have no quarrel with any assertion that transference occurs in the hypnotic setting, independently of therapy, even during the induction phase. The universality of this statement might be questioned, but only for lack of clear factual evidence.

I have observed indubitable transference-like manifestations in many nontherapeutic hypnotic sessions. Furthermore, these appeared within such a short period of time as to lend much credence to Macalpine's view mentioned earlier. It is conceivable that the presence of transference, or the greater speed of its arousal in my subjects (and those of other investigators) may have been due to a specific diathesis, since individuals who *volunteer* to be hypnotized, as mine did, may well possess specific personality traits which are manifested not only in this tendency to volunteer, but also in such a diathesis. Macalpine points out that possibly patients go to the therapist because of a pre-existing "sympathetic transference." She also remarks that the best hypnotic subjects are those who respond best to psychoanalysis, the implication being that whatever is responsible for the one is also responsible for the other. She sees transference as the common factor, but one can just as well assume a less direct interrelationship.

On the other hand, it is difficult to imagine that an interpersonal relationship such as that involved in hypnosis would not give rise to something of the sort, and that the resulting manifestations would not reflect the qualities of the hypnotic setting. Conversely, any transference which is present should affect the outcome of suggestions. Positive transference should aid, whereas negative transference should hinder. Here too, I have observed a number of instances of such interference. In such cases, resolution of the resulting resistance by the usual techniques has always re-established the hypnotic status quo.

I do disagree, however, with orthodox analysts in regard to the identity of transference and hypnosis and even to the necessity of a causal relation between the two. I am willing to admit theoretically that psychoanalysis does have a model which accounts for hypnotic phenomena, at least in their coarser manifestations. I am not certain, however, that the model is fully capable of handling all the details of the phenomena. In this respect Wolberg is quite right when he insists that a psychological explanation by itself is insufficient to account for all of the phenomena of hypnosis. Finally, I am not entirely convinced that the present analytic model of hypnosis is entirely consistent. Certain logical and conceptual difficulties seem to arise from it. In any event, at the empirical level, whatever little we have available does not support the main claim of the theory. Although it does not disprove the proposition, it *at best* only suggests that transference might be one of the dimensions of suggestibility, or rather of hypnotic hypersuggestibility. Only by stretching facts more than is warranted could we assert that it is the one and only dimension.

It may be of interest to note that Freud admitted the possibility that *there is more to hypnosis than transference*. Thus, after concluding[64] that hypnosis is a state of being in love with the directly sexual tendency removed, he admits that it possesses certain other features which cannot be accounted for in these terms. For one thing, hypnosis seems to possess an additional element of paralysis which has as its genesis an interaction between someone who is powerless or helpless and someone in a position of great power. Perhaps, he adds, this element constitutes the link between the paralysis of terror seen in animals, and human hypnosis. A second aspect of hypnosis he found to still need clarification is the relationship of hypnosis to sleep. Finally, he pondered upon the fact that susceptibility to hypnosis seems to be so much a matter of the individual subject. ". . .The puzzling way in which some individuals are subject to it, while others resist it completely, points to some factor still unknown which is realized in it and which perhaps alone makes possible the purity of the attitude of the libido which is exhibited."

It is true that somewhat later Freud gives the impression that he feels he has resolved these questions by means of his "primal horde" hypothesis, although it is not made clear whether it supersedes the previous notion regarding love, is meant to supplement it, or how general is its applicability. Accordingly, the hypnotic situation reactivates archaic reaction patterns of submission to the father-image. There are, however, reasons for disregarding this. First the hypothesis is of dubious character. Secondly, in summing up his thoughts in the last chapter, Freud rather significantly ignores all but the "being in love" aspect of hypnosis. Finally, his treatment of the "primal horde" notion in this connection has a quality about it which makes me feel he used it more as an afterthought than as a seriously considered solution.

If we are dealing here with such a dimension as just suggested, many of the similarities reported to exist between transference manifestations and hypnosis would be accounted for. In particular, it becomes understandable, as remarked by Wolstein, that manifestations of therapeutic transference should at times take on the quality of posthypnotic suggestions. There is a possibility that, independently of any transference, a true hypnotic condition develops for one reason or another during an analytic session. Fliess[60] has reported such an instance as a defensive reaction. In addition, there may be elements in the analytic setting which are capable of bringing about hypnosis in some individuals. An intriguing alternative to the traditional picture is to consider transference as an offshoot of hypnosis as Macalpine has suggested.

It is also entirely possible that enhanced suggestibility is a characteristic of transference, just as it is a characteristic of "hypnosis" induced by fixation of a bright object alone. At the process level, the two situations are not necessarily the same or reducible to one another. It must be kept in mind that there are many apparent paths to hypnosis, and furthermore, that what we call hypnosis today appears to be more of the nature of a compound than a pure element. On the other hand, one should not sell short the idea that hypnosis and transference are two distinct conditions which tend to develop in parallel because the conditions favorable to one are also favorable to the other.

Macalpine, for instance, has described the basic elements conducive to the production of transference. There is little question that they tend to overlap those conducive to hypnosis. Fisher has made a quite relevant remark: "The hypothesis may be advanced that increased suggestibility is one of the properties of states of induced regression, both hypnotic and analytic transference being included in this designation." Presumably the specific patterns of ego and superego changes are what differentiate hypnosis from transference. This concept of many nonidentical states of regression would go a long way toward clarifying the present issue. Hypnosis and transference could be related, could have many points of similarity, and yet still be different. This is a view which I am particularly tempted to favor. Although this notion might at first seem to be incompatible with hypnosis and transference considered as merely a matter of relative intensity of regression, a view which Fisher also espouses, this is not necessarily so because one may be looking at the two phenomena at different observational levels. On the other hand, it may be that only hypnosis is associated with hypersuggestibility.

Another likely theory is that the end result of the trance-inducing procedure is the production, not only of hypnosis as we know it, but also of a condition not unlike an infantile regression state which facilitates, maybe even brings about, a transference relationship. This transference aspect may serve as a final basis for hypersuggestibility, or may be a manifestation of it. In this eventuality, Macalpine's remark that transference is a "slow motion hypnosis" acquires special significance. But it is not so much a question of a slowly developing hypnotic state, as one of hypnosis being present and facilitating transference whereas in the analytic situation transference is allowed to progress on its own. I think Macalpine may have had something of the sort in mind when she remarked: "One may speculate that analytic transference is a derivative of hypnosis motivated by instinctual (libidinal) drives, and, *mutatis mutandis*, produced in a way comparable to the hypnotic trance.''

Up to this point we have spoken of transference primarily in terms of its direct relationship to suggestibility. That is, the implicit and at times explicit assumption was that it either was suggestibility itself or accounted for it in a very direct manner. However, it could very well be that the action of transference is much more one of molding and giving content to the behavioral expression of suggestibility. Except at the purely reflex level, most responses are much more than what they started out to be by the time they reach completion. As they develop, they become affected and shaped by a multitude of factors. Granted that infantile behavior patterns are reactivated in the hypnotic situation, this may mean nothing more than that a tendency is established for responses to follow one pattern more than another without affecting, of necessity, the intrinsic capacity for responsiveness. Furthermore, certain characteristics, such as emotional overtones, may become attached to a response after its initiation through a simple process of association, favored by the existence of transference. Whereas without the transference the response might have been carried out without any particular feeling tone, with transference its carrying out acquires a host of meanings to the subject and in feed-back fashion is thereby influenced. In either case, it must be re-emphasized, the initial impulse to act would not depend on the presence or absence of a transference.

To summarize then, the exact status of transference in its relation to hypnosis is by no means clearly established. That transference is found associated with hypnosis at times is clear. Its presence in all cases remains a surmise. In any event, it is a phenomenon which cannot be ignored in any study or use of hypnosis. Regardless of the outcome, its presence, even as a factor and not a causal agent, is bound to affect the result of suggestions and the general behavior of the subject. Of all the factors which can affect this outcome and behavior, transference is one of the most influential.

Inevitably the question must arise as to what is the exact relationship of the psychoanalytic theory to the psychophysiological theory of hypnosis presented earlier in this chapter. As I see it, psychoanalysis has evolved a model which deals primarily with the later stages in the formation of the hypnotic state, but not with the initial steps. Except, possibly, for certain special circumstances in which the individual to be hypnotized comes to the hypnotist physiologically preset or preconditioned, so to speak, the fully developed transference observed in hypnosis does not make its appearance until certain psychophysiological changes have been brought about. No matter how we look at it, the conclusion seems inescapable that the initial step in any suggestion situation is a physical interaction between a physical environment and a physical organism. The initial phase in hypnosis is the setting into motion of a pattern of neural activity. It is this which is subsequently expressed as changes in the psychic structure. Whatever isomorphism exists between the psychoanalytic and psychophysiological model seems, at present, to be partial at best. On the other hand, there is no incompatibility between the two—in some respects they tend to complement each other rather well.

Part II.
Waking Suggestions

Preliminary Exercises and Demonstrations
In Waking Suggestions

I T IS CUSTOMARY, if not traditional, to speak of the condition of in-dividuals responding to waking suggestions as "waking hypnosis," although a few writers such as Brenman and Gill[21] have reserved the term to denote situations when a trance-inducing technique is used which does not contain any references to sleep. I doubt very much whether any such dis-tinctions between "waking hypnosis" and hypnosis proper (or "sleep hypnosis") are particularly meaningful or useful, and they may in fact be misleading. The expression "waking hypnosis" is certainly inappropriate and self-contradictory since "waking" and "hypnosis" are polar terms. For this reason I prefer to speak of waking suggestions.

The beginner is often considerably irritated by any amount of space and time devoted to this topic. Quite understandably, he is anxious to get on to the major topic of hypnosis proper. Therefore, it may not be superfluous to point out a few of the reasons for spending time on waking suggestions at this stage.

In the first place, waking suggestions play a central role in modern methods of producing hypnosis. They are the basic tools used to predict the probable outcome of any attempt to use hypnosis on an individual. Many of the properties of suggestibility are best exhibited by waking suggestions, whereas hypnosis tends to mask them. From an applied standpoint, waking suggestions are also of importance in that many individuals who cannot be hypnotized can still benefit considerably from their use. For these reasons, it is unfortunate that in recent times so much emphasis has been placed on hypnosis, to the near exclusion of waking suggestions. It cannot be over-emphasized that a thorough familiarity with and an understanding of the properties of waking suggestibility are of the greatest importance and value in the practice of hypnosis.

In many of the experiments or demonstrations which follow, you will find a number of variations in procedure described. Hereafter we shall call the first procedure under any experiment the *principal procedure* or *model* distinguished by its more frequent use, its wider applicability and greater ease of administration. Other alternatives will be referred to as *variation procedures*.* In general, you should start with and practice the *model*, but you are *not* expected to perform all the variations included under a given experiment before you go on to the next. On the contrary, you should first try the principal procedure, then come back to the variations and try them out at different times. Of course, there is no fixed rule here. One reason why you usually will not want to try all variations of each demonstration at a time is that the experiments are described more or less in order of the increasing amount of suggestibility required to get a response. For maximum effectiveness when you are performing a series of experiments, *it is a good rule to begin with the experiment calling for the least amount of suggestibility and to proceed gradually to experiments calling for an increasing amount.*

FIRST RULES OF SUGGESTION

From here on you are going to be using suggestions. You may save yourself both embarrassment and anxiety by *always* observing the following basic rule: *Always make sure to properly and specifically cancel, i.e., terminate, any suggestion with which you are through, making certain that the termination is clearly distinguished by the subject from a challenge.*

The importance of this rule as well as what it means in practice can probably be best shown by the following true anecdotes.

Some time ago, one of my students learning to hypnotize, and whom we shall call "John," decided to suggest eye catalepsy. Briefly, this consists in telling the subject that his eyes are stuck fast and that he cannot open them. When it is deemed that the suggestion has taken sufficient effect, the subject is challenged to "break" the suggestion, that is, to overcome it. In this case it would be to open his eyes. "You cannot open your eyes," he is told. "Try to open your eyes, you cannot. . ."

Now, when John did this he was much gratified to find that his subject could not open his eyes in spite of all his efforts. Having allowed the subject to give the strength of the suggestion a good test, John decided to end the suggestion by saying to the subject, "Now open your eyes." The latter tried, but in vain. "Open your eyes!" reiterated John, a little worried. "I can't!" replied the subject making obvious efforts to do so. "Try real hard," John ordered. More of the same ensued with the subject continuing to be unable to open his eyes. Fearing that John or the subject might become

*Of course, this does not mean that some of the variations discussed have no points of superiority of their own. It is rather that the principal procedures will usually be found to satisfactorily meet most of the requirements of the majority of situations.

panicked I soon decided to step into the picture and help out our apprentice hypnotist, which was not difficult.

What happened? A very simple thing: John had never made it clear to the subject that the effect of the suggestion was canceled. Although John did not intend it to be so, as far as the subject was concerned every time John told him to open his eyes or to try it, it was a challenge, a further test of the efficacy of the suggestion. John would have saved himself much anxiety had he been careful to say to the subject, "Alright, now you can open your eyes.—Open your eyes!"

A surer way of preventing the above unpleasantness would have been for John to have told his subject prior to the challenge and in addition to the usual instructions something like: "You will not be able to open your eyes until I tell you that you can. . .," or again, ". . .You will not be able to open your eyes until I clap my hands again like this [*demonstrates*]. . ." Either one of these instructions would have introduced a demarcation between challenge and termination.

It cannot be overemphasized that it is not sufficient just to cancel the suggestion: the subject must be made clearly aware of this. Otherwise one is likely to encounter the sort of thing which happened to John.

Let us suppose, however, that for one reason or another you get yourself into this type of situation. Maybe you forgot to cancel the suggestion, or maybe you thought you did, but did it improperly. What should you do? Above all keep calm. Tell your subject to remain as he is and to relax for the next few minutes. Now think back carefully over each step you followed to see if you can pick up the cause of difficulty. If and when you find it, go right ahead and give the subject appropriate instructions *as if nothing wrong had ever happened*.

But suppose now that you fail to find the source of difficulty. What then? Address your subject in a conversational manner and ask him why he did not do whatever it is that he was supposed to do. Thus, John could have asked his subject, "Why can't you open your eyes?" Most likely the latter would have replied, "You told me that I would not be able to do this." Upon which John would only have had to say, "Alright. Now you will be able to open your eyes when I tell you to open them. You will have no difficulty doing this. You can open your eyes. Open them!" Or he might have said, "I shall now count to three and at the count of three you will be able to open your eyes without difficulty. One, two, three! Open your eyes!"

Once I gave a subject the posthypnotic suggestion that he would not be able to get out of his chair until I clapped my hands. Now it just so happened that I was talking in a relatively low voice and just as I mentioned the condition which would terminate the effect of the posthypnotic suggestion a very large and noisy powered lawn mower came under the open window of my laboratory. Unaware that the subject had not heard the canceling instructions I proceeded to dehypnotize him and test the posthypnotic suggestion which proved to be extremely effective. Eventually I clapped my hands. "Now try to get up," I told the subject. Which he did with no success. "Try again," I said, clapping my hands a second time. Still no success. Puzzled, I asked the subject why he could not get up. He explained that his legs felt strange, numb-like, and that he could not move them at all. In fact this condition seemed to extend up to his thigh. Could it be, I wondered, that inadvertently I had triggered an hysterical paralysis? Quickly I rehypnotized the subject. I told him that the numbness in his legs was going away, that he could move his legs which now felt quite normal. I had him do so under hypnosis, then stand up and move a bit. I ended this by asserting that he would have the full use of his legs after he woke up, that he would be able to get out of the chair at any time and that his legs would feel perfectly normal. I still did not know why the clapping of my hands had been ineffective. I therefore next proceeded to find this out by questioning him. This presented no problem.

As we shall see later, difficulty in removing the effects of a suggestion may arise for reasons other than the one considered here. But with waking suggestions, faulty termination of the suggestion is nearly always the principal reason. In any event one should always check this possibility first in all cases of perseverating suggestions. With a little care and forethought no one should have this difficulty.

It is extremely important that every suggestion be canceled *regardless of whether or not the subject has given evidence of responding to it*. Many hypnotists assume that if the suggested response is not produced the suggestion has had no effect upon the subject and, consequently, they do not bother to cancel the suggestion. This assumption should never be made. Each suggestion should always be canceled at the appropriate time even if the subject has not shown the least reaction to it. A few examples will make it clear why this rule is important.

On one occasion I had a subject who, when tested for his susceptibility to hypnosis by means of the Friedlander-Sarbin technique, turned out to be totally insusceptible. As will be seen later, this means, among other things, that the subject was able to lift her left hand (resting on her lap) in spite of being told that it was heavy and that she could not do this, and that she was able to bend her extended right arm in spite of being told that it was stiff and rigid and could not be bent. She had not the least difficulty in counteracting either suggestion. The next day, I had an unexpected visit from this subject. She was rather perturbed by the fact that on awakening that morning she had found herself unable to lift her left hand from on top of her blanket upon which it rested, and she had found a few moments later that she could not bend her right arm. This condition had lasted a few moments, then vanished. Now, it just happens that the wording used in the Friedlander-Sarbin instructions does not contain any clear statement to the subject that the suggestions which have been given have been canceled. Each suggestion is simply terminated with the instruction, "Now relax," which may or may not be understood by the subject as indicating that the suggested effect has been canceled. In this particular instance the suggestions had apparently influenced the subject in spite of outward evidence, and had acted in a delayed manner when conditions were more favorable. I shall not attempt to discuss the possible dynamics of this case. I would, however, like to point out a few things. First, this subject definitely was of a hysterical type and this may have been an important factor in her subsequent behavior which was not typical of most subjects. Secondly, it is worth noting the condition under which the suggestions became effective. This was right upon awakening from her night sleep, presumably in the borderline state between wakefulness and sleep, a state which is perhaps related to hypnosis. Lastly, the manner in which the suggestions became effective reminds one of the proehypnotic effect to be taken up later (page 350).

My second example, of a somewhat different nature, is taken from an article by Jolowicz[*] in which he tells of the following incident. On one occasion, when he had hypnotized one of his patients, a maid, he attempted to produce a blister on her right forearm by suggesting that he was applying a piece of red-hot metal to it. This had no particular effect at the time and the patient went home (without any countersuggestion being given). Several days later the patient came back suffering from a burn on her right forearm where a blister had formed on the very spot previously chosen by the experimenter. The patient had no awareness of the suggestion and reported that she had accidentally spilled scalding water on her arm when she had lifted a pot of boiling water with her left hand preparatory to making coffee. As far as she was concerned this was purely an accident. As Jolowicz points out, here is an instance in which a suggestion which has not been acted upon and which has been allowed to remain in force has led at a later date to an unconsciously premeditated accident effectively terminating it. I do not know

[*]Jolowicz, E.: Consciousness in dream and in the hypnotic state. Amer. J. Psychother. 1947, *1*, 2-24.

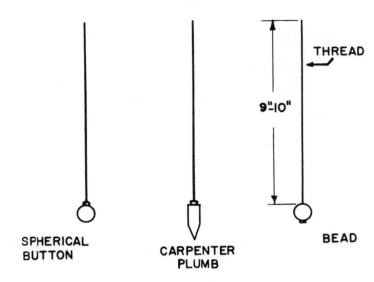

FIG. 2. Typical pendulums for the Chevreul demonstration.

how many similar delayed effects have occurred in subjects in the past because of non-cancelation of apparently ineffective suggestions. Perhaps this
is an atypical reaction to be found only in hysterical or potentially hysterical
individuals. My guess is that it is not. In any case these two examples should
clearly demonstrate the dangers inherent in not canceling each and every
suggestion one gives a subject regardless of the immediate outcome.

CHEVREUL PENDULUM

This is one of the oldest demonstrations of suggestibility and a rather
fascinating one. It is named after Chevreul who, in 1812, was the first to
recognize the true nature of the phenomenon involved.[26] It is of particular
interest because: first of all, it is one of the simplest experiments, ideal for
beginning—yet in spite of its simplicity it can be used to demonstrate a
great many properties of suggestibility; secondly, it can be used to get an
indication of a person's susceptibility to hypnosis; and thirdly, it throws
some interesting light upon the nature of dowsing (water divination).

Before doing any part of this experiment, read the entire demonstration
through. There are many ways of doing it and later on, when you become
more familiar with it, you may wish to work out your own adaptation.

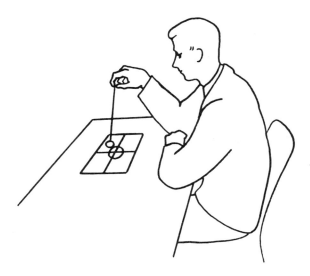

FIG. 3. The Chevreul pendulum demonstration.

First, you must make yourself a pendulum, that is, a small bob hanging to a thread or string. Just about any small object will do. Some of the older hypnotists used their watch and chain. I have found that an excellent pendulum is made with a spherical button about 3/8 to 1/2 inch in diameter tied to the end of an ordinary piece of thread 9 to 10 inches long (fig. 2). I like to use a white pearl button, however, the color as well as the size and shape is really immaterial in most instances. Sit at a table, rest your left forearm near the edge in front of you, rest your right elbow with your right arm lifted near the vertical, a little forward of your left arm, holding the end of the thread between your finger tips. Adjust yourself so as to be comfortable. If you are sitting properly, the pendulum should hang in front of the center of your body (median plane) and the bob should be about 1/2 inch from the top of the table (fig. 3). You must understand that none of these details are crucial. As long as you approximate them, the experiment is nearly certain to succeed.

The bob probably will be swinging about after you have adjusted your position. With your left hand, bring it to a standstill (later you can do this by "willing" it), then gently bring your left hand back to position. It is usually not possible, especially at first, to start out with a perfectly still pendulum; this is immaterial. Now fix your eyes on the bob and *will* it to move in a circle, say clockwise. This question of willing has never been properly described anywhere and, because of the very nature of the process, it is likely that it will not be for some time to come. Although merely desiring or wanting the bob to move in the proper manner is often sufficient, better results are obtained by simultaneously imagining the motion of the bob, by seeing it move in your own mind. Think of it going round and round. Two helpful aids are to keep saying to yourself, over and over, "It is going around, going around, round and round," and to actually follow with your eyes an imaginary bob going in a small circle. In the latter case you may have to take your eyes off the real bob, although if you make the imaginary circle small enough at first you will still be able to keep your eyes on it; then as it begins to move, you can slowly enlarge the size of the circle in your mind. Keep your mind and attention on the bob and the desired motion at all times. Try not to think about anything else and do not try to analyze what is happening. Usually, the bob first begins to be agitated by a slight motion that takes the form of a small (precessional) swinging in various directions. If you keep concentrating on the idea of a circular motion, and particularly, as soon as you notice any definite movement in your bob concentrate on this motion and on improving or elaborating it into a circular pattern, you should very quickly get the desired motion. As soon as you get some motion, try to enlarge it by thinking of it growing larger, wanting it to do so, see it getting larger in your mind and so on. Incidentally, do not be concerned if at first your circle is irregular, elliptical or wobbly. At first it may be a very narrow ellipse; in time you will be able to improve it—indeed, it will tend to correct itself as the motion gains amplitude or momentum.

In the process of willing the motion, some individuals tend to get muscularly tense. This is entirely unnecessary and often impedes the production of the desired effect. Try to be relaxed instead. Very often, after you have obtained the desired motion, if you relax your willing, you find that the bob acquires greater motion and seems to swing more freely and more regularly.

The Chevreul pendulum experiment is a fine demonstration of the phenomenon of ideomotor action discussed in chapter 2. Ideomotor action is rather weak, particularly in its initial phase. Presumably, the presence of another pattern of strong muscular action or tension involving the same muscles, or part of them, will either mask or block the weak pattern induced by thoughts. In any event, interference will arise which, at the least, will tend to distort the thought-induced pattern. This is probably one reason why a certain amount of relaxation seems to favor ideomotor action. Conversely, too much relaxation can be detrimental. A certain amount of general tonus is desirable for optimal effect. The reason for this is not fully understood. It appears to involve the question of readiness to respond on the part of the neuromuscular system. This, in turn, would seem to be a function of the presence of certain central excitatory and inhibitory states, as well as of their equivalents at myoneural junctions. Optimal tonus is presumably associated with a condition of maximal readiness for muscular response. In addition, deep relaxation may involve an active inhibitory effect which serves as a blocking agent in respect to muscular activity.

You will probably succeed with this experiment to some degree, for few people fail. If you do not get any results do not despair. Some individuals have to try it several times; often they can get only a very small and irregular motion at first. Try again a number of times on several consecutive days. Try the other direction of rotation. You may also want to try different bobs, heavier or lighter, smaller or larger, and also different lengths of thread. In general, the amount of swing you can get, hence the sensitivity, depends upon the length of the string. If you should happen to be one of those who can only get very small motions at first, a longer string will increase the amplitude of motion. However, if you do increase the length of string you may have to modify your position. The exact position used is not essential. If you use a longer pendulum you can dispense with the table, holding your arm and hand out and letting the pendulum swing over the floor; you can even work standing up. I have found, however, that the method described earlier contains the most favorable factors for the production of the effect for the majority of people.

Whether or not you have succeeded, try the next effect. Holding your pendulum the same as at the start of the experiment, will it to swing in a straight line in front of you, back and forth, away from and toward you. Do exactly as before. Try the same thing for a motion from right and left. Try other directions of swing.

Once you have succeeded in these various motions, set your pendulum in motion any way you want, either by willing it, or by hand, then will it to come to a standstill. Very often, if you have difficulty doing this at first, you can help by willing the pendulum to change its motion to a completely different one, e.g., a sidewise swing if it is rotating. Similarly, having set the bob into motion, will it to change its type of motion or its direction. When you do this it may come to a standstill before making the desired movement.

Beginning with the rotary motion is recommended since it is frequently the easiest movement to produce at first. However, some people have better

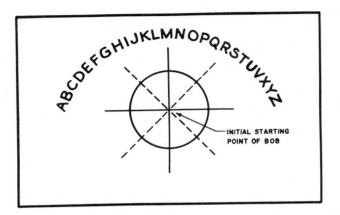

FIG. 4. Guide board for the Chevreul pendulum.

success with rectilinear motions. As a matter of fact, a very useful "trick"* to use at first is to observe how the bob is moving after willing it to rotate a few moments, then to switch to willing it to move more strongly in the direction it is already moving. The reason is that the bob must move sideways from its position of rest in order to get into a circular orbit, hence it nearly always begins by swinging sideways as a result of your willing.

Another trick which some people find helpful, particularly if they have difficulty in visualizing the motion, is to place a piece of paper on the table with a circle about two inches in diameter drawn on it. Hold the bob over its center and imagine that the bob is following the contour of the circle. Follow the circle with your eyes as if you were following the bob around it. Similarly, you may draw a line on the paper and use it as a guide to produce sideways swinging. As a matter of fact, you can combine all of these on a single paper (fig. 4).

An interesting variation of the above experiment is to write the letters of the alphabet or a series of numbers in a line or, better still, along the arc of a circle on a large piece of paper. Then hold the pendulum near the center of the arc and will it to move toward any given letter. In this manner you can make the bob spell out words, names and so on (fig. 4). This experiment may bring to mind the Ouija board of occult fame. Indeed, there is a close relationship between these two.

*By "trick" is meant "helpful device," no implication of misdirection, subterfuge, etc., being intended.

Regardless of the results you may have obtained to date, proceed with the following experiment using a subject. Give him the pendulum and have him sit at a table as already described. Instruct him to concentrate on the bob and to pay close attention to what you tell him. Then say*:

I want you to look at the small bob. Pay close attention to it. Don't think about anything but the bob and what I am going to tell you. Be relaxed. Don't tense yourself. . .In a moment, as you watch this bob closely, you will notice that it moves a little. Just which way is un-important, but it will move. . .It is going to move, a little at first, then more and more. Watch the bob. . .It is beginning to move a little now, it is beginning to swing. . .See it is moving a little. . .it is moving . . .moving. Just keep watching it. . .Think of it as moving. As you do so, it will move more and more. . .[*By this time the bob should definitely be moving. As soon as you have an idea as to its most likely direction and fashion of moving, proceed as follows.*] It is now moving in—*State here the manner or direction of motion you observe. If you have some doubts about the exact motion, it is usually safe at this stage to call it a sideways motion. Let us suppose that it then does swing sideways. Continue by saying:*] See, it is moving sideways. It is moving back and forth. . .back. . .and forth. . .[*If possible, syn-chronize your speech with the actual motion of the bob.*] It is swinging, more and more. . .It is swinging more strongly. . .swinging more strongly . . .back . . .and forth. . .back. . .and forth. You cannot stop the bob from moving now. The more you try to stop it the harder it will swing. [*This part concerning the subject's inability to stop the pendulum should be tried only if a good response has been obtained. It will probably be best for the beginner to wait until he has had more experience to try this.*]

Sometimes when a weak rectilinear motion is imparted to the pendulum, it tends to change into a circular motion. Should you notice that the bob begins to follow a definitely elliptical or circular trajectory after you have stated it is moving rectilinearly, just go on as if this was fully anticipated by saying: "Now it is beginning to move in a circle. . .more and more in a circle. . .It is moving in a circle. . .stronger. . .and stronger."

*The suggestions given here and elsewhere in this book are intended to be taken only as models. Every situation in which suggestions are given tends to be unique in various respects. For this reason no single universal suggestion can be designed. The best that can be done in a text of this kind is to offer models that incorporate the best and most important features of sug-gestions. It is largely up to the reader to adapt the models to each situation. This is why hyp-notism remains something of an art.

Let us stop here a moment and consider certain features of these procedures and suggestions. It is important that you should understand clearly the reasons for each step that you have been told to follow. This will also help you to better relate practice to theory and facts. An obvious application of theory and fact is the request to the subject to fixate the bob of the pendulum. If this induces any degree of hypnosis the effect of the suggestions will be enhanced. In any case the resulting focus of attention will probably tend to prevent stray thoughts from competing with those that are being suggested.

The effects of suggestions depend on a variety of factors. First, there is the subject's *innate* capacity for ideomotor action, or what we may also call his innate suggestibility. Another factor consists of his *attitudes*. It is believed that this factor can probably alter to a considerable extent the degree to which the individual's innate suggestibility will manifest itself. A negative attitude will hinder while a positive attitude will help. It is not hard to see why this should be. Attitudes can be expected to set up muscular tension patterns which interact with those set up by the suggestions. One might also suspect that abstract conditioning, which is also a part of suggestibility, as seen earlier, is relatively sensitive to attitudes. This is one reason why besides the proper choice of words *proper timing* is one of the most important factors in giving effective suggestions. If one tells the subject, contrary to facts, that something is happening or is going to happen, he is likely to form a set unfavorable to the manifestations of suggestibility. By the same token, if he experiences events taking place in accordance with the suggestions, he tends to form a positive set for subsequent suggestions, quite independent of the true causation of events. Consequently in the Chevreul pendulum experiment you do not want to tell your subject that the bob is moving in a circle if it is actually moving sideways—at least not without preparing him for such a contradictory statement. If you do want the subject to make the bob move in a circle under these conditions, then tell him: "The bob is now moving strongly. Very shortly it will begin to move in a circle. . .It is going to move in a circle. . .See, it is beginning to change its motion some. Soon it will move in a circle, a perfect circle. . .There, it is beginning to move in a circle."

This is also why it is best at the start of the experiment to tell the subject the bob *is going* to move, but not to specify the direction of motion.   This, however, is not a set rule and you could actually make such a specification in many cases with no bad effects; indeed, you may try this variation with some subjects if you wish to do so.   The main point to watch for is to be able to instruct the subject accordingly if the bob should move differently.

Proceeding in the above fashion probably helps in another way. Insuring that the subject has experiences only in accordance with what he is told will happen or is happening will be recognized as being the requisite for the production of abstract conditioning. Its effects are then probably added to those of positive attitude. On the other hand, if the operator's statements are contradicted by events, this conditioning will certainly not take place, and even a negative, inhibition-like effect may be induced.

The matter of timing and choosing proper wording means, among other things, that when you give suggestions you may have to alter the model suggestions given in this book to fit various situations, since subjects tend to react in an individual manner. Some will react slowly, others faster; some will produce motion of large amplitude, others only slight motion at the start, and so on. You will have to suggest accordingly. For instance, if there is a frank motion of the pendulum right after you have mentioned the idea of motion, then you may say right away: "See it is moving." Since in such a case the movement probably will be a sideways motion, you can continue by saying that it will be a sideways motion and build up the motion by suggestions such as: "It is moving sideways more and more. . .more. . . and more. . .It is swinging more and more strongly." Or you may decide to transform the motion into a rotation by saying: "Although it is moving somewhat sideways now, the bob will begin to go around in a circle very soon. . .it is going to rotate. . .round. . .and round. Think of a circle. . . See the motion is beginning to alter. The bob is moving irregularly. It is going to move in a circle. . .in a circle. . .Now it is beginning to really move in a circle. It is moving in a circle. In a larger and larger circle." On the other hand, the bob may at first merely oscillate irregularly, in which case you should emphasize this aspect of the motion and delay more specific suggestions. Very often too, the pendulum oscillates and even swings a little from the start, even before you have given any suggestions, because the subject's hand is not perfectly steady. Obviously, it would be absurd to tell the subject that the bob is going to move when it is already moving for all to see (unless the subject has not already noticed it). In this case, you should impress upon the subject that he is to relax and not be tense. You can also take hold of the bob and keep it still a few moments, which is usually a good way to begin in any event. If, in spite of everything, there is some motion, and usually there will be, then call the subject's attention to it in the following way: "You may notice that the bob is already moving a little. Do not pay attention to this. It is simply because your hand shakes a little. However, in a little while you will find that the bob is moving much more strongly and that it will move with increasing strength. You will also note that it will begin to move in a very definite direction, perhaps sideways, right and left, or round and round, in a circle. . .It will move. . .Already its motion is getting a little stronger. . .Yes, it definitely is getting stronger. It is now moving right and left [*or whatever else is appropriate*] right. . .and left. . . More and more strongly. There, now it is swinging real well. . .right. . . and left.''

You may, of course, have to cut these instructions short if the desired effect makes a strong appearance earlier than anticipated. Or, as remarked earlier, you may have to lengthen your suggestions.

Because of the necessity for proper timing, you do not usually want to go too fast in giving suggestions, otherwise you may tell the subject something is happening before it has happened. On the other hand, there are occasions when it is desirable to do this, but the time must be properly chosen and/or the statement made properly. A good rule is that if you see indications that a certain event is going to take place at any moment, then you can suggest that it is taking place. Otherwise, and probably this is preferable in all cases, you should introduce the event as a future possibility and work up, more or less gradually, to making a positive statement of its presence, as in the above example. Sometimes a suggested event makes its appearance so quickly after the suggestion of its future occurrence that one must pass without transition to a positive statement of its presence.

One way in which the hypnotist can prevent himself from getting ahead too fast is through the use of repetition in giving suggestions. However, there are other equally important reasons for using this device. Repetition enhances suggestibility through homoaction in a cumulative manner. Of special importance here is the fact that cumulative homoaction is probably not restricted to overt responses, but is also to be found present in connection with minute responses which through it become built up into gross, observable manifestations. Thus we may start out with a subject giving such weak responses to suggestions as to be unobservable, and through repetition alone of the same idea increase this response to the point where it can be clearly detected and be used as a basis for subsequent generalization of his suggestibility.[191] Another way in which repetition may help the effectiveness of suggestions is through monotony. As remarked earlier, monotony is believed by many hypnotists to have the ability in itself of bringing hypnosis about.

It may have occurred to the reader that if repetition is used as a way of allowing time for the suggestions to synchronize with the progress of their effects, one might also do this by using periods of silence of variable length between statements. This is usually not done in practice for a number of reasons. First it is imperative to focus the subject's attention on the suggested phenomena at all times. Periods of silence which are too lengthy would tend to allow the subject's attention to wander. Secondly, the enhancement caused by homoaction decays with time. This effect is particularly rapid immediately after cessation of the suggestion, hence is most prominent for relatively short time intervals. If you are to obtain maximum cumulation of homoaction by repetition, then the interval of time between statements must be quite short.

On the other hand, rapid fire suggestions are not always indicated. There is a need for short pauses because the response of a subject is not usually immediate. Not only must the subject overcome a certain amount of muscular inertia and even pre-existing muscular sets, but there are indications that a certain amount of neural reorganization may have to take place at times, introducing an additional latency. One can *overwhelm* the subject with suggestions to a point which is detrimental to the effectiveness of suggestions.

It is a standard procedure among hypnotists, particularly when giving waking suggestions, to tell their subjects, as was done in the case of the Chevreul pendulum experiment (page 89), that not only they will not be able to resist or counteract the suggested effects, but that the more they will try to resist, the less they will be able to do so. What this technique does is rather interesting because it makes use of the subject's very own resistance to overcome itself and to favor the suggestions instead of to hinder them. That is, it renders any resistance self-defeating.

The method is not without danger in regard to the effectiveness of the suggestions—it may suggest to the subject the possibility that he can resist, when otherwise this thought might never have entered his mind. It is therefore probably safer to say, "The more you *try* to resist," rather than "The more you resist," as I have often heard some hypnotists say. The first way has an implication of failure on the part of the subject, whereas the second does not, and even implies some success in resisting. Possibly an even safer way of stating this would be "If you try to resist. . ." Probably a good rule to follow is to use this particular approach only when you suspect the subject is actively attempting to resist or is intending to do so.

The reader who is familiar with some of the older literature has probably been reminded by the above of Baudouin's Law of Reversed Effort.[8] This law states that the suggested relationship between resistance and effectiveness of suggestions is a characteristic property of the latter. It must be clearly understood that when Baudouin formulated his principle he did not have in mind a suggested effect. For him, it was immaterial whether the subject was or was not aware of the existence of such a law because it expressed a characteristic property of all suggestions. Actually, the principle appears to be a typical undemonstrated lore of hypnotism and a pseudo-law. It is doubtful whether responsiveness to suggestion has such a property intrinsically. Where the law seems to act in the absence of specific suggestions by the operator, one would suspect that it is the product of self-suggestion, of a suggestion situation so structured as to suggest this very thing to the subject, or even of the subject's attitude. Frequently subjects submit to suggestions with the belief that they are all-powerful, irresistible and that any effort on their part is doomed to failure. Why increasing effort to overcome the suggestion should have an increasing countereffect is not too clear, unless one assumes that consistent failure to resist has a cumulative effect — as reasonable an explanation as any.

In any event whether or not Baudouin's original formulation is valid need not concern us, since with the technique we advocate the suggestor *deliberately suggests* the law to the subject.

There are many ways of doing the Chevreul pendulum experiment. In one very effective variation, as soon as you have positioned the subject with the bob hanging from his hand, take hold of the bob and hold it still. While still holding it, speak to the subject as follows: "I want you to look at this bob and to start thinking of it as moving. [*You should of course hold it in such a way that it can be seen by the subject.*] In a moment I will release it and you will find that as you keep thinking of it as moving, it will begin to move. At first it will move slightly, but soon it will move more strongly as you keep thinking of its moving and as you listen to me. [*At this point let go of the bob as gently as possible and continue:*] Keep looking at the bob. Pay close attention to it. Don't think about anything else but the bob and what I tell you. Now as you watch it you see it moving in your mind." Continue in this fashion and as instructed earlier. This variation is not essentially different from the previous one. However, it possibly does tend to capitalize a little more upon the spontaneous motions of the pendulum that are nearly certain to take place when it is released. It is important, however, that you do not immediately call the subject's attention to these movements, because he is very likely to recognize them for what they are. Instead, you should continue with a few suggestions that tend to prevent him from thinking about the motion so that when you do call his attention to it, he is more likely to feel it has been brought about through the suggestions. Also, in most instances, the suggestions already given will have tended to develop the motion into something more definite.

Once you have been able to get your subject to produce a given motion, stop the pendulum and say: "That was fine. You did very well. . .Let's try again. This time the pendulum will start to move sooner and more strongly.'' Then proceed as before, altering the suggestions as required. After this, stop the bob and try a different motion. Or, for example, simply tell the subject while the pendulum is swinging right and left: ''Good. Just keep your attention on the bob and listen to me. Very soon the pendulum will swing in a different direction. . .It is going to move in a circle. Think of a circle . . .As you do so, you will find the bob altering its motion so as to move more and more in a circle-like motion. See it is beginning to alter its motion. . . It is moving a little like in a circle. Keep watching and thinking about it. It is moving more and more as in a circle.''

Sometimes the pendulum at first tends to decrease its initial motion and may even come to a standstill when such suggestions are given. This is quite alright, but of course must be taken into consideration in the suggestions. Instead of proceeding as above and following ''See it is beginning to alter its motion,'' continue to speak of it moving in a circle in the future tense, emphasize that the bob is now changing its mode of motion in order to be able to move in a circle. If the motion is much decreased, refer at first to a small circular motion, then once such a movement is induced, build it up with suggestions.

As already mentioned, there are times when you can anticipate future events a little by stating their occurrence even though they are not yet happening. Thus, after saying a few times that the bob *will* move, you can assert quite early that it is now moving a little. This alone will often start a definite motion. The main thing is not to overdo this to the extent of giving a series of obviously false statements to the subject. Such a procedure is particularly indicated if the bob has oscillated a little even though you may suspect that this has been merely the result of the unsteadiness of the subject's hand. There are no set rules as to when one should proceed in this manner. Common sense, the ability to follow hunches and, especially, to judge the kind of subject an individual is likely to be are important. At first, it probably will be best for you to restrict yourself to the first set of instructions (page 89) until you have gained some familiarity with the use of suggestions and with the individual peculiarities of subjects. But once you have gone through this early training, it will be a good idea for you to experiment with the different variations. This remark applies equally well to any of the demonstrations and instructions given in the pages to come.

You may have noticed that in one of the variations discussed above instructions were given to the subject to specifically think of a circle. This may have brought to your mind the procedure you yourself followed when first introduced to the Chevreul pendulum demonstration. This procedure can equally well be used on other individuals. Just as you were instructed in the earlier pages to imagine the desired motion, to think about it, you can similarly instruct the subject at the same time you give him suggestions. This really becomes a part of your suggestions. Conversely, you might now try giving yourself the very same suggestions first used on the subject.

If you do this and compare the results you obtain with these two types of procedures you will be able to demonstrate to yourself that there is essentially no difference between the effects of imagining or thinking about the response to be produced and the initial action of heterosuggestions. This was first demonstrated experimentally by Hull. [85] The reason is simply that in both instances ideomotor action is the main process which is initiated. Since ideomotor action should be, mathematically speaking, a monotonically increasing function of vividness of imagining, it follows that the more vivid the imagining, the greater should be the response. This is one rationale for combining suggestions proper with instructions to imagine. This is also one reason for having the subject follow the imaginary trajectory of the bob or the drawn guide path with his eyes. Presumably this forced voluntary association of motor action with corresponding thoughts either facilitates ideomotor action or leads to some generalization of it.

Undoubtedly these procedures help in some cases, although their experimental validity remains to be shown. On theoretical grounds, one might expect a facilitating effect would probably come about in several other ways. First of all, the procedures are attention-getting, that is, they help focus and maintain attention upon the suggested phenomenon. Second, they may in themselves act as reinforcing nonverbal suggestions. For those individuals with weak imagery, the actual presence of a circle may be an aid in visualizing the motion, which may also be true of the eye motions. Indeed, such a motion, or abortive attempt at it, may arise from looking at the circle which, in a fashion, compels the eyes to follow it. Some facilitative motor interaction may take place between following the circle visually and muscular movements of the hand leading to circular motion of the pendulum, and finally, for some individuals these procedures may assume a sort of magical or ritualistic aspect which induces a more positive attitude which, in turn, increases suggestibility.

A question which always bothers the beginner is how to determine which method to use. There is no definite answer. As you continue your training and gain experience, you will find that subjects differ considerably in their responses to suggestions. It is not always very easy to foretell what is the most efficient way of giving suggestions to a specific individual. After you have had some experience with a person, you will be in a much better position to decide on the initial form of approach on succeeding occasions. In practice, you can only try one method and hope for the best, making use of all available clues. If this fails, try another one. You should keep in mind, however, that it is often a good idea to try the same method again before giving it up, because often the second attempt is successful. Furthermore, if you do find it necessary to use a different method and are successful, you often find that if you again try the one that failed, you will now have success with it also.

You should also keep in mind that you need not always change abruptly from one method to another, but can often make a gradual transition, or even combine several methods. For instance, you might begin as outlined, and if you see you are not getting any effect by merely giving suggestions, you can then continue by instructing the subject to imagine that the bob is moving. If this does not appear to be effective enough, you can add the instructions for the subject to follow the imaginary motion with his eyes. All of this can be done quite smoothly without starting over or giving the subject any indication that anything has gone wrong.

The effect of a successful change in procedure on a previously ineffective suggestion is probably due to generalization of suggestibility. The rationale for giving any complex suggestion at least two tries is that some homo-action may have been produced in quantity sufficient to lead to an appreciable improvement on the second or even third try, even though the subject's overt response may have been poor or nonexistent the first time. You should always keep in mind the possibility that the subject's attitude is responsible for his low suggestibility. In such instances try to find out the reason for the negative attitude and try to get around it. Very often if an individual comes to you insisting that he cannot be hypnotized, responds poorly or fails to respond to suggestions, you can overcome this attitude and resistance by simply asserting with assurance that there is no such thing as a person who is totally nonsuggestible. Proceed then to give the subject the same suggestion repeatedly, in order to build up by homoaction whatever suggestibility he has, and point out any overt response on his part as a proof of your contention as soon as it occurs. Do not stop at the first response, but continue building it up (within reason, of course). This is often all that is needed to get around an individual's belief that he is not responsive to suggestions.

It must be understood that we are concerned here mainly with individuals who merely believe they are not suggestible, and not with the persons who are determined not to be hypnotized. (Even these can often have their resistance broken down by the above procedure.) Such individuals often use this attitude as a defense against their fear of being hypnotized. Because of this it is best to take advantage of any break in their negative attitude and to try to hypnotize them in the same session, giving them suggestions to remove their fear at the same time (see page 395). Otherwise, they may develop greater anxiety and between sessions may build up a very high resistance against any further response to suggestions. This may be contraindicated in psychotherapy or when it is recognized that the subject sees hypnosis as a threat and is likely to react violently to its induction.

BACKWARD POSTURAL SWAY

The following experiment is not much harder to carry out than the preceding one. The procedures are essentially those given as examples in chapter 1. Some variations are introduced here and the reader may wish to compare the two approaches. Both ways of producing the phenomenon of suggested postural sway are equally acceptable. One reason the two descriptions were not duplicated was to demonstrate the general flexibility of suggestions and suggestive procedures.

Before taking up this suggestions, a few general words might be said concerning the approach to a prospective subject. Different situations call for different methods. It may depend upon whether you are giving a demonstration to a group, to one individual (the subject), are performing a scientific experiment, doing therapy, or applying suggestions in some other way. Again, it makes some difference whether you are dealing with individuals who have volunteered as subjects, who are prospective volunteers, are paid subjects, and so on. For the present, we shall assume that you have secured the collaboration of a person who has little if any knowledge concerning the nature of hypnosis. I like to start by saying something like the following to the subject: "I do not know how much you know about hypnotism, so I will tell you a few things about what we are going to do to make sure you do not have any misconceptions about it. First of all, I am not going to put you to sleep. You need not be afraid of that. I will also tell you when I intend to hypnotize you. What we are going to do first, however, is to see how well you can respond to suggestions. Now this depends very much upon how well you cooperate with me. This is not a matter of finding how strong your will or my will is. Frankly, if you have made up your mind to resist, not to cooperate, we may as well call it a day, because I have no intention of trying to overcome your will. But if you are willing to cooperate, to do exactly as I instruct you, then we should be able to do some rather interesting things. I think you will find this not only a very interesting experience, but one which will be beneficial to you in the long run. Most subjects do. Now, do you have any questions? I will be glad to answer them." If the subject has some questions, try to answer them briefly. After this you may proceed with the experiment.

FIG. 5. Backward postural sway, pretesting.

First, if you are doing this demonstration or any variation of it with a woman subject wearing high-heeled shoes, before starting request her to remove them as the heels may snap when she sways backward. In any event, have the subject stand in front of you with his back to you and say:

I want you to stand with your heels and toes together, your hands at your sides. Look straight ahead. Be relaxed and just listen to me. In a few moments I will ask you to think of falling backward and after a little while you will find yourself falling backward. Do not be afraid. Just let yourself go. I will be right behind you to catch you. Let me show you how it will feel. [*At this point place yourself no more than a foot away from him, and placing your hands on his shoulders, pull him gently but firmly backward (fig. 5). If necessary, step back a little bit yourself. Nearly always the subject also steps backward to prevent himself from falling. If he does this, bring him back to an upright posture and keeping your hands on his shoulders, say:*] You stepped back. That is exactly what you must not do. You did it because you were afraid I might let you fall. But you see, I was right here to catch you. We will try it again. This time try to let yourself go. Don't be afraid. . .Alright now, just relax. [*Repeat the above procedure. Normally the subject will let himself fall this time, pivoting on his heels, or at least he will offer only very little resistance. Actually, regardless of whether or not he does step back again, go on and say:*] That was better. [*Or if he did not show any resistance say:*] Very good. You did real fine that time. [*Continue with:*] Now I want you to stand the same way again, heels and toes together, arms at your sides. . .Hold your head up straight [*with your hand under his chin tilt his head back slightly*], close your eyes and listen closely to what I say. [*Proceed similarly if the subject responds correctly the first time. Should he still show slight resistance or mistrust, point this out to him. Reassure him about falling, tell him that you will not let him fall any further than he fell just now. Then continue, repeating this if necessary. Then proceed as indicated, continuing as follows:*] Now I want you to think of falling backward. . .Imagine that you are falling backward, that a force is pulling you backward. In a few moments you will feel a force pulling you backward. There is a force pulling you backward. You feel a force pulling you backward. A force is pulling you backward, pulling you backward. You are falling backward, you are falling backward, backward. You are falling. You cannot help yourself. You are falling, *falling*, FALL!*

Most persons will fall backward when given the above suggestions. Some will waver or sway, but not fall completely. Some will tend to step backward. In the first case point out to the subject that he swayed. Say something like: "You did not quite fall this time. . .But you did sway quite a bit. You felt yourself being pulled back, didn't you? [*Continue immediately without letting the subject really answer the question.*] However, I think you were a little afraid to fall. Let's try it again, but this time let yourself go. Don't be afraid. I am right behind you ready to catch you. Now put your heels together." In the second case say: "Now you did not trust me. That is too bad because you would have fallen back had you not stepped back. Let us try it again, but this time try to be relaxed and try to let yourself fall when you feel yourself pulled back. Alright. Place your heels together."

Suppose now that your subject did not even sway. Speak to him in the following way:

---

*A variation of this experiment is to limit the subject's motion to swaying, falling becoming more an incidental effect. Since the detailed procedures for this effect are given in a later part of this book in connection with a technique of trance induction, the reader is referred to that section for details (chapter 8).

I am afraid that you are not cooperating fully. . .You must have resisted. Maybe you are afraid I will let you fall. I assure you I won't. I will be right behind you. You did feel something, didn't you?. . . [*Again do not allow the subject to fully answer you if you can help it, but go right on with:*] Now, let us try it again, but this time, relax. Think only of falling. *Try to imagine yourself falling. Feel yourself falling.* . . [*Use increasing emphasis as you say these words*] and whatever happens, don't resist. Just let yourself go. Now think of falling, only of falling. Keep thinking of falling.

How many times should you try this? Usually not more than twice, unless the subject shows definite evidence of responding to your suggestions the second time; then you can try a third time. In this regard you must be guided to some extent by the various considerations which will be brought up here and elsewhere in the book. Obviously, if you are only trying to get some practice, then short of boring and tiring your subject you can repeat this and other experiments as many times as you feel necessary. Again, if you feel that there is something to be gained by repeating the procedure, such as when the subject resists because of a fear of falling, then you may want to continue. On the other hand, it is often better to try out a different suggestion and come back to this one later, particularly after you have obtained other good results, because if the individual's resistance is caused by his fear of falling, not by low innate suggestibility, he may respond quite well to suggestions that do not cause him any anxiety. You may also guide yourself by the situation and your purpose for giving suggestions. In a demonstration, for instance, where a number of volunteer subjects are available and where one is primarily interested in getting good results quickly, it is best to stop using a poor subject entirely and go on to the next subject or to try one other suggestion on him, rather than repeat the falling back suggestion. But if your main concern is to get the most out of the subject's suggestibility, then you may want to try repeatedly to elicit a good response from him. Even if you decide on this course of action, you may find it well worth repeating the experiment with *variations*. Some possible ones will be given shortly.

Here as elsewhere it is essential to keep firing a continuous barrage of suggestions at the subject. *He must not be allowed to think of anything but the effect to be produced.* Speak normally, unless otherwise indicated. Pause approximately as indicated in the sample suggestions, but never very long. Keep firing suggestions at him. This is particularly important when he begins to respond. It is then that you should particularly hammer the suggestions at him, quickening your delivery and placing more emphasis on the words.

In doing this experiment you should watch out for three things. Sometimes, although rarely, the subject tends to fall in the direction opposite to the one suggested; always be ready to catch him no matter which way he may fall. Again, on rare occasions you may get a subject who responds strongly almost from the start; if you are not watching out for this, you may be caught off balance. Finally, there are certain disorders of the nervous system in which individuals lose their balance when they close their eyes. The direction of their fall is usually unpredictable. Be on watch for this.

Many variations of this experiment are possible and you may find it of interest to try some. For instance, the subject's eyes need not be closed, although it usually facilitates the response. (I rarely have my subjects close their eyes in practice.) Furthermore, the head need not be tilted back as instructed earlier, although again this can have a facilitating effect. If you choose to proceed this way, just tell the subject to look straight ahead.

Let us stop a moment and examine a few of the things that we have done. You will recall that in a number of places the subject was asked certain rhetorical questions. In brief we asked the subject to confirm an asserted fact but did not allow him time to do so. The purpose of this is multifold, as is quite often the case with various steps in a suggestion procedure. In the present case, there are reasons to believe that some of the responses of subjects are nonovert, hence the hypnotist cannot be certain that they took place. If they did occur, however, many hypnotists feel that calling the subject's attention to the event has a positive action upon his suggestibilty. Presumably this works through his attitude and possibly also through heteroaction. In some cases the subject may have had only a vague and weak experience and is not really aware of having responded. Asking him about it calls his attention to it and will often reinforce and bring this experience more fully into awareness. The question also may act as an additional indirect suggestion. On the other hand, because the response was weak or subliminal, the subject may have doubts that he experienced the suggested force, or he may have a critical mind and analyze the situation, concluding that his experience had nothing to do with the suggestions. This could have an adverse effect upon future suggestions, so one does not want to allow him too much time to think about the matter. In addition, in the absence of critical thinking, the question is more likely to function as a suggestion. Quite apart from this, many hypnotists believe that as long as the subject is unable to verbalize his doubts or deny the effect, there is little harm in asking the question. I do not know that there is any demonstrated basis for this view. Possibly the thinking of most individuals is clearest and most effective when it can be verbalized. In any case the rhetorical question is aimed at allowing the hypnotist to make the most use of the subject's possible non-overt responses without running too great a risk of eliciting a negative reaction by making an incorrect assertion or stimulating potential doubts. In many instances the entire matter may reduce to a question of successful bluffing.

As was pointed out, it is sometimes of help to have the subject close his eyes when postural sway suggestions are given. It is an observed fact that an individual with his eyes closed finds it more difficult to maintain his equilibrium and he will often sway appreciably. In any event he will be more likely to sway and fall if any tendency toward falling is induced. This effect is probably largely due to the fact that much of the normal spatial frame of reference used by the subject in orienting his body and in regulating his posture makes use of visual cues. Some years ago I met a subject who seemed to be quite impervious to suggestions. Yet, there were reasons to believe that he was innately suggestible. After trying every method of producing postural sway, I finally resorted to having the subject close his eyes. Not only was the response to postural sway suggestions powerful and immediate, but the induction of hypnosis, which until now had also been impossible, took place in record time and the subject entered a very deep trance state (chapter 15).

Similarly, when the subject's head is forcibly tilted back as part of the procedure for inducing postural sway, this shifts his center of gravity further back, consequently he is more easily thrown off balance. As a result, backward swaying and falling are favored. This and the use of eye closure as aids in the production of body sway raise the question of deception. First we must ask whether this is really deceiving the subject, and if so, whether it is justified. Does postural sway boil down to merely an illusion, a deception perpetrated upon the subject and not an expression of suggestibility? To begin with the last query first, there is considerable evidence that suggestions usually contribute something to the subject's motion quite apart from any effects of deception. What we are doing here, in most cases, is to set up certain physical conditions which allow us to magnify suggestion-induced effects which might otherwise be too weak to become evident. Thus, by shifting the subject's center of gravity, we make it possible to topple him backward with a much weaker suggested muscular reaction than would have been possible otherwise. There is no more deception in this than in the use of an optical lever to detect weak physical forces, as is done with galvanometers. In other words, suggestive phenomena can be produced without the use of deceiving devices or "hocus-pocus," as some have put it. The phenomena are real. There is a possibility that in using these devices a hypnotist might deceive himself into believing an individual is suggestible when he is not. There is no question that if one displaces the center of gravity too much, particularly if this is combined with the removal of visual cues, the subject may sway and even fall without the aid of suggestions. Misuse of a tool is always possible. Self-deception might also occur by using an ataxic individual who, with closed eyes, will tend to sway and fall anyway. On the whole, however, the occurrence of such accidents is rather unlikely.

There is another point to be considered here. *The chief aim of the hypnotist is to elicit maximum suggestibility in his subjects.* It is a matter of simple observation that very often, if the subject can be made to perform some suggested act, even abortively, his suggestibility will rise. This is true regardless of the actual mechanism through which it is done. As a matter of fact, there is evidence that something akin to homoaction takes place even as a result of voluntary response. However, this is not half as important as the fact already brought out that if a subject executes a response following a given suggestion, there occurs a *generalization* of whatever suggestibility he possesses at the time, *regardless of the true causation of the response.* Abstract conditioning does not depend specifically upon the true origin of the response. It therefore becomes a matter of expediency and practicality to use so-called "deception" methods as a means of increasing suggestibility. These are really no more deceptions than the use of any other artificial means of raising suggestibility (e.g., drugs) or than the use of a crutch to aid a person in walking until his ailing members become sufficiently strong to support him alone. Finally, provided the subject does not become aware of the exact nature of his response, his attitude and expectancies will be altered in a more positive direction and this will favor future truly suggestion-induced responses.

In any event, regardless of whether or not we speak of "deception" here, the important point to keep in mind is that such "deception" is a means of producing increased suggestibility, an adjuvant, not an end in itself.

One method I have found extremely effective, but which is somewhat more difficult to use, is as follows: Have the subject stand in front of you as before. Now move up very close to him, nearly touching him, and extend your arms outward on either side of his head as close as possible without touching him. Bring your hands to the level of his eyes, and curve your fingers slightly inward so that he may fix his eyes on them (fig. 6*A*). Extend your hands as far forward as possible and say: "Look at my fingers. I want you to think of falling backward, to imagine you are falling backward. In a moment I will pull my hands backward and as I do so, you will feel a force

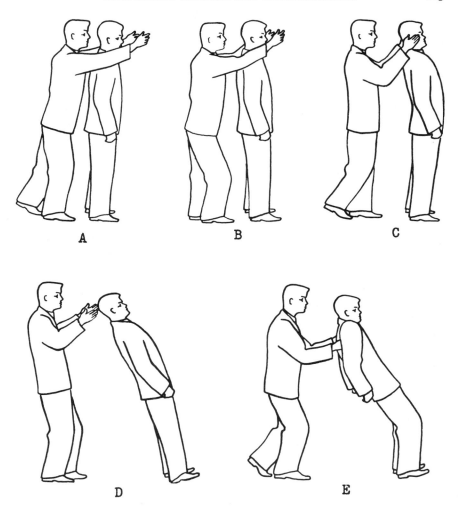

FIG. 6 *A-E*. Backward postural sway.

pulling you backward. Keep watching my fingers. As I pull my hands backward [*begin to do this rather slowly*], you will feel a force pulling you backward. You begin to feel a force pulling you backward. You feel a force pulling you backward. You are going to fall backward. A force is pulling you backward. You are falling backward. A force is pulling you . . . more and

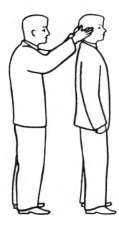

Fig. 7. Backward postural sway, variant of the initial step.

more. You are falling backward, falling, *falling*, FALLING, FALL!'' All the time you are speaking you are also moving your hands backward, at first rather slowly, then with increasing speed. This is done at first by flexing the elbows outward (fig. 6B). At the same time, you prepare yourself to step backward, beginning to actually step back as your hands approach the subject's face (fig. 6C). By this time, if you are at all successful, the subject should be swaying strongly backwards and you should near the end of the suggestion. As your hands now pass rapidly by the side of his face and you finish stepping backward (fig. 6D), you command emphatically "FALL!'' and immediately bring your hands in position to catch the subject (fig. 6E). Some hypnotists prefer to start with their hands placed at the level of the subject's eyes on either side of the face with the edge of the hands horizontal and the base of the palm at the level of the temple (fig. 7).

As you can see, this method requires considerable coordination between what you say and what you do. Timing is even more crucial here than before. However, it is a very effective method which combines a number of effects. The fixating of the subject's eyes upon your fingers is primarily used as a device for focusing attention. It is unlikely that it produces any degree of hypnosis of itself because it is not allowed to persist long enough. Indirectly, however, it probably aids in rendering the effect of the backward motion of the hands more effective. This movement most likely acts as an additional nonverbal suggestion. It may be too that the subject tends reflexively to avoid the approaching hands by leaning backward or at least tilting his

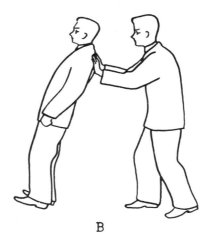

A   B

FIG. 8 *A, B.* Backward postural sway, a variation.

head further back, thus displacing his center of gravity and favoring sway. At the same time he probably does not recognize his avoidance response for what it is and confounds it with the expected suggested sway. Thus attitude and generalization of suggestibility may also be indirectly and positively influenced.

A much more subtle effect has also been used in this technique. It has already been remarked that the proper choice of words is of great importance in giving effective suggestions. The wording of the suggestion used here is a good example of what this means in practice. Consider the statement, "As I *pull* my hands *backward*" which was employed a few moments ago. This choice of words was no accident. We might have said, "As I bring my hands toward you," for instance. But note, "pull" and "backward" are two key words which describe the suggested effect and are used for that purpose in the suggestion. Although they are now employed in a different context, we may hope that through association they will also suggest this effect as well as enhance the indirect suggestion contained in the actual hand movements. At the same time the suggestion as a whole becomes more tightly knit and concentrated, so to speak.

A relatively simple variation involves your standing a foot or so behind the subject and placing your hands, palms flat against his shoulder blades (fig. 8*A*), your arms being partly extended straight in front of you. Your hands should be so oriented that the tips of your fingers point toward the top of his shoulders. It is quite common here to begin by hooking the fingers over the shoulder in order to be able to pull the subject gently backward. If this is the case, when you are ready to start suggesting, you should slide the hands further down. The remainder of the procedure is much the same as before, except that now after the introductory instructions you say: "As I pull my hands back (or away) from your shoulders, you will feel a force pulling you backward." When you do pull your hands away, do it very gently and slowly at first, trying to maintain contact with his body until you can detect a very definite sway (fig. 8B). Some hypnotists recommend hooking the fingers lightly over the shoulders and tugging gently backward, thus adding a purely mechanical effect to aid the initiation of the movement.

In olden days hypnotists, then more commonly known as magnetizers, believed that a magnetic-like influence was actually exerted by the hands. In addition to this effect, they believed that the subject, if susceptible to the influence of the hands, would also experience a peculiar sensation of warmth and even a tingling where the hands were applied. They would often tell the subject this was going to happen as a result of the magnetic emanations, more usually called "animal magnetism," supposedly coming from the hands. Many subjects would report having this sensation. Today it is believed that these effects were probably the result of suggestions, although many subjects will report such experiences even when this is not directly suggested to them. Some also feel a very definite force acting upon them, even when one omits the mention of force from the suggestions and regardless of the particular procedure used.

Excluding animal magnetism as an explanation, how are we to account for this phenomenon? To tell the truth one can only make guesses regarding both its nature and causation. 1. It may simply be a matter of self-suggested hallucinations where no suggestion of force is given or, in other instances, the hallucination would be a direct result of the suggestions given the subject. 2. Past experience associating the feeling of a force with the act of falling may give rise to a conditioned (or associated) hallucination. The production of this kind of hallucination has been demonstrated experimentally. Here, the falling response produces cues that in turn act in the capacity of conditioned stimuli for the sensory experience of a force. 3. The subject's need to avoid environmental ambiguity and his need for closure may make him perceive a force where there is none. 4. The nonspecificity of sensory impulses may be another mechanism. When an individual falls, he reflexively makes muscular adjustments intended to restore his position. Even with relaxed and cooperative individuals there must be some adjustive muscular tension patterns taking place in this manner. These adjustments give rise to patterns of proprioceptive impulses which are nearly the same in their dominant characteristics whether a force is or is not responsible for the subject's falling. In the absence of adequate supplementary information, the central nervous system cannot discriminate sufficiently between the proprioceptive patterns of stimulation resulting from falling as a result of a disturbing force or falling in the absence of a force. Because a force is usually involved, the nervous system interprets the information received in terms of the presence of a force and the subject experiences one. 5. Finally, the hallucinated force might arise as a result of a spontaneous alteration of body awareness, such as is known to arise during the induction of hypnosis.[191]

It is extremely difficult to say whether any one of these mechanisms is more likely than the others to account for the illusion of a force. I think it possible that all of them enter into the picture at one time or another. Some, like the proprioceptor element (4), would be expected to play a part in all cases. Others, like the alteration of body awareness (5), may play a more infrequent part. More generally, one might think of each process as being able to contribute in varying degrees, ranging from a maximum to none, to the illusion in any given situation.

The experience of heat emanating from the hands of the hypnotist is no better understood. This has been reported not only when the hands are used as described in the postural sway experiment, but also when "passes" of various kinds are employed. Possibly the situation focuses the subject's attention upon the hypnotist's hands, making him particularly aware of any body heat. The tingling which has been reported may very well be caused by reflex pilomotor action. Here again, self-suggestion or alterations of body awareness may be a causative agent.

Still another way of bringing about backward sway is to face the subject and ask him to look at your eyes. You should then steadily fixate your eyes upon the bridge of his nose and stand far enough from him to be able to take at least one step forward. You then proceed to say something like: "Keep looking at my eyes. In a few moments you will feel a force pushing you backward so that you will fall backward. Think of falling backward. . .You are going to feel a force pushing you backward. A force is pushing you backward, a force is pushing you. You are beginning to feel a force pushing you backward, forcing you to fall backward. You are going to fall. You are falling backward (etc.)." About this time you should begin to step forward very slowly and gently toward the subject. At the same time continue giving the suggestions. Many beginners feel rather uncomfortable having to "look the subject steadily in the eyes." Instead of eye fixation you may have the subject look at your finger held in front of him. You should hold your finger

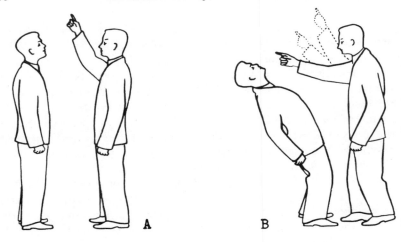

FIG. 9 *A, B.* Backward postural sway, still another variation.

above and slightly in front of your head, so that the subject has to look up-ward at it (fig. 9*A*). Give suggestions of falling backward as described earlier on page 104, and at the point where you begin to pull your hands toward the subject's face, now begin to move your finger very gently toward his face, increasing the pace rather slowly (fig. 9*B*).

In these variations you should make certain that an assistant is available to catch the subject since you may find it difficult to do this too, although it can be done.

In the above instructions you were told to have the subject look at your eyes and in turn you were to look steadily at the bridge of his nose. There are many procedures in the hypnotic literature which call for this step, seemingly implying that the eyes possess special suggestion enhancing powers. Indeed, the "hypnotic eye" myth is a classic. I do not know of anything specifically hypnotic about the eye in general other than the belief the subject may have that the eyes have such a property. Such a belief should certainly not be discounted as an important aid in giving suggestions when it is present. Possibly the myth reflects some specific aspect or element of the peculiar interpersonal relationship in the hypnotic situation. Thus far, however, the role of the eyes in suggestion phenomena appears to be merely that of an instrument for focusing the subject's attention. It is not even determined whether it is especially attention compelling.* Trainees are usual-

*Although there is a lack of experimental evidence in this respect, there is an abundance of material concerning the "hypnotic," magical, and attention compelling properties of the eyes to

ly recommended to maintain a steady, intent gaze. Actually, I have not found that moderate blinking ever caused any serious interference. As already stated, the subject looks into the hypnotist's eyes while the latter actually fixes his gaze on the bridge of the subject's nose. This is said to give the subject the impression of a very penetrating gaze being fixed on his eyes and to be easier on the hypnotist. It is also said to help if the hypnotist opens his eyes as wide as possible. Many hypnotists recommend that the trainee do certain exercises to develop a fixed, penetrating gaze. Whether these exercises really help, I could not say. The simplest way is for the individual to practice steadily fixating upon some point as long as possible. A black dot on a piece of paper will do very well. Another method, which is probably superior inasmuch as it is more lifelike, is to fixate on the reflection of the bridge of your nose in a mirror. You can practice giving appropriate suggestions at the same time.

Every so often someone asks me worriedly whether there is danger of the hypnotist becoming accidentally hypnotized either while doing this exercise or while fixating upon the subject. It is conceivable, but very unlikely. I do not know of any well authenticated case. The evidence seems to indicate that if hypnosis by eye-fixation alone is possible, it requires complete concentration upon the act of fixation, plus a certain mental set; since the hypnotist does not do this sort of intense mental concentration nor has he the appropriate set, the procedure appears relatively safe.

All of the suggestions which have been given as models up till now make considerable use of repetition. It is not always necessary to give the subject a lengthy repetition of suggestions to get the desired effects. Indeed, one single statement can sometimes be fully satisfactory. A surprisingly effective technique consists in saying to the subject: "I want you to listen carefully to what I am going to tell you. I am going to count to three and at three you will feel an irresistible urge to fall backward. Do not be afraid to fall, I will catch you. Alright now. One. . .two. . .THREE! FALL!" The degree of success one may expect to have here is a function of the degree of suggestibility of the subject. Therefore this technique usually is most successful if used after the subject has responded to a variety of suggestions or, even better, has been hypnotized since in either case his suggestibility will have been increased.

A rather uncommon occurrence which may take place with the falling response is the subject going into a trance or semitrance state. This can

be found in folklores. Whether this is an indication that the eyes do have properties not recognized to date, simply reflects the unconscious recognition of the importance of vision, or has a deeper psychoanalytic meaning, must remain a question.

happen when giving *any* waking suggestion, although I have seen it occur most often in connection with the falling response and the eye catalepsy suggestion. In most instances, the subject appears to be unstable on his legs when he is helped back to his feet after falling. He may sway a little or move "drunkenly." He may appear somewhat dazed. Sometimes he tends to remain standing passively wherever you last left him. In such cases, unless you want to take advantage of the situation to produce a deep trance, you should approach the subject, snap your fingers near his face and say in a positive tone of voice: "Wake up! You are wide awake, you feel fine." Talk with him a few moments to make sure that he is fully awake. A good rule to apply in all cases when you use suggestions is to *never allow your subject to leave you until you make sure that he is fully awake and that there are no aftereffects of your suggestions.* This is true regardless of the kind of suggestion you have used. Of course, it is more crucial in the case of hypnotic suggestions.

You will also find it edifying to try this experiment on yourself and this is strongly recommended. You should get a friend to stand behind you ready to catch you if you fall. The procedure is essentially the same as with a subject. Stand in the same manner as you instruct your subjects. You may either close your eyes or keep them open. If you suspect you may have some difficulty in responding, closing your eyes may help, otherwise look straight ahead of you. Then think of falling backward. Imagine yourself falling. Think how it feels to be falling backward. At the same time tell yourself that you are falling backward, that a force is pulling you, etc. In other words, tell yourself what you would tell a subject.

FORWARD POSTURAL SWAY

The following experiment is really nothing more than a variation of the one just described. The simplest way of proceeding is merely to have the subject stand as in the previous experiment, with his eyes closed, and then to give him suggestions like those for falling back, using the word "forward" wherever "backward" occurs. Of course, you should be close at hand in front of the subject to catch him if he falls (or have someone else do that.)

Another very effective way of giving these suggestions is as follows: Stand in front of the subject quite close to him. Lean forward so as to bring your face close to his, telling him: "I want you to look into my eyes." At the same time you fix your gaze on the bridge of his nose,* and raise your elbows

---

*Henceforth when we say "have the subject look at your eyes," "look into the subject's eyes," or "fixate the subject" we will mean having the subject look at your eyes and you fixate upon the bridge of his nose.

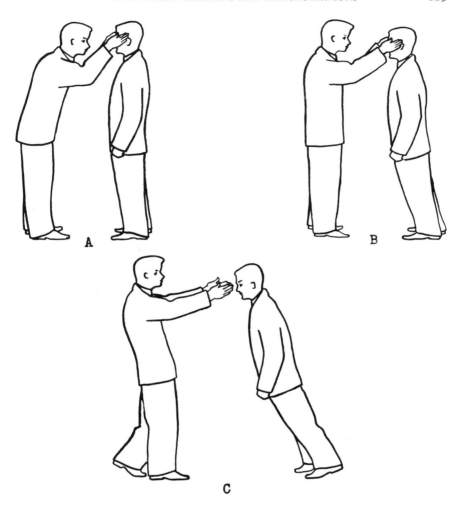

Fig. 10 *A-C.* Forward postural sway.

horizontally, bringing the tips of your extended hands to either side of his head so they nearly touch his temples (fig. 10*A*). Your elbows should be flexed. Now tell the subject that he is going to fall forward, that in a moment he will feel a force pulling him forward, that he will fall forward, and so on. Very often the subject will tend to sway forward a little. If he does, so much the better. You can take advantage of this by timing your suggestions with this effect. In any event, after a few moments of these suggestions, slowly move your body and head away from the subject, keeping your hand in the same position. You merely straighten your arms as you do this (fig. 10B). Continue giving suggestions of falling forward, of feeling a force pulling forward. You will have to step back slowly while you are doing this. You should not straighten your arms completely but instead, while they are still partially flexed, you stiffen them in this position so that your hands begin to pull away from the subject as you keep moving back (fig. 10C). Do not allow the subject to fall too far.

An alternative to this procedure is having the subject fixate on your upraised finger as described earlier. You then move your finger away from the subject, partially by moving it away and partly by stepping away. Do not hold your finger too close (not less than 8 to 10 inches) otherwise the subject will have difficulty focusing both eyes on it. You can either stand a little to the side of the subject and move your hand and finger sideways, or you can stand squarely in front of him and move your finger away by backing slowly (figs. 11 A, B, C).

Still another variation is as follows: Place your fingers over the subject's shoulders with your palms lightly pressing against the upper front part of the shoulders. Look the subject in the eyes and proceed as before. Presently you let go of his shoulders and very gently and gradually pull back your hands.

Here again there are many occasions when you can bring about the falling response by a single suggestion-statement. Thus you may simply tell the subject: "As soon as I clap my hands, if you let yourself be relaxed, you will be attracted forward and you will fall forward." Still another variation is to face the subject, look him in the eyes, and after making the above statement move quickly backward.

As previously recommended, you can also try this demonstration using autosuggestions. Be sure to have someone available to catch you if you fall.

SIDEWAYS POSTURAL SWAY

If you have succeeded in causing your subject to fall forward, you should have no difficulty with the following demonstration. Face your subject and fixate upon the bridge of his nose. Speak to him firmly as follows: "Look at my eyes. . .In a moment you are going to feel a force pulling you to the right. Just relax and think of falling to the right. Look steadily at my eyes. You are going to fall to the right. A force is now pulling you to the right, more and more to the right. An irresistible force is attracting you. You are being

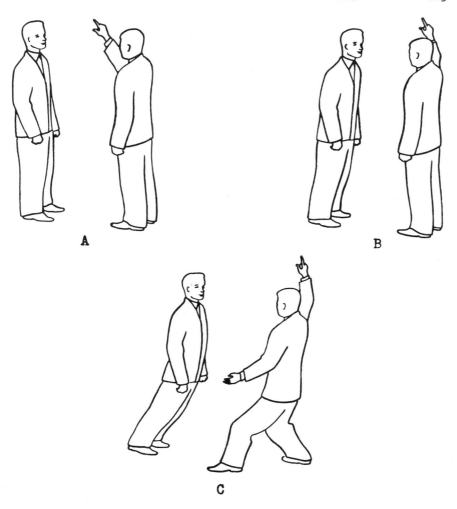

A

B

C

FIG. 11 *A-C.* Forward postural sway, variation.

pulled to the right. You are falling to the right, *falling*, FALLING, FALL!''

If the subject seems to show some delay in responding to the suggestions it often helps if you lean slowly toward your left while you talk. Keep your eyes focused upon the bridge of the subject's nose at all times.

Actually, you can get very good results by merely giving the suggestions without fixating upon the subject. Another variant is to have the subject fixate on your upraised finger, which is then moved sideways and downward in an arc toward your left at the proper moment. A similar procedure can be employed to make the subject sway and fall to the left.

FORCED WALK

If you have found a subject who is definitely responsive to postural sway suggestions, particularly one who falls completely, then you can proceed with the following interesting experiment. You will be most likely to succeed with it if you do it immediately after the subject has responded to the postural sway suggestions. Face the subject, fixating him, and say:

> Look at my eyes. In a moment you will find yourself pulled (or pushed)* backward. A force will pull you backward. You will find it impossible to resist, and you will have to walk backward to prevent yourself from falling. You will have to walk backward because an irresistible force will pull you backward. . .Keep looking at my eyes. As you do so you feel a force pulling you backward. In a moment you will have to step backward to keep from falling. You are going to walk backward. You will take one step back. . .and another. . .and another . . .You are being pulled backward and you are now stepping back. . . [*saying this you advance slowly toward the subject*] and stepping back again . . .and again. . .You cannot help yourself. . .Each step that you take will make you take another. . .(etc.).

All this time you are advancing forward toward the subject. Usually, if he is responding well, you will be able to stop walking and merely keep on suggesting at this stage. In many instances you will find that you can now say: "You are going to keep on walking backward until I tell you to stop. You will not be able to help yourself." You can then stop talking and merely keep fixating the subject; even this may often be discontinued. When doing this experiment you should make sure that you have enough space and that there are no obstacles with which the subject might collide.

It is also possible to do this experiment standing behind the subject. The procedure does not differ essentially, except that you cannot make use of the additional effects of advancing toward the subject or of eye fixation. This method is safer since you can easily catch the subject should he fall backward. However, by gaging your suggestions this accident is unlikely to

---

*Either word is usually satisfactory. If the subject has experienced a pull previously with the postural sway suggestions he is most likely to experience the same here and to speak of a push would be incongruous.

occur. In any event, it is always a good idea to instruct someone to stand ready to catch the subject should he fall.

In the same manner you can force the subject to walk forward. Face your subject and as you fixate upon the bridge of his nose say in a positive tone of voice: "Look into my eyes. You are going to find yourself thinking only of coming forward. No matter how hard you resist, you will find a force pulling you forward and you will have to step forward, to walk forward in order not to fall. You are now being pulled forward. A force is pulling you forward. You are beginning to lean forward. You cannot prevent yourself from doing so. . .the more you try to resist the less you will be able to and the more you will lean. You are falling. . .STEP forward so as not to fall. You are going to follow me, to follow me. You are walking forward, stepping forward. You cannot help yourself. A force is pulling you forward . . .FOLLOW ME!" At the same time you should slowly step back keeping your eyes fixed on the subject.

To end this effect, snap your fingers or clap your hands saying in a positive tone: "Alright, you may stop now. . .Everything is fine. You feel perfectly normal. . .very well. . .(etc.)."

The same demonstrations can be done by having the subject look at your upraised finger. Tell him that he is being attracted or repulsed by the finger. One way to introduce the suggestions in this case is as follows: "Look steadily at my finger. I am going to count to three, and as soon as I have done so you will be forced to walk backward. You will not be able to resist, you will be strongly pulled backward and you will have to step backward again and again. . .You will have to walk backward. [*Allow the subject to fixate for a few seconds, then count.*] One. . .two. . .*three*. You are now being pulled backward. You are stepping backward, backward. You are walking backward . . .(etc.)." As you say these last words move your finger quickly toward the subject and continue to move it toward him as he walks backward.

Still another variation consists in fixating the subject and saying to him: "As soon as I show you my finger you will find yourself pushed back by it. You will not be able to prevent yourself from being pushed back. You will step backward, and you will step back again and again. You will walk backward. . .Think of walking backward. . .(etc.)." At this point briskly bring your finger in front of the subject's face and he will step back.

Those readers who are familiar with the older literature will be reminded by the forced walk experiment of the classical demonstration of "fascination" by Donato and other early investigators. The main difference is that in the traditional demonstration no suggestions were given, at least outwardly. The hypnotist would simply stare hard into the subject's eyes, usually doing this rather abruptly. If he then backed away without a word, the subject appeared to be forced to follow him until the visual link was broken in some fashion. "Fascination" at one time held a special place among hypnotic phenomena, being ascribed to some mysterious emanations from the eyes and being said to be the means by which some wild beasts overpowered their prey. The snake, in particular, was thought to have great powers of fascination and there are tales of these reptiles forcing birds perched on the branches of trees to fall into their open jaws by merely looking at them. In Europe and other parts of the world there used to be (and probably still are) beliefs that certain "thieves of women and children" made a practice of kidnapping by merely looking the victims in the eyes and fascinating them into following wherever they led. What truth there is in this I cannot say, but I have never encountered an authentic case. It is conceivable that in a culture where such a belief was prevalent and taught to its members from infancy, such fascination would be a reality, a product of social suggestion.

As the notion of "fascination" evolved, it ceased to be the sole property of the "fascinator's" eyes. It soon came to be identified with the action of any powerful attention compelling device, usually acting through or upon the subject's vision. It most commonly had the property of attracting or of immobilizing him, of paralyzing his volition, and more generally of placing the will of the "fascinated" individual under the domination of the device or agent operating it. In time, such a power was ascribed even to inanimate objects. Thus it was said, for instance, that individuals "fascinated" by a stone falling over a precipice might be compelled to follow it.

Brémaud[20] seems to have been the first scientific investigator to have observed, studied and reported upon the so-called "state of fascination." Indeed, according to Cullerre[34] he named it. According to both of these investigators, this condition precedes the other three classical states of the Charcot School (see chapter 9) in the sense that these can be derived from it by means of various physical manipulations of the subject, but the converse is apparently not true. The state is best described as one of paralysis of the will, exaltation of the intellectual faculties and an overpowering tendency for perfect imitation of all of the acts of the hypnotist on the part of the subject.

Whether there is such a phenomenon as "fascination" remains uncertain. By Brémaud's own admission, only certain individuals could go into this condition. Interestingly enough, it cannot be brought about in women, whether "hysterics" or "normal." According to Cullerre, this is not because the condition cannot exist in them, but simply because they have a much greater diathesis for the "cataleptic state" and tend to pass immediately into it whenever any fascination-inducing procedures are used. Actually, he adds, fascination is a precursor of catalepsy and does occur fleetingly when catalepsy is induced in women. All in all, this is rather reminiscent of the situation existing in the other three classical states of hypnosis. In looking over various reports it would seem that in some cases "animal hypnosis" was really involved. In others, one has the impression of actually dealing with the Braid effect. This may indeed be, for as Cullerre points out, in the initial stage of the Braid effect one does briefly observe certain symptoms characteristic of the fascination state. However, it would seem likely that in many instances one is dealing with a suggested effect, and if one goes along with the Nancy School, this would presumably always be the case. As with the symptoms of the "grande hystérie," a few instances of fascination may have been pathological individuals whose responses became the prototype for other suggestible individuals. As Cullerre points out, a number of "imitative" disorders have been described in the past, and are still found. Echolalia was not only known as pathological, but was also described as one of the ways in which fascination manifested itself. It is possible that this condition was really a mixture of the various phenomena just mentioned. In general, the impression one gets from the literature is that fascination is not a phenomenon distinct from those that have just been mentioned.

FORCED IMBALANCE

This is still another application of postural sway suggestions. Fixate the subject and say:

> I want you to think that it is impossible for you to hold yourself straight. As soon as I have counted to three you will find it is impossible to stand straight. You will find yourself being pulled forward. . .backward. . .to the left. . .to the right and in every direction. It will be impossible for you to remain standing straight. It will be as if you were drunk. You will find it impossible to maintain your balance. I shall now count to three and then you will be pulled in every direction. One. . . two. . .*three*. Now you cannot hold yourself straight any longer. . .See . . .you are leaning to the right. . .Now to the left. . .You cannot remain straight. . .Now you are leaning backward. . .forward. . .You cannot retain your balance. . .the more you try the less you can. . . (etc.).

The subject may dislike behaving as if drunk, this word being objectionable to him. Often he will tell you so. In this case, you can substitute the word "dizzy" for "drunk" after starting over again. Some operators also like to add suggestions at the start that the subject's feet are stuck to the floor in order to decrease the possibility of the subject's falling.

Be ready to catch the subject should he really lose his balance. A method often quite effective is to have the subject fixate on your finger, and to slowly move your finger forward, backward, sideways, etc., in accord with the suggestions. The subject will appear to follow your finger.

Instead of using your finger, you can have the subject fixate on an object held in your hand in all of these experiments. Some hypnotists have devised all sorts of so-called "hypnotic balls" or "disks" for this purpose. Actually a pencil will do just as well, although it is better to use a bright metallic object. A quarter held between two fingers will work very nicely. For greater flexibility it is probably preferable to use some object having some sort of stem. For this purpose I have often employed a hat pin with an artificial pearl at one end.

The use of an object or your finger as a focus for visual fixation has certain advantages over the use of your eyes for the same purpose. First, it may be easier for the hypnotist. More important it allows the hypnotist more freedom to watch the progress of his suggestions. With eye fixation, the hypnotist is limited to seeing what falls within his field of vision. Although one can see an amazing amount with peripheral vision, it remains limited. In the case of sway suggestions, forced walk, the induction of hypnosis, etc., this is not important; on the other hand, with such suggestions as hand levitation and as hand clasping, to be discussed later, this is some disadvantage. The main advantage of eye fixation over other fixation methods is that it appears to be more effective, more compelling, probably because of the subject's attitude. To a large extent a bright object seems to have some of these advantages too.

ARM OR HAND LEVITATION

We will take up one more demonstration in this chapter. As with the other experiments, there is no single way of carrying it out. The following method is one of the simpler ones. As you will see later, this particular demonstration can be made an integral part of a very effective method for inducing hypnosis.

Have your subject sit in a chair and place his right hand on his lap. He can use his left hand if he prefers. Now speak to him as follows:

> I want you to sit in this chair and be as relaxed as possible. . .Just relax and look at your right hand. Think of your hand and listen to my voice. In a few moments you may notice a strange feeling in your hand.

It may be like a sort of numbness, or a tingling, or some other sensation. It does not matter which. In any case, your hand is going to move very soon. Just how, I do not know, but it will move. Maybe it will be just the tip of a finger, maybe a whole finger, or possibly the whole hand that moves. It does not matter which, but your hand is going to move. Just watch and think of your hand. . .Think of it moving. . .Very shortly your hand is going to move. . .You feel as if your hand is about to move. Your hand is going to move. It is moving a little. . .[*If it moves, add immediately:* "THERE, *it is moving some more.*"] Very soon you will begin to feel a sort of lightness in your hand and in your arm. As you keep listening to me think of your hand and arm becoming light . . .lighter and lighter. As you do so your hand and arm will become light, lighter. . .and lighter, and your hand will begin to rise from your lap. Your hand and your arm will rise from your lap and keep rising because they are going to become very light, without weight. It will be as if a balloon was attached to your hand and lifting, pulling it up in the air. . .Your hand is becoming lighter. It is becoming increasingly light. It weighs less and less. It is as if a force is pulling it upward, pulling your hand and your arm away from your lap. You can feel your hand getting light. It is going to be as light as a feather and will float up like a feather. . .There is a force pulling your hand and arm up. . . up. Your hand is beginning to rise, your hand is rising, rising. It is getting lighter all the time and rising. Your arm is rising. Your arm and hand are rising. . .rising. . .more and more. . .They are going up. . . . . .*up*. . .UP. . .UP!

If you are successful with this experiment, you will see the subject's hand and arm rise up in the air; if you question him later he will nearly always report having actually felt a lightness or that he felt a force pulling his arm and hand upward. It is usually quite helpful when giving these suggestions to watch for any sort of motion of the hand or arm and to point this out to the subject. For instance, very often at the start, a finger will twitch slightly. If this happens remark immediately: "There. . .one of your fingers just moved. This is going to spread. . .soon your entire hand will move (etc.)." If, following this, other fingers move, remark "See, it is now spreading." Similarly, as soon as you see his hand is not fully resting upon his lap you should say: "There, your hand is beginning to rise a little. It is going to rise much more than that. It will rise all the way. . .up. . .above your head. It is continuing to rise."

There are two variations of this experiment worthy of brief attention.

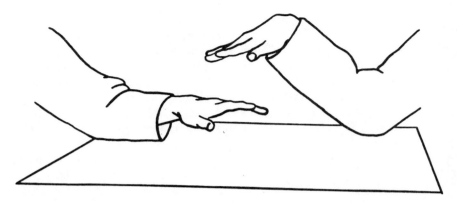

Fig. 12. The hand levitation, first method.

In the first, seat your subject opposite you at a small table or desk with his elbow and palm down flat on the top. Place your hand slightly above his (fig. 12) and speak as follows:

> I want you to relax. Make yourself comfortable and relax. . .Look at your hand. In a moment your hand is going to rise from the table as if it were attracted to my hand. . .You may even feel a force pulling your hand upward toward mine. Your hand is going to rise. You will follow it with your eyes. A force is now pulling your hand upward. . . You will not be able to resist it. Your hand is rising, your hand is rising slowly but surely. You cannot keep your hand on the table because an irresistible force is pulling it up. . .toward my hand. Your hand is slowly moving, rising up. [*As soon as it begins to rise, add "Keep looking at your hand, follow it with your eyes (etc.)."*] It is rising higher and higher . . .You cannot keep your hand down. . .It is rising higher and *higher*, faster and *faster*. It is going *up*. . .*up*. . .UP. . .(etc.).

Instead of having the subject look at his hand, you can have him look at your eyes; with some this is more effective.

A second variation consists of making use of "passes" or other suggestive motions of your own hand. The simplest of these is to proceed as before, only do not place your hand above the subject's at the start, wait until you have reiterated a number of times that the hand is going to rise or, even better, until you see signs of a response. Then bring your hand just above the subject's forearm behind his wrist. Move your hand forward, swooping it upward when it is directly above his hand (fig. 13). Repeat this

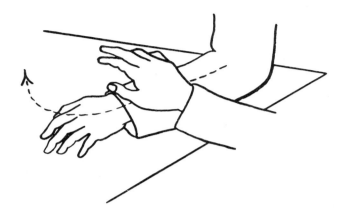

FIG. 13. The hand levitation, second method.

a number of times, saying: "As my hand passes over yours a force attracts yours to mine and will make it follow my hand upward.·. .Your hand is going to follow my hand upward. . .(etc.)." Or instead of swooping your hand, after it is directly above the subject's hand you can say: "A force is going to attract your hand to mine. . .A force is now attracting your hand to my hand. As I slowly lift my hand upward, your hand will begin to rise because it is attracted to my hand. . .As I lift my hand up, your hand rises . . .your hand is following my hand." As you say these words, slowly begin to raise your hand.

Some hypnotists prefer to seat the subject as described above and ask him to be relaxed. They then speak as follows:

> I want you to think of your arm and hand. I am going to pass my hand over your arm and hand like this. . .[*Placing their hand in front of the subject's upper arm, they proceed to follow his arms downward, swoop above his hand and then return to his upper arm. This is repeated.*] As I do so, you will begin to feel a sort of lightness in your arm and hand. . .You may also feel a tingling, or a peculiar warmth. . .Your arm and hand will become lighter and lighter and your hand will begin to rise. . .Very shortly you will feel a force pulling your hand up, pulling your hand and your arm up. . .Your hand and arm are getting lighter and lighter . . .(etc.).

It is not necessary that you be seated at the table too. You may find

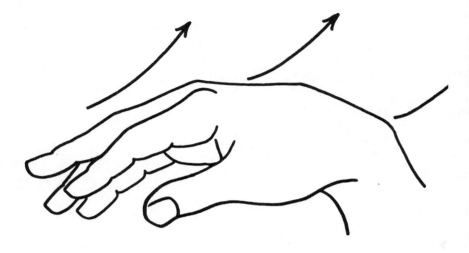

FIG. 14.

it more convenient to stand by the subject in doing this demonstration. Also, the suggestions can often be made more effective if, instead of merely raising your hand above the subject's, you tilt your hand somewhat, fingers downward, and move it as if some invisible threads connected your fingers to the subject's hand and were pulling it up (fig. 14). This is an instance of the use of nonverbal suggestions.

You may wonder at this point what to do when the subject's arm has risen as far as possible or as far as desired. All you have to say is: "That's fine. Now you can bring your arm down. It feels normal. Your hand feels normal. You feel fine." It is possible that you may encounter a subject whose muscles lock or who, for other reasons, is unable or unwilling to bring his arm down. If this should happen, have him close his eyes and tell him to listen to you closely. Then proceed to tell him that his arm and hand are becoming relaxed, that they are getting heavier and becoming quite normal again. Continue by telling him, if necessary, that they are moving down back to his lap and that he will be able to use and move them as usual. This kind of occurrence is very unusual. In any event, never get panicky. *Remember that what one suggestion can do, other suggestions can undo.*

It is needless to add that you should try this experiment on yourself too. You will be quite surprised by the results you get.

The suggestions described in this chapter are only a few of the kinds of simple suggestions you can give. You may wonder on what basis we say they are *simple*; it will be best to delay answering this for a short while. Leaving out the hand levitation suggestion, those experiments we have discussed have been presented about in order of increasing complexity, insofar as getting the subject to respond is concerned. The hand levitation suggestion holds a somewhat ambiguous position. Some hypnotists consider it to be next to the Chevreul pendulum suggestions in simplicity, others place it further along the scale toward complexity. Where it falls seems to be largely dependent upon the subject himself. Consequently, do not feel particularly perturbed if you find a subject responding well to all other suggestions but poorly to this one, or conversely.

There is some evidence that all suggestions are not entirely alike in their mechanisms of action. Those that have been discussed and those which will be taken up in the remainder of this book all belong to the same group which I call *primary suggestions*, because they elicit responses through primary suggestibility. This recognition is important because the production of hypnotic phenomena depends largely upon the use of primary suggestions, so that one should not expect all suggestions to be equally effective in this respect.

As you try these procedures, you should notice and, if possible, keep a record of the way your subjects react to suggestions. You should concentrate on how long it takes before the subject begins to show any sign of response (latency); how soon he reaches an arbitrary strength of response, such as actual fall, maximum displacement, etc. (response time); and how fully he carries out the suggestion (strength of response). Other measures could be the number of abortive responses, vigor of response and so on. Notice, in terms of these measures, whether there are differences in the way subjects respond to your suggestions. It is also suggested you do the additional following experiments. Take a subject who you know will respond to the postural sway suggestions, making sure he has not been given these suggestions or any others for at least 24 hours. Also make sure that he has not been hypnotized before. Now give him the postural sway suggestions and keep a record of one or all of the above measures. You may want to have someone keep this record for you. Repeat the procedure four or five times allowing only a few seconds between trials. What do you observe? Now allow the subject to rest without suggestions for an hour. Try the suggestion again. What do you find? If you can, test him in this manner about 12 to 24 hours later. Try this with a number of different subjects. If you are interested, you can also try using different intervals between trials. As a further experiment proceed essentially as you have just done, but this time instead of repeatedly using the same suggestion, use different suggestions, each once. Compare your results with those you obtained in the first experiment. The reading of chapters 3 and 11 in Hull's[85] work is highly recommended in connection with the above.

In concluding, it should be emphasized that many of the explanations that have been given in previous pages and which will be given in the remainder, are merely restatements of observed properties, and in this respect are "true" regardless of the particular theoretical schema in which one may choose to operate. Thus, for instance, it is a well established fact that repetition of suggestions increases their effectiveness. It is my particular bias to consider this an expression of homoactive cumulation, but one could conceivably argue in Tolmanian terminology that this effect arises because of the increasing confirmation of the subject's "expectancies" or "hypotheses." The fact remains that no matter what ultimate explanation we choose, repetition does enhance suggestions and one may make good use of this fact when working with them. All this is not to say that theory is useless here. On the contrary, it has a very definite place if, for no other reason, than it affords closure. But I believe the student should realize that his acceptance of the theoretical position presented here is not a requisite for his becoming a skilled hypnotist. Similarly, it is not important whether one accepts Eysencks three-fold factor analytical decomposition of suggestibility which I have used as a basis for partitioning suggestions. Suggestions fall into the same disjoint categories quite independently of the validity of Eysenck's results and one still finds the same category is specifically related to the induction of hypnosis.[191] I add this remark because some question has recently been raised regarding the correctness of Eysenck's findings and a reader aware of this might become unduly worried.

More Waking Suggestions

A S HAS ALREADY been mentioned, suggestions can be graded in terms of the ease with which one can get individuals to respond to them; of course the skill with which a suggestion is given is always a factor. However, when everything else has been equated, this still holds true. Some suggestions are "easier" than others. Those we considered in the last chapter are thought to be quite easy. In this chapter we shall take up more "difficult" and more elaborate suggestions. Actually, only a few of these have been ranked empirically, and one can only guess as to the status of the others. There are probably some here which are as easy as those we described in the last chapter. Then too, there are always individual differences among subjects and it is not uncommon to find a subject responding poorly to a suggestion previously graded as easy and doing very well on one rated as more difficult. We shall discuss some of the other possible suggestions one may give in the waking state.

HAND CLASPING

Before you begin this experiment, request the subject to remove any ring he may be wearing from his fingers, otherwise he might subsequently bruise them. Face your subject and say:

> I want you to clasp your hands like this. . .[*You demonstrate to the subject by clasping your own hands in front of you, fingers interlocked (fig. 15).*] Now look at my eyes and clasp your hands tight. [*Saying this you take hold of his hands. Pull them forward, unless they are already extended, maintain your hold momentarily and squeeze his hands together (fig. 16) saying:*] Make them real tight, *as tight as you can!* As you do so, you will soon find that your fingers are becoming locked together, that your hands are becoming stuck together. Your fingers are locking together more and more, your hands and fingers are sticking together more and more. Your hands are becoming more and more tightly clasped together. Your fingers are sticking together. Your hands are sticking together.

127

FIG. 15. The hand clasping suggestion.

Your fingers are locked fast. YOUR HANDS ARE STUCK FAST, YOU
CANNOT TAKE THEM APART. In a moment I will tell you to try
to take your hands apart, but *you will not be able to do this*. Your fingers
are *so completely locked* together, your hands are *so completely stuck* together
that YOU CANNOT PULL THEM APART. Try. You cannot take
your hands apart. The more you try the less you can. Your hands are
stuck fast. . .Try hard, you *cannot* take your hands apart, you CANNOT,
you CAN'T take them apart.

For best results it is important that you should keep fixating the subject
throughout, and you should at first give the suggestions in rapid succession
while the subject is trying to meet the challenge. This remark applies to
any other situation where a challenge is made. However, if the subject
responds well to the suggestions, you will usually be able after a few moments to stop giving suggestions, and the subject will still not be able to overcome them.

It is very important that you should not allow the subject to feel at any

Fig. 16. The hand clasping suggestion (continued).

time that he has been able to meet your challenge successfully. If you see that he is having some success pulling his hands apart or suspect that he will, immediately say: "Now you can take your hands apart, everything is as before." Then immediately, looking intently at the subject, go on by saying in a positive tone of voice, "You had a little bit of trouble getting your hands apart, didn't you. . .They felt kind of stuck. Let's try it again." It is particularly important to say this if the subject did have some difficulty. In any case, you should never appear to be dismayed. It should always appear that whatever happens was exactly what you expected and wanted.

If the subject begins to try to pull his hands apart before you give your challenge, as he may do, you should point this out to him before starting again and emphasize that he is to listen closely to what you say and do exactly as directed and that he is not to anticipate instructions. This anticipatory reaction is often a sign of resistance or noncooperation on the part of the subject. If you have reason to believe that the subject was not cooperating, you should point this out, explaining to him that the success of the suggestions depends upon his cooperation. Another way subjects often resist is by weakly clasping their hands. This is one reason for holding their hands at the start. This enables you to tell how tightly they are clasping their hands. If the subject fails to follow your instructions, you may have to be more emphatic. Say something like "Come on now, you can do better than that! Clasp your hands real tight, *tighter*, AS TIGHT AS YOU CAN!" At the same time give his hands a strong squeeze to emphasize your instructions. Even if your subject does clasp his hands tightly as instructed, this is no guarantee that he will maintain them this way. Some noncooperative individuals proceed to relax their hands prior to, or at the time of the challenge, and have little difficulty in meeting it. If this is the case, you should again point out to the subject his obvious resistance to the suggestions. Some subjects tend to respond passively to suggestions and may behave in a seemingly noncooperative manner in spite of their desire to cooperate. The following variation in procedure often works very nicely with them. You should use it in your second trial, should you be faced with this sort of situation.

Begin exactly as you did above, telling the subject:

> I want you to clasp your hands like this. . .Now look at my eyes and clasp your hand tight. . . Make them real tight, AS TIGHT AS YOU CAN! Think of your hand as tightly clasped together, think of your fingers pressing down upon the back of your hands, of your hands becoming more and more tightly clenched together. [*You are still holding the subject's hands. If they are still not clasped tightly, continue with:* "*as you do so and as you listen to what I say you will find that your fingers tend to close, to press against the back of your hands, that your hands are being pressed tightly together. You cannot help yourself.*" *Otherwise go on with what follows, gently letting go of the subject's hands.*] Your hands are becoming tightly clasped together, your fingers are pressing your hands tightly together. Your fingers and your hands are becoming *stiff, rigid. . . more and more stiff. Your hands are pressed tightly together. So tightly, so firmly, that you cannot take them apart.* THEY ARE STUCK FAST TOGETHER! YOUR HANDS ARE STUCK FAST! YOU CANNOT TAKE THEM APART! Try! YOU CANNOT! YOU CAN'T TAKE YOUR HANDS APART! THE MORE YOU TRY THE LESS YOU CAN!

There are several features of these procedures which merit discussion. You were instructed to make certain that the subject's arms were well extended out when doing the hand clasping experiment. This is a matter of leverage. The muscles involved are those used in the rotation of the arm about the shoulder. This means that the further the arms are extended, the less leverage these muscles have against any force preventing the hands to be moved laterally outward (pulled apart). There is another mechanical feature to this experiment. When the hands are tightly clasped together, the finger joints, because of their shape, tend to lock the hands together and prevent the fingers from sliding apart. This is why you should always make sure that the subject's hands are clasped in such a way that the bases of the fingers are against each other. With the fingers meshed in any other way the subject will meet relatively little resistance in trying to pull his hands apart.

In spite of the fact that this entire experiment appears to be based upon a mechanical illusion or "deception," nothing is further from the truth. If the subject is not suggestible, when challenged he will simply relax his hands before or shortly after trying to pull them apart. This is not the case if he is responding. In other instances you will observe that the subject tightens his hands considerably as you give the suggestions. As a matter of fact, if you want to more fully demonstrate the effects of suggestions in this experiment, just have the subject clasp his hands loosely in front of him, fairly close to his body. Suggest to him that the muscles of his fingers and hands are progressively tightening, that the fingers of his hands are bending inward as if he were going to close his hands into fists. They press against the back of his hands and force his hands close together. His hands are going to become tightly clasped, so tightly that he will not be able to pull them apart. They will be stuck, etc. Keep repeating this with variations. You and your subject will be surprised at the results.

Whether or not you make use of such mechanical aids depends upon your feelings in this regard, and upon what aim you are trying to achieve. If your purpose is to investigate or to demonstrate the properties of pure waking suggestibility, you probably will not want to make use of such aids. But even here you may wish to keep in mind the fact that if you are studying the properties of the generalization of suggestibility it might be desirable to consider the effects of these aids. On the other hand, if your main purpose is to enhance the subject's general suggestibility with a view to subsequently inducing hypnosis, then you want to make use of all available tools, and the aids we have been speaking about come under this heading.

The proper wording of a suggestion is frequently a matter of decision in the face of uncertainty. Both this fact and some of the considerations one must take into account in constructing suggestions are well demonstrated in the hand clasping experiment. The challenge to the subject revolves around the concept of "*taking* his hands apart." Now there are other alternatives in wording, for instance the challenge could have been centered about the notion of "*pulling* his hands apart." Would it really make any difference which of these we used? One can argue equally well in favor of either alternative, although I tend to favor the first, as is obvious from my choice. Let us look a little at the arguments which I think are edifying. The first proposition, of "taking" the hands apart, has in its favor the fact that it is ambiguous and relatively neutral with regard to *modus operandi*. On the other hand, when the subject is specifically told to "pull" his hands apart we may actually be solving for him half of the problem of overcoming the suggestion, if it is correct, as some believe, that the suggestion partly acts by inhibiting the subject's ability to think independently on how to proceed. In any event, by focusing his attention and efforts upon the specific act of pulling we may help him to concentrate his energies sufficiently in this direction to overcome the suggestion. Finally, prohibiting the subject from "pulling" his hands apart does not prohibit separation by other means, such as sliding the fingers against each other in certain fashions, thus allowing the subject a way out, as I have seen happen. The word "taking," however, is much more general or inclusive in its prohibitions.

Unfortunately it can be also pointed out that if we specifically and properly suggest to the subject that he cannot "pull" his hands apart this should effectively restrict him to this one act. This might have considerable advantage to it. In spite of this I somehow cannot help but feel that the first alternative is the safer of the two, particularly for the beginner. Any further decision shall be left to the reader.

Many subjects respond quite strongly to the hand clasping suggestion. They may respond so strongly that you can challenge them repeatedly and forcefully to pull their hands apart. They will go through all sorts of contortions to no avail, even though you have ceased fixating them and giving them suggestions. They will not be able to take their hands apart *until you tell them that they can*. One good way of ending this effect is to snap your fingers close to the subject and to say firmly: "Alright now, relax. You can take your hands apart. Your hands are not stuck anymore." Sometimes the subject still has some difficulty pulling his hands apart. If so, taking hold of his wrists pull his hands apart saying again: "Your hands are free now. . .Relax. You are as before." Such a subject, incidentally, will nearly always make a very good subject for hypnotic experiments. As a matter of fact, many who respond well to hand clasping suggestions can be hypnotized fairly deeply without too much difficulty.

The reader should be cautioned that it is usually not a good idea to permit the subject to struggle too long against the suggestion. If you see any indication that he may be able to pull his hands apart, you should immediately end the effect. In any event, you should only allow the effect to last long enough to demonstrate the power of the suggestion to the subject and to the audience, if one is present.* A responsive subject will often clasp his

---

*I wish to make it clear that my occasional use of the words "audience," "spectators," and even "stage," are not to be misconstrued as approval of stage hypnotism on my part. There are

hands so tightly as to stop the circulation in his fingers, and may even bruise his hands.

There is usually no problem in deciding that the suggestion has been ineffective when the subject takes his hands apart without signs of difficulty as soon as he is challenged or sooner. If the subject is able to "break" the suggestion, but only after some visible effort, this indicates the suggestion has had some effects. The magnitude of this effect is presumably roughly proportional to the amount of effort or the time required to break the suggestion. Occasionally, a subject responds to the challenge by straightening out his fingers, but keeping his palms more or less juxtaposed. How is one to interpret this rather ambiguous response and how should one proceed thereon? Unless there are other reasons for doing so, one should never assume in this instance that the subject is refractory to the suggestion because actually the challenge is that he cannot *take his hands apart* and not that he cannot straighten his fingers out. The obvious way to test the situation further is to again challenge the subject to take his hands apart. One can be more explicit if necessary by challenging him to "move" his hands apart or again to "pull" them apart or away from each other.

To return to procedures, a variation of the hand clasping demonstration is as follows. Tell your subject to extend his hands and arms in front of him, palms facing each other. Next tell him to bend his hands so that the palms face him and the tips of the fingers are opposite each other (fig. 17A). Now have him spread his fingers apart and bring his hands together so that the fingers interlock and touch at the base (palms still apart) (fig. 17B). Next, tell him to rotate his interlocked hands so that he sees the back of his hands (fig. 17C). Finally, have him elevate his hands above his head, palms outward with his arms outstretched as much as possible (fig. 17D). Demonstrate this to him as you tell him what to do, making him proceed step by step. Now speak to him as follows:

> Please look at my eyes and listen closely to what I tell you. . .
> Keep your hands above your head, fingers interlocked, arms extended.
> Think of your hands and fingers becoming tight. . .of your arms stiffen-
> ing. As I speak to you your hands and fingers are becoming tight. Your
> arms are becoming stiff. . .Think of nothing else. . .The muscles of
> your hands and arms are becoming more and more tight, stiff. Your
> hands are getting tighter and tighter, your arms are becoming stiffer
> and stiffer. I am going to count to three and at the count of three you

circumstances when a *professional* man is justified in giving demonstrations, and in this case will have an audience and something akin to a stage, be it only the end of a room.

FIG. 17 *A-D*. The hand clasping suggestion, a variation.

will not be able to unlock your hands and fingers. One. . .Your hands
are getting tight, very tight, so tight you will not be able to take them
apart. Two. . .your hands and arms are getting stiff, very stiff, so stiff
you cannot move them. THREE. . .*Your hands are stuck fast. Your fingers
are locked together.* YOU CANNOT TAKE YOUR HANDS APART,
no matter how hard you try. Try. . .You CANNOT. . .*The more you try,
the less you can.*

Some hypnotists prefer to give the above suggestions with the subject
keeping his eyes closed. Both methods seem equally effective. There may be

Fig. 18. The hand clasping suggestion, another suggestion.

some argument for advocating eye fixation when suggestions are given individually; having the subject close his eyes may be preferable when giving group (mass) suggestions. The important thing is that nothing distract the subject's attention from the suggestions. By having him close his eyes after his hands are in position, or having him look at your eyes (or some object such as your finger) you prevent various stimuli from distracting him. It is possible that for some individuals closing the eyes has a suggestive effect which induces a mild trance state, but this could occur with visual fixation. On the other hand some subjects may become anxious if asked to close their eyes because they interpret this as a sign that hypnosis is going to be induced and are not yet ready for it.

Another interesting and useful technique has been described by Wolberg.[203] It differs from other methods described thus far in the fact that it makes considerable use of the subject's imagining. As earlier, the subject, usually sitting down, is asked to clasp his hands, this being demonstrated to him. Wolberg then has the hypnotist say:

> I want you to close your eyes for a moment and visualize a vise, a heavy metal vise whose jaws clamp together with a screw. Imagine that your hands are like the jaws of the vise, and as you press them together tighter, they are just like the jaws of the vise tightening. I am going to count from one to five. As I count your hands will press together tighter, and tighter, and tighter. When I reach the count of five, your hands will be pressed together so firmly that it will be difficult or impossible to separate them. One, tight; two, tighter, and

tighter and tighter; three, very tight, your hands feel glued together; four, your hands are clamped tight, tight; five, so tight that even though you try to separate them, they remain clasped together, until I give you the command to open them—Now open them slowly.

As has been noted, the methods given thus far involve the use of certain mechanical aids. The next method is one that depends entirely on suggestions. Instruct the subject to place his hands crosswise against each other palm against palm and to close the fingers over the backs, thus clasping his hands and to hold them this way tightly (fig. 18). From here on you proceed along lines already indicated, giving suggestions of increasing tightening, of sticking together, of stiffening and of inability to take the hands apart. If you prefer, you can start with the subject holding his hands clasped lightly in the above manner and progressively tighten them with suggestions. This is a very convincing manner of demonstrating the hand clasping suggestions, although in my opinion it requires an individual of greater suggestibility than do the other methods to be successful.

EYE CATALEPSY

Many hypnotists use the term "catalepsy" rather indiscriminately to cover a number of situations which are by no means identical. In its strict sense the word refers to a state of muscular rigidity in which the individual's body retains any position it may be given. This is the so-called waxy flexibility. In hypnotic practice "catalepsy" is commonly and loosely employed to refer to any muscular condition in which the subject is unable to voluntarily move any of his members or his entire body, usually as a result of the presence of muscular contractures. In any event, we shall speak of "eye catalepsy" and other "catalepsies" regardless of their true nature since this is a well established terminology.

Standing next to your subject say the following:

I want you to close your eyes. . .[*As soon as he has done this place your finger on the top of his forehead.*] Keeping your eyes closed tight, turn your eyes upward as if you were looking through the top of your forehead at the tip of my finger. Keep your eyes closed tight and keep looking upward. As you do so you will find that your eyelids are becoming heavy and that they are closing more tightly. They are closing more and more tightly, they are becoming heavy, very heavy. They are sticking. In a few moments I will tell you to try and open your eyes, but you will find this very difficult to do, very hard, because your eyelids are becoming stuck as if they were glued. They feel heavy, like lead. They are stiff. They are stuck. Your eyelids are sticking. They are heavy as lead. Your eyes are sticking fast, as if they were glued solid. They are stuck closed. Your eyes are sticking fast, *are stuck fast*, YOU CANNOT OPEN YOUR EYES! Try. YOU CANNOT OPEN YOUR EYES!. . .THE MORE YOU TRY THE MORE THEY STICK.

Quite often when a person looks upward with his eyes closed he cannot close his eyes completely. Consequently, you may find that some of your subjects show an appreciable slit, or that after they begin to respond to your suggestions they tend to lift their eyelids a small amount. You should not worry about this. Just reiterate your request that the subject keep his eyes closed and keep looking upward. You can usually tell how well the subject is looking upward by watching the rolling of his eyes under the eyelids. Sometimes too, a subject will say that he cannot do both, that is, look upward and keep his eyes closed tight. Others will say that it hurts their eyes. In such cases instruct the subject to look up as well as he can without discomfort while keeping his eyes closed. Actually I am rather dubious as to the real value of having the subject look upward. I have heard many hypnotists explain that it is much more difficult, even impossible, to open one's eyes if one turns his eyes upward while they are closed, but I have not been able to find satisfactory evidence that this is true. Looking upward may, however, have some value in forcing the subject to concentrate his attention more fully upon his eyes and the suggestions relating to them.

A person who is fairly suggestible will have considerable difficulty opening his eyes. If he succeeds in doing this, but shows some difficulty, you should call this to his attention. As with the handclasping suggestions if it looks like the subject is going to overcome the suggestion, it is best to quickly say: "Alright, stop trying, you can now open your eyes," snapping your finger at the same time. A very suggestible person will not be able to open his eyes and you will have to say this to enable him to do so.

A variation of the above demonstration which is a better test of suggestibility and which you may prefer proceeds as follows. Address the subject thus:

> I want you to close your eyes and just relax. [*The subject can be standing, sitting, or even lying down. This also applies to the previous method.*] Don't be afraid, I am not going to hypnotize you yet. Now just listen to my voice and relax. As you do so your eyelids are going to become heavy. . . very heavy. Soon you will find it difficult to open your eyes because they will be so heavy. But now just listen to me. Your eyes are becoming heavy, heavier and heavier. Your eyelids are becoming very heavy, heavy like lead. You will find it very hard to open your eyes

when I tell you to try. Now your eyes are becoming more tightly closed. They are beginning to stick. Your eyelids are very heavy, they are tightly closed, they are becoming more and more tightly closed, heavier and heavier. They are sticking tightly. *Your eyes are shut tight. They are stuck fast.* THEY ARE STICKING TIGHT. YOU CANNOT OPEN YOUR EYES, THEY ARE STUCK FAST! Try. YOU CANNOT OPEN YOUR EYES!

It should be noted that in all these suggestions, particularly the one above, it is relatively easy to tell how well your suggestions are taking effect by merely watching the subject's eyes. Sometimes, however, the subject may give very little evidence that anything is happening until he is challenged. And here again, whereas some subjects may strenuously attempt to open their eyes, others may show only slight muscular effort involving as little as raising the eyebrows. This does not mean, however, that the suggestion has been ineffective. We have already seen this with the hand clasping suggestions.

Quite frequently, when told to close their eyes, subjects infer that this is the immediate preliminary to the induction of hypnosis and if they are unprepared for this event they may build up resistance because of anxiety. It is for this reason that the subject is told right at the start that he is not going to be hypnotized. Notice, however, that we said: "I am not going to hypnotize you *yet*. . ." This is not the same as telling him "I am not going to hypnotize you," or "I won't hypnotize you without telling you first." The first statement has reassurance value, yet in no way makes any commitments about the near future. If you do hypnotize the subject later there will be less likelihood that he will feel he has been tricked and that you cannot be trusted. Furthermore, if you tell the subject "I am not going to hypnotize you," this may act as a counter-suggestion to any later suggestions aimed at inducing hypnosis, whereas the statement we used actually prepares the subject for possible induction of the trance state. As will be seen later, eye catalepsy can be made a part of the trance induction procedure. Although the wording that has been used does not preclude your passing on to the induction of hypnosis without transition, you may prefer not to make this sort of statement when using this induction technique.

ARM CATALEPSY

Tell your subject to hold his arm horizontally straight out at his side (or forward if you prefer), to form a tight fist and to look into your eyes. Take hold of his fist and, squeezing it lightly, give his arm an outward pull. At the same time, with your other hand grasp his forearm and speak to him in the following manner: "Think of your arm as becoming stiff and rigid. Your arm is becoming stiff, *stiffer* and *stiffer*. It is becoming *stiff* like a bar of iron, *rigid* as a piece of steel. In a moment it will be so *stiff* and *rigid* that you will not be able to bend it or move it. Your arm is now *stiff* and *rigid*. . . *like a rod of iron. You cannot bend your arm*, YOU CAN'T MOVE IT. TRY. YOU CAN'T!. . .(etc.)."

Some hypnotists like to make passes with contact over the subject's arm while they suggest its stiffening. This is done by bringing your hand near the subject's shoulder and circling his arm lightly with your fingers. Slide your hand toward his wrist. Then you let go and bring your hand back near the shoulder and repeat this a number of times, each time applying a little pressure upon the arm so as to exert a little pull upon it as you move outward. As a variation, you may prefer to have the subject initially hold his hand in a relaxed fist and to suggest tightening the fist. One variant of this I like is to have the subject extend his hand horizontally, palm down, when he stretches his arm out. I begin by suggesting that his hand is closing into a fist, then when this has occurred, that his fist is becoming tight— from there on everything proceeds as described above.

Thus far, the experiments which we have discussed are in order of the increasing difficulty encountered in getting subjects to respond. The remainder of the experiments to be discussed here cannot be ranked in this fashion with any certainty because the necessary experimental data are not available An attempt will be made, however, to give them in a rough order of their presumed difficulty.

In general, you are most likely to succeed with the remaining suggestions if you first run your subjects through the ten simple suggestions we have already considered, in the order in which they are listed. In effect this *pre-sensitizes* the subjects for the more difficult ones to come by raising their suggestibility, largely through heteroaction, but also undoubtedly by creating a positive attitude. In general one may say that the degree of pre-sensitization is in proportion to the number of successful suggestions which have been given. The one exception to this is hypnosis, which as a pre-sensitizing agent holds a unique position.

The sequence in which you should use the suggestions described in the remainder of this chapter is somewhat arbitrary. Two partial criteria one may apply are that, generally, you should proceed from suggestions involving limited and simple muscular movements to suggestions requiring increasingly complex motions (e.g., preventing the subject from rising from his chair would come before having him walk around the room with a limp) and that suggestions aimed at motor effects should precede suggestions of sensory effects. This is an application of the general rule that for any given degree of suggestibility the strength and completeness of a subject's response is inversely related to the difficulty and complexity of the suggested task. This holds for both waking and hypnotic suggestions. To have a clear understanding of what this rule means one must think of each subject as possessing a certain response threshold such that any suggestion having a degree of difficulty or complexity less than a certain "value" is fully carried out, whereas all other suggestions have their effectiveness reduced in proportion to their excess difficulty or complexity. Obviously then, we expect and do find certain individuals to have so much suggestibility that no "reasonable" suggestion is able to task their ability to carry it out. Presumably some suggestions could be found that do.

STICKING THE SUBJECT'S FOOT TO THE FLOOR

To carry out the present demonstration, fixate the subject (who may be standing or sitting) and speak as follows: "Look at my eyes. . .Your feet are going to become heavy, very heavy. As I speak to you, you feel your feet getting heavy. . .heavier and heavier. . .They are becoming so heavy that you will not be able to move them from the floor when I tell you to try. Your feet are now v-e-r-y heavy. . .h-e-a-v-y like lead. . .*So* heavy you cannot lift them, *so* heavy that your feet are stuck fast to the floor. *Your feet are sticking to the floor. You cannot move your feet.* THEY ARE STUCK FAST TO THE FLOOR. YOU CANNOT MOVE THEM. Try! YOU CANNOT!"

MAKING THE HANDS HEAVY OR STUCK

Have the subject sit comfortably, his hand resting on his lap. Fixate on the bridge of his nose and tell him: "Look at my eyes and listen closely to what I tell you. As you do so you will find that your [right or left] hand becomes heavy. It will get heavier and heavier, so heavy that you will not be able to lift it when I tell you to try. But now, just listen to my voice. Your hand is beginning to feel heavy. A feeling of heaviness is coming over your hand, over your arm. Your arm and hand are becoming heavy. . . heavier and heavier. You feel a great heaviness in your hand. . .in your arm. They are now very heavy. . .v-e-r-y h-e-a-v-y, like lead. They are s-o h-e-a-v-y that now you cannot lift your hand. *Your hand feels as if it is stuck to your lap.* YOU CANNOT LIFT IT! YOU CANNOT. Try! YOU CAN'T! THE MORE YOU TRY, THE LESS YOU CAN."

A variation of this experiment is to start by telling the subject that his hand is going to stick to his lap (or some object, such as the surface of a table on which you have him lay his hand). Tell him that a force is attracting his hand to his lap, that it is holding it tight against his lap, etc.

MAKING THE SUBJECT UNABLE TO LET GO OF AN OBJECT

If you have succeeded in obtaining a strong response in the hand clasping experiment, you will nearly always succeed with the following one, particularly if you have also been able to obtain strong eye catalepsy or arm rigidity. Give the subject a piece of broomstick to hold in one hand in such a way that if he opens his hand it will fall. If you prefer, have the subject hold the stick in both hands in the same manner. (We shall assume only one hand is used here.) Have him look you in the eyes and speak to him firmly: "Hold this stick tightly. In a moment I am going to count to three* and at the count of three you will find it impossible to let go of the broomstick. You will not be able to drop it. Your hands, your fingers are going to become stuck to the stick. . .One. . .your hand is sticking to the wood, your fingers are becoming stuck to the stick. You will not be able to let go of the stick when I tell you to try. Two. . .Your hands and your fingers are now stuck fast to the stick. They are sticking tight, so tight that you cannot open your hand no matter how hard you try. THREE!. . .*Your hand is stuck fast to the stick,* YOUR FINGERS ARE STUCK TO IT! YOU CANNOT DROP IT. Try! YOU CAN'T. YOU CAN'T OPEN YOUR HAND."

A variation of this consists in suggesting to the subject that his hand and fingers are tightening about the stick and that he cannot unclench his hand.

FORCING THE RELEASE OF AN OBJECT

Have the subject hold a piece of broomstick as described above and tell him to hold it tightly. Fixate him, giving suggestions that he is not going to be able to hold on to the stick. That the more he tries, the less he will be able to hold it. Tell him that his hand is opening up, that the wood is repelling his fingers, forcing them to open, that he cannot hold on to the stick, etc.

FORCING THE SUBJECT'S HANDS APART

Have your subject hold his hands vertically in front of his chest, palm against palm, finger tips upward. Look him in the eyes and say: "When I count to three, a force is going to push your hands apart. Your hands will

---

*Counting as a signal is not specific to this suggestion and can be used with any. Furthermore, the figure three is arbitrary. Later we will have occasion to use different counts.

repel each other. At the count of three you will feel your hands being pushed apart and they will move apart. You will not be able to keep them together. One. . .a force is pushing your hands apart. . .You feel a force pushing your hands apart. This force is getting stronger and stronger. . .stronger and stronger. . .Two. . .Your hands are repelling each other so strongly that you cannot keep them together any longer. The force is increasing all the time. You cannot keep your hands together, they are being pushed apart. *Three.* . .Your hands are moving apart. *You cannot keep them together. A force is pushing them apart.* THEY ARE MOVING APART. . .FASTER and FASTER. . . THEY ARE MOVING (etc.)."

PREVENTING THE SUBJECT FROM TAKING HIS HANDS APART

With the subject holding his hands as in the above demonstration suggest that they are sticking together, that he cannot pull them apart, that the more he tries, the more they press against each other.

A variation of this is for you to hold your hand out flat at approximately waist level, palm up. Have the subject place his hand palm down on top of yours. Now look him in the eyes and tell him that in a moment, when you count to three, he will not be able to lift his hand from yours because it will be stuck (or, alternatively, because it weighs too much) or is strongly attracted to your hand.

As soon as you have ascertained that the subject's hand is stuck to yours, tell him that it will remain thus until you tell him otherwise. Now if you slowly move your hand in any direction, the subject's hand will follow it faithfully, and if you attempt to move any distance away from the subject, he will be forced to follow you.

FORCING THE SUBJECT'S HANDS TOGETHER

This is exactly the opposite of forcing the subject's hands apart. Have the subject hold his hands as in that demonstration, palm facing palm, but some distance away from each other. Now suggest that a force is going to pull the hands together, that they are going to be strongly attracted to each other, etc.

I often like to combine all three last demonstrations. For example, I begin with the hands apart, force them together, then stick them together, and finally force them apart, or conversely. To show you how it is done in a continuous fashion the entire suggestion follows:

I want you to place your hands like this. . .[*Demonstrate position*]

Now look at my eyes and think of a force pulling your hands together. Think of your hands being strongly attracted toward each other. . . A force is beginning to pull your hands together. . .It is growing stronger and stronger. Your hands are being pulled together, they are beginning to move toward each other. You cannot prevent them from moving. They are going to move until they touch each other. They are moving . . .*more* and *more*, *faster* and *faster*. . .They are coming closer and closer. Soon they will touch. . .*Closer* and *closer*. . .*They are nearly touching now* . . . NOW THEY ARE TOUCHING! They are pressing against each other. They are pressing hard. . .*harder. Now you can't pull them apart.* THEY ARE STUCK FAST. YOU CANNOT PULL THEM APART. Try! YOU CAN'T! . . .Stop trying. Now, you are not going to be able to keep them together because a force is pushing them apart. . .You feel a force pushing them apart. They are repelling each other. . .*more and more.* . .*You cannot keep them together.* They are moving apart, *faster and faster.* . .*flying apart.* . .(etc.).

OTHER EXPERIMENTS USING THE HANDS

There are a great many other suggestions you can give using the subject's hands. For instance, you can have him hold his hand out flat, palm down, fingers tightly closed, and suggest to him that his fingers will spread apart and that he cannot keep them together. Conversely, you can have him hold his hands in the same position but with fingers apart, and suggest that he cannot keep them this way and that they will close. Or again, with his fingers together, you can suggest that when you count to three he will not be able to spread them apart. You can force the subject to make a fist, to be unable to open his fist, or to be unable to make one. You can make any number of his fingers become stiff, unbending, etc.

A combined variation is the *Forced Hand Clapping* experiment. The easiest way of doing it is to have the subject start to clap his hands lightly. Then as he does this, you suggest to him that at the count of three he will find it impossible to stop clapping, that on the contrary the more he tries to stop, the harder he will clap. An alternative way is to force the hands apart, then force them back together alternately, progressively increasing the speed until the subject is clapping. At this point say: "Now you are clapping your hands. You are going to find it impossible to stop clapping until I tell you to stop. . .You are *clapping.* . .*clapping.* . .YOU CANNOT STOP. THE MORE YOU TRY, THE HARDER YOU CLAP. . .(etc.)."

Still another effect is the *Arm Twirl*. Have the subject hold his arms and

FIG. 19. The arm twirl.

hands as shown in figure 19. Tell him to twirl them away from himself* and around each other slowly as he would do in twiddling his thumbs. (You can do this experiment using the thumbs instead of the arms.) As in the hand clapping demonstration, suggest that when he tries to stop he will be unable to do so. Suggest that his arms are twirling faster and faster, and so on.

MAKING THE SUBJECT WALK WITH A LIMP

There are two ways of doing this. One is to suggest to the subject that one of his legs is stiff and that he cannot bend it as he walks. The other is to suggest that one of his legs is weak and folds under him every time he shifts his weight to it.

FORCING THE SUBJECT TO SIT DOWN

Have the subject stand in front of a chair in such a position that he can easily sit in it when desired. Now fixate upon him and firmly say: "Think of sitting down. In a moment when I count three you will find your legs feeling weak, your knees will fold, you will feel heavy, and get heavier and heavier, and you will have to sit down. . .One. . .two. . .*three*! Now you are becoming heavy. . .heavier and heavier. . .Your knees are folding. . .

*It is best to use a rotation away from the body, otherwise the subject may hit himself when the motion gets too powerful, as it often does.

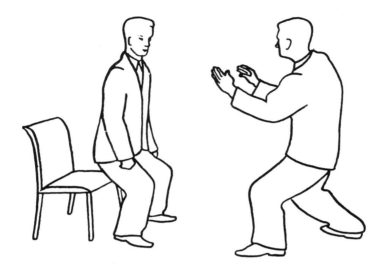

Fig. 20. Forcing the subject to sit down.

your legs are getting weak. . .You are going to sit down. You cannot remain standing. . .Your knees are folding, folding. . .Your body is going down, down. . .You are sitting down. . .sitting down. . .(etc.).''

As soon as you see any signs that the subject is responding, you should partially bend your knees and lower your body downward very slowly. It is often very effective to hold your hands up, palms facing the subject and at the appropriate moment to lower them slowly in a suggestive manner. These two procedures can be combined to enhance each other (fig. 20). Very often if the subject does not show any signs of responding, it is helpful to use these devices about the time you tell the subject that his body is going down.

You should keep in mind when you give suggestions of heaviness of the body to an overweight individual that it may evoke resistance. In such cases it is best not to refer to body weight.

FORCING A SITTING SUBJECT TO STAND UP

Look at the subject and tell him: "You cannot remain sitting. You feel a force pushing you up. . .A force is pushing you up. . .u-p. You cannot remain in your seat. The more you try, the less you can. You are rising. . . *more and more*. . .FASTER AND FASTER. . .(etc.).'' Here too you can use hand motions to add effectiveness to your suggestions.

PREVENTING THE SUBJECT FROM SITTING DOWN

Fixate the subject and tell him: "Hold your legs stiff. As stiff as you can. Now your legs are getting stiff. . .*stiffer and stiffer*. In a moment, you will not be able to bend your legs. Your knees, your legs are going to be so stiff that you will be completely unable to bend them and to sit down. I will count to three and at the count of three you will find it impossible to sit down. . .One. . .two. . .THREE! *You cannot sit down*. YOU CAN'T. Try. THE MORE YOU TRY, THE LESS YOU CAN. YOU CAN'T. . .(etc.)."

PREVENTING THE SUBJECT FROM STANDING UP

With the subject sitting in a chair, suggest to him that his entire body is getting heavy, that his body is sticking to his chair, and that he is going to be unable to get out of the chair. Many moderately suggestible individuals respond rather well to this suggestion and its position in the present sequence is not to be taken to indicate its relative difficulty.

MAKING THE SUBJECT KNEEL THEN GET ON ALL FOURS

Fixate the subject and suggest to him that his legs are becoming weak, that his body is getting heavy, that his knees are bending, that a force is pulling his body down and that shortly he will be forced to kneel down on the floor. As soon as the subject begins to respond or show signs that he is going to respond, move your body slowly downward or gesture with your hands as described earlier. It is often a good idea to place a cushion in front of the subject where he will kneel—in any event be ready to lend a hand as it is not uncommon for the subject to fall on his knees rather hard. Now with the subject on his knees, continue by suggesting that a force is pulling him forward, that his body is leaning forward* and that in a moment he will not be able to keep from falling on his hands and knees, etc. At the same time, in a semi-squatting position, move away from the subject, using your hands to give additional emphasis to the suggestion (fig. 21*A-C*).

PREVENTING THE SUBJECT FROM PICKING UP AN OBJECT

Place a coin, for instance a quarter or a half dollar, on a table and tell the subject to look at it steadily. Now tell him: "In a moment I am going to ask you to pick up this coin, but when you try you will be unable to do so

---

*You may wonder here what happens to the eye fixation. It is difficult to maintain under these conditions. You need not worry about it as long as you keep giving a steady flow of suggestions. Should you feel that visual fixation is important, you can start with the subject fixating on your finger and guide him through the responses in this way.

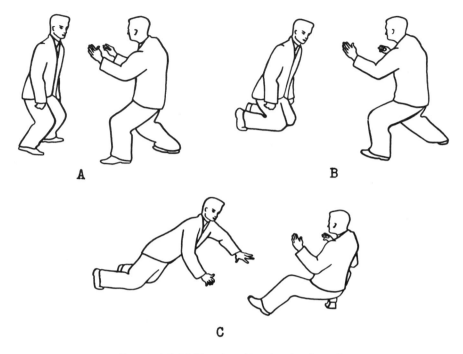

A   B

C

Fig. 21 *A-C:* Making the subject kneel and crawl.

because you will find that it is stuck fast to the table. You will find that it is
stuck so firmly that you will not be able to lift it up. Now try to pick up the
coin. *It is stuck fast,* you cannot lift it up. YOU CANNOT PICK IT UP,
IT IS STUCK (etc.)."

There are all sorts of variations of this experiment. Objects other than
coins can be used, but the effect is particularly easy to bring about with a
coin. The reason for this lies in part in a mechanical aspect of the situation.
A coin, particularly a thin coin, which is lying flat on the surface of a table,
is relatively difficult to pick up compared to other objects. This feature is
important here because when the subject is responding to the influence of
the suggestion his response is often the actual application of pressure on the
coin, defeating any attempt to lift it.

One demonstration which is usually quite easy to carry out is to have
the subject lift a light chair and hold it at about chest level. It is best if he
holds the chair by the seat or by the seat and back. Demonstrate this to him.
Here again a mechanical aid is involved. Holding a chair up at or near chest

level is conducive to rapid muscular fatigue, hence the subject has a perfectly natural increasing tendency to lower the chair as subsequently suggested. Now looking him steadily in the eyes, proceed to suggest that the chair is getting progressively heavier. That a force is pulling it down to the floor. That shortly he will not be able to hold it up and will be forced to put it down. Continue in this fashion, suggesting that the chair is moving down, and so on. As soon as he has put it down continue by telling him that the chair has now become so heavy that no matter how hard he tries he will not be able to lift it up. Tell him it is stuck fast to the floor, giving appropriate suggestions. As soon as he has shown his inability to lift the chair add that his hands are stuck fast to the chair and that the chair is stuck fast to the floor, that he can neither lift the chair nor let go of it. Finally, tell him that his hands will remain stuck to the chair, but that the chair itself is once more of normal weight and that he can move it anyway he wants, but that his hands are still stuck to it.

One word of caution: whenever you have a subject pull on a supposedly immovable object and you nullify the stability of the object, be ready to catch the subject as he may be thrown off balance. Of course you can tell the subject to stop pulling or pushing before you remove the suggestion that the object is immovable.

Another very simple demonstration is to give the subject a pencil and paper. Have him hold the pencil as if he were going to write with it. Tell him to fixate on the point of the pencil. Now suggest that he is going to be unable to move the pencil at all. That the pencil is stuck to the paper and that he can neither lift it or move it on the paper, hence cannot write with it. With a highly suggestible subject you can have him start writing a word or sentence over and over while you tell him that he will find it increasingly difficult to write because his pencil will more and more tend to stick to the paper, and that after a while he will have to stop. Continue to suggest increasing difficulty and, eventually, that the pencil is stuck fast and is immovable.

FORCING THE SUBJECT TO OPEN HIS MOUTH

Fixate the subject and state firmly: "Think of your mouth opening by itself. In a moment your mouth is going to open. . .It will open wide. Now your mouth is beginning to open. Your jaws are separating, a force is pushing them apart, you cannot keep your mouth closed. Your lips are parting, your jaws are being pushed apart, you cannot keep your jaws together. *Your mouth is open. . .it is opening more and more. . .*MORE AND MORE. . .IT IS NOW OPENING COMPLETELY, WIDE OPEN!"

FORCING THE SUBJECT TO CLOSE HIS MOUTH

You ask the subject to open his mouth wide. Then looking him in the eyes, give him suggestions to the effect that he cannot keep his mouth open. A force is pulling his jaws together, his mouth is closing.

PREVENTING THE SUBJECT FROM EITHER CLOSING OR OPENING HIS MOUTH

With the subject holding his mouth closed, you can suggest that he will not be able to open it. That his jaw muscles are becoming stiff. That his jaws are becoming locked, stiff, rigid, etc. Conversely, you can start with the subject holding his mouth wide open, and give similar suggestions. Very often I combine this last group of experiments doing them in rapid succession proceeding as described before.

OTHER SUGGESTIONS INVOLVING THE MOUTH

Proceeding along similar lines you can force the subject to put his tongue out, then prevent him from pulling it back in. You can force him to keep saying over and over a simple sound such as "da. . .da. . .da." This is most easily done by having the subject repeat this sound, then suggest that as he continues he will find it impossible to stop until you tell him to. It is relatively easy to prevent a person from whistling by telling him that he will be unable to do so, in spite of the fact that he may be able to pucker his lips as if he were going to whistle. Similarly, you can prevent a good subject from saying any words in spite of the fact that he is able to open and close his mouth. You can make him stutter, and so on.

CAUSING THE SUBJECT TO HALLUCINATE HEAT

It is claimed by some hypnotists that any suggestion that can be given to a subject in the hypnotic state can also be given in the waking state, and be carried out successfully. I am inclined to doubt that *all* hypnotic suggestions can be given successfully in the waking state, but certainly a great many can. Responses to motor suggestions are by far the easiest to bring about. Sensory hallucinations and distortions can also be produced but are more difficult. One of the easier sensory effects to induce is the illusion of heat. Use a subject who has given good responses to the earlier suggestions and preferably one whom you have used successfully to produce other effects, ask him to hold his hand out horizontally, palm up. Place a small coin in it, then have him look at your eyes (or at the coin) and say: "In a moment this coin is going to begin to get warm. You will feel it get warm. . .warmer. . . and warmer, even hot! [*Sometimes, if your subject is very suggestible, this will be quite sufficient to produce the effect and he will throw the coin and report that it got very hot. If this does not happen then continue.*] Now the coin is beginning to warm up. It is getting warmer. . .warmer. . .warmer. . .You feel it getting warm, don't you? *It is now quite warm, very warm. . .in fact, it is getting hot. . . uncomfortably hot.* . .HOTTER. . .HOTTER. . .RED HOT!''

PRODUCING ANESTHESIA

The above hallucination is called a *positive* hallucination. The converse, in which a subject is rendered unable to perceive a given stimulus is called a *negative* hallucination. One of the easier negative hallucinations to produce is suggested anesthesia for pain. One way of proceeding is as follows: Have the subject sitting comfortably, his hand on his lap. Now fixate on him and tell him that shortly his hand is going to become numb and that he will be unable to feel any pain. Then say:

Now I want you to close your eyes and to listen carefully to my voice. Pay attention to nothing but my voice. In a little while all feeling will be gone from your hand. You will not be able to feel anything with it. Think of your hand getting numb. . .like when it goes to sleep. As you do so, you will find that it is becoming numb. As I speak to you your hand is becoming more and more numb. . .You can feel less and less with it, it is losing all feeling. Very soon now you will not be able to feel any pain in it. You will feel absolutely no pain. I shall count to three and at the count of three your hand will be completely insensible to pain. You will be unable to feel pain. . .One. . .your hand is losing all feeling, all sense of pain. It is getting more and more numb, you can feel less and less with it and you are losing your awareness of it. Soon you will be unable to feel anything at all with it. Two. . .*Your hand is quite numb now.* There is hardly any feeling in it. It is as if it were asleep. *You cannot feel any pain in it, it is completely insensible.* Three. . .*Your hand is now without feeling.* YOU CANNOT FEEL ANY PAIN. . .NO MATTER WHAT I DO YOU CANNOT FEEL ANY PAIN.

The standard test for anesthesia is to lift up a flap of skin on the back of the subject's hand and to pierce the fold with a hat pin or a large hypodermic needle. When using waking suggestions I find it is usually best to keep telling the subject that he feels no pain, that his hand has no feeling, and so on, while I am doing this. Preferably there should be *no interruptions* in giving the suggestions until the needle has been passed through the skin. It is also advisable to give suggestions to the effect that there will be no after-pain or sequelae after removal of the pin. Of course, you should observe sterile techniques as much as possible. This means using a sterile needle and swabbing the subject's hand with alcohol before and after the test. I prefer to do this before starting the suggestions. The chance of contamination is minimal, and, if you use a needle that has been immersed in alcohol before puncturing the skin, it is probably safe to dispense with the initial swabbing. The advantage in this is that the swabbing often tends to create anxiety in the subject or, if done just prior to piercing the skin, it may cause a breaking down of the suggestions. This is much less likely when the subject is hypnotized. Some hypnotists flame the needle with a match. My own experience has been that this often causes a deposit of carbon black to form on the needle. Subsequently this substance is deposited under the subject's skin and leaves an objectionable temporary mark.

A less drastic test consists of pressing the point of the needle rather firmly in a number of spots on the back of the hand. It is not necessary to break the skin to produce appreciable pain. As a check I like to either test the subject's hand in the same manner after the suggestion has been removed, or test his other hand immediately after the anesthetized hand. The suggestions sometimes affect both hands in spite of the fact that you may have given them for only one hand, hence the latter check may be misleadingly negative.

Still another test of anesthesia which is often used is the flame test. For this you can use a burning candle or even a flaming match. Lift the subject's hand by the wrist and move the flame back and forth under his palm and fingers. You must be careful not to leave the flame in any one spot too long since you could cause tissue injury. On the other hand, if you move the flame too fast, you will invalidate the test because the subject would normally only perceive heat of a nonpainful kind. Incidentally, some stage hypnotists make use of this fact to demonstrate anesthesia when actually there may not be any. You can easily determine the correct speed by trying it on yourself. (See also chapter 15 under "Simulation.")

OTHER SUGGESTED SENSORY ALTERATIONS

It is possible to induce many other kinds of hallucinations in the waking state. However, since the best results can be obtained with hypnotized subjects, we will leave a further discussion of procedures for inducing hallucinations until later. In general, the suggestions used for the waking state and hypnosis are essentially the same, with the difference that usually in the waking state it is necessary to give longer and more elaborate suggestions than in hypnosis. You can often tell a hypnotized individual: "When I snap my fingers you will feel extremely warm—very hot," and get results, but with the waking individual you will usually have to proceed more slowly, although again there are exceptions. Waking individuals tend to give weaker responses to suggestions in general. Another point of difference is that the effects of waking suggestions are usually more temporary than the effects of hypnotic suggestions, so the suggestor must often keep repeating the suggestions while the subject carries them out to get maximum effect. This need for continued repetition of waking suggestions as contrasted to the hypnotic situation involves more than the production of homoaction and heteroaction. In the waking state influences due to various internal and external stimuli are much more likely to interfere with the effects of suggestions than in hypnosis, unless the subject's attention can be maintained on the suggested response. As suggestibility increases, the effect of interference decreases, and with good subjects one can often dispense with verbal repetition. This is also probably one of the reasons why a considerable degree of suggestibility is required to produce delayed responses to waking suggestions (see next section). Finally, waking individuals are much less prone to spontaneously elaborate upon suggestions, particularly where hallucinations are involved. As a consequence, to obtain the same degree of participation of the subject in the suggested situation as one gets in hypnosis, one must suggest many of the desired elaborations to the waking individual.

Some of the other sensory effects which can be produced in the waking state follow.

1. Gustatory Effects:
   (a) Tasting of salt
   (b) Tasting a glass of plain water as sweet
   (c) Anesthesia of taste for sweet (a piece of sugar rendered tasteless)
2. Olfactory Effects:
   (a) Smelling the odor of roses
   (b) Perceiving the odor of violets in a plain piece of paper
   (c) Smelling a pungent odor which makes the subject sneeze
   (d) Anosmia
3. Visual Effects:
   (a) Seeing the color red
   (b) Seeing everything in the room illuminated in red
   (c) Visualizing a scene
4. Tactile effects other than those already discussed:
   (a) Causing an object held by the subject to become ice cold
   (b) Making the subject feel very hot or very cold
   (c) Experiencing an itch

When producing sensory alterations, you need not restrict yourself to only one modality at a time. As a matter of fact, by including two or more modalities in your suggestions you may be able to reinforce one suggested effect with another. For instance, if you suggest to an individual that a glass of water is a glass of beer, you can reinforce this suggestion by also suggesting that he smells the odor of beer. Similarly, you can reinforce the hallucination that a potato tastes like an apple by making it also look and smell like an apple. Compounding various sensory hallucinations as done here is unnecessary with a highly suggestible subject because he tends to elaborate and to supplement the suggestions spontaneously. This is particularly frequent with hypnotic suggestions. Thus, telling the hypnotized subject that a potato tastes like an apple will often lead him to see, smell, and feel it as one. His entire perception is altered.

OTHER TYPES OF SUGGESTIONS

If you can produce hallucinations in your subjects you may want to try other kinds of suggested phenomena. Among these are disturbances of ideation. For instance, you may try to make the subject forget the correct order of the cardinal numbers and hence make him unable to count properly. You can do the same in regard to the alphabet. You can render him incapable of using certain words, and so on. These are rather difficult suggestions to use in the waking state and your chances of success are rather small except with the most suggestible individuals.

It is also possible to produce the equivalent of posthypnotic suggestions in the waking state, although they are rarely as effective or last as long as true posthypnotic suggestions. To distinguish between the two, I usually refer to the first as *waking delayed suggestions*, or simply delayed suggestions. Essentially, when you tell a subject that at the count of three (or some other number) he will do or feel something specific, you are giving a delayed suggestion. A variation of this is to tell the subject that when you clap your hands, snap your fingers or give some other signal the suggestion will become effective. In some of the demonstrations that we have discussed, there has been a combination of delayed and present suggestions. Thus, we tell the subject that he will find that a coin is stuck when he tries to pick it up. This in itself is a delayed suggestion. To it we add a suggestion in the present by telling the subject that the coin is stuck, at the time he actually tries to lift it. It is entirely possible to perform this demonstration also by giving all the suggestions prior to the subject's attempt to pick up the coin. More typically like a posthypnotic suggestion would be to tell the subject who is sitting in a chair that when he tries to get out of his chair he will be unable to do so, that he will not be able to get up until you clap your hands. (See also page 346.)

5

Practical Considerations
Concerning Suggestion in General

BEFORE GOING on to the production of hypnosis and hypnotic phenomena we shall discuss a number of techniques and topics which are applicable to both waking suggestions and hypnotic suggestions.

COMBINING AND INTEGRATING SUGGESTIONS

Although you can give any suggestion singly, independently of others, there is often value in combining several suggestions sequentially into a continuous unit. It makes for more effective demonstrations and often has a facilitating effect upon some of the suggestions which are a part of the unit, as well as on subsequent suggestions. This may be likened to the subject's acquiring a sort of momentum which you make use of. More accurately, increasing sensitization is brought about through homoaction, heteroaction, and possibly other factors such as increased prestige, expectancy, etc.

The integration of suggestions goes beyond sequential combinations, and can also involve the simultaneous use of several suggestions as a means of enhancing a given effect. This was shown earlier in the case of sensory hallucinations. A more subtle aspect of this lies in a suggestion like the one used to prevent the subject from rising from his chair. We not only suggest that his body is too heavy to lift, but we eventually tell him that he is stuck to the chair. These are really two different effects which are synergic. Again, in this same experiment, we merely told the subject he was stuck to the chair. We could have elaborated this effect and increased it by combining additional suggestions to the effect that the subject was stuck to the back of the chair, that his upper legs were stuck to the seat of the chair, and that he was extremely weak and tired, in addition to being very heavy. When we give the subject an object to hold such as the broomstick, and make it impossible for him to let go of it, we could merely suggest that he cannot let go. It is more effective to add the additional suggestion that his hand contracts and freezes around the stick. As a last example, consider the suggested hallucination of a hot coin. You can use additional suggestions as an adjunct in the following manner. Place the coin in the subject's palm as indicated earlier or have him hold it between his thumb and index finger, in his closed fist, or some other way. Tell him that in a moment the coin will be too hot to hold and that he will not be able to keep it in his hand (or hold it). Go on suggesting that soon he will not be able to hold it, that when you count to three he will have to get rid of it no matter how hard he tries to hold it. Then you start counting. When you say "Two" begin to say, "the coin is getting warm, warmer. . .soon it will be too hot for you to hold, you will have to let go of it. . .it is getting hot. . .*hotter*. THREE. . .IT'S RED HOT!"

"TRAINING" THE SUBJECT

Every individual has a certain maximal potentiality for response to suggestions. Part of this suggestibility is innate, and part of it is acquired. Few individuals, if any, normally manifest their potential suggestibility at its maximum. As we have seen this is partly because of various interfering factors, such as attitudes, beliefs, and anxiety, and partly because normally the effective innate component of suggestibility is mainly that which initially manifests itself. The induction of hypnosis by the Standard method requires that a certain degree of suggestibility be present at the start. Similarly, the success of each waking suggestion calls for a minimal amount of suggestibility. In either case, it may be necessary to increase the subject's initial suggestibility, if possible, before the desired effects can be had. This preliminary step is what is usually referred to in the literature as "training" the subject, although as we saw in chapter 2 this notion can be given a much wider meaning. Homoaction and heteroaction are the two basic processes which are used for this purpose and from this fact and their properties certain procedural rules evolve: Whenever you begin working with a subject, particularly the first time, you should give him a number of different suggestions in rapid succession. Each one should contain many repetitions of the suggested idea, and if the response is weak or absent, it should be given at least once again. Always progress from the simpler to the more complex suggestion, or from the easier to the more difficult. In particular, give motor suggestions first and sensory suggestions later, since the former seem to require less suggestibility than the latter for their successful elicitation. You should always aim for strong, well-defined, and complete responses. For this reason it is always important that you do not tax the subject's suggestibility. If you begin with a suggestion which calls for greater suggestibility than the subject has, and therefore he fails to respond, you will get neither homoaction or heteroaction; if he responds weakly or incompletely, the heteroaction if not the homoaction will suffer. This is also true if the inadequate response occurs somewhere in a sequence of successful suggestions. As a matter of fact, because of the surmized nature of heteroaction we would expect that failure to respond would tend to "extinguish" or decrease the heteroaction gained thus far.

There are other desirable effects which accrue from observing the above rules. They have already been mentioned in various parts of the text and will be presented again here for review purpose. A successful suggestion always tends to increase the operator's prestige and to create in the subject a more positive attitude toward his ability to affect the subject. A rapid succession of suggestions helps to keep the subject's attention focused upon the operator and his role of subject.

Insofar as raising the subject's suggestibility through responding to suggestions is concerned one could simply use a set of suggestions of equal difficulty and complexity and such as not to tax the subject's responsiveness. One difficulty with this approach is that one very quickly runs out of suggestions. Furthermore, since the aim is to increase his suggestibility, it is desirable to have an idea as one goes on as to what the suggestibility is at any given time. Both problems are solved in practice by using a set of suggestions graded in terms of the amount of suggestibility they each require for the elicitation of a satisfactory response. One starts with the suggestion having the lowest requirement and progresses more or less routinely to the one with the highest. Any time the subject gives no response, or a weak, unsatisfactory one, this is taken as indication that his suggestibility has not or has barely reached the level characteristic of the suggestion being used. If the response is weak one can then repeat previous suggestions or introduce new ones of similar difficulty, eventually retesting the subject with the failed suggestion.

The suggestions which were used to demonstrate the Chevreul pendulum, backward postural sway, forward postural sway, hand levitation, hand clasping, eye catalepsy, and catalepsy of the arm, constitute a set of graded suggestions in the order low to high suggestibility. The recommended procedure in general is to begin with the Chevreul pendulum and to work up rapidly through the remainder of the above suggestions. Unless you have reasons for not doing so, you should use the principal model suggestions rather than the variations, since the former were designed to have maximum effectiveness. This schedule is, of course, not as rigid as it sounds. Many hypnotists dispense with the Chevreul pendulum suggestion, and not a few are of the opinion that backward and forward postural sway are of equal difficulty, hence that one of these (usually forward postural sway) can be eliminated. It should also be remarked that some feel the hand levitation suggestion is the easiest of all. I have had too many failures with it with subjects responding to other suggestions to agree with this point of view. Aside from this, there will be cases where you will not want to use as many suggestions, for example when you induce hypnosis or want to get a rough estimate of an individual's susceptibility to it. (See chapter 6.) With a little experience you may find it convenient to skip certain suggestions when you have subjects who are obviously very suggestible. As a rule, unless there is evidence that the subject is very suggestible, I always go rapidly through the postural sway, hand clasping, and eye catalepsy suggestions in preparation for further suggestions, particularly those intended for trance-induction.

ENHANCEMENT OF SUGGESTIBILITY THROUGH VOLUNTARY ACTION. RHYTHMIC DEEP BREATHING.

There is another way of making use of the processes responsible for homoaction. There is some evidence that not only responding to a suggestion enhances the capacity to respond to it again, but *voluntarily* executing a given action appears to facilitate its subsequent re-execution. This means that your suggestion is likely to be more effective if, shortly before giving it, you have been able to get the subject to cooperate to the extent of voluntarily performing the suggested act or parts of it. This is probably one of the factors involved in the hand clasping experiment when you begin by having the subject voluntarily stiffen his hands, although conceivably muscular set and inertia could account for the apparent enhancement, and in fact, it may well be that all these effects are involved here and elsewhere.

Can we also get a heteroactive-like effect in this manner? There seems to be reason to believe that we can. Many hypnotists, myself included, feel that getting the subject to voluntarily do a number of simple things can facilitate not only repeated responses, but also the future use of all suggestions on him. A very simple trick for doing this is to move the subject about under the guise of procedure. Thus, you request him to stand here. . .or better there. . .no, turned like this, etc. You can make him sit down as soon as you are through with an experiment, then ask him shortly afterward to stand up again to submit to another suggestion. If you are going to hypnotize the subject you can have him move to a different chair or to a couch. Again, if the subject crosses his legs after sitting down, you can request that he uncross them. Of course this must be done quite naturally and must not be overdone.

Some hypnotists feel that it is important to give the subject a rationale for these requests. I do not think this is true in most cases. On the contrary, a major aim in giving suggestions is to have the subject accept them *uncritically*, and to give reasons when not requested seems to me to be contrary to this. On the other hand, with certain subjects it may be necessary.

The evidence that this has an effect comes from practice. It would also be expected on theoretical grounds. There is evidence that acts which are voluntarily elicited, as well as thoughts, can take part in conditioning, either in the capacity of stimuli or of responses. If, as postulated earlier, heteroaction is a conditioned response type of phenomenon it can easily be shown that a sort of heteroactive-like effect should arise if you get an individual to respond voluntarily to various commands and then go on to use suggestions. This sort of enhancement is probably small, although large enough to be used effectively as an aid. In this connection it might be pointed out there is a belief that, on the whole, servicemen make particularly good subjects. A really adequate test of this proposition is still lacking. However, along similar lines of thinking, one might expect that army training could predispose individuals to greater suggestibility, or at least make it easier to train them as subjects. In particular, one might suspect that an authoritarian type of suggesting would be more effective than a nonauthoritarian one here. However, this does not in any way mean that time spent in the armed forces makes people more likely to succumb to suggestions of all kinds under all circumstances, and hence that army training has undesirable aftereffects of this sort. It must be remembered that the setting, the attitude, especially the degree of cooperation of the subject are also basic factors in determining when a suggestion will act as such.

It may be of some interest to speculate whether this effect might first occur when an individual volunteers to be a subject, particularly when the hypnotist directly asks for volunteers, as when demonstrations are given or when an experiment is carried out. As I have pointed out[191] people who volunteer may do so partly in response to a suggestion inherent in the hypnotist's request. If this is true, we certainly would expect the act of volunteering to have a small enhancing effect. The line between what is a suggestion and what is not may become very tenuous, indeed!

The efficient use of voluntary responses and other effects is nicely demonstrated in the following procedure for the production of the hand clasping effect in the manner described earlier (page 133), but now using mass or group suggestions. It was employed by the late stage hypnotist Konradi Leitner as a means of testing the suggestibility of groups of individuals as well as conditioning them for further suggestions. His aim was to *insensibly* *transform* voluntary responses into responses to waking suggestions and these eventually into responses in a light to medium state of hypnosis.*

Leitner would begin with some brief introductory remarks to his audience aimed at creating a receptive attitude and at establishing a preliminary rapport. The audience was then requested to stand up, ample time being allowed for everybody to get squarely upon their feet. Simultaneously, with the instruction to stand up, he would straighten himself, thus suggesting nonverbally to the audience to do the same. The participants were next instructed to remove everything from their hands and to relax. Having allowed ample time for handbags, purses, cigars, etc., to be disposed of, Leitner then told the audience to inhale deeply and to hold its breath for 10 seconds, timing mentally from the moment the inhalation was completed. At the count of ten he would say, "Exhale slowly." This was repeated three times in succession. Leitner himself inhaled, held his breath, and exhaled, carefully doing this in unison with the audience. To accentuate this process he would also hold his hands and arms outstretched in front of his chest, horizontal and parallel to each other, fingers spread apart palms down. With each inhalation he raised both arms to slightly above the level of his forehead, keeping them parallel. They were held in this position for the 10 second pause, then lowered to the horizontal in unison with the exhalation. Doing this had two functions: it introduced a nonverbal suggestion by example (imitation) of the voluntary act of breathing called for earlier, as well as helped to show the participants what was desired of them; and the arm motion served both as a suggestion and as a means of emphasizing and controlling the action called for.

At the termination of the third command to exhale, Leitner would proceed through essentially the same instructions for the hand clasping suggestion described earlier (page 133), slowly going through each motion himself. He did make use of one additional feature. When the participants had their arms extended with their fingers spread open (fig. 17*A*) he would instruct them to breathe deeply and then to exhale slowly. In the next step he instructed them to again breath deeply, but this time he would add, "as you inhale, raise your arms." Simultaneously he raised his own, then as soon as this had been accomplished by the others he would order them to lower their arms slowly and exhale. According to him synchronization of breathing and arm motion is very important—the deep indrawn breath being completed when

*I do not believe that Leitner was clearly aware of the exact modus operandi of his technique. Like many other successful stage hypnotists he seemed to have an intuitive grasp of hypnotic fundamentals, possibly the result of trial-and-error lerning throughout his many years of experience.

the arms reach their maximum height, and the exhalation terminating as the arms come back to their horizontal position.

This process was also repeated three times, then the next step was undertaken. The audience was told to interlock their fingers and turn their palms outward (with interlocked fingers), this being demonstrated to them slowly step by step. Proceeding in this fashion reduces, for one thing, the chance that any subject might misunderstand what he is to do, but the greater value resides in the fact that the technique makes use of a sequence of clearly defined voluntary responses to serve as a foundation upon which to build up the participants's suggestibility. Properly done it allows the hypnotist to pass insensibly from the elicitation of voluntary acts to suggestion proper. Leitner felt that one of the most important factors was for the audience to be in "harmony" with the hypnotist and in rhythm with his movements. It was his recommendation that at all times the hypnotist should lead and dominate the movements. He emphasized this idea of leading as contrasted to dictating. The hypnotist should be authoritative, yes, even commanding, but never a dictator.

With their fingers interlocked and their hands turned palms outward, the subjects were then told to take another deep breath, hold it for ten seconds, then exhale. Now they were told to harmonize their breathing with the movement of their arms from horizontal to above their heads, keeping the hands and fingers interlocked. Having gotten the participants to perform this exercise a few times, Leitner would tell them that in a few moments they would be asked to close their eyes, upon which he would in quick succession command them sharply to raise their arms overhead, to breath deeply, and to close their eyes slowly. Following this another command to breath deeply was issued.

It was usual for Leitner at this point to add certain remarks to the subjects to the effect that they had complete control over their arms and hands. Although this has a certain value for some individuals because it removes the threatening aspect of loss of control associated with hypnosis, it more often runs the risk of defeating the entire purpose of the procedures (which is to displace the subject's control over his body). Indeed, it seems to me that it contradicts the assertion that the subjects cannot take their hands apart.

In any event, Leitner would go on by asserting to the subjects that their eyes are closed. "Now breath deeply—in unison," he would continue. "Keep your hands over your head—Your hands and fingers are interlocked— Breath deeply, in harmony—Now your hands are beginning to become tight —I shall begin to count to three. As I count your hands will get tighter and tighter and when I reach the count of three you will not be able to unlock your hands and fingers. . .Breathe in unison—I shall now begin to count.''

"One—Your hands begin to feel tight."

"Two—Your arms and your hands are becoming stiff."

"Three—You cannot take your hands apart. Try. You cannot unlock your hands."

This then in essence was Leitner's way of handling this phase in his demonstrations. One should note how well he blended actual suggestions with other instructions. It is an excellent technique admirably suited for mass hypnosis. It is a relatively slow procedure, yet it is not as slow as it may appear. Furthermore, in the long run, it may actually be a time saver because it may better prepare the subject for future suggestions than do the more rapid methods. It is also to be noted that Leitner usually passed from the production of the hand clasping effect to the induction of hypnosis proper. We will have more to say about this procedure later. For the time being, other features of the method should be pointed out. One is that the entire procedure is designed to secure the maximum attention from the subject and to keep it focused upon the suggestions and instruction. Another point to note is how Leitner keeps the subjects executing voluntary actions (or at least what initially were voluntary actions) through the entire proceedings.

Thus far we have said little regarding the deep rhythmic breathing which he used so extensively and which is also used by others, including myself. While it is one of the voluntary responses used in conjunction with the suggestions, there is more to it. There are actually two aspects to consider. The first is that rhythmic movements are among the easiest to transform into involuntary automatic movements. Binet[13] and many other psychologists have demonstrated this point very nicely. Considering the fact that respiration is normally involuntary, its use here is particularly appropriate. In terms of our present understanding of abstract conditioning and its relationship to suggestibility, this use of rhythmic movements may be of some significance since, presumably, it eventually associates the subject's involuntary action with the hypnotist's commands.

The second aspect is that many hypnotists feel, often without a sound basis for it, that deep breathing directly helps in inducing and deepening the trance state. There is some experimental evidence that deep breathing (hyperventilation) does have a positive effect upon a person's suggestibility provided the person is already suggestible; but as a whole the available evidence is poor. Furthermore, although we have a rather good understanding of the biochemical changes brought about in the body by hyperventilation and what some of their effects on the nervous system are, it must be admitted that our notions concerning how they affect suggestibility are rather hazy, to say the least. In any event, if deep breathing does cause increased suggestibility, then there is an additional rationale for Leitner's use of it. Just how much hyperventilation is actually required is not fully known. Leitner certainly uses it long enough to have a definite effect. In fact, it is well worth noting how he manages to use it to the end of the suggestions.

COUNTING TECHNIQUE IN THE HANDLING OF DIFFICULT SUBJECTS

There are few reasons for trying to use waking suggestions with recalcitrant subjects. There are occasions, however, when what appears to be a potentially good subject responds poorly or not at all to a suggestion. Such is the case with passive subjects (see below). This is where the so-called "counting technique" is often effective. Its use has already been demonstrated, and it may be used in any situation. With highly suggestible subjects it can be very effective. You often only have to say: "At the count of three you will do thus-and-thus. . .One. . .Two. . .Three." and the suggestion takes effect. With subjects who have failed to give a response, or who have given a weak or abortive one, better success can often be obtained by stating very positively and firmly: "Now I am going to count to three and when I say three, such-and-such will happen. You will not be able to prevent it. In fact, if you did try, you would find that it happens even more strongly. However, you will not want to prevent it from taking place, and at the count of three it will take place. Alright now, One. . .Two. . .THREE!" In some instances you may want to add certain suggestions after each count as was done earlier. Or again, you may feel that a longer count is necessary. Varying situations call for varying methods. We will have more to say concerning resistance in subjects in the second part of this book.

PASSIVE SUBJECTS—THE SMILING SUBJECT

Not infrequently, one encounters individuals who appear to be potentially excellent subjects, yet who do rather poorly when given many of the suggestions. They respond very well in the falling back or falling forward experiments, they are readily hypnotized, yet in other respects they are rather unresponsive. These individuals are known as *passive* subjects. They are often recognizable by the fact that they show a disinclination to exert any muscular effort when told to do so, as is done initially in the hand clasping demonstration. Furthermore, when challenged, they are likely to do nothing at all. For purposes of demonstration or for experimental work it is best not to use them. On the other hand, regarding therapy, it must be emphasized that in spite of their passivity these individuals can be extremely suggestible and the use of hypnosis for therapeutic purposes can be very effective. I do not know of any specific way of handling such subjects. The use of a more positive, commanding, authoritarian approach will often overcome their passivity, at least partially. The counting technique outlined is often effective. The subject may react passively for certain personal reasons which can be uncovered by questioning him. By proper subsequent manipulations the causes can then be eliminated, or at least circumvented. This will be taken up in greater detail in connection with the production of hypnotic phenomena. The main point to be emphasized is that unresponsiveness, or what appears to be unresponsiveness on the part of a subject is not always an indication of low suggestibility. This may be of some importance from a practical standpoint in certain situations.

Sometimes subjects react to suggestions in a manner which may be rather disconcerting to the hypnotist. One particular reaction which may occur with waking suggestions is that the subject smiles, often broadly, as you give your suggestions. This usually occurs as a result of the subject experiencing, much to his surprise, the actual sensations and events you are suggesting. His smiling is nothing more than an expression of his surprise. Rarely does the subject smile because the situation appears ludicrous to him. In any event, it is best to ignore the reaction and to continue with the suggestions as if nothing unusual had occurred. While there are exceptions, it is a good rule not to let any action of the subject disconcert you, at least not apparently so. If possible, you should integrate the subject's actions into the procedures, otherwise ignore them. If you feel that you must interrupt the procedures, then you should start over rather than continue from where you quit. It is always a good idea to inquire from the subject at the end of the experiment why he acted as he did, e.g., why he smiled. Furthermore, you can often make use of the subject's answer to reinforce your influence on him. Thus, for instance, if in answer to your query: "Why were you smiling a few moments ago?" he says that it was because he was experiencing what you were suggesting, you should follow up with such a remark as: "You had not expected it would really work?" or: "You felt that pretty strongly, didn't you?" or something to that effect. Sometimes you can inject the question in the suggestion without seriously disrupting the procedure. If you get the above response, you can effectively use this admission to reinforce your suggestions.

On the other hand, suppose you happen to have a subject who finds the situation funny. Actually, he may not be able to help himself—it just strikes him as funny. If you ask him why he is smiling and he answers that the situation is funny, tell him quite calmly and firmly that he must be serious and cooperate with you and to please try to do so; then continue. If it appears that in spite of this he cannot overcome his amusement, then you have the choice of going on, or of dismissing him and trying another subject. The danger in an early dismissal is that the subject may smile after your request to be serious because he now is beginning to experience the suggested effect. If so, it would be desirable to go on. Should you guess wrong and the suggestions fail, your risk is small because you can always point out to the subject (and any audience) that the subject was obviously not cooperating.

NONVERBAL AND EXTRAVERBAL SUGGESTIONS*

In the previous pages we have indicated how certain gestures can have an intrinsic suggestive power. For instance in the backward postural sway the motion of the operator's hands may act in this fashion. Again, the downward motion of the operator's hands and body when suggesting to the subject that he is going to be forced to sit down or to kneel down is an example of what can best be called a *nonverbal* suggestion.

Nonverbal suggestions are an important adjunct in giving suggestions. They vary considerably in nature and can consist of anything from a facial expression, a posture, a tonal quality of the voice, to a motion of the entire body. We will have many further occasions to make use of them; but like other useful tools, they are double-edged and can also cause undesirable effects. This is particularly apt to happen with facial expressions which may be used quite unconsciously and unintentionally by the operator, leading the subject to respond in unexpected and undesirable ways.

Some years ago Hull[85] showed that one could obtain the same motor effects by "empathy" as one obtains by suggestions of postural sway. He did not show, however, whether characteristic properties of suggestibility such as homoaction, held for "empathy"-induced movements. Consequently, the full relationship between "empathy" and suggestibility is not known; nor is it clear to what extent "empathy" is generally involved in nonverbal suggestions. Indeed, the area of nonverbal suggestions is a rather unexplored one in spite of its practical and theoretical importance. For instance, a very fundamental question in connection with the nature of "animal hypnosis" is whether it is possible to give suggestions to an animal. Does a dog enter a state of immobilization through some reflex-like response to enforced immobility, or because holding the dog immobile communicates to him the

---

*I have previously[191] called these marginal and contextual suggestions. The present designation has been suggested by Meares.[121]

idea of immobility in the same way the hypnotist's words, "In a moment you are going to be unable to move. . ." do to a human subject? We really do not know. In any event, there does not appear to be any equivalent to human waking hypnosis among animals, although "animal hypnosis" may parallel "human hypnosis."

We might also consider with this topic of nonverbal suggestion the matter of vocal expression—inflection, stressing, modulation, change in rate of delivery, use of a monotone, variations in volume and other aspects of speech which can influence the information which is communicated. Unfortunately, there has been no study made of this aspect of suggestion, the individual must learn through experience how to make effective use of these various factors. In general, they do not seem to represent essential elements, since a suggestion given in a perfectly flat monotone can be quite productive. Although the structure and verbal content of a suggestion is far more important, the effectiveness of suggestions can be greatly improved by a proper use of vocal expression. It is my impression that introducing a quickening of the delivery combined with increasing stress upon critical words in the last half or last third of a suggestion will often speed up the response and lead to a larger reaction. This is particularly true if some signs of response are already evident. Similarly, passing to an assertive, affective, dynamic expression that these events are beginning to take place, seems to be more effective than continuing in a flat tone of voice. The transition itself has an effect of its own, appearing to reinforce the idea that now something is really happening. We not only tell the subject that what we have been predicting is now taking place, but also the change in vocal expression indicates to him our awareness of this change, possibly making it more real to him. If the transition per se is important, this would indicate that there is a definite time and place for the use of a monotone in spite of its apparent overall ineffectiveness. Sometimes it is possible to suggest a very specific effect through proper voicing. Thus, in suggesting to the subject that something, say his hand, is getting heavy, one can put a quality of "heaviness" in one's voice. This is what I have tried to indicate by writing "heavy" as "h-e-a-v-y" in a number of suggestions where this word occurred.

Another factor which must also be taken into consideration are those aspects of vocal expression which reflect the hypnotist's feelings, emotions, attitudes and so on. It is important that suggestions be given in a tone of conviction, of self-assurance, of confidence in their effectiveness. It used to be a rule among hypnotists of old that suggestions were effective to the extent the hypnotist could "will" the desired effect as he gave the suggestions. In the past many a text on hypnotism has carried special exercises for developing and projecting one's "will." This notion has since been discarded. Possibly the rule may have had its genesis in the fact that the act of "willing" added some of the nonverbal elements we have been talking about to the suggestions. In any event, I would be inclined to state instead the rule that, within limits, a suggestion will be effective in proportion to the degree to which the hypnotist believes in its effectiveness and in the reality of the phenomena it evokes. Just as the suggestor's true feelings reflected in the delivery of a suggestion can influence the subject, so can any feeling or emotion expressed in the delivery of the suggestion, regardless of whether or not it is experienced by the suggestor. For instance, the hypnotist who wants to suggest disgust can do this more effectively if he can also make his tone of voice express this (and even more if this is reinforced by facial expressions, posture and so on), although he himself may not actually be experiencing disgust. In brief, the control of vocal expression is of importance in giving suggestions for two reasons, it prevents the suggestor's personal feelings, attitudes and so on, from counteracting the verbal suggestions he gives and it permits him to reinforce verbal suggestions in various ways.

More generally, suggestions, as a communication of ideas to the subject, are not restricted to words but can make use of *any* medium. Furthermore, the effectiveness of suggestions would appear to increase with the number of such media used simultaneously. Why should this be? A little thought shows the direction in which the answer probably lies. Consider the example from above. The suggestor says "You feel disgusted!" At the same time he expresses disgust by his tone of voice and shows it by facial expression and body posture. We have here essentially three and maybe four different stimuli, each of which has the power to evoke the same response in the subject. They are all acting at the same time, mutually reinforcing each other.

Another aspect which should be mentioned is what may best be referred to as an *extraverbal* suggestion, that which is conveyed by the implied meaning of a statement as contrasted to that which is contained in its literal meaning. Implied suggestions can play an important part in suggestions in three ways. One may make a statement not intended to suggest anything to the subject, but which in effect does. Because the nature of an implied suggestion depends upon both the context in which it occurs and upon the suggestee's personal perceptions, it is not uncommon to find different subjects responding differently to the same structured groups of words. This can be a cause of much confusion, particularly in experimental work. Finally, and by far the more important, is the fact that hypnotized subjects tend to be very literal-minded. Much of conversational language communicates through implied rather than through literal meaning, and the tendency is to use conversational language when giving suggestions. As a consequence one frequently obtains rather bizarre and certainly unexpected and unwanted responses from subjects unless one is very careful to say exactly what one means. For this reason the use of simple, brief, concise statements employing words of few syllables is much to be recommended in constructing suggestions.

MASS (GROUP) SUGGESTIONS

Thus far in our treatment of suggestions we have dealt with the situation where the hypnotist works with only one subject. There are situations where it is desirable to give suggestions to many individuals at the same time. The technique is essentially the same as that already outlined—the same rules apply. In most instances it will be quite obvious where deletions or other changes must be made. In general, the range of waking phenomena which can be obtained is smaller as the means available for reinforcing suggestions are considerably limited. Thus the use of nonverbal suggestions is more restricted, and when a large number of subjects is used it is not possible to judge as accurately how well the suggested effects are progressing. Even if this could be done, it would be impossible to design the suggestion to meet the needs of every individual. The suggestion situation can be optimal only for some and not all of the participants; some potentially good subjects may be missed when mass suggestions are used. In addition, mass suggesting probably places greater emphasis upon the hypnotist's verbal ability to deliver a convincing and effective suggestion and hence it is preferable that it be undertaken by the reader only after he has had some experience with individual suggesting.

Usually it is not practical to give anything but the simpler waking suggestions to groups.* Many hypnotists restrict themselves to the hand clasping and the eye catalepsy suggestions, although some include the arm rigidity experiment. Actually, the postural sway experiment can also be given provided certain precautions are taken. Let us consider some of the waking suggestions used most frequently for mass effects and see what changes have to be made.

Postural Sway. Backward sway is most indicated here. I like to have alternate members of the audience act as subjects, and the others help prevent any mishaps in case a subject does fall. Backward sway is indicated because if the subjects should fall, there usually are chairs behind them to help break the fall. With small groups, it is entirely feasible to have the members who

---

*That is, in so far as waking suggestions are concerned; with hypnosis induced in a group of individuals, extremely complex suggestions can be given.

are observing stand directly behind those acting as the subjects. The following is a sample of how to proceed. We shall assume that you have a small audience sitting in rows in front of you and have given a short introductory address (see chapter 7). Tell the audience the following:

> Please count off, starting with the first person on my right in the front row. [*With a large audience this is not practical and should be discarded. As soon as this is done, go on with*:] Now will every person with an odd number rise and turn toward his neighbor on the right. Will the persons with even numbers rise and look at my fingers. . . [*At this point raise your right arm with the index and middle fingers making a V.*] Now, I want those of you who are not looking at my fingers, that is the persons with odd numbers, to watch your neighbors. In a little while they are going to sway backward. . .some may even fall backward. . .I want you to be ready to catch them if they start to fall and ease them gently into their chairs. . .Alright. . .those of you who are looking at my fingers, keep on looking at them steadily. Soon you will begin to sway backward. You are going to feel a force pulling you backward and you will sway backward. . .You feel a force pulling you back. . .You are beginning to sway backward. . .You are swaying backward. . .(etc.).

As soon as you detect strong swaying among a fair number of subjects, stop the suggestions. It is preferable not to bring about actual fall, but should some individuals fall quite early do not let this interrupt the suggesting. Note that you use the word "sway" in preference to "fall," for the express purpose of bringing about the former rather than the latter. Also, at the start of this experiment it is a good idea to quickly make sure that no subject is so much larger than his neighbor that a problem would arise if he fell. In such a case you might ask them to trade places. Take note of the subjects who show a good response, particularly those who fall. They will be potentially good subjects. After this trial is over you can request the people with odd numbers to act as subjects while the others stand by to help.

Hand Clasping. This can be done with the subjects sitting or standing. If you intend to use this as part of your trance-inducing procedure (as will be discussed later) you will prefer to have the subject sitting. Many hypnotists seem to favor the method described on page 133, in which the hands are held above the head, over the one in which the hands are held horizontally. It usually does not seem to make much difference which method one uses.

Eye Catalepsy. The only difference here is that you have the subjects look upward without putting your finger on their foreheads. It sometimes helps to tell them to imagine a spot on their foreheads and to look upward toward it.

Arm Rigidity. For reasons of space, it is usual to have the subject hold his arm vertically, fist above his head. In other respects the experiment is carried out as already described.

Arm Twirl. Essentially unchanged. Make certain that there is ample room between subjects so that they do not hit each other.

As in the sway experiment, it is usual to have the subjects look at your finger or fingers. Many hypnotists instruct the subjects to look them in the eyes or to look at their nose. Obviously the hypnotist cannot fixate on all of them at the same time. Furthermore, you do not want to do this since you usually want to watch as many subjects as you can.

At this point you may wonder just when mass suggestions are indicated and when you should use individual suggestions. Mass suggestion is an excellent method for quickly selecting suggestible subjects from an audience, particularly if there are few volunteers. Many hypnotists rarely use anything other than hand clasping or arm rigidity suggestions, although some use mass suggestions on volunteers to simultaneously prepare them for the induction of hypnosis. This also can be rather impressive from the viewpoint of an audience. Mass suggestions are always indicated where time is at a premium. If your main objective is to use waking suggestions as a preliminary to producing hypnosis, it is often not worthwhile or even feasible to work with each potential subject individually.

In giving demonstrations, a very effective way of proceeding is to combine individual and mass suggestions. For instance, you can give the postural sway suggestions individually to a few volunteers, then do the same by mass suggestions to the remainder of the audience. If you are careful you will nearly always have good results with the individual suggestions and this will enhance the effectiveness of your mass suggestions. Or, if you have a small group of volunteers, you can give the postural sway suggestions individually then give hand clasping or arm twirl suggestions as a group to the three or more who gave the best responses.

CHOOSING A PROCEDURE

It is obvious that there are many ways of giving a suggestion. Which procedure are you to use? Should you consistently use the same approach in all cases or should you vary the procedures? This is largely a matter you must decide for yourself. Experiment with different procedures, then, if you find one which seems particularly well suited to you, use it consistently. How ever, you should never be too rigid, because there are always times when another procedure may be more effective and it is best to have some versatility. The beginner is usually wise to use one method until he has become quite adept with it. Then it may be a good idea for him to try other approaches. For lecture-demonstration purposes it is best to have a standard approach and to use it consistently, since this is not the place to experiment with methods. On the other hand, in individual therapy where the major aim is to get a response from the patient by any available means and not to impress an audience, one has considerably more leeway and the hypnotist may find it worthwhile for himself and his patient to experiment a little. When using suggestions in research it is often advantageous to be somewhat flexible with procedures, although problems of controls, standardization, and comparability may impose certain limitations.

COMPARATIVE STRENGTH OF WAKING AND HYPNOTIC SUGGESTIBILITY

Inasmuch as from here on we shall deal nearly exclusively with hypnotic suggestions, we may conclude this part by considering whether waking suggestibility can ever be as high as hypnotic suggestibility. This question is related to that of the suggestibility continuum discussed in chapter 2. The answer to it is a little more complex than it might appear. First of all, if suggestibility does increase with the number of basic processes called into action, and the full hypnotic state (hypnosis proper) is present only when *all* processes in question have been *fully* activated, then waking hypnosis can never be as great as hypnotic suggestibility. On the other hand, if we identify waking suggestibility with pure ideomotor action and enhancement, then waking suggestibility may reach the same height as hypnotic suggestibility insofar as the ideomotor component is concerned (if we are dealing with an individual in whom the basic processes cannot be elicited). Generally, if we are dealing with an individual in whom only some of the basic processes can be elicited, or one in whom all may be brought about, but only to a limited degree, then as we give waking suggestions the subject will tend to attain the same maximum degree of suggestibility he can attain when hypnotized. In practice most individuals attain a much greater suggestibility when deeply or even moderately hypnotized than when not hypnotized. This is the reason why hypnosis is of primary concern to us.

CONTINUITY AND DISCONTINUITY OF IDEAS IN SUGGESTIONS

It is not uncommon when giving suggestions to not only present the idea of the desired effect to the subject, but to either precede or accompany it with one or more subsidiary ideas which suggest this effect indirectly in varying degrees. One of the most common ways in which this is done is by using the additional ideas in metaphores. For instance, when suggesting to an individual whose eyes are closed that he cannot open them, one may assert that his eyelids are heavy, heavy as lead, and that when he tries to open them he will find it impossible to do so; it will be as if his eyes were glued tightly shut. Similarly, when suggesting to an individual that he is falling backward, we often tell him not only that he is going to fall or that he is falling, but that this is because a force is pulling him backward. There are certain advantages to doing this. Since the subsidiary ideas indirectly suggest the same end-effect as the principal idea, it is assumed that there will be some sort of synergic action. Also, it is always possible that the subject will misinterpret what effect is expected and stating it in several different ways may help to prevent misunderstandings. Sometimes, too, the subject is incapable of conceptualizing or visualizing a certain effect when it is presented to him in one way, yet he can do it if it is worded somewhat differently. About the best one can do to circumvent it, should it occur, is to offer the subject a choice of concepts as a matter of course. There is a final advantage to proceeding in this manner, it affords the subject an opportunity to participate more actively in the production of the suggested effect by choosing which idea to act upon. In cases where resistance arises out of the subject's reluctance to relinquish his control over reality, such a procedure is particularly useful in overcoming the resistance.

Some hypnotists, however, feel that this technique is harmful because it introduces discontinuities in the subject's thoughts. If monoideism or sustained attention is basic to the production of suggestion phenomena, this is certainly a reasonable position to take. To first call the subject's attention to the notion, for instance, of his eyelids being too heavy to open, then to the idea of their being glued closed does appear at first sight to be incompatible with the above conditions. And yet, a little thought on the matter also indicates that this might not be so. If, for instance, as some investigators have maintained, the all-important factor in suggestion is not just concentration but concentration upon the idea or person of the suggestor, as contrasted with concentration on any singled-out word, the above argument loses force.

Actually, what happens in practice is that some subjects appear to respond best to suggestions when one adheres to strict continuity of ideas, whereas others do seem to benefit from the introduction of subsidiary ideas. In general, the situation here appears to be one which must be maximized in order to establish the most profitable balance between the good and bad effects of introducing subsidiary notions. Perhaps this situation is not too difficult to understand. Words connote as well as denote ideas. The effectiveness of subsidiary ideas depends upon connotation and difficulties seem to arise mainly when the subject is more sensitive to denotations. It is then that one finds the ideas presented to the subject competing for his attention. The key to the successful use of subsidiary ideas would appear to reside ideally in preventing denoted ideas from being stimulated when only connoted ones are desired. A more practical way of looking at the problem, however, is in terms of whether or not all ideas induced by the words of a suggestion act together as a well-integrated and patterned ideational complex, that is, in a unitary way. Does the suggestion as a whole convey a single idea to the subject or does each word in it act separately, giving rise to its own set of specific and associated ideas? Each and every time this happens one has essentially a discontinuity introduced in the suggestion. Actually, then, when we speak of a lack of continuity in suggestions we really are speaking of the presence of one or more distinct, localized discontinuities. It is most likely that individuals possess a variable perceptual threshold as well as tolerance for discontinuities of this sort, so that in practice the main task one has here is to insure that the number of discontinuities and the degree to which they stand out is below the threshold and tolerance level of the subject. As long as this condition is satisfied one can use subsidiary ideas or introduce discontinuities in other ways and profit from whatever they may add to the effectiveness of the suggestion. One can go about meeting the above requirement by means of what may be best described as a smoothing out of discontinuities through the judicious use of closely related words, and the gradual step-wise passage from one idea to a more remote one via a sequence of such words. By proceeding in this manner one helps to create or to preserve an over-all continuity in the suggestion. In other words, one approximates continuity.

As I have indicated, experience shows that there are individual differences with regard to subjects' reactions to discontinuities. Both the threshold and the tolerance varies. Indeed, even the form the reaction takes shows variations. From a purely practical standpoint it would be useful to be able to predict who is likely to require special attention to continuity and to what degree. It is my impression that in general individuals who are literal-minded, who have critical or analytical minds, who place a high value on words, who are prone or trained to use a highly precise language, or who, in the course of their professional activities, are called upon to critically examine the words of others, are frequently the ones who cannot tolerate discontinuity or will tolerate only a small amount of it. These individuals, interestingly enough, often perceive the subsidiary ideas as being incompatible with one another as well as with the central idea of the suggestion, even though no logical or linguistic incompatibility really exists. Their tendency to literalness with regard to the words of the suggestion often shows up in a different way which is worth calling attention to. Whereas it is immaterial for most people whether one says in a suggestion, for instance, "Your eyelids are heavy," or "Your eyes are heavy," with these individuals this becomes quite important. Typically they will report that when told that their eyes were heavy they found it impossible to conceive of their *eyeballs* being heavy. On the other hand, it should be noted that not all individuals who perceive incompatibilities between ideas proposed in a suggestion give this reaction or even show any ill effects insofar as their suggestibility is concerned. Some simply ignore all but the idea which appeals most to them and allow it to have its effects upon them. My experience has been that the use of subsidiary ideas is most likely to cause difficulties when the subjects are professional scientists, and more particularly psychologists. On the other hand, I must admit that I have not as yet attempted to make a specific study of this problem and would not want to make any generalizations at this time.

To summarize this matter of continuity, it would appear that one is dealing here with a matter of relative rather than absolute discontinuity. As a matter of course one should always aim at giving one's suggestions as much over-all continuity as is feasible, at the same time keeping in mind that complete continuity is usually not required nor even desirable. However, when dealing with individuals falling in the category described a few moments ago, or when in doubt, it probably is a good rule to adhere to strict continuity, at least in the initial contact. It will often be possible with such subjects to introduce with advantage a certain amount of discontinuity at a later date. One should never forget in this connection that difficulties arising out of the use of subsidiary ideas may be signs of resistance, and part of the way of handling the situation will consist in dealing directly with the resistance.

The emphasis in this discussion has been upon apparent or real discontinuities which the use of subsidiary ideas introduces in suggestions. Discontinuity can probably arise in other ways. Although I have never encountered this situation, it is conceivable that when one attempts to integrate or combine several suggested effects into one suggestion, a discontinuity is created. In general this should be preventable through the same means as have been recommended in connection with the use of subsidiary ideas. Smoothing the transition point or points is probably the most basic technique here.

Part III.
Hypnosis and Hypnotic Suggestions

6

Hypnotic Susceptibility
And the Depth of Hypnosis

B Y SUSCEPTIBILITY to hypnosis we mean how well an individual responds to procedures aimed at inducing hypnosis. In practice it is
estimated by finding out what is the maximum depth of hypnosis or the
greatest suggestibility he is able to attain as a result of such procedures.
Some hypnotists also include under this term the speed or ease with which
a certain degree of hypnosis can be produced. As I pointed out,[191] it is better
to distinguish between the two measures and I reserve the name *hypnotizability* for the second.

SUSCEPTIBILITY TO HYPNOSIS—ITS PREDICTION

Clearly, the most direct way of finding out how susceptible an individual
may be is to simply attempt to hypnotize him. However, in practice there
are occasions when one would like to predict susceptibility. One of the simplest and most accurate ways is to use waking suggestions. It has been shown
by various investigators that there is a high correlation between an individual's response to certain suggestions and his capacity for going into a trance
state. The better he responds to these suggestions, the more likely it is that
he can be hypnotized to a given depth. Furthermore, the maximum depth
of hypnosis and the speed of induction tend to be in direct relation to the
effectiveness of these waking suggestions. When given to an individual to
predict his susceptibility, these suggestions are called *test suggestions*.

Undoubtedly the best known and most used test suggestion is the postural
sway suggestion,* usually called the postural sway test. It is particularly
useful because you can attach a string to the subject, connect it to a lever
through a system of pulleys, and get accurate graphical records of the amount
and rate of sway produced by a given suggestion. Obtaining such records is
rather important in many phases of experimental work. The reader who is
interested in looking further into this technique will find details in Hull's

*With a test-retest reliability of the order of 0.90.

classic study.[95] For most practical purposes, it is sufficient to give the postural sway test without benefit of recording apparatus or stop watch; with a little experience one can do a rather good job of estimation. Furthermore, it is easy to supplement the postural sway test with other readily administered tests.

Another test suggestion which gives a good prediction of hypnotic susceptibility is the heat illusion test, to be described shortly. There is reason to believe that this suggestion brings about responses through a somewhat different mechanism than the postural sway suggestion. Although it is a good test, it has the disadvantage of requiring an apparatus for administration. Furthermore, it is much less impressive than the postural sway test for demonstration purposes and it cannot be given easily to a group. Consequently, it is primarily relegated to the laboratory or office and to situations in which the subject alone is involved. On the other hand, experimental evidence shows that the heat illusion test given in conjunction with the postural sway test results in a two-test battery which constitutes to date the best existing predictor of susceptibility. Because of this, we shall describe the heat illusion test in some detail.

You need a small heating element which the subject can either apply to his forehead or hold in one hand. This heater should be connected to a potentiometer or some other device allowing you to regulate the amount of current flowing into the heater by means of a graduated knob. The potentiometer should permit a relatively slow variation in heat production and it should be mounted in a box. A switch should also be incorporated in the circuit so that the experimenter can interrupt the current flow in the heating element without the subject's knowledge.

The subject is shown beforehand how the heating element becomes hot as he turns the calibrated knob. He is next asked to turn the knob slowly (from the zero position) until he detects the first sign of heat in the element. He is instructed to immediately remove the element from his forehead or to let go of it when this happens, and to call out the reading on the dial. He is then asked to repeat the procedure and this time, unknown to him, the current is interrupted by means of the hidden switch. As the dial approaches the previous reading it is called to his attention by a statement such as: "Pay close attention now, you should soon feel the heat." If he is suggestible he will report detection of heat.

You might expect that any waking suggestion should be able to serve as a test of hypnotic susceptibility since the induction of hypnosis usually begins with waking suggestions, but only certain types of suggestions can be used in this manner. The reason is that suggestibility does not appear to be a unitary trait, but as seen earlier consists of at least three kinds: primary, secondary, and tertiary suggestibility, which together define the general trait complex. Different suggestibilities are evoked by different kinds of suggestions which I have called primary, secondary, and tertiary respectively. Postural sway, and in general, simple motor responses are brought about through primary suggestibility which in turn is directly a function of ideomotor action. The heat illusion effect, on the other hand, depends upon tertiary suggestibility.

As was explained primary suggestibility, hence ideomotor action, is believed to be mainly involved in the initiation of hypnosis by the Standard method; subsequently any waking test of the subject's capacity for primary suggestibility or ideomotor action is also a test of the likelihood that hypnosis can be initiated by trance-inducing suggestions. The heat illusion test creates somewhat of a puzzle here because there is no evidence that it depends directly upon any of the basic processes of hypnosis, and indeed, most data deny this possibility.[191] The most reasonable explanation for the high correlation between hypnotic susceptibility and this test is that the subject's ability to vividly imagine is highly favorable to both the test and to the elicitation of ideomotor action.

It should be clear that a high capacity for ideomotor action is not necessarily a sure index of high hypnotic susceptibility since development of the full hypnotic condition also depends upon other processes. A really adequate test should tap the subject's capacity for these other processes. That the tests which are available do not do this is one of their weaknesses.

As was indicated in the case of the heat illusion test, some test suggestions may serve as indices of hypnotic susceptibility, not because they depend upon one of the basic processes for their effectiveness, but because some factor which affects the processes underlying the response to the test suggestions also affects the processes responsible for the response to trance-inducing suggestions. This is a rather important point to keep in mind when working with tests of susceptibility to hypnosis.

Many hypnotists, particularly stage hypnotists, often make use of the hand clasping suggestion as a test of susceptibility. Although this has not been tested under laboratory conditions, there is good reason to expect that it would be a good test. Similarly, we would expect eye catalepsy suggestions and arm rigidity suggestions to be good tests of hypnotic susceptibility, and they are often used by stage hypnotists for this purpose. An excellent estimate results from giving the subject postural sway, hand clasping, and eye catalepsy suggestions (in this order, this being the order of relative difficulty). Thus one places increasing pressure upon the subject's suggestibility, ability to concentrate and cooperation. If he fails to respond to the easier suggestions, it is unlikely he will respond to the harder ones. It saves time and effort and gives a better estimate of the subject's waking suggestibility. Furthermore, heteroaction is an essential characteristic of trance induction and giving these suggestions in this order allows for the production of some heteroaction. This is an excellent sign of hypnotic susceptibility if it occurs. Although this procedure does not allow the direct detection of heteroaction, the latter will manifest itself in the manner and ease with which the subject responds. In this respect, one would expect this procedure to be a better indicator of trance susceptibility than the use of any one of the three suggestion tests singly. It remains to be shown under controlled conditions that this is true. Another reason why this may be a superior test is that if it allows for the generalization of suggestibility, then it more closely duplicates the essential conditions present in the production of hypnosis by means of suggestions and allows a test of the subject's ability to develop the heteroactive component of hypersuggestibility. In line with this, it is probably preferable to follow the rule given earlier in regard to giving a subject at least two trials on any given suggestion since this allows for the possibility of homoaction. If the formation of hypnotic hypersuggestibility depends upon three (or more) basic processes, then the more a waking procedure can test the subject's capacity to form all of the processes rather than any single one, the better predictor it should be.

One last reason for using this testing procedure is that it can be made part of the trance-induction process or it can at least be used to prepare the subject for hypnosis by raising his suggestibility through homoaction and heteroaction. If we quickly follow the testing with trance inducing suggestions, it is likely to lead to a successful hypnotization, provided, of course, that we have not come close to the subject's limiting capacity for developing the basic processes.

Before concluding this section, a few words of caution must be given. Predictive tests of hypnotic susceptibility are not perfect by any means. The correlation between test suggestions and hypnotic susceptibility is not unity, hence not all factors have been taken into consideration. If the hypnotist and subject have the time, it will often pay them to consider training, and to attempt hypnosis by several methods even should the test results be unfavorable. A subject may give a poor response initially, yet with training eventually develop a very deep trance. He may even develop a relatively deep trance at first, although he did poorly on some or all of the pretests. Conversely, some individuals do very well on the pretests, yet develop only a light to medium hypnosis. As hypnosis is multidimensional, it is easy to see how tests might tap only a few, maybe only one of the dimensions which are involved.

There are many things the tests of susceptibility do not tell us. They do not provide any information concerning the type of responses the subject will give once he is hypnotized, (whether he will be a passive or active subject); nor the most effective way of inducing hypnosis. They can only give us a rough idea of the depth attainable and of the rate of induction. They tell us very little or nothing concerning the outcome of training; and they do not usually tell us what factors may interfere with the manifestation of the subject's suggestibility.

These tests are valuable when one must quickly pick out the individuals most likely to be good subjects or when one has an ample supply of subjects. They are also valuable when made a part of the preinduction preparatory period and for certain kinds of experimental studies.

Thus far we have spoken of tests which involve giving obvious suggestions. In situations where this is contraindicated, it would be of value to have tests which do not depend on obvious suggestions. We can consider two such types: a situation involving a hidden suggestion and one where the subject's suggestibility or susceptibility is not directly tested, but some correlated function of it is. Some attempts have been made to find such indicators, but thus far they have not been very successful.[191] Some investigators have tried to use the Rorschach test, but the results have been rather ambiguous. Presumably this would be an indirect test of susceptibility or suggestibility. Another test that seems to have more promise consists of showing the subject card 12M of the Thematic Apperception Test. He is required to tell a story about the card (exactly as instructed in giving the TAT). It has been found that if the subject shows positive attitudes toward hypnosis in his story, he will most likely be susceptible to hypnosis and, conversely, if he shows a negative attitude, his susceptibility will be low. There is some disagreement concerning what is involved here. It may be that only the attitude factor in suggestibility is tapped. It is my opinion, however, that there is a hidden suggestion in card 12M and that in most cases this is the main element functioning in this test. Because of its simplicity, I believe further research on it is indicated.

Meares[121] has pointed out that the standard tests of suggestibility, such as the hand clasping test and the postural sway test, are not entirely suitable in the clinical setting. He lists the following objections: they tend to be too spectacular and "savour" of the variety show stage, they require introducing an authoritarian attitude right at the start of the treatment, which is not always good, and it is not always wise for the patient to know that he is being tested, especially for suggestibility.

In order to circumvent these objections he has developed a simple test of suggestibility which may be of interest to the reader, although very little is known about its actual reliability or validity.

Meares makes the test of suggestibility a part of the physical examination he gives his patients. When he tests the tendon reflexes he tells the patient to relax his whole body and to loosen all of his muscles so that the reflexes can be tested. He goes about examining the tendon reflexes while at the same time suggesting relaxation indirectly. He adds that one can modify the suggestions in various ways as one progresses with the test. Thus one may say to the patient, "You don't move your legs, they are quite loose, it is I that moves them." At the same time he moves the legs about passively or through the knee-jerk reflex.

There are three types of reactions to this. In the *positive* response complete relaxation with flacidity of the muscles takes place. The limbs can be moved passively without causing tension in them. This relaxation often extends to the face. Such individuals are suggestible and easy to hypnotize. Secondly, there may be very little response or no response at all, but no obvious resistance either. Such individuals can usually be hypnotized, according to Meares, but not as easily as those giving a positive response. Finally, the patient may give a *negative* response whereby he becomes more tense instead of relaxing. This tenseness spreads over the entire body and is usually accompanied by discomfort, fidgeting, restlessness and so forth. This, however, does not mean that the subject is not suggestible. On the contrary, Meares emphasizes that if the patient gives any response it shows he is being influenced by the suggestions and that he can be hypnotized. Negative reactions are not the same as negativistic behavior, but the latter may give rise to the negative reactions in which case different techniques must be used to induce hypnosis. Exactly what sort of techniques are used in these instances will be taken up in chapter 14.

MEASUREMENT OF THE DEPTH OF HYPNOSIS

In theory, measuring the depth of hypnosis is an easy matter since, by definition, it is nothing more than the amount of suggestibility the individual attains as a result of submitting to trance-inducing procedures. No assumption is made here that hypnosis is necessarily equated to suggestibility. All that is assumed is that various degrees of suggestibility are to be found associated with hypnosis, and we arbitrarily use this assumption to define depth of hypnosis. The resulting ordering of degrees of suggestibility may very well have no correlation whatsoever with other conceivable measures characteristic of hypnosis. As a matter of fact, a number of schemes of hypnotic depth built upon different principles or assumptions were proposed as early as 1884 and possibly earlier. Some of these will be found described in the works of Grasset,[73] of Bernheim,[10] and of Schilder.[151] If we have a set of suggestions of different difficulties, we can obtain an idea of the subject's relative suggestibility. By ordering these suggestions and assigning numbers to them we can establish a scale of hypnotic depth. In practice, however, constructing an adequate scale of this kind is not so simple. Of those that have been designed, two stand out and will be described.

The first is the Davis-Husband scale of hypnotic susceptibility.[36] It is easy to use and, although it does not fully meet all of the criteria of a perfect scale, it is entirely satisfactory for all practical purposes. It divides hypnosis into five major depths, each of which is further subdivided into a total of 30 degrees to which numerical values (ranging from 0 to 30) are assigned. The scale is given below:

DEPTH	SCORE	TEST SUGGESTION AND RESPONSES
Insusceptible	0	
Hypnoidal	1	
	2	Relaxation
	3	Fluttering of the eyelids
	4	Closing of the eyes
	5	Complete physical relaxation
Light Trance	6	Catalepsy of the eyes
	7	Limb catalepsies
	10	Rigid catalepsies
	11	Glove anesthesia
Medium Trance	13	Partial amnesia
	15	Posthypnotic anesthesia
	17	Personality changes
	18	Simple posthypnotic suggestions
	20	Kinesthetic delusions; complete amnesia
Deep Trance	21	Ability to open the eyes without affecting the trance
(Somnambulism)	23	Bizarre posthypnotic suggestions
	25	Complete somnambulism
	26	Positive visual hallucinations, posthypnotic
	27	Positive auditory hallucinations, posthypnotic
	28	Systematized posthypnotic amnesias
	29	Negative auditory hallucinations
	30	Negative visual hallucinations, hyperesthesia

With the exception of the insusceptible and the hypnoidal divisions, testing for the remainder of the depths simply consists of giving the subject the suggestions in listed order, beginning with catalepsy of the eyes. If he responds satisfactorily, you go on to the next, and so on. The measurement is terminated the first time he fails to respond to a suggestion. His depth of hypnosis is determined by the score corresponding to the last suggestion to which the subject responded satisfactorily. Thus, if the subject responds to "simple posthypnotic suggestions" but does not show "kinesthetic delusions," and "complete amnesia," he is assigned a depth of 18 and he is in a medium trance. As will be seen shortly test suggestions and responses for the hypnoidal condition are nothing less than those which make up the induction of hypnosis proper. Rather than testing the subject for the lighter degrees of hypnosis one simply notes the behavior as an *indicator* of the progress of the induction process. Of course, if a subject never goes beyond closing the eyes or fluttering the eyelids then we say that he has attained a hypnoidal state or has reached a depth of value 3 or 4 as the case may be.

As will become clear in the next chapter, testing for depth of hypnosis can be a part of the deepening phase of induction since deepening the trance is partly done by having the subject respond to graded suggestions. It is clear that if we give the subject suggestions in accordance with the above list we will be testing depth as well as increasing the depth of hypnosis, but this enhancement will be limited because it does make some difference in procedure whether we are only testing depth or also deepening the trance. In the first case one tests the subject with one suggestion after another. In the second case one would usually give one or two suggestions from the list, then deepen the trance further by other means and follow with more test suggestions. Furthermore, if the subject did poorly or failed completely on any given test suggestion, one would not stop, but would instead make an effort to get him over this hurdle by using other techniques for increasing the depth of hypnosis, then test him again with the same suggestion. Even if he still did not respond satisfactorily you might try other more difficult suggestions, but when testing merely for depth, the subject is allowed only one trial and the test stops when he fails the first time.

The Davis-Husband scale has a number of weaknesses. For one thing, the measure involved here is reactive. Each measurement tends to alter future measurements and to be affected by previous ones. The general effect is to cause an overestimation of the trance depth at the time of measurement. Of course, this is not a weakness of this scale alone; any other scale built on the same principles suffers from the same defect. Another weakness lies in the fact that the discriminating power of each item is not as good as one would desire. An individual can fail on one item, yet pass the next. This is particularly true in the range of the lesser depths. However, the biggest deficiency of the scale is probably that the suggestions used are not standardized. This makes it impossible to accurately compare data reported by different individuals. As a matter of fact, because the same hypnotist will often not use identical suggestions twice, data reported by a given individual on two occasions may not be comparable. Furthermore, since in designing and calibrating their scale Davis and Husband used suggestions which may or may not be comparable to those used by other hypnotists, there is no guarantee that others will meet the conditions this scale should obey. The weaknesses of the scale show up primarily when the subdivisions are used or when an individual is a borderline case. Since it otherwise appears to place subjects satisfactorily in the five main categories, it is probably all right where high precision and replicability are not requisites, the situation in many everyday cases.

Two variations of the scale have been offered since its publication. Watkins[188] has added to it four objective symptoms and corresponding scores: hypermnesia, slight = 8; hypermnesia, marked = 16; regression = 19; negative visual hallucination, posthypnotic = 32. A more extensive variation involving an expansion of the scale has been made by LeCron and Bordeaux[170] who use 50 items (as against 22 in the Davis-Husband scale) and assign 2 points for each symptom exhibited. On this scale a person can then have a maximum suggestibility score of 100. One important feature of this scale is that it includes a sixth major division, the *plenary trance* which the authors describe as a "stuporous condition in which all spontaneous activity is inhibited." According to them, somnambulism can be developed from this condition by suggestions to that effect. This is an important addition since there is increasing evidence that such a condition exists and that it is essential that it be induced for certain critical experiments and effects. Unfortunately, there is no evidence that the scale was constructed in accordance with accepted methods of scale construction, no information of reliability or validity is available, the method of scoring is rather ambiguously described and, finally, it seems to possess the same defects as the Davis-Husband scale (which served as a prototype). Some of these criticisms also apply to Watkin's scale.

In spite of weaknesses, the LeCron-Bordeaux scale may be of interest to some readers because of its attempt to find a greater number of symptoms which would allow construction of a more finely subdivided scale. This list may be of value to those who would like to devise more adequate scales of this kind. The scale follows:

DEPTH OF HYPNOSIS	WEIGHT	CRITERION SYMPTOM
Insusceptible	0	Subject fails to react in any way
Hypnoidal	1	Physical relaxation
	2	Drowsiness apparent
	3	Fluttering of the eyelids
	4	Closing of the eyes
	5	Mental relaxation, partial lethargy of the mind
	6	Heaviness of limbs
Light trance	7	Catalepsy of the eyes
	8	Partial limb catalepsy
	9	Inhibition of small muscle groups
	10	Slower and deeper breathing, slower pulse
	11	Strong lassitude (disinclination to move, speak, think, or act)
	12	Twitching of mouth or jaw during induction
	13	Rapport between subject and operator
	14	Simple posthypnotic suggestions heeded
	15	Involuntary start or eye twitch on waking
	16	Personality changes
	17	Feeling of heaviness throughout entire body
	18	Partial feeling of detachment
Medium trance	19	Recognition of trance (difficult to describe but definitely felt)
	20	Complete muscular inhibitions (kinaesthetic delusions)
	21	Partial amnesia
	22	Glove anesthesia
	23	Tactile illusions
	24	Gustatory illusions
	25	Olfactory illusions
	26	Hyperacuity to atmospheric conditions
	27	Complete catalepsy of limbs or body
Deep or somnambulistic trance	28	Ability to open eyes without affecting trance
	29	Fixed stare when eyes are open; pupilary dilation
	30	Somnambulism
	31	Complete amnesia
	32	Systematized posthypnotic amnesias
	33	Complete anaesthesia
	34	Posthypnotic anaesthesia

	35	Bizarre posthypnotic suggestions heeded
	36	Uncontrolled movements of eyeballs— eye coordination lost
	37	Sensation of lightness, floating, swinging, or being bloated or swollen, detached feeling
	38	Rigidity and lag in muscular movements and reactions
	39	Fading and increase in cycles of the sound of the operator's voice (like radio station fading in and out)
	40	Control of organic body functions (heart beat, blood pressure, digestion, etc.)
	41	Recall of lost memories (hypermnesia)
	42	Age regression
	43	Positive visual hallucinations; posthypnotic
	44	Negative visual hallucinations; posthypnotic
	45	Positive auditory hallucinations; posthypnotic
	46	Negative auditory hallucinations; posthypnotic
	47	Stimulation of dreams (in trance or posthypnotic in natural sleep)
	48	Hyperesthesias
	49	Color sensations experienced
Plenary trance	50	Stuporous condition in which all spontaneous activity is inhibited. Somnambulism can be developed by suggestion to that effect.

As already remarked it is not entirely clear from the author's account how to score with this scale. Two points are assigned to each symptom shown by the subject so that someone showing all of these would get 100 points. Apparently there is no way to account for the possibility that an individual may fail to show a number of symptoms. In contrast, the Davis-Husband scale has been constructed on the principle that no one will show a given symptom unless he has also shown all those preceding it on the scale and, conversely, no one will produce symptoms lying beyond the one he failed to show. LeCron and Bordeaux state that persons making a score from 2 to 12 on their scale are hypnoidal, from 14 to 36 are in a light trance, and so on. However, it is conceivable that an individual might get a score between

2 and 12 points by giving only symptoms listed under light trance or some other stage. The authors do admit that their scale may not apply perfectly to individual cases and that a subject in one degree of hypnosis may show symptoms belonging to other degrees and fail to show some of those specific to his own trance depth. They feel, however, that the total score will usually place the subject fairly accurately. Since the scale seems to agree fairly well with other scales reported in the literature, and with observations made from everyday practice, it is probably satisfactory where high precision is not a requirement. It may even be quite accurate; personally, I doubt that it is an improvement over the Davis-Husband scale, aside from its recognition of the plenary trance, and this can easily be included in the latter scheme.

Just exactly what state the plenary trance is remains to be determined. In some respects it reminds us of Braid's stuporous phase. It also resembles the state of "lethargy" described by the Salpêtrière school (chapter 9). It would be a relatively easy matter to test this condition to see if the many symptoms described by Charcot can be found. Until this is done one can only call attention to the possibility that one is dealing with a related state. The Charcot group did admit that all the symptoms they described could be brought about by suggestions, including those of lethargy. They contended, however, that these were pseudo-states because the subjects remained somnambulistic, merely producing the suggested symptoms.

Before going on to the next type of scale it will be of interest to relate the different depths of hypnosis we have been discussing to the induction process described in chapter 2. The correspondence which exists between the Husband-Davis divisions and the types of processes which are activated by the trance induction process as it progresses is outlined below:

Insusceptible	Poor ideomotor action and/or homoaction; and/or presence of interfering factors.
Hypnoidal	Primarily homoaction — possibly a small amount of generalization.
Light trance	Homoaction and definite generalization.
Medium trance	Primarily generalization — possibly some dissociation.
Deep trance	Dissociation fully established.

At any stage, of course, it is assumed that the processes which precede in the sequence leading to it are also active. For the medium trance, we assume that ideomotor action and homoaction are present. In addition, transference may be present at any step, although theory suggests that it would not become fully developed until the medium trance appeared. It must be re-emphasized that these various processes are both sequential and partially concurrent. Dissociation of awareness rarely appears in its final form during the development of homoaction. This also is true of heteroaction. On the other hand, these processes can be said to be developing, often from the very start of the induction process.

It is interesting to note that Kluge, Dessoir, and later Moll, felt that the various stages of hypnosis fell into two basic groups in terms of the extent to which functional disturbances could be elicited. Group I consisted of all states showing only changes in the voluntary movements; whereas Group II consisted of all of these as well as states in which the changes were in the sensory functions. In terms of the above, Group I would consist of persons who have well-developed ideomotor suggestibility but who have little of the heteroactive component. In contrast, Group II consists of persons with well-developed heteroactive suggestibility and a high degree of dissociative suggestibility.

In spite of some major defects, the best available scale by far is the one developed by Friedlander and Sarbin.[66] It is the only one which has been validated, in this instance by a test of internal consistency, and for which the reliability (test-retest) is known, this being 0.80.

The scale is built around a standardized procedure made up of a trance-inducing suggestion and a series of suggestions of various effects. The trance-inducing suggestions are divided into eight sections for purposes of scoring (the instructions for which will follow later).

Originally the investigators hypnotized subjects in a small portable booth illuminated by a 10-watt red-glow bulb. A cardboard cylinder was suspended from the ceiling with a 3/8 inch glass-covered apperture through which a white light bulb in the cylinder could shine. The subject was asked to look at this spot of light and to keep staring at it. This particular portion of the procedure is probably not too critical and those wishing to make use of the Friedlander-Sarbin scale can probably safely use a more convenient variant. However, they should approximate these conditions as closely as possible. The experimenter then recites the following material in a low monotonous tone. It is absolutely essential that you use exactly the same words in the same order as are given below, and that you deliver the suggestions as indicated if you wish to make use of this scale.

I.   Keep your eyes on that little light and listen carefully to what I say. Your ability to be hypnotized depends entirely on your willingness to cooperate. It has nothing to do with your intelligence. As for your will-power—if you want, you can remain awake all the time and pay no attention to me. In that case you might make me look silly, but you are only wasting time. On the other hand, if you pay close attention to what I say, and follow what I tell you, you can easily learn to fall into a hypnotic sleep.* In that case you will be helping this experiment and not wasting any time. Hypnosis is nothing fearful or mysterious. It is merely a state of strong interest in some particular thing. In a sense you are hypnotized whenever you see a good show and forget you are part of the audience, but instead feel you are part of the story. Your cooperation, your interest is what I ask you. Your ability to be hypnotized is a measure of your willingness to cooperate. Nothing will be done that will in any way cause you the least embarrassment.

II.   Now relax and make yourself entirely comfortable. Keep your eyes on that little light. Keep staring at it all the time. Keep staring as hard as you can, as long as you can.

III.   Relax completely. Relax every muscle of your body. Relax the muscles of your leg. Relax the muscles in your arms. Make yourself perfectly comfortable. Let yourself be limp, limp, limp. Relax more and more, more and more. Relax completely. Relax completely. Relax completely.

IV.   Your legs feel heavy and limp, heavy and limp. Your arms are heavy, heavy, heavy, heavy as lead. Your whole body feels heavy, heavier and heavier. You feel tired and sleepy, tired and sleepy. You feel drowsy and sleepy, drowsy and sleepy. Your breathing is slow and regular, slow and regular.

V.   Your eyes are tired from staring. Your eyes are wet from straining. The strain in your eyes is getting greater and greater, greater and greater. You would like to close your eyes and relax completely, relax completely (but keep your eyes open just a little longer, just a little longer).† You will soon reach your limit. The strain will be so great, your eyes will be so tired, your lids will become so heavy, your eyes will close of themselves, close of themselves.

VI.   And then you will be completely relaxed, completely relaxed. Warm and comfortable, warm and comfortable. Tired and drowsy. Tired and sleepy. Sleepy. Sleepy. Sleepy. You are paying attention to nothing but the sound of my voice. You hear nothing but the sound of my voice.

VII.   Your eyes are blurred. You can hardly see, hardly see. Your eyes are wet and uncomfortable. Your eyes are strained. The strain is getting greater and greater, greater and and greater. Your lids are heavy. Heavy as lead. Getting heavier and heavier, heavier and heavier. They're pushing down, down, down. Your lids seem weighted, weighted with lead, heavy as lead, your eyes are blinking, blinking, closing, closing.

VIII. You feel drowsy and sleepy, drowsy and sleepy. I shall now begin counting. At each count you will feel yourself going down, down, down into a deep comfortable, a deep restful sleep. Listen carefully. One—down, down, down. Two—three—four—more and more, more and more. Five—six—seven—eight—you are sinking, sinking. Nine—ten—eleven—twelve—deeper and deeper, deeper and deeper. Thirteen—fourteen—fifteen—sixteen—(If eyes

*Note this interesting way of getting the subject to actively participate in the process. He is told that this is a skill he can learn. It also implies that it is something desirable. This is often an excellent approach—to tell the subject that he is going to be taught how to relax, make himself go to sleep, and so on. This is particularly effective with young children, to whom you can often present the process as a game.

†As will be explained shortly, these suggestions may have to be read a second time. This is omitted on the second reading.

closed): You are falling fast asleep. (If open): Your eyes are closing, closing. Seventeen— eighteen—nineteen—twenty—(If closed): You are sound asleep, fast asleep. (If open): Begin at II and repeat.

If the subject should close his eyes before the end of this eight-minute recital, one notes the paragraph in which this occurs, it is completed and then the last paragraph is recited. If the subject's eyes are still open at the end of the last paragraph, the procedure is repeated, omitting the introductory paragraph (I). If the subject's eyes are open at the end of the second reading, he is given the command to close them while the experimenter simultaneously forces the lids down with his fingers. In this manner the authors estimate that the total duration of the induction never exceeds 14 minutes.

Although the next group of suggestions are continuous with those given above, we shall stop here and explain the system used by Friedlander and Sarbin to score this part of the induction process. They define *five periods* as follows:

Period I—Paragraph one to five inclusive.
Period II—Ends with paragraph seven.
Period III—Ends with paragraph eight.
Period IV—Involves repeating to the end of paragraph five.
Period V—Involves repetition beyond paragraph five.

The scoring is done on the basis of the period in which eyelid closure takes place, in accordance with the following key:

PERIOD IN WHICH EYES CLOSED	SCORE VALUE
I	5
II	4
III	3
IV	2
V	1
Eyes do not close	0

The second phase of the procedure consists of giving the subject six suggestions following the last step described above. These suggestions follow in the order in which they should be given. The subject should be timed in all cases so that if he overcomes a suggestion you have a measure of the required time.

1. Your eyes are tightly shut, tightly shut. Your lids are glued together, glued together, tightly shut. No matter how hard you try, you cannot open your eyes, you cannot open your eyes. Try to open your eyes. Try hard as you can (ten seconds pause). Now relax completely, relax completely.

2. Your left arm is heavy, heavy as lead. Your arm is heavy as lead. You cannot raise

your arm. Try hard as you can, hard as you can. You cannot bend your arm. Try hard as you can, hard as you can (pause ten seconds). Now relax completely.

    3. Extend your right arm, straight out, straight out. Your arm is rigid. Rigid and stiff. Stiff as a board. No matter how hard you try, you cannot bend your right arm. Try to bend your arm. Try hard as you can, hard as you can (pause ten seconds). Now relax completely, completely.

    4. Put your fingers together. Interlock your fingers. Your fingers are interlocked, tightly interlocked. You cannot separate your fingers. Try hard as you can (pause ten seconds). Now relax completely, relax completely.

    5. You cannot say your name. No matter how hard you try, you cannot say your name. Try to say your name. Try as hard as you can (pause ten seconds).

    6. Now relax completely. I am going to wake you up. When you awake, you will remember nothing of what has happened, nothing of what has happened. I shall count to ten. At eight you will open your eyes. At ten you will be wide awake and feeling cheerful. But you will remember nothing of what has happened. After you awake, you will hear someone calling your name. Ready now, one, two, etc. . . . .

    7. (When the subject awakens, wait ten seconds. If no response, ask: "Do you hear anything?" If the reply is "Yes," ask, "What?" If "No," ask, "Did you hear your name being called?")

This part is scored on the basis of the responses to the negative suggestions, the response to the suggested hallucination and the amount of amnesia present. The scoring key for each of these follows:

A. *Negative Suggestions*

    In addition to the values given under "Score," the total time required to resist "failed" items is taken into account *by adding* one point to the score values for each multiple of 10 seconds.

CRITERION	SCORE VALUE
Number of suggestions passed	
5	5
4	4
3	3
2	2
1	1
0	0

B. *Suggested Hallucination*

CRITERION	SCORE VALUE
Distinct hallucination, no prodding necessary	5
Faint hallucination, prodding necessary	3
No hallucination	0

C. *Suggested Amnesia*

CRITERION	SCORE VALUE
No items recalled	5
One item recalled	4
Two items recalled	3
Three items recalled	2
Four or five items recalled	1
More than five items recalled	0

The final total score of the subject is simply the sum of the four subscores obtained in the above fashion. The greater it is, the greater is the depth of hypnosis, the maximum being 20.

As was remarked earlier, this procedure is the most satisfactory one available today from the standpoint of reliability, standardization and, to some extent, validation. Unfortunately, it is relatively inelastic, requiring a specific procedure of induction and even of testing for suggestibility which is both not always applicable, nor the best in all instances. The resulting weakness does not really become apparent until one has used the scale extensively. Too few alternative procedures are allowed. I have found a subject hardly able to keep his eyes open, by the time period VIII is reached; yet as his eyes were not *completely* closed, it was necessary to start again and give suggestions which tended to counteract the effects already obtained. This was shown time and again by the subjects and mentioned in their own reports. It is my personal conviction that if an alternative procedure had been available, many who scored relatively low on this scale would have attained a deeper trance. Similarly, from my own experience as well as from theoretical considerations, the instructions to keep the eyes open a little longer in parenthesis in period V often tend to counteract the progress of the trance induction. Here too, an alternative procedure is needed.

An analogous observation can be made with regard to the instructions to blink at the end of period VII. Such instructions, and others in this period, are inconsistent and certainly unnecessary when the eyes have closed early in VII and remained closed. Two other sources of difficulty may lie in the suggestion of heaviness which may give rise to resistance in some subjects, and in the suggestion of sinking which may have unpleasant associations for some individuals. Another important weakness is to be found in the instructions to the subject at the very beginning "to keep staring *all the time*," and to "keep staring as hard as you can, *as long as you can*." Some subjects perceive this as an instruction to keep the eyes open, if at all possible, despite anything else that may be said or which happens. Thus these instructions tend to counteract the effects of the rest of the procedures. Since a person can become hypnotized with his eyes remaining open, one may improperly rate the subject. Furthermore, if the subject has at all become hypnotized during the first reading, these instructions on second reading now acquire the compulsive power of a suggestion and tend to be even more detrimental with regard to obtaining eye closure. Here too, subjective reports from subjects support this contention.

The scale proper has certain other weaknesses. For one thing, in the light of recent developments, it does not appear to cover a sufficiently large range of suggestibility, primarily on the side of the deeper trance states. It is also my belief that the scale fails to test properly for what we might call the medium to deep trance level. Of the six test suggestions, five tap the motor level. Generally speaking the motor phenomena called for are elicitable with a relatively low degree of suggestibility, indeed, in the absence of any evidence of hypnosis. On the other hand, the only hallucinatory test used is a posthypnotic auditory hallucination, one of the more severe tests of suggestibility. There is, therefore, a large gap on the suggestibility continuum which is not tested. To some degree this is remedied by the amnesia test, but not sufficiently so. At least one test of hypnotic hallucination would be desirable. However, since there are indications that individuals equally hypnotized are not equally capable of hallucinating in a given sense modality and show a selective effect in this respect, it would appear desirable to test for hallucinations in at least two sense modalities.

Two last criticisms of a different order which might be made are the lack of provisions enabling the experimenter to insert certain instructions or suggestions to the subject, as may be called for by an experiment. Furthermore, sufficient suggestions are not included to offset undesirable aftereffects such as headaches.

Special attention should be called to one part of the procedure which can lead to underscoring the subject. The posthypnotic test calls for the subject hallucinating immediately upon waking that he hears someone calling his name. To get a maximum score on this he must spontaneously show evidence of having had this hallucination. Now it occasionally happens, possibly more often than suspected, that the subject has the hallucination quite vividly, but in such a manner that it seems entirely natural to him that he should hear his name called. In such a case he may even give a negative answer to light probing. A typical instance is the situation where he hallucinates the experimenter as terminating the count to ten with such a command as "Wake up, Roger." This hallucination is so consistent with the entire setting that the subject may not even connect this experience with such a question as "Did you hear your name called?" and particularly with "Did you hear anything?"

For normal, everyday use, the Davis-Husband scale is probably ample. Indeed, most hypnotists do not bother to test for depth accurately. For reasons already given, the induction process can easily be combined with the testing procedure. On the other hand, wherever accurate research is to be done, particularly where the depth of hypnosis may be an important factor, the use of the Friedlander-Sarbin scale may be preferable.

A somewhat different and novel approach to the gaging of hypnotic depth consists of a self-rating by the subject. LeCron,[105] in describing one form of this method, gives as the rationale behind it the belief that the subject's unconscious mind is capable of giving accurate estimates of the trance depth when contacted, and that under hypnosis it can be contacted directly. He describes his technique as follows:

> A brief explanation is given the hypnotized subjects as to the stages of hypnosis.* It is stated that the subconscious mind can determine accurately the depth of trance when questioned "How deep are you?" and can reply verbally. A variation would be to have the subject visualize a blackboard on which the answer will appear in writing. It is fully explained that there are no well-differentiated stages of hypnosis, each merging into the next.
>
> For the yardstick with which to measure, a scoring system of 100% is used, percentages being arbitrarily assigned to the different stages. This is carefully explained to the subject. The hypnoidal stage is omitted as not being a trance state. He is told to consider from 1 to 20 in percentage as a light trance, 20–40% as a medium trance, 40–60% as a deep or somnambulistic trance, 60–80% as a still deeper trance (previously designated as plenary), and that 80 to 100% represents a deep stuporous state which may even approach something similar to suspended animation. In it a subject would probably be unable to answer at all.
>
> When such a yardstick has been described, the subject is told that, during the trance, the question may be asked at various times, "How deep are you?" The subconscious is directed to make an immediate reply with the proper figure.

LeCron states that his method is very quick and astonishingly accurate. He reports having validated it by comparing the self-ratings against trance depth determined in terms of the various phenomena which could be elicited in 30 subjects. However, the validation may not be adequate inasmuch as extensive exploration of the trance depth was limited to five of these subjects. One is hampered in evaluating this technique in other respects by the lack of certain essential information in regard to procedures. The method is interesting and certainly bears further investigation, but it cannot be recommended at this stage for use in any serious work with hypnosis.

*Whether symptoms characteristic of the different stages are described, and which ones, is not stated in the article.

Israeli[89] has described another self-rating technique. His method consists of telling the subjects during an orientation period (it is not clear whether they are hypnotized or not) that they will rate themselves according to a ten-point scale in which step 1 is defined as "out of trance," step 2 as "near trance," step 3 as "in trance," and step 10 as "maximum trance depth." The other six steps, 4 through 9, are left undefined. When a rating is desired the subject is told: "Upon signal, rate yourself (according to the scale) and describe your condition briefly." No rationale or validation is offered for this method. A major criticism which must be made in the absence of more detailed information is that it is doubtful if a subject can meaningfully estimate his trance depth in this manner. It is one thing to indicate to the subject what criteria he is to use in his rating, as presumably LeCron does, and another to let him make up his own criteria. Even if a subject is consistent from rating to rating, it seems unlikely that any two subjects picked at random (who did not possess common preconceptions regarding trance depth, would rate themselves the same when in similar depths, nor would one expect their ratings to coincide with those obtainable by external means. It is true that in Israeli's method the hypnotist has brief descriptions of the subject's self-perception and should therefore be able to make his own rating. However, if the samples given by Israeli are typical, it is my opinion that they are not likely to give a satisfactory estimate of the subject's depth of hypnosis.

As in the case of predicting hypnotic susceptibility, it would be very desirable to have a way of gaging trance depth which did not depend directly upon suggestibility measurements. Some sort of physiological test would be ideal. Unfortunately, it has been very difficult to establish any correlation between hypnosis and a specific physiological sign and even more so between such signs and the various levels of hypnosis. Recently a promising report was made by Doust[39] of a correlation between oximetric measurements and the level of awareness or "depth of hypnosis." The technique is simple and well suited for rapid determination of trance depth any time this is desired. Briefly described, it consists of applying a histamine preparation to the subject's fingernail fold. Then, following sudden occlusion of the peripheral circulation by means of a sphygmomanometer bandage connected to a pressure bottle, the blood in the dilated vessels of the fingernail fold is studied with a pocket spectroscope under standard lighting and heating conditions. The reduction time of the oxyhemoglobin can thus be obtained and from this, the arterial oxygen saturation level can be calculated. This procedure has adequate sensitivity.

Although the technique looks promising, it needs confirmation and further study. For one thing, Doust obtained his results from four mentally ill patients. Data from more and, especially, from normal individuals are desirable. There is no evidence in Doust's report that he attempted to measure trance depth in terms of hypersuggestibility; in fact there is some uncertainty concerning what Doust's criteria were, consequently his data remain somewhat ambiguous. Although what he calls "depth" of hypnosis and what we are referring to by this name are probably the same thing, this remains to be shown. A correlation with the degrees of hypersuggestibility associated with trance depth is needed before the method can serve satisfactorily to monitor the depth of hypnosis. It also should be noted that Doust has not demonstrated that the oximetric variations he reports are specific to hypnosis alone; as a matter of fact he has found depressions of oxygen level of comparable magnitudes occurring in deep hypnosis, affective experiences and sleep—whether sleep can be differentiated from hypnosis in terms of oximetric measures is not indicated. All that Doust is measuring is the effect of change in level of awareness upon oxygen tension, using hypnosis to affect the former. If a correlation between suggestibility and oximetric measurements is found, then the method will be a very valuable tool for measuring trance depth whether or not the basic effect is specific to hypnosis.

VALIDITY OF DEPTH MEASURES

By the validity of a test or scale is meant the extent or degree to which it measures what it purports to measure. The ideal way of estimating validity is to compare measurements obtained with the test against those obtained with an independent measure of the same quantity being studied (an external criterion). This procedure is often not possible and one must turn to some other form of validation, often using an internal criterion. When this is done, one obtains what is known as a test of internal consistency, another way of saying that structurally speaking the test or scale is satisfactory. This type of approach never actually answers the question whether the test or scale measures what it is designed to measure, but it does give a guarantee that the measuring instrument is logically and mathematically sound. The problem of rigorous validation of test instruments is rather complex and the reader who is interested in further details should consult such texts as those of Guilford[75, 76] and of Gulliksen.[77]

A less rigorous but more practical approach to this question is to ask how well does the concept and measure of hypnotic depth work in practice? Does it lead to meaningful information? In recent times, Conn,[29] Kline[100] and de Milechnin,[123] among others, have indicated their discontent in this respect. They have pointed out that too often the depth of hypnosis, as defined in the previous pages, is not consistent with the therapeutic results which are achieved through suggestions. More specifically, many therapeutic suggestions can be extremely effective even though only a relatively light hypnosis is found when one of the available scales of hypnotic depth is used. They feel this indicates a basic failure on the part of the scales to adequately measure the depth of hypnosis. This failure, they add, results from the fact that the scales in use do not sufficiently take into account, if at all, the psychodynamics of the hypnotic situation—the degree of involvement of the personality structure of the hypnotized person.

Although I would agree that our present scales have their weaknesses and that better scales might result were other criteria used, I do not feel that this criticism is entirely cogent. To begin, these investigators have failed to separate the possible contributions to the outcome of hypnotherapy of the therapeutic setting per se from those of the hypnotic suggestions. Suggestions often appear to be more effective than one might have expected on the basis of the measured depth of hypnosis and, conversely, some suggestions appear to be surprisingly ineffective, but is this because the depth of hypnosis was improperly gaged, or because certain situational or other factors had been disregarded? As I have pointed out, some individuals can produce vivid hallucinations with greater ease in one sense modality than others in a presumably equally deep trance. This may be a function of some intrinsic property of the subject's nervous system and not particularly relevant to the depth of hypnosis present, except in the sense that a greater depth is necessary if vivid hallucinations of a given type are to be induced in the refractory individuals. In any event, until this type of confounding is eliminated, one can only keep in mind that available scales of hypnotic depth may be faulty, but this is by no means proven.

Quite apart from this consideration, there is a basic weakness in these criticisms. They are apparently based upon the a priori decision by the writers that the effectiveness of certain therapeutic suggestions should require a certain specific degree of suggestibility *as already defined on a pre-existing scale*. But, to the best of my knowledge, there are at present no logical or empirical reasons why a given therapeutic suggestion should a priori be assigned to a specific point on any of the available scales. All that we are entitled to say is that it is an observed fact that such-and-such a therapeutic suggestion corresponds or is equivalent to such-and-such a nontherapeutic suggestion as used to define a given depth of hypnosis on a given scale. It is important to keep in mind that in constructing a scale of depth of hypnosis we can define the steps in many ways. One way, for instance, is to use the set of suggestions that Husband and Davis used, or the set of criteria that Friedlander and

Sarbin preferred; another possibility would be a set of therapeutic suggestions properly selected and ranked, producing a scale that would undoubtedly be more useful and "meaningful" to psychotherapists, but by no means invalidating other existing scales. Once we had such a scale, we would establish an equivalence relationship between the two scales.* At this point we might be able to show that one of the two scales was basically inconsistent with regard to empirical data; even then additional data would be required to decide which of the two scales was faulty.

As an alternative to the independent construction of a "therapeutic" scale, we can make the assumption that the existing scales are valid and empirically establish what values on these correspond to the effective action of a given therapeutic suggestion. This is essentially what was done by Wolberg[203] in setting up the equivalence relationship shown on page 425. Here we have a table showing what hypnotherapeutic technique is most likely to be successful for a given depth of hypnosis as measured on a scale of the Davis-Husband type. One could use the resulting therapeutic scale as an independent scale of hypnotic depth, although it would be rather impractical.

There are no reasons for assuming that hypnotic depth (as measured on the Friedlander-Sarbin or similar scales) does not take psychodynamic or other factors into account. At the basis of such scales is the observation that there exists at least one set of suggestions which may be uniquely ranked on the degree to which they affect an individual. No limitations are imposed upon what processes will be allowed to manifest themselves in the responses of the individuals being tested. Presumably, when a person responds to the test suggestions, all of the factors which determine the effectiveness of a suggestion are active. The only basis on which the criticism could be leveled against the existing scales would be that the test situation created by the use of the scale somehow prevents certain processes from taking part in the test-responses or that the therapeutic situation introduces additional factors which are not taken into account by the scales. It is possible that the induction technique prescribed by Friedlander and Sarbin tends, by virtue of being standardized, to de-emphasize certain elements in the hypnotic situation whereas the psychotherapeutic setting might well tend to overemphasize others. An advantage of the Davis-Husband scale is that it does not place any restrictions upon the trance-induction and trance-utilization procedures one may use, but one should keep in mind that the use of any test of hyp-

*This is essentially what is being done when the 31 steps on the Davis-Husband scale, for instance, are grouped in order to obtain a correspondence with the usual five-fold division of hypnotic depth.

notic depth always creates a new relationship which differs from the one established through the induction process. This point has been justifiably emphasized by Conn.[30]

Superior scales of hypnotic depth might be constructed on the basis of different principles or by using different concomitants of hypnosis. Doust's oxymetric measure is an example. Watkins[190] sees increasing trance depth as a process of "de-egotization" and relates it to the success of various psychotherapeutic procedures. Were we to find an independent measure of this "de-egotization" we might be able to derive a valuable new scale of hypnotic depth. To date, however, hypersuggestibility remains the most accessible and most meaningful concomitant of hypnosis.

On the other hand, hypersuggestibility is not an absolute criterion of hypnosis, except possibly under the condition that the subject's waking suggestibility has been accurately established prior to the induction of hypnosis. If we can demonstrate that a definite increase in suggestibility has resulted from the use of a recognized trance-induction technique, then, regardless of what other symptoms may be present, we probably are always justified in saying that the individual is hypnotized. By extension, if we can show that some particular agent or procedure not commonly accepted as trance inducing leads to an increase in suggestibility equal to or greater than that produced by an accepted technique, there is justification for calling the resulting state hypnosis. Where, on the other hand, some or all of the so-called symptoms of hypnosis listed on pages 17 and 210 are observed to be present, but for one reason or another hypersuggestibility cannot be demonstrated, it is not justifiable to state that hypnosis has occured. We can speculate that we are dealing with such a condition or, better, we can speak of a hypnosis-like state, but we cannot categorically call it hypnosis. Statements that "fugues," "day-dreaming" and other assorted conditions are hypnosis may be correct but do not seem to be warranted by the present state of knowledge; neither is the expression "highway hypnosis." This may seem to be a rather narrow and dogmatic position, but it seems to me that if the scientific study and use of hypnotism is to progress, it requires a clear cut, precise definition and delimitation of the subject matter.

In concluding, it is not superfluous to make a few remarks pertaining to the design and construction of scales should some reader wish to do this. First of all, to take over an already existing scale and to add or subtract items as has been done by some investigators is a very dangerous procedure. No matter how excellent the original scale may have been, the final results may be completely invalid and unreliable. No scale is ever fully acceptable unless it has been pretested, standardized (and this means some sort of standardized procedure for administering and scoring it must be given), tested for reliability and validated in some adequate fashion. These are minimum requirements—validation on an intuitive basis is definitely not acceptable. To be really useful, a scale should also be at least additive and preferably multiplicative.[31,195] Equality of intervals is also an important consideration, as well as the sort of distribution of scores it gives rise to. Neither the Friedlander-Sarbin nor the Davis-Husband scale gives rise to normal distributions, but with the increasing use of nonparametric statistics this may not be as much of a deterrent as it once was. Finally, the resulting measure should preferably be nonreactive.

7

The Induction of Hypnosis:
I. Introduction

THE INDUCTION of hypnosis consists of three phases, preparation, induction proper and deepening the trance. The first phase eliminates as many unfavorable factors and activates as many favorable ones as feasible. The second is concerned with inducing a change in condition that characterizes passing from the waking state into the hypnotic state. The last aims at maximizing this change. The three phases are not separate and distinct; actually there is considerable overlapping and we should think of them as processes which may occur simultaneously, although in practice it is customary to progress sequentially from one phase to the next.

Since the preparatory phase and the deepening of hypnosis generally involve the same procedures regardless of the method of induction used, we shall describe them once in connection with the first induction method discussed. Following this we shall discuss other procedures of the second phase and the reader is expected to carry over what has been said concerning the other phases to each new technique.

A SIMPLE METHOD OF INDUCTION*

PREPARATORY PHASE

If you have had access to a number of subjects in previous exercises pick out a subject who gave strong and rapid responses to your waking suggestions, particularly those of postural sway, hand clasping and eye catalepsy. For this experiment begin with the subject standing near you with a chair easily accessible to him. Now tell him that very soon you are going to hypnotize him. Say this positively and with conviction. Never use expressions like "I am going to *try*" or "I shall now *attempt*" since this often implies doubt concerning your ability to induce a trance. Sometimes the subject will

---

*An equally simple method is the one described by Friedlander and Sarbin as part of their technique for determining trance depth. While it belongs as well here, because of its intimate connection with the topic of measuring the depth of hypnosis, it has already been covered.

show signs of nervousness or uneasiness. If so, explain that there is nothing to fear, that he will find this a pleasant and interesting experience and one which will benefit him greatly. If he still seems bothered, ask him what worries him. Knowing what it is, you can then talk reassuringly to him about it. Often the subject worries about losing consciousness, in which case you can assure him that he will not be unconscious when he is hypnotized, but will be aware of everything that goes on. As will be seen later, there are times when a subject, consciously or unconsciously, sets certain conditions for his entering the trance state and in such instances these conditions must be incorporated into the procedures. For the time being, however, you need not be concerned with this eventuality. It is also a good idea to instruct the subject to remain as *passive* as possible—just to listen to what you say, but not to try to help in any way. He should neither help nor resist. Tell him to allow any urge he feels to develop. The subject should be instructed not to try to think about or analyze what he is told or what happens, but to just let it happen. Tell the subject "Don't try to do anything or not to do anything—just let yourself go."

It is often worth repeating these last instructions as the induction proceeds, particularly if there seems to be evidence that the subject may be resisting or interfering with the process in other ways. A frequent source of difficulty arises from the subject's active thinking and analysis of his experiences. This sometimes results when the hypnotist uses instructions and words which are not clearly defined for the subject. For instance, telling him to make his mind "blank" often leaves the subject uncertain as to how to do this and he may not know exactly what you want. He may voice his question in this regard and your problem becomes one of teaching him what is desired. Even such a simple matter as relaxing sometimes causes much trouble because the subject does not know how to relax and in trying to do this tenses his muscles. Here too some pretrance education may be necessary. After this give him in quick succession the postural sway suggestion, then the hand clasping suggestion, and finally the eye catalepsy suggestions. I have found it useful to introduce these to the subject by saying something like: "I am now going to give you a few suggestions so that you can get a better idea of what I have been telling you."

The main purpose of the preparatory phase is to facilitate the induction proper of hypnosis. Since the first technique, to be taken up shortly, is quite typical of the Standard method, suggestions play an important part in it from the start. It stands to reason that the more suggestible the subject is the more successful we should be in hypnotizing him, and it behooves us there-fore to raise his suggestibility by any means we have at hand. One of these is to give the subject a set of suggestions carefully graded with respect to dif-ficulty and complexity.

It is essential to give the subject only suggestions to which he will re-spond, preferably with a strong response. This is one reason for using a graded series. If we start with the easiest suggestions first we stand a better chance of getting a response. At the same time, if the subject responds, then the chances of his responding to the next harder suggestions may be improved because some heteroaction has taken place. Since, theoretically, one would not expect appreciable heteroaction to take place with the first or even the second successful suggestion, the first few suggestions must be so chosen that they will either evoke responses or be associated with activities which are present at the time. In this way, then, we can gradually build up the subject's suggestibility. A second reason for using a graded series is that it also allows us to have an idea of how suggestible the subject is at any stage of the proc-ess. It is not known whether greater heteroaction occurs if each successive suggestion is more difficult than the preceding one or when the series is made up of equally difficult suggestions. My own guess is that the first alternative is true. If so, this furnishes a third reason for using a set of suggestions of increasing difficulty.

From observations made earlier it might be expected that getting the subject to do various things on a voluntary basis could also be used in the preparation for hypnosis. Some hypnotists do make use of this.

As has been pointed out, there is no well-defined boundary between wak-ing and hypnotic suggestibility. According to the theory that has been outlined in previous pages, essentially the same processes that are responsible for the development of hypnotic hypersuggestibility can and do become active when a series of waking suggestions is given. Thus the preparatory phase tends to merge with the induction phase proper and it is not uncommon to find that the subject is "partially" hypnotized at the termination of the preparatory phase. Actually the expression "partial hypnosis" is ambiguous and vague and it probably would be more correct to speak here of a low to. medium degree of hypnosis. However, inasmuch as it is presumed that all of the basic processes are not yet active, or if so, are not fully active, the expression has a certain descriptive value.

This matter of hypnosis developing before the induction proper is even started brings up another matter. Subjects who become hypnotized at this early stage usually do not close their eyes. In spite of the fact that eye closure is suggested in the Standard method, it must be emphasized that it is by no means a requirement for hypnosis, nor, indeed, a specific symptom of this condition. It is a well known fact that a hypnotized subject can have his eyes open without affecting the trance when the hypnosis is deep enough. Actually, eye closure takes place only because it is directly or indirectly suggested, but individuals can be readily hypnotized with their eyes remaining open. The reports of Braid, Charcot and many others show this quite clearly. Indeed, they seem to indicate that a fixed stare with the eyes wide open was originally much more characteristic of hypnosis than closed eyes. Whether eye closure plays any essential role is not at all clear; certainly it is a poor criterion of hypnosis. Practical experience and some theoretical considerations lead us to feel that it can be a useful aid in light and medium hypnosis insofar as it eliminates distracting visual stimuli in a purely mechanical way. It is also helpful as a relatively easy response to suggestion and hence is a useful contributor to the generalization of suggestibility.

Sometimes a subject will unexpectedly open his eyes during hypnosis for no obvious reason. This may even occur with deeply hypnotized subjects, despite previous instructions to the contrary. Unless the trance state was relatively light in the first place (although this action may cause or be caused by a decrease in hypnotic depth) the subject is usually *still hypnotized*. This must be emphasized because too often the novice is ready to interpret this result as a failure. A simple command to the subject to close his eyes or to sleep is usually sufficient to restore the status quo, although it is a good idea to follow this up with a few additional suggestions aimed at deepening the trance. In some cases the subject appears definitely to be awake; even then it is often possible to bring the trance back to its former depth if suggestions are given quickly. As was pointed out earlier, Janet[91] found evidence that hypnosis perseveres for a short while after sudden waking, a fact partially substantiated by others.[191] In other instances, the subject, although seeming awake, is really in a light or even medium trance.

Just what causes these actions is not clear. Most often the subject himself does not know. This last may be partly caused by interstage amnesia, which Janet reported can occur when a subject passes from one level of hypnosis to another. Repression seems to be involved frequently, suggesting that the subject's actions are an attempt to ward off sudden anxiety. There is other evidence to support this notion; how general it is, is another question.

Induction Phase

Arons[3] suggests that the induction phase can itself be broken into three sequential stages. These should be kept in mind as a guide in any procedure. There is usually a first step in which the symptoms the subject *is about to* experience are described. Next, suggestions of these symptoms are given in the *present tense* as actually happening. This is normally done in a gentle manner using a relatively monotonous low toned voice. The third step really merges into the third phase to be discussed and introduces it. As soon as you have reasonable evidence that the subject is hypnotized, the suggestions are given in a more *direct and emphatic* way. This description is particularly suited to the "sleep suggestion" method, but applies with a few alterations to many other techniques. The most outstanding exception to this is the case of "instantaneous hypnosis" to be taken up later.

Regardless of the subject's responses to the preparatory phase, tell him that he can open his eyes again, ask him to sit down in the chair, and speak to him in a conversational manner:

I want you to look upward at a spot on the ceiling and to fixate your eyes on it. Any spot will do. You may imagine one that you can look at comfortably. Do not worry if your eyes stray away or you blink. That is all right. If you do, just bring your eyes right back to the spot and keep looking at it as steadily as you can. Don't be tense. Just relax and listen closely to my voice, to what I say. I want you to relax. . .Think of relaxing. Feel your body relaxing. . .As you do so you will find that your body becomes relaxed. . .You will relax more and more. As you keep looking at the spot above your head and listen to my voice you will find that your entire body becomes relaxed. Your feet are becoming relaxed, your legs are becoming relaxed, your arms and your hands are becoming relaxed, your entire body is becoming relaxed, and now you will find that you are also becoming drowsy. You are going to get more and more drowsy. Just listen to my voice. . .it makes you feel drowsy, sleepy. . .You feel a heaviness coming over your body. Your body is getting heavy, very h-e-a-v-y. Your hands are getting h-e-a-v-y. Your arms are becoming h-e-a-v-y. Your arms and your hands are heavy. Your feet are getting h-e-a-v-y. Your legs are getting h-e-a-v-y. Your entire body is becoming h-e-a-v-y, v-e-r-y h-e-a-v-y. You are d-r-o-w-s-y . . .s-l-e-e-p-y. A feeling of pleasant, drowsy warmth is coming over you. Soon you are going to sleep. . .deeply. . .soundly. . .A pleasant warmth is coming all over your body, just like when you fall asleep . . .Your eyes are getting heavy. You are becoming sleepy. Your eyes are getting heavier and h-e-a-v-i-e-r, s-o heavy and you are feeling s-o s-l-e-e-p-y. . .Think of sleep, of nothing but sleep. . .You are going to go to sleep very soon. . .My voice makes you sleepy. . .makes you want to sleep. . .Your eyes are heavy, they are closing. You cannot keep your eyes open. They are closing. In a moment you find it impossible to keep your eyes open and they blink. . .They will blink more and more and shortly they will close because they are getting heavier and heavier and you find it harder and harder to keep them open. [*It is best to coordinate this suggestion with actual blinking of the subject's eyes. Some subjects are able to keep a very steady unblinking stare and the above suggestions will often lead to their blinking. If they do not, it is best not to insist on this since it is actually not essential.*] You are now v-e-r-y s-l-e-e-p-y. . .Your eyes are s-o h-e-a-v-y you cannot keep them open. They are closing, closing more and more, more and more . . . [*If you find that the subject is not showing any indication of closing his eyes at this point, tell him in a firm tone of voice:*] All right, now close your eyes and keep listening closely to what I say. [*Then go on with:*] Your eyes are now closed and you are going deep asleep. . ." [*Very often a subject who has responded poorly to eye-closure suggestions may nevertheless develop some degree of hypnosis after closing his eyes to the command. Also, some individuals pass into a relatively deep hypnosis quite early in the process but maintain their eyes open and for some reason do not respond well to suggestions of eye closure. In any case, continue with:*]. . .They are now closed and you are going into a deep sleep. . .a d-e-e-p-e-r and d-e-e-p-e-r sleep. . .a sounder and sounder sleep. . .You will pay attention to nothing but the sound of my voice. You will not awaken until I tell you to. Nothing will bother you. Any time in the future I suggest sleep or say the word 'sleep' to you, you will immediately pass into a deep sleep. You are now going to sleep deeply . . .v-e-r-y d-e-e-p-l-y. [*These last few suggestions are important and should be given to the subject soon after his eyes close. They should be reiterated a number of times subsequently. They will give you a much better control over the subject than you would have otherwise.*]

Another suggestion I like to give my subjects before deepening the trance is that if anything should happen to me or anything endanger their lives, they will be able to wake up immediately by themselves ready to cope with the situation. Aside from just being fair to the subject I believe it helps to overcome unconscious anxieties the subject may have which interfere with the induction of a deeper trance. A few subjects have told me that they felt this instruction caused them to become anxious because of its implication of a possible danger and that it had prevented them from attaining a deeper trance. I question this last assertion, although it is conceivable that anxiety may have been produced in this manner. In my opinion this part of the instructions seems to be much more likely to allay fears on the part of the subject. In any case, I think of it as an important safeguard. Possibly it would be better to prepare the subject for it in the preparatory phase or to wait until a deeper trance has been induced. In many cases one could instruct the subject instead that he will wake up of his own within a certain time interval unless otherwise instructed, or again, that he will wake up if any one else tells him to wake up.

For a slight variation of the above method, stand close to the subject, lift your own hand above your head with the index and middle fingers spread apart in a V, and request the subject to fixate on the fingers (instead of the imaginary spot). The suggestions are no different, with the exception that if the subject appears to show some resistance to closing his eyes or is slow in doing so, continue by saying:". . .your eyes are closing. . .closing, closing . . .*They're closed!*" At the same time as you say this bring your hand down rapidly and suddenly in an arc toward the subject's face in such a way that each of your two fingers which are spread apart, comes close to one eye. You may either continue in a downward arc without touching the subject's eyes, or stop and press gently on the subject's closed eyes to emphasize your statement of closure. Obviously, by bringing your fingers so near the subject's eyes in a sudden manner you force him to close his eyes reflexedly. However, if the subject is suggestible and has been responding to your suggestions even partially, this response becomes integrated into the suggested response pattern in the manner which we have indicated in earlier discussions. For your first few inductions of hypnosis you should not attempt more than this.

In giving the above suggestions you should generally speak in a rather quiet monotone although you will find it helpful to make use of inflections and other effects from time to time, some of which have been indicated. When suggesting that the eyes are closing, if you see that some response is being given, it is very often helpful to quicken your speech, to raise your voice somewhat, putting urgency and some excitement in it, and to reaffirm the suggestion over and over rapidly. All this suggests to the subject that something important is indeed happening. A decisive "*They're closed!*" will often overcome any remaining tendency of the subject to retain his eyes partly open. Note, however, that some subjects may never completely close their eyes and you may see the white of the eyes through the small slit which remains. In addition, the eyelids may show a rapid trembling which may give the impression that the subject is resisting or about to reopen his eyes. Actually these subjects may be in a very deep hypnosis.

It should be obvious that the effectiveness of trance-inducing suggestions will be affected by various nonverbal and extraverbal elements, by the sequential arrangement of suggested ideas, the amount of repetition, and the length of the suggestions. One occasionally hears of a successful operator having a "hypnotic voice." I have had subjects make this remark in connection with my own voice. Whether there is any basis for this I do not know. Perhaps some voices are more attention-compelling than others, more persuasive, or possess some other unidentifiable quality. One particular effect which may be of influence and which is not so much a matter of voice per se as of the manner of delivery is rhythm. Snyder[170] has called attention to it.

According to him, certain poems have been found to actually produce a trance state when read. These poems have an unusual pattern of sound which, among other thing, is particularly soothing. They are characterized by what he calls a "hypnotic rhythm." He finds that reading iambic pentameters produces such a rhythm. In these the spacing of the accented beat is just a little less than a half second interval. (This estimate is based upon a reading rate of 25 lines of iambic pentameter a minute.) This, Snyder remarks, is just about the metronome setting of 2 per second which Brown[24] has reported as being particularly effective in inducing a trance.

Snyder goes on to say that although iambic and trochaic rhythm is just a little less than half a second for the heavy syllabic beat, in the anapaestic and dactylic rhythm, the rhythm is just a little more than half a second. Consequently he states, "If now we combine this half second time interval with the regularity of rhythm so obvious in the spellweaving poems. . . we have the almost perfect parallel to the stimulus of rhythm used by hypnotists."

Snyder finds a number of features in so-called hypnotic poems which he believes permits them to duplicate the hypnotic situation. Such poems stay away from what is "startling"—from any abrupt changes which would tend to break the spell, or from any ideas which might compel mental alertness—and preserve the regularity of rhythm. The ornamentation and elaboration of the pattern with rhyme helps in fixating the reader on the rhythm. This is also done with consonant return, and with regularity of pattern of rising and falling pitch. He sums this up by saying: "Hypnotic poems in general give us heavy stresses falling regularly at half second intervals, and so ornamented that the rhythmically inclined listener has his attention drawn to the sound rather than to the sense."

They have a vagueness of imagery. These poems present soft, shadowy outlines which act as a projective device for one's own fancy, fostering a dream state. They are also responsible for an effect akin to fatigue which Snyder calls "ear-strain." This is brought about by introducing a number of difficulties in the poems. These are not so much structural sentence difficulties or other similar verbal ones (i.e., inversions, complicated sentences, long sentences, etc.), as the use of foreign words, an obscure word or phrase, or some other slight difficulty which by recurring tends to fatigue the reader and to break down his resistance.* Lastly, hypnotic poems make use of refrain or of frequent repetition which may act as mere physical stimuli producing rhythmic monotony. Some repetitions, however, may take the form of key phrases or refrains of special significance.

Before going further, it may be well to stop a moment and talk a little more about what a hypnotized person looks like. Some sixty or so years ago, Moll[126] made the following noteworthy statement on the symptoms of hypnosis:

> This concludes my review of the symptomatology of hypnosis. We have seen that the symptoms are of manifold kinds, and I may add that they are hardly ever identical in two different persons. In spite of conformity to law, one human body is never exactly like another, the mental state of one man is never exactly like another's. It is the same in hypnosis; one man displays this symptom with great clearness, another that one. We shall never be able to find a subject in whom all the symptoms are united, just as we cannot find a patient who has all the symptoms of an illness as they are theoretically described.

Things have changed very little since this was written. The typical and traditional picture of the hypnotized individual one usually finds illustrated in books is that of an individual who appears to have fallen fast asleep and, in some instances, to be in a dead faint. It is certainly true that the subject often appears to be soundly asleep by the time the induction phase is terminated. His eyes are closed, the muscles of his face are rather loose, his entire body is quite relaxed and, if he is sitting in a chair, he often will have slumped down it. The head often falls forward on the subject's chest, sometimes far backward or, again, sideways over his shoulder. The arms and hands usually rest limply on a support or hang limply by his sides. The onset of this condition may be a gradual, progressive process which one can follow as the induction progresses; or it may have a sudden and rapid appearance.

This particular description, unfortunately, fails to apply in many cases. An appreciable number of individuals do not show these characteristics, even when deeply hypnotized. Conversely, their presence is not necessarily a criterion of deep hypnosis. Muscular relaxation is certainly not an essential correlate of hypnosis. Many people remain upright when hypnotized while

*This may bear some relation to Erickson's "confusion" technique discussed in chapter 8.

sitting. They may show considerable stiffness, and even an abnormal amount of muscular rigidity. Even closure of the eyes is not an essential criterion or requirement.

Yet, in spite of all this, nearly all hypnotists somehow feel that there is an elusive quality which distinguishes the hypnotized subject from the non-hypnotized person. What we are dealing with is probably a pattern or even several patterns of signs which remain to be isolated by a technique like factor or dispersion analysis. In the meantime, we might try to point to certain features which can be seen most often singly or in groups. The most characteristic symptom immediately following the induction of hypnosis seems to be a tendency toward *protracted immobility*. The subject may be tensed or relaxed, his eyes may be closed or open, he may be comfortable or not or he may show other signs, but nearly always, if not always, he shows an amazing degree of immobility in the absence of suggestions calling for movement. Some subjects may show spontaneous movements, but these are usually very limited in extent and duration, relatively infrequent and, as Moll has pointed out, most likely reflex in origin. There is usually a lack of facial expression and, if the eyes are open, the gaze is fixed and blank.

The subject has a strong *disinclination to talk*. It is often necessary to address him several times before obtaining an answer. Sometimes it is necessary to order him to answer questions. Even then the subject often favors nods and shakes of the head over words. When conversation of a sort has been established the subject is usually found to show a lack of spontaneity and initiative. His speech tends to be low in volume and rather flat and expressionless, he mumbles his answers and must be ordered to speak louder and more distinctly. At other times the speech of the subject can be best described as "thick."

When other motor responses are elicited, they tend to be overly slow and stiff. *Psychomotor retardation* is often evident, as well as a certain degree of *automatism*. Were we to describe the hypnotized subject in a word, I believe that we could best say that a general *passivity* seems to be the underlying motif.

The above best describes hypnotized individuals immediately following the appearance of hypnosis. With many subjects, as they are made to carry out an increasing number of suggestions, these various characteristics tend to decrease in intensity and even to vanish. Whether they ever vanish completely is a moot question. In many instances there is little which distinguishes the overt behavior of the hypnotized subject from that of the normal waking individual, and only an expert hypnotist is capable of detecting the presence of hypnosis. There seems to be some agreement that hypnotized individuals, even when behaving in a most natural manner, still show a constriction of awareness, a characteristic literal-mindedness, some psychomotor retardation and possibly a degree of automatism. To this list might be added a relative lack of humor or self-consciousness.

The appearance of the subject following the induction of hypnosis is partly a function of the manner in which hypnosis is induced and of the subject's expectations or pre-education. As will be seen in a later chapter, much of the famous Bernheim-Charcot controversy centered around this point. It should be clear, for instance, that complete relaxation is not consistent with the act of standing up. As contrasted to sitting or reclining subjects, individuals who are hypnotized while standing up show a minimal degree of muscular relaxation. This is necessary if they are to remain standing up. Occasionally one encounters a subject whose conception of hypnosis as a state of complete muscular relaxation is so dominant that when hypnotized in a standing position he collapses to the floor. But even with sitting subjects, the initial conditions at the start of the induction may prevent a relaxed state from occuring. Subjects who for one reason or another tense all or part of their body at the start of the induction often retain this condition and may even develop more or less generalized muscular rigidity. Braid reported this very sort of thing. As just remarked, the subject's expectation or conception of hypnosis may play an important part. If he expects to become muscularly relaxed, relaxation is most likely to be a symptom of hypnosis in his case; if he expects to behave in a zombie-like fashion, one may end up with exactly this sort of behavior. Finally, the type of instructions given the subject, the manner in which they are given, and his own interpretation of them, are also strong determinants of the way in which the subject will appear when hypnotized.

By far the best criterion of hypnosis is *hypersuggestibility*. However, the reader should always remember that it is much more an indicator of the degree to which the subject is hypnotized than an absolute indicator of the presence or absence of hypnosis.

DEEPENING THE TRANCE

Once the subject's eyes have closed, you are ready to deepen the trance. At this stage it may be anywhere from very light to very deep. For our present purpose we will assume that it is moderately deep, as it usually will be. The deepening process generally consists of giving suggestions to the effect that the trance is getting progressively deeper, allowing silent periods in which, presumably, the hypnotic condition deepens spontaneously (or at least gets consolidated), and giving the subject a variety of graded responses to execute. In addition, as will be discussed in the next chapter, there are special techniques for deepening the trance.

The most general procedure is to combine all three methods and we shall see an example of this shortly. The first method is fairly obvious and needs no further discussion. The second is best employed following suggestions of deeper hypnosis. The periods of silence can last from a few seconds to 30 minutes and more. Unless the period of silence is natural and needs no introduction, it is usually introduced by such a statement as: "In a moment I shall stop talking to you for a while. You will continue to sleep deeply. In fact, you will keep going into deeper and deeper sleep so that when I talk to you again you will be very deeply asleep. . .much more so than you are now. You will pay attention to nothing until I speak to you again. You are very comfortable and nothing will bother you. You will not wake up until I tell you. When I next speak to you, you will not be startled by my voice. Now I shall stop talking to you, but you will continue to go into a deeper and deeper sleep. With each breath that you take your sleep will deepen. . ." At this point stop talking for the length of time you have chosen. If you have good reason to believe that your subject is already in a fairly deep trance you can alter the above suggestion by telling him that from the time you say "now" until you touch him on the shoulder he will be unable to hear anything. It is best to begin with, "As soon as I say 'now'. . ."or, "Until I touch you on the shoulder. . ." (or if you have your hand on his shoulder, "As soon as I remove my hand from your shoulder. . .") rather than by saying first, "You will be unable to hear. . ." or, "You will not pay attention. . ." because there is always the slight possibility of a subject responding to these words as soon as they are said with the result that the remainder of the suggestion is rendered ineffective. It should be noted that to suggest inability to hear and to suggest not to pay attention are not necessarily the same thing for the subject and will often lead to different results. As soon as you are through suggesting, say "now." When you are ready to resume speaking, touch his shoulder. Some investigators say that such periods of silence allow the suggestions to take their full effect and permit the hypnotic state to develop more fully. Presumably the processes that are involved in the induction of hypnosis or the response to suggestions are not instantaneous. There is some evidence that they may involve a radical change in neural organization which is true not only of trance-inducing suggestions, but also of any suggestion.

The question of just how long the period of silence should be is always bothersome and I know of no satisfactory answer. Unfortunately, there is no adequate experimental data on this question. One possible danger when the silence is too long is that the subject may pass into a state of natural sleep. Because of this possibility I prefer to use more frequent but shorter intervals of time, rarely exceeding 15 minutes and usually limiting them to 10 minutes. Just how many periods of silence you should use is again a moot question. It depends partly upon how deep a trance you want and on how the subject responds.

The third procedure might be called the active method as contrasted with the previous one, the passive method. It consists of giving the subject a series of graded suggestions. As the subject carries out a variety of suggestions, he often appears to become increasingly responsive. Actually there is no reason to believe that the various processes which enter into the production of the hypnotic state stop with the closure of the eyes. On the contrary there is considerable evidence that eye closure can be brought about with a relatively small amount of suggestibility, much less than the subject's potential. Thus there is a rationale for continuing what was done in the preparatory phase and in the induction proper. As was pointed out earlier, the use of graded suggestions is important in order to avoid creating negative attitudes through failure to respond adequately, and also in order to bring about homoaction and heteroaction.

Most hypnotists follow eye closure with suggested eye catalepsy, leaving out the instructions to turn the eyes upward. If you have been successful in obtaining eye catalepsy in the waking state or if you are confident that the subject is sufficiently hypnotized you may terminate this suggestion with the usual challenge. But if there is any doubt about the outcome it is best not to actually challenge since the trance might be broken if the subject is able to open his eyes. More generally speaking, although rejection of a suggestion does not necessarily mean that the state of hypnosis is nullified, a good rule to follow is that when there is doubt concerning the strength of any hypnotic suggestion, one should not challenge the subject to overcome it unless there are good reasons for doing so. Instead, try to deepen the trance some more.

If you decide not to challenge the eye catalepsy, you may then proceed in one of two ways. You may simply say nothing concerning attempts to open the eyes, but go on to the next suggestion, or you may say something like: "Your eyes are stuck tight. . .so tight that *if* you tried to open them *you could not*. But you will *not* try to open them. *You have no desire* to open your eyes, but only want to sleep deeper."

Note the strategy employed here. If the suggestion is ineffective the subject will not have an opportunity to discover it or to respond in a way which would break the hypnosis. If the suggestion is effective, it probably will enhance the trance to some extent, although presumably not as much as if there had been a successful challenge. Furthermore, there is the possibility that if done skillfully the last procedure may carry a suggestion of success which may have an enhancing effect upon the subject's suggestibility. Notice that we do not tell the subject that he is unable to open his eyes or to try to open them, but we make it conditional. This is immediately followed by a suggestion aimed at preventing the subject from testing the suggestion's strength. Finally, note the suggested rationalization.

The suggestion which is usually given next is arm rigidity. Some hypnotists give it first, either before the eye catalepsy suggestion, or instead of it. Arm rigidity is one suggestion with which I *always* use a challenge. If the subject is not in a trance deep enough to make this suggestion effective I might as well start hypnotizing him all over again, preferably using a different method. Conceivably the trance could be deepened, but this would take more work than is desirable and the results would be doubtful. The subject probably will not go into a much deeper trance anyway, at least without extensive training and, if he can, a different approach is more likely to give satisfactory results Furthermore, if the subject should meet the challenge successfully you can usually give a countersuggestion fast enough to circumvent any bad effects and still take advantage of any positive effect that may be present. As will be seen shortly, the removal of this suggestion can be used very effectively to deepen the trance.

Let us now see a sample procedure for deepening hypnosis. This should be made continuous with the suggestions of the induction phase and follow eye closure immediately (or shortly after if you give the extra suggestions mentioned earlier). Now you go on with:

Sleep. . .deeply. . .profoundly. . .sleep. Your eyes are heavy. . . v-e-r-y h-e-a-v-y. . .They are stuck tight, so completely stuck that you cannot open them however hard you may try. YOU CANNOT OPEN YOUR EYES NOW. TRY! YOU CANNOT OPEN THEM. . .try hard. . .All right, now stop trying. You are going deeper asleep. . .much deeper. Lift your arm up [*as you say this take hold of his hand and gently guide his hand and arm straight out to the side at shoulder height or up above his head*]. Extend it straight. Make a fist . . . a tight fist . . . TIGHTER! Your arm is stiffening, your entire arm is becoming STIFF! RIGID! LIKE A BAR OF IRON! YOU CANNOT BEND YOUR ARM, YOU CANNOT MOVE IT. Try. YOU CAN'T. . .*try hard*. . .All right now, you can move it. [*With some subjects you may have to give more countersuggestions than this.*] Slowly lower it to your lap. As you do so you sink into a very deep sleep. . .d-e-e-p-e-r and d-e-e-p-e-r. [*If the subject lowers his arm slowly enough you can add* "*When your hand touches your lap you will be in a very* D-E-E-P *sleep. . .* *You are going deeply asleep. . .d-e-e-p-l-y asleep.*" *In any case, as the subject's hand comes to rest on his lap, continue with:*] You are now d-e-e-p asleep. S-l-e-e-p! D-e-e-p, d-e-e-p asleep!. . .Your body is now very relaxed. You have no desire to move. You only want to s-l-e-e-p. . .d-e-e-p-l-y . . .s-o-u-n-d-l-y. . .You want to do whatever I tell you to do. You can hear me quite well. You will be able to answer my questions and do everything I tell you to do, but you will remain *deep* asleep. Even if I tell you to open your eyes you will not wake up until I tell you to. Each and every time in the future I tell you to sleep you will *immediately* go into a deep sleep. As soon as I say 'sleep' or mention the word 'sleep' your eyes will get very heavy, you will get very sleepy, your eyes will close, and you will go soundly asleep. . .This will happen each and every time I tell you to go to sleep. . .that I say the word 'sleep.' [*If you wish you can substitute here some other signal, or preferably add it to the above instruction. More about this later.*] But now sleep. . .d-e-e-p-l-y, s-o-u-n-d-l-y. . .I am going to stop talking to you for a few moments, but you will continue to go deeper asleep and will not let anything disturb you. . .You hear only the sound of my voice. When I speak again to you, you will not be startled. . .Now sleep. . .d-e-e-p-l-y. . .profound-ly. [*Stop talking now for 5 to 10 minutes, then in a very low voice, even a whisper, resume your suggestions, gradually but fairly rapidly increasing the volume of your voice.*] You are now deep asleep. You can hear everything quite well but you will pay attention only to the sound of my voice. [*Remember you said earlier that the subject would hear nothing but the sound of your voice. With a very suggestible subject this may have the effect of making him deaf to other sounds, so you must be careful to remove this effect, if present.*]

At this point, unless you want to deepen the trance further, you should proceed to give the subject more comp'ex suggestions to ascertain his depth of hypnosis. In some instances you may prefer to wake your subject up without further testing. But let us say now t.at you test him and find that he is not as deeply hypnotized as you want. The next step in deepening the trance is to speak to the subject as follows:

You are deep asleep, but you can go even deeper asleep than you are now. You want very much to be in the deepest sleep possible because it is a very pleasant experience, because it will be very beneficial to you. [*You should beware in giving any suggestion of pleasantness in connection with suggestions since this can have disturbing consequences with some subjects.*

This is particularly true with psychotics and psychoneurotics. It is important to consider this when using hypnosis in psychotherapy, especially if a positive transference has begun or is ready to begin.] You are going to sleep much more deeply and all the suggestions I shall give you will be very effective. [*It is possible that saying this may associate response to suggestions and deep sleep together. If the subject should then decide that he is not deeply hypnotized, it might tend to interfere with his response to suggestions. In view of this you may prefer not to associate the two.*] I shall now count to five [*any other number is suitable—although I find five a good figure.*] and as I do so you will begin to sink into a much deeper sleep and at the count of five you will be very, very sound asleep. So sound asleep that when I tell you to wake up later on [*It is preferable to say "when I tell you to wake up" rather than "when you wake up" because the former reaffirms the contingency of waking upon the hypnotist's command, whereas the latter does not and can be interpreted by the subject as giving him some control over the matter of waking.*] you will have no memory of anything that was said or done while you were asleep. It will be just as if no time had passed and you had not slept. [*Again it must be emphasized that there are circumstances in which these last statements are contraindicated. This is true, for instance, with therapy cases who have a tendency to be disoriented anyway.*] Now I shall start counting. One. . .You are going to go deeply, much more d-e-e-p-l-y asleep. Two . . .you are going d-e-e-p-e-r and d-e-e-p-e-r asleep. With each count you sink deeper asleep. With each word I say, with every breath that you take you go more deeply asleep. Three. . .S-l-e-e-p, d-e-e-p-ly, s-o-u-n-d-l-y, s-l-e-e-p. My voice makes you want to sleep, [*This associates sleep with a stimulus which is continuously present.*] always d-e-e-p-e-r and d-e-e-p-e-r. You can feel yourself s-i-n-k-i-n-g into a very, v-e-r-y deep sleep. . .sinking. . .s-i-n-k-i-n-g into a d-e-e-p-e-r and s-o-u-n-d-e-r sleep in which you hear nothing but my voice which sounds as if it were coming from far, far away. [*Starting with "three" begin to soften and lower your voice so that by the time you say the last "far away" you are speaking quite softly—but loud enough for the subject to hear you clearly.*] Four. . .You continue to go deeper asleep as I count, as I talk to you. All the suggestions I shall give you in the future will be very effective. You will do everything I tell you to do. You have *no* fear of hypnosis because it can only be beneficial for you. . .You know that it cannot harm you. You are very responsive to my suggestions and you will continue to become increasingly more responsive. Even as I talk to you, you go deeper and deeper asleep. . .Any time that I tell you to see, hear, smell or feel something you will see, hear, smell or feel it as a reality. You will experience it fully, realistically. You will have very real experiences. Every time in the future that I tell you to do something when you are hypnotized and only then [*This provision is added to eliminate the possibility of the subject posthypnotically becoming completely dominated by the hypnotist. This is a matter of ethics as well as a safeguard for both subject and hypnotist.*] you will carry it out without question. . .I will always be able to remove and change any suggestion that I give you now, have given you or shall give you. [*This is an extremely important point, and this suggestion should always be given quite early and reiterated on a number of occasions. If you do not use the particular phase of deepening under discussion, you should make a point of giving this suggestion earlier. Now allow a few moments of silence.*] . . .Continue to sleep. At the next count you will be deeply, soundly asleep. [*Again allow a few moments of silence.*] Five. . .Deep, d-e-e-p asleep! You are now *very* deeply and *soundly* asleep. You will not awaken until I tell you to ~~or unless something should happen to me or endanger your life~~. Otherwise you will remain deep asleep and will do everything I tell you. Anytime in the future that I say sleep or suggest sleep [*include mention of signal if you have given one*] you will *instantly, immediately* go into a deep sleep, even deeper than the one you are in now. When I wake you up later you will have no recollection of anything but having slept.

At this point you are ready to use the hypnotic state for whatever purpose you have induced it.

A note of caution should be injected here. With passive subjects the above procedure may cause them to go into a lethargic and even stuporous state which is difficult to remedy. Since they are already prone to passivity, it appears best to make use of procedures for deepening the trance which deemphasize passivity and maximize the use of activity. In particular, it is inadvisable to suggest with such subjects a desire for sleep, or that sleep is a desirable state. Instead any suggestion to deepen the trance should be aimed at emphasizing the desire to be active and to cooperate. The method of fractionation which will be taken up in chapter 8 seems particularly suited here.

But even with active subjects, continued use of the procedure just examined with its repeated emphasis upon sleep and the use of fairly long periods of silence will often lead to the stuporous condition described in chapter 6 and which some investigators call the deepest state of hypnosis possible. These investigators insist that the full effectiveness of suggestions can be obtained only when this condition has been produced. Whatever the case may be, it now appears possible to bring about in the hypnotized subject a condition no different from sleep insofar as electroencephalograms are concerned. Presumably this condition is not compatible with giving suggestions. For further details the reader should consult Weitzenhoffer.[191]

One technique for deepening the trance which I frequently use with considerable success involves an adaptation of the Hand Levitation method (chapter 9) in which an increasing depth of hypnosis is associated with the rising of the hand. In brief, the subject is told that his hand is going to rise and will keep on rising until it touches his face and that as it rises he will pass into a deeper and deeper sleep so that when the hand touches his face he will be in a very deep trance. Suggestions aimed at causing the hand to rise are then given in combination with suggestions of deepening sleep.

This first method involves a rather long procedure although it appears longer than it really is. It is applicable in all instances, in part or in its entirety. You should become thoroughly familiar with it because it is prototypical; keep in mind that it is primarily offered as a model or outline to be adapted to your own uses. It is the method you may want to use if you expect that your subject has relatively low susceptibility. On the other hand, you will often have subjects who go into a deep trance from the first. With such cases you can abbreviate your procedure considerably. In the next two techniques to be discussed you will see how a rapid method of induction can still incorporate many of the features described here.

Since many suggested phenomena do not require an extremely deep hypnosis, there are occasions when you need not deepen the trance, or at least you can abbreviate this part without danger of failing in your objective. You will note too that the phase of deepening contained a number of suggestions that had purposes other than to deepen the hypnotic state. These could, of course, have been given earlier, even as part of the second phase or induction proper. Our rule here is that if you plan on a relatively extended phase of deepening, it is best to wait until you have gone through some deepening before giving suggestions regarding future aspects of your relationship with the subject, as was done above. In addition, it is always a good idea to reiterate these suggestions throughout the phase of deepening, giving them in slightly different forms each time. This allows the subject to "work through" the suggestions, in a manner of speaking.

A technique of general applicability might be mentioned here, although it was not used in the model just discussed. This is the technique of having the subject repeat some or all of the suggestions as soon as they are given to him. One obvious reason for doing this is to ascertain the possibility of any gross misunderstanding. Many hypnotists believe that it also enhances the effect of the suggestions. Since no experimental study of this has been made it is hard to tell whether or not the belief is justified. There are, however, some theoretical arguments which favor it. In the first place, it is possible that the subject's repetition has a homoactive effect of some kind, inasmuch as it is then essentially autosuggestion. Second, by forcing the subject to repeat a suggestion he may be forced to pay closer attention to it while, at the same time, he is forced to take a more active part in the suggestion situation, which is believed to favor response to suggestion. Possibly too, this helps to make the subject identify the hypnotist's words with his own thoughts through the close association of the two statements of the suggestion which would be important in the process of ego-extension to which we have already referred (page 38). Finally, by asking the subject to repeat a suggestion we are getting him to make a voluntary response which would be expected to increase his suggestibility; this may even be the only way in which it works. So much for the positive side of the question. On the negative it seems to me that excessive use of the technique can lenghten trance induction unnecessarily. Furthermore, it may interfere with the deepening process. I have gathered evidence that some subjects become rather resentful of anything which tends to disturb them from the sleep-like lethargic state which is being brought about. To force the subject to think about what has been said, to recollect it and to verbalize it can be unwelcome. For this reason I prefer to use this technique discreetly, preferably for suggestions that are given after the last phase of trance induction is completed.

Let us examine in a little more detail certain important aspects of this technique. As you will recall, as part of the deepening process we instructed (page 215) the subject to lower his arm and told him that as he did so his trance would deepen and that he would be deeply asleep when his hand reached his lap. This procedure allows the subject to take a more active part in the process of trance induction. Some hypnotists believe that it is advantageous to use this kind of technique for a number of reasons. One is that defensive subjects gain the feeling that they do have a say in the matter because the hypnotic state is, in part, the result of their self-determination. Another reason is that for hypnotic suggestions to be maximally effective, the subject should participate as fully as possible in the responses. A subject who acts passively throughout the induction tends to remain passive and to fail to respond fully following induction. This is especially true of subjects who are prone to give passive responses anyway. By getting the subject to take an active part in the trance induction as early as possible, passivity tendencies will be minimized. This may also help to maintain a better focus of the subject's attention.

We have frequently brought up the subject's motivation as it relates to his suggestibility. One particular aspect of this relation to which I wish to call attention is the general problem of giving the subject a favorable motivation for accepting some suggestions and of overcoming already existing negative motives, especially in the production and deepening of the trance state. Actually motivating the subject begins before induction proper and is often made a part of the preparatory phase by a short introductory discussion in which the subject is allowed to ask a few questions. It is usually a good idea to talk reassuringly for a few moments concerning the usual misgivings most laymen have before attempting hypnosis. I have found that if a preparatory phase of waking suggestions is to be used it often helps to relax the subject if one assures him that no attempt at hypnotizing will be made yet. This gives him the chance to experience suggestions more fully and often gives him the incentive to find out what hypnosis is like. In any event, it eliminates interfering tensions where they could be very detrimental.

One might expect that if there is any chance of manipulating the subject's motivation it would be after some degree of hypnosis has been induced. Many subjects have an unconscious fear of hypnosis. This may not only interfere with induction, but it may prevent the trance from becoming as deep as it might otherwise. Suggesting as on page 217 that the subject has or will have no fear of hypnosis is therefore indicated. However, it is usually easier to create positive motivation and attitudes than to negate already existing motives and attitudes. Consequently, it is best not to limit yourself to negating the fear but, for example, you should also add references to benefits that can accrue from going into hypnosis. If the subject is a patient and has some particular habit he wants to eliminate, you can point out that hypnosis can be of much help in this connection.* Again, we can make hypnosis a desirable state by suggesting that it is pleasant, restful, beneficial (without saying in what way). Similarly, we can tell the subject that he wants to sleep, that he desires to sleep more deeply. This may be made more effective in some cases by giving a reason for it, namely, that he is tired. You may therefore suggest tiredness first in order to work up to suggestions of sleep. Too often hypnotists fail to make use of the subject's own motivation to go into a trance. Not only does giving motivation to the subject facilitate the trance induction, but it is also another way of getting the subject to participate actively in the production of the desired responses.

*This can also backfire, for instance, in therapy when the patient obtains secondary gains from his illness. Knowledge that hypnosis can remove his illness may motivate him away from hypnosis.

It pays the hypnotist to be a good psychologist and to thoroughly understand human motivation and behavior, particularly in his subjects.

Sooner or later the inexperienced hypnotist learns that subjects have a
tendency to take everything they are told quite literally, sometimes much to
his embarrassment. This makes it essential to word suggestions very carefully
and to specify exactly the limits within which they hold. Furthermore,
having the subject repeat the suggestion, even in his own words, is no
guarantee that he will not interpret it in a manner different from that intended. My observation on page 217 that it is better to say to the subject, "when
I tell you to wake up," rather than "when you wake up," was an application of the above. A few examples of what can happen when the subject
makes the wrong interpretation will help to clarify this matter. Some years
ago during a demonstration, a hypnotist of my acquaintance was faced with
a subject who would not relinquish a hallucination which had been suggested
to him at an earlier date. In an effort to overcome the subject's resistance,
the hypnotist decided to give him an ultimatum that he would not wake up
from his trance until he agreed to give up the hallucination. Then the hypnotist left him alone for the rest of the session. At the end of the demonstration
the subject was still deeply hypnotized. Admitting his failure, the hypnotist
proceeded to command the subject to wake up, but to no avail. The subject
persisted in remaining in a trance. After several attempts, all unsuccessful,
the hypnotist finally resorted to asking the subject the reason for his refusal
or inability to wake up. The answer was simple and most illuminating:
"You told me that I would not be able to wake up until I ceased to see [here
he described the hallucination]." This then was a rather embarrassing situation brought about inadvertently by the hypnotist's careless phrasing of his
ultimatum. He could have easily prevented it if he had simply added the
provision ". . .or until I tell you to wake up." This example also shows how
the subject, in spite of the fact that he had awakened time and time again
at the hypnotist's command in the past, had interpreted the ultimatum to
override even such a command.*

On a different occasion another hypnotist suggested that a subject would
go into instantaneous hypnosis at a given signal and that no one could
change or remove this suggestion. The hypnotist, however, had not meant
this to apply to himself, and usually this would not have been the case.
Unfortunately in this instance the subject interpreted "no one" to include

---

*Looking a little more deeply into the dynamics of the situation I strongly suspect that the
refusal to wake up was a way for the subject to punish the hypnotist for attempting to force him
to relinquish the hallucination. The subject's explanation could have been either conscious or
unconscious rationalization.

the hypnotist. Consequently, when he tried to make a change in the signal at a later date he found it was impossible to do. This is one reason why I always tell my subjects quite early that "I will always be able to change or remove any suggestion I give you, including this one." Note the added provision. This is to prevent the possibility of a subject's interpreting the above to apply to all suggestions except this particular one. It could happen!

The matter of placing limitations upon a suggestion is very important, particularly when a signal is used to induce hypnosis rapidly. You would not want to tell the subject "Whenever I wave my hand at you, you will go into a deep trance," because you might happen to see the subject in the street some day and wave at him with dire consequences. If you have to use this signal, limit its influence to specified settings. Better still, never use a gesture or word for a signal that you might use unintentionally in front of the subject when you had no desire to produce hypnosis. Either place certain strict restrictions on its applicability or use gestures and words you are not likely to use very often when the subject is present. Chinese and Sanskrit words are excellent for this.

Subjects' reactions to suggestions can never be fully predicted. You tell a subject, for instance, that the next cigarette he tries to smoke will taste terrible. You cannot predict that the subject will interpret this to mean that it will taste so bad that it will make him sick, but I have seen it occur.

Once, when giving suggestions to deepen a trance, I found the subject showing distress each time I used the work "sink." Upon inquiring what was the matter I found that this word was causing him to experience a very unpleasant sensation of physical sinking.

Some of the most unexpected responses often show up in subjects' elaboration of suggestions. I once told a subject that he was suffering from intense heat with the result that he began to disrobe of his own accord, apparently hoping to get cool in this manner. Another began showing all the signs of incipient heat prostration.

Several other factors, although they are not directly involved in the actual interpretation of suggestions, affect their outcome in very much the same way. As was most dramatically, although unwittingly, shown by early investigators such as Charcot and Luys, preconceived ideas, prior suggestion, sets and the like can exert a powerful influence. If, prior to receiving a suggestion, the subject is led to expect a certain effect, one is likely to see this effect arise. It must be emphasized that the basis for this influence can be laid at any time and, furthermore, that the subject needs not be particularly aware of it. The determinants of hypnotic behavior are often deeply imbedded in the subject's past as well as his psyche. Separating the effects of a suggestion proper from these factors is not always easy, particularly if one has no reasons to suspect the presence of contamination.

One is too often prone to forget that the same psychic processes which govern waking behavior are equally at work in hypnosis. One of these which may play a major part is that of association. A hypnotic situation, or even a suggestion, may be so structured that one or more element in it gives rise to responses purely through association or redintegration. I think that some side-effects observed in hypnosis need no other explanation. An interesting instance of associative influence occurred recently in one of my experiments. Subjects were instructed to hallucinate a clock and to report the time shown on it at the start of each experimental run. One subject invariably called out "3 o'clock," irrespective of the time of the day. Then, one day, for no obvious reason, he called out "4 o'clock." Inquiry into this change in behavior showed that his choice had been determined in each case by the fact that I had counted to three and to four respectively as the signal for the hallucination to take place. My last count in each case had served as cue for the hallucinated time.

"WAKING" THE SUBJECT

We shall now consider the matter of waking up the subject, or more precisely, his *dehypnotization*, which is *normally* one of the simplest parts of hypnotism. In most cases it is only necessary to order the subject, "Wake up!" in a firm but gentle tone. Or you can say: "When I next snap my fingers and tell you to wake up, you will be wide awake." This is followed by snapping your fingers accompanied by a command of "Wake up!" For subjects who have been in a deep trance, this manner of dehypnotizing may be somewhat brusque or unpleasant for them, especially if they have been in a passive state for some time preceding the dehypnotization. Therefore it is better to make the process gentle and gradual. An excellent way is the following: "In a moment you are slowly going to wake up. I shall count to five and at the count of five you will be wide awake. You will feel fine, very much refreshed by your sleep. You will have no headaches, no dizziness. You will feel rested, your mind will be clear and you will feel well in every way. Now I shall count and you will slowly awaken. One. . .you are going to awaken very soon. . .Two. . .you are slowly beginning to awaken. . . Three. . .you are becoming a little more awake. . .Four. . .at the next count you will be wide awake. You will feel fine. . .*Five! Wide awake!* You feel fine. Your mind is clear, you are not at all sleepy. You are wide awake."

Many hypnotists use the somewhat shorter method of merely counting in the above manner without giving any further suggestions at each count.

This is often satisfactory because in itself the counting prepares the subject for waking and suggests that he wake up slowly.

Sometimes when the subject opens his eyes after being awakened he appears somewhat dazed. If asked to stand up and move elsewhere he may be unsteady on his legs. This is usually an indication that the subject is not fully dehypnotized. It may result from too hasty a technique. In such a case you should take additional measures to wake the subject up completely. One way is to snap your fingers near his face and command in a firm tone of voice *"Wake up! Now, wide awake!"* Or you can have the subject close his eyes again and the procedure of dehypnotization is repeated with appropriate changes. There is one rule here that should always be followed: *never allow a subject to leave you until you have made certain that he is fully dehypnotized, no matter how light his trance state may have been.* It is a very good idea to have the subject sit nearby for a short while where you can keep an eye on him. Before letting him leave ask him a few questions regarding how he feels.

Every so often following hypnosis a subject develops headaches which may be quite severe. This may occur right away or quite a while later. Just what causes these headaches has not been clarified. It is not just a matter of eye strain brought about by the visual fixation technique because headaches also occur when this technique is not employed. Many believe that they are psychogenic in nature and are a reaction to the hypnotic experience. They often occur when the hypnotist tries to force the subject to do some task he does not want to do. They also seem to occur more often with neurotic individuals in which case they are probably neurotic symptoms. Giving a suggestion to ward off headache is a relatively easy matter and is often fully effective. Should the subject develop a headache in spite of this, it can be usually removed by suggestions when the subject is rehypnotized. Although I have never known this method to fail, situations may arise when other methods must be employed. Besides dizziness and headaches, subjects may suffer from shivering, confusion, persistent drowsiness, and nausea, following dehypnotization. They may also be hyperexcitable and hyperactive. There is little doubt that these effects are psychogenic. The simplest treatment is to hypnotize the subject again and suggest the symptoms away, making this carry over posthypnotically. When the source of the difficulty lies in the existence of an incompatible posthypnotic suggestion, it may be necessary to remove it although, according to Wolberg,[203] sometimes the only cure in such a case is for the subject to carry out the posthypnotic suggestion. Again, as he points out, these psychosomatic manifestations usually disappear of their own accord within a few hours after termination of the hypnotic state. When they are neurotic reactions, it may be necessary to treat them as one would treat any other neurotic symptom. In the case of a patient, these reactions should always be taken into account. Many hypnotherapists recommend that they be treated as a form of "acting out" when they occur. Such manifestations often throw light upon some of the patient's personality problems since they may be a form of resistance to or a defense against the threat of hypnosis (see also page 395ff.). If, on the other hand, the subject is not a patient under treatment when such psychosomatic effects occur, it is best not to use him again.

There is evidence that dehypnotization is by no means instantaneous. Long ago, Janet[91] was able to demonstrate to his own satisfaction that although the subject may open his eyes at the signal to wake, hypnotic hypersuggestibility if not the entire hypnosis tends to persist for a short while. This fact has been substantiated more recently by the research done in Hull's laboratory.[85] One consequence of it is that if one tests for posthypnotic amnesia too soon after dehypnotization, the subject will be found to have excellent recall for the trance experience since he is really still in a trance. Again, the hypnotist must be extremely careful of what he says to or in front of the subject immediately after dehypnotization since any statement he makes can have the full power of a hypnotic suggestion. The above brings to mind the remark of Erickson and Erickson[51] that when a subject "wakes up" following appropriate suggestions to do so, he may really only behave as if he were awake while actually remaining hypnotized. The theory of hypnosis presented earlier leads, however, to the opposing conclusion that the suggestion to "wake up" will usually lead to a true dehypnotization. Theories aside, a little consideration of the matter will show the reader that Erickson's position here is generally untenable, but it might account for a few occurrences of difficult dehypnotization.

Can a situation ever occur in which the subject will not wake up in spite of the hypnotist's commands? Unfortunately yes, but these are rather rare cases and usually result from some mistake in procedure made by the hypnotist, although there are also instances, particularly in psychotherapy, when the latter is not at fault. I have never encountered an instance where the subject could not be dehypnotized, although I have seen a few cases that taxed the hypnotist's ingenuity. We will refer to some of these cases in more detail in discussing methods of dealing with resistance. The only truly intractable case which has ever been reported to me resulted when a hypnotist attempted to dehypnotize a subject who had previously been given a posthypnotic suggestion by another hypnotist to the effect that he (the subject) would not "wake up" when the said hypnotist tried to dehypnotize him. This is, of course, a rather unusual situation which is not likely to happen in practice.

You should always remember that as far as it is known, in the absence of any suggestion to do so *a subject will normally wake up on his own after at most a few hours*, and usually, this is a matter of minutes. Reports of subjects that have remained hypnotized for days on end despite the hypnotist's efforts must be looked upon with great doubt, unless coming from reliable sources. It is possible that through some psychodynamic quirk a subject might occasionally remain in a true hypnotic state for two or more days. But one may suspect that if the poorly authenticated reports which exist have any truth they more likely represent cases in which subjects entered some other condition than that of protracted and uncontrolled hypnosis. For instance, we know that some individuals will spontaneously enter a fugue state which may last for many days and bear strong resemblance to hypnosis.

It may be that hypnosis can become converted into a fugue. The condition might become established at any instant and, particularly, the command to "wake up" might act as a signal. The hypnotist would not be aware of this change and would be likely to report on a case of persistent hypnosis. Fugue conversion is probably a neurotic manifestation. Transformation of hypnosis into a hysterical coma has also been reported. In addition, the hypnotic experience may trigger the formation of a catatonic state in psychotic or potentially psychotic subjects.

Resistance to dehypnotization can take other forms than a frank refusal to awaken. Sometimes the subject appears to come out of the trance but remains in a dazed or semi-stuporous condition, or carries over into the presumed waking state behavioral elements which had been evoked in the hypnotic state. Such individuals can be considered to still be hypnotized. In other instances, the subject does seem to become fully dehypnotized, but presently relapses into a hypnotic state. This too is a resistance to dehypnotization.

Why do some individuals resist dehypnotization? In some cases, as we have seen, this may be the result of the waking response becoming incompatible with certain suggestions previously given, of hostility toward the hypnotist, of self-suggestion by the subject or of an explicit or implicit posthypnotic suggestion which the subject does not want to carry out. As has also been indicated, the subject's resistance may reflect some important psychodynamic aspects of his personality: a need for dependency and submission, a need for passivity, or it may even represent a flight from reality, an escape from conflict.* The trance state can have many functions, ranging from a highly threatening event to one which affords relief from tension and

*Fliess[60] has pointed out that a type of resistance which takes the form of a flight into hypnosis has been observed during therapy.

threats, or which, in itself, may be highly pleasurable to the subject. The resistance to dehypnotization may reflect reluctance to relinquish a condition which has need-reducing properties. When hypnosis is used in therapy, a refusal to "wake up" may be part of the subject's resistance, that is, an "acting out." A refusal acting as a neurotic symptom should be treated as any other neurotic symptom.

Williams[201] in his excellent discussion of this problem lists the following additional causes of resistance to dehypnotization: (a) The subject may be testing the hypnotist's ability to control him; (b) errors and ambiguities in the instructions, in particular, the fact that in spontaneous and suggested regressions loss of contact with the hypnotist is the only logical outcome; (c) redintegration of previous experiences caused by some element in a suggested experience or activity; (d) transformation of hypnosis into hysterical sleep and spontaneous somnambulism.

Williams also makes the important remark that difficulties with this sort of resistance often occur only with the second or even later trance induction, when the subject has learned how the hypnotic state can serve his needs. Consequently, success in dehypnotizing an individual after the first or even after a number of hypnotizations is no guarantee that difficulties will not arise subsequently. From our earlier discussion there are obviously other reasons too for saying this.

How does one go about waking a subject who resists dehypnotization? The simplest way of proceeding is to ask him why he does not wake up. Most subjects are quite willing to explain why. If the subject is uncooperative you may have to request an answer more forcefully. Usually the answer tells the hypnotist what to do. If it does not, it is sometimes possible to get the subject to specifically tell you what to do to wake him up, by merely asking him about it. Rosen[101] recommends the use of automatic writing, crystal gazing, and hypnotic dream induction to help in identifying, overcoming, or at least circumventing the causes of resistance to dehypnotization. An excellent way to dehypnotize an intractable subject is simply to say to him in a final tone: "Very well then, if you will not wake up I will just have to leave you as you are." You then ignore the subject entirely and go on to other things. If you absolutely have to absent yourself, arrange for someone to watch the subject. This need not be done in a continuous manner, but frequent checks of the subject's condition should be made, say every half hour. Whatever the case may be, the subject should never be allowed to leave the room in which he has presumably wakened without a competent person checking his condition.

In summing up methods of handling this problem, Williams points out quite pertinently that most of the methods which have been recommended to date are primarily opportunistic. They are more a reflection of the hypnotist's quickness of thinking and ingenuity than procedures derived from the theory and function of hypnosis. He recommends the following: (a) Using methods the subject believes will dehypnotize him; (b) correcting ambiguous instructions; (c) inducing a secondary trance (trance within a trance) using another hypnotist for this; (d) controlling redintegration by suggesting various experiences leading to the logical termination of the redintegrated experience; (e) acceding to some of the subject's demands, if he stipulates certain conditions for his cooperation; (f) using sophistry to circumvent the resistance.

Rosen[147] has also reported that Erickson found it efficacious to utilize the subject's own behavior to further the therapeutic goal and that through this he has been able to overcome resistance to dehypnotization. On the other hand it is *not* advisable to resort to slapping the subject's face or other relatively drastic methods unless all other measures have been exhausted. These last resort methods are more indicated when there is evidence that the subject is no longer in the hypnotic state, but is probably in a hysterical coma or something similar. In such cases some therapists will even use Metrazole injections and electroshock.

A QUICK METHOD OF INDUCTION*

With your subject standing in front of you place your hands on his shoulders, bring your face fairly close to his, about 8 or 9 inches away and fixate the bridge of his nose (fig. 22). As you do so, say: "Look at my eyes and think of sleep. You are going to go to sleep, quickly, soundly. . . You are going to go into a deep, sound sleep. Keep looking at my eyes. As you do so you feel a heaviness coming over your body. . .You are growing heavy. . .Your legs are heavy, very heavy. Your arms are heavy, very heavy. Your arms and your hands are very heavy, like lead. Your entire body is heavy. . . s-o heavy. . .s-o heavy. Your eyelids are getting heavy. . .You are getting drowsy. . .sleepy. . .You are tired. . .your body is so heavy. . . You want to sleep. Your eyes are so heavy you can't keep them open. They are closing. . .closing. . .closing. . .You cannot keep them open. . .You're going to sleep. . .Your eyes are closed, *Sleep!* DEEP ASLEEP!"

---

*Other techniques of rapid induction will be found in chapter 9 (page 299).

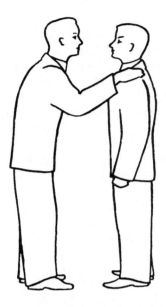

FIG. 22. One technique for hypnotizing.

ANOTHER RAPID METHOD OF INDUCING HYPNOSIS

This method is ideal when a preparatory phase is employed or when you want to combine testing for hypnotic susceptibility with the induction of hypnosis. You should proceed rapidly through the postural sway suggestion, the hand clasping suggestion and the eye catalepsy suggestion in this order. If the subject has given good strong responses to each of these, then as soon as you are satisfied that the subject cannot open his eyes, instead of telling him as usual that he can open them, proceed as follows:

All right, stop trying to open your eyes, you are now going to go to sleep. SLEEP! . . .DEEP ASLEEP! [*Following eye catalepsy suggestions your hand will be above the subject's forehead. Now, moving your hand downward in front of his face, form a V with the index and middle fingers and gently press the subject's closed eyes for a brief moment. Then place both hands on the subject's shoulders. All of this should take only a moment and produce no obvious break in the suggestions. In many cases the subject will now be in a relatively deep state of hypnosis, but it is best to carry the induction a little further before testing for depth. You may regard the remainder of this procedure* *as part of the induction proper or as part of the deepening phase; in any case we give it here because it makes use of a different approach. With your hands lightly grasping the subject's shoulders, very gently move his body in a slight, slow rotary swing with his feet as pivot. At the same time give further suggestions:]* You are now sinking into a deep. . .d-e-e-p sleep. You will not wake up until I tell you to. . .Waves of sleep are coming over you. . .You are going deeper and deeper asleep. . .There is a heaviness in your body. . . Your arms and hands are heavy, v-e-r-y heavy. . .Your feet and legs are s-o heavy. . .Your entire body is getting so h-e-a-v-y. You feel yourself sinking into a d-e-e-p, sound sleep. Sleep. . .deeply. . .soundly . . .S-l-e-e-p. *[At this point take hold of his forearm, raise it horizontally to his side saying at the same time:]* Now raise your arm. . .Make a tight fist. *[Proceed to give the arm rigidity suggestions for deepening the hypnosis as was done in the first method. After the challenge, have the subject lower his arm slowly, guiding it if necessary, and suggest that the trance is deepening. As soon as his arm is by his side, continue as follows:]* You are now deep asleep and you are going to go into an even deeper sleep. . .Take deep breaths. . .That's right, breathe deeply and slowly. . .With each breath that you take you sink* into a deeper and sounder sleep. . .a d-e-e-p, d-e-e-p, sound sleep. . .Continue to breathe deeply. . .Sleep. . .You have but one desire. . .one thought. . .to sleep deeply. . .Breathe deeply. . .sleep deeply. . .More and more deeply. . .Each and every time in the future that I tell you to sleep, suggest sleep, or say the word 'sleep' you will instantly go into a deep, sound sleep, deeper and sounder than you are now. You will not wake up until I tell you to unless something happens to me or your life is endangered. You will remain deep asleep. Nothing will bother you. Listen only to the sound of my voice.

SOME COMMENTS ON METHODS

In this chapter you have been given three methods for hypnotizing. Before you attempt any of the methods given in chapters 8 and 9 *you should make a definite effort to master the procedures of this chapter.* Between them lies the greatest portion of the elements which are used in any technique.

As you will note, you have not done anything here that differs essentially from what you did in handling waking suggestions, for good reason, since the initial portion of the induction involves waking suggestions, and since, according to all the evidence available today, much of what goes on in the

---

*This word sometimes causes anxiety.

remainder of the induction involves the same processes that are active in the waking state. Indeed, the main value of trance induction seems to be that it is a relatively rapid method for bringing about a condition of hypersuggestibility. How this is done has already been discussed. Certain procedural features appear to run through all modern trance-inducing techniques. Namely, a combination of attention focusing (usually involving visual and auditory fixation) with suggestions of some of the more superficial symptoms of the appearance of sleep and of sleep itself, culminating in suggested eye closure. As we shall see, introducing the notion of sleep and its symptoms is not always necessary. For the present, however, we are talking about standard methods. Theoretically then, it should be possible to make use of only one method of induction in all cases, at least where the subjects are normal individuals. In a way this surmise is essentially correct. The first method (page 206) would appear to have this sort of universality.*

Why bother then with other techniques? As pointed out, hypnotism today remains somewhat of an art. It is an art in that there is no single method of hypnosis, but there is always at least one technique which is better suited for a given setting, a given subject, a given hypnotist and a given problem. The art is in knowing how and when to choose the right one. It is equally an art to know how to adapt the chosen technique to the situation. I think most hypnotists, whether on the stage, in the laboratory or in the clinic would prefer to continually use the quickest most effective method. Would not the third method (page 229) be the one of choice then? The answer at present is a categorical no. In the first place, we shall show in chapter 9 that *under proper conditions* even faster methods exist. Second, success with this method depends largely upon having a subject of sufficient suggestibility to start with, but even with such a subject the method may fail to induce as deep a trance as desired in the time allotted for induction and, in the final outcome, one might have done better with the first method. If we only wish to rapidly induce a relatively light to medium hypnosis, the third method is very satisfactory in most cases in which waking eye-catalepsy can be produced. But suppose we do not have such a subject. Maybe the best we can obtain is the hand clasping response. Then certainly we have to resort to the first or second method (page 230), or to some other procedure. Again, if your subject is of sufficient suggestibility, the second method is very effective, although it does not guarantee a very deep trance. It is particularly effective in initiating hypnosis in individuals who, in addition to having sufficient suggestibility, believe strongly in the hypnotic eye myth or for some other

*I have always had success with it.

reason are particularly susceptible to this authoritarian form of relating.*
When used properly, the second method can be more attention-compelling
than many other methods. On the other hand, some hypnotists never get to
feel quite at home staring in a subject's eyes (or even at the bridge of h s
nose) and some subjects tend to be upset by this in a way which is detrimental to future interaction between subject and hypnotist.

It is not possible to set down all of the pros and cons, many of which w ll
be obvious to the reader. Others can be learned only through experience.
However, a few rules can be stated:

1. If it is not essential that you obtain a deep trance, a rapid method
   will often be satisfactory, but if a deep trance is desired, then it is
   safer to use the slower method.
2. Rapid methods are more impressive on an audience than slow methods.
   Judicious use of rapid methods where you have access to a fair number of subjects can often enhance the effectiveness of a demonstration,
   even though deep hypnosis is not produced in all subjects.
3. Failure to induce a trance by one method can hinder subsequent
   attempts to hypnotize by other methods which would have been
   otherwise successful. Since the likelihood of failure is greater with
   rapid methods (which usually depend upon certain ideal or semi-
   ideal conditions) the slower method is indicated in cases where subjects are not expendable.
4. For therapeutic and experimental purposes the slow method is usually
   to be preferred because it allows for better control and for a greater
   overall yield of successful trance inductions; yet some individuals
   only respond well to certain techniques which for a particular person
   may turn out to be what are normally considered rapid methods.

*For this reason it is contraindicated in certain forms of psychotherapy.

The Induction of Hypnosis:
II. Advanced Techniques

A MAJORITY of the innumerable techniques for the induction of hypnosis are merely variations of the procedures we have already considered. It would not be practical to discuss them all, nor is that really necessary,
since there are only a small number of techniques worth describing. Others
of less merit but still of interest can be briefly outlined without impairing
the reader's ability to use them. These will comprise the next chapter.
The reader should try each of the methods of this chapter; the order in which
this is done is not particularly important, but you should master these
techniques completely if they are to be used effectively.

HAND LEVITATION METHOD

While M. H. Erickson first described this procedure, one of the best
descriptions of it is given by Wolberg.[203] (The suggestions are a verbatim
report of a recorded induction session with a patient.) He says: "I believe
this is the best of all induction procedures. It permits of a participation in
the induction process by the patient and lends itself to nondirective and
analytic technics. It is, however, the most difficult of methods and calls
for greater endurance on the part of the hypnotist."

Wolberg states that following a brief preparatory phase he continues as
follows, telling the subject:

> I want you to sit comfortably in your chair and relax. As you sit there, bring both hands
> palms down on your thigh—just like that. Keep watching your hands, and you will notice
> that you are able to observe them closely.
>
> What you will do is sit in the chair and relax. Then you will notice that certain things
> happen in the course of relaxing. They always have happened while relaxing, but you have
> not noticed them so closely before. I am going to point them out to you. I'd like to have you
> concentrate on all sensations and feelings in your hands no matter what they may be. Perhaps
> you may feel the heaviness of your hand as it lies on your thigh, or you may feel pressure.
> Perhaps you will feel the texture of your trousers as they press against the palm of your hand;
> or the warmth of your hand on your thigh. Perhaps you may feel tingling. No matter what

sensations there are, I want you to observe them. Keep watching your hand, and you will notice how quiet it is, how it remains in one position. There is motion there, but it is not yet noticeable. I want you to keep watching your hand. Your attention may wander from the hand, but it will always return back to the hand, and you keep watching the hand and wondering when the motion that is there will show itself.

(At this point the patient's attention is fixed on his hand. He is curious about what will happen, and sensations such as any person might experience are suggested to him as possibilities. No attempt is being made to force any suggestions on him, and if he observes any sensations or feelings, he incorporates them as a product of his own experience. The object eventually is to get him to respond to the suggestions of the hypnotist as if these too are part of his own experiences. A subtle attempt is being made to get him to associate his sensations with the words spoken to him so that words or commands uttered by the hypnotist will evoke sensory or motor responses later on. Unless the patient is consciously resisting, a slight motion or jerking will develop in one of the fingers or in the hand. As soon as this happens, the hypnotist mentions it and remarks that the motion will probably increase. The hypnotist must also comment on any other objective reaction of the patient, such as motion of the legs or deep breathing. The result of this linking of the patient's reactions with comments of the hypnotist is an association of the two in the patient's mind.)

It will be interesting to see which one of the fingers will move first. It may be the middle finger, or the forefinger, or the ring finger, or the little finger, or the thumb. One of the fingers is going to jerk or move. You don't know exactly when or in which hand. Keep watching and you will begin to notice a slight movement, possibly in the right hand. There, the thumb jerks and moves, just like that.

As the movement begins you will notice an interesting thing. Very slowly the spaces between the fingers will widen, the fingers will slowly move apart, and you'll notice that the spaces will get wider and wider and wider. They'll move apart slowly; the fingers will seem to be spreading apart, wider and wider and wider. The fingers are spreading, wider and wider apart, just like that.

(This is the first real suggestion to which the patient is expected to respond. If the fingers start spreading apart, they do so because the patient is reacting to suggestion. The hypnotist continues to talk as if the response is one that would have come about by itself in the natural course of events.)

As the fingers spread apart, you will notice that the fingers will soon want to arch up from the thigh, as if they wanted to lift, higher and higher. *(The patient's index finger starts moving upward slightly.)* Notice how the index finger lifts. As it does the other fingers want to follow—up, up, slowly rising. *(The other fingers start lifting.)*

As the fingers lift you'll become aware of a lightness in the hand, a feeling of lightness, so much so that the fingers will arch up, and the whole hand will slowly lift and rise as if it feels like a feather, as if a balloon is lifting it up in the air, lifting, lifting,—up—up—up, pulling up higher and higher and higher, the hand becoming very light. *(The hand starts rising.)* As you watch your hand rise, you'll notice that the arm comes up, up, up in the air, a little higher—and higher—and higher—and higher, up—up—up. *(The arm has lifted about five inches above the thigh and the patient is gazing at it fixedly.)*

Keep watching the hand and arm as it rises straight up, and as it does you will soon become aware of how drowsy and tired your eyes become. As your arm continues to rise, you will get tired and relaxed and sleepy, very sleepy. Your eyes will get heavy and your lids may want to close. And as your arm rises higher and higher, you will want to feel more relaxed and sleepy, and you will want to enjoy the peaceful relaxed feeling of letting your eyes close and of being sleepy.

(*It will be noticed that as the patient executes one suggestion, his positive response is used to reinforce the next suggestion. For instance, as his arm rises, it is suggested in essence that he will get drowsy because his arm is rising.*)

Your arm lifts—up—up—and you are getting very drowsy; your lids get very heavy, your breathing gets slow and regular. Breathe deeply—in and out. (*The patient holds his arm stretched out directly in front of him, his eyes are blinking and his breathing is deep and regular.*) As you keep watching your hand and arm and feeling more and more drowsy and relaxed, you will notice that the direction of the hand will change. The arm will bend, and the hand will move closer and closer to your face—up—up—up—and as it rises you will slowly but steadily go into a deep, deep, sleep in which you relax deeply and to your satisfaction. The arm will continue to rise up—up—lifting, lifting—up in the air until it touches your face, and you will get sleepier and sleepier, but you must not go to sleep until your hand touches your face. When your hand touches your face you will be asleep, deeply asleep.

(*The patient here is requested to choose his own pace in falling asleep, so that when his hand touches his face, he feels himself to be asleep to his own satisfaction. Hand levitation and sleepiness continue to reinforce each other. When the patient finally does close his eyes, he will have entered a trance with his own participation. He will later be less inclined to deny that he has been in a trance.*)

Your hand is now changing its direction. It moves up—up—up—up toward your face. Your eyelids are getting heavy. You are getting sleepier, and sleepier, and sleepier. (*The patient's hand is approaching his face, his eyelids are blinking more rapidly.*) Your eyes get heavy, very heavy, and the hand moves straight up toward your face. You get very tired and drowsy. Your eyes are closing, are closing. When your hand touches your face you'll be asleep, deeply asleep. You'll feel very drowsy. You feel drowsier and drowsier and drowsier, very sleepy, very tired. Your eyes are like lead, and your hand moves up, up, up, right toward your face, and when it reaches your face, you will be asleep. (*Patient's hand touches his face and his eyes close.*) Go to sleep, go to sleep, just asleep. And as you sleep you feel very tired and relaxed. I want you to concentrate on relaxation, a state of tensionless relaxation. Think of nothing else, but sleep, deep sleep.

Wolberg adds that this technique is applicable to almost all subjects, although modifications may be made to fit individual cases, examples of which can be found in the second volume of his Medical Hypnosis. The reader should re-examine this procedure in terms of earlier material regarding factors making for effective suggestions. Wolberg's comments are also extremely pertinent and very basic.

Arons[4] has described an interesting variation of the Wolberg technique which possesses some of its advantages and is said to be more rapid in effect.* The subject is instructed to stand facing the hypnotist at a five foot distance, to stretch out his right arm and point at the hypnotist's feet while fixing his gaze upon his pointing finger.

*This gain in speed is probably at the cost of effectiveness in terms of percentage of successful inductions and of depth attained (see also chapter 9).

These instructions are followed by suggestions of lightness and of rising of the arm. The subject is told that his arm will rise upward toward the hypnotist's eyes and that the subject's eyes will remain focused upon his finger during this motion. The hypnotist continues his suggestion by telling the subject that his hand will rise until his finger points at the hypnotist's eyes and that when this happens their gaze will meet. The subject is told that as soon as this occurs he will instantly fall into a deep hypnotic sleep. When the subject begins to show some response to this suggestion, Arons says the hypnotist should change his suggestions accordingly. As soon as the subject's finger points to the hypnotist's eyes and their gaze meets, the hypnotist should forcefully command the subject to sleep.

FOLDING HAND METHOD

This method was first described by Wagner.[185] He has found that it is sometimes difficult to get the subject's hand up to his face in Wolberg's technique, largely because of mechanical factors and also that the abnormal protracted position which ensues may be painfully tiring for some subjects. Therefore, he has modified the procedure so that the last phase of the trance induction is replaced by the hand clasping response. In this manner only the forearms and hands are involved. In describing it Wagner says:

> In short the method is as follows: After careful preparation, hypnosis commences as in the hand levitation method. The initial position is the same (see fig. 1).* First, the fingers of one hand are induced to spread out (fig. 2); secondly, the flexing of the fingers and simultaneously spreading of the fingers of the other hand (fig. 3).† When both hands have been raised from the thigh (fig. 4), suggestions are given that the palms will turn to each other (fig. 5); and that they will be attracted to each other like opposite poles of a magnet (fig. 6). Gradually, as the hands get closer together, general suggestions are given of increasing drowsiness, deeper breathing and sensations of heaviness of the eyelids. These suggestions are enforced while the fingers interlace (fig. 7). The hands are clenched simultaneously with eyelids drooping. When the clenching of the hands reaches its maximum (fig. 8), general relaxing and heaviness of the whole body including arms and eyelids is suggested; the hands slip apart (fig. 9). Then the trance may be deepened in the usual manner, or the patient may be wakened if a fractional technique is preferred.

Wagner adds that most people get a very intense feeling of mutual attraction of the hands, a fact that I have also found to be generally true. This, he says, considerably intensifies the suggestibility. This effect directly follows from some of the principles discussed earlier. Wagner also remarks that anxiety which may be aroused during the hypnotic session tends to

*Since this is quoted material, the original numbering of the illustrations as given in the article has been preserved. As a group, these illustrations constitute figure 23 of this text.

†This figure has been excluded.

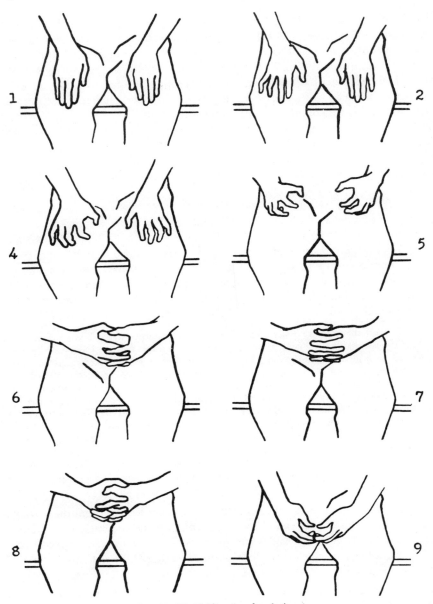

Fig. 23. The folding hand technique.

vanish as soon as the hands are folded. He proposes that this might have something to do with the religious significance of folded hands.

POSTURAL SWAY METHODS

I first came across this method in Watkins' textbook of hypnotherapy, [88] although I have seen a very abbreviated variation of it used on the stage. It can be an extraordinarily rapid method and it can also insensibly follow the postural sway test of suggestibility when the subject responds well to the initial suggestions. We will now quote Watkins:

The therapist speaks to the patient as follows: "Now Jones, I'd like to have you stand here with your heels and your toes together and your body erect, shoulders back. That's right. Breathe comfortably and easily with your hands at your sides. Now close your eyes. Just imagine that your feet are hinged to the floor and your body is like a stick pointing upward in the air, free to move back and forth. You will probably find after a while, you will become unsteady. Don't worry, if you should fall, I'll catch you." (This last remark is given in a rather matter-of-fact way, almost as a side comment. If previous suggestibility tests have been given, and the therapist is quite certain the patient will enter the trance, he may modify this statement by saying, "Don't worry, I will catch you *when* you fall.")

The therapist then continues: "Now while you are standing there, breathe very calmly and easily. Just imagine that your body is floating up into space. Don't try to do anything, and don't try *not* to do anything. Just stand there and let yourself drift." The therapist is then silent for a time, perhaps fifteen seconds up to a minute. If the patient is suggestible he will sway back and forth slightly.

The therapist should place himself at the side of the patient where he can line the back of the patient's head or the tip of his nose against a mark on the opposite wall so that a slight backward or forward swaying movement can be easily detected and measured. It is even convenient to have a card against the wall on which black vertical lines have been ruled about an inch apart, thus making it easier to determine the amount of sway. Usually the therapist will soon detect the rhythm of the swaying, since it is almost impossible for anybody to stand perfectly still. There will always be some swaying, although it may be slight in the more unsuggestible patients. One will generally find that the more suggestible the patient, the greater will be the amplitude of the swaying arc.

The therapist next begins to reinforce this swaying by timing his remarks to coincide with it. As soon as the patient has reached the extreme forward part of the arc and begins to sway backward the therapist says, "Now you are drifting backward." Frequently this will cause the patient immediately to catch himself and to reverse the direction, whereupon the therapist instantly follows it with, "Now you are drifting over forward." As the swaying continues the therapist reinforces it with "Drifting forward, drifting backward and forward, backward, forward, backward," etc. The tone is low, soft, and firm. The therapist should be about one to two feet away from the patient's ear and should repeat the suggestions in a low, soft monotone from which all harshness has been deleted. It should have an almost pleading quality, monotonous like the drone of a bee. There should be no change in pitch, and the patter should be continued steadily. Occasionally it may be varied from "drifting forward" to "swaying forward, swaying backward, swaying over backward, now swaying forward," or "leaning forward, backward, forward, backward," etc.—on and on in a monotonous, repetitious voice.

As the therapist observes the amplitude of the swaying arc increasing, he may make the voice somewhat less pleading, less soft, and more dominant and controlling, even injecting some emotional pitch into the "forward, backward, forward, backward."

When the amplitude of the swaying arc has become quite substantial—six or more inches —it is probable that some light degree of trance has been induced.* Suggestibility should then be checked by beginning a command of "forward, backward" a little before the patient has reached the maximum sway of the arc. If the patient is suggestible, and there is a degree of hypnotic trance, he will interrupt the natural sway in order to follow the therapist's suggestions. The past remarks of the therapist have so closely followed the patient's swaying behavior that the patient begins to think to himself, "What this man says is true, I am swaying backward. Then I do sway forward." Consequently, the therapist's prestige is increased, and the patient begins to follow the suggestions instead of leading them.† From this point on the therapist can usually assume the more dominating role and direct rather than follow the swaying of the patient.

To induce deeper trance the voice tone is now made much firmer and the swaying suggestions are given somewhat more rapidly. "*Swaying forward, swaying backward, forward, backward,*" the volume of the voice growing stronger and stronger. Finally, attempt is made to induce the patient to fall over backward into a deep trance. The emphasis on the "backward" is increased, and on the "forward" diminished, and the verb is changed from "drifting" or "swaying" to Falling, *falling backward,* falling forward, *falling backward,* falling forward, *falling over backward,* falling, falling, *falling, falling*" rather rapidly and in a higher-pitched and more emotional tone. If a deep trance has been induced, the patient will increase the amplitude of his sway until he can no longer stand erect. He will then fall over backward in a deep trance where he may be caught by the therapist and eased into a waiting chair.

If the patient is in a light trance only he may start to fall backward, but catch himself by placing one of his feet back, or attempt to sway sideways or steady himself voluntarily in some manner. This indicates to the therapist that a deep trance has not yet been induced and he can then do one of two things: he may either continue the monotonous repetition of "falling forward, falling backward," etc., to induce a deeper degree of trance; or he may reassure the patient that he will not fall by placing a hand lightly behind his shoulder. This allays fears which might arise and interrupt the hypnotic process. After the patient realizes that he will not be permitted to fall and hurt himself, he tends to lose the signs of anxiety which may have begun to appear. He may then allow himself to fall back against the therapist's arm, whereupon the therapist continues the suggestions, "Falling over backward, falling backward, falling back into a deep sleep, back into a deep sleep, deep sleep, deep sleep," and then eases the patient gradually over into a chair. This, preferably an arm

---

*Note that in this procedure the suggestions of sleep do not come up until quite late, after the subject has already presumably attained a deep trance. We will have more to say later concerning the induction of hypnosis without mention of sleep.

†This explanation, although essentially correct, seems to me to be incomplete. Some of the above effects may take place at the level of awareness; however, the most important effects are taking place, I believe, at a much deeper level and the subject need not have any awareness of what is happening.

chair, should have been placed behind the patient. He can also be gradually lowered back upon a couch which has been located conveniently near.

If the patient is either completely limp or in a stiff catatonic state when he is placed back on the chair or cot, it is evident that a fairly deep degree of trance has been induced. If, however, he is able to help himself either by taking steps backward or by putting his hands on the arm chair and guiding himself into it, then only a light hypnoidal trance has been induced.

In any event, the trance may be deepened by various means. Watkins gives several advantages of this technique: it appears inoffensive to the subject, particularly since the hypnotist may present the procedure merely as a test of reflexes, etc., and the method is not generally known to the public and consequently its use is not as likely to cause anxiety or apprehension as do the standard techniques.

The next method to be considered can be used for inducing the trance from the beginning although it is given here primarily as an effective way of deepening the trance state. Watkins [188] speaks of two variations of it which are given below and I have added others which I believe are equally effective.

METRONOME METHOD

A metronome should be placed near the subject, but out of sight. Watkins recommends a slow rate—fifty beats to the minute. He also finds that it is wise to muffle the sound by inclosing it in a cabinet or box, since some subjects are disturbed by a loud click. There are electronic metronomes available which can be adjusted for volume and pitch.* We will assume that the first phase of trance induction has been completed. Now, to quote Watkins:

> He [the patient or subject] is told, "Now I am going to turn on a slow ticking sound. This will help you to go to sleep. Listen very carefully to it and to nothing else. It goes like this." The metronome is turned on. Then the therapist continues, "Just imagine each tick saying to you, 'deep—sleep—deep—sleep,' and the deeper you go into sleep the deeper you will want to go. How comfortable you will feel all over. Just keep on listening to this ticking sound which says over and over again, 'deep—sleep—deep—sleep.' The therapist may even continue speaking the words 'deep—sleep' for a little while, timing them to coincide with the ticking.

The second variation given by Watkins is:

> Suggest to the patient that as he listens to the ticking he will imagine himself slowly

---

*In addition they are equipped with a small light which flashes with each beat, therefore visual fixation on the light can also be used.

going down a ladder or stairway. "Each tick is saying "step—down,—step—down," or "deep—sleep,—step—down," etc. He may be told, "As you go down this ladder you will feel that you are going down into a deeper and deeper sleep."

After a few moments he often leaves the patient to listen to the metronome for 10 to 30 minutes. He adds a number of other minor variations. In one he tells the patient that he is going to leave him for a short time while the patient listens to the ticking, and that when he comes back he will be in the deepest possible sleep. The patient may also be told that when he reaches the deepest sleep he can attain, his hand will slowly rise and touch his forehead. The hypnotist then checks at intervals to observe whether this has taken place.

I like to give the latter suggestion a little differently. I tell the subject: "Now imagine that you are going down a ladder without end. At each tick (or count) you step down one rung of the ladder and each time you do you will go deeper asleep. One — step — down, you are going to sleep deeply. Two — step again — down. As you sink lower and lower down the ladder you sink deeper and deeper asleep. Three — step — down, sleep, deeply . . . (etc.)." (See also chapter 9 under Counting Method.)

As Watkins points out, the use of a metronome has the advantage that, when coupled with suggestions as in the above, it is less fatiguing for the hypnotist, but the ticking of a watch or of a clock can often be used in lieu of a metronome. It is not difficult for the subject to focus his attention on a slow rhythmic beat in the ticking. One may also tap regularly with a pencil or ruler on a table top. One can also count slowly in a uniformly low, monotonous tone, following each count with appropriate suggestions.

Two other variations might be mentioned here. A thin cardboard or paper disk is attached to the top of the beating arm of the metronome. Some hypnotists like to cover the disk with tinfoil. The metronome is then placed so that the disk is slightly above eye level and the subject is asked to fixate the disk while listening to the beats. Appropriate suggestions are then given. Or, the subject is told to imagine a pendulum swinging back and forth in time with the ticking or beat.

FRACTIONATION METHOD

This method, first described by Vogt,[183] is one of the most effective methods for inducing a very deep trance state, and it often succeeds when every other method has failed. It is especially indicated when you expect the subject to enter a light to medium trance at best. It also offers an effective method for handling subjects who, because they experience at first only a light hypnosis, doubt that they have been hypnotized. In essence the method involves hypnotizing and waking the subject in rapid consecutive successions. The observation as well as the theory is that each hypnotization makes the subjects a little more suggestible and favors the induction of a deeper hypnosis on the next trial. As we have seen, Janet reported a tendency for the hypnotic state to perseverate a short while after the subject "wakens," particularly if the wakening process were sudden. Data has been reported which supports this contention, in so far as homoactive hypersuggestibility resulting from the trance induction is found to perseverate into the waking state for better than 30 minutes.[191]

I have found that this principle can be used even more effectively in the following manner: As soon as you are ready to awaken the subject tell him the following: "In a moment I will tell you to awaken. When I do so you will awake, but you will immediately begin to feel very sleepy again. You will find it hard to keep your eyes open and to stay awake. Your eyes will feel very heavy, and they will get heavier and heavier until you will not be able to keep them open any longer and you will not be able to prevent yourself from blinking and closing them. You will get sleepier and drowsier by the moment, your eyes will close, and you will go soundly asleep, much more deeply than you are now. I shall now count to three, and at three you will be awake and will open your eyes. But you will be drowsy and sleepy, and your eyes will be so heavy that you will not be able to keep them open long and will go back to sleep . . . Now, one . . . two . . . three . . . Awake!'' Usually the subject will remain sitting rather passively in his chair (or reclining on the couch if one is used). He may start to blink his eyes or show a sleepy countenance, eyes half closed. Ask him what is the matter with his eyes. He may tell you that he feels sleepy, although more often he will seem puzzled about it saying that he doesn't know what the trouble is, or again he may say that the light is bothering them. Whatever the case may be, and regardless of whether or not you ask the question (if you don't, wait 10 or 15 seconds), go on and say to the subject: "You feel kind of sleepy, don't you? It's hard to keep your eyes open?[*Nearly always this is enough to start the subject blinking or even closing his eyes. Whatever he does you should attempt to follow it up and incorporate it in your next suggestions or statements, which might be:*]* Your eyes are getting rather heavy, you feel drowsy and sleepy. Close your eyes, you are going asleep. *Sleep!*'' If the subject closes his eyes before this, then of course you should make the proper alterations in the suggestions, something like: "Your eyes are closed, *sleep, deep, deep asleep!*'' Or as the eyes close, say commandingly "SLEEP! DEEP ASLEEP! . . . You are going deeply, soundly asleep.''

You may then deepen the trance somewhat by methods previously described, although this is usually not done since the method you are using is aimed at doing this. Instead, one customarily gives the subject only such suggestions as are deemed essential, waking him up very soon (at least for the first few repetitions of the induction). This procedure is repeated a number of times. Following eye closure you might give a few additional suggestions to deepen the trance, then suggestions mainly to the effect that whenever you suggest sleep or say the word sleep, he will go quickly and deeply asleep, and will not wake up until you tell him. Then instruct him again in regard to the next waking period, this time telling him that he will be awake and will feel fine, but that as soon as you begin to talk to him, no matter what you say, he will find that his eyes are getting heavy, hard to keep open, that he feels tired and is getting very drowsy and sleepy and that his eyes will close and he will go into a very deep sleep, much deeper than he is in now. Then you wake him up and after a few moments ask him how he feels. He may or may not reply. In any case the conversation should be pretty much one-sided and might run something like this:

> *Hypnotist*: How do you feel?
> *Subject*: All right . . . I guess.
> *Hypnotist*: Feel at all sleepy? . . . You look kind of sleepy.
> *Subject*: (Says nothing but passes hand over eyes and forehead in the typical gesture of a tired person.)
> *Hypnotist*: Your eyes feel sort of tired and heavy, hard to keep open, aren't they? . . . You are getting sleepy, you would like to sleep . . . Why don't you close your eyes . . . *Close your eyes* . . . and go to sleep. *Deep*, DEEP ASLEEP . . . [*The subject has now closed his eyes and is relaxing.*] You are now going deeply asleep, very soundly asleep.

This time, after deepening the trance with a few more suggestions, give the subject the eye catalepsy and the arm rigidity suggestions, but don't challenge him in either case. Instead say something like: "You cannot open your eyes now (or you cannot bend your arm now). If you tried you would be unable to do so, but you have no desire to try* . . . Now you are relaxing . . . relaxing more and more and sinking into a very deep and sound sleep." You then follow with suggestions regarding waking as previously done, or you can tell him that you will talk with him after he wakes up and that as soon as you mention the word "sleep," or anything that has to do with sleep, he will feel an overpowering urge to close his eyes and to go to

---

*If you suspect that the subject is not too cooperative, you may prefer to leave such suggestions until later, since the subject might take this as a challenge which he may be able to meet.

sleep, that he will be unable to resist, and that he will go soundly asleep

In general, how long you want to keep this up and exactly how you want to proceed each time depends upon the type of subject you have and how much time you have to spend with him. Let us say that you proceed as described and this is your fourth hypnotization. You find that the subject goes to sleep readily. This time, as soon as he has done so and you have given a few additional suggestions of greater depth, give the suggestion that each and every time in the future you say "sleep" or that you snap your fingers and say "sleep" to him, he will immediately go soundly asleep. That he will become very sleepy, his eyes will close immediately and he will go deeply asleep. Now wake him up and shortly after he has opened his eyes (within about 5 seconds) snap your fingers near his face and in a commanding tone of voice say "SLEEP! DEEP ASLEEP!" If you see any hesitation, snap your fingers repeatedly and at the same time say quickly "SLEEP! SLEEP . . . DEEP ASLEEP!" or, as you say this, bring your hand downward toward the subject's face and apply gentle pressure on his eyelids.

Repeat this a few more times or until the subject immediately responds to your command. Sometimes a subject shows a kind of inertia in spite of the fact that he is a good subject. He is just slow, not resisting. It is usually not possible to speed up his responses and you should not attempt to do so. After a few more rapid responses, you may test for depth of hypnosis. Often, if time permits, I make use of the last induction in the series to deepen the trance state, letting the subject sleep in silence for 15 minutes or more.

This procedure, like others, has variations. Many hypnotists do not bother to give any suggestions, but merely dehypnotize and rehypnotize the subject by the same method they have used. They keep doing this repeatedly until the subject passes into hypnosis shortly after the induction has begun.

Although successive rapid dehypnotization and hypnotization is usually employed, it is not absolutely necessary that the interval of time between inductions be very short. Sometimes, if the subject is capable of attaining a trance depth sufficient for some of the hypnotist's purposes, he can be used for these, then awakened to be rehypnotized and used again. Indeed, there is considerable evidence that hypnotization on successive days leads to improvement in many instances. In such cases, however, it is not called fractionation.

An excellent variation of the Vogt method which often succeeds with subjects who fail to attain a deep trance is to ask them to describe the sensations they experience when going into the trance. You will find great diversity among subjects in this regard. In the next induction include suggestions describing these various feelings in the order the subject gave them to you. This feedback technique is often extremely effective because it prevents you from suggesting experiences which the subject will not have, to which he may even have unconscious or conscious resistance. In addition, you can suggest events which will happen or are happening. As we have seen, this is a basic part of hypnotization. Finally, if these symptoms are part of the trance state, then obviously they are the ones to bring about rather than effects which have nothing to do with it.

Some hypnotists make it a practice to ask the subject for a description of his sensations after the first induction regardless of the method used. Then, on subsequent occasions, weeks or months later, these symptoms are used when a trance is again induced.

One particularly effective variation of the fractionation method consists in using the hand levitation method for the second and even subsequent inductions. It can be used even when hand levitation is employed in the deepening phase of the previous hypnotization.

A SEMI-INDIRECT METHOD OF TRANCE INDUCTION— PICTURE VISUALIZATION

Kline[99] has reported a rather interesting and ingenious technique of induction which he finds to be particularly effective with refractory subjects. Using this method he claims that light to medium trance can be brought about in such subjects in about 10 minutes on the average. Kline refers to it as a "visual imagery technique." I have included it here as a semi-indirect method because it serves as a link between the direct methods of induction in which the subject is told directly that he is going to sleep, and the techniques we shall see in the next section in which the subject is hypnotized unknowingly. It is possible that this also takes place here with some subjects, although suggestions of sleep are used.

We shall quote Kline in his own description of the method. He divides the procedure into five steps as follows:

> 1. In the waking state with the eyes open, each subject was asked to visualize in "his mind's eye" certain familiar objects. In order these were: (a) a house, (b) a tree, (c) a person, and (d) an animal. The psychodiagnostic value of this imagery production will be dealt with elsewhere. This step was continued until each stimulus had been achieved. In this population of 15 subjects,* all were able to achieve the requested images readily and easily. For subjects who may have difficulty in visual imagery, other methods may have to be devised based upon the principles described here.
>
> 2. Following the attainment of image formation in the waking state, each subject was

*All of whom had proven refractory to the usual techniques.

told, "Close your eyes and in your mind's eye visualize yourself as you are here; sitting in the chair (or lying on the couch) *except the image of yourself has his (her) eyes open.*

3. At this point the subject was told to concentrate on the image and that all the therapist's (experimenter's) comments would be directed toward the subject's *image* and *not* toward the subject.

4. Then, a simple ocular-fixation technique was described and related to the eye-closure of the *image.* Close clinical observation of the subject will reveal subtle response patterns indicating the associative effect upon him directly. The subject can be asked to confirm eye-closure in the image, though often his straining to raise his eyebrows will reveal the situation. The image can be challenged on the lid catalepsy depending on the value that this mechanism may have in the total hypnotic relationship. Following eye-closure in the *image,* suggestions for "deepening" the trance are given in the usual manner.

5. The next step involves moving directly into the induction relationship with the *subject.* This may be done by saying, "Now you are feeling just like the image, going deeper and deeper asleep (or an equated word) and the image is disappearing." Within a few minutes, depending on the subject's personality, you will have obtained a light to medium hypnotic trance. Further depth may be secured in the usual manner, but the patient is now ready for hypnotherapeutic work.

A somewhat similar technique combined with the hand levitation method has been described by Moss.[128] He asks the subject to choose something he has seen happen such as a movie, television show, football game, etc., to try to recall it in exact details and to keep it in his mind. The subject is also instructed that his right arm will rise when he sees a faithful reproduction of the scene he has chosen. Then Moss waits a short while. If nothing happens, he urges the patient to concentrate more, telling him again that his hand will rise when he sees the picture. He follows this immediately with suggestions of hand levitation, then, as soon as the hand begins to rise, he urges the patient to keep the picture in his mind and pay attention to nothing else. Now, he also adds suggestions of sleep: " . . . as you keep looking at the picture you are going into a pleasant deep sleep. Deeper and deeper. Sleep! Deeply! Deep sleep!" Moss follows this by taking the subject's right arm and raising it up and forward. At the same time he tells the subject that his arm will bend and his hand will approach his face and touch it, and that when this happens, he will go into a deep sleep. He also suggests that he will continue to see the picture. He then gives suggestions that the arm is bending, etc. When the hand touches the face, he says firmly: "Deep sleep! Deep sleep!" and returns the hand to the subject's lap if the subject does not do this himself.

This method appears to be eminently suitable for the induction of hypnosis in children who, usually, have vivid imaginations.

Another form of hypnotization by picture visualization is described by Powers.[140] The subject with his eyes closed first visualizes a large blackboard. As soon as he reports success he is told to visualize himself drawing a large circle on this board. Following this, the hypnotist asks him to mentally draw a large "X" in the center of the circle. If he succeeds, he is next requested to erase the whole picture from his mind. Then again the subject is requested to visualize the empty circle and is told to visualize then erase each letter of the alphabet in consecutive order. The hypnotist checks the subject for the first few letters, then instructs him to continue, no further check being made. The subject is told that when he reaches the end of the alphabet he will be deeply hypnotized. While the subject continues with the letters, suggestions of deep hypnotic sleep are given. Powers claims that this method is particularly effective with individuals who have a low attention span, as it helps them to concentrate.

The simplest form of the visualization technique I have seen is to place a coin on the center of the subject's forehead and ask him to feel and "see" it mentally. Suggestions are then given in conjunction with this.

I suspect that the visualization method can probably be made extremely effective by choosing scenes or experiences which have deep psychological significance for the subject. Furthermore, I believe that visual imagery is not the only form of imagery that can be thus used, nor is it necessarily the most effective; any of the other senses might be used too. There are individuals in whom the other senses are much more developed in regard to imagery. Impressions in several senses could be combined.

This technique appears to be an excellent way of dealing with subjects who are blind.

HYPNOTIZING WITHOUT SUGGESTIONS OF SLEEP— SENSORIMOTOR METHOD

This is a method whereby an individual is hypnotized not only without reference to sleep, but essentially without his awareness that he is being hypnotized.* This method requires a hypnotist with considerable skill, possibly one reason why the literature concerning it is limited. As was mentioned earlier, the postural sway method can be considered a form of the sensorimotor method of trance induction. I have found it an excellent way of bringing about a hypnotic state without suggesting sleep or even relaxation. Pattie[137] has described one variant of this method. This is not surprising in view of the fact that subjects sometimes pass into a condition no

*Probably the reader will immediately think in this connection of Braid's classical method. But we have in mind a somewhat different type of procedure. There is no reason why Braid's method could not be discussed in this section but, because of its rather special position in hypnotism, it is taken up separately in the next chapter.

different from hypnosis when they are submitted to a series of progressively more complex waking suggestions. Wells,[198] who speaks of "waking hypnosis" in this connection, begins by talking to his subjects about involuntary ideomotor action and about phenomena which happen naturally to persons in their everyday life (dissociation phenomena). He follows this with a few preliminary experiments, then usually asks the subject to fix his visual attention upon some small and simple object. He then gives the subject suggestions of eyelid catalepsy essentially following the pattern used earlier, except that he does not place his finger on the subject's forehead. If this is successful, Wells goes on to produce other muscular contractures such as the hand clasping or the arm rigidity effects. If the eye closure suggestion fails, he recommends that one should go on to other suggestions and then come back to it. At the end of the "waking hypnosis" session, dehypnotization is brought about by telling the subject that at a given signal he will return to his normal self. In the case of patients, it is particualrly important to say this rather than to use such expressions as "you will be just as you were earlier." A counting technique can be used here as was described earlier, "waking," of course, never being mentioned.

Adler and Secunda[1] have approached the problem of hypnotization in terms of the concept that in therapy the hypnotic situation expresses an already existing interrelationship between doctor and patient. Thus, they conclude, it is unnecessary for the physician to assume any sort of a pose or for the patient to be prepared for an occurrence out of the ordinary, as is the case in the usual approach to this method of treatment. They feel that undesirable changes and tensions are created when the patient must be prepared for an unusual situation. To circumvent this possibility they evolved a method of trance induction which they claim assures more uniform success because it is least suggestive of such changes. They call it an indirect method because no direct suggestion of hypnotizing the patient or of putting him to sleep is made. Although the authors have described the method in the very specific and limited setting of therapy, I believe that it can be adapted to other situations. It will be given here as originally described.

We made use of two frequent complaints—inability to relax and to concentrate—as the only orientation to the hypnosis. After the preliminary case study, the procedure is introduced saying: "I shall teach you to relax and concentrate." The patient is interested in learning this procedure for it offers relief from symptoms in an objective manner. The patient is seated in a comfortable arm chair and is told to let all of his muscles go limp; the head should be inclined slightly forward; the arms rest fully on the chair arms with hands hanging limply over the edges. He is then asked to fix his glance on the thumb and forefinger of one of his hands. The physician then states: "I am going to ask you to close your eyes soon, but continue to concentrate on your thumb and forefinger. As you concentrate I shall count, and as I count you will become more and more relaxed. As you do so you will feel your thumb and forefinger draw closer and closer together. When they touch you will then know you are in a deep state of relaxation."

After this explanation, the patient is requested to close his eyes and concentrate on his thumb and forefinger. The physician repeats: "I shall start to count. As I count you will feel your thumb and forefinger draw closer and closer together as you become more and more relaxed. When your fingers touch, you will know that you are in a deep state of relaxation." The count is synchronized with the patient's respirations, and continued indefinitely. At one hundred the formula is usually repeated. "Continue to concentrate on your thumb and forefinger. As I count you will feel your thumb and forefinger draw closer and closer together as you become more and more relaxed. When they touch you will know that you are in a deep state of relaxation." When the thumb and forefinger are in contact, the patient is told, "Now you know you are in a deep state of relaxation."

The movement of a larger muscle group is then undertaken. The physician continues: "As I count further you go into a deeper state of relaxation. As you do so, your left hand gradually, and without effort on your part, moves from the arm rest and comes to rest on the chair beside you." When this occurs, the patient is told: "Now you know you are in a deeper state of relaxation." At this point the patient is at least in light hypnosis, i.e., inability to move a limb at suggestion of heaviness and hypesthesia to pin prick.

To bridge the gap between light hypnosis and deep trance, the suggestion of Erickson is followed. It differs only in that the words "sleep" and "trance" are omitted: "Without further counting you will continue to relax more and more, as you do so, your hand will rise without effort, and touch your face. However, your hand will not and must not touch your face until you are in the deepest state of relaxation. Then the touching of your face will be a signal that you are in a profound state of relaxation."

When this has been accomplished, a brief orientation procedure is gone through, i.e., "What is your name?" "What are you doing?" At this point the patient can be tested for depth of trance; however, deep hypnosis is not required for therapeutic results.

The patient is then trained for future induction into the same depth of trance he had attained by suggesting to him that from now on, as the physician counts from 1 to 20, he will go into this depth of relaxation and at this point his hand will rise automatically and touch his face, as a signal that he has reached the required depth of trance.

To return the patient to his non-hypnotic state the physician says: "As I count from 1 to 5, you will gradually awaken—at 5 you will be wide awake."

After the patient wakens he usually asks whether he has been asleep or hypnotized. Whichever term he uses is then accepted by the physician who then confirms what has occurred, using the phenomena as reassurance for the patient's ability to relax under adverse circumstances. Then a discussion follows on the use of the technique to obtain subconscious and repressed material, and an opportunity is given the patient to express his opinions on what has occurred. Since no attempts are made in the first session to produce hypnotic or posthypnotic amnesia, the patient recollects the entire process. No patient has ever expressed objections to the manner in which he was introduced to hypnotherapy.

Conn[29] described a somewhat similar technique. After a satisfactory transference relationship ("rapport") has been established, the topic of relaxation and its therapeutic effects is introduced and the patient is induced to attempt to become more relaxed. He is requested to move to a more comfortable chair and once seated he is asked to look up at a bright object placed several inches from his eyes and just above the horizontal line of vision. Conn emphasizes that at this point he *"carefully defines how he expects the patient to act"* by telling him first that he will *not* fall asleep so that they can talk matters over when complete relaxation has taken place. Progressive relaxation is then suggested, followed by suggestion of eye closure. At the same time, the bright object is gradually lowered to below the line of vision. Progressively deeper relaxation is suggested, but the word sleep is *never* mentioned again. In some instances the eyes remain open and staring, in which case the hypnotist should direct the patient to close them. The whole procedure takes 3 to 5 minutes.

It should be noted that Conn uses the resulting state mainly to facilitate free association. Once he has obtained some of the overt signs of hypnosis mentioned earlier (page 210 ff.) he brings up the matter of free association by telling the patient that if anything comes to his mind while he is relaxed and he feels like talking, he should do so, but that he should let it come without making any effort, just as easily *as breathing.* At this point Conn shifts from this mention of breathing to instructions to the patient to "breathe in" and "breathe out" in a rhythmic manner. This, he remarks to the subject, will keep him "listening" and close to the waking state. From here on the procedure is directed at obtaining free association. The reader is referred to Conn's paper for further details.

Should the method fail to produce the desired state, an attempt should be made to remove the resistance; then the induction process should be tried again. This may be done up to three times. In case of persisting failure, the subject or patient can be told that he is not yet ready for the technique but will be later on, or that the production of a relaxed state is not a necessity, that what is important is to work out a method of treatment best suited to him and his specific problem.

The initiation of a state of hypersuggestibility, presumably hypnotic in character, can be even more indirect. In its most extreme form the technique used for this has been referred to by Rosen[147] as the sensorimotor method. No truly adequate definition or description of the technique has yet been given by its originator, and that presented here is my interpretation of what has been written none too clearly elsewhere. In essence, it consists of unobtrusively getting the subject to relax and to concentrate his attention on some idea or object. Then by a skillful manipulation of the subject's own spontaneous reactions (in a manner reminiscent of the procedure in Wolberg's hand levitation technique) he is slowly conditioned to respond to suggestions with increasing strength and frequency. Ways of proceeding vary. For instance, as Rosen explains, speaking in the context of therapy, the subject may have difficulty in relaxing. One can then begin by telling him that one wishes to test his ability to relax. The patient may have a problem in concentrating, or suffer from tenseness. He can then be told that the first step will be to see how much the tension can be reduced, or how well he can do with less tension. Where organic symptoms form the basis of the complaint, the patient should preferably be instructed to concentrate on the symptom and its site. Whatever one does at this point in the procedures, one should try to make use, as much as possible, of the words which the patient used in describing his problem. From there on it is a matter of capitalizing on every reaction of the patient. Each and every one of these should be carefully observed and utilized. Since few individuals can keep their attention from wandering for long, the patient can be told as a start that this very thing will happen, but that he will return his attention to its focus. Subsequently, whatever manifestations appear, motor or autonomic, they are commented upon as soon as perceived *by the hypnotist*, preferably before the patient himself becomes aware of them. Such manifestations may consist of foot tapping, nervous movements of the hands and fingers or of the whole body, crossing of the legs, postural changes, flushing of the face, noticeable perspiration, and so forth. All of these are used by being brought to the attention of the patient. However, they are spoken of as though they had a physiological basis, rather than as being the result of suggestions. Whatever these reactions turn out to be, the patient is next told that individuals who exhibit them usually develop other motor manifestations as well. These predicted phenomena are then carefully described in minute detail and in very specific terms. The choice of phenomena here is guided by the criteria that they must not have a physiological nor an anatomical basis, and that they must manifest themselves solely because the therapist or hypnotist has concretely, specifically and directly suggested their occurrence. In general, the cadence of the hypnotist's speech should be timed to the patient's respiratory rhythm. The word "sleep" should never be mentioned. Nor is it usual to suggest eye-closure with or without lid paralysis. Since the aim is to gradually and unobtrusively lead the patient to accept suggestions, it is probably best to phrase all suggestions permissively. Because of this feature, the sensorimotor method is probably most readily adapted to permissive types of therapies.

Although this technique was originally developed for use in therapy situations and is described in such a context, there is no reason why it cannot be adapted, with a little ingenuity, to other situations.

These procedures follow directly from the principles discussed earlier.

The reader should analyze this section in terms of these principles and make certain that he understands the mechanics involved.

The sensorimotor and related methods can be employed in conjunction with methods described earlier. If this is done, you usually begin with the sensorimotor approach and introduce sleep suggestions later. Note that visual fixation is not used in the sensorimotor method, a feature that distinguishes it from Wells' "waking hypnosis." Features from other techniques can be more intimately combined with sensorimotor methods. As a matter of fact, if you re-examine some of the procedures for the induction of hypnosis described earlier, you will see evidence of this in some of them.

AN INDIRECT METHOD OF TRANCE INDUCTION

Erickson and Kubie[53] reported an ingenious procedure used to induce hypnosis without the subject's knowledge under circumstances when it is probable that the subject would not have been willing to be hypnotized. The subject was a patient and was known to have a roommate. The first step in the procedure was to contact the roommate and obtain her cooperation in the enterprise. After some preliminary setting the patient was requested, as a special favor, to act as chaperone while her roommate, who she believed was under treatment by Erickson, was being hypnotized. This, says Erickson, gave the patient an active giving role in the procedures. At the time of the first hypnotization Erickson suggested matter of factly to the patient that she pay close attention to the hypnotic work since she herself might sometime wish to try it too. The remainder of the procedure is described in the author's words:

> Upon entering the office, the two girls were seated in adjacent chairs and a prolonged, tedious, and laborious series of suggestions were given to the roommate who soon developed an excellent trance, thereby setting an effective example for the intended patient. During the course of the trance, suggestions were given to the roommate in such a way that by imperceptible degrees they were accepted by the patient as applying to her. The two girls were seated not far apart in identical chairs, and in such a manner that they adopted more or less similar postures as they faced the hypnotist; also they were so placed that inconspicuously the hypnotist could observe either or both of them continuously. In this way it was possible to give a suggestion to the roommate that she inhale or exhale more deeply, so timing the suggestion as to coincide with the patient's respiratory movements. By repeating this carefully many times it was possible finally to see that any suggestion given to the roommate with regard to her respiration was automatically performed by the patient as well. Similarly, the patient having been observed placing her hand on her thigh, the suggestion was given to the roommate that she place her hand upon her thigh and that she should feel it resting there. Such maneuvers gradually and cumulatively brought the patient into a close indentification with her roommate, so that gradually anything said to the roommate applied to the patient as well.

Interspersed with this were other maneuvers. For instance, the hypnotist would turn to the patient and say casually, "I hope you are not getting too tired waiting." In subsequent suggestions to the roommate that she was tired, the patient herself would thereupon feel increasing fatigue without any realization that this was because of a suggestion which had been given to her. Gradually, it then became possible for the hypnotist to make suggestions to the roommate, while looking directly at the patient, thus creating in the patient an impulse to respond, just as anyone feels when someone looks at one, while addressing a question or comment to another person.

Once deep hypnosis was induced, which, incidentally, took an hour and a half, the writers took a number of measures to insure continuance of the present trance, cooperation of the subject while in it, and that there would be future opportunity to use hypnotherapy. To begin with, the patient was gently made aware of the fact that she was hypnotized. She was then told that nothing would be done to her that she did not want done, hence that there was no need for a chaperone in the future. She was, in fact, told that that she could break the trance should the hypnotist offend her. At the same time suggestions were added to the effect that she would continue to sleep deeply for an indefinite time and that she would listen to and obey only every legitimate suggestion. In this manner, the authors feel, the patient was given the reassuring, although illusory, feeling that she was a free agent. Finally, precaution was taken to insure that the patient felt friendly toward the hypnotist and a promise was obtained from her that she would enter into a deep trance any time in the future for any legitimate purpose.

Further on in their discussion of the case the authors say the following in regard to suggestions concerning future trance induction which were given just before waking the subject.

Finally, technical suggestions were given to the patient to the effect that she should allow herself to be hypnotized again, that she should go into a sound and deep trance, that if she had any resistances toward such a trance she would make the hypnotist aware of it *after* the trance had developed, whereupon she could then decide whether or not to continue in the trance. The purpose of these suggestions was merely to make certain that the patient would again allow herself to be hypnotized with full confidence that she could if she chose disrupt the trance at any time. This illusion of self-determination made it certain that the hypnotist would be able to swing the patient into a trance. Once in that condition, he was confident that he could keep her there until his therapeutic aims had been achieved.

Further comments on the technique need hardly be given. As will be realized, it contains some of the elements of the sensorimotor method, but differs in at least two respects: (1) the subject is not addressed directly, and (2) suggestions of sleep, relaxation, fatigue, and so forth are used.

Although the method is described in a therapeutic setting and involves a rather special condition, the cooperation of a roommate, it can be adapted to other situations. It is not uncommon, as will be seen in the next chapter, while giving hypnotic demonstrations before groups, to find some members of the audience responding to the suggestions quite unintentionally. This can be used effectively to obtain additional hypnotic subjects. Often a sudden shift of attention to some of these individuals with a strong command of "Sleep!" will put them in a trance. Bernheim's custom of hypnotizing patients in the presence of potential subjects may have partly been an attempt to capitalize on this sort of effect.

"DRUG HYPNOSIS"

What we know about the effects of drugs on suggestibility and hypnosis, especially in regard to mechanisms of action, is far from satisfactory. Three things can be said concerning what we do know: 1. Narcotics of all sorts can seemingly increase waking suggestibility if given in proper dosage. 2. It is often much easier to induce hypnosis following administration of these drugs. In some cases the drugs allow induction of hypnosis in individuals who otherwise appear refractory. 3. These same drugs produce a number of other effects when given in similar dosages, such as release of emotional material, breakdown of inhibition, hypermnesia, regressions and amnesia which usually follows recovery from the effects of the drug. These effects may or may not be related to hypnosis, although it too can produce them. Possibly this is because, as Wolberg[203] suggested, hypnosis and drugs partially act upon the same cortical loci. It may be significant in this connection that barbiturates have been shown by Brazier and Finesinger[19] to depress the frontal lobes first, then the motor cortex and occipital lobes.

Nowhere has it been shown conclusively that any drug induces a hypnotic state by itself. Until it can be demonstrated that pharmacological agents can *directly* cause an increase in suggestibility comparable to that which hypnosis can bring in a given individual, it does not seem justifiable to speak of "drug hypnosis" except in a loose sense. At present all we can really say is that certain drugs, more specifically, any strong depressant of the nervous system, can be used as an aid in inducing hypnosis by the Standard method or related techniques. Assuming that it is correct they do not directly produce hypnosis, but do increase waking suggestibility, these drugs could obviously be used to increase the effectiveness of waking suggestions in general. Thus far, with the exception of the induction of hypnosis by suggestions, this has not been common practice, perhaps because there has been a tendency in the past to give preference to hypnotic suggestions over waking suggestions.

The exact action of these drugs on suggestibility is far from clear. If three or more basic processes are involved in the full manifestation of hypnosis, it might be at the level of any or all of them. Eysenck has suggested that the effect may be at the level of ideomotor action, the drugs removing or at least neutralizing the effects of negative, interfering attitudes. Possibly there is an inhibition of the capacity for critical thinking or conscious volition. On the other hand, action at the level of abstract conditioning does not appear to be a likely explanation at present, although this conclusion may be more a reflection of our inadequate information than an actual fact. This leaves the process of dissociation of awareness as the most likely level at which the main action under consideration may take place. Presumably the drugs initiate or lay the ground for a dissociation of awareness. If this is true and if the Braid effect does have an existence apart from suggestion there would be some basis for speaking of "drug hypnosis" in a restricted sense.

Indirectly, narcotics may aid in the production of hypnosis because they produce many of the symptoms of sleep that we suggest to the subject in the verbal part of the induction procedure. As has often been pointed out, *it is not so much what brings about a response that is important in the early induction of hypnosis as the temporal contiguous association of the response with the suggestion that the response is taking place or will take place.* If drugs will produce the suggested symptoms in correct temporal relation to the suggestion, then we can well expect that drugs will help in the production of hypnosis. Attitude and self suggestion, a belief by the subject that the drug will produce or help to produce hypnosis, may also be involved.

What are some of the specific drugs in question and how are they used? In the early history of hypnotism, chloroform and *Cannabis indica* were first used as adjuncts to suggestions. With the development of the barbiturates the shift has been to them, not only because they are safer, but also because they have a rapid action and their effect wears off quickly. Also their effects on the subject can be better graded; this is very important since the optimal range of dosage for obtaining the best results is highly critical. Too small a dose does not sufficiently affect the subject's suggestibility, whereas too large a dose depresses him too much. There is no full agreement upon which drugs to use or upon dosages. The best we can do here is to list the preferences of those who have had considerable experience with this technique.

Schilder and Kauders[151] among earlier experts in the field found that 0.5 to 1 Gm. (maximum 1.5 Gm.) of Medinal was satisfactory. Quicker action can be obtained with 4 to 12 Gm. Of course, with too rapid induction of narcosis you are more likely to miss the critical range, or you may have insufficient time to produce hypnosis.

Stungo[179] uses Evipal sodium, using a 10 per cent solution which he injects intravenously at the rate of 1 cc./min. He finds that 1 to 3 cc. are required. To tell when the subject has reached the proper stage he has him count backward. When the patient begins to show confusion this is taken as the desired stage. Stungo then tries to maintain this level of sedation by continuous injection.

Wolberg[203] recommends 6 to 9 gr. of Sodium Amytal taken orally 30 minutes prior to hypnosis; or 1 to 2 drams of paraldehyde 5 to 10 minutes before induction of the trance. If these methods fail he suggests using intravenous injections of other drugs. He recommends 1 Gm. Sodium Amytal in 30 or 40 cc. of distilled water injected at a rate of 1 to 2 cc./min.; or 7 ½ gr. Sodium Pentothal in 20 cc. distilled water given in a similar manner.

Horsley[82] in an early paper stated that 3 to 20 gr. of Sodium Pentothal injected at the maximum rate of 1 cc/min. as a 2.5 per cent solution was satisfactory. In his book[84] he states that 2 cc. of Sodium Pentothal (presumably a 2.5 per cent solution) is usually sufficient, although with overanxious individuals 4 cc. may be necessary; with resistant patients a full narcotic dose may be called for. In such a case *the stage of confusion* which appears early in the action of the drug should be used to give suggestions. Elsewhere,[83] he also recommends giving orally 3 gr. of Nembutal about 30 minutes prior to the induction of hypnosis. According to him, the choice of drug used depends largely upon whether you are dealing with in- or outpatients. Long-acting drugs like Nembutal are recommended with inpatients, particularly if it is desired to follow hypnosis with a prolonged state of narcosis. With outpatients short-acting drugs like Pentothal are preferred.

In general the barbiturates used intravenously should be injected slowly with the patient counting backward. As soon as he becomes incoherent in counting the injection should be interrupted. The patient should be kept at this level of sedation. Efforts to maintain rapport should be made prior to the injection and should continue during it and throughout the narcosis. It is clear that the use of intravenous procedures has a great advantage over oral sedation in regard to control and regulation of the sedation.

Some investigators have attempted to use nitrous oxide inhalation as an adjunct to the induction of hypnosis. There is little information on this other than that suggestibility can be raised in this way. The oxygen to nitrous oxide ratio as well as the amount of inhalation necessary to bring the subject to a critical stage is rather variable. Further investigations may furnish more definite information. Certainly nitrous oxide inhalation would appear to be an ideal method and particularly suited for the dental office.

The standard practice in using these drugs to induce hypnosis is to give a subanesthetic dose just sufficient to cause a state of confusion and relaxation. Horsley,[83] however, has questioned the adequacy of the backward counting method for determination of the critical depth of narcosis. He prefers to carry on a conversation with the subject throughout the induction procedure taking note of the point where confusion first arises and the nature of the confusion, and recommends using Vogt's fractionation method discussed on page 242. This should be used during the period when the drug effect decreases, especially if a large dose is used, to circumvent the amnesic gap, to afford an intensive training of the subject, and to permit the most efficient use of the drug. The minimal dose of Pentothal combined with the Vogt technique is very effective. He also points out that if the effect of the narcotic becomes too strong, one of the standard analeptics should be used to bring the subject back to the proper level of narcosis.

We might expect that a critical range would also exist during the recovery from the drugs. This does appear to be true, and some hypnotists prefer to induce a deep narcosis in the subject first, then wait until he reaches the proper stage of recovery. Whatever means are used to attain the proper sedation, once it is obtained, the technique usually consists of giving the subject suggestions aimed at inducing hypnosis proper, and testing and deepening the trance as usual. Some hypnotists prefer to begin by producing some easy suggested effects, then they progress to the trance induction proper.

Although those who use drug hypnosis usually claim that it allows the induction of hypnosis in many individuals who are otherwise not susceptible, it has also been claimed that there are cases where the situation is reversed. In my opinion one should always try standard procedures before resorting to the use of drugs, unless of course they have to be employed for other reasons.

There seems to be general agreement that once a deep hypnosis has been obtained by means of drugs, it is possible to induce it thereafter by verbal means alone without difficulty. Horsley[83] states that at least 60 per cent of the refractory cases in whom he had originally induced hypnosis with the help of drugs were successfully hypnotized by standard methods on subsequent occasions.

Some hypnotists do not attempt to induce hypnosis during narcosis, but limit themselves to using it to give the patient postnarcotic suggestions aimed at facilitating the future induction of hypnosis without aid of drugs. The suggestions are that the patient will henceforth be susceptible to hypnosis. It is important to proceed slowly and to give very detailed and specific instructions to the patient. Every feature of the future induction of hypnosis should be covered. If, for instance, one plans to use the Braid technique, the subject should be told that he will be asked later to fixate upon a certain object (which is described to him) and that when he does so his eyes will quickly become tired; they will tend to water, his eyelids will become heavy and his eyes will close. At the same time, it is suggested, his breathing will deepen and become more regular and he will pass into a deep sleep which will deepen until it is at least as deep as that in which he is presently. It is good practice to ask the patient if he has understood these suggestions and to have him repeat them. Sometimes the narcosis is too deep and the subject shows confusion. In such an event one should allow the effects of the drug to wear off a little and repeat the instructions, again asking the patient to repeat them. In any case, it is a good idea to restate the suggestions once or twice as a matter of course. The fractionation technique can be very effectively used here. As soon as the patient is *partially* awake, the technique of induction for which he has been prepared is used on him. After eye-closure has been obtained, one should give additional suggestions that in the future the patient will fall much more quickly and deeply asleep. This procedure may be repeated several times.

The induction of hypnosis with the help of drugs does not always succeed. With too deep a narcosis and with some psychotics a breakdown in communication may be the cause. With other individuals their resistance may be simply too great. According to Wolberg[203] the technique works best when the narcosis is accompanied by a positive transference.

I stated earlier that no drug had been conclusively demonstrated to directly produce a trance state. There exists, however, one pharmacological compound which shows some promise of possibly having such a power. Since 1928 Brotteaux[23] has extensively used a mixture of scopolamine hydrobromide and chloralose which he calls scopochloralose. He claims that even in refractory individuals he is able to readily bring about a condition in no way different from the somnambulistic trance obtained by standard hypnotic procedures. Scopochloralose has been successfully used by an appreciable number of French medical men in a variety of situations and has been the subject of a number of pharmacological studies. The use of this drug appears to have merit and, in my opinion, it might be worth more consideration in America.

The discovery of the drug by Brotteaux was not an accident, for he was seeking such a drug. In doing this he was guided by the assumption that hypnosis is a paralysis or inhibition of the higher centers, suggestions being entirely subconscious phenomena. According to him, deep sleep is the ideal condition for suggestions to have full effectiveness. There are many drugs that can inhibit the higher centers, but unfortunately they also tend to paralyze the subconscious much too readily. Is it possible, asked Brotteaux, to find a combination of drugs that would sufficiently inhibit the higher centers, yet leave the subconscious effectively unaffected over a wide range of dosages? A drug causing natural sleep or something akin to it was indicated. Scopolamine in this respect seemed very satisfactory, particularly since scopolamine-induced sleep shows such phenomena as waxy flexibility, automaticism and increased suggestibility. But this effect is rather limited, and Brotteaux felt that the use of a potentiating agent, if one existed, would be desirable. He believed that chloralose might do just this. Just how he decided on chloralose is hard to tell, seemingly the only clue was that chloralose was said to produce somnambulism. In any case, scopochloralose originated in this manner.

Some limited research has been done in regard to the pharmacodynamical action of the mixture. Baruk and Massaut, for instance, find that ergographic recordings made following the administration of scopochloralose show the same characteristics as those obtained during cataleptic sleep and catalepsy of spontaneous origin as well as that resulting from the effects of bulbocapnine. Unfortunately, our understanding of catalepsy is still very poor, especially in its relation to hypnosis. At present, it appears more closely related to "animal hypnosis" or states of immobilization than to "human hypnosis." On the whole, because of this, Baruk's data are not particularly informative at this stage.

In my opinion, Brotteaux has greatly oversimplified the problems of the nature of hypnosis and suggestibility. As has been shown earlier, they are quite complex. For obvious reasons, Brotteaux has attached great importance to the fact that the two components of scopochloralose can cause "somnambulistic" manifestations. Unfortunately, this is another rather ambiguous term. Brotteaux appears to be using it not to designate a certain trance depth, but in its old medical meaning, synonymous with sleep-walking. We cannot deny that sleep-walking bears some resemblance to deep hypnosis insofar as the ambulatory aspects are concerned. Indeed, our modern use of the expression "somnambulistic state" to describe deep hypnosis is derived from these and other resemblances, but whether or not we are dealing with identical states is a big question. We might come closer to the truth by saying that somnambulistic behavior (old meaning) can be created when hypnosis has been induced, but until the postulated identity is demonstrated the term should be used with extreme caution.

In contrast to the emphasis on the somnambulistic aspect of the drug effect, Brotteaux pretty well ignores the better established pharmaco-dynamic properties of chloralose and scopolamine. In the case of chloralose, these properties appear to be particularly significant. It is known that chloralose has a double action. In small to medium doses it depresses the psychic functions. "Perception," "the will" and "attention" are probably more affected than the imagination and cerebral motor functions. At the same time, chloralose increases the reflex functions through some facilita-tion effect at the spinal level.[74] Unfortunately, details concerning these effects are not readily available. Furthermore, there is some ambiguity of meaning of "perception," "will," "attention" and "imagination." Whether pharmacologists use these terms to mean the same things that psychologists have in mind when using them is unknown. In most instances no adequate study of these aspects has been made. Scopochloralose probably facilitates motor responses at the spinal level and cortically. This is particularly true for the reflexes. We might expect, therefore, that ideomotor action, neuro-motor enhancement and abstract conditioning would benefit. Since other psychic functions are also depressed, interference from these parts should be minimized; the fact that imagination tends to persist is also significant. The result should be increased suggestibility up to and including medium hyp-nosis. There is obviously an alteration of awareness and possibly of volition. The ambiguity and lack of adequate data does not allow anything more specific to be said. But in view of the apparent role played by such alterations in the production of hypnosis, the observation is suggestive, particularly the possible depression of "volition," since the absence of an initial volition-al act seems characteristic of responses to suggestions.

Assuming that all this is correct, just what would be the function of scopolamine in scopochloralose-induced hypnosis? In general, scopolamine is a depressant of the central nervous system, causing drowsiness and a natural sleep-like condition, although its exact role remains hazy. It is said that it produces somnambulistic phenomena,[74] leading us to suspect it has other more specific effects. One possible role it may play is that of a moderat-ing agent for the action of chloralose. In large doses chloralose tends to produce convulsions by inducing hyperexcitability in the lower centers. Whether these convulsions are intrinsic properties of chloralose action or are caused by impurities alone, as suggested by Brotteaux, is not clear.

Scopolamine is believed to affect the peripheral system by paralyzing the interoceptors and causing a depression of the termination of the sensory nerves.[74] If awareness is truly a function of interoceptive discharges,[67] this may be a significant property. In particular, we may have a partial explanation for Brotteaux's observation that amnesia is characteristic of the recovery from scopochloralose action. This is an important point because, contrary to Brotteaux's belief, the evidence does not indicate that amnesia is a criterion of hypnosis. We find it characteristic of scopochloralose narcosis, which would seem to indicate that the latter is not hypnosis in the sense we have been using the term, or, at least, that it is a mixture of hypnosis and something else. There is, however, an alternative. This may be a side-effect independent of the drug-induced hypnotic state, which is quite plausible in the light of what has just been said about the action of scopolamine. Another possibility is that the drug induces a "dissociation" of cortical and subcortical functions analogous to that of curare. Let us now consider how it is used.

Brotteaux recommends using a mixture of 0.75 Gm. chloralose and 0.75 mg. scopolamine hydrobromide for most cases. The required dosage will vary with the subject. Some respond to as little as 0.50 Gm. chloralose and 0.50 mg. scopolamine whereas, in many instances, as much as 1.50 Gm. chloralose and 0.50 mg. scopolamine may be necessary. Individuals vary in their susceptibility to the mixture. Body weight is, of course, an important factor in determining the dose. One way of proceeding when the actual necessary dosage is unknown, according to Brotteaux, is to begin with the smallest dose (0.50 Gm. and 0.50 mg.) then to increase it if insufficient. He also adds that with individuals who are innately suggestible, adding 0.50 to 1.00 mg. of Eserine Sulfate has a strong potentiating effect. Administration may be orally or parenterally.

Brotteaux says that in spite of the size of the doses, neither he nor his colleagues have ever had any ill effects from using the mixture. In his earlier work, Brotteaux had observed that some patients became hyperexcitable and showed tremors. He later found that this was due to impurities in the chloralose, more specifically, parachloralose. Although these side effects never proved deleterious or a hindrance, it seems best to eliminate them if possible, which can be done if very pure chloralose is used.

Brotteaux also remarks that the kind of scopolamine used is very important. It should be extracted either from members of the duboisia or scopolia species and should not be hyoscine.* If these conditions are not satisfied only weak effects will result. According to him, all failures have been traced

*This is a rather puzzling statement inasmuch as in the United States hyoscine and scopolamine are synonymous, and I have not been able to find any evidence that they denote different substances in Europe. It may be that I have misread Brotteaux, or that he meant to write something else.

to either the use of the wrong kind of scopolamine, impure chloralose, an improper ratio of the components or too small a dose.

There are two ways of using scopochloralose. One consists of simply administering it to the subject, then waiting until he falls into a deep sleep, which usually takes about two hours, but may take as long as three and even four hours. As soon as deep sleep is obtained suggestions are given. With a 0.75 Gm./0.75 mg. mixture, Brotteaux says that the effect begins in about 2 minutes. At this time it is possible to give suggestions aimed at inducing somnambulism and it is unnecessary to wait for the full effect of the drugs.

In another method Brotteaux gives the proper dosage to the subject and as soon as he reports or shows symptoms of sleep, he is made to recline and gentle pressure is exerted with the fingers on his eyeballs. At the same time suggestions of hypnotic sleep are given as in the standard method. This has the advantage that it can be employed with doses as small as 0.50 Gm. chloralose and 0.50 mg. scopolamine which normally will not produce the typical somnambulistic state available with the larger doses. This method is very effective with individuals who are cooperative and have some definite suggestibility, and is particularly indicated when the subject cannot be hospitalized. With refractory subjects, the first method is preferred.

In general, the duration of the sleep is proportional to the dosage. On the average one can figure on four to five hours for full recovery with dosages of 0.75 Gm. chloralose and 0.75 mg. scopolamine, or greater. Where the subject cannot be kept under surveillance or where it is necessary for him to be in a normal condition within a shorter time, smaller doses combined with trance-inducing suggestions are indicated, provided other conditions are satisfied. As Brotteaux remarks, once the drug is given, its effects must run their full course (unless counteracted with some other drugs, a point he did not discuss); and although it is possible to wake the subject by suggestions, this may be difficult and in any event he will go back to sleep. Therefore Brotteaux advises suggesting to the subject that he will sleep for 2 or 3 more hours as a terminating suggestion.

NATURAL SLEEP AND HYPNOSIS

Many of the earlier writers on hypnosis (and some in modern times)[192] spoke of natural sleep being converted or passing into the hypnotic state. Others spoke of giving suggestions directly to the sleeping individual who, presumably, remained asleep. The technique has been particularly recommended for children, although no experimental data are available.

Suggestions can be given effectively to an individual who is initially asleep. The question is what is the real condition of the individual at the time the suggestion takes effect? Furthermore, even if suggestions can be given and be effective when the subject is asleep, we must still inquire whether or not sleep can be converted into hypnosis. Our main reason for answering these questions negatively comes from Hull[85] who presents arguments that when a suggestion is given to a sleeper and it is effective, he always wakes up to some degree and then passes into a hypnotic state. Hull goes on to say that sleep is never converted directly into hypnosis, nor are suggestions ever effective if natural sleep is present. Data reported by Barker and Burgwin[6] lend some support to this position.

The method consists of speaking to the sleeping person in a soft whispered monotone so as not to awaken him. He is told something like: "Sleep. Remain deep asleep. You are sleeping deeply but you can hear me. You will not wake up, but you will listen to what I tell you. You are comfortable. My voice does not bother or disturb you. You are going deeper asleep, deeper all the time. But you keep hearing me. You can understand everything I tell you although you are going more deeply asleep all the time. You will not wake up until I tell you. Remain deep asleep. You hear everything I say. You will now raise your hand to show me that you can hear me. You are now raising your hand, but you will remain deep asleep." After the subject has responded to a few simple suggestions, you can tell him that even though you are going to speak louder, he will remain deep asleep. Continue to suggest sleep, and so on, at the same time raising your voice gradually until you speak normally. After this you can proceed with whatever suggestions you want to give.

COLOR CONTRAST METHOD

The following method, recently described by Stokvis,[177] is a rather ingenious and interesting technique which may prove valuable. A piece of plain gray cardboard 14 x 23 cm. is used and on it two strips of paper 8 x 3.2 cm. are pasted parallel to each other with a space of 5 mm. between them. One strip, pasted on the right, should be light blue, the one on the left light yellow. Both should have a dull finish (fig. 24), and Stokvis recommends rounding the bottom right hand corner where the subject will hold the board.

The subject lying on a couch is given the apparatus to hold at arm's length (if he has normal eyesight). The couch should be in such a position that the light falls on the strips. The subject is requested to look at the slit between the two strips without interruption. While he is doing this, Stokvis says:

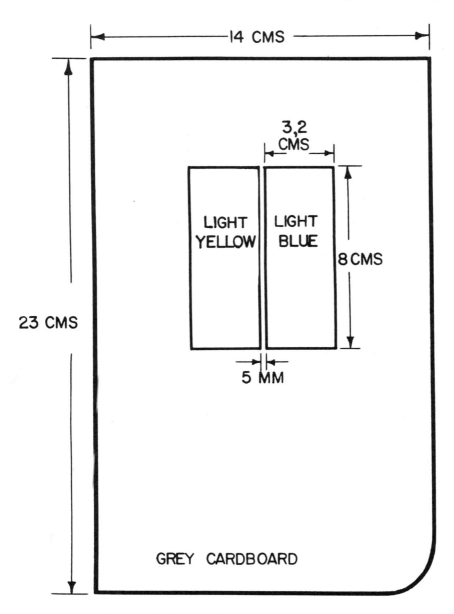

FIG. 24. Fixation target for the color contrast method.

. . .he is asked what exactly he sees there. He will naturally reply "A piece of grey cardboard on which a yellow strip is pasted on the left, and a blue one on the right of it, with a grey slit between." The patient* is told that, as he continues to watch the picture, especially the slit, he will soon observe some additional colours appearing. These chromatic phenomena, as a general rule, will be observed physiologically by any normal person, including the so-called "red-green dichromatics," and by all "anomalous trichromatics"; they consist in appearance of the respective complementary colours along the outside edges of the yellow and blue strips.

"When you have seen the colour phenomena appear, that will be proof that the hypnotic state is going to set in," I tell the patient. "In fact the appearance of the colours is the first sign of the effect of the hypnotic influence; it is a kind of fatigue phenomenon of the eyes," I assure him.

"In the same way as you have seen these colour phenomena, you will observe some other signs of the approaching hypnotic state. Do keep looking at the slit; then you will soon see that the inner edge of the blue strip, that is to say, the edge bordering on the slit, becomes more intensely blue, while the rest of the blue strip will be a much duller shade. In precisely the same manner you will notice that the part of the yellow immediately bordering on the grey slit becomes more intensely yellow, while the rest of the yellow strip becomes more faintly yellow. Just keep watching sharply. . .keep looking fixedly at the slit. . .look very closely; you will see something else happen as well. You will also see colours appear in the slit; you will see a yellow border appear along the edge of the blue strip, and a blue border along the edge of the yellow strip. These two newly made colours will touch at about the centre of the slit; now and then they will overlap; they may even disappear for a moment or two; perhaps because your consciousness is now beginning to waver, owing to the hypnotic condition, which is on the point of setting in." I continue in this (purposely longwinded) strain.

Although the patient may perhaps feel somewhat skeptical at first toward this method of treatment, there is no doubt that by this time he will have abandoned this attitude; for he now sees before his eyes, point for point, that what is being told to him is also actually happening, with the result that his confidence in the physician will increase correspondingly.

"You remember what I told you just now" (I continue very softly and monotonously) "that, as you observed the colour phenomena, you will find that your eyelids are getting heavier and heavier. . .still heavier all the time. . .you will feel that you are getting more and more tired. . .tired and weary. . .and you will soon get so tired that you would just love to shut your eyes. When you feel like that don't resist. . .don't resist. . .you may close your eyes."

From here on, Stokvis' technique does not differ from others'. Note that he *does not mention sleep* anywhere in his procedure, even when dehypnotizing the subject. Also right after the subject's eyes have closed, he is instructed to *breathe deeply and regularly*.

Clearly, this procedure also belongs under the topic of induction of hypnosis without sleep suggestions. Comments Stokvis made indicate that it is apparently well suited for negative subjects. Although it does not usually

---

*The term "patient" is used here rather than "subject" because Stokvis is primarily concerned with therapy.

bring about a very deep hypnosis, there are many situations in therapy where this is not essential. Also, the possibilities of deepening the trance after induction are often quite good. Then too, after one method of hypnotization has been successful, other methods more suited for inducing a deep trance can often be substituted.

The reader should analyze this procedure in terms of the remarks that have been made regarding the mechanism of trance induction. This method makes a very interesting use of many of the facts and principles discussed earlier.

A method which bears some similarity to the color contrast method has been described by Powers.[140] He says the hypnotist should use a pencil flashlight and aim its light into one of the subject's eyes, asking him to concentrate his gaze upon the light until his eyes become heavy with fatigue. The hypnotist also says that he will count to five, at which time the subject will close his eyes and go into a deep trance. A slow count to five is given. If the subject has not closed his eyes by then, he is encouraged to close them at his convenience. Then it is suggested to him that he will soon see a red spot inside the one eye exposed to the light. He is asked to look for it and to report as soon as he notices it. This is repeated a number of times. As soon as the subject reports seeing the spot, it is suggested that it will disappear in a flash and that in its place a purple spot will appear. If the subject responds to this suggestion other color changes can be suggested. As the subject watches for the changes, relaxation is suggested as well as the fact that the subject will soon be in a deep hypnosis. From there on the technique is one of deepening hypnosis.

This technique is not as subtle as Stokvis' and is not likely to work too well with individuals who have some elementary knowledge of sensory phenomena.

The principle involved here, that of using and suggesting a real sensory or perceptual effect concerning which the subject is naive, then suggesting a very similar effect which normally would not occur, appears promising. Another approach is to have the subject fixate on a ground glass plate and try to visualize some simple geometrical design on it, which can be merely a colored spot. Unknown to the subject, a faint image of the suggested object is projected on the back of the screen, first with a subthreshold intensity raised until the subject reports a faint image. At the same time suggestions are given that the subject will see the image, is seeing it, etc. It is then suggested that the screen is becoming blank again. Following this the hypnotist suggests that the subject try to visualize the same object more clearly. This time the image is projected a little brighter. This can be repeated a third time, or the next step may be undertaken, that is either making some color changes in the same object, or visualizing a different object. This time, however, when a stronger image is suggested, a subthreshold brightness is used. If the subject reports seeing something you should try to get him to visualize the image more clearly by giving suggestions. In any case a third trial is made without the projector. If this is successful, as it normally will be, the subject is then told to hold the image in his mind and that in a few moments it will begin to fade very slowly and that as it does he will become very sleepy and that when he ceases to see the image he will be sound asleep.

I once knew a hypnotist who used a simple variation of the above procedure. After the subject's eyes were closed either by a command or suggestion, suggestions were given to deepen the trance. At this point he would begin to gradually dim the light in the room, all the time suggesting increasing darkness in association with increasing sleep.

These methods are well worth trying on subjects who are difficult to hypnotize. The reader should be warned, however, that they are not as simple as they may seem and that they require considerable skill. The main problem is to prevent the subject from suspecting the true nature of his initial "hallucinations."

DEPTH HYPNOSIS AND ITS INDUCTION

Although the lesser depths of hypnosis can be very useful in many cases, most hypnotists usually hope and aim to produce a deep to a very deep state of hypnosis in their subjects. There are situations when such a trance is necessary. Most hypnotists agree that deep hypnosis is far too often impossible to attain. Some investigators find only 5 per cent of their subjects reach a deep trance, and no investigator has reported better than 29 per cent. When averaged the reported figures lead to a mean of 20 per cent, which is not very encouraging!

Actually, these figures are not too accurate for a number of reasons. First, nothing is said in the reports regarding *stability* of the depth of hypnosis. This is a point about which Erickson[44] has justifiably been very emphatic. Once a subject has reached a given trance depth he will usually tend to drift away from it, generally toward the lighter stages. Thus it is rather meaningless to state that X per cent of subjects will attain deep hypnosis, if they cannot be kept at that level. Second, "deep hypnosis" and "somnambulism" tend to denote a condition in which the lower limit is fairly well established, but the upper limit seems to extend nebulously upward. Erickson was one of the first to point out that hypnosis could be made much deeper than the available scales indicated, and he spoke of deep hypnosis as consisting of a somnambulistic and a stuporous phase. (This last is what LeCron and Bordeaux have referred to as the plenary trance.) Actually, I see no reason why we should stop there, except that further subdividing defies qualitative descriptions. Doust's oximetric technique may help to clarify this situation. Studies such as those of Barker and Burgwin[6] lend support to the statement that a stuporous state can be produced. Whether hypersuggestibility is still higher in this condition is another matter. Erickson states that control of body functions and other effects usually produced with difficulty through suggestions are best obtained in this state. However, this does not necessarily mean that increased suggestibility is responsible. Instead it may be a question of the psychic level at which the subject is able to function.

Failure to recognize the above has led many hypnotists to overestimate the overall quality of the trance reached by their subjects. This is largely compensated for by the fact that the percentage figures referred to are underestimations of the true state of affairs. Many of these figures were determined on the basis of one trial, generally using some standard technique of trance induction. Furthermore, the time the hypnotist devoted to each subject was limited and attempts to deepen the trance state were minimal. On the basis of my own experience, I would claim that success in producing any given depth of hypnosis depends very much upon choosing the proper technique for each subject and upon the amount of time devoted to the process. Other hypnotists concur with this. Erickson, who claims to have hypnotized over 3500 individuals, sums up the situation well by stating that although one of his subjects had reached a profound trance on the first induction in less than 30 seconds, he had also had one who had required 300 hours of systematic work before the first signs of any trance were produced! On the basis of these considerations, I would estimate that the percentage of people who can reach a relatively stable deep trance may be as high as 70 to 80 per cent, and at least 50 per cent or better—provided of course that hypnotizing is made an individual problem and the proper amount of time is allowed.

We shall now proceed to the exposition of depth hypnosis. For this I shall closely follow Erickson's own exposition.[44]

According to Erickson, hypnosis is a highly individualistic process because it is a function of intrapersonal (or intrapsychic) relationships and of interpersonal relationships, themselves contingent and dependent upon the former. Every individual has a unique personality, and his behavior, including that in the trance inducing situation, is a function of his personality, the time, the situation and the purposes which are served. Thus, it is invalid to assume that under identical conditions of administration, identical suggestions must invariably yield identical responses in different subjects or in the same subject at different times.

Intrapsychic factors are considered very important by Erickson, who maintains that far too much weight has been placed upon external factors. Instead the intrapsychic behavior of the subject should be primarily employed. Thus, sensory fixation by means of crystal balls, metronomes and the like is of secondary importance. At best, they are incidental aids to initiate behavior, but do not develop it. Utilization of the subject's behavior is the key to successful hypnosis. He points out that superior trance induction can be obtained if the subject visualizes such apparatus as a crystal ball or a pendulum instead of seeing a real one. The reason for this is that the subject uses actual capacities and does not have to adjust to nonessentials in the external environment. Instead, the imaginary apparatus and the effects it produces adjust themselves to the needs of the subject. This use of imaginary devices in the induction of hypnosis appears also to facilitate the development of similar and related hypnotic behavior that is more complex.

Erickson also considers the temporal factor of great importance in the production of hypnosis and hypnotic behavior. The hypnotic subject, he remarks, is no different from other persons in possessing a latency or reaction time. Why expect the hypnotized person to go through a complete physiological and psychological reorientation instantaneously, and to perform the most complex behavior when this is impossible in the waking state? Conceivably hypnosis might speed up the process, however some latency would still have to be present because the nervous system, inherently, has a specific limiting latency which is highly variable for suggestions. It differs between individuals for the same suggestions, as well as with the same individual for different suggestions and for the same suggestion at different times.

Furthermore, one should make a distinction between the *trance induction* process itself and *trance utilization*. Not only is time required for the psychophysiological reorganization leading to the full trance state, but after this has been established, each suggestion given to the subject must presumably involve a similar reorganization of varying degrees with its own latency period. There is no necessary relation between rate of induction and subsequent performance because trance induction and trance utilization are two different types of behavior. It is important to recognize that trance utilization is less a function of the trance inducing procedure and more a function of whatever behavioral responses arise out of the trance state and subsequent to it. Erickson remarks that when psychophysiological reorganization is not allowed the subject's behavior seems to become mere role-playing, a fact which has led to much controversy in the interpretation of hypnotic phenomena.

This matter of reorganization is important in another way. He points out that if it is not sufficient, the subject may shift to a lighter trance state in spite of having attained a deep one with apparent ease. This, he says, is an attempt of the subject to secure the aid of conscious mental processes to assure adequate functioning. Furthermore, he remarks that ease in hypnotizing may be an indication that the subject needs more time for reorientation before a full and sustained response can take place.

Time is not the only factor which must be taken into consideration; the situation itself may have to be manipulated. As an example, Erickson cites the case of an otherwise excellent subject who could not perform satisfactorily unless he was in a laboratory setting. However, it was entirely all right if this setting was hallucinated. The possibility of substituting hallucinations for real events as part of the instrumentality for the induction of hypnosis and the production of hypnotic phenomena appears to be of considerable generality.

We have mentioned the matter of training individuals to be good subjects. For a long time it has been believed that the more a subject is used in hypnotic experiments, the better subject he usually becomes, which has often been misinterpreted as an indication that repeated hypnosis had deleterious effects upon the subject's "will" and other faculties. It has long since been decided that there is no basis for such fears and that whatever mechanism was involved in the subject's improvement ought to be sought elsewhere. Erickson finds that subjects who have experienced hypnosis many times over a long period of time, and who have also produced a great variety of hypnotic phenomena, are by far the better subjects. This phenomenon he sees as a learning process in which the subject learns to operate with increasing effectiveness in the hypnotic state. Subjects who lack such experience can be systematically taught various kinds of hypnotic behavior. Unfortunately, he does not give a *modus operandi* for this. On the basis of an example which he discusses, it would appear that the technique is to analyze the more complex desired effect into simpler elements of behavior which the subject is made to produce first individually, then later in combination. Thus, anesthesia can be decomposed into a dissociation of body parts and a disregard of stimuli. The subject can be given a foundation for this by having him experience automatic writing and negative visual hallucinations, respectively.

Up to this point we have been discussing various aspects of hypnosis which play important roles in the determination of the hypnotic state as well as the hypnotic behavior of the subject, but we have not said much concerning deep hypnosis itself as yet. According to Erickson, "*deep hypnosis is that level of hypnosis that permits the subject to function adequately and directly at an unconscious level of awareness without interference by the conscious mind.*"

As he explains it, it would appear that in deep hypnosis the unconscious as controlled and directed by the hypnotist holds sway over reality testing. The subject behaves only in terms of the reality which exists in the hypnotic situation for his unconscious. This is an important point because the real world is not the subject's reality, and it possesses no intrinsic value for him. The subject need not deal with it, which is in contrast to light hypnosis. In spite of this, the reality of the deep trance has certain restrictions, one of which is that it must agree with the basic needs and structure of the subject's total personality. Erickson thus emphasizes the importance of respecting the subject as an individual, even though he may be in deep hypnosis.

It was remarked earlier that Erickson classifies the deep trance as somnambulistic or stuporous. According to him the somnambulistic subject fully participates in the hypnotic situation, interacting freely and adequately with his environment, real and imaginary, very much as a nonhypnotized person would with his real surroundings. To all intents and purposes, this type of subject behaves as if he were awake.* The well-trained somnambulistic subject is one who relies entirely upon his unconscious response patterns, while passivity, implying psychological and physiologic retardation, underlies the stuporous trance. The stuporous subject shows neither spontaneity nor initiative, self-perception seems to be lacking, and he perseverates in the production of incomplete responses.

Erickson believes that there are six major aspects which must be considered in connection with the induction of deep hypnosis because they are most likely to give rise to problems:

1. *Trance induction must be distinguished from trance utilization.*

2. *Trance behavior must be distinguished from ordinary conscious behavior.*

3. *All hypnotic procedure must be oriented about the subject.* The subject's psychological needs must *all* be met as fully as possible in the trance. Thus, whatever hypnotic work is required of the subject should be adapted to him, and not the converse.

4. *The need for protection of the subject must be recognized.* The subject has a strong need for protection against infringement of his rights and privacy

---

*This is not a contradiction of what was stated earlier regarding the symptoms of hypnosis as we are speaking now of *trained* hypnotic subjects and not of subjects who have just attained the hypnotic state for the first time.

in what appears to him as a very vulnerable position. It is essential that the subject should be made to feel protected if his full participation in the hypnotic work is to be secured.

5. *All of the subject's specific responses as well as his spontaneous behavior during trance induction should be utilized.* The role of the hypnotist should be minimized and that of the subject enlarged. What the hypnotist does should only serve to facilitate trance induction. The subject, on the other hand, should be allowed freedom of action, the hypnotist adapting his technique to the behavioral activities of the subject, that is, he should incorporate and make use of them for the induction itself. Even resistance of the subject should be so treated. In general, no matter what behavior is shown by the subject, it should be accepted by the hypnotist and used to develop further responsive behavior. One should never attempt to correct or alter the subject's behavior or force other responses on him (see also page 395 ff.).

6. *Each progressive step of trance induction should be based upon actual successful performances by the subject.* These may arise as a result of the hypnotic situation, or belong to the subject's everyday experiences, thus emphasizing the utilization of behavior that can be interpreted as a successful response of the subject. This may often tax the hypnotist's ingenuity, but as Erickson points out, even absence of a response can often be turned into an accomplishment.

These two last aspects are very important and are of general application. Thus if you re-examine the instructions on the production of hypnosis without the mention of sleep, particularly the sensorimotor method, you will see that the methodology is essentially centered about points 5 and 6. You will also find other instances of the application of these two "principles" in many other techniques of induction. Wolberg's hand levitation method is a good example of this, as is Stokvis' color contrast technique.

Erickson's *modus operandi* for the production and use of the deep trance state is nicely and concisely described in the following quote taken from one of his case histories.[48] There are three separate but overlapping steps.

1. *The development of a deep trance state.* Approximately twenty minutes were spent in giving her instructions to sleep deeply, soundly, continuously and more and more profoundly. This was done to insure a deep trance rigidly established by long continuance so that it might not easily be disturbed or disrupted.

2. *The development of a stuporous trance state.* Approximately twenty minutes were spent suggesting a profoundly stuporous state, of stuporous absorption in "just sleeping without interests, desires, feeling," and "thinking, sensing, feeling nothing but a stuporous lethargic sleep in a timeless, endless way." The purpose of this was to establish firmly an extremely passive receptive yielding mental state and attitude.

3. *The development of a somnambulistic state.* Approximately fifteen minutes more were

spent suggesting that the subject, now in a profound stuporous trance, remain so but at the same time recover slowly and gradually her ability to think, to move, to feel and to respond as if she were awake but only to that exact degree required by whatever instructions she must be given. Thus she was permitted to become passively responsive but only within the hypnotic situation.

Erickson adds that, "In such a state the subject presents very much the behavior of a person heavily drugged but not yet fully in the narcotized state and has been so described by subjects who have experienced both conditions."

In addition to this general procedure and the principles listed earlier, Erickson[44] developed four specialized techniques of trance induction which he claims are particularly suited for producing deep trance. We shall now describe each of these briefly, using his nomenclature.

1. *Method of Confusion.* The key to this technique is the giving of suggestions and instructions which literally confuse the subject by calling for a constant reorientation on his part. It essentially consists of the use of a rapid sequence of suggestions forcing him to continuously shift from one task or idea to another which is often just the opposite, thereby creating increasing uncertainty regarding what is expected of him.

The rationale is apparently threefold: First, the subject is led to respond by an attempt to accommodate himself to the confusion. Unwitting as it may be, this response is most important since getting the subject to respond in any fashion leads to eventual enhancement of suggestibilty. Second, in his effort to cooperate, the subject is forced to intensely concentrate upon the suggestions in order to carry out the instructions correctly. Lastly, if the confusion is great enough, the subject feels a need to escape from it; if the hypnotist times himself properly and offers the subject a positive suggestion to which he can respond, the pressure of the need to escape the confusion will give the act of fully accepting the suggestion a high positive valence. In the end the lethargy of deep hypnosis itself becomes the ultimate escape.

The procedure used here is not an easy one. Its success depends upon the hypnotist's ability to convincingly deliver what amounts to suggestions in the form of double-talk. The hypnotist must make contradictory statements in such a way that the subject feels something very meaningful and precise is being said to him, and has insufficient time to establish the illogical character of the suggestions. As an example, Erickson describes how one would proceed in regard to hand levitation. He would emphatically suggest levitation of the right hand and concurrent immobility of the left hand. This is immediately followed by suggestions of levitation of the left hand and immobility of the right hand. Upon this immobility of both hands is suggested, and is followed by suggestions that one hand is lifting while the other is pressing down. The hypnotist then returns to the initial suggestion. It is essential that these suggestions be given rapidly, with insistence and confidence.

According to him the method works well with highly intelligent subjects who are interested in the hypnotic process and with those who, in spite of having an unconscious desire to be hypnotized, are consciously unwilling.

LeCron[106] described a variation which he claims to be equally effective in spite of being simpler and quicker. The subject is first asked to slowly count backward aloud from 100 and to pay a minimum of attention to what the hypnotist says while he counts. After the subject has begun counting the hypnotist starts giving suggestions of relaxation, heaviness of the eyelids and eye closure. He adds that before the subject reaches 0 he will be sound asleep. As the subject continues, arm levitation is suggested. Presently he becomes confused and when this happens, the hypnotist tells him that he will lose track of his count by the time he has called 10 more numbers. If the subject is standing up this technique can be further enhanced by facing him and taking hold of his shoulders, gently imparting a circular sway to his body.

The confusion technique is not only useful in inducing the trance state, but can also be employed to bring about various hypnotic phenomena, as for instance, regressions (chapter 13).

2. *Method of Rehearsing.* Briefly, the method involves picking a response or form of behavior shown by the subject which seems likely to develop well and having him rehearse it mentally in various ways. Then he is asked to repeat the response in actuality. As an example Erickson speaks of a subject who seems to be a potentially good one, but who responds poorly to hypnosis. In testing him it is observed that he makes abortive responses to suggestions of automatic writing. Any partial, tentative response is considered successful by Erickson and is taken as a likely response for rehearsal. By means of suggestions the subject is led to mentally rehearse what must have occurred to bring about his success, then he is requested to rehearse how it would be done using various kinds of writing material and implements. This is followed by actual performance of the different variations which were rehearsed, and is succeeded by additional rehearsals and actual performances in which new elements such as various hallucinated writing materials and instruments are introduced. (New words, letters, sentences, drawings might also be suggested.) As this sequence of events progresses, an increasingly deeper hypnosis develops. One should not limit the procedure to a single hypnotic behavior, but should use as many as possible.

This technique has many refinements and extensions. Erickson gives an excellent example of how it can be employed to overcome expected resistance to a specific suggestion. For details the reader should refer to the appropriate chapter in LeCron.[106]

The method can also be used to deepen the subject's trance once it is established. Erickson uses a variation of having the subject repeatedly experience a dream (initially spontaneous or induced) or a fantasy* in different guises which are continuously changed. He adds that one should preferably make use of dreams and fantasies which have a pleasant character. If this is not possible, he says that one can often limit the extent of the unpleasant effect by implanting an artificial complex.

Another variation is to have the subject visualize himself carrying out some hypnotic performance step by step in detail, adding to this additional sensory images. This can be used very effectively *before* the actual trance induction or prior to the specific utilization of the trance and may be related to Stembo's proe-hypnotic technique (page 350). Erickson points out that as a means of planning future hypnotic work with the subject's participation it is a very valuable technique since it enables the hypnotist to meet the subject's needs more satisfactorily and often permits correction of errors and oversights.

According to its originator, this method is suitable for both the induction of hypnosis and the production of hypnotic phenomena. The reader might be interested in comparing it with Kline's method (page 246).

3. *Method of Multiple-Dissociation*. Erickson briefly states that this method consists of the repetitious use of dissociation phenomena, either of artificial or spontaneous origin, to create a "psychological momentum" to which the subject readily yields. That is, if you can lead the subject to have such experiences, they are often so compelling that he becomes totally absorbed in them, and a deep trance readily ensues. The induction of dissociated phenomena may start with a perfectly normal everyday event such as having the subject vividly recall some experience.† If this is successful, one may suggest the recall of similar experiences.

Erickson states that this method is used for inducing, maintaining and utilizing deep trances.

4. *The Posthypnotic Technique.* In this technique Erickson makes logical

*He says fantasies are less preferable.

†A light trance usually facilitates this considerably. Crystal gazing can also often be taught to light trance subjects and can then be used for subsequent deepening of the trance or for certain effects in therapy. The important point is that, because the method is adaptable to a light trance, it is eminently suited for deepening the hypnosis.

and ingenious use of the fact that a spontaneous trance seems to develop whenever a posthypnotic act is carried out. The method is simply to give the subject a simple, unobtrusive posthypnotic suggestion. As soon as it is initiated, the hypnotist can deepen the associated spontaneous trance. The process is repeated over and over, the trance being increasingly deepened each time. The reader should compare this with our earlier discussion of the method of fractionation (page 242).

This procedure seems particularly suited to subjects who enter only a light trance when induction is attempted. (Contrary to the beliefs of many people, simple posthypnotic phenomena can be readily produced with a relatively light trance.) Because of the lightness of trance or the fact that the procedure may have to be used to circumvent resistance, the unobtrusive character of the suggestion, of the signal used and of the act is very important. Erickson suggests that the required act be some casual activity rather than an attention-compelling overt behavior. He proposes, for instance, watching someone light his cigarette, noting what happens to the match when tossed toward the waste basket. Or again, it might be noticing that an object on a table is about so-many inches from its border. The signal can be anything. Erickson usually tells his subject that when he takes hold of his wrist and moves his arm in a certain manner (he demonstrates at the same time), this will be the signal for him "to do something." Here, however, in contrast to the usual posthypnotic suggestion, Erickson tries not to be too specific about the expected response, allowing the subject some leeway in his subsequent action. Also, when a similar technique is used in another connection, it permits the hypnotist to make use of a response which is likely to occur spontaneously anyway, and in any event, decreases the possibility of the subject's failing to carry out the suggestion, consequently building up a negative attitude.

For these reasons he gives the subject a choice of possible responses. He continues his instructions by telling the subject that *perhaps* the signal will be for him to move his other hand, or maybe to turn his head, or again to sleep more soundly. In any event, he impresses upon the subject that the latter will become ready to carry out the suggestion whenever the signal occurs.

Erickson claims that, interestingly enough, although the subject takes the signal to apply only to the immediate situation, it usually carries over to much later dates when the signal may often bring about a deep hypnosis. I agree with him that there is often a carry-over of a posthypnotic signal; however, I seriously question that this is possible if the subject has *clearly* understood that this effect was to be limited to a specific interval of time.

9

The Induction of Hypnosis
III. Miscellaneous Methods

THREE CLASSICAL METHODS

MESMERISM OR THE MAGNETIC METHOD

MESMERISM, like psychoanalysis, describes a theory, a set of phenomena, and a form of therapy. Hypnotism is primarily a group of phenomena, and although it can include the phenomena of mesmerism, it is questionable whether all of the results reported by Mesmer and his students were true hypnotic manifestations. For instance, for Mesmer, a successful treatment by animal magnetism ended in what he called the "crisis," a convulsive attack often accompanied by crying and laughing which looked every bit like its hysteric counterparts. Looking back, one cannot help concluding that hysteria must have played a large part in some of Mesmer's experiences.

The germ of mesmerism is to be found in his doctoral dissertation in which he expounded upon the influence of emanations from heavenly bodies upon the health of human beings. Not long after writing this, he was introduced to the work of a priest who was said to obtain miraculous effects in the art of healing by exposing his patients to the influence of a magnet. Whether Mesmer originally identified the physical magnetism inherent in the magnet as the source of organic influence is not entirely clear. However, it is certain that he later decided that there were two sources of influence in magnets: the physical magnetism which he called "mineral magnetism" and another, just as subtle emanation, having analogous properties which he named "animal magnetism" and identified with the universal emanation he had postulated in his dissertation. Accordingly, animal magnetism had, among others, the following properties: it can be communicated to animate and inanimate bodies; it can be concentrated or diffused by such bodies; it can act at a distance; it is reflected by mirrors; it is communicated, propagated, and increased by sound; it can be accumulated in bodies; and it has two polarities* which produce opposite effects and which can decrease or destroy each other's effects.

Mesmer's interest in animal magnetism was solely in terms of its curative powers. Ill health was apparently the result of an excess or a deficiency of animal magnetism in the patient as a whole, or in specific parts of his body. The rationale of the treatment was therefore to give, remove or redistribute the animal magnetism in the patient.

Later magnetizers evolved these notions into a rather impressive body of pseudo-scientific knowledge which is best summarized in Durville's works [41] and extensively treated by Barety. [5] Eventually negative or positive animal magnetism came to be associated with every known physical phenomenon and object. Furthermore, it became capable of acting as a transmission medium for various properties characteristic of the objects from which it came. For instance, various drug effects were said to be transported at a distance by their animal magnetism. Human thought and the will could also affect it or be carried by it. Some people, called "sensitives," were said to be able to see animal magnetism as a luminous emanation, the "aura" surrounding individuals and objects. The color, intensity, and other aspects of this "aura" were said to be specific for each individual, his thoughts, emotions, etc. As this doctrine was elaborated, it was used to account for various purported supranormal phenomena. For instance, phantasms or "astral projections" were nothing else than exteriorized animal magnetism or that which had become separated from its owner's body by death. Of course, animal magnetism offered an excellent medium for the communication of thoughts. One of the most spectacular applications of the doctrine was made by de Rochas, a follower of the Salpêtrière school. He claimed to have found proof that under hypnosis one could extract or project the subject's sensory capacities with his animal magnetism and by impregnating objects with the latter, transfer these capacities to the object. Anything done to the object was felt, so he claimed, by the subject, no matter how far apart they were. Furthermore, alterations of the object would become duplicated in the subject. In particular, if the object was a photograph or drawing of the subject, or a figurine, it became possible to strictly localize these effects on the subject's body. Thus the voodoo doll came to be considered a scientific reality in certain circles. Similarly, de Rochas claimed that the motoric

---

*Mesmer and later mesmerists, or "magnetizers" as they are often called, appear to have thought not only in terms of two polarities, but actually of two kinds of magnetisms. This notion plays an important part in mesmeric theories and practice.

capacities of the subject could also be "exteriorized" via his animal magnetism and made to act upon objects, thereby giving rise to telekinetic phenomena.

This is only a very brief and very incomplete account of the doctrine of animal magnetism and its various ramifications. It is an extremely fascinating topic if for no other reason than that it represents one of the most complete misinterpretations of facts under the guise of science. It shows how suggestibility and the wish to believe can lead to a fantastic adulteration of data.

One of the clearest expositions of Mesmer's technique was given by his student, Deleuze. His description as quoted by Binet and Féré[15] follows:

Have the patient seat himself as comfortably as possible. Face him sitting yourself on a seat slightly higher than his, and in such a way that his knees be between yours and your feet be next to his. Instruct him to be passive, not to think about anything, not to distract himself by examining the effects he may feel, not to have any fear, to be confident, and not to worry or be discouraged if the action of the magnetism causes him some temporary pains.

Following a few moments of silent meditation on your part, take hold of his thumbs between your two fingers, in such a way that the inside of your thumbs touch the inside of his and fixate your eyes on him. You will remain two to five minutes in this position or until you feel that the temperature of your and his thumbs have become the same.

This done, take your hands away by moving them apart to the right and to the left, and turning them in such a way that their inside surface be on the outside, at the same time lifting them to the level of the head. Then you will place them upon the two shoulders, allowing them there about a minute, following which you bring them back along the arms to the end of the fingers, touching lightly. Repeat these passes five or six times, always turning your hands and taking them away a little from the body when coming up again. Next, you place your hands above the head. Hold them there a moment, then carry them downward, passing in front of the face a couple of inches away, until the pit of the stomach is reached. There you stop again for about two minutes, placing your thumbs upon the pit of the stomach, and the other fingers below the ribs. Then you go downward slowly the length of the body to the knees. Repeat this process for the greater part of the session. Sometimes you should come close to the patient in such a way as to place your hands behind his shoulders, then moving them slowly down the length of the spine and, from there over the hips and along the thigh, to the knee and even the feet.

When you wish to terminate the session, you will take great care to *attract* toward the end of the feet, by continuing your passes beyond these extremities, shaking your fingers after each pass. Finally, you will make in front of the face, and even over the chest, a few crosswise passes, at a distance of three or four inches.

It is essential to magnetize always by going downward from the head to the extremities, and never by going up in the opposite direction.

The downward passes are magnetic, that is, are accompanied by the intention of the magnetizer. Upward passes are not.

When the magnetizer acts upon the magnetized person, one says that they are in *rapport*, that is, there is acquired a peculiar state of affairs that is such as to allow the magnetizer to exercise an influence upon the magnetized person, or again, that effects between them a communication of the vital principles.

Once rapport is well established, the magnetic influence is renewed in the subsequent sessions at the moment one begins to magnetize.

This procedure has many variations but in essence they are no different. The mesmerists firmly believed that the state they provoked in this way resulted from transmission and concentration of animal magnetism. The eyes and finger tips were said to be particularly powerful emitters, and the hands were particularly capable of directing and controlling it through the process of passes discussed later (page 295). There are many fascinating aspects of this subject, of which this description represents only one phase. Inasmuch as it appears today to be based upon false premises and is, in any case, obsolete, we shall not go into greater detail.

BRAIDISM

Deleuze's instructions to look the patient in the eyes strongly brings to mind Braid's method, which was conceived as a result of attending a demonstration by Lafontaine, a contemporary of Deleuze and also a mesmerist. Braid's reasoning was straightforward: Assuming that there was no such thing as animal magnetism the effects which he saw Lafontaine produce had to result from the situation as a whole or from some aspect of it. Braid eliminated all but the visual fixation required of the subjects and found from the very first that his guess was correct, or so it seemed for a long time. Let us look at Braid's own account.[18]

> Take any bright object (I generally use my lancet case) between the thumb and forefinger and middle fingers of the left hand; hold it from about eight to fifteen inches from the eyes, at such position above the forehead as may be necessary to produce the greatest strain upon the eyes and eyelids, and enable the patient to maintain a steady fixed stare on the object. The patient must be made to understand that he is to keep the eyes steadily fixed on the object, and the mind riveted on the idea of the object. It will be observed, that owing to the consensual adjustment of the eyes, the pupils will be at first contracted: they will shortly begin to dilate, and after they have done so to a considerable extent, and have assumed a wavy motion, if the fore and middle fingers of the right hand, extended and a little separated, are carried from the object towards the eyes, most probably the eyelids will close involuntarily, with a vibratory motion. If this is not the case, or the patient allows the *eyeballs* to *move*, desire him to begin anew, giving him to understand that he is to allow the eyelids to close when the fingers are again carried towards the eyes, but that the *eyeballs must be kept fixed in the same position*, and the *mind riveted to the one idea of the object held above the eyes*. It will generally be found that the eyelids close with a *vibratory* motion, or become spasmodically closed.

He states that after the hypnotic state is obtained, one can place the limbs of the subject in a given position and they will remain that way, or requesting him to keep them in such a position will have this effect. After a while, he adds, the limbs tend to become rigid and involuntarily fixed. Also, all of the sense organs (except sight), muscular motion, resistance and certain mental faculties *first* become extremely *exalted*. Later there is a very large *depression* which takes the form of a profound *torpor* with tonic rigidity of the muscles. Braid interestingly remarks in this connection that it is possible to "dehypnotize any specific sense," muscle, or part of the subject's body by stimulating it; a gentle current of air will do this.

Braid also points out that hypnosis can be produced regardless of the actual direction in which the patient's eyes are focused, but the induction is slowest and weakest when the eyes are directed straight ahead, and is most rapid and intense when the eyes are held in the position of a "double internal and upward squint."

Braid found that many of his subjects, particularly those he used in his initial research, had a tendency to exhibit tonic rigidity, muscular spasms and even convulsions. At first he believed this was one of the essential characteristics of the hypnotic state. Later he concluded that the appearance of these symptoms was connected to the position of the eyes during hypnosis, and could be eliminated by having the patient close his eyes and gently turn them upward as if looking at an object at a great distance. At the same time the limbs were placed in a position which would relax the muscles as much as possible.

Regarding dehypnotization, Braid states that a clap of the hands, an abrupt shock on the arm or leg by striking them sharply with the flat of the hand, pressure and friction over the eyelids, and a current of air wafted against the face, will suffice for this. The choice of method depends partly upon what effects the operator desires to obtain following the trance. If he wishes that changes induced in hypnosis persist into the waking state Braid recommends that he use a sudden clap near the subject's ear when the desired effect has reached its full height. But if tranquilization of the subject is desired, then a gentler technique, such as light fanning should be used.

Charcot and Hypnotism

Charcot, the famous French neurologist and anatomist, played a very important, although controversial part in the history of scientific hypnotism, beginning his research in 1878. At that time he strongly felt that the first and most important step in establishing hypnosis on a sound scientific basis was to isolate as many invariant and unique somatic characteristics of hypnosis as possible; and of such a nature as to be proof against simulation.

The results of his search culminated in the delivery in 1882 of his famous nosographic paper before the Paris Academy of Science. In it he describes three fundamental "stages" of hypnosis, which might best be called Charcot's *hypnotic syndromes*, and the methods for eliciting them. The following is a translation of this paper.[25]

The numerous and varied phenomena which are observed in hypnotic subjects do not occur in one and the same nervous state. In reality, hypnotism clinically represents a natural group, including a series of nervous states, differing from each other, and each distinguished by peculiar symptoms. We ought, therefore, to follow the example of nosographists in endeavoring to make a clear definition of these different nervous states, according to their generic character, before entering on the closer study of the phenomena presented by each of them. It is owing to not having begun by defining the special state of the subject under observation that observers so often misunderstand and contradict one another without sufficient cause. These different states which, taken as a whole, include all the symptoms of hypnotism, may be referred to three fundamental types: 1st, the cataleptic state; 2nd, the lethargic state; 3rd, the state of artificial somnambulism. Each of these states, including moreover a certain number of secondary forms, and leaving room for mixed states, may be displayed suddenly, originally, and separately. They may also, in the course of a single observation, and in one subject, be produced in succession, in varying order, at the will of the observer, by the employment of certain methods. In this latter case, the different states mentioned above may be said to represent the phases or periods of a single process.

Setting aside the variations, the imperfect forms, and the mixed states, we do not propose in this account to do more than indicate briefly the general features of these three fundamental states, which may be said to dominate the complex history of the symptoms of hypnosis.

1. *The Cataleptic State*—This may be produced: (a) primarily, under the influence of an intense and unsuspected noise, of a bright light presented to the gaze or, again, in some subjects, by the more or less prolonged fixing of the eyes on a given object; (b) consecutive to the lethargic state, when the eyes, which up to that moment had been closed, are exposed to the light by raising the eyelids. The subject thus rendered cataleptic is motionless and, as it were, fascinated. The eyes are open, the gaze is fixed, the eyelids do not quiver, the tears soon gather and flow down the cheeks. Often there is anesthesia of the conjunctiva, and even of the cornea. The limbs and all parts of the body may retain the position in which they are placed for a considerable period, even when the attitude is one which is difficult to maintain. The limbs appear to be extremely light when raised or displaced, and there is no *flexibilitas cereas*, nor yet what is termed the stiffness of a clay figure. The tendon reflex disappears. Neuromuscular hyperexcitability is absent. There is complete insensibility to pain, but some senses retain their activity at any rate in part—the muscular sense, and those of sight and hearing. This continuance of sensorial activity often enables the experimenter to influence the cataleptic subject in various ways, and to develop in him by means of suggestion automatic impulses, and also to produce hallucinations. When this is the case, the fixed attitudes artificially impressed on the limbs, or, in a more general way, on different parts of the body, give place to more or less complex movements, perfectly coordinated and in agreement with the nature of the hallucinations and of the impulses which have been produced. If left to himself, the subject soon falls back into the state in which he was placed at the moment when he was influenced by the suggestion.

2. *The Lethargic State.*—This is displayed: (a) primarily, under the influence of a fixed

gaze at some object placed within a certain distance of the eyes; (b) in succession to the cataleptic state, simply by closing the eyelids, or by leading the subject in a perfectly dark place.

At the moment when he falls into the lethargic state, the subject often emits a peculiar sound from the larynx, and at the same time a little foam gathers at the lips. He then becomes flaccid, as if plunged in deep sleep; there is complete insensibility to pain in the skin, and in the mucous membrane in proximity with it. The organs of the senses sometimes, however, retain a certain amount of activity; but the various attempts which may be made to affect the subject by means of suggestion or intimidation are generally fruitless. The limbs are relaxed, flaccid, and pendant, and when raised, they fall back again as soon as they are left to themselves. The pupils are, on the other hand, contracted, the eyes are closed or half-closed, and an almost incessant quivering of the eyelids may usually be observed. There is an exaggeration of the tendon reflex; neuromuscular hyperexcitability is always present, although it varies in intensity. It may be general, extending to all the muscles of the animal system, the face, the trunk, and the limbs; and it may also be partial, only present, for instance, in the upper limbs, and not in the face. This phenomenon is displayed when mechanical excitement is applied to a nerve-trunk by means of pressure with a rod or quill; this causes the muscles supplied by this nerve to contract.

The muscles themselves may be directly excited in the same way; somewhat intense and prolonged excitement of the muscles of the limbs, trunk, and neck produce contracture of the muscles in question; on the face, however, the contractions are transitory, and do not become established in a state of permanent contracture. Contracture may also be produced in the limbs by means of repeated percussion of the tendons. These contractures, whether produced by excitement of the nerves or muscles, or by percussion of the tendons, are rapidly relaxed by exciting the antagonist muscles. As it has been already said, the cataleptic state can be instantaneously developed in a subject plunged in lethargy, if while in a lighted room the upper eyelids are raised so as to expose the eyes.

3. *The State of Artificial Somnambulism.* —This state may, in some subjects, be immediately produced by fixity of gaze, and also in other ways which it is not necessary to enumerate. It may be produced at will in subjects who have first been thrown in a state of lethargy or catalepsy, by exerting a simple pressure on the scalp, or by a slight friction. This state seems to correspond with what has been termed magnetic sleep.

It is difficult to analyze the very complex phenomena which are presented under this form. In the researches made at the Salpêtrière, many of them have been provisionally set aside. The chief aim has been to define, as far as possible, the characteristics which distinguish somnambulism from the lethargic and cataleptic states, and to demonstrate the relation which exists between it and the two latter.

The eyes are closed or half-closed; the eyelids generally quiver; when left to himself the subject seems to be asleep, but even in this case the limbs are not in such a pronounced state of relaxation as when we have to do with lethargy. Neuro-muscular hyperexcitability, as it has been defined above, does not exist; in other words, excitement of the nerves or of the muscles themselves, and percussion of the tendons do not produce contracture. On the other hand, various methods, among others, passing the hand lightly and repeatedly over the surface of the limb (mesmeric passes), or again breathing gently on the skin, cause the limb to become rigid, but in a way which differs from the contracture due to muscular hyperexcitability, since it cannot, like the latter, be relaxed by mechanical excitement of the antagonist muscles; it also differs from cataleptic immobility in the resistance encountered in the region of the joints, when the attempt is made to give a change of attitude to the stiffened limb. To distinguish this state from cataleptic immobility, strictly so-called, it is proposed to distinguish the rigidity peculiar to the somnambulistic state by the name of *cataleptoid*; it might also be called *pseudo-catalepsy*.

The skin is insensible to pain, but this is combined with hyperesthesia of some forms of cutaneous sensibility, of the muscular sense, and of the special senses of sight, hearing, and smell. It is generally easy, by the employment of commands or suggestions, to induce the subject to perform very complex automatic actions. We may then observe what is strictly called artificial somnambulism.

In the case of a subject in a state of somnambulism, a slight pressure on the cornea, made by applying the fingers to the eyelids, will change that state into a lethargy accompanied by neuro-muscular hyperexcitability; if, on the other hand, the eyes are kept open in a lighted room by raising their lids, the cataleptic state is now produced.

These three states are the forerunners of our modern conception of hypnotic depth, although in considering them and a fourth, fascination, introduced by Brémaud (page 118) it should be kept in mind they were not meant initially to represent different depths of hypnosis, but were seen as different kinds of hypnoses. The concept of depth does not appear to have entered Charcot's mind at this stage, if it ever did. Later, Cullerre[34] pointed out a possible ranking of the Charcot-Brémaud stages on a single continuum in the order fascination, somnambulism, catalepsy and lethargy on the basis that, "there is a more or less complete and progressive suppression of the intellectual functions, starting with the highest ones, volition first, then consciousness, then self-awareness, and finally, subconscious activity." This progressive suppression he believed to be correlated with a progressive inhibition of cortical activity. Cullerre speaks of "degrees of hypnotic sleep" very much as we speak of depth of hypnosis, but in this instance suggestibility is not taken as its basis. In terms of this scaling somnambulism appears as a condition of relatively light hypnosis, as contrasted to our present day conception. The reason for such a set of diametrically opposed conclusions will become clear shortly.

The main difficulty with Charcot's nosography was that it did not agree with the experience of many of his contemporaries any more than it does with our present day experiences. Bernheim, the principal voice for the opposition, insisted that he had never witnessed the spontaneous occurrence of Charcot's syndromes. Even more damaging was his contention that the only way he could obtain the various symptoms in question was by suggesting them. His eventual conclusion and accusation was that the three stages reported by Charcot were artifacts created by the pre-"education" of the subjects or by unwitting suggestions to them. Thus arose the now famous, often violent, controversy between the Salpêtrière and the Nancy schools of hypnotism.

Now in all fairness to Charcot, it must be said that he worked exclusively with patients suffering from the so-called "grande hystérie," a point which is specifically emphasized in the later work of the Salpêtrière. Furthermore, Charcot and his co-workers strongly emphasized that his three syndromes, comprising "grand hypnotisme," could be elicited only in such individuals, for which reason Richer[144] also calls it "hypnotisme hystérique." In other words, "grand hypnotisme" was symptomatic of "grande hystérie," although not of hysteria in general. In any event, it was a pathological manifestation. On the other hand, there is no evidence that Bernheim ever actually worked with fully developed cases of "grande hystérie," although one would assume that such a serious investigator would have made a point to do so. There is evidence from his writings that he did have some "hysterics" among his subjects, but they were probably not of the "grande hystérie" type.

Bernheim claimed that he could produce Charcot's various stages entirely, and as a matter of fact, only by suggestion. There is no question that something which outwardly looks like these stages can thus be brought into being. The question, however, is whether the resemblance holds at the level of detailed and finer examination which Charcot used. The Salpêtrière contended that it did not, and that, with the exception of somnambulism, the "petit hypnotisme" of the Nancy school never led to anything more than an imperfect copy of the syndromes. In Charcot's terms "petit hypnotisme" was only a "forme fruste" of the "grand hypnotisme." Now the significance of the exception is that, as Richer has explained and as is most clearly expressed by Cullerre, "petit hypnotisme" (and hence modern hypnosis) turns out to be *nothing else than Charcot's state of somnambulism*. Indeed, if one examines the characteristics of modern hypnosis and compares them to those of the three stages described by Charcot, there is little doubt that Charcot's somnambulism *is the only* condition comparable to our present conception of hypnosis, regardless of whether we are dealing with (suggested) pseudo-catalepsy, pseudo-lethargy, or "somnambulism." Thus, if Charcot's syndromes had any reality, it would mean that modern hypnotism and its precursor, "petit hypnotisme," are a suggested condition which mimics or is identical to only one aspect of *a potentially more inclusive and pathological phenomenon* and that when we talk of the depth of hypnosis we are quantifying only one aspect, not hypnosis as a whole. This is why there is no incompatibility between Cullerre's view that "somnambulism" is a relatively light state of hypnosis and the modern conception of "somnambulism" as the deepest or one of the deepest states of hypnosis; the two somnambulisms are quite different things. It would be much better if a totally different term were used in our modern nomenclature, but like the term "hypnoidal," it is probably here to stay.

The big question, of course, is whether Charcot's syndromes ever had any reality of their own or were they mere suggested artifacts as Bernheim contended? I think that many of the phenomena Charcot and his co-workers observed were most likely the results of unwitting suggestions and possibly the attempt to defraud on the part of some subjects. The remarkable effects of magnets, for instance, which they reported must certainly fall in this category. On the other hand I do not believe this gives just cause for rejecting all of the observations made at the Salpêtrière, although it is good reason for carefully sifting all material reported by this group of investigators and not accepting it purely on Charcot's say so. It would be a grave mistake to assume that there is nothing of value to be found in the records of the Salpêtrière. Richer's account of the research and results of the Charcot group is anything but amateurish, and is obviously written by a man with no mean training in experimental physiology. Some of his research can be favorably compared to that reported in Hull's[86] work, all of which does not settle the question raised a few moments ago.

In attempting to answer it, it is important to keep in mind that it is immaterial here whether or not "grande hystérie" was itself a suggested phenomenon, hence an artifact, as has been contended. If we forget that there was ever any name given to the condition predisposing individuals to exhibiting "grand hypnotisme," Charcot's findings boil down simply to the assertion that a small number of individuals exhibited this phenomenon. Was this a suggested effect or did it have some other basis? Now, even granting that all subsequent cases were artifacts, there must have been, as Grasset[73] remarks, a first instance of "grand hypnotisme" for which it is unlikely that pre-education or suggestion can be invoked as the cause of the observed somatic symptoms. Neither Charcot nor the subject could have known about the symptoms of "grand hypnotisme" until after they had been produced *for the first time*. Until then there was nothing to model, hence to specifically suggest. What other alternatives are there? Charcot or the subject might have deliberately created the three syndromes. Charcot might have unwittingly and more or less by chance suggested the symptoms. Or again, was it pure chance that his first case gave forth the particular set of symptoms in question, and might equally well have given some other set? Finally, is it possible that Charcot, making use of a number of isolated occurrences of various symptoms, extrapolated from them and in good faith presented their combination as "grand hypnotisme?" Undoubtedly other alternatives· exist, but I will limit myself to the above more obvious and conceivable ones. After a careful examination I cannot accept the above as satisfactory explanations. For one thing, other investigators whose integrity cannot be questioned independently obtained similar data. Then too, when one examines the details of the somatic data on which the Salpêtrière relied, it is difficult to believe that it could all have been many times duplicated only through the influence of pre-education or of unwitting suggestions. Bernheim does not appear to have ever examined his hypnotized subjects with the care and detail of the Salpêtrière. Finally, if pre-education or suggestion could have brought into being the Charcot syndromes in his subjects, could the converse not be equally true (that pre-education and suggestion could have prevented the appearance of these syndromes in Bernheim's subjects)? If the modern investigators who hold to the role-taking theory of hypnosis are right, there is no more reality to Bernheim's findings than there is to Charcot's or anyone else's.

I believe that there is a much simpler answer than all this. Charcot's true cases of "grand hypnotisme" were probably atypical cases, as were those studied by independent investigators. According to Binet and Féré, the Salpêtrière averaged, over a period of 10 years, only slightly more than one case of "grand hypnotisme" per year! It is my understanding that the 1882 paper was based on only three cases. It was one of Charcot's great mistakes and fault to have generalized from so small a sample.* To my way of thinking these figures are the best argument against the claims of Bernheim and others that suggestion created the symptoms. Had this been so, why should there have been so few cases when by Bernheim's own admission deep hypnosis could be induced in 13 per cent of the cases, and 45 per cent of the people could be hypnotized to a fair degree?

It is not my intention to prove that Charcot was right, nor to suggest a "return to Charcot." Even if one could convincingly demonstrate that the first proposition is correct, the fact would remain that there are apparently no more cases of "grande hystérie" to be had, so that for the time being this is a closed area. Furthermore, besides being atypical "grand hypnotisme" was, presumably, a pathological manifestation which could be elicited only in certain cases, as contrasted with the greater universality and non-pathological character of modern hypnosis. There is no question that the latter should have our main attention. On the other hand, for a clear understanding of the nature of hypnosis, it seems important to know what was involved in "grand hypnotisme" and, particularly, its relation to modern hypnosis.

*Another important oversight of Charcot was that of not using normal, or at least, non-hysterical controls.

In spite of the fact that the Charcot syndromes are largely of historic and, at best, academic interest today, there is one feature which may not be without significance for the elucidation of the nature of hypnosis. This is that Cullerre's detailed description of the hypnosis continuum bears a strong resemblance to what, psychoanalytically speaking, might be described as a continuum of progressively increasing regression. But whereas analysts have conceived the regression underlying hypnosis as being partial and limited, Cullerre's description implies that, under presumably pathological circumstances, the induced regression can progress much further than has been assumed and become quasi-, if not totally complete; the individual reaching a quasi-fetal-like psychic state or vegetative condition (Charcot's lethargy). Nothing like this is yet provided for by the psychophysiological theory of chapter 2.

COUNTING METHOD

The subject is comfortably seated and is asked to fixate upon an object held up in front of him or to look straight ahead of him at the wall. He is then told:

> I am going to count and I want you to follow me closely. When I say 'one' you will close your eyes and keep them closed until I say 'two.' When I say 'two' you will open your eyes. Then when I say 'three' you will close them again and keep them closed until I say 'four.' Do you understand?. . .[*If the subject seems to show some confusion, you can demonstrate for him what you want. Some hypnotists make it a standard practice to demonstrate these instructions while giving them.*] You will keep on opening and closing your eyes as I count until they get very tired. You will find it increasingly difficult to open your eyes. They will get heavier and heavier. You will find yourself becoming more and more drowsy and sleepy. After a while your eyes will have become so-o-o heavy and you will be so-o-o sleepy that your eyes will close and remain closed and you will go into a deep, sound sleep. You will have no desire to open your eyes, you will only want to sleep, to sleep deeply and soundly.

Then begin to count in a monotonous voice, pausing after each number. How high to count is immaterial—many hypnotists prefer to count up to 10 or 20, then start over, at the rate of one or two integers per second. Watch your subject's reactions closely, since they can tell you much concerning the progress of the trance induction. If he consistently anticipates your count, especially on opening his eyes, you may suspect that he is either not paying close attention or that he is resisting. On the other hand, if he has difficulty opening his eyes or keeping them open, he may be entering the trance state. Although you can produce hypnosis by using only the counting part of the procedure, it is more effective to use the suggestions of heaviness of eyelids, drowsiness, etc. Interjection of similar suggestions between counts is particularly helpful. One usually continues counting for a short time after the eyes remain closed. At first, the subject may raise and lower his eyebrows in time with the count although the eyes remain closed.

In some cases the subject may continue to open and close his eyes despite becoming deeply hypnotized. This may result when the subject does not clearly understand the instructions, or from the fact that each count acts through association as a command-suggestion. In such cases it is rarely difficult to determine whether hypnosis is present or not. Usually the subject acquires a characteristic fixed and vacant stare. His posture assumes a rigid appearance, and the motion of his eyes becomes typically automatic. Another way of ascertaining the condition of the subject is to alter the rate of counting. If he follows these changes faithfully it is nearly certain that he is hypnotized, probably deeply. As soon as you have decided that the subject is hypnotized, wait until he closes his eyes again, then stop counting and say something like "Now your eyes are closed and you are deep asleep. Your eyes are very heavy. . .like lead. They are stuck fast. . .so fast that you cannot open them."

One noteworthy feature of these suggestions is that the subject is told not to open his eyes until the next count, but he is not told not to close them before the next count. This is because he may fall into a deep hypnosis and his eyes may close any time in the induction; to specify conditions for closing the eyes might interfere. This is another example of the importance of careful wording in suggestion.

CLASSICAL METRONOME AND ALLIED METHODS

This procedure, which is closely related to the previous one, consists mainly of having the subject listen intently to a metronome, a clock, a watch, or to a steady hum. The subject may be comfortably seated or reclining on a couch. Preferably the subject should close his eyes and the room should be dimly lit. One disadvantage of starting with the subject's eyes closed is that there is no way of knowing when he has passed into hypnosis, but even with opened eyes you cannot always tell for sure. Since the time required for induction by this method is highly variable, you may assume when time is at a premium that if the subject has not passed into hypnosis within 5 to 10 minutes, he will either not respond or will require considerably more time. Consequently, you should begin suggestions after 5 or 10 minutes. Where ample time is available, however, you can allow 30 minutes or more to pass before attempting suggestions. The main difficulty is that the subject may simply fall into a natural sleep. Often, individuals who are potentially hypnotizable by this method fail to go into a trance in a short time because they do not concentrate properly on the sound. For this reason I often talk the matter over with the subject at the end of 10 minutes and try again. Sometimes a specific rate of counting is found to be more effective than another.

One variation is to have the subject alternately close and open his eyes with consecutive beats of a metronome, essentially the method just described.

In the classical metronome method the subject presumably had no knowledge of what was to happen as he concentrated on the beats. Most hypnotists today find it more efficient to give suggestions regarding the effects of the metronome prior to using it. Some hypnotists also instruct their subjects to repeat to themselves the word "sleep" every time they hear a beat. The most effective use of the metronome is in combination with suggestions, usually allowing an initial period of up to 10 minutes without suggestions. If the subject should be responsive to the metronome sound alone, he will have an opportunity to manifest it. Watkins' method (page 241) is an excellent example of this use of the metronome.

One interesting variation consists of using a small microphone to amplify the subject's heart or respiratory sounds, and conducting these to his ears by means of earphones. According to Kubie and Margolin[102] this technique makes use of two separate effects. One is the use of rhythm as a monotonous fixating stimulus, the other that the rhythm of respiration acts as a conditioned stimulus for sleep. Some hypnotists state that the metronome technique works best when its rate is adjusted to some body rhythm, such as the heart beat or the respiration.* If you use respiration, and if the subject is at all responsive, it is possible to decrease the metronome rate and the subject's respiration will slow down to match the metronome. A way to use this for the induction of hypnosis is as follows: Start out with the metronome beating at a rate slightly lower than the subject's normal breathing. He is asked to breathe in unison with the metronome and to pay close attention to it. This last admonition should be repeated a number of times at various intervals, at first. After a few moments the rate of the metronome is imperceptibly decreased. If the subject follows, it is raised to its initial value then shifted in the other direction. If properly done, it will be found that the subject follows the variations quite faithfully and, as this is contin-

---

*Brown[24] says a rate of about 2 beats per second is optimal.

ued, he will pass into a progressively deeper trance. Once this control is established, suggestions of sleep can be introduced. It is important, however, that the first suggestions given be concerned with his respiration and its variation in rate.

It is also possible to use what might be described as a visual metronome, a flashing light upon which the subject fixates. (The flashes can easily be controlled by a metronome.) As a matter of fact, a combination of intermittent visual and auditory stimuli can be used to advantage.

PENDULUM AND ROTATING MIRROR METHOD

These are two closely related procedures. The pendulum method makes use of a bright object suspended at the end of a string or chain. Some of the older hypnotists used their pocket watches which were carried at the end of a chain. Hold the bob in front of the subject, slightly above eye level, and allow it to slowly swing back and forth. Preferably the hypnotist should stand to the side of the subject. Suggestions as well as the sound of a metronome can be combined with this method.

The original rotating mirror technique developed by Luys used an old-fashioned lure for meadow larks which consisted of a vertical wooden support with many small mirrors imbedded in the surface, revolving about a central axis at a fairly slow rate. Subjects were asked to concentrate upon the lure. Many adaptations have been made of this apparatus, one of these consisting of one or more small glass spheres on one or more rotating arms. The subject is instructed to fixate upon and follow the spheres with his eyes. As with the previous methods, suggestions can be combined with this technique.

"HYPNODISKS" AND OTHER DEVICES

As with drugs, many a hypnotist has hoped to find some automatic, easy and sure method of inducing hypnosis by using various physical devices. This hope has been supported by the fact that Braid and Charcot had recourse to purely physical means to produce hypnosis. As a consequence of this quest for more certain techniques, a rash of gimmicks and gadgets have been proposed and even marketed, sometimes with rather deceptive descriptions. It is doubtful that any device exists that will facilitate the induction of hypnosis *in every use*. The existence of any device that *induces* hypnosis by purely physical means without the conscious participation and/or cooperation of the subject is only speculative. It is possible that with increased knowledge of hypnotism and how the nervous system functions such a device might eventually be invented or discovered. For instance, the fact that the alpha wave can be "driven" by intermittent photic and auditory stimulation and that a slowing down of the alpha rhythm is symptomatic of the appearance of sleep might be used as a basis for such an apparatus. It suggests that if the same cortical and subcortical changes are associated with the onset of sleep and with such a slowing down of alpha activity as might be brought about by photic "driving," a flickering light, properly used, might induce a "drowsy" or "dissociated" state of greater receptivity to suggestions. Walter, Dovey, and Shipton[186] have reported findings which may be of significance here. They found that flicker induces mental confusion, hallucinations, and various other disturbed states in many people, and that in every case the disturbances were associated with specific electrical response patterns. Conceivably the effects of such devices as whirling spirals are reducible to a similar phenomenon. Current research being done by such men as Magoun, Lindsley, and other neurophysiologists on the functions of the reticular system and on the alpha wave, particularly in their relation to attention and consciousness, may hold the key to the further development of hypnosis-inducing devices.

In any event, if the theory developed in chapter 2 is correct, hypnosis could conceivably be helped in many ways and even induced to a certain degree by physical means. It is my guess that such devices as might prove effective would most likely be those capable of bringing about "dissociative" states.

Assuming that focusing of attention is an essential factor in the induction of hypnosis, it is theoretically possible that some fixation stimuli are more efficacious than others, by having greater attention-catching or compelling power. They may also differ in quality in other ways. For instance, one device, often called a hypnosphere or a hypnoscope, consists of a small polished metal sphere inclosed within a larger hollow glass sphere. The presence of multiple spherical surfaces supposedly causes light placed anywhere in the room to be reflected in the subject's eyes. Furthermore, the spherical nature of the reflecting surfaces allows the reflected lights to appear steady and relatively undisturbed by movements of the person holding the apparatus.[85]

Another device, sometimes called a hypnodisk or hypnotron, is a disk with one or more spirals drawn from the center. This disk is placed on a turntable or on a shaft of some sort and rotated at a moderate speed. The subject is requested to look at the disk while he is given suggestions aimed at inducing hypnosis. The rationale is that the apparent contracting or expanding movement, often giving the illusion of an axial flow, is particularly attention compelling. Also, many subjects claim that watching the disk makes them dizzy and some hypnotists capitalize upon this. In any case, this device appears to be one of the more effective. Wolberg[203] recommends it for dealing with refractory subjects. He repeats the following suggestions until the subject's eyes are closed. "Keep your eyes fastened on the wheel. As you watch it, you will notice that it vibrates. The white circles become more prominent, then the black. Then it seems to recede in the distance and you feel as if you are drawn into it. Your breathing becomes deep and regular. You get drowsy, very drowsy. Soon you will be asleep."

A variant of this device is a disk on which a number of concentric rings are drawn. It is held up for the subject to fixate upon while the hypnotist rotates it, resulting in the illusion that the concentric rings are turning. Another variation consists of a background of spirals covered by a piece of plastic molded in such a way that its surface consists of a large number of tiny parallel hemicylindrical lenses. Any slight motion of the disk causes the spirals to shimmer and change.

It is also said that a disk with a black ring painted on it and a white spot or a bright metal sphere imbedded in the center makes a very effective fixation object, probably as a result of a contrast effect.

Another device used by one hypnotist is a small hourglass.[140] He instructs the subject to watch the moving level of the sand in the upper compartment and to reverse the hourglass every time the top half is empty. Meanwhile he gives suggestions that the subject will become deeply hypnotized as he watches the sand. I believe that the hourglass can be used more effectively by having the subject closely watch the upper level of the sand and telling him that as it moves downward his eyes will be pulled downward, will become heavy and that by the time the upper receptacle has emptied, his eyes will have closed and he will have gone into a deep trance. By doing this you allow the moving sand level to act as a nonverbal suggestion of eye closure. Suggestions can be given during the sand flow.

Another method often described in books for the layman is called the "candle method" and requires the subject to watch the flame of a candle. Probably the only feature that gives it effectiveness, besides the mysterious and dramatic, is the continually moving and changing shape of the flame. It is said that dancing flames exert a peculiar fascination on people.

There is apparently no limit to the devices that have been found to be successful. For instance, one medical hypnotist reports that the hum of his office air conditioner is an effective source of monotonous auditory stimulation. Another reports under the somewhat questionable designation of "faradohypnosis" the use of the hum of a faradic machine for auditory stimulation.

It is difficult to evaluate these various devices in the absence of adequate data. Theoretically some instruments might better facilitate hypnosis by being more attention-arresting and maintaining than others, and many of the devices that have just been discussed probably owe their efficaciousness to their novel and often impressive nature. It is doubtful that they are superior in speed, depth attained, or percentage of individuals successfully hypnotized to a given degree, and they have the disadvantage of necessitating sometimes quite bulky equipment. However, any professional hypnotist should keep these instruments in mind because where other methods may fail, one of these devices may succeed.

HYPNOSIS BY PASSES

Passes are hand gestures made by the hypnotist over the subject's body with or without contact. Originally, they were introduced by the mesmerists on the assumption that these motions directed, concentrated or dispersed the animal magnetism upon and within the subject, thus bringing about various general or localized phenomena. Although there never was general agreement regarding how many types there were, Deleuze's description (page 280) of how he used them is quite typical. Today they are used almost entirely for their theatrical effect. Of course, if a subject believes in their effectiveness, there is a certain value in using them. To supplement Deleuze's description we might add that, according to past and present mesmerists, passes are very important and must be used properly or not at all. This involves special ways of holding the hands and fingers, certain mental attitudes to take, certain ways of moving the hands, and so on. There are at least six major types of passes:

1. *Longitudinal passes* are made from head to foot a few inches from the body surface. Their main object is to dissipate the magnetic fluid throughout the body, and they are extensively used to induce "magnetic sleep."

2. *Passes "a grand courant."* These are similar to the ones above, but they are made more rapidly and with wider motions at a somewhat greater distance from the subject. They are said to have a greater effect upon the subject than the longitudinal passes.

3. *Oblique passes* are a variation of (2) differing in that the two arms more or less describe arcs of circles in front of the subject. This is supposed to remove or dissipate whatever animal magnetism is present in the chest and head. They are used to awaken the subject gently from induced magnetic somnambulism.

4. *Transverse passes.* The arms are crossed scissor fashion in front of the hypnotist's chest, the palms forward facing the subject. The arms are then

simultaneously rapidly stretched forward and outward, right and left. These passes constitute the most radical method of dissipating any magnetism accumulated at any point in the subject's body. According to the mesmerists, they constituted an excellent method for awakening the subject.

5. *Vibratory passes* are supposed to be the most powerful of all passes in regard to the emission of animal magnetism from the magnetizer. They are made in a variety of ways allowing different parts of the hand to come in contact with the subject, the hands either remaining in one position, or moving in one of the manners already described. At the same time the hands are imparted with a continuous vibratory motion.

6. *Circular passes* consist of short or large circular motions of the hands and arms and have different properties depending upon whether done clockwise or counterclockwise.

There is nothing to indicate that passes have any special properties, and whether one uses them is strictly a matter of personal choice, belief, expediency and showmanship. They can be quite effective if one goes by past records. One of the most complete discussions of passes is given by Baréty. [5] In a private communication, Milton H. Erickson called my attention to Eliotson's specific use of passes to produce deep states of hypnosis, and he believes that some of the resulting conditions may have been similar to the plenary trance. A rather interesting observation made by de Rochas [145] might also be mentioned here. Entirely by accident, he discovered that he could bring about age regressions through prolonged use of longitudinal passes, there being a direct relationship between the degree of regression and the time spent on making the passes. My interest in this arose from the fact that it appears unlikely that the observed regressions could have resulted from any specific suggestion. But how else account for the phenomenon? Spontaneous regressions are of course known but this does not entirely account for de Rochas' results. A possible clue is that de Rochas' primary use of longitudinal passes was initially to induce and later *deepen* the trance state. There is little question that for de Rochas, deepening of the trance and age regression went together. As was seen earlier, modern psychoanalytic thinking views hypnosis as a regression in which there is also a relation between depth of hypnosis and degree of regression obtained. It is possible that de Rochas discovered over fifty years ago something that we are only beginning to realize. I must emphasize that all of this is only tentatively advanced and should not be misconstrued as a general acceptance of de Rochas' work. There is, unfortunately, much in his writings which is questionable with regard both to adequate controls and with respect to interpretation.

HYPERVENTILATION

We saw earlier (page 157) that voluntary hyperventilation, (forced deep breathing *without forced expiration*) appears to raise a person's suggestibility. One might therefore use it to facilitate the induction of hypnosis, as have many hypnotists. However, it should be realized that to be effective, it usually must be sustained and not limited to a few deep breaths. There are a variety of ways of proceeding. The induction of hypnosis can be preceded by 2 to 4 minutes of hyperventilation, after which suggestions are begun. Another excellent method is to have the subject concentrate on his breathing (visual fixation can also be used here) and take rhythmic breaths as deeply as possible in regular and rapid succession. It is a good idea for the hypnotist to set the pace at first by indicating the rhythm with movements of his hand, or by saying in a monotonous voice, "in—out," or "breathe in—breathe out." Not only does this set the pace, but the effect of the subject responding voluntarily to the words of the hypnotist adds to his suggestibility.

While a metronome can also be used, I question whether or not requiring fixation of too many senses may be detrimental to trance induction. My own experience seems to indicate that this is so.

After the rhythm is established, standard suggestions can be integrated with the breathing. That is, as part of the suggestions the subject should be told at various times that the deep breathing is related to the induction, that the progress of the two is related, etc. At intervals the hypnotist should reinforce the instructions and maintain the rhythm by giving a verbal cadence. One can also induce the first stage of hypnosis, then have the subject hyperventilate as part of the deepening procedure, a technique I have found quite effective.

Can hyperventilation alone induce hypnosis? Sargant and Frazer[150] believe so, although the hypnosis is light. However, examination of their method shows that another factor may be at least partly, if not entirely, responsible for the hypnosis. They require the subject to concentrate on his breathing and, as we have seen, this alone may be conducive to hypnosis. Thus the question remains unresolved. In any event, they state that if a subject lies on a couch and concentrates on breathing as deeply and rapidly as possible with a regular rhythm, a condition of light hypnosis will appear after 2 to 4 minutes and will be maintained as long as the hyperventilation* is

---

*Actually the authors say as long as "regular breathing" is maintained. Whether they mean continuation of deep breathing or merely maintaining the rhythm is unclear.

continued. They add that the increase in suggestibility is evident about the time the subject reports feeling dizzy and confused, which is interesting but ambiguous, because we do not know whether this results from the onset of hypnosis or is an effect of hyperventilation. We may favor the second alternative on the basis of what we know about hyperventilation. This brings up an important point, that clinical unconsciousness can result from hyperventilation. Indeed, the symptoms they describe may be precursors of a syncope or an abortive one. Although it would not be particularly dangerous, it most likely would interfere with attempts at hypnotization. Normally, you may expect subjects to enter the hypnotic state before hyperventilation has reached the syncope-producing stage. However, some individuals are particularly susceptible to this effect and you will occasionally encounter a case of fainting before hypnosis has been induced. Unconsciousness might also occur if the hypnosis had not been detected and the subject was allowed to continue hyperventilating. It is really an easy matter to check on both the state of awareness and the suggestibility of the subject and hence to discontinue overbreathing with the onset of hypnosis or if there are indications that fainting is imminent. In regard to testing the progress of suggestibility, Sargant and Frazer offer some fairly simple criteria: increased readiness to follow a quickly moving finger, a more automatic quality in the respiration and greater willingness of response to requests to breathe deeply.

What should you do if the subject faints? He will shortly recover alone because the fainting automatically brings an end to the hyperventilation and also brings about a reversal of the condition which caused the syncope. In addition to fainting, a number of other effects may be observed during hyperventilation. Among these are sweating, cold, clammy skin, more rapid heart beat, muscular weakness and fatigue. These are prefectly normal reactions and you need not worry about them. However, the subject may need reassurance. Sometimes while using hyperventilation unnecessary worry is caused when the subject temporarily stops breathing altogether. At worst this will only interfere with the procedure. A more serious reaction is when the subject develops muscular spasms and even convulsions. Although these are more frightening than serious, they are a good indication against further use of the method.

THE CAROTID SINUS METHOD

One of the chief attractions of this method, besides its *apparent* simplicity and the *false* assumption that it is a sure fire technique requiring little skill of the hypnotist, is its great speed of action.

Like the last method discussed, the carotid sinus technique is based upon a known physiologic phenomenon which also often leads to a state of unconsciousness when carried to completion. In my opinion it is ONE OF THE MOST DANGEROUS PROCEDURES AND HAS ABSOLUTELY NO PLACE IN THE ARMAMENTARIUM OF THE HYPNOTIST. One reason that it is so dangerous is that, among many things, it can cause the heart to stop, which, coupled with other effects, can be fatal. There are numerous records of instantaneous deaths caused through elicitation of the carotid sinus reflexes. In any event, it is difficult to use these reflexes to produce hypnosis because their action is often too rapid, uncertain and difficult to control, and it is doubtful, even when used by an expert, that it has anything but "show" value. One fact is certain, the collapse of the subject following the elicitation of the reflexes in question is not hypnosis but a syncope, although some poorly informed or not so honest stage hypnotists have often indicated otherwise.

The actual production of hypnosis with this technique involves giving the subject proper suggestions while he is passing from consciousness to unconsciousness. With many individuals this in-between state can be maintained fairly readily. With others it is extremely brief in duration.

RAPID METHODS OF TRANCE INDUCTION

In modern times stage and lay hypnotists have placed much emphasis upon techniques of "speed hypnosis," "ultra-rapid hypnosis" and, particularly, "instantaneous hypnosis." It may be worth while to devote some space to this rather confused area.

First of all, there is a basis for distinguishing between *rapid* and *instantaneous* induction. The instantaneous method, as best exemplified by the use of a posthypnotic signal, will produce hypnosis in a fraction of a second. It is probable that this figure comes close to the limiting speed of induction because a certain innate lag is always associated with any response. In contrast, many of the techniques of so-called "instantaneous hypnosis" usually require a minute or more. They are better described as "rapid methods." In many instances claims of rapid or instantaneous hypnosis are deceptive because they neglect to take into account the time used to prepare the subject or to "set the stage," nor is any specification given of the depth of trance attained or of the percentage of successes obtained with the method. Many subjects can be rapidly brought to a light or medium state, whereas getting a deep trance in these same subjects may require appreciable time or may even be impossible. Finally, it should be pointed out that some hypnotists confuse "rapid hypnosis" with economy of manipulations without saving of time.

Invariably, when we examine these methods it turns out that they are quite limited. The best we can say about them is that they are very "quick" *when they work*. When they fail one is no better off, and often one is worse off, than if a slower technique had been used in the beginning. There is no question, however, that under the proper conditions, rapid and even "instantaneous" hypnosis is possible. By maximizing the various factors contributing to effective trance induction which have been described throughout this volume, such conditions are created. Arons[4] lists the following factors as being crucial: expectation, prestige, mass psychology (or suggestion), imitativeness and prehypnotic suggestions (intentionally or unintentionally given). Unquestionably, all of these play a part, but to what extent is not known. Furthermore, we may suspect that in many instances their role may have been overrated. In any event, it may be instructive to describe a small number of so-called methods of rapid and "instantaneous" hypnosis in addition to those outlined in chapter 7 and to see how some of these are used.

One of these might be referred to as the prestige method. If a person has a high to very high suggestibility and he feels that you are a "powerful" hypnotist, a sudden look from you with a firm command of "sleep!" will sometimes be sufficient to bring about hypnosis. This is particularly successful if the subject has just witnessed the induction of hypnosis in others at a signal or command by you. Individuals who appear awed or afraid of you often respond in this manner. Another kind is the one who volunteers as a subject yet at the same time seems to be reluctant to submit himself, or seems to wish he had not volunteered.

Sometimes a subject who has given strong responses to a few waking suggestions appears a little dazed, eyes glazed, unstable on his feet and so on. This is particularly noticeable after postural sway suggestions. If you suddenly look at the subject and command "sleep," he will often pass into a hypnotic state. An excellent way of enhancing this is to extend your arm and point your finger at the subject's face, or better, extend your hand and arm, index and middle fingers forming a V at the level of the subject's forehead or eyebrows. At the same time move your arm downward so that your fingers pass very close to the subject's eyes or even brush them. This will of course cause the subject to close his eyes reflexively, a fact of which he may not be aware. For reasons already discussed, this reaction will have suggestive value. As soon as the eyes close, or even as soon as they are partially closed, some hypnotists immediately apply a gentle pressure upon the eyeballs, while at the same time giving appropriate suggestions to reinforce the eye closure and deepen hypnosis. All of this should be done in a continuous integrated manner.

A simpler technique, but one which is quite effective, is merely to quickly extend your hand toward the subject's face, snap your fingers near his eyes and at the same time command "*Sleep! Deep asleep!*" If done properly, the eyelids will close by reflex if not as a result of hypnosis and will then remain closed if the subject is sufficiently suggestible. Like the previous method, this one works best when a subject or prospective subject shows evidence of high suggestibility or appears to be in the process of becoming hypnotized and can be used rather effectively in certain situations. Not infrequently you may find a subject responding very strongly from the start. It is usually feasible to shorten the procedures by introducing one of the above maneuvers.* Another place where these techniques can also be used effectively is in demonstrations. While hypnotizing or even giving waking suggestions to a subject, it is not uncommon to find that some nearby member of the audience is showing strong evidence of being influenced. Very often if you turn toward him, snap your fingers and command sleep, he will be deeply hypnotized.

The following method is one I have seen used very effectively by several stage hypnotists. Start giving the postural sway suggestions and as the subject begins to fall, step backward so that your chest will support the head and shoulders of the subject when you catch him. As he comes to rest against your chest slide one hand down over his eyes thus forcing them closed. At the same time command "*Sleep! Deep, deep asleep!*" You may continue with suggestions to deepen the trance before helping the subject back to a normal standing position.

Many vaunted methods of rapid or instantaneous hypnosis are merely short-circuited standard inductions in which various steps have been omitted or collapsed together. Under proper conditions, you can start outright with eye-catalepsy suggestions and while the subject is struggling to open his eyes, give a sharp command of "SLEEP!" In a similar way you may start with the hand clasping suggestion then, while the subject struggles with his hands, command "SLEEP!" at the same time making a downward pass over the subject's eyes. This method and others described in these pages will work well only if the subject is essentially already hypnotized or is rapidly becoming so. The ability to detect whether a subject is ready for this is somewhat of an art. A tense, fixed expression, bodily tenseness, expectancy

---

*Skillful shifting in techniques is a general method which often will help to appreciably shorten trance induction.

and glazed eyes are among the cues the experienced hypnotist watches for.

Still another method of rapid hypnosis is to have the subject clasp his hands in yours, apply a slight pressure as you tell him to hold his hands tight, but do not stretch his arms out as in the hand clasping test. Now say the following:

> In a few moments your hands are going to become tightly stuck together, stuck so tightly that if you tried to take them apart you would not be able to do so. But you will not try. Now your hands are beginning to stick together, they are stiffening, getting stiffer and stiffer, tighter and tighter. They are sticking together, sticking tight. . .tighter. . . still tighter. . .THEY ARE STUCK TIGHT! Now your eyes are becoming heavy, heavier and heavier, very heavy. In a few moments when I tell you, you will be able to take your hands apart, but your eyes will be so completely stuck closed that you will not be able to open them. Now your eyes are sticking fast. They are tightly stuck. You can take your hands apart, but your eyes are completely stuck. You can take your hands apart, but your eyes are completely stuck and you cannot open them. The more you try the harder it is. You can't open your eyes. [*Usually by now the subject will have tried, but if he does not, challenge him.*] You CAN'T. . .Stop trying. DEEP ASLEEP! DEEP, DEEP ASLEEP! [*As you say this apply gentle pressure with your fingers upon his eyes.*] Just relax, you are going to go deeply asleep. You are sinking, sinking into a very deep sleep.

You can even use the Chevreul pendulum demonstration as a way into hypnosis. The subject is instructed to concentrate on the bob and its motion. Once movement is obtained, he is told that he cannot stop it and he is challenged to do so. Depending upon the reaction, you can command sleep or begin a slower induction of hypnosis. A method often effective with a subject who fails to meet the challenge is to state positively "All right, now you can stop it if you want, but you are getting very sleepy. *Sleep!* DEEP ASLEEP!" This may be emphasized by snapping your fingers next to his eyes. A less authoritative procedure would be "Stop trying and just relax. . .You are going to go deep asleep now. [*The subject often closes his eyes here. If he does not, continue with*] Now close your eyes."

The difficulty with all of these methods is that they are very uncertain and their success depends too much upon the hypnotist's sensitivity, his ability to pick out proper subjects and to adequately set the stage, so to speak, for the induction. They are rarely indicated for the beginner's use. The only true method of instantaneous hypnosis is the use of a posthypnotic signal. While the subject is hypnotized, you simply suggest before waking him that the next time you give a particular signal he will immediately go into a deep sleep. Any signal will do. It is a good idea to follow this by suggesting that he will not recall this. This is a simple and effective technique. But it is not foolproof, nor is it applicable in all cases. First, clearly, the subject must be hypnotized a first time before it can be used. Second, although posthypnotic suggestions can be effective with a light trance, to be fully effective, especially to be lasting, the subject must be in a deep hypnosis or at least in moderately deep hypnosis.* When using this method *you should be very careful not to use as a signal a word, gesture, etc. which you are likely to use in the normal course of communication with the subject*, otherwise the subject may fall into a trance when this is not intended, and possibly when it might be dangerous. I remember a case where a hypnotist had used the name "John" for a signal. Later while descending a stairway with the subject and several other persons (myself included) he mentioned someone by the name of John in the course of conversation. Immediately the subject began to collapse and she would have fallen down the stairs if there had not been someone nearby to catch her in time. Another thing which should be remembered is to place proper limitations upon the suggestion. Never say, "Anytime you hear the word 'fume' you will go into a trance," or even "Anytime someone says 'fume' to you." In the first instance this could mean that the subjects should become hypnotized any time anyone said this word, whether addressed to them or not. In the second case, it would mean the same for anyone addressing them. Instead, the suggestion should be so worded that only those entitled to hypnotize the subject by the signal should be able to do so. As a rule only the hypnotist should be empowered to hypnotize at a signal. If, for purposes of demonstration, this power is also given to others, the hypnotist should make it a point to nullify this before concluding the session, as a precaution. An exception to this rule is when post-hypnotic instructions are given to a subject in order to enable other professionals (dentists, surgeons, etc.) to use hypnosis on this subject as part of therapy.

The position taken in this section may puzzle readers who have been impressed by the apparent high rate of success stage hypnotists seem to have in using the methods just discussed. One reason for the apparent success is that stage hypnotists pick subjects who appear to be most likely to respond. The ability to do this seems to come partly with experience and to be partly innate. To some extent they are probably helped by the fact that volunteers most likely represent the more suggestible members of the

---

*This does not apply to posthypnotic suggestions as used in the fractionation method (see page 242).

audience and they are often already "hypnotized" by the time they reach the hypnotist. Second, stage hypnotists are proficient at using every favorable aspect of a situation and at setting the stage. A factor which probably plays an important part here is the hypnotist's prestige. Also, the audience is often led to believe that the effect produced is greater than it actually is, so that the stage hypnotist can content himself with the rapid induction of a light hypnosis to impress the audience with his mastery. Later, to demonstrate various phenomena requiring deep hypnosis, he uses only sub-jects who have been deeply hypnotized by the rapid method or, if necessary, by a slower method. The number of such subjects may be small, but if skill-fully done, this "switch" is not perceived by the audience which remains under the impression that the hypnotist is quite adept at rapid and effective hypnosis. The reader interested in looking further into instantaneous hyp-nosis will find other variations and methods in Aron's small book on speed hypnosis.

MASS OR GROUP HYPNOSIS

Hypnotizing a large number of subjects at the same time is not particular-ly difficult. It can be done with either a selected or an unselected group. In the first case the subjects are either individuals who have submitted to a few tests of suggestibility, such as the postural sway test and the hand clasp-ing test and proved to be potential hypnotic subjects, or they may be un-tested volunteers. In general, volunteers may be expected to have greater susceptibility to hypnosis than nonvolunteers. In the second case, no testing or calling of volunteers is made, but the entire audience is used.

How to proceed is more a matter of personal preference than anything else. Let us first consider the case of a group selected on the basis of sugges-tibility tests. In this situation you can proceed in two ways. You can pick out a few individuals who you feel are highly suggestible, and hypnotize them individually before the remainder of the group. Not infrequently you will find that other members of the group have also gone to "sleep," or you will notice one or two have become partially hypnotized. If so, as soon as you have finished hypnotizing the one, turn to the other subjects and either finish hypnotizing them or deepen their trance a little. When you do this tell each subject, including the one with whom you were working individually: "You will remain as you are, deep asleep, until I tell you otherwise. You will not wake up until I tell you." It is a good idea to touch each subject lightly on the shoulder or the arm as you address him, thus making your suggestions more emphatic and personal. In any event, whether or not other members of the group go into a trance after you have hypnotized a couple of subjects individually, you can then turn to the group as a whole and say something like: "Hypnotizing is just as simple as that. Now, I want you to all look at my eyes."

The other mode of proceeding is simply to hypnotize the group without further demonstration.

Should the subjects be seated or standing? This is not too important, particularly if you are working with a selected group. If they are standing you should place less emphasis on relaxation. Also, it is a good idea, especially after you detect signs of incipient hypnosis, to instruct the subjects to remain standing in spite of going to sleep and that they will be very comfortable this way. This eliminates the possibility that a subject might collapse and helps to counteract the feeling of some subjects that standing is inconsistent with going into a trance. Personally, I prefer to have my subjects seated, mainly because I can then make full use of suggested relaxation. Occasionally, however, some subjects become so relaxed while being hypnotized that even when on a chair they fall. You should always watch out for this, and if necessary, while still giving suggestions, gently straighten up the subject. Often this alone is sufficient to suggest what you want. If necessary, you can interrupt your suggestions briefly and give quick instructions in a low voice to the subject in question. Some hypnotists prefer to take care of these occasions by introducing appropriate suggestions to the group as a whole. Thus you can say: "You will remain seated in your chair. You will not fall off at any time." Finally, when using visual fixation it is desirable to have the subject look upward. If your eyes, fingers, etc. are used for this, a sitting position is better than a standing one unless you are very tall.

You may start with a group of volunteers or with the total audience by demonstrating waking suggestions and even hypnosis with a few subjects picked from the group, or you can give group waking suggestions to all present as explained in chapter 5. Most hypnotists restrict themselves to giving the hand clasping test to the entire audience. If you are dealing with a group of volunteers, you can be most effective by making this part of the trance-inducing procedure so that when this test is terminated you can go on directly to suggestions of sleep. With the total audience one usually requests all those who had difficulty in separating their hands to come forth and act as subjects. Whether you will want to give a few more waking suggestions to them then is optional. If the production of hypnosis is your main concern, you probably will not want to take more time with waking phenomena.

Many hypnotists mistakenly think that the potentialities of the audience have been exhausted once volunteers have been called or subjects selected by means of a test. This is certainly not correct. Some of the best subjects may still be in the audience. Consequently, when you are ready to hypnotize the selected group, address the audience before starting and tell it: "In a few moments I am going to ask those who have volunteered to perform an exercise in relaxation. You may try it too if you wish. I think you will find it very interesting. All you have to do is close your eyes and listen to what I tell you and do what I tell you to do. Now just close your eyes." Then turn toward your volunteer group and say "Those of you who volunteered will now please look at my eyes."

Or, you can first address the volunteer group and give them some preliminary instructions. "In a moment we will do an exercise in relaxation. I think you will find it very interesting. All you will have to do is to look at my eyes and listen to what I tell you." Now turn toward the audience and add: "Those of you who are watching may like to try this too. You will find that it is a very interesting experience. Just close your eyes and listen to what I say. Don't worry, you won't miss anything. All right now, close your eyes and just listen." Then turn again to the subjects and proceed to induce hypnosis.

At the end of the induction, you should add the following instructions: "Some of you in the audience are now sound asleep. You will remain asleep. You will not wake up until I tell you to. In a few moments I will ask someone next to you to bring you to me. You will follow him and remain deeply asleep. All others in the audience now may open your eyes. Please look around and if you notice anyone near you who is asleep, bring him to me. Just take hold of his arm and guide him gently out of his chair." You should always come forward to meet the subject.

Some people feel that this is unethical since, they argue, if these persons in the audience had wanted to be subjects they would have volunteered. This can be counterargued in a number of ways. The decision to use or not to use this part of the procedure must be left to each individual. I am neither advocating it nor repudiating it, my purpose being only to present impartially the standard procedures used in practice. In the event you decide against using this part of the procedure, keep in mind that some members of the audience may unintentionally become hypnotized. Although it is not usually done, it is a good idea at the end of the induction to ask the audience to notify you if anyone is hypnotized. You should then first ask the hypnotized person if he wants to join the volunteers. If he shows disinclination, you should awaken him.

In other respects the induction of hypnosis in a group does not differ from that in single individuals, although obviously certain techniques cannot be used. One method which can be readily used with hardly any alterations at all is the first technique described in chapter 7.

A few examples of mass hypnosis might now be given. The instructions which follow assume that an audience is being addressed. Actually, except for the last part, they are equally applicable to groups of volunteers assembled on a stage or elsewhere in the room. When volunteers are used there are occasions when they may not all be seated. Make a rough estimate of how many volunteers you expect from the audience and try to have available a sufficient number of chairs. Of course, there is no reason why some subjects cannot be kept standing. You may have more volunteers than there are chairs. *Never turn down volunteers for such a reason.* Simply arrange the extra subjects in rows behind or in line with the chairs and go ahead with the suggestions, making a few appropriate changes where needed. For instance, you can alter the instructions something like: ". . .Those of you who are standing be as relaxed as possible, but hold yourself straight, hands by your sides." Later when you instruct the subjects to clasp their hands, again specify that the sitting subjects hold them in their laps, and those standing just keep them clasped in front of them.

After dimming the lights* and making some introductory remarks to the audience, say:

I would like to ask you now to participate in an interesting experiment. Please place both of your feet flat on the floor. If you have any rings on your fingers it would be best for you to remove them and place them in your pocket or handbag. Now clasp your hands together like this [*demonstrate*] and keep them this way in your lap. Breathe deeply, just like I do [*demonstrate*]. Keep breathing deeply and just listen to my voice. As you keep breathing deeply imagine that every muscle in your body is relaxing, think of your entire body relaxing. As you do this your arms and hands are relaxing, your legs are relaxing, your entire body is becoming relaxed, very relaxed, and you keep breathing deeply, regularly. Now close your eyes. With your eyes closed keep breathing deeply and relaxing. Your arms and hands are beginning to feel heavy, your legs are growing heavy, your entire body is growing heavy, heavier and heavier, and you feel yourself becoming pleasantly drowsy, sleepy. . .Just listen to my voice. Think of nothing but what I tell you. As you keep relaxing more and more and getting drowsier and

*This is strictly optional. Some hypnotists feel that it helps, others do not. I usually do not bother with it.

sleepier you will find that your hands are becoming stuck together. In a little while they will be so tightly stuck that you will not be able to take them apart until I tell you that you can. But right now you just listen to my voice. Your hands are heavy, very heavy. Your arms are heavy, very heavy. Your legs and your feet are very heavy. Your entire body is very heavy, so-o heavy. . .and you are so drowsy, so-o sleepy. Just let yourself go to sleep. You feel yourself drifting away into a pleasant, restful sleep. You can hear everything I say and you will keep listening to me. Nothing will bother you. You will pay attention to nothing but my voice. You are comfortable and going into a deep sleep. And now as I speak to you, you will find that your hands are stuck together, that they are so completely stuck together that you cannot pull them apart. The more you will try the more completely stuck they will get. You will remain asleep, your eyes closed and as I count your hands will get still more tightly stuck together. One. . .they are sticking even more. Two. . .they are stuck tight. Three. . .tighter. . .Four . . .still tighter. Five. . .They're stuck tight, you can't take them apart; *they're stuck fast and you can't take them apart*. Try. You CAN'T. You CAN'T!. . .Now stop trying, and just relax. You can now take your hands apart, but now your eyes are sticking, sticking more and more. *They are stuck fast and now you can't open your eyes, no matter how hard you try*. YOU CANNOT OPEN YOUR EYES, THEY ARE STUCK TIGHTLY CLOSED . . .All right, now stop trying and relax. You are going deep asleep, deep asleep. You are sinking into a deep sound sleep. Deeper and deeper.

The next suggestion you should give to the subjects is to raise their right arms above their heads and to make a tight fist. Reassert that they will remain soundly asleep, but will hear and do everything you say. Suggest stiffening of the arm and inability to bend it down until told that they can. This will have the triple purpose of testing suggestibility, deepening the trance and allowing you to get an idea of who in the audience has responded to your suggestions. You can now do one of three things. Have members of the audience guide these subjects to you as described earlier. If feasible you can go to each one, give him a few additional suggestions to deepen his trance, and conduct him to the place where you will give the rest of the demonstration. Or, finally, you can instruct the subjects that in the future they will become quickly hypnotized when you command them to sleep or use trance-inducing suggestions, wake them up and ask them to come forward as subjects. You can then very quickly reinduce the trance individually or as a group.

An effective variation of this technique is as follows. The audience or a group of volunteers are again instructed to clasp their hands. Tell them to look at your eyes or some other fixation object which they can all see. Have the lights dimmed. Now ask them to breathe deeply and rhythmically and tell them that you are going to count and that they are to pay close attention to the counts and what you say, that they are not to think about anything but what you tell them. At all times speak smoothly in a low tone of voice. Your count then goes somewhat as follows:

One—As I count you will find yourself relaxing and soon you will fall asleep.

Two—You will find this a pleasant and interesting experience.

Three—As you relax more and more, a feeling of heaviness comes over you.

Four—You feel yourself getting pleasantly drowsy. Soon you will sleep.

Five—As you become increasingly sleepy and relaxed your hands are becoming stuck together.

Six—Your hands are sticking fast together.

Seven—Tight.

Eight—Tighter.

Nine—Your hands are stuck. You cannot take them apart. Try!

Ten—Stop trying and as you do so you go deeply asleep.

Eleven—If your eyes are not closed, close them.

Twelve—You go deeper and deeper asleep.

Thirteen—You are soundly asleep.

Fourteen—I may waken some of you later, but if I do, you will go right back to sleep as soon as I tell you to do so.

Fifteen—Sleep deeply. . .soundly. You will not awaken until I tell you. Stay as you are until I speak to you again.

At this point, as explained earlier, instruct the nonhypnotized audience regarding those among it who have entered a trance. Then, as soon as it is feasible, dismiss the subjects that obviously are not hypnotized. Watch for those that are lightly asleep and may tend to wake. If you see a subject waking up you can usually get him back in the trance by giving him a few suggestions of sleep. It is a good idea to give individual attention to each subject that is hypnotized by touching him on the shoulder or the arm. You should deepen his trance a little, at the same time reiterating that he will not wake up until you tell him to and that anytime he wakes up he will go back to sleep quickly at your command. In general, this method will rapidly hypnotize a rather large group of individuals; however, with the exception of a few, most of the subjects will be in a light to medium hypnosis.* A good way to deepen the trance is to apply a variation of the fractionation method by waking up the subjects, all at once or only a few at a time, under some pretext, then rehypnotizing them, having them carry out simple tasks and so on. You need not have all the subjects participate at the same time, but you can allow some to remain sitting or standing while working with others. It is a good idea to suggest to those who are remaining inactive that their trance will deepen while they wait, also that they will not pay attention to what you say until you address them again or give them some signal such as touching them on the right shoulder. With small groups you can learn the subjects' names or assign numbers to them and thereafter refer to their names or numbers as a signal. In general, the best results are obtained with mass hypnosis if you work quickly but smoothly and keep your subjects performing most of the time.

The fractionation procedure can also be used effectively when performing group hypnosis by telling the subjects who appear to be sufficiently hypnotized that you are going to awaken them and send them back to their chairs but that shortly after they have resumed their seats they will feel sleepy†; that as they watch you they will get sleepier as time passes, that their eyes will get progressively heavier, so heavy that they will close and they will fall soundly asleep; and that they will not awaken until you tell them to. Then awaken them and send them back to their chairs. As you proceed to work with those subjects who went into satisfactory trances, keep an eye on those who were given the suggestions. After a short time, you will often notice one of these subjects nodding or showing difficulty in keeping his eyes open. Point your finger at him in a rapid, sudden motion, try to catch his eye and say commandingly, "SLEEP!" This will frequently put him in a deep trance state. In many instances these subjects will become hypnotized without this, and you can give them your attention later.

The uses of mass hypnosis are somewhat limited; nevertheless, it has its place in hypnotic practice. It is a useful technique when giving demonstrations. It is a way of increasing the hypnotic susceptibility of prospective subjects or patients. Finally, it is a form of psychotherapy. Mass sugges-

---

*Gaining speed of induction at the expense of losing depth of hypnosis is a rather typical effect, thus the usual necessity for making a compromise.

†We have assumed that you are working with a small group. With large groups you may find it advisable to have chairs available nearby to which you can send these subjects, or, if they are already seated, as they will often be, you may keep them where they are, making appropriate changes in your suggestions.

tion presumably is at the bottom of the mass cures which have been reported to occur in temples, at holy sites and so forth since ancient times. Mesmer was one of the first physicians to make use of the technique on a large scale. Mass hypnosis was also a standard practice with Bernheim, although he seems to have used it primarily to increase the susceptibility of his patients. According to Wolberg, the types of psychotherapies which are best combined with group hypnosis are those involving guidance, reassurance, desensitization and persuasion, those using a directive approach. This form of therapy differs essentially from the usual, nondirective, group psychotherapy, for in contrast, psychotherapy with group hypnosis is characterized by the presence of a leader who, as Wolberg believes, acts in the capacity of the authoritative, magical figure, a parental substitute. This results in a situation wherein the group exists largely as an appendage of the leader. As a technique of therapy, mass hypnosis has serious limitations and should always be replaced by individual psychotherapy at the first opportunity. On the other hand, it is often the only form of therapy that stands some chance of success with individuals who have very weak egos. Unfortunately, its results often are impermanent and lead to increased dependency on the part of the patient.

HYPNOIDIZATION

In chapter 2 we discussed a borderline condition known as the hypnoidal state. It is useful in two ways. The dreamy condition associated with it has been found valuable in psychotherapy as a means of securing free associations and early memories and, because of the enhanced suggestibility of the hypnoidized* subject, it is possible to give a large variety of suggestions successfully. It can be used in psychotherapy with advantage, in conjunction with persuasion, relaxation and reassurance. It is said to be a useful tool for the removal of mild obsessions and phobias relative to various aspects of the individual's treatment by dentists, physicians and even psychotherapists. In any event, the hypnoidal state *makes an excellent starting point* for the training of difficult subjects or subjects with low initial suggestibility. Not only does it often permit uncovering and removal of factors hindering the progress of trance induction, but it also permits the use of posthypnoidal suggestions to facilitate the future induction of deep hypnosis. Far too

---

*It is convenient to speak of "hypnoidization" and related terms by analogy with the nomenclature of hypnotism. It should, however, be kept in mind that there is little evidence for thinking that it is not a mild state of hypnosis. It certainly lies on the continuum of progressive effects which are obtained when hypnosis is induced. Nevertheless, there have been some investigators who believe otherwise and the question remains unsettled.

many hypnotists are prone to reject a potentially good subject because he does not go beyond the hypnoidal state at the first trial, or because the hypnoidal state is not recognized as being present. In fact, *in many instances success or failure to hypnotize depends critically upon how the hypnotist handles the subject as he reaches and passes through the hypnoidal state.*

One particular advantage of the hypnoidal state is that it can be induced without reference to hypnosis, a fact of some importance in handling certain difficult subjects. Another advantage is that in most cases it involves a simpler procedure than hypnosis. Finally, it is possible to hypnoidize far more individuals than can be hypnotized to any other degree.

From our discussion in chapter 2 it is obvious the hypnoidal state can be brought about by any method used to induce hypnosis. Some investigators have found a few simple techniques particularly effective which they say are specific to the production of the hypnoidal state. One of these is the breathing method of Kubie and Margolin[102] discussed on page 291. In general, the use of concentration on a monotonous sound tends to bring about the hypnoidal condition, and can be combined with visual fixation if desired. It is best to have the subject reclining on a couch and to have the room dimly lit. Some investigators have used the ticking of a watch or the sound of a metronome as stimulus. Several of them have reported that reading newspaper clippings of indifferent content to the subject is very effective. The most basic rule of hypnoidization is that *suggestions are never given during the induction of the hypnoidal state.* If suggestions are to be used, they must be given after this state has been induced and, of course, they have nothing to do with the production of the condition itself.

It may be instructive to quote Sidis[168] regarding several typical methods of hypnoidization. He says:

> The patient is asked to close his eyes and keep as quiet as possible, without, however, making any special effort to put himself in such a state. He is then asked to attend to some stimulus such as reading or singing (or the monotonous beat of a metronome). When the reading is over, the patient, with his eyes shut, is asked to repeat it and tell what comes to his mind during the reading, or during the repetition, or immediately after it. Sometimes the patient is simply asked to tell the nature of ideas and images that have entered his mind. This should be carried out in a quiet place, and the room, if possible, should be darkened so as not to disturb the patient and bring him out of the state in which he has been put.
>
> As modifications of the same method, the patient is asked to fixate his attention on some object while at the same time listening to the beats of a metronome; the patient's eyes are then closed; he is to keep very quiet, while the metronome or some other monotonous stimulus is kept going. After some time, when his respiration and pulse are found somewhat lowered, and he declares that he thinks of nothing in particular, he is asked to concentrate his attention on a subject closely related to the symptoms of his malady or to the submerged subconscious state.

The patient again may be asked to keep quiet, to move or change position as little as possible, and he is then required to look steadily into a glass of water on a white background, with a light shining through the contents of the glass; a mechanism producing monotonous sounds is set going, and after a time, when the patient is observed to have become unusually quiet, he is asked to tell what he thinks in regard to a subject relating to his symptoms. He may be asked to write the stray ideas down, if speaking aloud disturbs the induced state favorable to the emergence of the dissociated states.

In some cases it is sufficient to put the patient in a quiet condition; have his eyes shut and command him to think hard of the particular dissociated state.

These methods clearly are special applications of the general conditions listed earlier in chapter 2.

Are there different levels of hypnoidization? Some investigators say there are, but no criteria or scales are available for their determination.

One obvious question which comes to mind is how does one tell when the hypnoidal state has been induced? Strangely enough, very little can be found in the literature in this regard. There is, of course, no problem if a hypnotic technique has been used and it is known that the subject does not go beyond this stage. In general, the best way to tell is to watch the subject for signs of progressive general relaxation, to allow at least 5 to 10 minutes for the development of the condition* and, as soon as it is estimated that the subject is hypnoidized, to speak to him gently and ask him how he feels, or to tell whatever comes to his mind, and so forth. From his answers and the way he responds one can, with a little practice, tell whether or not he is hypnoidized.

*The main thing to watch out for is that the subject does not fall into a natural sleep.

10

Self-Suggestion and Self-Hypnosis

SELF-HYPNOSIS THROUGH POSTHYPNOTIC SUGGESTIONS

GENERAL CONSIDERATIONS

BY DEFINITION *autosuggestion* is the giving of suggestions to one's self. It was first made popular by Émile Coué[33] who seems to have felt that it was the universal panacea. The best account of Coué's teachings will be found in Baudouin's work.[8] That suggestions can be given by an individual to himself is a well attested fact. Most of the readers who have tried the various autosuggestion experiments given in the early parts of this book will have experienced some of the effects that may be obtained. The reality of autosuggestive effects follows directly from the theory of hypnosis outlined in this book. Other theories also predict their existence. From the standpoint of theory, autosuggestion and heterosuggestion should have the same properties and, within limits, Hull[85] has presented evidence supporting this. It would be desirable for further data to be gathered upon this question, however, as many properties remain to be examined.

The administration and use of autosuggestions is in no essential way different from the giving and use of heterosuggestions and should present no difficulties to the reader who has progressed thus far. Essentially the same rules apply here as earlier. In addition, a number of observations which will be made in regard to self-hypnosis in the following pages can be regarded as largely applicable to autosuggestion in general. The use of waking autosuggestion is straightforward, but self-hypnosis does present major problems. Since it is, of course, the condition of choice for the administration of autosuggestions, we shall devote this chapter to it exclusively.

There is evidence that self-hypnosis can be induced by Braid's method or variations of it, and that the same can probably be said for self-hypnosis through suggestion. Indeed, although some writers state that self-hypnosis may occur in our daily life without our realization, and we frequently enter such a condition unknowingly, I think these statements are made without support of experimental evidence or, for that matter, any evidence other

314

than a striking resemblance and some theoretical biases. Actually, the only true criterion of hypnosis to date is hypersuggestibility. Unless this is demonstrated, any claim that a condition is hypnosis or self-hypnosis must be considered a guess and nothing more. This is one reason why a satisfactory proof of self-hypnosis is usually not available in most reported cases. We usually must rely upon subjective reports of the individuals, their objective behavior when in self-hypnosis and parallelism between methods used. This is fair proof, but not absolutely conclusive and possibly misleading in some cases. In any event, it is within these limitations that we will speak of self-hypnosis.

In spite of the glib assertions of some writers of popular pamphlets on hypnosis, the production of autohypnosis is not easy—as many who have tried it will attest. It is true that mild states are relatively easy to obtain, even medium hypnosis is not too difficult, but deep hypnosis is! The difference in difficulty is much greater than for heterohypnosis. As yet we do not know why this is so in all cases. When we say that deep self-hypnosis is far more difficult to induce than lesser depths and that we do not know why, we must consider two situations. When self-hypnosis is taught by post-hypnotic suggestion (in the manner to be described shortly) there is theoretically no reason to expect that the percentage of success for various depths of self-hypnosis would be different than in the case of heterohypnosis, and the data reported by various investigators, particularly Salter,[148] substantiate this. The reasons are the same as those determining the distribution of heterohypnotic depth. When self-training is employed the matter is quite different. There is a considerable drop in the percentage of successful self-inductions which are really the exceptions. It is in regard to this situation that our understanding seriously fails.

Part of the difficulty seems to lie in the fact that the subject must also be the hypnotist. As such he is faced with the difficult problem of being passive yet taking an active role. We may therefore wonder if we are not dealing with a self-contradictory condition, hence one which cannot exist. It may be argued that after all we do know self-hypnosis takes place. True, but there is a question whether "self-hypnosis" learned by posthypnotic suggestions is truly self-hypnosis; so that whatever success may have been obtained in this manner cannot be used as counter-argument.

This leaves for consideration the only other form of self-hypnotism, that in which the individual learns to hypnotize himself strictly by using some trance-inducing method without benefit of any suggestions from another person. But what are the facts? I have known many individuals who could bring about suggestion phenomena of the medium trance level without the help of heterosuggestions, but I do not know of any well authenticated cases of self-induced *deep* hypnosis (the Braid effect excluded) in which suggestions were used in the induction, or in which the subject gave himself suggestions. I know of only one instance of self-hypnotism in which the authenticity and identity of the induced condition as the Braid effect was fairly certain. Other cases have come to my attention which, in spite of inconclusive evidence, seemed to be typical of the Braid effect. In none of these was there evidence that the subjects gave themselves any suggestions during the trance. In the one case with which I was closely associated, this would have been impossible for the subject, thus it would appear that self-induced hypnosis in the proper sense of the term is possible. The percentage of success is not known. Nor has it been adequately demonstrated that it is possible to bring about *deep* hypnosis by means of only autosuggestions or giving one's self suggestions while in the trance without the help of heterosuggestions or posthypnotic suggestions. It may seem strange that it should be relatively easy to produce light to medium self-hypnosis, but that there should be so much doubt regarding deep self-hypnosis. I think if the reader will go back to the theory presented earlier, the reason will become much clearer. This does not mean that self-hypnosis can be derived from the theory as one would derive a theorem from a set of axioms. If self-hypnosis and autosuggestion are mainly like heterohypnosis and heterosuggestion, and if the theory presented earlier is correct, then this theory should extend to the present group of phenomena. The ideomotor and generalization aspects do not seem to present any particular problem, but "dissociation" does, possibly because it is itself a poorly defined and poorly understood concept. Psychoanalysis proposes that a splitting of the self takes place, at least at the level of the executive functions (ego), but this leaves much unsaid. On the other hand, Stembo's proe-hypnotic suggestions (page 276), which do not necessarily eliminate the notion of the splitting of the self, may contain a solution to the problem. This notion suggests the initiation of the suggestion occurs prior to the induction of a full hypnotic state instead of after, and thus the question of "who" is the executive during the self-induced hypnotic state does not arise. Unconscious ideation, unconscious problem solving and so forth* which often manifest themselves overtly as delayed responses lend some support to this notion. If such is the

---

*It can be argued that to speak of unconscious and conscious ideation and the like is doing nothing more than splitting the self. Granted, but this is a normal split present at all times in the waking individual; whereas we are concerned here with an induced split, above and beyond this, presumably involving a different type and order of partitioning.

situation, then the main role of hypnosis would be to facilitate or inhibit certain processes with the over-all effect of favoring the manifestation of the proe-hypnotic self-suggestion. In this case any split of the self could well be the consequence of the subject's own conception of the nature of self-hypnosis, a conception which may have forced itself into his mind as a result of his unconscious attempt to resolve the paradox of "who" is the hypnotist and "who" is the subject in the self-hypnotic situation.

The best and most detailed treatment of the psychoanalytic solution to this question is that of Jones.[95] The approach essentially extends hetero-hypnosis and heterosuggestion to include the present case. The main difference is the postulation of a split of the self whereby one half takes over the functions of the superego as the hypnotist does and dictates to the other half.

Let us now examine some of the methods used to produce self-hypnosis. There is one sure way for an individual to acquire the ability to hypnotize himself. This is to be put into a deep hypnotic trance by a hypnotist and to be given a posthypnotic suggestion to the effect that self-hypnosis will henceforth be possible.* A typical posthypnotic suggestion of this sort could be worded as follows:

Any time in the future that you wish to induce a deep state of hypnosis in yourself, even deeper than the one in which you are now, you will be able to do so. All you will need to do is to place yourself in a comfortable position and relax by taking a few deep breaths and think of relaxing as you did when I hypnotized you a while ago. When you are relaxed, tell yourself mentally that you are going to go into a deep hypnotic state, then take three deep breaths and as soon as you have taken the third breath you will go into a very deep trance. During hypnosis you will be able to think and will have full command of yourself. You will be able to give yourself any suggestion you wish while hypnotized and you will be able to bring about any hypnotic phenomena you desire. To awaken you will only need to tell yourself that you are going to wake up. You will then count to three, and at the last count you will be wide awake. Should any emergency arise while you are hypnotized you will immediately and automatically awaken ready to take whatever action is necessary. Until I tell you otherwise, any time that you have hypnotized yourself, you will always be able to hear me and you will carry out any suggestions I give you, even if they are contradictory to some you have given yourself. But

---

*It is rather remarkable that this simple method was not described in the scientific literature until 1941 in an article by Salter,[148] although it had been used in Europe prior to this date.

you will not listen to anyone else or accept suggestions from others unless you have previously decided to do so. You will always employ good judgment in using self-hypnosis, and will not use it excessively. You can use it to remove any pains and aches from which you suffer, but you will always consult a physician if they are persistent. You can produce hallucinations if you wish, but you will be careful to do so only when others are not around, or if they are, only if they know what you are doing. You will never give yourself hallucinations that could lead you to harm yourself or others. These suggestions will be effective until I change or remove them. No one else, including you, can change or remove them.

This is, of course, only one of many kinds of such suggestions. It will not be satisfactory in all cases. In spite of the suggestion some individuals may at first have some difficulty hypnotizing themselves. It may be helpful in such cases to add later to the instructions that they will fixate their eyes on some object or point at the start of the induction. Also, instead of telling the subject to breathe three times and that hypnosis will set in at the third breath, he should be told to breathe ten or twelve times and that as he does so he will gradually pass into a trance so that by the time he takes his tenth or twelfth breath he will be deeply hypnotized.

Obviously, there is more to teaching self-hypnosis by means of post-hypnotic suggestions than in just giving them. It may involve a training situation in the true sense of the word. Furthermore, the suggestions have to be carefully planned.

First of all, there is the signal used to induce hypnosis. It can be anything from a word said aloud, willing one's self hypnotized, or actually going step by step, mentally or otherwise, through the procedure for induction. Whether the signal makes any difference in the production of hypnosis is not known. One precaution to observe in setting a signal: it should not be one that the subject is likely to encounter by accident and respond to at the wrong time. It is good to know the subject's habits and interests well before deciding on a signal. I know of one instance where it was thought that the word "yoga" was unusual enough not to be used commonly by the subject. But in the course of a conversation which followed when the subject came out of the trance, he unintentionally used this word on several occasions, and every time he went into a trance. The best way to get around such an eventuality is to clearly specify the conditions under which the signal will be effective. Thus we can tell the subject: "Whenever you say the word 'yoga' three times in rapid succession, and only if you say it three times in rapid succession, will you enter a deep state of hypnosis." Note that we said specifically "rapid succession" because if we had said merely "three times" this could have meant to the subject that any time he said this word three times irrespective of what came in between he would be hypnotized. Even to specify "in succession" still leaves some possible ambiguity. It should be clear that the more complex we make the signal and its associated conditions, the less likelihood there is that the subject will respond to it accidentally, but it must not be so complex that the subject might forget some part, get mixed up, or that it might require too much time for the subject to bring about hypnosis. The effectiveness of posthypnotic suggestions over time is inversely related to the complexity of the suggestion. Furthermore, the type of signal and conditions used are also determined by the ease with which the subject can enter the hypnotic state. In some cases, such as when an individual at first has difficulty hypnotizing himself, one signal may be specified for his early training and later changed when he becomes more proficient.

Second, there is the matter of what limitations, if any, should be imposed upon the subject's use of self-hypnosis. The hypnotist who gives an individual this ability has a responsibility to see that the subject does not harm himself with it. The indiscriminate training in self-hypnosis of disturbed individuals as a form of therapy must be strongly condemned. Only a normal, mature, intelligent individual who fully understands the limitations and dangers of hypnosis should be taught unrestricted self-hypnosis. Others should be trained only if appropriate limitations are imposed on its use and sometimes teaching self-hypnosis is definitely contraindicated.

Third, we need to realize that going into a trance state is one thing, and making use of it is another. The subject not only must be given a signal for the induction of hypnosis, but also must be instructed how to give himself hypnotic suggestions. He can be told that whenever he wants to give himself a hypnotic or posthypnotic suggestion he should first state the content of the suggestion to himself mentally, in writing, etc., then give himself whatever signal will induce hypnosis. It is also possible to combine the suggestion and the induction by instructing the subject that if he wishes to give himself a hypnotic or posthypnotic suggestion, he needs only to formulate it clearly, repeat it to himself, and that as soon as he has done so he will pass into a deep trance during which the suggestion will take effect. Thus the self-suggestion also acts as a trance-inducing signal.

Four, the subject must either be instructed how to awaken himself, or the self-induced trance must be made self-limiting. Thus you can instruct the subject that his trance will last exactly so many minutes, or you can instruct him to hold in his mind, repeat, or suggest to himself in some other way that he will wake up at a specified time, before giving himself the signal to produce hypnosis. This can be made a part of the suggestion he gives himself. There are two clauses which I think are important for the protection of the subject. One is that unless he specifies a different duration for his trance, it will always terminate by itself after, say, 5 minutes. The other provision is that if anything should occur which endangers the subject while he is in self-hypnosis, he will either wake up fully aware of the situation and ready to act accordingly, or he will take the proper measures while still hypnotized, whichever way is best for him.

This matter of protection of the subject leads to a fifth point. It is not known whether or not a person can give effective suggestions to a self-hypnotized individual when this has not been provided for, but should it be possible, as a safeguard for the subject your posthypnotic suggestions should include a provision to make it impossible for another person to give suggestions to the self-hypnotized subject unless he has given himself a suggestion to the contrary. Furthermore, as an added precaution, this provision can be so made that the hypnotist doing the training is the only one who can remove it. However, since it is often useful in training for the hypnotist to be able to give autohypnotized subjects suggestions and generally guide them while in a trance, provisions should be made for this for the length of time deemed necessary. Sometimes the subject will spontaneously lose rapport with the hypnotist when going into autohypnosis. To circumvent such a contingency it is good practice to emphasize by suggestions that the subject will be able to talk with the hypnotist and carry out his suggestions at all times.

A sixth point to consider is the fact that a deep hypnotic subject usually has spontaneous amnesia for the trance experience when dehypnotized. In any case, since posthypnotic suggestions seem to be most effective if amnesia is present, it is common practice to suggest amnesia. This means of course that the dehypnotized subject must again be told in the waking state what to do to hypnotize himself, how to give himself hypnotic suggestions, and what limitations have been imposed (unless this last knowledge is contraindicated).

Finally, a seventh point is that although giving the posthypnotic suggestion once is usually sufficient, it is sometimes necessary to give it several times, to "work through" the suggestion, or both. Having dehypnotized the subject and given him the waking instructions, he is told to try them. At first he should be allowed to try just producing hypnosis, then later hypnosis with suggestions. For one thing, this gives the subject a chance to ask any questions that may come to his mind and it also allows the hypnotist to make sure that the subject is proceeding correctly as well as to check on the effectiveness of the instructions. In some instances when the subject first tries the instructions it will be found that, although he shows some signs of being affected, he is not passing into a deep enough trance, is extremely slow in doing this or his suggestions lack effectiveness. The hypnotist can often help him by giving a strong command of "sleep" and other suggestions at the appropriate moment, to act as a booster and help the subject over the hump. Also the hypnotist is in a better position to determine what is hindering the subject and to make the necessary readjustments. In many instances the subject just has to "learn" how to make use of posthypnotic suggestions. With others it seems to take a little time for the suggestions to attain their full effect and actual usage helps. As will be seen later, this is generally true of any posthypnotic suggestion.

Salter's Techniques

So much for basic principles. We might now look briefly at Salter's three techniques. To begin, Salter says that unless the subject can respond to suggestions of limb catalepsy or inability to rise from the chair, it is not worthwhile trying to teach him autohypnosis. A depth score of 13 or better on the Davis-Husband scale is highly desirable. Salter first spends some time preparing the subject with what he calls pretrance instructions. These are aimed at giving the subject a set in regard to autohypnosis and the use of posthypnotic suggestions. He is told that he will soon be given a suggestion which will allow him to subsequently hypnotize himself, and it is described to him. Following this the postural sway suggestion is given to the subject as a heterosuggestion, then he is told to repeat the test by mentally giving himself suggestions of falling back. It is added that he need not exactly duplicate the hypnotist's suggestions, but he should merely follow the general pattern. He can either think to himself "I am falling, etc. . . ." or he can actually whisper or say these words in a low tone. In the next step, the subject is hypnotized and what he has been told in the waking state is reiterated. The subject is then awakened and questioned about his amnesia for the trance. If he remembers something, Salters advises passing it off lightly while suggesting in the waking state that the amnesia will be more complete presently. A short rest period is then allowed in which social conversation is undertaken and after about 5 minutes it is matter of factly proposed to the subject that he try to hypnotize himself as he was previously told he would (before hypnosis). As soon as the subject is hypnotized, he is requested to give himself suggestions aimed at bringing about such effects as glove anesthesia. (Salter points out that you should not ask the subject to produce an effect that he has not been able to produce when hypnotized on previous occasions by the hypnotist.) A test of the effectiveness of these self-induced responses is made, then the subject is told that he can wake up whenever he desires, a few minutes being hinted at as a good time.

Salter's second method is most successful with a good hypnotic subject. Having previously determined what forms of heterosuggestion are most effective for inducing hypnosis, the hypnotist types out these suggestions verbatim, the only alteration being that they are worded in the first person. These suggestions cover both the induction and deepening phases. They also contain self-suggestions aimed at allowing the hypnotist to have rapport with the subject as well as suggestions regarding his future ability to produce self-hypnosis. The hypnotist gives these to the subject to memorize, again explaining that it is the form rather than the content which is important. He is told not to try to hypnotize himself yet. The pretrance preparation used with the first method is then given, but it *excludes* any mention of the use of posthypnotic effects. In addition, the principles of suggestion are explained to the subject. Namely, that they are the result of ideomotor action and that the actual origin of the suggestions is immaterial for their effectiveness. This is emphasized. The subject is then asked to slowly repeat the memorized instruction to himself, preferably in a low voice (so that the hypnotist can follow him). Sometimes the subject has to do this several times, with variations to find the most effective way of using them to hypnotize himself. The hypnotist can help in this and within limits can help the subject along with a few heterosuggestions here and there. Once self-hypnosis is induced in this way the method proceeds as the first one did.

Salter's third method, which he calls the method of "fractional autohypnosis," appears to be particularly applicable to individuals of relatively low suggestibility who can produce limb catalepsy, inability to get out of a chair, etc. The basic idea behind this technique, according to Salter, is to teach autohypnosis part by part rather than as a whole.

Actually Salter's technique is not so much one of teaching by part as one of building up the subject's suggestibility in a gradual fashion by getting him to respond successfully to a variety of suggestions, for the mechanism of heteroaction is the same whether the subject gives the suggestions to himself or some one else does. Salter refers to Hull's work in support of his view, but I believe he has misinterpreted what Hull said.

In any case, the technique is essentially to give the subject a variety of waking heterosuggestions, roughly in order of increasing difficulty, each time having him repeat the suggested effect by autosuggestion. The subject is allowed to practice each suggestion a while and at the same time it is repeatedly impressed upon him that it is immaterial who gives the suggestions. Salter uses suggestions in this order: postural sway test, Chevreul pendulum, heaviness of the right arm, heaviness of the left arm, heaviness of the right leg, heaviness of the left leg, heaviness of the entire body and heaviness of the eyelids (eyelid catalepsy). The subject should be thoroughly drilled in each of these. This, Salter says, ends the first lesson. At its termination the subject is told to autosuggest away any fatigue. He is instructed to go home and practice autosuggesting first heaviness of both arms at the same time, then of the two legs together and, finally, of the whole body. Following this, with his body heavy, he is to induce catalepsy of the eyelids which he will terminate when he desires to do so. He is also to practice removing fatigue by autosuggestions.

When the subject is next seen, Salter says you should have him demonstrate how quickly he can produce the above effects. If he has practiced sufficiently he should have no difficulty. This is followed by a new pretrance preparation in which the subject is told that self-hypnosis is nothing but a state of high concentration. It is explained to him how one becomes unaware of certain stimuli when intensely concentrating on something else. Anesthesia is explained in this manner. Illusions and hallucinations are compared to dreams and amnesia is compared to the forgetfulness following sleep. The somnambulistic trance is then described, acted out or demonstrated with another subject. Next the subject is asked to hypnotize himself as deeply as possible and the hypnotist proceeds to bring about various hypnotic effects in the subject, allowing him to bring about each effect in his turn every time, just as was done with waking suggestions in the first lesson.

Hypnotists who have been using posthypnotic suggestions to teach individuals to hypnotize themselves have spoken of this method as auto- or self-hypnosis in the same sense as they would if the subject had truly induced the trance in himself entirely by his own self-application of the basic principles of hypnotism. But can we seriously call this self-hypnosis? The facts are: 1. The condition results from heterosuggestion, and as far as we know is no different from hypnosis resulting from any other posthypnotic signal used to induce a trance. The entire training procedure is nothing more than giving the subject a highly complex posthypnotic signal. 2. There is reason to believe that when a signal activates a posthypnotic response the subject spontaneously enters a trance state which can be considered a continuation of that in which he was initially when told about the signal; thus it is a heterosuggested state of hypnosis. 3. The ability of the subject to wake himself at will, induce hypnotic phenomena on his own and in general give himself suggestions while in hypnosis can be imparted to the subject equally well in any given heterohypnotic session. It is therefore not specifically characteristic of self-hypnosis, but is as much a heterosuggested behavior as any other heterosuggested phenomenon.

All of this brings numerous questions to mind. For instance, what happens to the spontaneous trance when a signal is used to produce hypnosis? More important to us theoretically is what happens to the trance (corresponding to the specific instructions of the posthypnotic suggestion) as the subject utilizes it more and more? Does it increasingly become a truly auto-induced effect? If so, how is this change affected by methods like Salter's that combine auto- and heterosuggestions during the training period? And finally, do these and other considerations make any difference from an applied point of view? We can only ask questions at this stage—the answers are yet to come. In the meantime, we will distinguish between *self-hypnosis proper* and *pseudo-self-hypnosis*, or *mediated self-hypnosis*.

INDUCTION OF SELF-HYPNOSIS PROPER

These methods all have one disadvantage—they require the help of a well trained hypnotist. Is it possible to train one's self without such help? Probably yes. At least it seems rather certain that self training can lead to the ability to create a medium to medium-deep trance. We can predict this on a theoretical basis, and facts support it. On the other hand, very little can definitely be said for or against the possibility of training one's self to go into a deep hypnosis. To date I have not found any authentic case.*

PHONOGRAPH RECORD TECHNIQUE

One method which immediately comes to mind is to listen to a recording of trance-inducing suggestions and instructions while doing whatever else is necessary for the production of hypnosis, such as deep breathing, visual fixation, etc. This method has become rather popular in recent years and such recordings have been made and offered on the market by some hypnotists. Although they are sold for the purpose of producing "self-hypnosis," this is not self-hypnosis. A little consideration of the principles of suggestion and hypnosis that have been discussed in previous pages will show quite

---

*Excluding yoga and similar practices. It is highly probable that yogis and others learn self-hypnosis or a state closely related to it. To what extent they learn alone is not clear. It is my understanding that a true yogi has a sort of guide or teacher called a *guru* during part of his training at least, and that the latter is supposed to be at hand to help the neophyte on certain exercises.

clearly that this is no more self-hypnosis than if the suggestions were being given by the hypnotist in person. It is still heterohypnosis. What if the subject makes his own record and speaks to himself? Would that be self-hypnosis? This is a more difficult question to answer. It certainly is closer to self-suggestion. Still the source of suggestions is outside and apart from the subject. The record is a surrogate hypnotist. From a practical standpoint this is probably immaterial. The use of recordings does make the subject rather independent of the presence of the hypnotist and it can be a highly useful device.

In general, using recordings is quite simple. Pick out one technique of induction, then make a recording of the exact instructions and suggestions the hypnotist would use. You can eliminate such things as instructions to relax or fixate on an object by using a timing device which turns the recording on after sufficient time has been allowed for the initial preparations. A tape recorder is best because of its great versatility and long run economy. One big disadvantage of the method is, of course, that the suggestions cannot be paced to the actual progress of the trance induction nor worded in the most appropriate way at each step. The use of suitable voice inflections and other vocal devices is largely eliminated, but with a little experience you can still make use of them within limits. Readers who make their own records will usually find it desirable to alter them for greater effectiveness after they have tried them out, for which a tape recorder is most advantageous.

Some hypnotists and lay persons believe that an excellent way of using these recordings is by playing them to one's self while asleep. Complete outfits including recorder, timer, and pillow-speakers have been put on the market. Although adequate experimental verification is lacking, suggestions given to individuals during the time they are passing from wakefulness to sleep and while awaking appear to be relatively effective. Suggestions given to an individual while he is in deep sleep appear to be rather ineffective. Reports of successful attempts of this kind rarely state how deeply asleep the individual was, and we may suspect that he was not in the deepest state of natural sleep. In general, the evidence I have been able to gather regarding the effectiveness of recorded suggestions during sleep has been disappointing.

RHODES' TECHNIQUE

One method of self-training in autohypnosis proper which has merit has been reported by Rhodes.[143] He says:

> The first stage of autohypnosis is "eye closure." By this I mean a condition in which, although you are awake, you cannot open your eyes. It may be achieved as follows: Sit in a comfortable chair, in a quiet room. Then:

1. Say *one* and as you say it, think, "My eyelids are getting very heavy." Repeat that thought, think only that thought, concentrate upon it, mean it and believe it as you think it. Exclude any other thoughts such as, "I'll see if this will work." Just repeat the one thought, "My lids are getting very heavy, very heavy." If you think only that thought, concentrate upon it, mean it and believe it as you think it, your lids will begin to feel heavy. Don't wait until they get very heavy. When they begin to get heavy, proceed to the next step.

2. Say *two* and as you say it, think, "My eyelids are getting so heavy now, they'll close by themselves." As in *one*, repeat that thought, think only that thought, concentrate upon it, believe it. Do not force your eyes closed, do not fight to keep them open; just concentrate on the one thought. "My eyelids are getting so heavy now, they'll close by themselves," and as you repeat that thought, that thought alone, let your eyelids do as they want to. If you really concentrate on that thought to the exclusion of any other, mean it and believe it as you think it, your eyelids will slowly close. When your lids are closed, allow them to remain shut and continue as follows:

3. Say *three* and as you say it, think "My lids are so tightly shut, I cannot open them no matter how hard I try." As above, repeat that thought, think only that thought, concentrate upon it, mean it and believe it. As you do so, try to open your eyes and you will find that you cannot until you say the word *open*, and then your lids will pop open.

Do not be discouraged by failure in your first attempts at self-taught autohypnosis. This is the type of experiment in which the average person will fail the first two or three times he tries it because the average person has not learned how to concentrate upon one thought alone, that is, to the exclusion of all others. This is not due to a lack of intelligence. Indeed, intelligent people have rather involved thought patterns and are accustomed to thinking more than one thought at a time. Concentration upon only one thought, to the exclusion of all others, involves a new discipline, and this requires determination and practice. So, if you fail the first time, try again. If you are intelligent enough to control your mental processes you can succeed in thinking only one thought at a time; and once you achieve that ability, autohypnosis is in your grasp.

Thus, when your eyes close after *two*, and you go on to *three* and think, "My lids are so tightly shut, I cannot open them no matter how hard I try," you must keep repeating that thought, that thought alone, and as you think it, try to open your eyes.

As long as you concentrate on that thought alone, your eyelids will remain shut. Your muscles will strain to open them, but your eyes will remain shut until you say *open*, either out loud or mentally.

Once you have achieved eye closure, the next step is to speed up the process. Try it two or three times to make sure the eye closure is good. Every time you do it, the effect will be stronger. Now for the acceleration. Do *one* as above, and the moment your lids get heavy, go on to *two*. As you say *two*, think the requisite thought only once, or twice at the most, but think it exclusively. By now you will have acquired that ability. As your lids close, say *three*, and again think the requisite thought only once, or twice at most, but think it exclusively. Your lids will remain shut. Release them by the command, *open*.

Now go through the procedure once again, but instead of saying, *one*, *two*, and *three*, just think those numbers, following each one with its appropriate thought. Finally go through the entire procedure without the numbers; just think the thought for *one* once, the thought for *two* once, and then the thought for *three* once. With practice you may be able to get almost instantaneous eye closure by merely letting your lids close and thinking the thought for *three* once.

You will find that as you acquire speed, you achieve stronger and stronger control. Having mastered the discipline of concentrating upon one simple thought at a time (steps *one* and *two*), you will be able to attain step *three*, a complex thought, almost instantaneously. The touchstone of your success with autohypnosis is rapid eye closure.* Once you have achieved that, you can proceed to the depth of trance necessary to meet your particular problem or problems.

The next step is relaxation. Keep your eyes closed, and think, "I'm going to take a deep breath and relax all over." Take a *deep* breath, and as you exhale you will relax all over. Think, "I'll breathe normally and deeply and relax more and more with every breath." After that, as you breathe, you will relax more and more.

With good eye closure and relaxation (which in a short time comes with the eye closure), you will have attained the first degree of autohypnotic trance. Your mind is now ready to accept suggestions you make to it with both hypnotic and posthypnotic effect. But just as in the case of the eye closure itself, where the total rapid result was built up through repetition, so also the succeeding steps sometimes need practice. The secret of success is concentration—the ability to think one thought at a time, to the exclusion of all others, and to mean and believe it.

Try simple suggestions first. For example: Grasp your left index finger with your right fist. Think, "I cannot pull my finger out." As above concentrate on that thought alone, mean it, believe it, and as you think it, try to pull your finger out. It will remain stuck until you think, "Now I can release it," or use some other word or phrase with similar import.

Rhodes goes on to list a number of other simple suggestions that can be used in the same manner, for example arm rigidity, hand clasping, being stuck to a chair, glove anesthesia, illusion of heat and so forth.

The Author's Technique

My own procedure of self training resembles both Rhodes' method and Salter's third method. It differs primarily in the fact that the trainee works entirely alone.

Insure yourself privacy for a minimum of 1 hour at a time. Then begin by doing the Chevreul pendulum experiment with as many variations as possible. At first control of the direction of movement is more important than amplitude of motion. If you get only slight motion the first time, don't worry about it. Later you can try to improve it. It is quite easy to spend an hour with the pendulum, and if you are at all successful you should go ahead and practice until you have perfect control over it. Don't be satisfied with one trial, but repeat various motions over and over. If you do not have much success after half an hour, you should stop and try the postural sway test. Of course, if you succeed with the pendulum test you should plan on doing the postural sway test right after it. If possible someone should be present when you are using the postural sway suggestions. However, it can be safely

*I cannot agree entirely with Rhodes on this point. Satisfactory eye closure is not always necessarily related to satisfactory trance depth.

done alone, as follows. Place your back against a wall, then move forward no more than one foot. By placing your hand back against the wall from this position, you can gently ease yourself backward against the wall a few times in order to make sure you will not fall too far or too hard against the wall. It is a good idea to hold the head slightly forward so that the shoulders hit the wall first. It is also possible to hang a small cushion on the wall at head level, although I have never found a real need for it. Again, do not be discouraged if you do not fall the first time. If you notice any backward sway, you can feel satisfied that you have responded. Remember also that even when no overt act is observed, a suggestion may still have had some effect which will eventually make itself felt.

As soon as you have succeeded with the backward sway suggestion, try variations of it. Actually, once you are satisfied that you can fall backward as a result of suggestions you can limit yourself to strong swaying in other directions without falling.

If you have time, you can try the hand levitation suggestion, but it is best to proceed slowly and master each step rather than to half complete many suggestions. In your study period you should repeat the suggestions done the previous time before trying any new ones. Usually you will find that you can do the first suggestions much better. If not, spend some time practicing them, making sure to save at least half of your time for the new exercises. Seat yourself comfortably, preferably in an armchair, letting your arms rest on the arms of the chair. Close your eyes and try to levitate one hand and arm. After you have succeeded in getting it up a few times, suggest to yourself that you cannot bring it down again. Do this a few times too, then having returned your arm back to normal position by telling yourself that you can (or something of this sort), suggest that your hand is heavy, that you cannot lift it, that it is stuck to the arm of the chair. If you do not have too much success with the arm levitation, do not insist on it at this stage, but go on to the suggestion of heaviness of your hand. After you have succeeded with this, try the hand levitation again. Alternate these for a few trials then, when you feel you have mastered them, repeat with your other hand; then try both hands at the same time.

The next exercise you should try is to suggest heaviness of one foot, then of both feet while sitting in a chair with both feet flat on the floor. If this works well then suggest heaviness of your entire body. In doing this, it is best to do it part by part at first. Begin with the hands, next the arms, the feet, the legs and so forth. Next in line is the hand clasping test which you can follow with arm rigidity suggestions. Also try causing your hand alone to stiffen, then each finger in turn. Finally, do the eye catalepsy test.

Once again you may find it desirable to change the order of these suggestions.

Regardless of your success or failure with any of the suggestions, you should practice inducing relaxation by autosuggestions. Relaxation is usually obtained primarily by suggesting heaviness of the entire body, either as a whole or by parts. You will quickly find this relatively easy to do. When using suggestions of heaviness to induce relaxation, it is best not to attempt to test the effectiveness of the suggestion since this will produce tension and defeat your purpose. If you are relaxing properly you will be able to feel it. As soon as this process is fairly well controlled, particularly if you have been successful with the eye catalepsy suggestion, give yourself suggestions of relaxation with your eyes open. As soon as you feel reasonably relaxed, begin giving yourself suggestions of heaviness of the eyelids and eye closure. As soon as they close, suggest eye catalepsy. At this point take a slow deep breath, hold it briefly and, as you slowly exhale, think of sleep, while you relax more if possible. Do this five times, then let your mind go blank for as long as possible. *It is essential in doing this that you make no active effort and are as passive as possible.* If thoughts intrude, as they probably will at first, just allow them to do so without pursuing them. You may pass into a dreamy condition which is characteristic of the hypnoidal state. This is probably an indication that you are on the road to deeper self-hypnosis, but is not to be interpreted as the desired end.

At this point there is little else that can be added regarding procedures for attaining deeper hypnosis, except that you should try as many different types of waking and hypnotic suggestions as possible, always working up from the simpler to the more complex. Even such a complex process as automatic writing can be brought about rather easily in many individuals. This, I suspect, would be an excellent exercise toward the production of the dissociation-like phenomena characteristic of hypnosis. Excellent accounts of procedures for bringing about automatic writing in the waking state have been described by Binet,[13] Solomon and Stein,[171] Stein[175] and Mühl.[129] Make liberal use of posthypnotic autosuggestions aimed at bringing about a faster induction and a deeper trance on future trials.

General Rules for Practice

1. You should devote as much time as possible to these exercises, but do not tire yourself. Two hours at a time is suitable. You should try to practice every day. I believe it is better to do this, even if it means spending less time on any given day, than to spend more time on each occasion, but to practice only a few times a week. As a matter of fact, you should try these suggestions as often as possible whenever you have a chance.

2. At the start of any practice period you should begin by quickly going through as many previous exercises as feasible. Later on, of course, there will be too many exercises for you to repeat. When this time comes select a few, but always end with eye catalepsy, unless you want to go beyond it. A good series is: hand heaviness, hand levitation, hand clasping, arm rigidity, eye catalepsy, inability to get out of the chair. Those which are still troublesome should be singled out for additional practice. Then go on to new suggestions. By starting out with suggestions to which you can respond your suggestibility builds up; this will enable you to more successfully tackle the newer and more difficult suggestions.

3. Do not let failure with one or more exercises prevent you from going on to the next. Just make sure you get back to the ineffective suggestions at the first opportunity.

4. Make it a regular habit at the end of each practice period to give yourself autosuggestions that the following time you will do better with the exercises which caused you difficulty and that your overall suggestibility will be highly improved. You should also do this at night as you fall asleep and in the morning when you have just awakened. In all these situations your suggestibility will be at its highest point.

5. Don't be afraid to try variations of the procedures described here. You may find one that is far more effective for yourself. In particular, you may find it more helpful to fixate your gaze on some object or to look straight ahead of you as at a distance, rather than to keep your eyes closed.

6. When you are suggesting an effect, keep your attention concentrated on this effect *for as long as you want it to act*. This is a very important point which is well presented in Rhodes' discussion of his method.

7. Use your powers to visualize and to imagine actual experiences as much as possible. The more vividly you can do this not only in respect to the effect you want to produce, but also with respect to the sensations which must be associated with it, the more potent your autosuggestions will be.

What is Hypnosis Like?

One question is probably uppermost in your mind: What does it feel like to be hypnotized? How do I know that I am in a trance? There is no completely satisfactory or unique answer, since different individuals experience hypnosis in different ways. Furthermore, the experience partly depends upon the depth of trance attained. Probably your best criterion of hypnosis is our standard one, the sort of phenomena you are able to bring about by suggestions. *However, one effect which is not necessarily present even in deep hypnosis is amnesia.* For this reason you may hypnotize yourself and not detect any difference but if amnesia is present, you will often be aware of a blank period, particularly if you had noticed the time shortly before hypnotizing yourself and note it on awakening. There are many instances when the hypnotized subject awakens unaware of any passage of time. Of course you can always suggest the presence or absence of these effects. I strongly recommend, purely on theoretical grounds, that you do not suggest amnesia for your trance experiences at first. Do not suggest its absence either, unless you have specific reasons for doing so. This way, if it is spontaneously present so much the better; and if you are not able to reach a deep enough trance early in your training, you will not run the risk of adversely affecting your progress through the failure of a suggestion. When you do feel that you have progressed sufficiently, you can try to induce amnesia. You should be warned that you may find at first that this suggestion acts more as a compulsion not to make an active act of recall than as a true inability to recall material at will. You should not attempt to test yourself for recall of trance material until you have allowed some time to pass while you turn your attention to something not related to hypnosis (page 347). Another experience often reported by self-hypnotized individuals is that they felt like a sort of detached observer of their own behavior. They were aware of a kind of dissociation. Their body seemed to execute various acts on its own. This particular feeling can also be observed while executing certain waking suggestions.

The Method of Schultz, "Autogenic Training"*

Introduction

A method of training in autohypnosis called "autogenic training" or "self-relaxation through concentration" was developed by the German psychiatrist J. H. Schultz[158, 159] and his collaborators. Autogenic training is well known among European psychiatrists and psychotherapists and an extensive literature exists on the subject. The standard work by Schultz is his book *Das Autogene Training* first published in 1932 and subsequently reissued in seven editions. He defines autogenic training as a method of rational physiologic conditioning designed to produce a general psycho-biological alteration in the subject in which all the manifestations obtained through heterohypnosis are made possible. It is thus a method of systematic

*This section was especially written at the author's request by Doctor Bernard E. Gorton, M.D., Senior Psychiatrist at the Syracuse Psychopathic Hospital, Syracuse, New York. Doctor Gorton's long interest in Schultz's work as well as his thorough knowledge of the German language makes him eminently suited to write this exposition. Doctor Gorton has also long been actively interested in hypnotism and has made a number of important contributions.

autohypnotic training which Schultz compares to a graduated series of mental exercises or gymnastics. Autogenic training can be used to bring about an improved level of functioning and life performance in normal individuals; or in control, and occasional removal, of maladaptive behavior patterns or symptoms in patients.

The purpose of autogenic training is defined by Schultz as the capacity to develop by means of a definite prescribed series of exercises the capacity to attain inner relaxation and introspective ability. This is supposed to lead to a self-directed organism which permits the strengthening of healthy biologic potentials and reduction or abolition of malfunction or disease. Schultz mentions the following specific attainments possible through autogenic training.

1. Ability to rest and restore energy.
2. Ability to relax oneself, not through "will power" but through the dissolution of inner tensions.
3. Self regulation of ordinarily autonomous body functions (e.g., circulation).
4. Heightened capacity for voluntary performance (e.g., memory).
5. Ability to abolish painful sensation (analgesia).
6. Capacity for self-mastery through concentration on resolutions expressed in various formulas (e.g., "order is freedom") which take effect in a manner analogous to that seen in posthypnotic suggestion obtained by in various formulas (e.g., "order is freedom") which take effect in a manner analogous to that seen in posthypnotic suggestion obtained by heterohypnosis.
7. Ability to develop self-criticism and self-control through introspection in the autohypnotic state.

Method of Training

Schultz states that autogenic training is based on ideomotor action obtained through systematic autosuggestive training on the part of the subject. His aim is to develop such training through a progressively graded series of exercises which will be described. The subject starts by attaining control over the voluntary muscles since this is most familiar to him. Later, he progressively develops control over the circulatory system, heart, respiration, bodily organs and finally the head. Schultz recommends that the exercises be performed in a relaxed sitting position, preferably in an easy chair with arm rests, although they may also be performed in a supine position.

First Exercise, Muscle Relaxation. The subject assumes one of the positions described and formulates in his mind the following suggestions.

1. "I am completely relaxed." (Basic goal of the entire training.)
2. "The right (left) arm is completely heavy." (First formula of exercises.)

He recommends that in a right-handed individual the right arm be used in beginning the training process; conversely, left-handed individuals should concentrate on the left arm. After 1 to 2 minutes "termination" of the exercise is performed by concentrating on the following suggestions which are to be used whenever a progressive exercise is terminated.

1. "The arm is stiff!"
2. "Breathe deeply!"
3. "Open the eyes!"

Schultz recommends that for the first 1 to 2 weeks there should be two or three brief daily exercise sessions, at all times under conscientious control. If the exercise is successfully carried out, the sensation of heaviness is markedly felt first in the arm and eventually it becomes spontaneously generalized into all four extremities.

Second Exercise, Feeling of Warmth (Vasomotor Relaxation).

1. "I am completely relaxed."
2. "The arms (legs) are completely heavy."
3. "The right (left) arm is very warm."

No "termination" is needed for the experience of warmth since this subsides spontaneously, but the previous standard termination formula is used. Schultz recommends that this exercise be continued for 2 weeks or until the feeling of warmth is felt in all extremities. He states that a rise of body temperature of 1°C. can be demonstrated if the exercise is successful.

Third Exercise, Heart Regulation. This exercise is started by placing the right hand over the heart so that the subject learns to develop "heart consciousness." In addition to the three formulas already described, the following is now used.

4. "The heart beats quietly and strongly."

Ultimately, control of the pulse rate is made possible through autosuggestion, but Schultz warns against any attempt to produce undue slowing of the pulse.

Fourth Exercise, Control of Respiration. After the previous three exercises have been mastered, control of the respiratory function is attained through the formula.

5. "I am breathing slowly and easily."

If necessary the supplementary thought "I breathe with no conscious effort" is used.

When the subject has practiced each of these four exercises for 10 to 14 days each (i.e., after a total of 6 to 10 weeks of training), he goes on to the next exercise.

Fifth Exercise, Control of the Abdomen. The formula used is

    6. "The solar plexus is warm."

When this exercise has been mastered, the subject is able to be completely relaxed, breathing quietly with a regular pulse and a sensation of streaming warmth throughout the entire body.

Sixth Exercise, Control of the Cerebral Region. The formula used here is

    7. "The forehead feels pleasantly cool."

The development of the experience of a cool forehead requires 1 to 2 weeks. When this has been attained, it is possible to carry out the complete set of exercises, using all seven formulas as a unit.

    1. "I am completely relaxed."
    2. "The arms (legs) are completely heavy."
    3. "The right (left) arm is very warm."
    4. "The heart beats quietly and strongly."
    5. "I am breathing slowly and easily."
    6. "The solar plexus is warm."
    7. "The forehead feels pleasantly cool."

After 2 to 3 months, the average person is able to master the seven exercises. It is necessary to practice them once, preferably twice, daily in the following 4 to 6 months until the subjective feeling becomes progressively more intense and is developed more and more promptly. Each set of exercises is terminated according to the standard formula.

Comments

At the present time Schultz's autogenic training is practically unknown in this country. There is no other comparable method of autohypnotic training in use; Salter's method of hypnotic conditioning comes closest to it. The approach used by Schultz is in definite contrast to the hypnotherapeutic methods which have gained general acceptance in this country which are based upon a "dynamic" approach designed to help the patient gain an understanding of the unconscious factors in his behavior.

It is noteworthy that autogenic training has found a wide acceptance in Europe and that there is an extensive clinical and experimental literature devoted to the subject which suggests that this method has produced definite results and has been helpful in many cases. Schultz himself points out the close relationship of his work to the "progressive relaxation" advocated by Jacobson and also to the methods employed in yoga. It may be concluded that autogenic training deserves more study and investigation in this country than it has yet received.

UTILIZATION OF SELF-HYPNOSIS

How should you go about using self-hypnotic suggestions? Most hypnotists instruct the student to give himself whatever suggestion he has in mind after he has obtained the trance state. Although some peculiar dissociation of personality might be taking place which resolves the problem, it seems to me that for the subject to assume this much initiative is not compatible with the essential passivity which is presumably one aspect of hypnosis. Furthermore, this technique is not likely to work very well for individuals who have difficulty in attaining a medium or medium-deep hypnosis. Instead a technique which seems to work equally well and which does not have this defect is to give yourself the suggestions just prior to inducing hypnosis. I am acquainted with one hypnotist who recommends writing down the suggestion on a piece of paper, folding or crumpling the paper, and keeping it in one hand. He proposes that the piece of paper acts through association as a constant reminder of the suggestion after the trance is induced. This procedure only needs to be temporary. By using it you can give yourself a suggestion, for instance, to turn on a recording which contains further and more complex suggestions. You may instruct yourself to read such suggestions on a paper prepared ahead of time. You can even give yourself posthypnotic instructions in regard to future trance inductions in this manner. This approach to self-hypnotic suggestions is particularly recommended to those who have difficulty producing a deep autohypnosis or who "go blank" when the hypnotic state appears and hence who are unable to make use of it for suggestions.

Another solution is to use a phonograph or tape recording which is automatically turned on by a timing device which you have previously set to operate after induction of the trance. Although I have not heard of this method failing, it could conceivably do so if the trance state brought about a sufficient loss of rapport with the environment. Of course, the induction of self-hypnosis and the acceptance and carrying out of autosuggestions are subject to the same counter-forces and vicissitudes that heterohypnosis and heterosuggestion encounter, and what we have said earlier and will consider later regarding resistance, simulation and related effects applies equally here.

In spite of the enthusiastic claims of the new Nancy school founded by

Coué and of a number of present day hypnotists, self-hypnosis is at present of limited application. This is particularly true in the area of psychotherapy, for no individual can long be his own psychotherapist. Inevitably, no matter how proficient he may be, he must encounter what Stekel has so aptly refered to as his psychic "scotoma," his inability to perceive and handle properly that which he has repressed. Actually, however, the greater percentage of potential users of self-hypnosis are far from being qualified therapists. Thus self-cure through hypnosis is not only a near, if not a total, impossibility, but it is also not advisable for the majority of individuals. The only efficient and safe use of self-hypnosis for psychotherapy is under the guidance and supervision of a qualified therapist. But then what is the advantage of self-hypnosis over heterohypnosis if a second person, a therapist, is still required? Actually, there is really no advantage, but there is some value in combining self-hypnosis with heterohypnosis in the handling of some psychotherapy cases, particularly those in which hypnotherapy is being used. Some individuals seem to respond better to self-hypnosis than to heterohypnosis, possibly because it allows them to participate more actively in the therapy and induction. In fact, in many instances, the main, and even the only, justification for teaching self-hypnosis to a patient undergoing psychotherapy is, as Wolberg [205] has pointed out, to enable him to acquire self-sufficiency, for self-hypnosis teaches the patient that he can do for himself what the therapist does for him, hence that there is no need for him to be dependent upon him. Eventually, the patient must learn to do entirely without hypnosis for it must never be allowed to become a crutch.

Besides the "scotoma" problem just mentioned, another limitation of self-hypnosis seems to lie in that the effective use of suggestion calls not only for careful planning, but also for on the spot alterations aimed to take advantage of, counteract and more generally take into account events *which cannot be anticipated*. Lack of empirical data does not allow an estimation of the extent of this limitation. It is possible that it is not as serious as I conceive it to be, and that with future developments it will be largely overcome. The answer may lie in the direction of the production of secondary personalities and dissociative phenomena in general.

Thus far we have been mainly concerned with self-hypnosis in its applications to psychotherapy. More generally speaking, within limits and with judicious use, self-hypnosis can be a useful instrument. It is an excellent means of re-enforcing posthypnotic heterosuggestions, thereby reducing the number of visits the patient must make to the therapist as well as his dependency upon him. It can serve as a palliative agent in many conditions, and is particularly useful in controlling anticipated pain in a large variety of situations in which the hypnotist cannot be available at the critical time. Self-hypnosis can also be a valuable aid in overcoming habits, acquiring desirable habits, creating motivation, changing attitudes, increasing concentration, marshaling one's mental and, possibly, physiological resources in stress situations, reducing tension and so forth. But it should always be used under the guidance of a competent professional person. Improper use of self-hypnosis will not only defeat its own purpose, but may have unfortunate results.

11

States of Immobilization ("Animal Hypnosis")

T HIS IS CERTAINLY a topic of no mean interest from a scientific standpoint, and in time it may even turn out to be of considerable value
for the practical side of hypnotism. In spite of the rather extensive work
that has been done in this area, relatively little is known about the phenomenon and there seems to be little agreement among investigators regarding
the facts that are known. Even the methods of induction are extremely
variable in their effectiveness. Certainly, very little can be done with these
states in animals, and there are no known applications for human management with the possible exception of hypnoidization should Sidis be right.
In a book which is essentially intended to be practical it is unwarranted to
devote any large amount of space to a topic of purely academic interest at
this time. Consequently, those who are particularly interested should see
Volgyesi's fine book[184] and the excellent paper by Gilman and Marcuse[70]
which includes a good up-to-date modern bibliography.* An excellent discussion of techniques will also be found in Mangold's article.[118] We will
content ourselves here with a quick summary of the four principal ways
in which states of immobilization can be induced in animals and a brief
examination of some critical questions. The methods are:

Repetitive Stimuli. These include stroking or scratching various body parts,
gazing into the eyes of the animal, suddenly presenting a light stimulus,
closing the eyes of the beast and swinging the animal back and forth. In
general, there are no rules governing the regions of the animal that must be
stimulated.

Pressure on Body Parts. Pressure on the abdominal region of the inverted
animal is often very effective. Here again the sensitive region differs with
the species.

Inversion. Sudden inversion of the animal has been found very successful
in some instances. Investigators have built special apparatus to bring about
the desired rapid inversion.

*This bibliography will also be found, slightly enlarged, in my previous book.[191]

338

Restraint of Movement. This appears to be an essential and common feature of all experimental productions of "animal hypnosis," so much so that one wonders if this might be, after all, the main factor producing "hypnosis." It appears nearly impossible to use any method without also introducing some restraint of motion.

Generally speaking, there is no definite way to decide which of these methods will work best for a given animal, nor how the method is to be applied. In fact, the same animal may not even respond twice in the same manner to a given method. Or again, one animal may respond well to several different procedures. In some instances the effect is so transient that one may have difficulty deciding whether "hypnosis" was ever produced. Furthermore, in some cases the state of immobilization persists only as long as the stimulus is allowed to act.

In general, the states of immobilization thus produced are accompanied by a condition of hypertonicity, often associated with a marked plasticity, but relaxation and great rigidity have also been reported. Usually the animals appear to be insensitive to most stimuli. Whether this be because of an inability to respond at the motor level or because of interference at some other level is not known. *The most characteristic feature of the condition is immobility,* and it may last as long as several hours. This is the only true and general symptom or criterion. Finally, there is some evidence that with successive repetitions of the induction process animals tend to go into the state more quickly and to remain in this condition longer. Any of these symptoms can be observed at times during the induction of hypnosis in humans, but there is little evidence that they are generally characteristic of human hypnosis, with the exception perhaps of immobility. The immobility, and the fact that the procedures used in animal hypnosis belong to the classical group, have probably been major factors leading investigators to identify animal with human hypnosis. Others have been the belief once held that insensibility was characteristic of hypnosis and the resemblance of Charcot's hypnotic catalepsy to the manifestations of animal hypnosis.

I am of the opinion that, aside from certain apparent similarities, there is little basis for thinking the two states are the same, although they may be related. The Braid effect appears to be a possible link between the two. As was explained on page 44, the combination of suggestions with sensory fixation presumably prevents the stupor phase from coming about. But in animal hypnosis produced by sensory fixation, suggestions are absent and the Braid effect is free to go to completion, or what I have called *terminal dissociation.* Further evidence that the Braid effect may serve to bridge animal and human hypnosis is to be found in Sidis' work. As we just saw he identifies the hypnoidal state with "animal hypnosis." In discussing the hypnoidal state he describes it as possessing a characteristic cataleptic condition which is more or less evanescent. He also states that the hypnoidal state tends to pass into one of hypnosis or of sleep (unresponsiveness to suggestions). As his induction technique would be expected to bring about the Braid effect, the above remarks acquire significance. It may also be quite significant that Braid observed a number of atypical manifestations such as contractures, increased pulse and respiration, congestion, and even convulsions. He eventually concluded that these were side-effects arising out of specific experimental conditions and that they were not characteristic of all inductions. This conclusion, if correct, and I am inclined to believe it is, would go a long way toward establishing the Braid effect as the link between animal and human hypnosis since it makes it possible for the Braid effect to be associated with the symptoms of animal hypnosis.

The main obstacle which lies in the way of fully accepting this theory is that it is difficult to derive the condition for the production of the Braid effect from all of the techniques used to induce animal hypnosis. It is not impossible to do it, but it cannot be done at present in a sufficiently convincing manner. Conceivably not all forms of animal hypnosis are basically alike and only some can be related to human hypnosis through the Braid effect.

One reason why I do not feel that we can identify states of immobilization with modern hypnosis is that there is no evidence that suggestions play a part. It has been pointed out as a counter-argument that mechanical manipulations of the animal could certainly act as suggestions of a nonverbal kind, and more specifically, that immobilizing the animal by mechanical means suggests immobility. This assertion, cannot be rebutted conclusively at present, but is a possibility primarily because we cannot prove its absence. A suggestion, by definition, involves the transmission of ideas. Whether verbal or not it contains meaning and it is this meaning which acts upon the individual and, presumably, gives rise to ideomotor action, among other effects. I doubt that anything of this sort can be present when a state of immobilization is produced in a cockroach or some other lower organism! I doubt that this is the case even with higher forms such as chickens, owls and storks, and higher mammals such as rats, rabbits and guinea pigs, particularly when they have not had extensive prior contact with humans. But if we are willing to concede that a given procedure, such as restraint of movement, which gives rise to a certain state in the lower forms, is not suggestive in nature, then are we justified, without additional evidence, in saying that when the same method gives rise to an identical state (within our means of comparing them) in higher organisms it is due to a suggestive property? There are further arguments. It is difficult to separate restraint of movement as a technique from the other three methods; but if the latter can independently produce states of immobilization, it is difficult to see how they could suggest immobility to the animal. Even if immobility is suggested in all cases, we must inquire where the suggestion of tonic rigidity or hypertonicity originates, which are present far more often than not. Could it be a nonsuggestive side effect? Is thinking differently of the immobility warranted?

A second reason I find for saying hypnosis and states of immobilization are probably different is that tonic rigidity is not typical of human hypnotism. This argument has been countered by at least one hypnotist who claims that he has often observed it in his human subjects. I grant that it may take place in *some* cases, but how does its frequency in humans compare to its frequency in animals? Assuming that the two conditions are the same, we must still show that the two types of rigidity are also the same. As was pointed out earlier in the discussion of the symptoms of hypnosis, tonic rigidity might arise simply as a result of specific nonessential factors associated with the induction process. For this reason, cases of tonic rigidity in human hypnosis may definitely be as atypical as some of Charcot's symptoms. Finally, if tonic rigidity or even hypertonicity are found in all instances of human hypnosis, we must wonder why it is so outstandingly characteristic in animals and such a minor manifestation in humans. Could this be an indication that there is a basic difference between the two conditions and could this difference indicate the presence of a suggestive element? Let us suppose for a moment that undisturbed visual fixation gives rise to a condition characterized at some stage of its development by immobility and tonic rigidity or hypertonicity. What would happen if it were disturbed by some other process? The resulting condition might be arrested or destroyed, and an entirely new condition appear, the two processes might cancel each other or a second contemporaneous condition might come into existence with the result that the two conditions would coexist, possibly with one tending to mask the other. Some of the early data reported by Braid suggest that the first alternative is likely. I think now that we should also consider the last one as a possibility too.

The reader may wonder why I have been so concerned in establishing the likelihood that "animal hypnosis" is different from human hypnosis. One reason is that if we can look at it in this manner it may throw some light upon the relationship of the Braid effect to hypnosis. If we accept the possibility that states of immobilization in animals are not the same as modern hypnotism in humans, we can then ask whether a state of immobilization can be produced in humans. After all, they are mammals too, and their nervous systems should be much the same as that of other mammals in this regard. According to Piéron,[139] Sidis reported the production of "animal hypnosis" in children (the exact reference is not given). In one of his books Sidis[168] speaks of the production of "hypnoidal states" in animals and children. I am led to believe that he actually was concerned with the production of "animal hypnosis" in children. Hoagland[81] also reported the production of a state of tonic immobility in man which, presumably, is the same as that characteristic of "animal hypnosis." He describes the method as follows: "If one bends forward from the waist through an angle of 90°, places the hands on the abdomen and after taking a deep breath, is thrown violently backward through 180° by a man on either side, the skeletal muscles contract vigorously and a state of pronounced immobility lasting for some seconds may result." Hoagland adds the following significant remark: "The condition is striking and of especial interest since this type of manipulation (sudden turning into a dorsal position) is the most common one used for producing tonic immobility in vertebrates." It seems to me that in view of this it becomes difficult to maintain that human hypnotism and "animal hypnotism" are the same or are even closely related.* The best we can say for the time being is that they may be related in at least some instances. The one crucial experiment which needs to be done is to attempt to hypnotize animals by what are clearly suggestions comparable to those used in human cases. This is not as impossible a task as it may seem. In the meantime, I believe it is best to stop talking of "hypnotism" in respect to what might be better designated as "states of immobilization."

---

*Hoagland is not too clear on just how many individuals have shown this effect, or what type of persons they were. That the sample was very small seems rather certain. One cannot help wondering if the subjects in question might not have possessed a diathesis for Charcot's "grande hysterie." One can probably still find such individuals, rare as they seem to be, and a study of some of these would be well worthwhile.

12

Hypnotic Phenomena
I. Principles and Simple Demonstrations

HYPNOTIC VS. WAKING SUGGESTIBILITY

A S HAS BEEN EMPHASIZED, there is no essential difference at the objective level between waking and hypnotic suggestibility except the increased amount of suggestibility. For this reason we have described hypnosis as a state of hypersuggestibility. A few investigators believe that another difference is that the hypnotic state per se makes normally unconscious processes more amenable to conscious control by either the subject or by the hypnotist. There is certainly greater access to unconscious processes in hypnosis, but it has not been clearly shown that this effect is independent of suggestions.

One consequence of the similarity of the two states is that giving hypnotic suggestions is essentially no different from giving waking suggestions. In general, all of the rules given earlier for the case of waking suggestions apply to hypnotic suggestions. Such differences as do exist are, for the most part, a matter of degree rather than of quality. This is of course a function of the depth of hypnosis attained. The lighter the trance, the more like waking suggestions the hypnotic suggestions will be, and conversely. Therefore we will be talking here and in the next chapter primarily about suggestions and phenomena produced with medium and especially deep hypnosis, unless otherwise indicated.

Because of the very great suggestibility of the hypnotized subject, one of the most striking differences between waking and hypnotic suggestions is that whereas repetition of the ideas in the suggestions is essential in the waking state, usually one statement of the idea is fully effective in hypnosis. Furthermore, for all practical purposes anything the hypnotist says to the hypnotized subject, or even says in his presence but not necessarily to him, often has the full power of a suggestion. This leads to our first rule of caution: always make sure that your subject clearly knows when he is being given a suggestion and when he is not. One standard practice mentioned earlier, which is used by hypnotists when it is necessary for them to give different suggestions to different subjects who are all present in the same room, or when they wish to say something to other persons present in the room, is to tell the subject that he will not pay attention to anything the hypnotist says unless he, the hypnotist, address the subject first by his name. Another technique is to touch the subject on the shoulder and to tell him that he will be unable to hear anything being said as soon as you lift your hand from his shoulder until you touch him again in the same way. Whenever you suggest deafness to a subject for some reason or other, always include some sort of nonverbal signal for the recovery of audition because if the suggestion is really effective, the subject may become completely unable to hear you and attempt to suggest verbally the return of hearing may fail.

This lack of responsiveness is not to be confused with a "break in rapport," where the subject is able to hear, but has lost his responsiveness itself. As a matter of fact, one can demonstrate that rapport is still present by making use of the unaffected sense modalities for the communication of suggestions.

Sometimes some subjects develop much anxiety on finding themselves deaf. Consequently it is a good idea to suggest to the subject that being deaf will not perturb him and will seem quite normal. This caution also applies to other situations of a similar kind, such as suggested blindness.

It is not uncommon to find that a subject rendered deaf by suggestion and who otherwise shows all of the symptoms of deafness may fail to exhibit it when the hypnotist gives further suggestions, at least when prearranged auditory signals are used. There are several reasons for this. Many hypnotists, including myself, as a matter of course, deliberately suggest rapport early in the hypnotization, for reasons already taken up. In addition, induction has the seed of rapport inherent in it. The laws of precedence (page 346) lead one to expect that prior conditions would hold sway over more recent instructions (of deafness) if these have not been made to specifically include the hypnotist. Similarly a set of signals which has been previously arranged should have priority.

It should be kept in mind that subjects very often tend to take everything they are told quite literally. This tendency, which is present to some extent in the waking state, is much greater in the hypnotic state and necessitates far greater care in the wording of suggestions.

If practical, the subject should repeat your suggestion as soon as it is given, particularly if it is long or complex. In order for him to do this, one should give, as part of the suggestion, a signal which will indicate to the subject when the suggestion is to become effective. This will enable you to make certain he has not misunderstood you. If he has, or seems to miss some point, you can correct him. In addition, many hypnotists feel that this reinforces the suggestion more than if the hypnotist had repeated it himself. There seems also to be a belief that if the subject repeats it, it is a sign of his acceptance of the suggestion. None of these beliefs, however, have been adequately tested. In any case, when a suggestion is long or complex it is a good idea to repeat it at least once. If you word it somewhat differently, you can make it less likely that the subject will have placed a different meaning on your words than you had intended.

Hypnotized subjects sometimes disconcertingly elaborate or simply change some aspect of a suggestion. These elaborations are a function of the subject's understanding of the hypnotic state, of the limitations placed upon him (the extent to which the hypnotic situation was defined), of his degree of participation and of various factors in the subject's personality, his attitudes, expectancies and so forth. It should be understood that, all other things being equal, elaborations are quite natural. They often fulfill the need of the subject for closure, stability, and definiteness or meaning. Indeed, the fact that the subject elaborates is often an excellent sign of his total participation in the hypnotic situation, that he is living it. For instance, as was remarked earlier, when we tell the subject to hallucinate that he is picking cherries from a tree, we may find him presently going through the motions of getting a ladder, setting it up against the imaginary tree, climbing it and picking more cherries. From time to time we may observe him putting an imaginary cherry to his mouth, eating it, and getting rid of the stem and pit. Yet none of these aspects of his behavior have been suggested to him. The hypnotist who encounters this sort of behavior for the first time may wonder whether the subject is not making a fool of him and, at the least, will be perturbed by such "unorthodox" behavior. A little thought about the matter will, however, show that it is really a natural outcome of the original suggestion. If the hallucination has any reality for the subject we must expect him to behave with respect to it as he would with respect to the corresponding real situation. The tendency to elaborate is not unique to hypnosis and can sometimes also be seen with waking suggestions, but rarely this clearly.

SOME GENERAL PRINCIPLES

Nothing can replace actual experience in the field of hypnosis, but it is possible to state a few helpful rules which may guide the beginner.

1. In general, hypnosis should always be as deep as possible. Failure to elicit deep hypnosis is probably the most common cause for partial or complete failure of suggestions.

2. The subject should always be given an opportunity to reorient himself

into the suggested situation. This is particularly true when the suggestion is complex or involves deep-seated changes in the subject. This means that the subject must not be pressed to produce the desired phenomenon too rapidly. Complex phenomena should be brought about gradually, step by step if necessary. Successive approximations to the desired condition are often useful. We will see how this is done in the next chapter.

3. The subject should be allowed to participate as fully and completely as possible in the hypnotic situation. It should become his sole reality.

4. When a subject fails to carry out a suggestion after several attempts, and the reason has not been discovered, ask him why he does not respond properly, or what must be done before he will carry out the suggestion.

5. When giving suggestions always keep in mind the following law which combines the three *rules of precedence* for suggestions into one: Whenever two or more suggestions conflict, the one which was given first, given in the greatest hypnotic depth, or was most deeply "impressed," is prepotent. For greater details regarding the laws see reference 191. Failure to take this rule into account may give rise to difficulty.

6. Always keep a record of suggestions given to a subject. Otherwise you may inadvertently give him a suggestion which will later prevent another suggestion from being effective because of the laws of precedence.

7. When using suggestions to bring about phenomena which transcend the subject's normal voluntary capacities, keep in mind that the following factors favor the production of these phenomena in decreasing order: Alterations of the perceived stimulus situation by suggestions; suggested emotionally toned experiences; the degree to which the altered capacity or function is normally amenable to voluntary control—the more it is, the greater the influence; the presence of other factors specific to the given test situation (such as meaningfulness of material recalled); set-producing (preparatory) suggestions; and the difficulty and nature of the suggested task—simpler, less difficult tasks favor improvement.

8. Whenever possible, integrate the subject's needs into the suggestions. The more a suggested act satisfies a subject's needs, the better he will carry it out. Conversely, by creating or manipulating the subject's needs, many suggestions can be made far more effective (see chapter 14).

POSTHYPNOTIC SUGGESTIONS

Because posthypnotic suggestions hold an important and rather unique position in hypnotism, they will be discussed separately. However, their properties are primarily the same as those of other suggestions.

A posthypnotic suggestion is one that is given to the subject while he is hypnotized, but which does not become effective until a predetermined time after the subject has been dehypnotized. Although it is certainly not essential posthypnotic suggestions are believed to be more effective if amnesia for them is present. Consequently, it is usual to emphasize before dehypnotizing the subject that he will have such an amnesia. Obviously, this will also be a posthypnotic phenomenon.

The above is a reasonable belief insofar as theory is concerned. As we know, attitudes, expectations, and the subject's will can have varying degrees of positive or negative influence upon the outcome of any suggestion. If the subject is not aware of the posthypnotic suggestion he will not be able to influence it at the conscious level through such factors, hence, any possible resistance is minimized. This will of course be at the expense of also losing any positive effect, should the subject be so inclined. On the whole, this loss is much less than the expected gain. It might be remarked that perhaps the sole reason it is possible to hypnotize a person against his will by using a posthypnotic signal is that the action of the signal takes place so suddenly and rapidly that the subject is hypnotized before he has time to become aware of what is happening and thus has no opportunity to muster his defenses. This probably is not the entire story. Quite independent of any attitude, expectation and so forth, some sort of interference seems to result in many cases from the subject's simply being aware of the existence of the suggestion.* In the absence of data one guess is as good as another, and further speculation does not seem justified. Posthypnotic suggestions can still be quite effective even though no amnesia or only partial amnesia is present.

How to know whether amnesia is present? The simplest way is to directly or indirectly ask the subject questions aimed at finding out. Many hypnotists will frankly ask the subject, "Do you remember my telling you such and such. . .?" This procedure is not always advisable, since it may tend to destroy whatever amnesia the subject may have, particularly with medium-trance subjects. Some deep-trance subjects may fail to have complete amnesia, usually because of resistance. In most instances I have found it helpful not to call the subject's attention to his presumed amnesia or to the extent of his amnesia; and, if I do, certainly not immediately after his waking. Instead, I like to turn his attention for a period of 5 to 10 minutes to something totally

---

*This interference may be related to my observation that some subjects, when told to hallucinate, are unable to do so until they have been distracted from the task. Then the hallucination occurs spontaneously. Such individuals subsequently reveal that they had felt compelled to make a strong effort of will to produce the hallucination, and had concentrated their energies in this act of will. Thus any conative act, even though it may be positive, would appear to be inimical to the manifestation of suggested effects.

unrelated to any of the suggestions given during hypnosis. This often allows the amnesia to consolidate. Another technique I have found very useful in consolidating suggested amnesia is to allow the subject to remain quiet for 5 minutes or more following suggestions that he sleep deeply until "I begin to count, at which time you will wake up slowly. At the count of three you will be wide awake and will have no memory of what I have said to you while you were hypnotized, but the suggestions will nevertheless be very effective." Many cases which are refractory to this method can be effectively handled by using a form of the fractionation method of trance induction. Either before or after amnesia has been suggested and the subject has been allowed to remain quiet for a short time (this latter step is not essential) a suggestion is given that as soon as he wakes up, or very shortly after, he will go back into a sound sleep. Nothing else is said. Usually it is not necessary to give any further suggestions in the second hypnotic state.

It is not uncommon for a subject to assert that he remembers everything that was said or done during his trance, this being said either spontaneously or when asked about his amnesia. Often a few well chosen questions will show that the subject's memory of the events is much less than he presumes. How to deal with such a subject largely depends upon the purpose for hypnotizing him. You might skillfully sidestep his remarks, but such evasion must be done with tact. Or you might pass them off lightly by saying something like, "That is fine. Most people do remember something right after awakening, but they soon forget, just as you do with dreams." In any event, never let the subject feel that you are disappointed or that this was not what you expected. This is a rule that applies in the case of *any* suggestion. *Whatever happens, you should always give the subject the impression that it was exactly what you expected and that you have full control of the situation.* If you are confident that the subject does have at least partial amnesia you can prove to him that he does not remember everything, and that in any case his memory is fuzzy. Although this last method is used by many hypnotists, I do not consider it usually very safe and do not recommend it.

Regarding posthypnotic suggestion other than that of amnesia, it is not uncommon that a generally responsive subject will fail to carry out a particular suggestion. In certain instances there is obvious resistance which may have to be removed before any such suggestions can be effective. Sometimes only an additional cue is needed. Just why is not entirely clear in all cases. For instance, the subject is told that presently, after he wakes up, he will find that one of his feet itches and that this will become so severe he will have to remove his shoe. It is added that as soon as he does this his foot will feel fine. The subject is then awakened and a conversation is begun. Nothing happens. Five, maybe 10, minutes pass and still nothing happens.

Has the posthypnotic suggestion failed? Not necessarily. At this point you might remark to the subject, "Is that a new pair of shoes you are wearing?" or, "Those are nice shoes you have on your feet." A still more pointed cue would be, "Are those new shoes you are wearing? They sure look comfortable."* It is likely that as soon as you have said this, your subject will begin to fidget, move his foot, and eventually will remove his shoe. In the meantime you can ask him what is the matter, thus focusing his attention upon the suggested effect. This example is based on an actual case. In this instance the probable reason the suggestion did not take effect sooner is fairly obvious. An expression like "presently" is too indefinite. It may be meaningless for the subject, it may mean a few minutes, an hour, or longer.

Even specifying the exact time by saying something like "5 minutes after you awaken. . ." may still be insufficient since the subject's perception of time may be poor.† Furthermore, he may become so engrossed in what is going on that he loses track of time. Here again a cue will often help. Once I suggested to one of my best subjects used for demonstration purposes that, at a certain signal, he would stand up and deliver, in the role of a pastor, a real rousing sermon. I added that after he had been speaking for 5 minutes he would suddenly find it difficult to speak and would stutter no matter how hard he tried not to. The subject got up at the proper time and began to deliver his sermon in fine style. However, when the 5 minutes were up no sign of speech difficulty appeared. I waited a minute or two, after which, acting in the capacity of a prompter, I said to him: "Reverend, you have only 5 more minutes for your sermon." Immediately he began to stutter. I cannot be sure, of course, why this particular cue was required, but my guess is that the subject's very complete participation in his role of pastor may have altered his perception of the flow of time.

Posthypnotic suggestions tend to lose effectiveness with time. The extent of loss is a direct function of the difficulty or complexity of the suggestion and is inversely a function of the subject's depth of hypnosis. Simple suggestions given only once to a deeply hypnotized subject may last many months, even years. But when suggesting a difficult task or one which meets resistance, or when using a subject in a medium-deep hypnosis, it is usually necessary to repeat the posthypnotic suggestion at intervals if there is any lapse of time before it is to be activated or if it is to remain effective over a long period (even though repeatedly elicited). A similar rule applies to the degree to which a suggestion, particularly a posthypnotic suggestion, can

---

*Of course these statements should be made an integral part of the general conversation.

†The ability of hypnotized subjects to estimate time intervals during hypnosis or posthypnotically is grossly overrated.[191]

be impressed upon the subject at any given time. An attempt should always be made to ascertain the subject's future activities, so that posthypnotic suggestions can be set to become effective at times when they are least likely to interfere or conflict with other, normal, activities (unless this is the aim). A suggestion does not necessarily have to be carried out for it to cause serious interference. It may be just strong enough to create a conflictful situation in which the subject, being equally motivated to carry out incompatible acts, becomes paralyzed in respect to them. In one dramatic instance I have witnessed the subject suffered an attack of hysterical fainting—the best way he could resolve the imposed dilemma. Conflicts, of course, may also arise if the demands of the posthypnotic suggestions on the subject are too much at variance with his personality.

In general, as can be seen from the scales of hypnotic depth in chapter 6, a greater depth of hypnosis is required to produce a specific phenomenon posthypnotically than to produce the same phenomenon in hypnosis. A good rule is to proceed slowly in giving posthypnotic suggestions unless you are certain that the subject is deeply hypnotized. The subject should first be tested with some simple posthypnotic suggestions, then progressively more difficult ones can be given. To be most effective, posthypnotic suggestions should be stated as specifically as possible and should be repeated several times, as well as recounted by the subject. Many posthypnotic suggestions, however, will be quite effective even though the subject has only a partial amnesia or none at all or was not in a deep trance at the time they were given. For this reason posthypnotic suggestions regarding future inductions of hypnosis, as used, for example, in the fractionation method, can be of great help in training the subject to attain deeper states. The subject develops a spontaneous trance state at the beginning of the posthypnotic response, affording a convenient manner of rehypnotizing him, particularly since this trance is a continuation of the original one. Often the subject can be put into a much deeper hypnosis by taking advantage of this new trance state. Many individuals who show resistance to deep trance induction discard their resistance during the formation of the spontaneous trance. Since the nature of the posthypnotic act is essentially irrelevant in this particular use of posthypnotic suggestions and since many subjects in light to medium hypnosis will carry out simple posthypnotic suggestions, the method is highly applicable in many instances.

PROE-HYPNOTIC SUGGESTION

This term was first introduced by Stembo.[174] It is the converse of a posthypnotic suggestion and operates essentially through the same mechanism.

That is, one can give a waking suggestion which is to become effective upon or during the first (or some other) occasion the subject is hypnotized. When subsequently the subject is hypnotized, no further suggestion is given. Being in the hypnotic state seems to act as a catalyst for the waking suggestion. Stembo considers this to be a useful technique with certain difficult therapy cases.

ENABLING THE SUBJECT TO OPEN HIS EYES WITHOUT AWAKENING

A deeply hypnotized subject, upon being told to open his eyes, usually will do so without coming out of the trance. With those who are less deeply hypnotized (medium or lesser depth) the trance tends to become lightened, or the subject may wake completely. This is increasingly true the lighter the hypnosis. Very often, however, a subject can be maintained in the hypnotic state with his eyes open even though he is not in a deep hypnotic state if care is taken to train him to do this beforehand. Occasionally even a deeply hypnotized subject enters a lighter trance or wakes when told to open his eyes. This is usually the result of the subject's identifying opened eyes with the waking state and closed eyes with hypnosis, so that closed eyes becomes a condition for the presence of hypnosis; a command to open the eyes is then equivalent to a command to wake up. Such difficulties can usually be avoided by the use of appropriate suggestions. Since one can never be certain how the subject will interpret the command to open his eyes, even though he is deeply hypnotized, it is best to suggest something like the following: "In a moment I am going to tell you to open your eyes. You will remain deeply hypnotized, even though your eyes will be open and you will be able to see everything around you quite clearly. You will remain asleep until I tell you to awaken. You will be able to open your eyes and to look around, but you will remain deep asleep at all times. Now, open your eyes but remain deep asleep." Keep repeating that the subject is deep asleep, etc., while he is in the process of opening his eyes and afterward. Note that the suggestion contains references to the ability to see clearly. Occasionally a subject opens his eyes but functionally is totally or partially blind because in his mind hypnosis is associated with loss of sensory contact with the external world. If the above suggestion fails to prevent this, it usually can easily be overcome by explaining to the subject under hypnosis that the hypnotic state does not necessarily mean a loss in sensory function, pointing out to him that just as he can hear you while he is hypnotized, so will he also be able to see.

Sometimes a subject persistently wakes up completely or partially when he opens his eyes. Usually the best way to deal with this is to rehypnotize him and while his eyes are closed question him about his resistance. The subject most likely will tell you the reason and may even suggest possible solutions to the difficulty. With other subjects, it is merely a matter of making a more gradual transition from closed to open eyes. For one thing, this means a longer giving of suggestions of the type indicated, repeating the essential ideas a number of times before having the subject open his eyes. Also, rather than having him see everything clearly as soon as he opens his eyes, suggest that everything will seem hazy or blurred at first, but that after a few moments his vision will clear up although he will remain asleep. It is also a good idea to tell him that he will see everything you point out to him or indicate. This last suggestion has a double function. It not only enables the subject to see actual objects clearly, but by its indefiniteness also includes any imaginary object to which you may point. This favors hallucinations with the eyes open.

A useful way of handling this type of subject is to suggest a number of hallucinations after the eyes have opened. The first hallucinations are made very simple, then progressively more difficult. An interesting technique has been described by Wolberg. [203] He primarily follows the procedure outlined, but suggests that the subject, while his eyes are still closed, hallucinate the hypnotist as holding a bottle of water close to the subject's eyes, the subject seeing the water change color, becoming pink and then gradually a reddish shade. The subject is requested to indicate when he sees this final effect by raising his left hand slightly. Wolberg then instructs the subject that the trance will persist after he opens his eyes, and tells him that when he does open his eyes he will have the same experience. A real bottle of clear water is actually placed in front of the subject's face, and the subject has only to hallucinate the change in color. As soon as the subject indicates that he sees the color change, some other simple hallucination is suggested by Wolberg.

It is usually a good idea, when giving suggestions regarding the ability of the subject to open his eyes and to see clearly while remaining deeply hypnotized, to also suggest the same thing about his ability to move about. Some subjects associate inability to move about with deep hypnosis, and some tend to wake when made to move if countersuggestions are not used.

It is one thing to have the subject remain hypnotized with his eyes open, seeing whatever is actually present, and another to have him hallucinate objects under the same conditions. In many cases these imaginary objects will be incongruous in the actual setting or will be incompatible with it, hence the subject needs to have positive and negative hallucinations simultaneously. For this reason, when training a subject to hallucinate with his eyes open, it is best to begin with simple hallucinations of objects which fit into the immediate setting, such as a fictitious vase of flowers on a real mantel-piece and, in some cases, even using partial hallucinations such as Wolberg suggests. A method I have found useful with subjects who hallucinate well with closed eyes but have difficulty hallucinating with their eyes open is to have them visualize some simple object, such a red index card. Then, when they see it clearly, I tell them that when I give the signal to open their eyes they will continue to see the card, that they will see it after their eyes are open and until I tell them otherwise. I add that they will remain deeply hypnotized. I repeatedly suggest during the transition and after that they continue seeing the card.

ENABLING THE HYPNOTIZED SUBJECT TO TALK WITHOUT AWAKENING

Many hypnotized subjects will readily answer questions, repeat suggestions and even hold complex conversations, without coming out of the trance. However, some wake up or their trance state lightens considerably, the minute they are made to talk. This often can be prevented by the simple expedient of giving suggestions, prior to making the subject talk, to the effect that, although he is deeply asleep, he will be able to hear your voice distinctly, to talk to you without awakening and to answer all of your questions. Then ask him a few simple questions such as his age, his name, etc., and give further suggestions to the effect that he can do this without waking. This procedure is particularly important of course in therapeutic work, where anxiety-provoking questions must be asked sooner or later. It is then that the subject or patient is most likely to become dehypnotized. In therapy a much longer period should be spent asking relatively innocuous questions, and slowly moving to anxiety-provoking questions.

PRODUCTION OF POSTHYPNOTIC AMNESIA

Many subjects, especially those who become deeply hypnotized, will show amnesia upon waking; in other cases, even deeply hypnotized subjects either fail to show amnesia or show only a partial amnesia. In many such instances the cause can be uncovered in the same way that other resistances to suggestions are uncovered, and can be dealt with accordingly. In a few cases nothing seems to help. The subject appears to have a need to retain some control over the situation, and retaining his memory is his solution. Hypnosis, and particularly the loss of memory, can be quite threatening to the subject. In such refractory cases, a solution proposed by Wolberg[203] is to suggest to the subject that he remember some minor aspect of the hypnotic session, but that he have amnesia for the bulk of it. This often satisfies the subject's need for control.

Wolberg also proposes that if the subject recalls everything, he should, in the next trance session, be told just before being awakened that: (a) he will imagine he is asleep at home and having a brief dream; (b) following this he will open his eyes and wake with a start; and (c) he will have the impression of waking from a profound sleep and will remember the dream quite clearly, but as soon as he has recounted it, his memory of other events of the trance will be hazy and he may even forget some of them if asked about his trance experience.

With subjects who have shown partial amnesia in the previous trance, Wolberg proposes telling them while they are hypnotized that forgetting is a normal process and that it can result simply from shifting attention. The subject's attention is then called to those items which he forgot in the previous session, with the instruction that this time he will forget many more items, possibly everything pertaining to the trance. Then, here also, the dream technique is used.

A similar procedure I have found effective is a sort of fractionation method consisting of repeatedly waking and rehypnotizing the subject, each time suggesting that he will forget more and more of the trance events. Since amnesia and depth of hypnosis usually go together, this is a convenient way of dealing with the two problems simultaneously.

SOME SIMPLE DEMONSTRATIONS

I shall briefly list a group of hypnotic phenomena with which you should become thoroughly familiar. You need not try them all at any given time, but you should practice them well before you attempt the demonstrations described in the next chapter or try to deal with complex situations. In order to perform these demonstrations you need not have mastered all the methods of hypnotizing discussed in the previous chapters. On the contrary, as soon as you have become thoroughly familiar with any one method and have found a subject who attains a sufficient hypnotic depth, you should proceed to do some or all of the following demonstrations. For convenience, they have been grouped into three categories. The order in which you do them is not particularly important, although it is suggested you proceed more or less as they are given here.

A WORD OF CAUTION

As was pointed out earlier, hypnosis per se is not dangerous. The dangers of hypnotism lie mainly in the *mismanagement* of the hypnotic subject before, after and, particularly, during hypnosis. This is especially relevant in the case of the production of neurotic behavior, complexes and regressions. No one should undertake the production of these phenomena who does not have some training in clinical psychology or psychiatry or who is not closely supervised by someone who has such training. Furthermore, such a third person should always be placed in rapport with the subject prior to the induction of the phenomena in question so that he may take over immediately if necessary. In my judgment, *regressions probably are potentially the most dangerous of all hypnotic phenomena* insofar as the mental health of the subject is concerned, for one usually does not know what sort of traumatic experiences the subject may have gone through in the past. Thus, as one explores the subject's past, there is always the danger of inadvertently regressing the subject to just such a nuclear point in his life. When this happens, anything can take place, but only the clinically trained person is competent to handle the situation adequately. Only sheer good luck and, in a few cases, an innate intuitive ability, will permit the untrained hypnotist to smooth over the resulting disturbance. *Once regression has returned the subject to a highly traumatic situation, it may become imperative to transform the hypnotic situation into a psychotherapeutic situation or else run the risk of having a seriously disturbed individual on one's hands.* (There are instances of this very thing on record.) I believe that, without exaggeration, every regression experiment should be labeled "DANGER—POTENTIAL HIGH TENSION."

Waking Suggestions as Hypnotic Suggestions

A good way to get acquainted with hypnotic phenomena is to use some or all of the various waking suggestions under hypnosis. You will find it instructive to compare the subject's behavior under hypnosis with his waking behavior in regard to these suggestions. I also suggest that you test for some of the differences I have indicated between waking and hypnotic suggestions and suggestibility.

Hypnotic Suggestions and Trance Depth

Using either waking suggestions or some of those listed further on, compare the subject's responses as a function of the depth of hypnosis attained. The best way to do this is to use various subjects who you know attain various limiting depths. It is possible to use one subject for this, but it may require considerable skill to arrest him momentarily at different depths. One word of warning here: You should not suggest to the subject that he will attain a particular depth, since he may very quickly go into a deep trance and will simply act out the suggested depth. However, I believe it is relatively safe to suggest to a subject that he will remain at a given level of hypnosis when he reaches it. In general, even deeply hypnotized subjects tend to fluctuate in depth throughout a hypnotic session, so that there is some variability in their suggestibility from moment to moment.

Selected Hypnotic Demonstrations

(In all of the following demonstrations it is understood that the subject is hypnotized.)

Body Rigidity (or Catalepsy). Before starting the demonstration arrange two chairs nearby facing each other at a distance of about five and a half feet. With the subject standing before you, tell him to place his toes and heels together and his hands by his sides. Now suggest that his entire body is becoming stiff, rigid, like a board. Some hypnotists like to make passes with contact from shoulder to thigh (some include even the legs to emphasize the effect); others begin by having the subject voluntarily stiffen himself as much as possible and then go on from there. Whatever method you use, continue to tell the subject he will remain completely rigid, no matter what happens, until you tell him otherwise. It is a good idea to add that he will not feel at all uncomfortable. Generally, as the subject becomes rigid, he will topple over, usually but not always backward. (It is advisable to have an assistant or two to help catch him. The demonstration can also be made, if you prefer, with the subject reclining on a couch or cot.) With the help of assistants, lift the subject as soon as he is sufficiently rigid (which, if he has been standing, will normally be when he falls over) and, adjusting the chairs, place the subject so that the nape of his neck lies on the back of one chair and his ankles on the back of the second chair. His body thus forms a bridge between the two chairs. This is a rather spectacular demonstration, although not the extraordinary feat of strength it may seem to be, even when someone climbs up on the subject and stands on him. This last part may well be omitted since the demonstration is spectacular enough without it and, if improperly done, it can lead to herniation of the subject. Although I have never seen this demonstration fail, it is advisable always to have assistants ready to catch the subject if he should collapse, as well as to hold the chairs stable.

General Illusions and Hallucinations. There is no limit to the number of things that can be suggested as hallucinations. You might tell the subject that he is at a movie watching an extremely funny picture or that he is watching a very sad and depressing scene. A very effective suggestion is that the subject is sitting outdoors, bothered by a swarm of mosquitoes. Another is that the subject is in a very warm place, say an Arizona desert in mid-summer, where the temperature is unbearable. Or he can be told that he is freezing from cold in the frozen wastes of the North. With some subjects a brief statement is all that is needed; they elaborate the rest. With others it may be necessary to give greater structure to the hallucinated situations, such as by telling the subject who is "freezing" that he is shivering from cold and that he is going to build a fire.

A question I am sometimes asked is: What should the role of the hypnotist be in the hallucinated setting? (We shall see in the next chapter that this is an important question in the case of regressions.) Very often the subject spontaneously incorporates the hypnotist into his hallucination and the question resolves itself. But if this does not happen, then one may have a definite problem on hand. Unfortunately, very little research has been done in this area and so no definite solution is known. My own preferred method, once the suggestions have begun to take effect, is to talk in an impersonal way to the subject, as if my words were his thoughts. Thus, with the "freezing" subject, instead of directing him by saying: "Now shiver. You are very cold. Find some wood. . .Pile it here. . .Now light a match, etc.," I prefer to say something like: "Oh. . .how cold it is!. . .It makes one shiver! . . .Let's build a fire. . .We'll have to get some wood. . .Ah. . .there's some wood. . ." Of course, you cannot be absolutely impersonal everywhere in the suggestion, but frequently you can be for a large portion of it. It is also possible for a hypnotist to suggest that he has such or such a role in the hallucination.

Specific Sensory Hallucinations and Illusions. This is essentially a variation of the preceding type of suggestion. The subject is told, for instance, that the back of a playing card is a picture of his mother. Or he can be shown a playing card and told that it is blank, or something else other than what it really is. The subject can also be told that he will be unable to hear (or else to touch or to see) certain persons in the room. It is quite instructive to observe how the subject reacts when he cannot see, but can hear or touch a person or object, or when the "invisible" person moves objects about the room. Some subjects are greatly mystified. Others develop interesting additional spontaneous selective anesthesias aimed at making their environment less ambiguous. The tendency for individuals to maintain consistency in their environment as well as to bring about closure is often very nicely demonstrated in this sort of situation.

Hallucinations of the taste sense are easy to produce. The subject can be given a potato and told that it is a delicious apple. Then while he is enjoying eating it, you can suggest that it is an extremely sour lemon. The subject can be given a glass of water and told that it is whiskey. Not only will he give indications of the effects of this hallucination on his gustatory sense, but he will often show signs of its effect on his sense of equilibrium and on his speech centers. In any event, a few additional suggestions can produce the latter results.

It is good practice when producing hallucinations to first inquire about the subject's likes, dislikes and other relevant idiosyncrasies. I know of a case where a hypnotized subject promptly fainted when told that a swarm of bees was after her. Unknown to the hypnotist she had a severe phobia of bees! The effects of this class of suggestions are more spectacular if the subject hallucinates things he either strongly likes or dislikes, depending upon the desired effect. A person who drinks merely to be sociable is not likely to show as much reaction to drinking "whiskey" as will someone who either likes or dislikes it very much. Again, whereas one large glass of "whiskey" may suffice to cause a subject to become very drunk, another subject who has a high capacity for drinks will show no effects at all. This can be disconcerting to the hypnotist if the cause is not known. Again, a subject may be neutral toward apples, but may particularly like peaches. It would be better in this case to suggest that a potato is a peach rather than an apple.

Perceptual Transcendence. A striking demonstration is as follows. Using a clean pack of playing cards (a new one is best), pick one card at random, note the face of the card, and show only its reverse side to a deeply hypnotized subject, preferably one who has been used several times for other demonstrations and who is good at developing hallucinations. Tell him that there is a black cross, or some other design, on the card you are showing him. When the subject agrees that this is so, add that whenever he sees this card he will always see the cross. Now place the card back in the pack and shuffle it. Give the deck to the subject, reverse side toward him, and ask him to go through it and hand you the card with the cross when he finds it. Add that it is the only one with this design and that he will have no difficulty in finding it. With a good subject this demonstration can be done with several cards thus hidden at the same time, each with a different hallucinated mark. Although some individuals can do this "trick" without the help of hypnosis, many who are incapable of doing so will do extremely well when hypnotized. Some subjects will perform better if, before hiding the card in the deck, you alternately show them a few times the reverse side of two or three other cards as well as of the chosen card, having them indicate each time which of the cards has the cross.

Synthetic Emotions. We have touched upon this in discussing hallucinations. By telling the subject that he is in a certain mood, or, better, by suggesting that he experiences some event which normally would lead to a given mood or emotion, you can cause the subject to exhibit the signs of these specific moods or emotions.

Simulation of Other Personalities. The subject can be told that he is some other person. A standard procedure used by stage hypnotists is to learn from the subject who his favorite actor or singer is. The hypnotist then suggests that the subject is the specified actor or singer and that he is making a public appearance. Also the subject, upon being told that he is a doctor, a nurse, a janitor, and so forth, can be given appropriate props to use in his suggested capacity in various suggested settings. Acts typical of his role may be suggested and structured to various degrees.

Regressions. Regressions are alterations of the personality such that the subject reexperiences an earlier period in his life, perceiving and behaving as he did at that time. He actually lives in the past, with all experiences subsequent to the regression age presumably ceasing to have any influence on his behavior. This is not always the case, but for the purposes of this chapter we need not be concerned with this point. We shall have more to say on the topic in the next chapter.

It is a good idea, first, to ask the subject to write his name or to draw a man or a house before hypnotizing him, or at least before regressing him. Then, having hypnotized the subject deeply, tell him that at a given signal he will once again be a certain age, say, 9 years old. It is usual to specify as the time of regression some special day such as a birthday, Christmas or Easter. The specific time of day is often suggested. The subject is told that he will feel exactly as he did on that occasion, that he will see the same things he did then, and so on. It is best to allow a few moments for these suggestions to "sink in." Then the signal is given. Allow a few moments for it to build up to full effect, then ask the subject such questions as what day it is, where he is, who is with him or who are the various persons near him. (This last is not always advisable since it may force the subject to introduce elements not originally present in the situation. On the other hand, the subject is often found to have spontaneously become functionally blind to various extraneous elements.) He should be asked to describe the place where he is and, in general, various questions to ascertain what sort of regression has been obtained. Further conversation suitable for the regression age usually will help to establish the regression more firmly. After a while, the subject should be asked to write his name or to draw a man or house. This can be compared with the waking or preregression material and that obtained at other regression levels. Often some rather remarkable changes will be observed.

To end any phase of a regression I usually command the subject to sleep, having conditioned him, prior to the regression, to respond instantaneously to this command. Having terminated a regression phase, you can then either cause a further regression, a "relative" progression,* or a return to the actual age. Of course, you should always do this before waking the subject. In general, it is advisable to have two extra sets of signals available when producing regressions. One is a nonverbal signal to produce instantaneous hypnosis, the other a similar type of signal for causing the subject to return to the present. If contact at the verbal level should be lost during the regression, these signals will usually be sufficient to regain control of the situation. A truly regressed individual should lose the ability to communicate by language or by any other sign system if regressed far enough. Because such signals as those mentioned here probably act at a reflex level, they tend to persist through the regression and hence to allow you to control the subject's state in spite of the regression. I do not know whether there are limitations to this. Conceivably there are.

Much better results can be obtained in producing a regression if it is done stepwise. That is, instead of regressing the subject from, say, 30 years of age to 9 in one step, first regress him to 28, then 25, then 20, etc. It is even better first to regress to the previous day, then to a week before, then 2 or 3 weeks, a month and so forth. We shall see in the next chapter that to get the ultimate form of regression, much more involved procedures, including the one just mentioned, must be employed. Finally, it is possible to carry a regression over into the posthypnotic state.

Posthypnotic Phenomena. This is one of the most interesting areas to experiment with. There is little else to be added to what has already been said about it. Many hypnotists, as a matter of routine, terminate each hypnotic session with a posthypnotic suggestion which is activated before the subject leaves. One advantage in doing this is that it automatically gages the subject's depth of hypnosis. If a demonstration is being given, this is of course the most natural and effective way of ending it.

Amnesias and Paramnesias. These are best done as posthypnotic phenomena. With the amnesias, the subject is told that when he wakes up he will not be able to remember certain things, such as his name, birthday, what day it is, the meaning of words. Phenomena resembling aphasias, agnosias, apraxias, and so forth can thus be brought about. With the paramnesias, the subject is told under hypnosis the fiction that a certain set of events has taken place and that when he wakes up he will remember these as actual facts.

*The term "progression" is used in hypnotic research to denote the result of telling a subject that he is now living in the future with respect to his actual age. To distinguish this from situations in which the subject is made to shift from one regression age to a time when he was older (but still a regression) I use the qualifier "relative."

13

Hypnotic Phenomena
II. Specialized Advanced Techniques

A LTHOUGH possibly all hypnotic phenomena can be brought about in some instances by a mere suggestion or command, more often it is necessary to use relatively involved and lengthy procedures to get the most out of a suggestion. This is particularly true when deep alterations of the subject's personality or physiology are desired or when you want to insure the reality of the phenomena to be brought about. Then is the time to follow exactly the principles given in previous chapters.

Need for the skillful use of hypnotic techniques is particularly great in such areas as the production of psychosomatic disturbances, regressions, sensory alterations, and experimental neuroses and psychoses. Fortunately, detailed procedures used in a number of investigations dealing with the last three topics are available to us. Not only are they of considerable value for anyone proposing to produce similar phenomena, they are fine examples of the sophisticated and effective use of hypnosis. This chapter will be devoted to a presentation of the more pertinent aspects of these studies.

INDUCTION OF COMPLEXES AND NEUROTIC BEHAVIOR

There are three basic ways of bringing about abnormal behavior by suggestion. One is to suggest the syndrome of interest element by element, or if you are interested only in some particular symptom, it alone may be suggested. This method usually leads to rather superficial changes. Another is to create a conflict situation by putting the subject in a position where he is compelled to carry out two incompatible modes of behavior. The main disadvantage in this is that it does not allow the experimenter much control over the type of manifestations which will arise, since they will almost entirely be determined by already existing complexes in the subject. However, it can be useful as a technique for investigating the specific modes of resolution of conflict used by a given individual. The third and last method, the most difficult but also the most powerful, is the implantation of an artificial complex in the subject. This we shall discuss fairly extensively.

361

We shall begin by very briefly outlining the important steps in the technique used by Erickson[45] to demonstrate by means of posthypnotic suggestions a large variety of psychopathological manifestations which occur in everyday life. The main requisites for success when doing this type of experiment are that the subject be deeply hypnotized, have posthypnotic amnesia and the posthypnotic setting be as natural as possible. Every effort should be made to give continuity to the hypnotic and posthypnotic states. The posthypnotic situations should be made as consistent with the suggestions as is feasible. Erickson used this approach to bring about a total of 10 different manifestations. Although each one called for the application of measures specific to it, there is a general underlying procedure which I believe can be abstracted by considering only a few of the experiments Erickson described.

The general manner of proceeding consists in giving the subject a posthypnotic suggestion such as to create in him certain sets, attitudes, needs and, especially, conflicts. In this process certain individuals, acts, or objects are transformed into key determinants of his future behavior. After he has been dehypnotized these key elements are allowed or made to act upon the subject who is otherwise allowed to operate freely in his environment.

Demonstration of Unconscious Determinants Of the Causal Content of a Conversation

The investigator gave the following posthypnotic suggestion to the subject: On awakening he would see one of the persons present during the experiment (Dr. D.) searching for cigarettes. He would offer his own pack. Dr. D. would absent-mindedly forget to return the cigarettes. The subject would feel eager to recover these because he had no others, but he would be too courteous to ask for them directly or indirectly. He would engage in a conversation which would cover any topic except cigarettes, although at the same time his desire for the return of his package would be on his mind constantly.

In accord with the procedural recommendations which were made, Dr. D. actually began to look for cigarettes when the subject awakened from the trance.

Demonstration of Ambivalence: Manifestations of Unconscious Conflict about Smoking in the Distortion of Simple, Daily Smoking Habits

The subject was instructed that smoking was a bad habit, that he both loved and hated it, that he wanted to get over the habit but felt it was too strong to break, that he would be very reluctant to smoke and would give anything not to smoke, but he would find himself compelled to smoke. After he was awakened he would experience all of these feelings.

While casually talking to the subject after he awakened, Erickson lighted a cigarette and offered him one.*

DEMONSTRATION OF LAPSUS LINGUAE AND UNCONSCIOUS IRONY

While in hypnosis the subject was told that after he awakened, Dr. D. would start talking to him about a difficult topic in which the subject had no interest but, although he would be profoundly bored by the conversation, he would try to pretend being interested. It was added that he would have a strong desire to close the conversation, he would wish for some way of "shutting off" this interminable flow of words, he would look around for some distraction and would feel that Dr. D. was extremely tiresome.

Of course, after the subject was awakened Dr. D. proceeded to address the subject accordingly. The use in the suggestion of such words as "close" and "shutting off" played an important part in the subject's subsequent behavior in the particular case reported by Erickson.

These three examples should give the reader an idea of the kind of procedure to be followed. There are so many possible psychodynamic manifestations of the kind being considered in this section that it would be impractical to attempt to outline specific procedures for each one. Other particular examples of mild behavioral disturbance not taken up here will be found discussed by Erickson. In general his procedures can readily be adapted to most other situations.

In one of Erickson's[46] most important papers he has analyzed in great detail the suggestion he employed to create a complex in one of his patients. This analysis is of far wider application than just to the case under consideration and contains a number of important lessons. It constitutes an excellent application of what I have pointed out to be important factors in the wording and the giving of optimal suggestion. It certainly should serve to emphasize that there is more to giving a suggestion than stating an idea. For these reasons I feel that the suggestion and its analysis as originally presented by Erickson should be included in this book. I should like to start out by quoting some of his very pertinent remarks:

> In considering how to devise or formulate a suitable complex applicable to the subject the task seems to be essentially a problem of "It is not only what you say, but how you say it." Under the proposed experimental conditions, "what" was to be said had to be a seemingly innocuous and credible but fictitious story of a past forgotten social error by the subject. The content of such a story was relatively simple to determine and required little imagination since the patient had been a hypnotic subject of mine for over a year and I knew him

*Inasmuch as this book is specifically about techniques and also because of the length of the material, I have refrained from describing the ensuing behavior of the subject. This, however, constitutes some extremely fascinating reading and the reader will be well repaid by reading Erickson's article.

intimately, was well acquainted with his family, and I also had professional knowledge of his neurosis.* Hence the content of the story was easily made to center around an imaginary visit to the home of an unidentified prominent man. There he was supposedly greeted by the man's wife, introduced to an attractive only daughter in whose presence he smoked a cigarette and accidentally broke a prize ash-tray.

The "how" of telling the story seemed primarily to be a task of so relating the fictitious account that it would become superimposed upon his actual experiential past in a manner that would cause him to react appropriately to it emotionally, to incorporate it into his real memories and, thus, to transform it into a vital part of his psychic life.

This could be done, it was reasoned, by taking the objective items contained in the essential content of the story and so weaving a narrative about them that they would stimulate a wealth and a variety of emotions, memories, and associations that would in turn give the story a second and much greater significance and validity than could its apparent content.

To do this would require a careful choice and use of words which would carry multiple meaning, or which would have various associations, connotations, and nuances of meaning which would serve to build up in a gradual, unrecognized, cumulative fashion a second more extensive but unrealized meaningfulness for the story.

Also, the words, by their arrangement into phrases, clauses, and sentences, and even their introductory, transitional, and repetitive uses, could be made to serve special purposes for building up emphasis or cutting it short, for establishing contrasts, similarities, parallelism, identifications, and equations of one idea to another, all of which would effect a building up of a series of associations and emotional responses stimulated, but not aroused directly, by the actual content of the complex. Additionally, sharp transitions from one idea to another, sequential relationships of various ideas and objects, shifts of responsibility and action from one character to another, the use of words that threatened, challenged, distracted, or served only to delay the development of the narrative were all employed to formulate a story possessing a significance beyond its formal content.

. . .The hypnotist, in administering the complex to the patient, was fully aware of what he hoped each item of the story might mean to the patient. Hence, the hypnotist's voice in administering that complex to the patient would carry a load of meaningful intonations, inflections, emphases, and pauses, all of which, as common daily experience constantly proved, so often convey more than spoken words.

Essentially, the task, as worked out, was comparable to that of composing music intended to produce a certain effect upon the listener. Words and ideas, rather than notes of music, were employed in selected sequences, patterns, rhythms, and other relationships and by this composition it was hoped to evoke profound responses in the subject. These responses were to be of a type not only hoped for in terms of what the story could mean but which would be in accord with the established patterns of behavior deriving from the patient's experiential past.

Erickson's acquaintance with the subject was undoubtedly of considerable help in making the suggestion successful. Provisions would have to be made with other subjects for differences in this regard. In general, however, one would try to follow Erickson's modus operandi as faithfully as possible. Furthermore, one must not expect to work out a satisfactory complex in

---

*It might be added here for subsequent clarity of the analysis of the suggestion that the patient was under treatment for ejaculatio praecox.

one sitting. It must be carefully conceived, written, and rewritten a number of times and, preferably, subjected to criticism by others, all of which Erickson was careful to do.

Since the suggestion used by Erickson has to be broken up into its individual elements for the purpose of analyzing it, it will first be presented in its entirety so that the reader may have a general overall view of its content and structure. The suggestion was an follows:

Now as you continue to sleep I'm going to recall to your mind an event which occurred not long ago. As I recount this event to you, you will recall fully and completely everything that happened. You have had good reason to forget this occurrence, but as I recall it, you will remember each and every detail fully. Now bear this in mind, that while I repeat what I know of this event, you will recall fully and completely everything just as it happened, and more than that, you will re-experience the various conflicting emotions which you had at the time and you will feel exactly as you did while this occurrence was taking place. Now the particular event of which I am going to tell you is this: Some time ago you met a man prominent in academic circles who manifested an interest in you and who was in a position to aid you in securing a certain research fellowship in which you were much interested. He made an appointment with you to see him at his home and on that day you called at the designated hour. When you knocked at the door you were met not by this gentleman but by his wife who greeted you cordially and was very friendly, making you feel that her husband had given a good account of you to her. She explained apologetically that her husband had been called away for a few moments but that he would return shortly and had asked that you be made comfortable in the library. You accompanied her to this room where she introduced you to a charming girl who was obviously shy and reserved and who, she explained, was their only daughter. The mother then requested your permission to go about her work, explaining that the daughter would be very happy to entertain you while you waited. You assured the mother that you would be very comfortable and even now you can recall the glow of pleasure you experienced at the thought of having the daughter as a hostess. As the mother left the room you set about conversing with the girl, and despite her shyness and bashfulness, you soon found that she was as attractive conversationally as she was pleasing to the eye. You soon learned that she was much interested in painting, had attended art school, and was really profoundly interested in art. She timidly showed you some vases she had painted. Finally she showed you a delicate little glass dish which she had painted in a very artistic manner, explaining that she had decorated it as an ash-tray for her father, to be used more as an ornament than as an actual ash-tray. You admired it very greatly. This mention of using the dish as an ash-tray made you desirous of smoking. Because of her youth you hesitated to give her a cigarette. Also, you did not know how her father might feel about such things and yet you wanted to observe the courtesies of smoking. As you debated this problem you became increasingly impatient. The girl did not offer you a cigarette and thus solve your problem and you kept wishing that you might offer her a cigarette. Finally in desperation you asked her permission to smoke which she granted very readily and you took a cigarette but did not offer her one. As you smoked you looked around for an ash-tray and the girl, noticing your glance, urged you to use the ash-tray she had designed for her father. Hesitantly you did so and began talking on various topics. As you talked you became aware of a rapidly mounting impatience for her father's return. Shortly you became so impatient that you could not enjoy smoking any longer, and so great was your impatience and distress that instead of carefully putting out your cigarette and then dropping it in the ash-tray, you simply dropped the lighted cigarette into the ash-tray and continued to converse with the girl. The girl apparently took no notice of the act but after a few minutes you suddenly heard a loud crack and you immediately realized that the cigarette you had dropped into the ash-tray had continued burning and had heated the glass unevenly, with the result that it had cracked in pieces. You felt very badly about this, but the girl very kindly and generously insisted that it was a matter of small moment, that she had not yet given the ash-tray to her father, that he would not know anything about it, and that he would not be disappointed. Nevertheless, you felt exceedingly guilty about your carelessness in breaking the ash-tray and you wondered about how her father would feel about it if he ever learned of it. Your concern was plainly evident, and when the mother came into the room you tried to explain, but she graciously reassured you and told you that it really did not matter. However, you felt most uncomfortable about it and it seemed to you that the girl felt badly too. Shortly after this a telephone call was received from the father stating that he was called away for the rest of the day and asking your permission to see you on a later day. You left the house very gladly, feeling most wretched about the whole situation and realizing at the time that there was really nothing you could do about it. Now after you are awakened this whole situation will be on your mind. You will not consciously know what it is but, nevertheless, it will be on your mind, it will worry you and govern your actions and your speech although you will not be aware that it is doing so. I have just told you of a recent experience of yours, and as I recounted it to you, you recalled it in detail, realizing the whole time that I gave you a fairly accurate account of the situation, that I gave the essential story. After you awaken the whole situation will be on your mind but you will not be conscious of what it is, you will not even be aware of what it might be, but it will worry you and it will govern your speech and your actions. Do you understand? And do you feel badly about this thing?

Erickson's analysis of this suggestion follows:

THE COMPLEX	EXPLANATORY REMARKS
Now	"Now" relates to the present, the immediate, circumscribed, highly limited present; it will not bear upon the past, nor upon the future; it is safe, secure.
as you	"You" is a soft word; the subject is introduced gently.
continue	"Continue" is a most important word, since it carries on into the future, it contradicts "now," which relates to the present, and it introduces an indefinite extension into the future. Hence, the subject unwittingly makes a change from the "now" situation into a continuing future situation.
to sleep	Thus he has the time situation changed and at the same moment is given a command to "continue to sleep," a command based upon the past, including the present and extending into the remote future.
I'm	First person pronoun, which means that anything

The complex	Explanatory remarks
	done is to be done by the hypnotist and that the subject can be safely passive.
going	"Going" carries on the future connotation of "continue," but enlarges it by bringing both the hypnotist and the subject into the continuation into the future.
to recall	"Recall" signifies the past, and we are both going into the future, taking with us the past.
to your	Second person pronoun; emphasizing that we are both going into the future taking with us the past.
mind	"Mind" is a selected, important, most important part of him, a part of him related to the past.
an	"An" means just one, a certain one and yet is at the same time so indefinite.
event	"Event" is a specific word; just one event, "an event," and yet, despite its seeming specificity, it is so general that one cannot seize upon it or resist or reject it or do anything but accept "an event."
which occurred	"Occurred" is a narrative word; lots of things occur, especially minor things.
not	If the subject wishes to reject, deny, or contradict, the word "not" gives him full opportunity. He can seize upon it and attach to it all of his resistances to an acceptance of the story; it is literally a decoy word to attract his resistances. The sequences are "occurred not," in other words, "did not occur," but, even should his resistances seize upon "not," that decoy is legitimately snatched away by the next two words, and thus his resistances are mustered, mobilized, but left unattached and frustrated.
long ago.	Actually "not long ago,"—"not" now destroys itself as a negative word; it is positive in that sequence. Furthermore, it is highly specific, but in a vague, general way; when is "not long ago"? Yesterday? Last week? Also "not long ago" is real, since we do have a "not long ago" in our lives: thus a weight of truth is given which will radiate.
As I	First person again, assuming responsibility.
recount	Previously, I was going "to recall," but in this phrase I immediately withdraw from that responsibility. Now, I am only going to "recount," and

The complex	Explanatory remarks
	"recount" and "recall" are totally different words. Thus, the responsibility for a "recall," which was the initial task, is rejected by the hypnotist, who assumes the responsibility only for recounting. Therefore, if the hypnotist recounts, the subject is thereby compelled to recall. Indeed if the hypnotist can recount, and there can be no doubt about that, then the subject can, actually can, recall; a sophistical but indisputable establishment of the truth of the story to be told.
this	"This" like "an" is a definitive word that cannot be disputed; and readiness to dispute or deny must be held in abeyance.
event	Again a specific word.
to you,	Second person; first it was recalled to "your mind," and now it is to recount "to you," that is, to him as a person. Thus he is introduced so that, in his passive acceptance of the recounting, he, as a person, can assume responsibility.
you will	The subject is called upon to act as a person, and at the same time is given a command.
recall	"Recall" completes the shift of responsibility from first to second person, with a final allocation of responsibility for recounting and for recalling.
fully and completely	These are distraction words since they attract attention not to the task, but to the size or quality of the task. Hence, he must first refuse to do it "fully and completely" before he can refuse to do the task at all, and if he refuses to do it "fully and completely," he is, by implication, obligating himself to do it at least in part, until he goes through the process of refusing to do it in toto. All this takes so much time that there is no opportunity to go through those mental processes permitting a logical rejection of the entire task. Additionally, if he still has resistances to the hypnotic situation, he can mobilize them against these distraction words.
everything	"Everything" is really a threatening word; to tell everything is something one just does not do. So here is an opportunity to mobilize resistance, since, if he is to accept this story, his resistances must first be mobilized as a preliminary to a dispersion. Also, if he refuses to tell "everything," he is thereby affirming that there is something to tell.

The complex	Explanatory remarks
that happened.	The command to tell "everything" is now seemingly qualified, since it is not "everything," but just the bald facts of "what happened," not the meanings or personal implications. Again there is an implication of other things.
You	Second person, reemphasizing the subject's role as someone involved.
have had good reason	There is not only a "reason," but a "good reason," at that! We all like to think we have a "good reason"; it vindicates.
to forget	Now the "good reason" becomes inexplicably transformed into a "bad" reason; "good" no longer is "good," but is really a bad sort of thing; the kind of reason one likes to forget. Also, "to forget" explains the need "to recall", and explains the recounting. But what does one forget? Bad things, especially!
this	Explicit word, intended to reemphasize the feeling of specificity.
occurrence,	"Occurred" was a narrative word, and now the word is "occurrence," so often a euphemism applied to bad things one forgets.
but	"But" always prefaces unpleasant things; "let's have no 'buts' about it," is so common an expression.
as I recall it,	This phrasing is a reprieve, since the first person assumes the responsibility, but he who can assume responsibility can also assign it. Thus, indirectly, the dominance of the hypnotist is assured, and the next words lead to active work for the subject.
you will remember each and every detail fully.	More than recall is wanted. Previously, it was "you will recall"; now it is more "you will remember"; furthermore, "remember" is in itself a simple, direct, hypnotic suggestion, similar to the suggestion of "sleep" in the opening sentence. Also, what is to be remembered is "each and every detail," so that refusal to remember has to be directed to each detail, not to the whole occurrence. Thus, "each" and "every" and "fully" are distraction words, directing refusal or rejection to a quality of performance.
Now	"Now" harks back to the first word of the first sentence, a word that could be fully accepted. Thus, utilization is made of that first attitude.

The complex	Explanatory remarks
bear this in mind,	"Mind" harks back to the first sentence again for a similar reason.
that while I repeat	"Repeat" is a word which relates to a factual experience in the past, one that really occurred and is known, since otherwise it could not be repeated by someone. Also, the role of the hypnotist is clearly defined and cannot be disputed.
what I know of this event,	"Repeat" and "know" affirm and establish the truth, but give an avenue of escape, because the qualification of what "I know" implies that there may be much that "I" don't know, and therefore something additional that he does know.
you will recall fully and completely	This phrasing harks back and reaffirms the original allocation of responsibility to "you." "Fully and completely" is again a repeated distraction, reinforcing the previous use of those words.
everything	That meaningful, even threatening word again.
just as it happened,	A qualification that limits and comforts since it excludes possible personal implications and meanings.
and more	Further threatening since "more," what "more," is wanted.
than that,	Still carrying the threat.
you will	A hypnotic command carrying compulsion.
re-experience the various conflicting emotions	The thing is now defined as conflicting and as emotional, of which things he had a plenty, all real, and, above all, emotional.
which you had at the time	A specific but unidentified "time" in the past, but a time related to "conflicting emotions."
and you will feel	A hypnotic command that he is to feel, which carries a threat since it follows "conflicting emotions."
exactly as you did while this occurrence was taking place.	The thing is defined and outlined, his course of action indicated to be a revivification, only that, of a past experience, not a confession, just a re-experiencing of something that took place.
Now	Harking back to the opening word, repeated later for its acceptance values immediately after the assignment of a task, and once again repeated here at a similar point.
the particular event	"An event," "an occurrence" now becomes a highly specific item.
of which I am going to tell you is this:	"I" can tell only what little "I know," a casual

The complex	Explanatory remarks
	statement, transitional in its use, reassuring in its implications.
Some time ago	"Not long ago" redefined, but still vague and elusive of contradiction.
you met a man	Indisputably true and acceptable.
prominent	We like to know "prominent" people, an initial appeal to narcissism.
in academic circles	A narrowing of the identification of the man, but safely so!
who manifested an interest in you	A strong appeal to narcissism.
and who was in a position	A tentative threat, because "position," synonym of power, can be used favorably or unfavorably.
to aid you	Narcissism reinforced and reassured, but more than that, the subject now wants to know, to identify, the man, and, hence, is open readily to suggestion.
in securing a certain	Highly specific but not definitive.
research fellowship in which you were much interested.	A true statement in that he was interested in a fellowship, actually any fellowship, but this statement offers no opportunity to take issue or dispute, since each item is progressively qualified, and each qualification requires dispute before the initial premise can be attacked, and his narcissism requires that he accept each item in the suggestions. Thus, resistance is dispersed. Additionally, the man is "interested," the subject is "interested," there is a common denominator, and the reality of the subject's interest radiates to and substantiates the man's interest.
He	A third person taking all responsibility. Therefore, the subject can listen receptively, since the story is about a third person.
made an appointment with you	This is a disputable statement, and hence is to be qualified in more and more detailed and specific fashion, thus to preclude any upsurge of resistance or rejection, and each little item to be added must have a cumulative effect that takes the subject even farther from the essential point.
to see him at his home	A qualification as to place.
and on that day	A qualification as to a specific day that must be selected out of the past.
you called at the designated	"Designated" is so specific, final, absolute, and yet so indefinite.
hour.	A final specific qualification for the appointment,

The complex	Explanatory remarks
	and it is most important to establish that appointment. Thus the subject is led to a home, to "that day," to a "designated hour." With such detail, not even a thought can flash obstructively in his mind since the only measure open to him in the hypnotic situation is to reject a "designated hour" of a specific day at a home of an interested man whom, narcissistically, he wanted. Thus, an idea has been offered, and its acceptance literally forced. Therefore an opportunity to resist something about this rapidly growing story must be given him in return for being forced to accept some ideas.
When	A challenging word, anything can happen "when."
you	Second person active, giving opportunity for him to get set for action.
knocked at the door	A brief item of detail, momentarily obstructing action.
you were met	"You" is the second person passive—thus he is forced from the active to the passive role. "Were met" a dogmatic declaration which is the opening for all resistance and rejection, an opportunity to interpolate from past experience, a wide open door for dismissal of the entire story, and thus, a chance for him to construct his own account.
not	A negative word, emphatically negative.
by this gentleman	Apparently, it is unnecessary to deny, reject or dispute the story, since the hypnotist is doing that by the implications of "you were not met." Thus, the subject's resistances have been built up and then lulled into inaction, and rendered futile by the negations employed.
but by his wife	"But" used a second time, this time in close association with a woman to reinforce possible previous unpleasant associations, since a wife is a sexualized woman. Also, this is another disputable statement, but before he can remobilize his resistances, the total situation is completely changed by the next words.
who greeted you cordially and was very friendly,	A tremendous appeal is made to his narcissism, already stimulated previously. One likes to be greeted cordially by a "prominent" man's wife.
making you feel	"Feel" means respond emotionally, a safe secure situation for responding to narcissism. Also, the word is a direct call for narcissistic response. At

The complex	Explanatory remarks
	the same time there is given the simple direct hypnotic command of "you feel."
that her husband had given a good account of you to her.	Full opportunity offered for unrestricted narcissism in a safe secure fashion. All that has been told now rests upon secure foundation of narcissistic satisfactions. He needs this story.
She explained apologetically	An indirect attack upon his narcissism—this gracious woman who flattered him now becoming apologetic? That must not be so, because whatever that cordial woman does must be right, and he will make it so. Apologies and praise in that combination are not good.
that her husband had been called away	A faint, remote realization that he was alone with a woman who was a wife and hence a recognized sexual object.
for a few moments	A limitation of the danger, and hence he is safe, although alone with a woman.
but that he would return shortly	"Shortly" is so specifically vague and reassuring.
and had asked that you	"You," the person, introduced again.
be made comfortable	Gracious man, gracious woman, narcissistic satisfactions reinforced.
in the library.	A distraction phrase. Yet, to be made comfortable by a lone woman in the safe confines of a library is like inviting a girl to meet you in the sitting room of your hotel suite—a faint suggestive implication.
You	Second person active.
accompanied her to this room where	Reduction of possible fear by specificity in mentioning only this room—but what is to happen?
she	A woman active in his company—something will happen!
introduced you to a charming girl	For him there can be no greater threat in all the world than a charming girl. A terrifying threatening situation, loaded with tension, firmly established by his past.
who was obviously rather shy and reserved	The threat castrated, and he was master. Thus his fears were aroused and immediately lessened.
and who, she explained	First she explained apologetically and unacceptably, now she explains in relation to a threat—will these displeasing explanations never end? A direct opportunity for relief of tension, directed against unnecessary social amenities conducted in such a terrifying situation, but serving to introduce mother antagonism.

The complex	Explanatory remarks
was their only daughter.	A very special kind of daughter, all the more threatening despite the castration. Thus a useless, only temporary castration was performed and while it did relieve his tension briefly, that tension has been revived and intensified.
The mother	An immediate shift from the threatening daughter to the displeasing mother, permitting his tension to increase.
then requested your permission	This cordial, gracious, apologetic woman, who led him into a trap, she was nice, certainly he would do anything for her, especially since it would change the total situation by letting him deal with the mother and not the daughter.
to go about her work,	Work is a far cry from social pleasures, remote and distant, and thus she was removing herself far from him, leaving him alone with danger.
explaining	That unpleasant word again, first used to rob him of narcissistic pleasure, then to lead him into a dangerous situation. What now?
that the daughter	Special, precious, only daughter—charming girl. A peculiar threat, challenge and danger all combined.
would be very happy to entertain you	To be entertained by a charming girl with the mother's connivance!
while you waited.	"Waited" for what? "Waited," a threatening word, expressive of his passive helplessness. He could only wait, and in the past he had so often "waited" in the company of a charming girl.
You assured	"Assured" carries connotations about risks and dangers.
the mother	Who led you into a trap, a danger situation—opportunity for intense resentment and tension relief.
that you would be very comfortable	"Comfortable," with a girl? Past history proves the mockery of that.
and even now	Harking back to the first "now" and neutrilizing its "present" values.
you can recall	Harking back to the first use of "recall" and thus tying tightly everything together.
the glow of pleasure	Harking back to "reexperience the various conflicting emotions."
you experienced	If there were conflicting emotions, some were glows of pleasure, and now his situation is

The complex	Explanatory remarks
	one of conflict, of attractive and shy, of charming and only daughter, of mother coming and not staying and praising and apologizing, pleasure and unpleasure.
at the thought of having the daughter	"Having the daughter," possessing the charming girl—synonymous phrases.
as a hostess.	Dance-hall hostess? He had had hostesses before, and now there is given the suggestion that he have the "daughter as a hostess."
As the mother left the room	A distraction by shifting attention away from the immediate threat of the girl, and hence readily accepted even though it leaves him alone with his danger.
you	Second person introduced.
set about	"Set about" implies action, doing something.
conversing	"Conversing" is a safe activity, but it is a euphemism, and what thinking one can do as he converses!
with the girl,	Alone with a dangerous girl brought to full realization.
and despite her shyness and bashfulness,	Despite those qualities, what else? What danger threatens?
you soon found	Continuation of the threat.
that she was	What was she? An only daughter, a charming girl, a daughter as a hostess?
as attractive conversationally as she was pleasing to the eye.	Safe, yet unsafe, physically pleasing, capable of conversation, capable as a hostess?
You	Second person again emphasized.
soon learned	He had learned much about her, too much, and now what more was to be learned about this charming girl so pleasing to the eye?
that she was much interested	Repetition of the word "interested." In what could she, in this danger situation, be interested?
in painting,	"Painting?" Painting the town red? A euphemism?
had attended art school, and was really profoundly interested in art.	He had done commercial art to pay his way through college, so there was something in common, a common interest—to be profoundly interested in art would mean that she was interested in *his* art and his art was part of him. A part of him?
She	A shift from him to her.
timidly	A dangerous girl being timid? Girl-boy behavior, coy, luring behavior?

The complex	Explanatory remarks
showed you	Presented to you.
some vases she had painted.	A symbol innocuously introduced, and with the word "painted" establishing their common interest in doing something.
Finally	This is a threatening word. It establishes a moment surcharged with finality, a grand finale is about to be!
she showed	Previously she timidly "showed," but now where is that timidity? The situation has changed!
you a delicate little glass dish	Fragile, precious thing, easily shattered by masculine strength so like the girl.
which she had painted	Something on which she had lavished attention.
in a very artistic manner,	Lavished care in a special sort of way that he and she together could both appreciate.
explaining	That word of previously unsatisfactory connotations.
that she had decorated it as an ashtray for her father,	Charming girl, precious possession, father's ownership and priority.
to be used	There is something in this danger situation to be used!
more as an ornament	An ornament can decorate a pleasing body.
than as an actual	It's not an ash-tray! It's something different.
ash-tray.	Thus, the symbolic value is clearly established. It is just called an ash-tray, but it is an ornament belonging to her and over which the father exercises some undetermined undefined authority.
You admired it	"It" was what she had, she was attractive, pleasing to the eye.
very greatly.	Redundant superlative! In other words a special significance is to be attached to this symbol, a significance in relation to admiration in the presence of a physically attractive girl.
This mention	Some things are just "mentioned," hinted at, not said in a forthright manner.
of using the dish as an ash-tray	But it is not a "dish," it is not a vase, it is not even an ash-tray, it is just an ornament that belongs to her and to her father in a peculiar sort of way.
made you desirous	One wishes to smoke, but becomes "desirous" in the presence of a pretty girl.
of smoking.	A euphemism, a safe conventional way of giving

The complex	Explanatory remarks
	expression to the feeling of being "desirous," actually a pattern of behavior taken out of his past, since smoking was used by him in his problem situation as a distraction.
Because of her youth	Not "youth" really, though she was fresh and pretty and youthful, but something that "youth" connoted, something not to be expressed.
you hesitated	One may eye an attractive girl and be "desirous" and "hesitate." Thus a sexual motif becomes more evident. Besides, one does not hesitate to smoke in the presence of youth.
to give her a cigarette.	A symbolic ash-tray, an ornament belonging to her in which both she and he were "interested" in a special way with a father lurking in the background. The words "desirous," "smoking," "youth," "hesitate" all constitute a background for a symbolic cigarette that fits a symbolic ash-tray.
Also,	There is something else left unsaid as yet, an implication repeatedly established by transitional words.
you did not know how her father	Father lurking in the background reinforced.
might feel about such things	What are "such things" in the presence of a youthful girl that might arouse a father's ire?
and yet you wanted	A long history of "wanting," "wanting," in the presence of every pretty girl.
to observe the courtesies of smoking.	A euphemism, since what else can be said?
As you debated	One does not debate about smoking, one debates for deep reasons, one strives against and tries to controvert the forces against him in a debate.
this problem	He had a "problem," a most troublesome problem in relation to girls and he is "debating" a "problem" in a girl's presence.
you became increasingly impatient.	Not over smoking does one become "increasingly impatient," but only over vital problems.
The girl	"The girl" follows "increasingly impatient" and by that juxtaposition a relationship is established between "the girl" and the feelings described.
did not offer you a cigarette and thus solve your problem	She failed him like all other girls he had known, equating her with those other girls who did not solve his "problem."

The complex	Explanatory remarks
and you kept wishing	"Wishing" just "wishing" in direct connection with a girl who had failed to solve his "problem," an old, old story for him.
that you might offer her a cigarette.	If only he "might," really "could" do something. "They satisfy," was one of his clichés, and he did want satisfaction. The conventional and the sexual motifs intermingled—satisfaction in relation to a girl, a symbolic ash-tray, being "desirous" and his "problem."
Finally in desperation	Another final moment, with implication of other things. Strong, bitter, frustrated emotions constitute desperation, and it does not derive from being deprived of a cigarette.
you asked her permission	The role of being miserable, a suppliant, incapable of self-determined action.
to smoke.	A long history of smoking in his "problem" situation to cover up and conceal his disability.
which she granted very readily	A permissive, willing girl, readily granting favors —another item taken out of his past history.
and you took a cigarette	That was all he could do, and which he had so often done in the past.
but did not offer her one.	She had no pleasure, she was unsatisfied. Past history still being utilized.
As you smoked	He couldn't do anything else, as he had proved many times.
you looked about	Did she notice? Did all those girls of the past notice your glance, your look?
for an ash-tray and the girl noticing your glance,	"For an ash-tray and the girl," making them in this juxtaposition a single object to be looked for. Also, another cliché was "ashes hauled."
urged you to use the ash-tray she had designed	Not only permissive, but urgent, active, aggressive. An "ash-tray she had designed" for what? She had only decorated it for father.
for her father.	Father's special thing, unused by him and not intended for his use, but only an ornament over which he exercises an undefined authority.
Hesitantly	Again he "hesitates," but more than that, the word "hesitantly" implies insecurity, uncertainty, even fears.
you did so	"Hesitantly, you did so," in other words disposed of "ashes" in a forbidden object.
and began talking on various topics.	A technique of self-distraction and of distraction for the girl often employed in the past.

The complex	Explanatory remarks
As you talked you became aware of a rapidly mounting impatience for her father's return.	"Mounting" is a word he often used with special significance. He was always "impatient to mount" before "something happened" that meant the end of the attempt to succeed. Incongruous words!
	What choice is there between "father's return" in a seduction situation and ejaculatio praecox? Any ending, however tragic, is needed to bring to a close an impotence situation.
Shortly you became so impatient that you could not enjoy smoking any longer,	This is only another "impatient" situation, thereby it is equated with other "impatient" situations. Past history repeated. Was that why the slogan "they satisfy" was his cliché?
and so great was your impatience and distress	Those words can describe only something more vital than smoking. They are pertinent to past experiences.
that instead of carefully putting out your cigarette and then dropping it in the ash-tray, you simply dropped the lighted cigarette into the ash-tray	The whole performance was of no value—it was futile, useless, hopeless, fraught with distressing emotions. "Lighted cigarette" and ashes just dropped futilely.
and continued to converse with the girl.	Past history, in that he could only conclude by conversing with the girl.
The girl apparently took no notice of the act	"Apparently" carries a weight of hope.
	There are acts and then, there is "the act," and this was an act that preceded his despairing resignation to mere conversation with a girl, a girl who "took no notice," a parallel of many previous instances.
but after a few minutes you suddenly heard a loud crack	"The crack that never heals" was a paraphrase from a song often employed by him to vent sadistic reactions.
and you immediately realized that the cigarette you had dropped into the ash-tray had continued burning and had heated the	He had often bitterly described his repeated efforts and failures on a single occasion as an attempt "to take a crack in pieces."

The complex	Explanatory remarks
glass unevenly, with the result that it had cracked in pieces.	
You felt very badly	Redundancy, strained superlative to carry extreme emotional weight.
about this, but the girl	"This" is one thing, "the girl" is another, another juxtaposition of two items that are to be equated.
very kindly and generously	Permissive, granting, urgent, now maternally kind and forgiving,—copied from past experiences.
insisted that it	An unnamed "it."
was a matter of small moment,	Past history again, carrying the same load of bitter ironic significance. What he did was of "small moment."
that she had not yet given the ash-tray	Further ironic truth.
to her father,	First maternal, now the girl speaks for her father, thus combining maternal and paternal attitudes in her forbearance.
that he would not know anything	"Not anything," a secret was to be kept, a guilty secret.
about it,	Still an unnamed "it."
and that he would not be disappointed.	A seriously tense situation does not warrant such a mild word as "disappointed." "Disappointed" is a euphemism and at the same time signifies that the situation warrants the mockery implied by "small moment."
Nevertheless, you felt exceedingly guilty	"Nevertheless" implies the existence of certain other facts. Fitting words, but not for the superficial content.
about your carelessness in breaking the ash-tray	A euphemism since exceeding guilt does not attach to an ash-tray.
and you wondered	How many times had he "wondered" in similarly emotionally charged situations?
about how her father	Man of power, authority, prior rights.
would feel about it	Not think but "feel," since this was a matter for profound emotion.
if he ever learned of it.	"Ever learned"—a continuing threat implied.
Your concern was plainly evident,	How many times in the past had his concern been evident?

The complex	Explanatory remarks
and when the mother	Maternal retribution, forgiveness, or what?
came into the room you tried	You really did try, you've always tried, but it always ends the same old way.
to explain, but she graciously	Forgiveness, not retribution, always forgiveness as in the past.
reassured you and told you that it really did not matter.	"Small moment" ironically brought home by the one who should be the most bitter.
However, you felt most uncomfortable about it	A conventional way of saying something too vital to be put into words.
and it seemed to you that the girl felt badly too.	Like other unsatisfied girls who masked their disappointment by maternal behavior, who did not reveal that they had been "badly" used.
Shortly after this a telephone call was received from the father stating that he was called away for the rest of the day	A reprieve, a postponement.
and asking your permission to see you on a later day.	"Your permission," when he has been wronged and violated in relation to his only daughter. The whole situation now radiates beyond the room; reaches out into the fabric of the social situation, the educational situation infringes upon and enters into everything, and continues to a "later day." Hence, it is not ended yet, but reaches indefinitely into the future.
You left the house very gladly, feeling most wretched about the whole situation	That was all it was, a "whole situation." A pun upon another cliché he employed when distressed about his disability.
and realizing at the time that there was really nothing you could do about it.	A final, despairing repetition of the teachings of the past.
Now after you are awakened	The original "now" situation continuing into the immediate future with the repetition of the word "now" re-establishing the original receptive attitude.
this whole situation	Pun repeated in relation to the immediate future.

The complex	Explanatory remarks
will be on your mind. You will not consciously know what it is but, nevertheless, it will be on your mind, it will worry you and govern your actions and your speech although you will not be aware that it is doing so.	Hypnotic suggestions, with careful emphasis upon the second person pronoun.
I have just told you of a recent experience of yours, and as I recounted it to you, you recalled it in detail, realizing the whole time that I gave you a fairly accurate account of the situation, that I gave the essential story.	A brief summary of first and second person activities with allocation of responsibilities and definition of roles reiterated.
After you awaken the whole situation will be on your mind but you will not be conscious of what it is, you will not even be aware of what it might be, but it will worry you and it will govern your speech and your actions.	A final shifting of all action upon the second person and repetition of hypnotic suggestions.
Do you understand?	A final command, request and plea that in itself signifies that there is much to be understood.
And you do feel badly about this thing.	A simple statement in the present tense that concludes with the ambiguous reproachful sounding phrase "this thing" of such utterly unpleasant connotations.

This material should make it clear that proper utilization of hypnosis is the most difficult and delicate part of hypnotism. Few hypnotists have taken as much care and trouble as Erickson has in his work with hypnosis. This may largely account for their inability to duplicate many of his remarkable demonstrations. He has written a number of other articles on the production and uses of hypnotic complexes; unfortunately space does not allow our taking these up in detail. Particular attention might, however, be called to one other very basic paper by him[48] in which an acute obsessional hysterical state was created in a subject through the systematic implantation of suggestions of obsessive compulsive ideation, affects and behavior. The technique used bears some resemblance to those already discussed, but is quite different in many ways. This article is an extremely important one and should be read by any person planning to do work in this area.

PRODUCTION OF HYPNOTIC REGRESSIONS AND REVIVIFICATIONS

Conceptually speaking, *a hypnotic regression is a reinstatement of earlier experiences and their associated behavioral patterns under the influence of hypnosis or of hypnotic suggestions.* That is, the hypnotized individual returns to an earlier age-level in thought and behavior. In practice, although most hypnotists accept this definition, there is a tendency for investigators to use the operational definition that a hypnotic regression is any alteration in behavior which results from and is consistent with the suggestion that a regression (in the conceptual sense) will take place. Now, what happens when such a suggestion is given is that many individuals who are presumed to be regressed are really only playing the part of an individual of the age to which they had been told to return. Such individuals act out what they as adults conceive to be the correct behavior for the suggested period of their life. The form and quality of these dramatizations or role playings depend upon the subject's beliefs, remembrances, adult understanding and imagining of the period to which he is being "regressed." In such instances there may be hypermnesia for some or all past events, but there is no true reinstatement. This is nevertheless what many writers have called a regression. There are reasons for believing, however, that when some individuals are regressed, not only is there a reactivation or reinstatement of experiences and behavior which existed at a past epoch in their life with all subsequent experiences "ablated," that is, prevented from having any influence upon the subject's behavior and from entering his awareness, but older organic conditions may even be re-established within limits. When this condition occurs, one has what has been called a "revivification." Wolberg[202] has described it as an actual organic reproduction of an earlier period of life in which past patterns of ideation and behavior are revived. Kubie and Margolin[103] interpret it as a channeling of the expression of all subsequent experiences through earlier redintegrated mechanisms.

If one had only to deal with one or the other of the above situations one could probably fairly easily agree to restrict the use of the term "regression" to the second event since it is the only one which can really be said to fit the conceptual definition. Unfortunately, the entire situation is very much complicated by the fact that often a "regressed" individual shows evidence of both role playing and the presence of some reinstated elements in his behavior. How are we to classify such mixtures? Most hypnotists who have encountered this situation have not recognized its true nature and have simply proceeded to call it a regression. A few who have realized what was happening have, nevertheless, also called it a regression. It is my firm belief that one should clearly distinguish between situations in which one has complete revivification, some, and none at all. Much of this confusion and controversy regarding "regressions" which is to be found in the literature would thereby be easily eliminated. To begin with, cases in which hypermnesia for previous experiences occurs without any clear-cut dramatization should never be called regressions. When the hypermnesic material is dramatized, I have previously recommended[191] that one speak of a *regression type* I. What has been called a revivification now becomes a *regression type* II, and a mixture of revivification and dramatization is to be called a *regression type* III. When this nomenclature is followed, the term "revivification" is used strictly to denote the actual psychophysiological process which brings about type II regressions; the term "regression" without reference to type is employed, when greater specification is not required, to refer to the occurrence of any one or all of the different types.

One also occasionally encounters, in both past and current literature on hypnosis, the use of the term "regression" to denote the recall with or without dramatization of "previous lives" or incarnations. If one must use the notion of regression in this sense I would strongly recommend that he specifically refer here to a "supranormal regression." Finally, whenever there is a possibility of confusion with "natural" or uninduced regressions, such as are observed in psychotics, one should always qualify the foregoing types of regressions as being "hypnotic regressions," for there is reason to believe that these are not identical phenomena. Possibly one could extend this classificatory system and speak of regressions of type IV, V, and so forth, to cover this and other situations. Alternatively, one might follow the suggestion of Barker, Dembo, and Lewin[6a] that all reinstatement processes be called "retrogressions," leaving the term "regression" to denote the "de-differentiation" and "primitivization" of the person. This step neverthe-less would still require making a distinction between three kinds of hypnotic-ally induced effects, one of which alone qualifies fully as a "retrogression." As the three authors have made clear, the problem is complex, too much for us to attempt to solve in these pages.

From the standpoint of induction, the demarcation between type I and type II regressions does not appear to be quite as definite as in the above discussion since one apparently is working with a continuum, at one end of which lies mere recall of past experiences, while at the other end are the type II regressions. Somewhere in between and shading off imperceptibly into these two extremes are the type I (and type III) regressions. The pro-cedure of induction is essentially the same for all points on this continuum. All other things being the same, the level of regression reached is largely determined by the depth of hypnosis, the amount of set which has been allowed and the length of the suggestions. Various factors will from one time to another favor one level more than another. But usually, when work-ing with regression phenomena, one aims for the highest point on the con-tinuum, a type II regression.* As progress is made toward this end the other stages tend to appear sequentially; however, the sequence is not always followed, or at least it progresses so rapidly that for all intents and purposes it has not been followed. Thus in practice, one sometimes sees individuals spontaneously revivifying, and not too uncommonly entering a regression type III without apparent transition. On the other hand, many individuals will normally not go beyond a certain level of regression, unless careful psychodynamic manipulation is used to get around the existing obstruction. There is evidence that with repeated regressions a subject tends to show an increasing amount of revivification. It seems as if the subject had learned how to regress.

A relatively simple method which often brings about a considerable degree of regression is the use of graded suggestions (page 37). As an exam-ple of this technique, we quote here from Wolberg.[202] Having hypnotized the patient deeply, he says:

> Now concentrate carefully upon what I have to say. I am going to suggest that you go back in time, back into the past. You will feel as if you were back in the period I suggest. Let us start with yesterday. What did you do yesterday morning? What did you have for breakfast? For lunch? Now we are going back to the first day you came to see me. Can you see yourself talking to me? How did you feel? Describe it. What clothes did you

---

* There probably are situations in therapy in which this is contraindicated, and a regression type I or at most type III is preferable.

wear? Now listen carefully. We are going back a period when you were little. You are getting smaller. You are getting smaller and smaller. Your arms and legs are getting smaller. I am someone you know and like. You are between ten and twelve. Can you see yourself? Describe what you see. Now you are getting even smaller. You are becoming very, very little. Your arms and legs are shrinking. Your body is shrinking. You are going back to a time when you were very, very little. Now you are a very little child. You are going back to the time when you entered school for the first time. Can you see yourself? Who is your teacher? How old are you? What are your friends' names? Now you are even smaller than that; you are very, very much smaller. Your mother is holding you. Do you see yourself with mother? What is she wearing? What is she saying?

By far the most powerful of the methods, one which we owe to Erickson,[44] is a combination of disorientation and reorientation. The subject is first gradually but completely disoriented with respect to time and place, then he is gradually reoriented. First a state of general confusion is suggested in regard to the exact day, then this is carried over step by step to include the week, the month and the year. You can merely suggest to the subject that he finds it increasingly difficult to remember the day, date, etc., that he feels mixed up about it, and so on.

Erickson also recommends the use of his "confusion technique." It is a slower and more difficult method, but possibly a more effective one. In it he sets out not only to suggest disorientation with regard to time, but also to confuse the subject by the very wording of his suggestions, as explained on page 274. As we saw, part of the aim of this procedure is to disorient the subject sufficiently so as to create in him a strong need for a definite, reassuring feeling of certainty about anything at all. Under these conditions he becomes extremely receptive to any suggestion which gives him a frame of reference. This is essentially what the reorientation phase which follows does, offering a new frame of reference laid in the subject's past. Both the disorientation and the reorientation are done gradually, step-by-step. At first one must be very careful not to word the suggestions as commands or instructions; they should be presented in a conversational manner, as thought-provoking comments. It is only after indications that the subject is beginning to respond that one makes a progressive shift to direct suggestions to recall past events with increasing vividness, and to increasingly forget all events subsequent to the selected regression age. All of this must be done slowly and unnoticeably. The method is probably extremely powerful in some cases, but it seems unnecessarily long and difficult for many others.

Regardless of the technique used it is essential, as Erickson points out, that the hypnotist be fitted into the regression situation. Although the reason is obvious, it is very often overlooked. If the subject has been reoriented to a period of his life which is prior to his meeting the hypnotist, the latter cannot exist for him as such. Very often the subject will spontaneously transform the hypnotist into a person who was present in the period to which the subject is being regressed. If the hypnotist has independently obtained sufficient information regarding the events which transpired at a certain regression date, he can bring about a suitable transformation of his identity by using various cues.

With regression to a time in the individual's life when he could neither speak nor understand words, there is always the possibility of losing verbal contact with the subject if an intense revivification is produced. Theoretically the revivification could be so complete that the capacity for communication in all forms would be lost. Evidence that this can happen has been reported by Dieterle and Koch.[37a] Therefore one should be very careful in working with regression phenomena. I have made a practice of setting up a system of simple nonverbal signals which I use to provoke the final step in the regression as well as to bring the subject back to his actual age or at least some age in which I can communicate with him. So far I have not encountered any difficulties. I have observed that subjects responding to such signals when regressed to a very early stage (1 or 2 months of age) tend to show a rather long latency, as if a definite reorganization was taking place. This would seem to fit in with Erickson's emphatic contention that one should always give the subject ample time for assimilation of suggestions and reorientation in the suggested setting. In connection with the use of nonverbal signals, one should keep in mind that, at very early ages, the individual's vision is poor, and that with the exception of certain "erogenous" zones which vary with age, tactual localization and discrimination is rather limited. Signals must be devised accordingly.

Sometimes the particular age to which the subject is regressed happens to be connected directly or indirectly with some traumatic event in his life. This may, in the first place, create difficulty in regressing the individual; then even if the hypnotist can bring about regression to the specific age and day, the resulting experience may be so unpleasant for the subject that future regressions will become difficult or impossible. This type of situation arises frequently in psychotherapy. The best way of dealing with such cases is to gradually reorient the subject to a vaguely defined period which lies between limits bounding the traumatic time. The subject is not asked to specifically name and identify the time of reorientation. Later, these limits can be narrowed down, and eventually the specific age evoked.

As I stated earlier, in a true regression (type II) the hypnotist cannot have any existence as such for the subject. Indeed, if revivification (which includes ablation) takes place, logically the subject should cease to be hypnotized! But then, would the regression persist? Obviously, from experience, we know that apparently it does. Furthermore I know of no cases where subjects in a type II regression have failed to respond to pre-arranged signals or have shown evidence that hypnosis has ceased. This is in essence what I have called[191] the *regression paradox*. Now, the existence of this paradox depends upon the assumption that not only does an ablation take place in the way we have described, but also that it is complete, that is, among other things, affects all levels of nervous activity. Perhaps then we must take this as evidence that either ablation does not occur or that it is never complete. It may be that ablation is a process which can occur only in connection with higher center functions; or it may simply be that no complete ablation has ever been observed because no complete regression of type II has ever been produced. There is evidence that the reflex level is the last level to become affected by suggestions, from which we can deduce that it is likely also to be the last one to be influenced by a regression. If this is the case it is unlikely that revivification has ever been observed going to completion. Presumably, with deep enough hypnosis and proper techniques, it is possible to attain such a goal. What the consequences would be is difficult to say, but anyone inclined to experiment in this direction is warned to do so with extreme caution.

PRODUCTION OF SENSORY ALTERATIONS

Here again we turn to the work of Erickson[47] for the most effective approach. One of the first requirements to be met is producing an adequate trance state. As has been remarked many times, this is essential if the effects are to be more than acting out. In general, the subject's behavior in so-called deep hypnosis can be expected to be a mixture of his reactions to the immediate hypnotic situation and reactions which are derived from his normal waking behavior. It is essential that no aspect of the subject's normal behavior patterns be able to influence the hypnotic behavior. In order to satisfy this condition, Erickson emphasizes the need to produce a much more complex change in the subject than normal deep-trance induction does. Consequently, his technique is first to induce a deep trance by standard means, then to induce a stuporous state through a systematic technique of graduated suggestions. This phase alone should take about 2 hours. Then a somnambulistic state is induced in which the subject is slowly and gradually adjusted to the demands of the somnambulistic trance. This may require another hour or more. The aim here is to inhibit all spontaneous activity, at the same time allowing complete freedom to all responsive activity. The procedure should be repeated until it is possible to obtain stupor and somnambulism within 10 or less minutes. The reader should re-examine the material on deep-trance induction in chapter 8.

The foregoing represents the preliminary training of the subject. Let us now look at the type of procedure Erickson follows in the production of, say, deafness. He outlines his method in the following steps, referring to the instructions given the subject:

1. A clear concise emphatic statement that it was proposed "to hypnotize" him into a "state of absolute deafness."

2. The statement that, as this was done, hypnotic suggestions would be given which would cause slight difficulty, and then more and more difficulty in hearing until finally all sounds, including the hypnotist's voice, "would fade to nothingness."

3. The statement that, as all sound faded away, he would receive a sharp slap on the shoulder which would cause "the utter silence of absolute deafness," and that *ever afterwards whenever he was in a deep trance* merely a blow on the shoulder would produce "instant and absolute deafness."

4. The statement that the deafness would persist *unchanged and complete* until his right wrist was squeezed, or until he was informed definitely in some way to recover his hearing, whereupon his hearing would return "instantly and completely."

5. The induction of a state of amnesia for all commands and instructions, the amnesia to be present continuously for all future trance, post-hypnotic and waking state.

Erickson states that all of these instructions were presented slowly, emphatically, and repeated many times to insure full comprehension and acceptance. After these, the following set of statements was given, likewise slowly, repetitiously and insistently, with the hypnotist progressing to the succeeding instruction only after each was accepted by the subject.

1. Realization that deafness *could* be achieved.
2. That it *would* be achieved.
3. That it was an absolute reality of the *future*.
4. That it was an *impending actuality* of the moment.
5. That the subject was now *preparing to become* totally deaf.
6. That he was *now prepared* and ready.
7. That he was now *awaiting the total deafness* to ensue upon suggestion.
8. That he was now *getting* deaf, that sounds *were fading out*, that the silence was *getting deeper*, that it was *harder and harder* to hear, that he *felt* himself *growing* more and more deaf.
9. Finally, he was given a rapid series of loud, emphatic and absolute instructions to become deaf, totally deaf, with the experimenter's voice gradually fading out as these instructions were concluded.

The cessation of verbal suggestions occurred with the prearranged signal. A few moments rest was allowed, then gradually increasing pressure was applied to the shoulder, until the subject showed discomfort, then it was slowly released.

After allowing another short rest, hearing was tested by clinical means.

Hearing was then restored, and again a short rest followed. The entire procedure was repeated with gradual diminishing of verbal suggestions, until the physical stimulus alone was sufficient. The time for the first induction was 20 to 40 minutes.

In discussing his results, Erickson reports a number of observations which are very pertinent to the question of methodology, and are also related to the question of dealing with difficult subjects. Moreover, they throw interesting light upon the nature of hypnosis. One observation was that some subjects appeared to hear everything when first examined, hence not to be deaf. However, further examination showed Erickson that there actually was a selective deafness and that the subjects heard only those sounds they expected to hear in the particular situation. The importance of the setting is demonstrated by the fact that when they were blindfolded, which created an entirely new situation, no deafness at all could be found.

In other cases, Erickson observed that the subjects would become deaf only if certain conditions were fulfilled. Some would not become deaf unless they were allowed to hear certain sounds. One subject had to have the assurance that no third party would be present before the auditory alteration could be induced. Erickson states that any hint that a third person might be present was sufficient to restore hearing in this case. In still another case, there was *spontaneous* total deafness to all sounds except the experimenter's voice; although it was not possible to bring about deafness to the experimenter's voice by direct suggestion, this was accomplished by a period of silence. Finally, there was one case in which deafness could be produced only if, at the subject's stipulation, he was permitted to hear a pendulum which he could also watch moving. An interesting feature of this case is that by using a complex procedure Erickson was later able to substitute a silent pendulum by inducing the hallucination of an accompanying click.

In a number of cases, Erickson observed that the subjects showed, in association with the suggested deafness, various sensory and motor effects which were not suggested. These various psychodynamic manifestations are of considerable interest in themselves since they are connected to the ego functions of the subjects. Their significance here is that attempts to remove them tended to cause a decrease in suggested deafness. Furthermore, some subjects who failed to develop deafness when the usual suggestions were given would develop it when the suggestions of deafness were combined with those of other sensory and motor disturbances.

Erickson observed three types of reactions to induced deafness. One was curiosity and is of no concern to us. Another was *panic*. This was found to have serious detrimental effects upon the progress of the experiment as well as upon further repetitions of it. The difficulty is that although one can allay the anxiety by suggestions, and this should be done as much as possible, it is difficult to do this without interfering with the experimental situation. The third type of reaction was *shock*. This occurred mainly in subjects who developed only partial deafness, and it always appeared following the restoration of hearing. It had profound physiological effects and tended to interfere with future reinductions of deafness. Since questioning showed that it was the result of a too rapid transition from silence into normal sound, Erickson eventually circumvented the problem by developing a technique of slow recovery of hearing which he used in the first few trials, subsequently gradually reducing the recovery time to 3 to 5 seconds.

As a second example of how to induce deep sensory alterations, we might look at the steps followed by Erickson in producing color blindness. [50] There are seven steps:

1. Slow, gradual induction of profound somnambulism.

2. Slow, gradual induction of *total* blindness to last through the trance and posthypnotically.

3. Awakening of the subject in the blind condition. Anxiety and distress allowed to develop spontaneously.

4. Induction of a second trance with reinforcement of blindness.

5. Alteration of total blindness into color blindness. This is merely proposed at this step. Suggestions are given that vision will be clear but that a neutral tone will be seen instead of colors. Actual restoration waits until step 7 is taken.

6. Induction of deep amnesia of indefinite duration for critical color (or colors). This amnesia should include all connotations and associations with color and should be vague and general.

7. Gradual partial restoration of vision. No mention of color is made, but the suggestions are that vision will be partial, hues altered, and a greater number of neutral tones will be present. Objects will have an altered appearance, quite indefinable, as a result of color blindness.

Note that color blindness is not directly suggested; such a suggestion would tend to be at variance with the subject's grasp of reality. Furthermore, it would require that the subject differentiate between "what is to be seen" and "what is not to be seen," and as Erickson points out this could be done only "if all were seen." This is not merely speculation. Erickson actually made a preliminary study in order to ascertain the best way of proceeding and found that direct suggestions were ineffective. This led him to introduce step 6 to circumvent the differentiation problem. As he explains it, the color blind individual probably has not only a lack of perception for the color, but also the conceptual deficiency which must result. The person who has never seen color can hardly have any real conception of it. Thus the suggestions should be aimed at creating a psychological state which approximates, as closely as possible, the state which is presumably associated with the true defect.

This is only half of the conceptual problem.

How does one get around the conflict which must arise between the subject's past knowledge of reality and the requirements of the immediate hypnotic situation? Here Erickson makes ingenious use of psychodynamics. He says:

> Accordingly the solution of this problem was attempted by first suggesting total blindness, intellectually an entirely conceivable state, and causing to develop in the subject a strong unpleasant affective reaction. This, in turn, would lead to a ready acceptance of any suggestion affording relief from the emotional distress arising from the subjective blindness. There followed a restoration of vision with the relief from the emotional distress of subjective blindness made indirectly and unnoticeably conditional upon the acceptance of direct suggestions of color blindness. Thus, any critical, intellectual tendencies would be held completely in abeyance by inner forces deriving from the emotional needs of the subject, these affective needs compelling the subject to accept color blindness suggestions in full as the only means of securing affective comfort. Hence there would develop neither the occasion nor any need to bring about an adjustment between the critical faculties and the suggestions of color blindness, since the subject's primary purpose and the object became the seeking of affective satisfaction and not the consideration of an intellectual problem. Thus, the color blindness suggestions became possessed of legitimate and essential values for the subject, enforcing their acceptance.

It was pointed out earlier that the effectiveness of suggestions can be considerably increased if they are related to the needs of the subject. Here then is a good example of the skillful use of the technique. However, it goes one step beyond the utilization of needs already present because, in this instance, Erickson *first creates* the need, then uses it to his own end. It hardly seems necessary to add that this sort of manipulation makes a high demand upon the knowledge and skill of the hypnotist and should not be attempted by the beginner. In particular, one must be careful not to create so intense a need in the individual that, falling short of being able to produce the desired effect, he will become compelled to produce an imitation of it (chapter 14). A fine balance is often involved in this kind of manipulation.

The problem of creating hypnotic blindness has been treated in a somewhat different and very clever manner by Erickson[48] in a paper mentioned earlier. Here too he makes extensive use of the psychodynamics of the situation and manipulates the subject's needs in a masterful way. This article is a must for any reader seriously interested in doing this type of experimentation.

Anesthesia of the skin senses is one of the less difficult effects to bring about by hypnotic suggestions. This seems to be particularly true for touch and pain. Nevertheless, one should not be misled into thinking that it is merely a matter of telling the subject that he is anesthetic. Even here a certain degree of skill is required. To begin, complete anesthesia is usually not obtained at the first attempt. In some cases the effect may be quite small, being more in the nature of light analgesia. Here the hypnotist must content himself with the subject's admission of the presence of a small differential in sensitivity between the part suggested to be anesthetic and other parts of his body, especially homologous parts. In this case, however, it is highly important to make certain that the subject really perceives such a differential and is convinced that a relative insensitivity has been brought about. In instances where the subject perceives no difference, he should be told in a positive manner that this sort of discrimination requires a certain amount of practice and that the next time this is tried he will surely detect a difference. In general, I believe it is best to end the attempt here and postpone further trial until the next hypnotic session.

Wolberg[203] apparently believes that cutaneous hyperesthesia is easier to produce than anesthesia and recommends doing this first. This has the advantage, if successful, of allowing the hypnotist to use the hypersensitive part of the subject's body as reference when asking the subject to make a discrimination. If the subject does develop a certain degree of anesthesia, it will be enhanced by comparison with the hypersensitive part; if none or very little anesthesia is brought about, he may be led to perceive some whereas otherwise he would not. The reader will find in Wolberg's work,[203] a very nice description of a procedure which not only incorporates many of these features, but has two other interesting aspects as well. One, he requests the subject to raise his hand when he first clearly experiences glove anesthesia, thus allowing greater participation of the subject in the production of this effect. Two, he uses the production of glove anesthesia as part of a trance deepening process.

As was remarked at the beginning of this book, hypnotism is, in a sense, an art. There are no set procedures that cover every possible situation. Instead, we have a number of principles and facts which must be employed variously in the combination that best suits a given situation. Many ingenious methods have been reported in the literature. It is impossible to cover all of these, so I have restricted myself, in this chapter, to the discussion of a few outstanding examples in order to give some idea of what can and should be done. I would urge the reader, in order to broaden his knowledge of methodology and as the next step in his training as a hypnotist, to become acquainted with the experimental and applied literature on the subject. A relatively comprehensive bibliography of experimental work will be found in my previous book. Other excellent sources of reference are the *Psychological Abstracts*, the *Index Medicus*, the *Catalogue of the Surgeon General*, and the *Army Medical Review of Current Literature*.

14

Special Problems of Hypnosis

HANDLING RESISTANCE

IN PREVIOUS chapters we have touched upon the problem of how to handle subjects who show resistance to the initial induction of hypnosis, to deepening of the trance, or to suggestions given either during hypnosis or posthypnotically. Here I will attempt to complement this earlier material. We will start with the matter of trance induction and deepening the trance in refractory subjects, then go on to the question of hypnotized subjects who reject a given suggestion. However, much of what will be said in one instance will be applicable to the others. The reader interested in a fuller understanding of the nature of resistance to hypnosis should look up Christenson's article[27] which approaches the topic in a different and instructive manner. Kline's article[97] will also be read profitably in this connection.

There is probably no such thing as an individual who is absolutely insusceptible to hypnosis. Every normal person probably has the *potentiality* for developing deep hypnosis and it is just a matter of finding a way to make use of this potential. In some instances the difficulty boils down to one of communicating to the subject just what is wanted of him, which frequently reduces to the inability of the subject to form the proper concepts. As I have remarked, this is not at all unusual when an individual is told to make his mind "blank." Even the concept of deep relaxation may be alien to the subject's way of thinking. A similar situation is often encountered by dentists when they suggest the presence of local anesthesia. Some patients have never experienced a drug-induced local anesthesia. The standard procedure for production of the suggested anesthesia requires the patient to imagine the typical numbness associated with local anesthetics. Obviously to expect the patient to vividly imagine something he has never experienced is courting failure. In this instance an easy solution is to allow the patient to have such a prior experience by actually injecting a small dose of anesthetic in a spot on his hand, or in his mouth. Even the unpleasantness of a small injection can be eliminated by using a small amount of cocaine swabbed on the gum or the surface of the tongue. Of course, this problem of teaching the subject

395

certain essential concepts is not always as simply solved and the hypnotist must often have recourse to his ingenuity.

Many normal individuals will approach hypnosis with some trepidations. The interfering anxiety can often be reduced by suitable suggestions early in the induction. In other cases it is best taken care of in the preliminary period of discussion and instruction which is often made a part of the preparatory phase of the induction. It should be realized that all cases of anxiety are not this easily managed, and in some instances, some form of psychotherapy, mild and brief as it may be, must first be undertaken. Sometimes anxiety contraindicates the use of hypnosis; in any case, it usually has analytical significance and should be explored if the subject is undergoing therapy. Conversely, an excessive lack of affect regarding the hypnotic induction is often equally significant.

Most cases of refractory behavior result from various, usually unconscious, resistances. According to Wolberg,[203] the most common resistances are defiance of the authority of the hypnotist, fear of yielding one's will or independence, need to prove oneself superior and fear of failure.

If the subject is aware of the sources of resistance and is willing to talk about them, they can often be overcome with the hypnotist giving reassurance wherever it is called for and introducing specific suggestions aimed at dealing with the resistances during the induction or deepening of the trance. Resistance due to defiance can sometimes be overcome if the subject ventilates his feelings to the hypnotist. Where the subject needs to show his superiority, an effective technique is to induce and deepen the trance so as to actually challenge the subject's aptitude. In such an instance the subject is prepared by being told that considerable intelligence and concentrative ability is necessary for anyone to be hypnotized, which is the opposite of what prospective subjects are usually told. The various suggestions are then given in a way which challenges the subject's ability to perform satisfactorily. Thus, says Wolberg, you do not command him to make his arm stiff and rigid, or even tell him that his arm is becoming so. Instead, say something like: "See if you can make your arm stiff and rigid so that you cannot bend it. It takes much effort and concentration to do this. Let's see if you have the necessary ability to do so . . . " Once hypnosis has been induced a few times in this manner, you can usually make use of the more standard methods.

An extremely effective way of dealing with resistances is to accept them and make use of them to reinforce the suggestions. This is essentially what we did when we told the subject in various suggestions that the more he tried to resist, the more he was impelled to carry out the suggestions. How this may be done in the induction of hypnosis is nicely demonstrated by the following sample suggestion used by Wolberg[203] in connection with the visual fixation method:

> As you sit here looking into my eyes, you begin to resist falling asleep. You say to yourself, "It isn't possible to fall asleep. I can't fall asleep." But you will find that the more you resist, the more difficult it is to keep from falling asleep. The harder you fight, the sleepier you get. Try it, and you will see that the more you resist falling asleep, the sleepier you are. Fight hard against falling asleep. Try not to fall asleep, and the harder you try, the sleepier you get. The more you fight, the sleepier you get. Fight hard to keep awake. Try to defy me, try to keep awake; but the more you defy me, the sleepier you get. Your eyelids are getting heavier and heavier until they close.

This method can be used in an extremely subtle manner, as Erickson has nicely demonstrated.[44] In discussing resistance he emphasizes that the best way of handling it is to accept and utilize the resistance in conjunction with the use of other types of behavioral responses produced by the subject. Properly used, *all* behavioral responses of a subject can be made to favor the production of the trance state. Resistance is best utilized by creating a situation in which it serves a purpose. One way of accomplishing this is to word the suggestions in such a way that no matter what the subject does, positive or negative, or does not do, it becomes an actual responsive behavior.

This kind of approach is well exemplified in the hand levitation method for inducing hypnosis which was described in chapter 8. In essence, we told the subject that one of his hands would do something. Maybe it would press down, or possibly it would move upward, or still again it might do nothing at all. The subject was told that he might feel a tingling in his hand, or maybe a sensation of warmth, but surely something would happen. Possibly, he was told, it would be a twitching of the muscles of his hands, or perhaps of a finger. Perhaps the middle finger would move, or maybe the little finger—possibly the whole hand. And so forth.

In this way all possible outcomes of the suggestions are included under the label of response without any specific commitments on the part of the hypnotist. If the subject shows resistance, it is now placed in the context of a constructive, cooperative response. Erickson emphasizes that the key to successful manipulation of the resistance consists in making an opportunity for its manifestations contingent upon suggested behavior. Furthermore, all resistance should be localized as much as possible upon irrelevant alternatives. As an example, one can suggest to a subject resisting hand levitation that his right hand will move upward, but that the left one will not. He has found this specific measure to be very satisfactory.

Erickson further emphasizes that one should never attempt to "correct" the subject's behavior, alter it or force him to produce a response. This can only interfere with trance induction and its deepening. On the contrary, acceptance and utilization of the subject's responses, regardless of their nature, to further trance behavior makes for effective hypnosis. As Erickson remarks, the fact that a subject volunteers to be hypnotized and simultaneously offers resistance is evidence of an ambivalence which, once recognized, can be made to serve the purposes of both the hypnotist and the subject. A subject is a functioning personality and should be treated as such in hypnosis as well as in the waking state.

This type of thinking has been nicely summarized by Watkins[189] who states, "A true *science of hypnotizing* must be based on a deep and intimate knowledge of the personality structure of the patient, his transference needs, ego defenses, and the cathexes (press-valence) of these factors."

He adds, "It would further require that the hypnotist be quite aware of his own countertransference needs, role abilities and limitations."

Watkins' article is a fundamental one and should be read by every serious student of hypnotism. One particularly important point he brings out is that if transference plays a basic part in the induction and utilization of hypnosis, transference reactions *of different orders* may be associated with *different levels of hypnosis* in the same subject. The inability of the subject or patient to develop a trance depth beyond a certain point may simply reflect a change in his transference needs as induction has progressed. The new need can be satisfied and hence greater depth attained only if the hypnotist takes on a different transference role. Thus, whereas at one stage of the induction a highly permissive approach succeeds best, at another depth a very authoritarian handling of the subject or patient may give the most results. And again, at still another stage of the induction process another approach may be required to overcome the new resistance, perhaps a return to the permissive role. There is no particular order in which this kind of structuring is to be done, nor any particular limits upon the number of times a given transference role must be assumed or upon the number of different transference roles which must be employed.

It is not always necessary to uncover the nature of the subject's resistance to overcome it. The nature of the resistance may center around such a minor point that the simplest solution is to accede, so to speak, to the subject's idiosyncrasy. The subject may come to the first hypnotic session with a preconceived notion of what the hypnotic induction should be like and any deviation from it will lead to a failure in the induction. The simplest way of solving this resistance is to inquire what the difficulty is, something you should always do in any case, and act accordingly—in this case, shift methods, although some hypnotists prefer to try and "sell" the subject on the idea that there are many equally successful methods. Sometimes the subject is very willing, cooperative and responsive on the various tests of suggestibility, but either does not go into a trance state or attains only a light state. This may be the result of a negative attitude toward hypnosis. With such cases an excellent mode of attack is to take the subject by surprise by using a strong authoritarian approach. For example, the various tests of suggestibility are administered and then without warning, a sudden command of "Sleep!" is given combined with a sudden pass of the hand over the subject's eyes. The exact moment at which this is done must be determined by the hypnotist.

Another example of how an easy change in condition can be effective is a case reported by Erickson.[44] In this situation the hypnotist was a stranger to the subject and this prevented her from going into a deep trance. By allowing the subject to identify the hypnotist with someone else, the difficulty was resolved.

One of my own subjects who appeared to be potentially capable of attaining a deep trance could not do so. Eventually, questioning brought out the fact that every time I hypnotized him he felt a tenseness in his epigastric region. He claimed that this prevented him from going into the trance more deeply. Once this was known, it was an easy matter to give him additional suggestions aimed at relieving this situation, as part of the induction. Note that we never went into the matter of why he initially reacted to trance induction in this manner. Had this been a deeply rooted defense against hypnosis which the subject felt as threatening, he might have developed some new manifestation of the resistance. Fortunately, this did not happen.

Another instance when hypnosis was induced without investigation or direct or indirect action upon the interfering resistance is one in which every attempt to elicit suggestibility from the subject had failed. Several hypnotists, including myself, had tried various waking suggestions and had tried to induce hypnosis, all to no avail. Then while trying the postural sway test I told the subject to close his eyes on the next trial. The most remarkable change took place and he responded very strongly to the falling suggestions. This was immediately followed with the hand clasping and eye catalepsy suggestions which had failed until then, and again a very strong response was elicited. Following this, deep hypnosis was induced in a matter of minutes. We can only guess what happened in this case. The subject was very willing and wanted to be hypnotized, yet in spite of this remained unresponsive until the solution was discovered. It is interesting that once postural sway was successfully induced, all resistance was broken down.

Did the resistance to other suggestions arise because the subject failed to respond to the postural sway suggestions, the first suggestions of any sort given to the subject? If so, he might have responded to the other suggestions had they been given first, and much time and effort would have been saved. I suspect this was the case. But, since the subject was so susceptible, why did he fail to respond to the first postural sway suggestions?

Meares[120] says that a very satisfactory method for dealing with negativistic subjects is to induce hypnosis by repetitive movements of the arm. Take hold of the arm by the cuff (or wrist) and move it back and forth. Simultaneously suggest "Your arm goes back and forth, back and forth, your arm goes back and forth, back and forth. Your arm automatically goes back and forth, automatically back and forth . . ." After a short while the negativistic subject will tend to spontaneously move his arm opposite to the direction suggested each time. When this happens, he is hypnotized, says Meares.

Inability to concentrate is very often the basis of resistance to hypnosis. Wolberg[203] recommends the counting technique with alternative opening and closing of the eyes in such cases (page 289).

Resistance to hypnosis may also arise simply out of the subject's fear of revealing personal data while hypnotized, or of being made to do something embarrassing. With some it is merely a fear of the unknown or mysterious. Verbal reassurance and education of the subject in regard to hypnotic phenomena often helps. An excellent way of handling the fear of embarrassment is to allow the subject to experience mild suggestion phenomena, that is, to sample them in small, mild doses. Waking suggestions and mild hypnosis are good ways of introducing the subject to hypnosis.

Although the techniques examined thus far are mainly for dealing with resistance to the initial induction of hypnosis, they have wider application. Sometimes a subject who has been responding quite well to trance-inducing procedures suddenly develops resistance to them in the course of therapy or of an experiment. This is particularly likely to happen if the hypnotist has used a permissive approach. Usually one can circumvent such resistance by taking the precaution of training the subject, as early as possible, to become hypnotized at one or more signals, at the same time suggesting that he will not become aware at any time of the manner in which the trance is produced when the signals are used. Then, when resistance does arise with respect to a given method, a sudden shift is made to one of the signals. Once hypnosis has been induced it is important to inquire into the cause of the resistance and to remove it. It is not uncommon, when a variety of induction procedures have been used on a subject, for him to develop a preference or a dislike, often quite strong, for one or more methods. When this is the case it is often possible to break the subject's resistance down, should it arise, by making him choose between the lesser of two evils, so to speak. A couple of examples will make this clearer.

In one instance the subject, S, was a particularly susceptible person and had gone through several sessions at the time the first incident took place. He had been readily hypnotized once before, on that occasion using the standard method, then dehypnotized. There was no particular evidence that anything was disturbing him. Now, however, when an attempt to rehypnotize S by the same method was made, he soon took his eyes off the fixation point and looking at me declared: "It's no use. I cannot be hypnotized." A second attempt was made with the same results. Questioned, S insisted that there was nothing wrong, that he did not know why, but that he knew he could not be hypnotized and that there was no use going on. Now, it has been my experience that whenever a subject interrupts a procedure, as S did, before any effect could be expected to have taken place, or anticipates a challenge, such behavior is usually symptomatic of resistance. The additional insistence on the part of the subject that it was useless to go on, as well as the fact that he was known to me to be highly susceptible, were additional clues supporting such a conclusion. Consequently, I pointed out to him that he had been easily hypnotized previously by the same method and that if he could not be hypnotized now this was obviously because he was not cooperating. Without waiting for any answer I very firmly said: "Actually it does not make any difference to me how we hypnotize you. There are many other ways of doing this. Now look at your right hand. . ." With this I proceeded to use the hand levitation method without further preamble. It should be added that it has been used previously and had turned out to be a very effective technique. S very quickly passed into a deep hypnotic state. Questioned about his resistance, he readily admitted that something was troubling him and disclosed what it was. The matter was easily taken care of and no further difficulties arose from it.

This particular example shows a number of interesting and important features. First, it is obvious that under *certain circumstances* a subject capable of developing a deep somnambulistic trance and who has been hypnotized a number of times can prevent himself from being hypnotized. Now I have emphasized "certain circumstances" because this probably does not hold for all instances. There were a number of factors involved here which made this kind of thing much more likely than it might otherwise have been. One of these was that the entire hypnotic relationship had been made very permissive from the start. Had the relationship been authoritarian, a totally different story would probably have been told. Furthermore, I am not certain that the subject could not have been hypnotized by the first method had insistence been placed upon it, but the permissive nature of the situation as well as other considerations did not allow the testing of this aspect.

Now it may be asked, why did the second method succeed when the first did not? Certainly the reason for resisting was still there. The situation was not favorable at the time, unfortunately, for inquiring too deeply into the subject's motives, so that one can only hazard a guess. For one thing, when the shift was made to the second method, it was done with finality and confidence which could not help but convey an assurance that this method would work, resistance or no resistance, while shifting the situation from a rather permissive one to a more authoritarian one. Now the use of a permissive approach was not guided initially by any thought that it might facilitate the induction process. On the contrary, had there not been other reasons, an authoritarian approach would probably have been used. Actually then, the above may simply have represented a change to the most effective method for this particular subject. On the other hand, he may have been testing to see how much control he retained, and having satisfied himself that he still had a say in the matter, however illusory this may really have been, he was willing to submit once more to my domination. A little thought will show that only a change in technique could have been satisfactory, since the basis of the resistance pertained to aspects of "free-will."

During a later session the same kind of thing happened, although for a different reason, and its handling took a different turn. At the start of the session, just as I was about to instruct the subject to fixate on the target, he turned toward me and declared matter-of-factly that he felt he was not going to be hypnotized. He could not give any reasons, just asserted he felt this was so. Since he was willing to try, the standard method was then begun, but very soon he interrupted the procedure and rather triumphantly pointed out its failure. Further questioning did not elicit any further information, but by then various signs of disguised hostility had become evident. There was little reason to doubt that this resistance had an aggressive element to it. S was asked whether he would like to have a different method used. No, he would not. He just could not be hypnotized today, that was all. After more of this interchange it became clear that the subject was behaving with a childish maliciousness and being "naughty." Presently, taking things more in hand, I reminded him that we knew from past experience that he could be readily hypnotized. Obviously if he could not be hypnotized now this was because he was resisting, possibly unconsciously. Actually I felt sure the subject had a pretty good idea of the reason.

I continued by pointing out that since the previous method did not work we would have to use another one. While we were thus talking I had taken hold of my pencil and was holding it in front of myself between the first three fingers in such a way as to be able to flip it over 180 degrees. I had previously instructed S while hypnotized that any time I flipped the pencil in this manner it would be a signal for him to go into a deep hypnotic state. Later I learned that S disliked this method, although it was extremely effective. Of those I used, he preferred the standard method. Having gotten my pencil ready, I commanded: "Look at my pencil!" In response, S quickly glanced at it sideways, then away. "I know what it'll do," he said. "What?" I inquired. "It'll put me to sleep, that's what it'll do." "Fine," I replied, "that's just what we want. Now look at it." All this time S was making a deliberate point of looking straight ahead and away from me and the pencil. In answer to my last request he shook his head, very much like a stubborn, negativistic child and added: "I don't like for you to put me to sleep that way!" "I am sorry," I said, "but you won't cooperate when I use the usual method, so I must use this one. Now look at the pencil!" This last was said sharply and commandingly. Immediately S, who had been sitting tense, leaned back in his chair, became noticeably relaxed, smiled sheepishly, and looking up at the usual target, said: "Alright—I'll go to sleep the other way," referring to the standard method. A deep somnambulistic trance ensued within less than a minute. I immediately questioned S about his resistance. What had happened was that he had expected that the witness (I nearly always have one whenever doing experimental work with hypnosis) would be a certain person. At the last moment he was unable to come and a substitution had to be made. I had not thought of consulting with, or even warning the subject about this switch. Upon his discovery of it, he had become very suspicious of, and resentful toward me; thus the whole episode. The matter was easily cleared up under hypnosis and no further difficulties took place.

This incident has been related in some detail because it has a number of interesting facets. First, it shows again that a "good" subject can become refractory. Secondly, it demonstrates how resistance can arise over what is essentially "nothing." And finally, it is a nice example of the technique of forcing the subject to choose between two alternatives, each one of which leads to the same end-result.

Now it may be asked why I did not force the issue and use the pencil, or some other signal. Although S probably would not have counteracted the pencil method, my overpowering him in this manner was likely, in this particular case, to have detrimental effects upon future interactions, and might have given rise to conflict and strong anxiety as well. As a matter of fact, this entire incident turned out to be related to a basic anxiety pattern possessed by the subject. Furthermore, I could not be certain that resistance might not generalize to this particular method of induction and therefore ran the risk, if S was able to resist with any degree of success, of laying the foundation for more effective and wide-spread resistance on his part at a later date. Had S been unaware of what would happen when I flipped the pencil, things might have been different. Obviously, knowing about it would enable him to consciously marshal his defenses against the expected action. As long as S believed in the efficacy of the method, could be led to make a choice, and made to *accept* being hypnotized by another method, this was by far the best procedure. It is always best, and certainly more pleasant, to work with rather than against the subject.

To conclude this discussion of resistance to the induction of hypnosis I would like to go back for a few moments to the remark made earlier that all behavioral responses can be made to facilitate the production of the trance state. This assertion can be easily derived from the theory of chapter 2. I believe one may go a step further and say that not only will facilitation result, but properly handled, a great many, perhaps all, behavioral responses can be used to *directly* induce hypnosis. The sensorimotor method is a perfect example of the application of this principle. Although it is indirect in the sense that the subject is hypnotized without his being aware that this is being done, and perhaps, in spite of his feelings about hypnosis, hypnosis is a direct consequence of the manipulation of the subject. Another potentially powerful technique which suggests itself here for use with resistant subjects who are overtly cooperative is to request the subjects to deliberately role-play the part, as they perceive it, of a person, first going into a trance, then carrying out hypnotic suggestions, all of course in synchrony with the hypnotist's suggestions and instructions. I suspect that in many instances such role-playing will be found to insensibly transform of its own into a true hypnotic state, and if not, that such a transformation can be brought about with relative ease. In any case, I would expect a definite increase in suggestibility would result and could be used to advantage.

To terminate this section I would like to take up a few actual cases of resistance to hypnotic suggestions which I have witnessed. I believe that they are particularly instructive both in regard to the nature of the resistance and to the way in which it was handled. In all these cases I was merely an observer. In each instance the subjects were deep trance subjects whom the hypnotist had used extensively over a period of many months. They were relatively sophisticated in regard to hypnotic phenomena and had themselves occasionally hypnotized others. In general, they were extremely cooperative. The following abbreviations will be used : S = subject, H = hypnotist, P = other participant.

Case 1. On one occasion S, an otherwise excellent subject trained in the use of self-hypnosis, was found to be unresponsive to certain post-hypnotic suggestions. Inquiry revealed that he was using self-hypnotic suggestions to counteract the posthypnotic suggestions. He had given himself the suggestions prior to the giving of the posthypnotic suggestions. In order to remedy this, H rehypnotized S and gave him various countersuggestions without success. S could not be induced to remove his self-suggestions. This particular resistance was finally overcome when H regressed S to a period of time just previous to the time when he had given the subject instructions in self-hypnosis. S was then given the suggestion that he knew nothing about self-hypnosis, had never heard of it until then, had no interest in it or its uses and would never have any such interest, that this would be so when he wakened. When S was awakened he had indeed forgotten everything he had known regarding self-hypnosis, and had lost his interest in it. No further interference followed. There was no evidence that he was in a regressed state when awakened, although this was not directly checked. It is probable that the same result could have been obtained by regressing S to any period prior to the time he had given himself the self-suggestions and then giving him various suggestions aimed at preventing the use of self-suggestions to oppose heterosuggestions.

Case 2. S was hypnotized by P who then attempted to give S a code word which would put him in a trance "any time" P said it in the future. Various attempts were made, but S persistently refused to accept the suggestion, merely shaking his head. On questioning he revealed that H had originally given him a suggestion that no one else would be able to hypnotize him outside of the laboratory.* P then suggested to S that upon waking S would perceive P as being H and conversely. S was then awakened and his behavior showed that the exchange had taken place.

All participants in this session were careful to behave in accordance with the suggested interchange in order not to create interference with the suggestion. Although such interference might not have occurred, it often does.

Now, P, taking the role of H, again hypnotized S and the code word was given. This time it was readily accepted.†

Case 3. S had been hypnotized and given a posthypnotic suggestion When awakened he carried out the suggestion, but then appeared to be highly perturbed. He seated himself at some distance from those present in the room. When one of the persons present addressed him, he was totally unresponsive and it was quickly discovered that he was in a trance-like state. Questioning revealed that S had been very upset by the posthypnotic suggestion and had induced a trance state in himself to prevent being used again as a subject during that session. H attempted in various ways to enter into rapport with S, but without success. Finally H used a code-word he usually employed to hypnotize S quickly. Rapport was immediately re-established and H was able to control S by suggestion from there on. This

*It is interesting to note that S was quick to catch on to the implications of the suggestion since to go into a trance "any time the suggestion was given" would include situations outside of the laboratory.

†Clearly there were other ways of dealing with the situation. For instance, the suggestion could have been limited to the laboratory situation, thus surmounting the subject's objection.

is an interesting aspect of "hypnosis within hypnosis" and presents some fascinating questions. (Some rather interesting material on this aspect will be found in Janet's writings.[91])

Sometimes the resistance may be more apparent than real. The following cases illustrate this point.

Case 4. S was hypnotized and told that he would be deaf when he woke up. He was then awakened and addressed by several persons whom he was facing. S replied quite intelligently, showing no evidence of deafness. Since he was a deep subject and had carried out very complex hallucinatory suggestions, this was rather surprising. The reason for this apparant resistance to the suggestion was made clear when questioning elicited the fact that S was lip-reading.*

Case 5. S was hypnotized by P and told that he would hear only P's voice, and only when P touched him on the shoulder. However, it was discovered that S persisted in hearing H's voice. When questioned with specific reference to this suggestion, S replied with obvious astonishment, "But it is H's voice. . . ." Unfortunately the matter was not cleared further, and we must guess what probably happened. When hypnotizing his subjects H always told them that they would pay attention only to the sound of his voice. Possibly this suggestion carried over to the new situation. We should also keep in mind the fact that H has extensively used S over a period of 4 months or more. Furthermore, S knew that he was being used as subject by P only on a "loan" basis. Finally, in this instance I suspect that there may have been a special interpersonal transference-like relationship existing between H and S which need not be discussed but which, in itself, might have caused the situation. In any case, it is clear that the subject had somehow acquired the understanding that rapport was to be maintained with H at all times, or this may have satisfied some particular need of his.

Case 6. This is really part of Case 2. I cite it here because it exemplifies the type of misunderstanding that may arise in hypnotic experiments and which might be interpreted as a form of resistance under other circumstances. After S had refused to accept a code word from P, the latter asked him what code word he would accept, not yet knowing the reasons for the refusal. S's succinct answer was "No." P, taking this to mean that "No" would be a satisfactory signal proceeded to repeat his former suggestion using this word. Again S emphatically refused it. This apparent inconsistency and continuation of resistance was finally resolved when it became clear that S had meant by "No" that he would not accept any signal under the conditions proposed by P.

Little more can be said about ways of handling resistance since each situation is highly individualistic and no definite rules can be set up. As has been pointed out, in some cases the resistance itself can be used; in others you must seek to understand its nature, and having done so act accordingly. In others, it may be a matter of circumventing the resistance. In still other cases, very little can be done about it.

THE PROBLEM OF SIMULATION

The simulation of hypnosis and of responses to suggestions in general is a very old problem which has, at one time or other, worried all those who have

---

*It was never fully clarified whether S had acquired this capacity at this time or prior to the session, or whether he was merely rationalizing his failure to carry out the suggestion.

worked in this area. This is a question which Freud himself raised early in his writings. He pointed out[64] that it is a remarkable fact that even when in all other respects there is evidence of total suggestive compliance the moral conscience of the hypnotized person may resist. Could this be, he asks, because the subject retains some sort of understanding that what is taking place is only make-believe? It is so real a problem that some, like White[199] and Sarbin,[149] substituting the expression "role playing," have essentially asserted that hypnosis is a form of simulation. In the final analysis, however, I do not believe this solves the problem (chapter 2). On the other hand, simulation does occur. What is its meaning with regard to the nature of hypnosis and what can we do about it? More precisely, how can we detect it and, when found, how should we deal with it? Finally, how can we prevent it from occurring? There is no satisfactory solution to the problem yet. The best we can do is to minimize simulation and, where we cannot eradicate it, at least keep it under some degree of control.

There has existed for a long time a rather widespread fallacy that a positive safeguard against simulation of hypnosis and of its phenomena was the ability of a subject to develop anesthesia. As early as 1889 Moll[126] recognized that suggested anesthesia was by no means an adequate test, but few hypnotists seem to have been willing to accept this. Now, anesthesia, like hypnosis, has many degrees. Unquestionably, deep surgical anesthesia would be, probably, a reliable and valid test against simulation. Unfortunately it is not very practical. The anesthesia usually referred to is so-called "glove anesthesia," which is relatively mild and superficial. If we look back at the Husband-Davis scale of hypnotic depth, it will be seen that glove anesthesia will occur when the subject is still in a light trance, although about to pass into a medium trance. It will also be noted that nearly all of the hypnotic manifestations of interest, such as hallucinations, personality changes, regressions and so forth, require the presence of a much deeper hypnosis. *At best*, the presence of glove anesthesia tells us that our subject is hypnotized to a depth of 11 or thereabout on the scale, and that it is unlikely that he will simulate any of the phenomena expected for this range of hypnosis. If, however, with this degree of hypnosis present we suggest a phenomenon requiring a greater depth, the subject may feel a strong compulsion to produce it when he is unable to do so. The result will often be a simulation of the required response. The presence of glove anesthesia tells us *nothing* regarding simulation or nonsimulation of phenomena belonging to the higher range of hypnotic depth.

There are other weaknesses in the anesthesia test. The pain threshold varies considerably among individuals. Furthermore, it is a function of the type of painful stimulation used. One individual may report pain where another will not, everything else being the same. The use of a pin prick on the dorsal surface of the hand, for instance, is a common test for anesthesia. This test, unfortunately, is not infrequently invalidated by the fact that an area free of pain receptors is involved. In this respect, a much more satisfactory test is the use of a faradic brush, an instrument once in wide usage, but rather rare nowadays. Personally, I have never felt that I was testing glove anesthesia satisfactorily with a pin or needle unless I was able to transpierce a raised fold of skin on the arm or hand of the subject. But this is not always feasible, desirable or a foolproof test. There is no question in my mind that given a *severe enough* test of anesthesia these weaknesses could be overcome. The only question is, just how severe a test can we justifiably use? In most cases there are very definite limits.

Further difficulties arise with the usual test of anesthesia in regard to what constitutes objective proof that anesthesia is absent when the subject claims he does not feel any pain. For flinching, the avoidance reflex and other reflex responses may be present to various degrees even when the subject really does not perceive pain. On the other hand, some individuals can do an excellent job of simulating anesthesia even in respect to some of these objective signs.

Suppose that we find that a subject who does not show evidence of anesthesia nevertheless produces other phenomena, particularly some requiring greater depth of hypnosis than anesthesia does. Are we to conclude that they are simulated? Definitely not. It may be that this subject has an unusually low pain threshold requiring a much deeper anesthesia to overcome it.

Some subjects who are only partially anesthetized often report pain when actually considerable *analgesia* is present. Others give pain "reactions," including verbal utterances, purely reflexively, when actually they can not perceive any pain. In other instances, the subject is sufficiently hypnotized but is unable to produce anesthesia because the necessary conceptual processes are lacking in his repertoire, or because some particular complex is interfering. These are but a few of the possibilities, but it should suffice to show the dangers of too hasty a conclusion.

In the situation described in the last paragraph, it was assumed that the subject did not pretend he was anesthetic, hence there is no basis for suspecting that he will simulate other phenomena if unable to produce them. But suppose that it is found that he has pretended anesthesia. What should we conclude with regard to future simulations? Even then we cannot deduce that he will simulate other phenomena. We can and should, however, expect that *if he is unable to produce a suggested phenomenon, he will very likely simulate it.* We should be on our guard and take proper precautions.

The main defect with anesthesia as a test of simulation is that glove anesthesia first occurs at too low a degree of hypnosis to be useful regarding most of the phenomena of interest, and deeper anesthesia, while presumably requiring greater hypnotic depth for its production, also requires too severe a test to demonstrate its presence. This suggests that if one could make use of a phenomenon requiring greater hypnotic depth one might have a more suitable way of testing for simulation.

One such phenomenon is at the basis of the card experiment described under perceptual transcendence (chapter 12). In spite of being more involved than the anesthesia test, in my experience it has been very satisfactory in those instances where it was crucial to determine whether deception was or was not present. Essentially, what one does is test the subject *before* trance induction for his ability to recognize a playing card, the reverse side of which he has been allowed to look at for one minute, when (1) it is presented to him, reverse side up, by *itself* once at random in five trials in which four other cards are used (reverse sides up), and (2) when it is presented to him mixed among five other cards (all reverse sides up), five trials also being allowed. Provided the subject can pick out the chosen card with less than perfect success, this test can be used. Of course, the closer to chance his success is, the better is the test. As soon as the subject has reached a point in his hypnotic training where he can produce hallucinations with his eyes open, he is again shown the card in question,* reverse side up, and is made to hallucinate this side as being of different appearance. He may be told to see a cross on it, someone's picture, etc. I usually tell the subject that it is blank and a deep blue in color. In any case, as soon as a stable hallucination is obtained, procedure 1 or 2 is used. If the subject is able to pick the card out significantly better than he could in the waking state, this can be taken as evidence that he is really hallucinating. The ideal situation, of course, is when he has only chance success when awake, and 100 per cent success when hallucinating. As a final check, one should repeat the procedure after the subject has been awakened.† From my experience with this test, it appears that procedure 2 requires somewhat greater depth of hypnosis than 1. As a result, this test

---

*I have not found any evidence that practice effect interferes with this test. The use of equivalent sets of cards would minimize this possibility.

†This is mainly to check for the possibility of practice effect. If equivalent sets of cards are used one can probably dispense with it. One should make sure that the suggestions are so worded that there can be no posthypnotic carry-over into the waking state.

offers a way of testing at two levels. A third level can easily be introduced by performing the test posthypnotically. A much greater depth of hypnosis is usually required for success under this condition. The test is rather flexible and can be altered to test at other levels or to test a greater number of levels. My experience has been that procedure 1 is frequently sufficient.

To use this test properly, it is important to keep in mind that many individuals achieve above chance, even attaining 100 per cent success without benefit of hypnosis or hallucinations.[194] This is a function, of course, of how alike the cards are. As a consequence one particular set of cards is usually not sufficient to take care of all cases. It is relatively easy to construct sets of five or more cards such that each set is of a different order of difficulty with respect to the discriminatory recognition of a card taken from it. By having a number of such sets available one can cover a sufficient range of difficulty to include most subjects. The prehypnotic test allows one not only to make sure that one is using a sufficiently difficult set, but it is also used to select such a set which is then used as described in the preceding pages. One should be careful not to use too difficult a set, for even though a subject may be fully capable of producing real posthypnotic hallucinations, his discriminatory skills may be tasked by too difficult a test. My own experience indicates that three sets of cards are ample for most practical applications, one set being relatively easy, one hard, and one very hard. In most cases the middle set alone is satisfactory, particularly since perfect chance and nonchance scores are desirable, but not an absolute requisite. Thus, if a subject passes 3 out of 5 trials when awake, and 5 out of 5 when hypnotized, or again, say, 1 out of 5 awake and 3 out of 5 hypnotized, these could be taken as evidence that some effect is present and that it probably can be increased.

It is more important in this test that the subject be able to pick the card out for any reason than for him to be able to report the presence of the suggested hallucination. Some subjects have difficulty maintaining a posthypnotic hallucination of this sort, especially at first, particularly when doing the second part of the test, yet they are able to pick the card out because somehow they know it is right, they feel there is something special about it.

For the same depth of hypnosis, some individuals have greater facility for producing hallucinations in one sense modality than in another. One can also have the subject hallucinate differences in weight, odor, temperature and so forth, provided one keeps in mind that the level of hypnosis involved is not necessarily quite the same in each case. Besides playing cards, one may use coins, index cards and other objects which come in sets of identical elements.

Undoubtedly, one could devise objective tests of this sort for the lesser depths of hypnosis. The value of doing so is questionable because when critical work has to be done using hypnosis, one is rarely interested in any thing but the deeper levels.

This test is by no means foolproof. If properly conducted, however, I do not believe it can be easily falsified. Positive results with it are not likely to cause trouble. On the other hand, negative results can be misleading unless properly evaluated. What was said regarding anesthesia is equally applicable here.

A test making use of physiological measures would probably be the ideal test. Occasionally someone suggests to me the use of so-called lie detectors, such as the Keeler or the Reid Polygraph. Quite recently, in fact, such a device was used in conjunction with a reported investigation[32] and on its basis the investigator concluded that falsification was improbable in his studies. Unfortunately, except for a minority of investigators, this is far from being a practical solution. The instrument is quite expensive, requires specialized training on the part of the examiner which cannot be obtained on short order; a qualified lie detector examiner must be a person who devotes his full time to its use, not only when the occasion calls for it. He must meet certain personal qualifications besides those of training. Modern lie detection methods require attaching various pieces of equipment to the subject who must often sit in a special chair in a certain position and finally, lie detection necessitates following a strict routine and is time consuming. These two last requirements are particularly incompatible with the requirements of many experiments.*

But let us assume momentarily that none of the above objections is a major obstacle. How successful can we expect the lie detection to be? Inbau and Reid[88] estimate, on the basis of a study of 4280 criminal cases that *"when applied under the most favorable conditions,"* the accuracy is 95 per cent. Four per cent of the cases give rise to indefinite determinations, and only one per cent are errors, that is, false diagnoses. These are fine and convincing figures. One should realize, however, that they are based on cases in which the individuals had presumably *knowingly* committed *crimes*, and who *knowingly lied*. Can we say that the italic words accurately describe the hypnotized individual who is simulating? I am of the opinion that they rarely

---

*I am assuming that the lie detector test is to be given during the hypnotic session. In many instances it probably could be given following the experiment, or at least, preliminary trials could be done for the purpose of determining the extent to which hypnotic phenomena can be produced. The last two aspects referred to would then not be so much of an obstacle. Other objections, however, remain.

do. Modern lie detectors are quite capable of detecting lies which have no connection whatsoever with crimes, but how successfully this can be done is another matter. No data seem available on this question, but one might guess that the percentage success would be much less than that listed.

However, it seems to me that the most serious weakness of lie detection in connection with hypnotic work is that many subjects who role-play *really believe* that they are carrying out the suggestions satisfactorily. Under this condition it may be that it is possible for them to unconsciously deceive the lie detector. This is only one way in which interference with lie detection may arise. Inbau and Reid have given an extensive list of interfering factors. Some of these are not particularly relevant here because they can be easily kept under control or are not likely to take place in the use which we are considering. Others are definitely relevant and are listed here:

1. Overanxiety to cooperate, in order to assure an accurate test result.
2. Anger and resentment over having to take a lie detector test.
3. Overanxiety regarding serious personal problems unrelated to the offense under investigation.
4. A guilt-complex or fear of detection regarding some other offense.
5. Attempts to "beat the machine" by controlled breathing or muscular flexing.
6. Unobserved applications of muscular pressures which produce ambiguity or misleading indications in the blood pressure tracing.
7. No fear of detection.
8. Apparent ability to consciously control responses by means of certain mental sets or attitudes.
9. Rationalization of the crime in advance of the test to such an extent that lying about the offense arouses little or no emotional disturbances.

In view of all of these considerations, any use of the lie detector in hypnotic research should be done with circumspection. Indeed, before lie detector methods are used more extensively in this area, specific studies of their applicability should be made.

Possibly the situation regarding simulation is not quite as bad as it first seems. One can usually get subjects to readily admit having role-played, provided they can distinguish an adequate response to suggestions, and provided also that they understand that this information is desired. Furthermore, in many instances subjects are led to role play because the suggestions leave the way open to such behavior, and because it has never been made clear that role playing is not an acceptable response.* In any case, it must

---

*There are circumstances, as in psychotherapy, where role playing has a definite place, both when resulting from specific instructions to role play and when occurring spontaneously.

be re-emphasized *that occasional role playing or role playing early in hypnotic training should never be taken as an indication that the subject will not be reliable, or again, that his potentialities for hypnotic manifestations are poor.*

Moll's[126] comments with which I shall conclude, although made over sixty years ago, seem as pertinent now as then:

> . . . when discussing simulation I have not to consider whether there is such a thing as hypnosis at all, but whether there is simulation in any particular case.
>
> In the first place, I think that simulation is much rarer than is generally believed. It has been too much the habit to look for one physical or objective symptom which could not be simulated, and settle the question of fraud from its presence or absence. And yet this is exactly the opposite of what is generally done in judging mental states. When we want to diagnose a case and decide whether it is insanity or not, no authority on mental disorders would suppose fraud simply because some bodily symptom was absent. He will consider and weigh the case as a whole. Even when each symptom taken separately might be fraudulent they would be weighed against one another and a diagnosis formed from them. If the doctor also finds some symptoms which cannot be simulated, he will weigh this too, but he will not conclude fraud from its absence. It is true that in this way the conviction may be only subjective, or rather it will be clear only to those who have studied mental disease. The outsider may often be able to raise the objection that this or that symptom may be feigned; but no specialist would allow himself to be influenced by this.
>
> If we apply this to hypnosis, which is also a mental state, it follows that only he who has studied hypnosis practically is in a position to diagnose it, although many a person who has no knowledge whatever of hypnotic experiments considers that he is able to judge of hypnotism, express an opinion on it, and demand considerations for his views. Kron and Sperling have very rightly contested this assumption. It is not correct to diagnose fraud in hypnotism from the absence of a certain physical symptom. Even if each separate symptom may be feigned, the experienced hypnotist will diagnose by summing up the different symptoms and comparing their relation to each other. It is satisfactory if he finds an unfeignable symptom besides; this is an objective proof, convincing even those who have no practical knowledge of hypnosis. But we must bear in mind that objective physical symptoms are less seldom found in hypnosis than in mental diseases. The first is a transitory mental state, in which objective physical change is less likely to occur than in mental disorders, which last for months and years. . . .

Moll continues that the various somatic and psychic signs of hypnosis which have been listed in the literature have only relative value. One is never justified in concluding that there is fraud because one or even all of these signs are absent. On the other hand one should not accept too readily as objective sign of hypnosis a symptom which may turn out not to be specific to it. He particularly warns his reader against assuming that hypnosis must invariably present an ideal and complete picture, hence assuming there is simulation when some symptom appears which does not fit that picture. As an example he points to the fact that a subject may laugh at his own actions. This is because even in a deep trance the subject may retain a trace of consciousness and, of course, it is even more true for lighter trances. In other cases, various reflexes such as an avoidance or scratch reflex, etc., are elicited by adequate stimuli occurring during the hypnosis. As Moll points out, the suggested act may be in conflict with the reflex, in which case, depending on various factors, one or the other will predominate. Sometimes there is a misunderstanding of the suggestion. In some cases one has to do with one of the lower degrees of hypnosis in which compulsion causes role playing. Finally, the presence of passive hypnosis may make the subject appear to be simulating because he verbally agrees that he is experiencing what is suggested but does not react adequately.

Moll concludes:

> All this makes it evident how difficult it is to decide the question with regard to fraud. It seems to me to occur relatively more often with children, but the transition from simulation to true hypnosis is so gradual that even an experienced experimenter is sometimes uncertain. For example, when a subject shuts his eyes to be obliging, it is not the same thing as if he shut them to deceive; or he shuts them because he is tired of fixing them on something, but could open them by a strong effort, though he keeps them shut because he is more comfortable. It would be a great mistake to identify this with simulation. Others do what the experimenter wishes, to please him, but not to deceive him. This, as I have already mentioned, is not pure fraud either; we can only speak of that when there is the deliberate intention to deceive.
>
> There is yet another complication: people in hypnosis sometimes pretend exactly as insane persons do. Thus, a hypnotic will say he sees something when he does not. It is, naturally, difficult to say where deceit begins and ends in such cases; but generally speaking, practice will enable us to judge the mental state of the subject with some certainty, or at least great probability. It occasionally happens that the most experienced deceive themselves or are deceived; the most experienced alienist or neurologist is in the same case. But that is no reason why we should deny the reality of hypnosis. Obersteiner justly observes: "A group of morbid symptoms, such as an epileptic fit, may be so exactly reproduced by clever simulation that even the most skilful expert (Esquirol, for example) may be deceived. And yet, unfortunately, we must still unconditionally recognize the existence of epileptic fits." The fear of being deceived has prevented many from interesting themselves in the subject; yet no other principles need be followed than those which guide us in the study of other mental states—psychopathic states, for example. Each case must be treated with scientific reserve, as mental cases are treated. We must not make impossible demands in order to exclude imposition; to do so would be to overstep the bounds of scientific scepticism, and would, in truth, only display an unscientific mind.

CRYING AND OTHER EMOTIONAL REACTIONS

Emotional reactions in individuals undergoing hypnotherapy are not uncommon. Many of these are unrelated to the use of hypnosis, others are specific to it. In either case they should be handled in the context of the therapy. Further treatment of this topic will be left to texts specifically concerned with psychotherapy and, particularly, with hypnotherapy. There are, however, occasions when individuals who are *not* undergoing therapy but who have submitted to hypnosis also exhibit various emotional reactions in the absence of any obvious causation. They may occur in spite of all precautions. For hypnotists with clinical training the handling of such situations will be largely a routine matter since individuals who react emotionally in hypnosis are essentially no different from individuals who show emotional reactions in their waking behavior. For the hypnotist lacking clinical experience, they may present some problems. Any person working with hypnosis should be prepared to handle spontaneous emotional reactions, infrequent as they are.

These reactions may take place at any stage in the use of hypnosis, during the induction of the trance, while it is present and in the absence of any suggestion, following suggestions or subsequent to dehypnotization. The most frequent occurrence appears to be during trance induction, the next during hypnosis while carrying out suggestions. Somewhat less frequent are the occurrences of reactions following the completion of a suggested act and immediately upon waking from hypnosis. Affective reactions observed in association with hypnosis include crying, laughter, anger, fear, general excitement, violent acting out, trembling, anxious perspiration and other signs of anxiety and posthypnotic depression. Other untoward reactions to hypnosis include spasms and convulsions, contractures and other forms of rigidity, paleness and other shock-like reactions and posthypnotic lethargy. Including all these under the heading of affective responses may be questioned by some; they certainly all appear to have a psychodynamic origin. In any case, their occurrence makes it imperative that every hypnotist be aware that such reactions will take place. Further details will be found in papers by Erickson,[52] Brenman, Gill, and Hackner,[22] and by Schneck.[152-156]

Although such a listing should stand as good argument against the indiscriminate use of hypnosis or its use by untrained individuals, lest it deters serious investigators and potential users of hypnosis let me reassert that the incidence of these reactions is rather low, particularly in the nontherapeutic setting. Furthermore, they can usually be handled satisfactorily and in such a way as to allow further use of hypnosis. With regard to incidence, in my own work I have observed such reactions in less than one per cent of many hundred cases. The most frequent reaction has been crying in women subjects. In a recent survey I made, of the twenty-five leading experts in this area who were questioned, the highest incidence reported was 5 per cent of cases.* The majority estimated a 1 per cent incidence. These percentages are based on several hundred to several thousand cases. With regard to crying, observed cases were reported as ranging from weak to violent,† strong crying being the most common observation.

There is no single accepted way of handling such reactions. Most authorities seem to feel that a permissive, accepting approach is best. The subject should be allowed to cry and ventilate his feelings. Many advise letting the subject terminate his crying on his own, although others recommend helping the subject do so by comforting approval and the use of anything which may help calm him. Reassurance is highly recommended. The subject may be told that his crying is brought about by unconscious factors, that it is a release of tension, that it will be beneficial, and that he will feel better when it is over. Generally one should attempt to determine the causes of the reaction after it is over, although the subject should never be forced to talk about it. Although one hypnotist advised immediate termination of the trance state and a few suggested eventual discontinuation, many seem to feel that there is no necessity for doing this and, indeed, that it is preferable to maintain the hypnotic state at least until the subject has been calmed down. Many hypnotists recommend waking the subject after the reaction has been controlled and then rehypnotizing him with suggestions added to prevent further recurrence of the unwanted response. In the case of crying, a suggestion may be given to the subject that he will have happy thoughts of his own choosing, or simply that his experience will be pleasurable.

My own feelings in this matter are that, as most hypnotists have advised, one should always *pass off* such reactions as regular, normal responses and de-emphasize their importance. In most instances keeping the subject in hypnosis until the reaction is terminated seems best. This permits the hypnotist to retain better control over the situation and to intercede more effectively when necessary. Whether one will want to dehypnotize the subject later depends largely upon the nature and intensity of the reaction. With weak to moderate reactions this will usually be unnecessary. Similarly, with weak to moderate reactions one should probably allow the subject to terminate them himself. With strong to violent responses, calming and partial control by the hypnotist seems desirable. Much depends, of course, on the nature of the reaction. One should certainly never allow spasms and convulsions to lead to physical trauma. On the other hand, with the possible exception of

*The 90 per cent who answered the questionnaire encountered crying. Nearly all observed emotional reactions of one kind or another in individuals whom they had hypnotized.

†This also describes the range of intensity of other reported reactions.

extremely violent sobbing, one is not likely to obtain any ill effects from crying; again professional acumen is of the essence.

If one is to continue using hypnosis with individuals who exhibit any of the above reactions *he should always try to ascertain the nature of the causes.* This may be done in a number of ways. Direct questioning of the hypnotized subject after the reaction has been controlled will often suffice; or, if the subject has been dehypnotized, rehypnotization may be necessary. By telling the subject prior to dehypnotizing him that he will not only remember what has happened but will understand why it did and will find it easy to talk about it after he wakes up, one often gets good results.

With individuals who show reactions following waking, it is advisable to rehypnotize them to uncover the causes, to control the present manifestations or to prevent further recurrences. This, however, is not an absolute rule. There will be occasions when further hypnotizing is absolutely contraindicated, such as when the hypnotic situation might trigger a psychotic episode.

As a general rule, outside of psychotherapy, unless there are *very good* reasons for not doing so, it is best *not to make further use* of individuals who show strong emotional reactions. With those exhibiting weak to moderate reactions one should work with prudence. In any case, one should not continue to use such people without finding out what the causes of their atypical behavior are and taking the steps necessary to prevent their recurrence (keeping in mind that it is not always advisable to block the expressions of a person's defenses). Again, one's decision in such matters must be partly determined by one's training and by the nature of the reactions which are involved. Investigators who are not trained in psychotherapy should not allow the situation to assume a psychotherapeutic character, which it can easily do. Usually one can assume that individuals who show emotional or other reactions in response to hypnosis have personality problems and might well benefit from some psychotherapy; this is particularly true of those exhibiting strong reactions.

15

Applications of Hypnotism

A GENERAL SURVEY

THE EFFECTS of hypnosis and of suggestions in general can be quite extensive, affecting just about every psychophysiologic function.[191] The recognition of this fact has led many a hypnotist to make suggestions a panacea for all the ailments of mankind. What easier method could there be, indeed, than suggesting away the ills no matter what they may be. This was largely the way hypnosis was originally applied. Unfortunately, it is one thing to remove symptoms, be they physical or mental, and another to treat the roots of the trouble. Here lies the great mistake of many past and present hypnotists.

The main area of application of hypnosis and suggestions has therefore been medicine, including psychiatry and dentistry. This particular use of hypnosis goes back to times immemorial. According to the Eber papyrus, suggestions in the form of the "laying on of the hands" were being used in Egypt 3500 years ago to cure a variety of ailments. As a matter of fact, most of the earlier investigations of hypnotic phenomena were made by physicians, such a Mesmer and Braid. It is only in the last 50 or so years that psychologists have begun to critically investigate the phenomena of hypnosis. As this research has progressed, it has become evident that hypnotism can be applied to the study of psychologic phenomena as a whole. Although progress has been slow, there has been a start and we may expect that the future will see hypnotism used much more extensively in psychologic research. Not only does the study of hypnotic phenomena promise to cast interesting and important light upon basic processes but, because of its apparently powerful and profound effects upon psychological and physiological functions, hypnotism appears to be an important instrument of investigation. It has already proven a valuable tool in the study of dreams, emotions, mental images and particularly, in the study of abnormal behavior. For instance, Leuba[109] used the hypnotic state to aid conditioning, Lundholm[114] studied the nature of the conditioned stimulus, Erickson[43,44] Lundholm,[115] and Luria,[116] produced artificial neuroses and psychoses,

Brenman[21] explored the Zeigarnik effect, Nagge[131] uncovered the nature of retroactive inhibition (hence of forgetting), Teitelbaum[180] studied body image distortions, Naruse and Obonai[132, 133] investigated the properties of mental images, and finally, Gidro-Frank[69] contributed to our knowledge of the emotions. Other studies could be cited, but these should suffice to indicate the sort of thing which has been and is being done.

Hypnotism as an Adjunct to Medicine and Dentistry

The most obvious application of hypnotism is its use as an anesthetic or analgesic. Past physicians used hypnotic anesthesia extensively for major surgical work. Before chloroform was introduced hypnosis was a boon to surgery, but with the development of modern anesthetics, it became outmoded. Recently there has been a renewed interest in this application for many reasons. Hypnosis does not require any apparatus, drugs, or anesthetist; it is absolutely safe, its side- and after-effects are not comparable to those of drug anesthesia, and can be used where anesthetic agents are contraindicated. Additionally it allows the patient to participate actively in his treatment by carrying out instructions which facilitate the surgeon's work. It is true that some of these features are also shown by local, spinal and caudal anesthesia, but some patients do not react well to the drugs used and others find that the injection itself is unpleasant or painful. For some persons local anesthetics fail for unknown reasons and often have only partial applicability, as in childbirth, where spinal and caudal anesthesia may interfere with the progress of labor and must be foregone for some time, much to the patient's discomfort.

In addition to the anesthetic power of hypnotic suggestions, hypnosis per se has been said to have some valuable side effects. Bleeding during surgery *seems* to be much decreased, and some say that it can be controlled to various extents by giving suggestions. Patients who have had hypnotic anesthesia during surgery are said to suffer much less from postoperative shock and to recover more rapidly from their operations. There is definitely no question that hypnosis is a valuable tool for removing preoperative anxieties and keeping the patient calm, comfortable and relaxed during the operation or even during the induction of drug anesthesia when suggested anesthesia is impossible.

Directed suggestions given in hypnosis have been used to advantage in many nonsurgical situations arising in the practice of dentistry, obstetrics and gynecology. Dentures as well as various temporary devices used in the oral cavity to correct faulty dentitions are often very uncomfortable at first.

Hypnotic suggestions have been found to be of great help here. Another use for suggestions is in training individuals, particularly children, in the proper care of their teeth. Similarly, many conditions treated by obstreticians and gynecologists involve considerable discomfort for the patient and sometimes require changes in living habits. For example, the nausea of pregnancy can often be relieved by suggestions and patients who must have a salt free diet during pregnancy can be helped considerably. Many patients find gynecological examinations extremely uncomfortable and here again hypnotism is found to be a great help.

Dentists and physicians meet a great many conditions every day which must be labeled psychosomatic. Many of these can be cured only through psychotherapy, but there are many minor conditions that can be alleviated by suggestions alone. Hence the usefulness of hypnotism in psychosomatic dentistry and medicine. It has found applications in internal medicine, in the treatment of skin conditions, asthma and various other allergies. It has been used effectively in various gastrointestinal disorders, cardiovascular disturbances, genitourinary reactions, headaches, joint and muscle pain and disturbances of nutrition. In the fields of gynecology and obstetrics, hypnosis has been applied to such conditions as morning sickness, the so-called abortion habit, heartburn of pregnancy, false pregnancy, lactation, frigidity, menstrual disorders of various kinds, premenstrual tension, sterility, menopause and other conditions.[157]

HYPNOSIS IN PSYCHOTHERAPY (HYPNOTHERAPY)

To date psychotherapy has been by far the widest and most extensive field of application of hypnotism. Although etymologically the term "hypnotherapy" should denote the application of hypnosis to all types of ailments, it has been exclusively used to denote its use in psychotherapy, and such a convention is followed here. This discussion will be limited to a brief general survey of this area. However, because of the increasing use of and interest in suggestion techniques for the treatment of mental illness and also because this use has raised some rather interesting and basically important questions we will take it up again in more detail in the next section and will attempt to point out certain important but rather technical issues.

There is nothing particularly new in this use of hypnosis; in fact, it was very much in vogue before the introduction of psychoanalysis. Freud himself used it for a while, but becoming dissatisfied with the results he sought another method of treatment and developed psychoanalysis. Since Freud's time it has become obvious that the failure of hypnosis did not lie so much in hypnosis per se as in its nonrational use by various practitioners. With today's greater understanding of both hypnotic phenomena and psychotherapy, suggestion methods have been regaining their rightful place in modern treatment of illness, particularly the behavior disorders. Hypnotism is being employed successfully in treating such major disorders as psychoneuroses, psychoses and drug addiction, particularly alcoholism. Other minor conditions which respond well to hypnotic treatment are insomnia, overweight, nail biting, excessive smoking, bed wetting, stage fright, speech disorders, and a number of psychosomatic conditions already discussed.

Generally speaking, in psychotherapy hypnosis is used not so much as a specific remedy for any single type of disturbance, but rather to facilitate therapy. Indeed, the great attraction of hypnosis for therapists is the possibility of speeding up therapy. Consider that psychoanalysis may take from 1 to 5 years, costing the patient thousands of dollars, not to mention many inconveniences. Furthermore, the psychoanalyst's time for other patients will be limited during this period. In contrast, the longest hypnotic psychotherapeutic technique, hypnoanalysis, often gives the same results obtained through essentially the same steps in 6 months or less. But how can this happen? The answer is that hypnosis permits the therapist to have much more direct access to the patient's mind and to more fully and precisely control its activity. Ordinarily the therapist must wait for the normal course of events to bring about certain effects, but with the help of hypnosis he can cause their occurrence more or less at will. For instance, rather than waiting months for the patient to have significant dreams to analyze, the therapist can stimulate the patient to have these dreams at any moment, even during interviews.

Such a use of hypnosis is a far cry from the popular notion of how hypnosis is used in the treatment of nervous and allied disorders. Many people believe that the hypnotist tells the patient that he is cured or that his symptoms are gone. Actually, this is only one of the many ways of using hypnosis. It is not the best method by far, and it can only be used successfully in certain situations. Often it is likely to cause more harm than good, since it removes the symptoms but not the cause.

Simple as this method of treatment is, there is one even simpler. It consists in keeping the subject in a deep hypnotic state for a period of a week or more. At no time are any suggestions given nor is the patient talked to except to maintain the trance. This type of therapy is believed to be sometimes effective in the treatment of certain neurotic disorders. However, it is a method of very limited application and value. Meares[122] recently introduced a variation of this technique which he calls "non-specific suggestion" therapy. It appears to differ from the above in two respects.

It involves from two to a half dozen or so hypnotic sessions of about a half hour each, and may include the giving of some sort of blanket suggestion of well-being.   Meares believes that this form of the technique is of considerable value in the treatment of neuroses which do not show any well-defined symptomatology.

As seen from one standpoint the behavior disorders not directly caused by organic lesions or deficiencies result from the patient's faulty attitudes concerning daily life.   Therapy aims at eliminating, or better, replacing these attitudes.   Hypnosis is an ideal tool for this, being used to discover what these faulty attitudes are, then to help the patient understand them and to accept new concepts in their stead.   This method is superior to the two just mentioned because it attempts to affect some of the underlying causes of the symptoms.

Many symptoms shown by psychoneurotic individuals, especially hysterics, are the result of traumatic experiences in the past life of the patient. The memories of such experiences are usually too painful for the patient, so without being aware of it he forcibly forgets them. The symptoms are the consequence of this repression.   It has been found that if the patient can be made to recall and preferably to re-experience the traumatic situations, the symptoms very often vanish permanently.   Hypnosis is a very powerful instrument here, partly because it appears to facilitate recall and partly because it can be used to help and even force the patient to re-experience.   This method has been found to be most useful with war neuroses, although it is applicable to other situations.

In these therapy techniques, the psychotherapist usually limits himself to a few hypnotic phenomena.   Some therapists, however, make an intensive use of as many hypnotic phenomena as appear to have a therapeutic effect. Any and all hypnotic phenomena are used.   Among those that are most often employed to uncover lost memories are crystal gazing and automatic writing. In the first instance the patient looks into a crystal ball or mirror and hallucinates events connected with his problem.   In the second case, he unconsciously writes information which pertains to his problem but which he cannot admit to consciousness.   Regressions are used to gain access to events of childhood or some other period of the patient's life.   Another use of hypnosis is to cause the patient to dream about specific events which will throw light upon his difficulties.   The patient can also be led to dramatize events which have had an important part in his life.   Not only does this disclose important information, but the patient often works out some of his emotional problems in this process and obtains a release of tension.   Finally, hypnosis can be used to create artificial neuroses which are very limited and carefully controlled. These can later be used to help the patient acquire insight into his true neurosis.

Although this approach to therapy often leads to dramatic and rapid cures, it frequently has the weakness of not getting at the deepest roots of the disorder. This has been overcome in hypnoanalysis which does not differ essentially from this method insofar as the hypnotic aspect is concerned. But hypnoanalysis is psychoanalytically oriented, that is, everything is done in accordance with the theory, methodology and rules of psychoanalysis. In consequence, the main aim in using hypnoanalysis is to overcome the factors preventing the patient from gaining insight into his difficulties. This method is probably one of the best, if not the best form of psychotherapy using hypnosis available to us today.

All of the techniques that have been discussed aim at the eventual disappearance of the patient's symptomatology. Not infrequently, however, situations arise in practice in which it is not practical or advisable to "cure" the patient. In such a case the goal of the therapist becomes one of aiding him to function as adequately and as constructively as possible while keeping his neuroticism. The general approach is to minimize in one way or another the handicapping and disabling aspects of the symptoms while still permitting the patient's neurotic needs to be served. For this purpose Erickson[49] developed a group of techniques which, with symptom removal, might be grouped under the general heading of *direct symptom manipulation*. Erickson's techniques, however, do not remove the symptoms but instead put them to various uses. These techniques include *symptom substitution, symptom transformation, symptom utilization, symptom amelioration* and *corrective emotional responses*. All of these are rather specialized techniques, some of which require considerable skill on the part of the hypnotherapist. For further details the reader should read Erickson.

An Evaluation

Thus far we have pointed primarily to the advantages of hypnotism in therapy. It would be grossly unfair not to say something about its possible disadvantages. Assuming that the therapist is competent there is really only one major drawback to the use of hypnosis. Everyone cannot be readily hypnotized. Of those who can develop a trance state many can attain deep hypnosis only with difficulty and after prolonged training. Unfortunately very deep hypnosis is often a prerequisite for treatment. This is particularly true when the three psychotherapeutic methods last discussed are considered. On the other hand, many more individuals can be deeply hypnotized than is commonly believed, provided the hypnotist is sufficiently skilled. In any case, many persons can benefit considerably from suggestions even in light and medium hypnosis. If nothing else then deep relaxation is obtained and anxiety is removed prior, during and after treatment, especially surgery, hypnosis is a valuable adjuvant.

That deep hypnosis often requires a relatively lengthy "training" period is considered objectionable by some individuals. However, once deep hypnosis has been induced it is an easy matter to reinduce it at any time in the future. When you consider that this "training" has life-long value, the cost and time involved are indeed quite small.

There have been claims made that hypnosis weakens the will, leads to overdependency, causes neuroticism and so forth. There is no foundation for any such beliefs. It is true that in the hands of incompetent persons latent neuroses and psychoses can be set off and overdependency created; improper use of hypnosis in symptom removal may cause the appearance of other, often more debilitating symptoms; or again, in the hands of incompetent individuals, symptoms may be removed but the true organic cause of the symptoms ignored and allowed to progress until it is too late to treat it. These are real dangers, but they exist quite independently of hypnosis and are not specific to it alone. Their source lies entirely in the competence and integrity of those using hypnosis, not in hypnosis per se.

HYPNOTHERAPY

Suggestion techniques can be classified in many ways. One of the more satisfactory of these, given by Wolberg,[204] is in terms of the kinds of therapeutic situations in which hypnosis has been used as an aid. According to him, one has:

A. Hypnosis in Symptom Removal
    (1) with strong authoritarian approach
    (2) with active participation of the patient
B. Hypnosis in Psychobiologic Therapy
    (3) in guidance
    (4) in reassurance
    (5) in persuasion
    (6) in desensitization
    (7) in re-education
    (8) in reconditioning
C. Hypnosis in Psychoanalytic Therapy
    (9) hypnoanalysis
    (10) hypnoanalysis with analysis of transference
    (11) hypnoanalytic desensitization
    (12) re-education through psychoanalytic insight

Thorne[181] has made somewhat different classification based upon the specific ways in which hypnosis or suggestion techniques can be used within each of the above mentioned therapeutic situations. It thus supplements Wolberg's table. According to him, suggestions can be used for:

(1) symptom removal through prestige suggestion
(2) abreaction through reliving traumatic experiences
(3) building confidence through positive reassurance
(4) modifying attitudes and values
(5) attacking the emotional sources of symptom
(6) hypnotic handling of transference
(7) hypnotic handling of resistance
(8) induction of experimental conflicts
(9) facilitation of the various psychoanalytic techniques (dreams, crystal gazing, automatic writing, desensitization, etc.)

The term hypnotherapy tends to be somewhat misleading, intimating as it does a brand new kind of therapy with its own characteristic techniques and principles. Actually, in hypnotherapy, hypnosis is merely used as an adjunct to already well known forms of psychotherapy whose governing rules remain largely unaltered. Thus, just as in palliative therapy or in symptom removal, analysis of the transference is not usually indicated, so it remains true when hypnosis is introduced into such forms of therapy. Similarly, where analysis of the transference plays an important role, this is done in the same way when hypnosis is used as when it is not. In general then, the main role of hypnosis in psychotherapy is to facilitate and enhance the therapeutic process, while at the same time remaining within the bounds of the particular therapeutic setting in question. This, then, appears to be the character of hypnotherapy as it stands today.

One's choice of hypnotherapeutic technique is not entirely free because each technique requires a specific minimum depth of hypnosis to be most effective, which should be kept clearly in mind in planning therapy with hypnosis. Wolberg[203] recommends the following table:

THERAPY TECHNIQUE	MINIMUM DEPTH
Psychobiologic therapy (Reassurance, persuasion, re-education, confession and ventilation) Hypnoanalysis (Free association, fantasy induction)	Hypnoidal State
Psychobiologic therapy (Guidance)	Light Hypnosis
Ability to learn auto-hypnosis Hypnoanalysis (Dream induction)	Medium Hypnosis

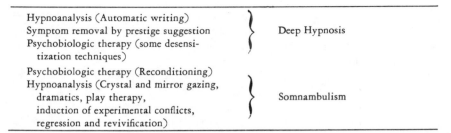

Hypnoanalysis (Automatic writing) Symptom removal by prestige suggestion Psychobiologic therapy (some desensi- tization techniques)	Deep Hypnosis
Psychobiologic therapy (Reconditioning) Hypnoanalysis (Crystal and mirror gazing, dramatics, play therapy, induction of experimental conflicts, regression and revivification)	Somnambulism

As Wolberg has pointed out, one should not take such a table literally because there are considerable individual variations in regard to the type of phenomena one can evoke with a given depth of hypnosis. It can, however, be a useful guide. As the table shows, much can be accomplished with a relatively low depth of hypnosis.

DYNAMICS OF HYPNOTHERAPY

There is little question in the minds of those who use hypnosis as an aid or adjunct that it is an invaluable aid in the therapeutic process, often acting as a catalyst, but, in any case, having strong facilitating and enhancing powers over crucial processes. It is somewhat disappointing, however, to find that there is very little experimental data which bears directly upon this matter. Clinical data, often of dubious value, is usually the best one has in this area. One cannot help but wonder at times whether one may not be dealing with a straw man. We do not know that many of the reported cases might not have been just as successfully treated without hypnosis. Even in those instances where hypnosis was used as a last resort, it cannot be shown for certain that it was not the cumulated influence of all previous therapeutic work done up to the time of the change in therapy that was mainly responsible. Indeed, for all we know, the change itself, or the novelty of the new technique, not to mention the magic-like quality of hypnosis, may have been the main factors in bringing about the dramatic results attributed to hypnosis and suggestions. This is not to say that hypnosis has not or cannot be responsible for some spectacular results. The question, however, is how many of these and under what conditions?

How does hypnosis function in the therapeutic setting? Since psychotherapy is, from one standpoint, a special kind of interpersonal relationship, it appears logical to approach the topic from this point of view, particularly since hypnosis itself constitutes a rather special type of interpersonal relationship. We shall first be concerned with what kind of relationship hypnosis is, then with the manner in which it interacts with the interpersonal relationship characteristic of therapy.

INTERPERSONAL ASPECT OF HYPNOSIS

Many years ago Freud[64] described hypnosis as "a group of two," thereby emphasizing that hypnosis involves a complex hypnotist-subject interaction which can be fully understood only in these terms. We discussed some of its objective characteristics in chapters 1 and 2. As we have seen, upon further analyzing the matter, Freud was able to reduce the matter to a question of transference. This topic was dealt with rather extensively in chapter 2 and needs no further treatment here. As remarked earlier, the acceptance or rejection of the Freudian hypothesis remains largely a matter of personal preference, since conclusive empirical verification is still lacking.

However, whatever orientation one may have, that transference reactions do take place with hypnosis, and that they are quite varied is not only clear from earlier reports and theorizing, but has been made emphatically so by modern therapists and investigators. Mazer,[119] for instance, has shown that the interpersonal relation in hypnosis varies considerably from subject to subject and that it can express itself in many ways other than through eroticism or dominance-submission. As seen earlier, Wolberg[203] has pointed out something of this kind. Not only this, but the same patient may react in many different, often mutually contradictory ways.

Obviously, if hypnosis is a transference phenomenon, it is not limited to a single kind of response as former investigators seem to have implied, although it is probably true that a given individual will have a preferred mode of response. Unfortunately, even this kind of consideration leaves the question open as to whether or not hypnosis is a transference reaction, a matter already taken up to some length (chapter 2). We shall now resume this earlier discussion in terms of its implications for psychotherapy. Transference is a very thorny topic, and if there is a tendency for some repetition, this may not be without some value in keeping our ideas on this question clear. The particular issue seems to have been obscured in a number of ways. To begin with, whatever else it may be, hypnosis involves a rather special and intimate inter-relationship between subject and hypnotist. It is even more intense when these two protagonists happen also to be patient and therapist. Whatever else occurs in this inter-relationship, it would be rather strange if some transference did not also take place. The danger of confounding one reaction (the formation of hypnosis) with another (the formation of transference) is great, and may have influenced therapists to conclude that hypnosis arose out of the transference. Second, in many cases, hypnoanalysis or hypnotherapy is not instituted at the first contact, but is often delayed. Consequently some transference, or at least its beginning, may be present by the time hypnosis is induced and, consequently, the resulting inter-relationship will tend to be colored by the incipient transference which may, indeed, be precipitated. Since much of the evidence reported by therapists is often the result of sampling at various stages of therapy, any matter relevant to hypnosis will most likely tend to take on considerable transference characteristics. Finally, one often tends to forget that hypnoanalysis (and this is also true of hypnotherapy in general) is not hypnosis, as Wolberg[202] has quite aptly expressed when he states that "Hypnoanalysis will bring out reactions that are in direct response to the trance state, to the interpersonal experience with the analyst, and to the recovered material."

Here again lies the danger of confounding reactions arising from very different sources. In particular, the patient's reactions to hypnosis may become a part of his general transference reaction without being necessarily responsible for the influence of suggestions. Furthermore, as hypnoanalysis progress an interaction probably occurs between the three areas Wolberg mentions.

Consequently, although the data undeniably show hypnosis to be closely associated with transference, the nature of this association remains in doubt. While hypnosis is not demonstrably a transference phenomenon, it is often accompanied by it, may initiate it, and probably facilitates it (although it may arise from other aspects of the situation). I would not go so far as to deny the possibility that some forms of hypnotic behavior might arise in the form of transference in some instances. Furthermore, it is likely that even if hypnosis and transference have different origins, the latter may at times become a component of the fully developed hypnotic state. The theory presented in chapter 2 does not exclude the possibility of transference being one of the dimensions of hypnotic hypersuggestibility. In any case, whatever the answer, it does not affect the fact that hypnosis is or involves a characteristic interpersonal relationship. That it is a rather special interrelationship is seen in the fact that hypnosis appears to involve, in the final stage of the induction process, a dissolution of the boundaries between the subject's ego and the external world, in such a way that, in the words of Kubie and Margolin[103] the voice of the hypnotist becomes an "extension of the subject's own psychic processes." This, it must be repeated, can take place without benefit of transference.* It is also quite significant that the available data indicate that, within the framework of the hypnotic situation, the hypnotized individual normally retains his basic personality structure, content and dynamics, as well as the capacity to react to stimuli in

---

*It is possible that Kubie and Margolin mean nothing more by this than that the hypnotist takes the place of the ego-ideal, which was Freud's way of identifying hypnosis with transference. This certainly is one possible interpretation of the phenomenon, but not necessarily the only one.

accordance with these. Consequently, the behavior of the hypnotized individual is to be understood exactly in the same terms as it would be in the waking state with the proviso that the presence of hypnosis be taken into account.

Inasmuch as hypnosis is an event experienced by the patient within the framework of an interpersonal relationship, we may expect him to react to it as he would to any other element of the situation. But what are the reactions of the patient to hypnosis? Something of their nature has already been intimated. A somewhat more detailed account can now be given in the words of Wolberg[203]:

> Reactions to hypnosis are conditioned by the way in which the trance fits into the subject's particular scheme of life. If he is compulsively dependent, he will attempt to utilize hypnosis to gratify his needs. He may seek from hypnosis complete support and fulfillment of all expressed and unexpressed wishes, as well as a magical abatement of his symptoms. If he has an impulse to detach himself from people, he may regard the hypnotic relationship as potentially dangerous, and he may then resist hypnosis, or he may strive to protect himself from fancied hurt by submitting himself masochistically. If he has a power drive he may try to gain strength through ingratiation and identification with the omnipotent analyst. One of the most common reactions is a feeling of having been forced to yield to hypnosis. The associated hostility may be expressed openly or internalized in depressive or psychosomatic manifestations. Strong submissive tendencies of which the patient is in terror may create a desire to dominate the situation by refusing to cooperate and by active resistance. Some patients feel free of anxiety only when they are fighting, and they may strive to make the treatment hour a battle, attacking the analyst and his attitudes or interpretations. There may be fears of being dominated, overpowered, attacked, seduced, and mutilated. At the same time, there may be a deep wish to be attacked or seduced.
>
> The patient will bring into the hypnoanalytic relationship his usual attitudes and defenses—his evasions, his disguises, and the rationalizations by which he wards off too intimate an interpersonal contact.

Such reactions are dealt with by the therapist in exactly the same fashion as other reactions encountered in therapy are manipulated. In brief then, hypnosis appears to become incorporated integrally into the total transference situation provided the transference is allowed to form. There are situations, of course, in which this is not the case. For instance, in palliative therapy, one usually aims at minimizing the transference. Nevertheless, even in such cases, the reactions to hypnosis are dealt with accordingly.

Interaction of Hypnosis with the Therapeutic Process

One might expect that if hypnosis is a transference process, interference might arise between it and the process of therapy. According to Wolberg[203] and others working in this field, this is not the case. For instance, one might expect that the analysis of the hypnotic relationship (as part of the analysis of the transference) would decrease the subject's hypnotizability by removing the motivation that makes hypnosis possible. Usually this does not happen. Again, it is very rare that the resistance caused by analyzing the transference affects the patient's suggestibility. He explains this apparent paradox by saying that in the first instance a peculiar dissociation takes place, and in the second the patient reacts to the therapist as if he were made up of different persons towards one of whom there is no resistance. These *ad hoc* explanations are unsatisfactory and are unnecessary if one takes the alternative position that hypnosis does not depend upon transference for its existence. One might also expect that hypnosis would tend to bring about a limitation of the patient's reactions. This does not occur because, as has already been seen, the patient always reacts to the hypnotist-therapist with the full range of his inner wishes, fears and impulses, the products of his character structure. Spontaneous feelings and emotions can develop here as freely as in psychoanalysis. The transference theory of hypnosis does not make it quite clear why this should be so, but it is no particular problem with the alternative approach.

Quite apart from any question of whether hypnosis is a transference phenomenon, it is sometimes asked whether the hypnotic relationship per se may not impede the effectiveness of transference interpretations whenever these are used as part of therapy. This question is of particular relevance in cases where transference reactions are utilized in the service of resistance. For instance, it is pointed out by some that it is usual for the hypnotist acting in the capacity of a therapist to assume a dominating role in the induction of hypnosis. If it should happen that the transference determined reactions of the patient cast the therapist-hypnotist in a dominating role as a defense, it becomes rather difficult to show the patient that he is distorting when he sees the therapist as dominating him. This objection can be understood in two ways. One, it refers to the fact that by creating a realistic basis for certain responses, the hypnotic situation prevents the therapist from having access to certain potential transference reactions, (somewhat analogously to giving additional structure to a projective situation). This is quite true. However, in my opinion, this loss is more than compensated for in other respects. Besides, the hypnotic situation affords ample freedom and opportunities for transference.

The second interpretation which may be placed upon this argument is that it proposes that the induction of hypnosis brings about a confounding of transference reactions with realistically based responses. Here the objection appears to be founded upon the misconception that if an individual has a tendency to distort in certain directions, he will always do so. But if one is prone to react in certain ways in the absence of an adequate stimulus-situation it does not mean that he cannot and will not make the same response when there is a realistic basis for it, hence, when it is adequate. Under such conditions there is no distortion, hence no cause for telling him that he is distorting. It is conceivable that this proneness has a sensitizing effect upon the patient so that he is more likely to focus upon certain real aspects of the hypnotic situation than he would be otherwise. It may even strengthen or facilitate his reactions. If so, an experienced therapist will perceive and analyze it accordingly, although he will not deal with the reaction itself. In conclusion, it seems to me that the only problem is the fact that a situation is created in which the inexperienced therapist is given a special opportunity to confound an adequate response with a transference reaction. Such situations, however, occur constantly in practice, whether or not hypnosis is used. At worst this might be taken as a warning that hypnotic psychotherapy should be undertaken only with the greatest of care, only by a therapist with considerable experience, and that the introduction of hypnosis in psychotherapy does not mean the process is made any simpler for the therapist.

Inasmuch as each type of therapy has its own particular characteristics, it is not possible to discuss the manner in which hypnosis and therapy interact in entirely general terms. Perforce it will be necessary to take this question up for each form of therapy in turn, which is a major endeavor. Fortunately Wolberg has already done this in some detail, and even more fortunate, his point of view appears to be representative of that of the majority of workers in the field. Consequently, our task is considerably simplified. The following is a very abbreviated version of the manner in which he believes hypnosis functions in specific individual therapies.

Symptom Removal

In suggestive therapy the therapist holds a position of omnipotence in the patient's mind. Symptoms are removed because the subject wants to comply with the therapist's commands. Motivation for this results from the wish to gratify security needs through archaic submission mechanisms to, and identification with, an omnipotent authority. It is only if this motivation is greater than that gained from symptom elaboration that the latter will be given up. This will persist only as long as the balance of motivation favors the therapist. Hostility generated by the dependency relationship inherent in the hypnotic situation may act against this motivation.

Psychobiologic Therapy

The chief value of hypnosis here is its effect upon the interpersonal rela-

tionship with the therapist.   Hypnosis acts very effectively as a catalyst to
the various psychobiologic techniques, all of which gain reinforcement with
its use.   This is because hypnosis expedites the positive relationship essential
for this sort of therapy.   It speeds up development of feelings of confidence
and closeness, leading to greater response on the part of the patient to persuasive and re-educational influences.   Furthermore, the hypnotic experience
itself tends to convince him something is being done for him in the immediate
present.

In addition to these general aspects of the way hypnosis works, there
are more specific ones for each kind of psychobiologic therapy as follows:

Guidance. Hypnosis can be used to compel the patient to comply with such
suggestions as are in line with the principles of guidance. In hypnosis the
patient may often experience a security feeling like that of a child toward a
parent, teacher and so on, and hence may assume the role of a demanding
infant who depends on the parent for love and support. Finally, hypnosis can
be used to externalize the patient's interests by stimulating him.

Reassurance. Reassurance is founded on the acceptance of the physician as a
sincere and omniscient authority. For this reason, reassurance given under
hypnosis will be accepted and acted upon more intensely than that given in
the waking state.

Persuasion. Hypnosis reinforces persuasive arguments because the trance
relationship facilitates absorption and acceptance of suggestions. Hypnosis
also facilitates the learning of certain techniques the patient must acquire in
this form of therapy. Finally, posthypnotic suggestions may help the patient
to carry out directions with more power and determination.

Desensitization. Hypnosis helps by producing a relation of such confidence
and intimacy that the patient is enabled to talk about matters he could not
divulge in the waking state. Repressed memories can be recaptured in the
deep trance because the induction of hypnosis dissolves resistance to recall.
Catharsis and desensitization are often associated with this process. Specialized hypnotic techniques such as crystal gazing, automatic writing, etc., can
be used to advantage here. Substitutive reactions can be suggested. Finally,
the basis of the patient's inadequate behavior can be demonstrated to him
through such techniques as experimental conflict production.

Re-education. Hypnosis is mainly used to produce experimental conflicts in
order to creat situations reminiscent of the original source of trauma. The
patient is thus able to acquire some understanding, or at least to become
aware, of the origins of his character drives.

Reconditioning. Hypnosis can intensify emotional stimuli and can render
the patient more susceptible to the establishment of conditioned reflexes.

Hypnoanalysis

Hypnosis facilitates the psychoanalytic process. One way it accomplishes this is by removing resistance hence allowing repressed material to come into consciousness. Hypnosis can also catalyze feelings. Finally, hypnosis tends to stimulate expressiveness and assertiveness, and also tends to disinhibit. In addition, there exist a great number of so-called specialized hypnoanalytic techniques or procedures. In summarizing the uses of hypnoanalysis, Wolberg[205] says it can be used in three major ways:

(a) to permit the development of a transference neurosis with its analysis in the traditional psychoanalytic sense;

(b) to desensitize the patient thus allowing him to become aware of and to adjust to repressed elements of his personality;

(c) to re-educate the patient through psychoanalytic insight.

Wolberg feels that it is essential that the physician using hypnoanalysis in forms which depend upon the analysis of the transference as the predominant technique have undergone a personal analysis. On the other hand this is not a necessary requirement when using hypnoanalysis in the form of desensitization or of re-education.

Specialized Hypnotherapeutic Procedures

These techniques are primarily techniques for uncovering* the unconscious motivational patterns which determine the individual's values and behavior. A number of these offer a means for bringing about abreaction. One method, that of the induction of experimental conflicts, is mainly used to demonstrate to the patient how his unconscious works. The other techniques are free-association in hypnosis, dream induction and interpretation, automatic writing, hypnotic drawing, play therapy in hypnosis, hypnodrama, induced hypermnesia, regression and revivification, and crystal and mirror gazing. Although these techniques are usually referred to as hypnoanalytic, they are applicable to many other forms of psychotherapy. For the most part they depend in a straightforward manner for their functioning upon known properties of hypnosis in relation to motor and nonmotor responses, although some are also partly dependent upon the patient's emotions toward hypnosis itself and upon his transference reactions.

The picture in regard to the experimental foundations of these techniques is somewhat better than it is in other areas of hypnotherapy. A number of interesting studies have been made in relation to the phenomena character-

*Although, because of posthypnotic amnesia, material uncovered during hypnosis remains inaccessible to the patient's waking consciousness, according to Wolberg, something does persist into the waking state and facilitates eventual waking recall and insight.

istic of many of the techniques which have been listed. A review and analysis of these investigations will be found elsewhere.[194] In brief, the results which have been obtained show, in general, that there is a definite basis for employing these techniques. Of special interest may be the fact that many appear to function as projective devices. Also, that in the recall of past experiences in hypnosis there is a considerable tendency to confabulate on the part of the hypnotized individual, with a consequence that the use of hypnotic hypermnesia and of regressions may thereby be more limited than might at first have appeared. It is fairly certain that the way in which these various techniques function therapeutically is no different from the way in which techniques characteristic of therapy in the waking state do.

RECOMMENDED BOOKS FOR THE SPECIALIST

This book, as emphasized earlier, has been about general techniques of hypnosis. The reader should not have any difficulty applying them to specific problems occurring in his specialty. For those who wish to do some additional reading in their field of specialization a few pertinent books selected from among many other worthwhile ones might be recommended.

For the Psychotherapist

Wolberg, L. R.: Medical Hypnosis. Vol. I and II. New York, Grune and Stratton, Inc., 1948.

For the Dentist

Moss, A. A.: Hypnodontics. Hypnosis in Dentistry. Brooklyn, Dental Items of Interest Publishing Co., 1952.

For the General Practitioner and Other Specialties not Listed Here

Schneck, J. M.: Hypnotism in Modern Medicine. Springfield, Charles C Thomas, 1953.

For the Psychologist

Kline, M. V.: Hypnodynamic Psychology. New York, Julian Press, 1955.
Weitzenhoffer, A. M.: Hypnotism. An Objective Study in Suggestibility. New York, John Wiley and Sons, Inc., 1953.

Part IV.
Appendix

References

1. ADLER, M.H. AND SECUNDA, L.: An indirect technique to induce hypnosis. J. Nerv. & Ment. Dis., 1947, *106*, 190-193.
2. ALEXANDER, F. AND FRENCH, T.M.: Psychoanalytic Therapy. New York: The Ronald Press, 1946.
3. ARONS, H.: Master Course in Hypnotism. Newark: Power Publishers, 1948.
4. ——: Techniques of Speed Hypnosis. Newark: Power Publishers, 1953.
5. BARETY, A.: Le Magnétisme Animal Étudié Sous le Nom de Force Neurique Rayonnante et Circulante. Paris: O. Douin, 1887.
6. BARKER, N. AND BURGWIN, S.: Brain wave patterns during hypnosis, hypnotic sleep, and normal sleep. Arch. Neurol. Psychiat., 1949, *62*, 412-420.
6a. BARKER, R.G., DEMBO,. AND LEWIN, K.: Frustration and Regression: An experiment with young children. Studies in topological and vector psychology. II. University of Iowa studies in child welfare, Vol. 18, No. 1. University of Iowa Studies No. 386. Iowa City: University of Iowa Press, 1941.
7. BARUK, H. AND MASSAUT, C.: Action physiologique experimentale et clinique du scopochloralose. Ann. Med. Psychol., 1936, *94*, 702-712.
8. BAUDOUIN, C.: Suggestion and Autosuggestion. London: George Allen and Unwin, Ltd., 1920.
9. BECHTEREW, V.M.: Die Bedeutung der Suggestion in sozialen Leben. Granzfr. Nervenleben. Wiesbaden, 1905.
10. BERNHEIM, H.: Suggestive Therapeutics (1886). New York: London Book Co., 1947.
11. BERTRAND A.: Traite du Somnambulisme et des Differentes Modes qu'il Presente. Paris, 1823.
12. BEXTON, W.H., HERON, W. AND SCOTT, T.H.: Effects of decreased variation in the sensory environment. Canadian J. Psychol., 1954, *8*, 70-76.
13. BINET, A.: La Suggestibilité. Paris: Schleicher Frères, 1900.
14. ——: Les Altérations de la Personalité. Paris: Felix Alcan, 1892.
15. —— AND FÉRÉ, C.: Animal Magnetism. London: Kegan Paul, Trench, and Trübner, and Co., 1905.
16. BIRD, C.: Suggestion and suggestibility: A bibliography. Psychol. Bull., 1939, *36*, 264-283.
17. BRAMWELL, M.J.: Hypnotism: Its History, Practice, and Theory (1921). Philadelphia: J. B. Lippincott Co., 1930.
18. BRAID, J.: Neurypnology: or the Rationale of Nervous Sleep considered in Relation with Animal Magnetism. London: John Churchill, 1843.
19. BRAZIER, M.A.B. AND FINESINGER, J.E.: Action of barbiturates on the cerebral cortex. Arch. Neurol. Psychiat., 1945, *53*, 31-38.
20. BREMAUD, P.: Des différentes phases de l'hypnotisme et en particulier de la fascination. Bull. du Cercle Scient. Simon, No. 1, 1885.
21. BRENMAN, M. AND GILL, M.M.: Hypnotherapy. New York: International Universities Press, 1947.
22. ——AND HACKNER, F.J.: Alterations in the state of the ego in hypnosis. Bull. Menninger Clin., 1943, *7*, 183-187.

437

23. BROTTEAUX, P.: Hypnotisme et Scopochloralose. Paris: Vigot Frères, 1936.
24. BROWN, W.: Suggestion and Mental Analysis, 2 nd. ed., New York: G. H. Doran Co., 1922.
25. CHARCOT, J.M.: Note sur les divers états nerveux déterminés par l'hypnotization sur les hystéro-épileptiques. C.R. de l'Acad. des Sciences, Paris, 13 février, 1882.
26. CHEVREUL: De la Baguette Divinatoire, du Pendule dit Explorateur et des Tables Tournantes au Point de Vue de l'Histoire, de la Critique et de le Méthode Experimentale. Paris: Mallet-Richelieu, 1854.
27. CHRISTENSON, J.A.: Dynamic of Hypnotic Induction. Chapter in (106).
28. COFFIN, T.E.: Some conditions of suggestion and suggestibility: A study of certain attitudinal and situational factors influencing the process of suggestion. Psychol. Monog., 1941, 53, No. 4.
29. CONN, J.H.: Hypnosynthesis: Hypnosis as a unifying interpersonal experience. J. Nerv. and Ment. Dis., 1949, 109, 9-24.
30. —— : Paper presented at the Round Table on Current Practices in Hypnosis. 112th Annual Meeting of the American Psychiatric Association, 1956.
31. COOMBS, C.H.: A Theory of Psychological Scaling. Engng. Res. Bull., (University of Michigan), 1952, No. 34.
32. COOPER, L.F. AND ERICKSON, M.H.: Time Distortion in Hypnosis. Baltimore: Williams and Wilkins, 1954.
33. COUÉ, E.: Self-mastery Through Conscious Autosuggestion (1922). London: G. Allen and Unwin, Ltd., 1951.
34. CULLERRE, A.: Magnétisme et Hypnotisme. Paris: J.B. Baillière et Fils, 1886.
35. DALBIEZ, R.: Psychoanalytical Method and the Doctrine of Freud. Vol. II. New York: Green and Co., 1941.
36. DAVIS, L.W. AND HUSBAND, R.W.: A study of hypnotic susceptibility in relation to personality traits. J. abnorm. soc. Psychol., 1931, 26, 175-182.
37. DESSOIR, M.: Bibliographie des modernen Hypnotismus. Berlin: C. Dunker, 1888.
37a. DIETERLE, R.R. AND KOCH, E.J.: Experimental induction of infantile behavior in major hysteria. J. Nerv. & Ment. Dis., 1937, 86, 688-710.
38. DORCUS, R.M.: Hypnosis and its Therapeutic Applications. New York: McGraw-Hill, 1956.
39. DOUST, J.W.L.: Studies on the physiology of awareness: Oximetric analysis of emotion and the differential planes of consciousness seen in hypnosis. J. Clin. Exper. Psychopath., 1953, 14, 113-126.
40. DURAND DE GROS: See (138).
41. DURVILLE, H.: Traité Experimental de Magnétisme. 2 vols. Paris: Chamuel, 1895.
42. ENNOMOSER, J.: Der Magnetismus. Leipzig, 1819.
43. ERICKSON, M.H.: Hypnosis: A general review. Dis. Nerv. Syst., 1941, 2, 13-18.
44. —— : Deep hypnosis and its induction. Chapter in (106).
45. —— : An experimental demonstration of the psychopathology of everyday life. Psychoanal. Quart., 1939, 8, 338-353.
46. —— : The method employed to formulate a complex story for the induction of an experimental neurosis in a hypnotic subject. J. gen. Psychol., 1944, 31, 67-84.
47. —— : A study of clinical and experimental findings on hypnotic deafness: I. Clinical experimentation and findings. J. gen. Psychol., 1938, 19, 127-150.
48. —— : The development of an actual limited obsessional hysterical state in a normal hypnotic subject. J. Clin. Exper. Hypnosis, 1954, 2, 27-41.

49. ——: Special techniques of brief hypnotherapy. J. Clin. Exper. Hypnosis, 1954, 2, 102-129.

50. ——: The induction of color blindness by a technique of hypnotic suggestion. J. gen. Psychol., 1939, 20, 61-89.

51. ——AND ERICKSON, E.M.: Concerning the nature and character of posthypnotic behavior. J. gen. Psychol., 1941, 24, 95-133.

52. ——AND——: Hypnotic investigation of psychosomatic phenomena: I. Psychosomatic interrelationships studied by experimental hypnosis. Psychosom. Med., 1943, 5, 51-58.

53. ——AND KUBIE, L.S.: The successful treatment of a case of acute hysterical depression by a return under hypnosis to a critical phase of childhood. Psychoanal. Quarter., 1941, 10, 583-609.

54. EYSENCK, H.J.: Suggestibility and hysteria. J. Neurol. Psychiat., 1943, 6, 22-31.

55. ——: Book review. Psychol. Bull., 1954, 51, 593-595.

56. FENICHEL, O.: The Psychoanalytic Theory of Neuroses. New York: Norton, 1945.

57. FERENCZI, S.: Introjection and Transference. In: Sex and Psychoanalysis. New York: Basic Books, 1950.

58. FISHER, C.: Studies on the nature of suggestions. Part I. Experimental induction of dreams by direct suggestion. J. Amer. Psychoanalytic Ass., 1953, 1, 222-255.

59. ——: Idem. Part II. The transference meaning of giving suggestions. J. Amer. Psychoanalytic Ass., 1953, 1, 406-437.

60. FLIES, R.: The hypnotic evasion: A clinical observation. Psychoanal. Quarter., 1953, 22, 497-511.

61. FOREL, A.: Hypnotism. New York: Allied Publications, 1949.

62. FREUD, S.: Three Contributions to the Theory of Sex. In: The Basic Writings of Freud. New York: Modern Library, 1938.

63. ——: A General Introduction to Psychoanalysis. New York: Garden City Publishing Co., Inc., 1938.

64. ——: Group Psychology and the Analysis of the Ego. International Psycho-analytical Library, No. 6. New York: Liveright Publishing Corp., 1949.

65. ——: Psychical (or mental) treatment. Standard Edition. Collected Psychological Works of S. Freud. Vol. VII. London: The Hogarth Press, 1953.

66. FRIEDLANDER, J.W. AND SARBIN, T.R.: The depth of hypnosis. J. abnorm. soc. Psychol., 1938, 33, 281-294.

67. GELLHORN, E.: The Physiological Foundations of Neurology and Psychiatry. Minneapolis: Univ. of Minnesota Press, 1953.

68. GIBIER, P.: L'Analyse des Choses. Paris: Durville, 1922.

69. GIDRO-FRANK, L. AND BULL, N.: Emotions induced and studied in hypnotic subjects. Part I. The method. J. nerv. ment. Dis., 1950, 111, 91-100.

70. GILLMAN, T. AND MARCUSE, F.L.: Animal hypnosis. Psychol. Bull., 1949, 46, 151-165.

71. GLOVER, E.: The Technique of Psycho-analysis. New York: International Universities Press, Inc., 1955.

72. GORTON, B.E.: The physiology of hypnosis—A review of the literature. Parts I and II. Psychiat. Quart., 1949, 23, 317-343, 457-485.

73. GRASSET, P.: L'Hypnotisme et la Suggestion. 2 eme ed. Paris: O. Douin, 1904.

74. GROLLMAN, A.: Pharmacology and Therapeutics. Philadelphia: Lea and Febiger, 1951.

75. GUILFORD, J.P.: Psychometric Methods. New York: McGraw-Hill, 1954.

76. ——: Fundamental Statistics in Psychology and Education. New York: McGraw-Hill, 1950.

77. GULLIKSEN, H.: Theory of Mental Tests. New York: John Wiley and Sons, 1950.
77a. GURNEY, E.: Peculiarities of certain posthypnotic states. Proc. Soc. Psychic. Res., London, 1886-87, 4, 268-323.
78. GUZE, H.: Hypnosis as an emotional response. A Theoretical approach. J. Clin. Exper. Hypnosis, 1953, 35, 313-328.
79. HENDRIK, I.: Facts and Theories of Psycho-analysis. New York: A. Knopf, 1935.
80. HERON, W.T.: Clinical Applications of Suggestions and Hypnosis. Springfield: Charles C Thomas, 1950.
81. HOAGLAND, H.: The mechanism of tonic immobility ("animal hypnosis"). J. gen. Psychol., 1928, 1, 426-447.
82. HORSLEY, J.S.: Pentothal sodium in mental hospital practice. Brit. M. J., 1936, 1, 938-940.
83. ———: Narcotic hypnosis. Chapter in (106).
84. ———: Narco-analysis. New York: Oxford University Press, 1943.
85. HULL, C.L.: Hypnosis and Suggestibility. An Experimental Approach. New York: D. Appleton-Century Co., 1933.
86. HULL, C.L.: Hypnotism and scientific perspective. Scient. Month., 1929, 29, 170-185.
87. HUNT, J. McV.: Personality and the Behavior Disorders. New York: The Ronald Press, 1944.
88. INBAU, F.E. AND REID, J.E.: Lie Detection and Clinical Interrogation. 3rd ed. Baltimore: William and Wilkins, 1953.
89. ISRAELI, N.: Experimental study of hypnotic imagination and dreams of projection in time: I. Outlook upon the remote future—Extending through the quintillionth year. J. Clin. Exper. Hypnosis, 1953, 1, 49-60.
90. JANET, P.: Psychological Healing. Vol. I. London: George Allen and Unwin, 1925.
91. ———: L'Automatisme Psychologique. Paris: F. Alcan, 1889.
92. ———: Névroses et Idées Fixes. Paris: F. Alcan, 1898.
93. ———: État Mental des Hystériques: Les Accidents Mentaux. Paris: F. Alcan, 1894.
94. JENNESS, A.: Hypnotism. Chapter in (87).
95. JONES, E.: The Nature of Auto-suggestion. In Papers on Psycho-analysis. 5th ed., Baltimore: Williams and Wilkins Co., 1948.
96. ———: The action of suggestion in psychotherapy. J. abnorm. soc. Psychol., 1910-11, 5, 217-254.
97. KLINE, M.V.: Toward a theoretical understanding of the nature of resistance to the induction of hypnosis and depth hypnosis. J. Clin. Exper. Hypnosis, 1953, 1, 32-41.
98. ———: Hypnodynamic Psychology. New York: The Julian Press, 1955.
99. ———: A visual imagery technique for the induction of hypnosis in certain refractory subjects. J. Psychol., 1953, 35, 227-228.
100. ———: Hypnotic retrogression: A neurophysiological theory of Age regression and progression. J. Clin. Exper. Hypnosis, 1953, 1, 21-28.
101. ———: The application of hypnosis to non-directive psychotherapy. J. Clin. Psychol., 1951, 7, 283.
102. KUBIE, L.S. AND MARGOLIN, S.: A physiological method for the induction of states of partial sleep, and securing free association and early memories in such states. Trans. Am. Neurol. Ass., 1942, 136-139.
103. ———AND———: The process of hypnotism and the nature of the hypnotic state. Amer. J. Psychiat., 1944, 100, 611-622.
104. KUHN, L. AND RUSSO, S.: Modern Hypnosis. New York: Psychological Library Publishers, 1947.

105. LeCron, L.M.: A method of measuring the depth of hypnosis. J. Clin. Exper. Hypnosis, 1953, *1*, 4-7.
106. ———: Experimental Hypnosis. New York: Macmillan Co., 1952.
107. ———and Bordeaux, J.: Hypnotism Today. New York: Grune and Stratton, Inc., 1947.
108. Leitner, K.: How to Hypnotize. A Master Key to Hypnotism. New York: Stravon Publishers, 1950.
109. Leuba, C.: Images as conditioned sensations. J. exper. Psychol., 1940, *26*, 338-355.
110. Levy-Suhl, M.: Die hypnotische Beeinflussung der Farbenwahrnemung und die Helmholtzsche Theorie vom Simultankontrast. Ztschr. f. Psychol. u. Physiol. d. Sinnesorg., Leipz., 1909, *53*, 179-205.
111. Liégeois, M.J.: De la Suggestion et du Somnambulisme dans leurs Rapports avec la Jurisprudence et la Médecine Légale. Paris: F. Alcan, 1899.
112. Lipps, T.: Suggestion und Hypnose. Ein psychologische Untersuchung. Sitzungsbericht der bayerischen Akademie der Wissenschaft, 1897 (1898), 391-522. [This comes under: Munich Akademie. Philosophische-Philologische-und Historische Classe, 1897].
112a. Lorand, S.: Hypnotic suggestion: its dynamics, indications, and limitations in the therapy of neurosis. J. Nerv. Ment. Dis., 1941, *94*, 64-75.
113. Lovell, G.D. and Morgan, J.J.B.: Physiological and motor responses to a regularly recurring sound: A study in monotony. J. exper. Psychol., 1942, *30*, 435-451.
114. Lundholm, H.: An experimental study of functional anesthesia as induced by suggestions in hypnosis. J. abnorm. soc. Psychol., 1928, *23*, 338-355.
115. ———: A new laboratory neurosis. Charact. and Person., 1940, *9*, 111-121.
116. Luria, A.R.: The Nature of Human Conflicts. New York: Liveright, 1932.
117. Macalpine, I.: The development of the transference. Psychoanal. Quart., 1950, *19*, 501-537.
118. Mangold, E.: Methodik der Versuche über tierische Hypnose. Handbuch der biologischen Arbeitsmethoden Abt. VI. Methoden der experimentellen Psychologie. Teil C^1, Heft 5 (Reine Psychologie): Hypnose. Berlin: Urban und Schwarzenberg, 1925.
119. Mazer, M.: An experimental study of the hypnotic dream. Psychiatry, 1951, *14*, 265-277.
120. Meares, A.: The clinical estimation of suggestibility. J. Clin. Exper. Hypnosis, 1954, *2*, 106-108.
121. ———: Non-verbal and extra-verbal suggestion in the induction of hypnosis, Parts I and II. Brit. J. Med. Hypnotism, 1954, *5*, 2-6; 1954, *6*, 51-54.
122. ———: Non-specific suggestion. Brit. J. Med. Hypnotism, 1956, *7*, 16-19.
123. Milechnin, G.S. de: Concerning the concept of hypnotic depth. J. Clin. Exper. Hypnosis, 1955, *3*, 243-252.
124. ———: Concerning a theory of hypnosis. J. Clin. Exper. Hypnosis, 1956, *4*, 37-45.
125. Mesmer, F.A.: Mesmerism. (Introduction by J. Frankau). London: Macdonald and Co., 1948.
126. Moll, A.: Hypnotism. London: Walter-Scott, 1890.
127. ———: Der Rapport in der Hypnose. Untersuchungen über den thierischen Magnetismus. Schriften d. ges. f. psychol. Forsch. I, Leipzig: 1892.
128. Moss, A.A.: Hypnodontics. Hypnosis in Dentistry. Brooklyn: Dental Items of Interest Publishing Co., 1952.
129. Muhl, A.M.: Automatic Writing and hypnosis. Chapter in (106).
130. Murray, H.S.: Explorations in Personality. Cambridge: Harvard University Press, 1938.
131. Nagge, J.W.: An experimental test of the theory of associative interference. J. exper. Psychol., 1935, *18*, 663-681.

132. NARUSE, G. AND OBONAI, T.: Decomposition and fusion of mental images in a drowsy and a post-hypnotic hallucinatory state, (I). J. Clin. Exp. Hypnosis, 1953, *1*, 23-42.

133. ——AND——: Decomposition and fusion of mental images in the posthypnotic hallucinatory state, (II): Mechanism of image composing activity. J. Clin. Exp. Hypnosis, 1955, *3*, 2-23.

134. NUNBERG, H.: Transference and reality. Internat. J. Psychoanalysis, 1951, *32*, 1-9.

135. OTIS, M.: A study of suggestibility in children. Arch. Psychol., 1924, *11*, No. 70.

136. PATTI, F.A., JR.: The production of blisters by hypnotic suggestions: A review. J. abnorm. soc. Psychol., 1941, *36*, 62-72.

137. ——: Chapter on induction techniques in Dorcus (38).

138. PHILIPS, J.P.: Cours Théoriques et Pratiques de Braidisme ou.Hypnotisme Nerveux. Paris: J.B. Baillière et fils, 1860.

139. PIERON, H.: Le Problème Physiologique du Sommeil. Paris: Masson et Cie., 1931.

140. POWERS, M. Advanced Techniques of Hypnosis. Los Angeles: Wilshire Book Co., 1953.

141. PREYER, W.: Die Kataplexie und der tierische Hypnotismus. Sammlung physiologischen Abhandlungen, 2te Reihe, H.¹, Jena: G. Fisher, 1878.

142. RADO, S.: The economic principle in psycho-analytic technique. Internat. J. Psychoanalysis, 1925, *6*, 35-44.

143. RHODES, R.H.: Therapy through Hypnosis. New York: Citadel Press, 1952.

144. RICHER, P.: Études Cliniques de la Grande Hystérie ou Hystéro-epilepsie. Paris: Delahaye et Le Crosnier, 1885.

145. ROCHAS (D'AIGLUN), A. DE: Les Vies Successives. 2 ed., Paris: Chacornac Frères, 1924.

146. ROSENZWEIG, S. AND SARASON, S.: An experimental study of the triadic hypothesis in relation to frustration, ego-defense, and hypnotic ability. Character and Pers., 1942, *11*, 1-14, 150-165.

147. ROSEN, H.: Hypnotherapy in Clinical Psychiatry. New York: Julian Press, 1953.

148. SALTER, A.: Three techniques of autohypnosis. J. gen. Psychol., 1941, *24*, 423-438.

149. SARBIN, T.R.: Contributions to role-taking theory: I. Hypnotic Behavior. Psychol. Rev., 1950, *5*, 255-270.

150. SARGANT, W. AND FRAZER, R.: Inducing light hypnosis by hyperventilation. Lancet, 1938, *235*, 778-779.

151. SCHILDER, P.: The Nature of Hypnosis (1921, 1926). New York: International Universities Press, 1956.

152. SCHMIDKUNZ, H.: Psychologie der Suggestion. Stuttgart; F. Enke, 1892.

153. SCHNECK, J.M.: Psychosomatic reactions to the induction of hypnosis. Dis. nerv. Syst., 1950, *11*, 118-121.

154. ——: A note on spontaneous hallucinations during hypnosis. Psychiat. Quarter., 1950, *24*, 1-3.

155. ——: Spontaneous homonymous hemianopsia in hypnotic imagery. Brit. J. Med. Hypnotism, 1951, 2, 2-3.

156. ——: The elucidation of spontaneous sensory and motor phenomena during hypnoanalysis. Psychoanal. Rev., 1952, *39*, 79-89.

157. ——: Hypnotism in Modern Medicine. Springfield: Charles C Thomas, 1953.

158. SCHULTZ, J.J: Das Autogene Training. 8th Edition. Stuttgart: George Thieme Verlag, 1953.

159. SCHULTZ, J.H.: Uebungsheft für das Autogene Training. 6th Edition. Stuttgart: George Thieme Verlag, 1947.

160. SCOTT, W.D.: Suggestion. Psychol. Bull, 1910, 7, 369-372.

161. ——: *Idem* 1911, *8*, 309-311.

162. ——: *Idem*. 1912, *9*, 269-273.
163. ——: *Idem*. 1913, *10*, 269-270.
164. ——: *Idem*. 1914, *11*, 250-252.
165. ——: *Idem*. 1915, *12*, 225-226.
166. ——: *Idem*. 1916, *13*, 266-268.
167. Sidis, B.: The Psychology of Suggestion. New York: D. Appleton Co., 1910.
168. ——: Symptomatology, Psychogenesis, and Diagnosis of Psychopathic Diseases. Edinburgh: E. and S. Livingston, 1921.
169. ——: The value of the method of hypnoidization in the diagnosis and treatment of psychopathic disorders. Medical Times. 1919, *47*, 245-250.
170. Snyder, E.D.: Hypnotic Poetry. Philadelphia: The University of Pennsylvania, 1930.
171. Solomon, L.M. and Stein, G.: Normal motor automaticism. Psychol. Rev., 1896, 3, 492-512.
172. Speyer, N. and Stokvis, B.: The psycho-analytical factor in hypnosis. Brit. J. med. Psychol., 1938, *17*, 217-222.
173. Steger, M.: Hypnoidal Therapy. New York: Froben, 1951.
174. Stembo, L.: Applications thérapeutiques de la suggestion proe-hypnotique. Rev. Hypnotisme, 1893, 7, 276.
175. Stein, G.: Cultivated motor automatism: A study of character in relation to attention. Psychol. Rev. 1898, *5*, 295-306.
176. Stein, M.R.: A critical review of an investigation in the psychology of suggestion and hypnosis. J. abnorm. soc. Psychol., 1930, *25*, 49-56.
177. Stokvis, B.: A simple hypnotizing technique with the aid of colour-contrast action. Amer. J. Psychiat., 1952, *109*, 380-381.
178. Stoll, O.: Suggestion und Hypnotismus in der Völkerpsychologie. Leipzig. Veit u. Co., 1904.
179. Stungo, E.: Evipan hypnosis in psychiatric outpatients. Lancet, 1941, *240*, 507-509.
180. Teitelbaum, H.A.: Psychogenic body-image disturbances associated with psychogenic aphasia and agnosia. J. Nerv. Ment. Dis., 1941, *93*, 581-591.
181. Thorne, F.C.: Principles of Personality Counseling. Brandon (Vermont): Journal of Clinical Psychology, 1950.
182. Verworn, M.: Beitrage zur Physiologie des Zentralnervensystems. I. Theil: Die sogenannte Hypnose der Tiere. Jena: G. Fisher, 1898.
183. Vogt, O.: Zur Kenntnis des Wesens und der psychologischen Bedeutung des Hypnotismus. Zeitschrift fuer Hypnotismus, 1894-95, 3, 277; 1896, 4, 32, 122, 229.
184. Volgyesi, F.: Menschen-und Tierhypnose. Leipzig: Orell Füsali Verlag, 1938.
185. Wagner, F.F.: Hypnotic induction by means of folding hands. Acta Psychiatrica et Neurologica Scandinavica, 1951, *26*, 90-94.
186. Walter, W.G. Dovey, V.J. and Shipton, H.: Analysis of electrical response of human cortex to photic stimulation. Nature, 1946, *158*, 340-541.
187. Warren, H.C.: Dictionary of Psychology. New York: Houghton Mifflin Co., 1934.
188. Watkins, J.G.: Hypnotherapy of War Neuroses. New York: The Ronald Press Co., 1949.
189. ——: Trance and transference. J. Clin. Exper. Hypnosis, 1954, 2, 284-290.
190. ——: Paper presented at the Round Table on Current Practices in Hypnosis. 112th Annual Meeting of the American Psychiatric Association, 1956.
191. Weitzenhoffer, A.M.: Hypnotism: An Objective Study in Suggestibility. New York: John Wiley and Sons, Inc., 1953.
192. ——: The Induction of Hypnosis. Chapter in (98).

193.   ——: The transcendence of normal voluntary capacities in hypnosis: An evaluation.
        Personality, 1951, *1*, 272-282.
194.   ——: The discriminatory recognition of visual patterns under hypnosis. J. abnorm. soc.
        Psychol., 1951, *46*, 388-397.
195.   ——: Mathematical structure and psychological measurements. Psychometrika, 1951,
        16, 398-496.
196.   ——: Learning, motivation, and hypnosis. In press.
197.   ——: and WEITZENHOFFER, G.B.: Toward a verification of the psychoanalytic concept of
        hypnosis: Part I. Hypnotic susceptibility as related to masculinity-femininity.
        In: Current Practice in Hypnosis. Edited by Wolberg, L.R. and Rosen, H. New
        York: Grune and Stratton, Inc., In press.
197a.   ——: Posthypnotic behavior and the recall of suggestion. J. Clin. Exper. Hypnosis. In
        press.
198.   WELLS, W.R.: Experiments in waking hypnosis for instructional purposes. J. abnorm.
        soc. Psychol., 1924, *18*, 389-404.
199.   WHITE, R.W.: A preface to the theory of hypnotism. J. abnorm. soc. Psychol., 1941,
        36, 477-505.
200.   ——: An analysis of motivation in hypnosis. J. gen. Psychol., 1941, *24*, 145-162.
201.   WILLIAMS, G.W.: Difficulty in dehypnotizing. J. Clin. Exper. Psychol., 1953, *1*, 3-12.
202.   WOLBERG, L.R.: Hypnoanalysis. New York: Grune and Stratton, Inc., 1945.
203.   ——: Medical Hypnosis. Volume I. New York: Grune and Stratton, Inc., 1948.
204.   ——: Medical Hypnosis. Volume II. New York: Grune and Stratton, Inc., 1948.
205.   ——: The Technique of Psychotherapy. New York: Grune and Stratton, Inc., 1954.
206.   WOLSTEIN, B.: Transference. Its Meaning and Function in Psychoanalytic Therapy. New
        York: Grune and Stratton, Inc., 1954.
207.   YOUNG, P.C.: A general review of the literature of hypnotism. Psychol. Bull., 1927,
        24, 540-560.
208.   ——: A general review of the literature on hypnotism and suggestion. Psychol. Bull.,
        1931, *28*, 367-391.
209.   ——: Experimental hypnosis: A review. Psychol. Bull., 1941, *38*, 92-104.

Author Index

Subject Index

and fascination, 119
hypnoidal state and, 340
and modern hypnosis, 42-45, 47, 256
and suggestion, 43
Braid's method, 248, 259, 281
Blindness
    induced, 391ff.
    spontaneous, 351

Cancellation of suggestions
        (See: Termination.)
Canibis indica, 254
Catalepsy, 118, 260, 283, 285, 339, 340 (See
        also: Rigidity.)
    defined, 136
    suggested, of the arm, 138
        of the body, 356
        of the eyelids, 136
Cataleptoid state, 285
Challenge
    to break a suggestion, 128, 214
    to overcome resistance, use of, 396
Charcot syndrome
    as an artifact, 285, 287
    authenticity of, 287f.
    defined and described, 283f.
    fascination and, 118, 185
    and modern hypnotism, 185
Chevreul pendulum
    experiment with, 84, 98
    as a suggestibility test, 84
    to induce hypnotism, 302
Chloralose (See: Scopochloralose.)
Chloroform, 254
Choosing between techniques, 96f.
Clasping of the hands, suggested, 127
Color contrast technique, 264, 273
Commands and suggestion, 23
Complexes, production of neurotic, 361-383
Complexity of suggestions, effectiveness as a
        function of, 155f., 319, 349
Compulsive behavior and suggestion, 30, 31,
        36
Conditioning and hypnosis, 36, 331 (See also:
        Abstract conditioning.)
Conditions for hypnosis, 33-34
Conflicts, inducing, 361, 383

Confusion technique, 274
    use in regressions, 275, 386
Connation
    interference of, with suggestions, 347
    and suggestions, 22
Consciousness, limitation of, and hypnosis, 33
Continuity—discontinuity in suggestions, 170-
        173
Continuum of hypnosis, 285, 289
Continuum of regression, 289, 385
Continuum, suggestibility, 45-47, 204
Convulsions in hypnosis, 282, 298, 340, 415
        (See also: Rigidity.)
Corrective emotional responses, 423
Countertransference, 6, 398
Counting, use of, in giving suggestions, 162
Criteria of hypnosis (See: Symptoms.)
Critical ideation, 256
    suggestions and, 23
Crying, during and following hypnosis, 414f.
Crystal gazing, 276
    in psychotherapy 422, 426, 431

Dangers of hypnotism, 4, 5, 8, 9, 354f., 424
Davis-Husband scale of hypnotic depth, 183
Deafness
    producing, 344, 389
    use of suggested, 344
Decay with time of the effectiveness of sugges-
        tions, 349
Deception of subject, suggestion, in using,
        103f., 131, 137, 147, 151, 300
De-differentiation, 385
Deep breathing, use and effects of, 161
Deep hypnosis
    defined, 272
    as psychotherapy, 421
    somnambulistic vs. stuporous trance, 272
    statistics regarding, 268, 269, 395
    symptoms of, 272, 274
    technique for the production of, 273, 274-
        277
    uses of (See: Depth of hypnosis, required.)
Deep trance, defined, 183
Deepening hypnosis (See: Hypnosis.)
Deepening phase in the induction of hypnosis,
        212ff.